SECOND EDITION

CREATING AND
KEEPING CUSTOMERS

Effective Marketing

William G. Zikmund
Oklahoma State University

Michael d'Amico
University of Akron

SOUTH-WESTERN College Publishing

An International Thomson Publishing Company

Publishing Team Leader: John Szilagyi
Sponsoring Editor: Dreis Van Landuyt
Developmental Editor: Atietie Tonwe
Production Editor: Barbara Fuller Jacobsen
Production House: Litten Editing and Production
Composition: GGS Information Services
Internal Design: Craig LaGesse Ramsdell and Michael Stratton
Cover Design: Barbara Matulionis
Cover Painting: *Boston Public Gardens* silkscreen by Thomas McKnight.
  Copyright © 1997 Thomas McKnight.
Marketing Manager: Sarah Woelfel

Library of Congress Cataloging-in-Publication Data:

Zikmund, William G.
    Effective marketing : creating and keeping customers / William G.
Zikmund. Michael d'Amico. — 2nd ed.
      p.   cm.
    Includes index.
    ISBN 0-538-87848-7 (alk. paper)
    1. Marketing.   2. Consumer behavior.   3. Export marketing.
I. D'Amico, Michael.   II. Title.
HF5415.Z53   1997
  658.8—dc21   97-30024
                                                                  CIP

International Thomson Publishing

South-Western College Publishing is an ITP Company.
The ITP trademark is used under license.

ISBN 0-538-87848-7

      5 6 7 8 9 D4 5 4 3 2 1 0 9

Printed in the United States of America

To Tobin and Noah Zikmund
Kathy and Alyse d'Amico

Brief Contents

PART 1

Introduction

1 The Nature of Marketing   2
2 Marketing Management: Strategy
  and Ethical Behavior   26
3 Environmental Forces in a Diverse
  World: The Macroenvironment   56
4 The Microenvironment in an Era
  of Global Competition   82

PART 2

Analysis of Market and Consumer Behavior

5 Global Information Systems and
  Marketing Research   104
6 Consumer Behavior: Decision-Making
  Processes and Sociocultural Forces   134
7 Business Markets and
  Organizational Buying   164
8 Market Segmentation, Targeting,
  and Positioning Strategies   182

PART 3

Product Strategy

9 Basic Concepts About Goods,
  Services, and Ideas   214
10 New Products and Product Life
  Cycle Strategies   246

PART 4

Distribution Strategy

11 The Nature of the Value Chain
  and Distribution   286

12 Retailing and Wholesaling of
  Goods and Services   318

PART 5

Integrated Marketing Communications

13 Marketing Communications
  and Promotion Strategy   350
14 Advertising and Public Relations   372
15 Personal Selling, Sales Management,
  and Sales Promotion   408

PART 6

Pricing Strategy

16 Introduction to Pricing Concepts   440
17 Pricing Strategies and Tactics   462

Appendix A Careers and the Internet   491

Appendix B The Marketing Audit   494

**Appendix C Marketing Arithmetic for
        Business Analysis   496**

Glossary   502

Endnotes   523

Acknowledgments   530

Photo Credits   535

Name Index   537

Company/Product Index   541

Subject Index   547

v

Contents

PART 1 INTRODUCTION

1 The Nature of Marketing 2

Marketing Affects our Daily Lives 4
Marketing—What Is it? 4
Not-for-Profit Organizations Are Marketers Too 6
A Definition of Marketing 7
Keeping Customers and Building Relationships 7
What Is a Market? 8
The Marketing Mix 8
The First Element—Product 8
The Second Element—Place 9
The Third Element—Price 11
The Fourth Element—Promotion 11
The Art of Blending the Elements 12
The Marketing Environment—Coping With the Uncontrollable 13
Modern Marketers Use the Marketing Concept 14
Production Orientation—"As Long as It's Black" 15
Sales Orientation—Changing Their Minds 15
The Marketing Concept—The Foundation of a Marketing Orientation 15
COMPETITIVE STRATEGY: WHAT WENT RIGHT?
   Fletcher Music Centers   16
Integrated Marketing Effort 17
Total Quality Management (TQM) 18
Marketing and Society 18

**FOCUS ON TRENDS Marriott: Marketing-Oriented
        and Future-Oriented   19**
The Societal Marketing Concept 19
Why Study Marketing? 20
Summary 21
Key Terms 22
Questions for Review and Critical Thinking 22
INTERNET INSIGHTS   23
ETHICS IN PRACTICE: TAKE A STAND   23
VIDEO CASE 1–1 The Minnesota Twins (A)   24
VIDEO CASE 1–2 Lawn Care of Wisconsin   25

2 Marketing Management: Strategy and Ethical Behavior   26

Marketing Management 28
What Is a Marketing Strategy? 29
Planning—Designing a Framework for the Future 30
Top Management Makes Corporate Strategic Plans 31
   Defining the Organizational Mission 31
   Establishing Strategic Business Units 33
Middle Managers Plan Strategies for SBUs 34
   Business-Unit Strategies for Competitive Advantage 34
   Total Quality Management to Achieve Differentiation 35
**COMPETITIVE STRATEGY: WHAT WENT WRONG?
        Trouble-Shooter Barbie   37**
   Planning Business-Unit Growth Strategies 38
FOCUS ON RELATIONSHIPS 3M   40
The Strategic Marketing Process 40
   Stage 1: Identifying and Evaluating Opportunities 41
FOCUS ON GLOBAL COMPETITION General Electric Lighting   43
   Stage 2: Analyzing Market Segments and Selecting Target Markets 43
   *Stage 3: Planning a Market Position and Developing
        a Marketing Mix Strategy 44*
   Stage 4: Preparing a Formal Marketing Plan 44
   Stage 5: Executing the Plan 45
   Stage 6: Controlling Efforts and Evaluating Results 46
COMPETITIVE STRATEGY: WHAT WENT WRONG? Play 'n Learn   47
Planning, Execution, and Control Are Interrelated 47
Managerial Ethics and Socially Responsible Behavior 48
Summary 51
Key Terms 52
Questions for Review and Critical Thinking 52
INTERNET INSIGHTS   53
ETHICS IN PRACTICE: TAKE A STAND   53
CASE 2–1 Lanier   54
VIDEO CASE 2–2 Shingobee Builders—Focus on Small Business   55

3 Environmental Forces in a Diverse World: The Macroenvironment   56

A World Perspective 57
The Macroenvironment 58

The Physical Environment 58
Sociocultural Forces 59
**COMPETITIVE STRATEGY: WHAT WENT RIGHT? Japanese
    Like Seafood Really Fresh   61**
Demographics 62
The U.S. Population 62
FOCUS ON TRENDS American Eating Patterns   67
World Population 68
Economic and Competitive Forces 69
Economic Systems 69
Economic Conditions 70
Science and Technology 71
FOCUS ON TRENDS High-Tech Packaging   73
Politics and Laws 73
FOCUS ON GLOBAL COMPETITION Pepsi   74
Three Levels of U.S. Law 75
International Laws 78
Summary 78
Key Terms 79
Questions for Review and Critical Thinking 79
INTERNET INSIGHTS   80
ETHICS IN PRACTICE: TAKE A STAND   80
VIDEO CASE 3–1 LION Coffee   80
CASE 3–2 Thirty Years of Freshman   81

4 The Microenvironment in an Era of Global Competition   82

The Microenvironment—The Four Cs 83
Company 84
Customers 84
Competitors 85
Collaborators 87
The Value Chain 88
Core Competencies 88
Relationship Management 90
Microenvironments and the Four Cs in a Global Economy 90
Customers—The Era of the Global Consumer 91
**COMPETITIVE STRATEGY: WHAT WENT WRONG?
    Gestures Speak Louder Than Words   93**
Competitors in a Worldwide Arena 93
The Company as an International Marketer 95
Global Collaborations 97
FOCUS ON RELATIONSHIPS Nike   98
Summary 99
Key Terms 99
Questions for Review and Critical Thinking 100
INTERNET INSIGHTS   100
ETHICS IN PRACTICE: TAKE A STAND   101
VIDEO CASE 4–1 Sonic Drive-Ins   101
VIDEO CASE 4–2 Gaston's White River Resort   102
Enhance Your Marketing Skills With CD-ROM   103

PART 2   ANALYSIS OF MARKET AND CONSUMER BEHAVIOR

5 Global Information Systems and Marketing Research   104

Information—The Basis of Effective Marketing 106
Global Information Systems in the 21st Century 106
Data and Information 107
The Internet—A New Means of Global Communication 107
Decision Support Systems and Intranets 109
FOCUS ON TRENDS Silicon Graphics   111
Data-Based Marketing 112
FOCUS ON RELATIONSHIPS Manhattan East Suite Hotels   112
What Is Marketing Research? 112
Stages in the Research Process 113
  Stage One: Defining the Problem 114
COMPETITIVE STRATEGY: WHAT WENT RIGHT?
    Fisher-Price's Play Laboratory   117
  Stage Two: Planning the Research Design 118
FOCUS ON TRENDS Information Resources   119
  Stage Three: Selecting a Sample 122
COMPETITIVE STRATEGY: WHAT WENT
    WRONG? The Fiasco of 1936   123
  Stage Four: Collecting Data 124
  Stage Five: Analyzing the Data 124
  Stage Six: Drawing Conclusions and Preparing the Report 125
  Stage Seven: Following Up 125
Marketing Research Is a Global Activity 125
FOCUS ON GLOBAL COMPETITION Domino's   126
Sales Forecasting—Research About the Future 127
  Break-Down and Build-Up Forecasting 127
  The Three Levels of Forecasting 127
  Conditional Forecasting—"What If?" 128
  Forecasting by Time Periods 128
  Forecasting Options 128
Summary 129
Key Terms 130
Questions for Review and Critical Thinking 131
INTERNET INSIGHTS   131
ETHICS IN PRACTICE: TAKE A STAND   132
CASE 5–1 Space Wheyfers   132
CASE 5–2 First Bank Systems of Minneapolis   133

6 Consumer Behavior: Decision-Making Processes and Sociocultural Forces   134

What Is Consumer Behavior? 136
A Simple Start: Some Behavioral Fundamentals 136
The Decision-Making Process 136
  Step 1: Problem Recognition 138
  Step 2: Search for Alternative Solutions and Information 139
COMPETITIVE STRATEGY: WHAT WENT RIGHT? You'll Be Brilliant   140

Step 3: Evaluation of Alternatives 141
Step 4: Choice: Purchase Decisions and the Act of Buying 141
Step 5: Postpurchase Consumption and Evaluation 141
FOCUS ON QUALITY Packard Bell   142
Individual Factors That Shape the Decision-Making Process 142
Motivation 142
Perception 145
FOCUS ON GLOBAL COMPETITION Copying in Korea   148
Learning 149
Attitudes 150
Personality and Self-Concept 151
Interpersonal Influences on the Decision-Making Process 152
Social Values, Norms, and Roles 152
FOCUS ON GLOBAL COMPETITION Children in China   153
Culture 154
Subcultures: Cultures within Cultures 154
Social Classes 155
Reference Groups 156
FOCUS ON RELATIONSHIPS Harley-Davidson   157
The Family 157
Social Situations 158
Joint Decision Making 158
Summary 159
Key Terms 160
Questions for Review and Critical Thinking 161
INTERNET INSIGHTS   162
ETHICS IN PRACTICE: TAKE A STAND   162
VIDEO CASE 6–1 Minnesota Twins (B)   163

7 Business Markets and Organizational Buying   164

Organizational Buying Behavior 166
Characteristics of the Business Market 167
Three Kinds of Buying 169
The Cross-Functional Buying Center 170
Why Do Organizations Buy? 172
COMPETITIVE STRATEGY: WHAT WENT WRONG?
   Electronic Ticketing by Airlines   173
Product Quality 173
FOCUS ON GLOBAL COMPETITION ISO 9000 and ISO 14000   174
Related Services 174
FOCUS ON QUALITY Digital Equipment Corp.   175
Prices 175
Reliable Delivery and Inventory Management: Opportunities for
   Organizational Collaboration 175
The Bottom Line 176
The North American Industry Classification System 176
Summary 178
Key Terms 178
Questions for Review and Critical Thinking 179
INTERNET INSIGHTS   179
ETHICS IN PRACTICE: TAKE A STAND   179
VIDEO CASE 7–1 Weather or Not, Inc.   180
VIDEO CASE 7–2 Nypro   181

8 Market Segmentation, Targeting, and Positioning Strategies   182

What Is a Market? What Is Market Segmentation? 184
    Not All Buyers Are Alike 184
    Choosing Meaningful Market Segments 185
FOCUS ON TRENDS National Basketball Association—The NBA   186
    The Market Segment Cross-Classification Matrix 187
    Matching the Mix to the Target Market 188
Four Strategies for Target Marketing 188
    Undifferentiated Marketing: Everyone Is a Customer 189
    Concentrated Marketing: Zeroing in on a Single Target 189
    Differentiated Marketing: Different Buyers, Different Strategies 191
    Custom Marketing and Data-Based Marketing: To Each His Own 191
COMPETITIVE STRATEGY: WHAT WENT RIGHT? Lexus   194
Identifying Market Differences 194
    Geographic Segmentation 195
    Demographic Segmentation 196
FOCUS ON GLOBAL COMPETITION Barbie   196
    Socioeconomic Bases of Segmentation 198
    Lifestyle and Psychographic Segmentation 199
COMPETITIVE STRATEGY: WHAT WENT WRONG? Porsche   201
    Segmentation by Behavioral Patterns 201
    Geodemographic Segmentation 202
Segmenting Business Markets 202
Positioning: The Basic Focus for the Marketing Mix 203
Summary 205
Key Terms 206
Questions for Review and Critical Thinking 206
INTERNET INSIGHTS   207
ETHICS IN PRACTICE: TAKE A STAND   207
CASE 8–1 VALS™ 2   208
CASE 8–2 The Point—105.7   210
Enhance Your Marketing Skills With CD-ROM   213

PART 3   PRODUCT STRATEGY

9 Basic Concepts About Goods, Services, and Ideas   214

What Is a Product? 215
    The Total Product 216
    Product Strategy and the Product Concept 216
    Product Differentiation 217
Classifying Products by the Nature of the Market 217
    Classifying Consumer Products 218
    Consumer Behavior 219
    Classifying Organizational Products 221
The Product Line and the Product Mix 223
The Marketer's Product Portfolio 223
COMPETITIVE STRATEGY: WHAT WENT RIGHT? Quidel Corp.   224
Branding—What's in a Name? 225
    Brands and Trademarks 226
COMPETITIVE STRATEGY: WHAT WENT WRONG? Toyota   227

Generic Names 227
FOCUS ON QUALITY Minnesota Moose   228
A "Good" Brand Name? 228
Manufacturer Brands versus Distributor Brands 229
FOCUS ON GLOBAL COMPETITION Sony   230
Generic Brands 230
Family Brands and Individual Brands 230
Co-Branding 231
Licensing 232
Packaging and Packing 232
Labeling—Telling about the Product 233
Legal Guidelines for Packaging 233
Product Warranties 233
Customer Service 234
Services Are Products Too! 234
Characteristics of Services 234
FOCUS ON GLOBAL COMPETITION British Airways   236
The Total Service Product 239
Summary 239
Key Terms 240
Questions for Review and Critical Thinking 241
INTERNET INSIGHTS   242
ETHICS IN PRACTICE: TAKE A STAND   242
VIDEO CASE 9–1 Yawgoo Valley Ski Area   243
CASE 9–2 Dirty Potato Chips   244

10 New Products and Product Life Cycle Strategies   246

What is a New Product? 248
Management's Perspective on New Product 248
The Consumer's Perspective on Newness 249
Discontinuous Innovation 249
Dynamically Continuous Innovation 249
Continuous Innovation 250
The Slim Chances of Success 250
The Characteristics of Success 250
Relative Advantage 251
Compatibility with Existing Consumption Patterns 251
Trialability—The Opportunity for Buyer Testing 251
Observability—The Chance to See the Newness 251
Simplicity versus Complexity 252
New Product Development 252
Idea Generation 253
FOCUS ON GLOBAL COMPETITION Yamaha   254
Screening 254
Business Analysis 255
Development 255
Commercialization 256
Why Do New Products Fail? 257
The Role of the Entrepreneur 258
The Product Life Cycle 259
The Introduction Stage 259
The Growth Stage 260
The Maturity Stage 261
The Decline Stage 262

FOCUS ON TRENDS The Recording Industry   263
Do All Products Follow a Product Life Cycle? 263
Is There Life after Decline? 264
The Adoption and Diffusion Processes 265
Innovators—Being Venturesome 266
Early Adopters—Following the Lead 266
Early and Late Majorities—Riding the Bandwagon 266
Laggards—Bringing Up the Rear 267
Nonadopters—Holding Out 267
Use of the Adopter Categories 267
Strategies for Modifying Existing Products 267
Cost Reduction Strategies 268
Repositioning Strategies 268
Total Quality Management Strategies 268
**COMPETITIVE STRATEGY: WHAT WENT RIGHT? Silicon Graphics, Inc.,
        Cultivates Its Most Demanding Customers   269**
FOCUS ON QUALITY Jeep   270
Matching Products to Markets—Product Line Strategy 273
COMPETITIVE STRATEGY: WHAT WENT RIGHT? Merry Maids   274
Strategies for Expanding the Product Line or the Product Mix 274
Modifying Product Offerings for International Markets 275
Eliminating Old Products 276
Ethical Considerations Associated With Product Strategy 276
The Right to Safety 276
The Right to Be Informed 276
Quality of Life and Ecology 277
Product Obsolescence 278
Summary 279
Key Terms 280
Questions for Review and Critical Thinking 281
INTERNET INSIGHTS   282
ETHICS IN PRACTICE: TAKE A STAND   282
CASE 10–1 Water Joe—Johnny Beverages Inc.   283
VIDEO CASE 10–2 Spanier & Bourne Sailmakers   284
Enhance Your Marketing Skills With CD-ROM   285

PART 4   DISTRIBUTION STRATEGY

11 The Nature of the Value Chain and Distribution   286

Distribution Delivers a Standard of Living to Society 288
Logistics and Physical Distribution Defined 288
The Objectives of Physical Distribution 289
COMPETITIVE STRATEGY: WHAT WENT WRONG? A Triple Treat?   290
Channel of Distribution—Defined 290
Marketing Functions Performed by Intermediaries 292
How Intermediaries Fit in Channels 292
Physical Distribution Functions 293
Breaking Bulk 293
Accumulating Bulk 293
Creating Assortments 294
Reducing Transactions 295

Transportation and Storage 296
Integration of the Physical Distribution Functions 299
Communication Functions 300
Facilitating Functions 301
FOCUS ON GLOBAL COMPETITION ATM Services   302
Typical Channels of Distribution 302
Channels of Distribution for Consumer Goods and Services 302
Channels of Distribution for Business-to-Business Marketing 304
Vertical Marketing Systems 306
Corporate Systems—Total Ownership 306
Administered Strategic Alliances—Strong Leadership 306
FOCUS ON RELATIONSHIPS Caterpillar   307
Contractual Systems—Legal Relationships 307
Managing the Channel of Distribution 308
Determining the Structure of the Channel 308
COMPETITIVE STRATEGY: WHAT WENT RIGHT? American Greetings   310
The Extent of Distribution: How Many Outlets? 310
Channels of Distribution: A System of Interdependency 311
Channel Cooperation 312
Channel Conflict 312
Channel Power 312
Reverse Distribution 313
Ethical, Political, and Legal Forces in Distribution Management 313
Does Distribution Cost Too Much? 313
Summary 313
Key Terms 315
Questions for Review and Critical Thinking 315
INTERNET INSIGHTS   316
ETHICS IN PRACTICE: TAKE A STAND   316
VIDEO CASE 11–1 StockPot Soups   317
VIDEO CASE 11–2 Aquathin Corporation   317

12 Retailing and Wholesaling of Goods and Services   318

Retailing and Its Importance 320
Retailing Institutions—Toward A System of Classifications 320
Classifying Retailers by Ownership 320
Classifying Retailers by Prominent Strategy 321
FOCUS ON GLOBAL COMPETITION European Direct Marketing   327
FOCUS ON TRENDS Buying a Car on the Internet   328
**COMPETITIVE STRATEGY: WHAT WENT
    WRONG? American Greetings   329**
The Wheel of Retailing 329
Retail Management Strategies 330
Merchandise Assortment 331
Location, Location, and Location 332
**COMPETITIVE STRATEGY: WHAT WENT
    RIGHT? McDonald's International   333**
Atmospherics 333
Customer Service 333
Database Management 334
Wholesaling 335
Classifying Wholesalers 335
Merchant Wholesalers 335

     Agents 337
     Manufacturers That Do Their Own Wholesaling 339
     Wholesalers That Distribute Services 340
   Wholesale Management Strategies 340
     Selecting Target Markets and Creating Assortments 340
     Organizational Collaborations for Long-Term Relationships 340
   Regulation of Retail and Wholesale Distribution 341
     Exclusive Dealing 341
     Exclusive Territories 341
     Tying Contracts 342
     Legalities of International Distribution 342
   Summary 342
   Key Terms 343
   Questions for Review and Critical Thinking 344
   INTERNET INSIGHTS   345
   ETHICS IN PRACTICE: TAKE A STAND   345
   CASE 12–1 EatZi's   346
   VIDEO CASE 12–2 Muebleria la Unica   347
   Enhance Your Marketing Skills With CD-ROM   349

PART 5   INTEGRATED MARKETING COMMUNICATIONS

13 Marketing Communications and Promotion Strategy   350

Promotion: Communication With a Purpose 351
The Elements of Promotion 352
   Personal Selling 352
   Advertising 352
   Publicity and Public Relations 353
COMPETITIVE STRATEGY: WHAT WENT WRONG? Scope   354
   Sales Promotion 354
FOCUS ON GLOBAL COMPETITION Intel   354
   Integrated Marketing Communications—The Promotional Mix 355
The Communication Process 355
   Encoding the Message 355
   Transmitting the Message through a Channel 356
   Decoding the Message 357
   Feedback 357
   Perfect Communication 358
The Hierarchy of Communication Effects 358
Push and Pull Strategies 361
Promotional Campaigns 362
   Image Building 362
   Product Differentiation 364
   Positioning 364
   Direct-Response Campaigns 365
COMPETITIVE STRATEGY: WHAT WENT RIGHT? Got Milk?   366
The Ethics of Persuasion 366
Summary 367
Key Terms 368
Questions for Review and Critical Thinking 368

INTERNET INSIGHTS 369
ETHICS IN PRACTICE: TAKE A STAND 369
VIDEO CASE 13–1 International Management Group 370

14 Advertising and Public Relations 372

The Nature of Advertising 374
  Product Advertising 374
COMPETITIVE STRATEGY: WHAT WENT RIGHT? Purina Dog Chow   375
  Institutional Advertising 375
Planning and Developing Advertising Campaigns 376
  Communication Goals for Advertising 376
  Specific Advertising Objectives 377
  Advertising Objectives and Product Life Cycle 377
Creative Strategy 378
  What to Say—The Appeal 378
  How to Say It—Execution of the Appeal 379
FOCUS ON QUALITY Scotch-Brite Never Rust   381
Producing an Effective Advertisement 382
  Copy—The Verbal Appeal 383
  Art—The Visual Appeal 383
  Copy and Art Working Together—The AIDA Formula 383
Media Selection 385
  Mass Media, Direct-Marketing Media, and Interactive Media 385
  Which Media? 387
  Media Advantages and Disadvantages 388
FOCUS ON TRENDS Narrowcasting   390
  What Scheduling? 390
Measuring the Effectiveness of Advertising 390
  Developing Messages and Pretesting Advertisements 391
  Posttesting Advertisements 391
  Sales as a Measure of Advertisement Effectiveness 392
Public Relations 393
  News Releases 393
  Press Conferences 394
  Appearances 394
COMPETITIVE STRATEGY: WHAT WENT RIGHT?
    Chemical Bank Corporate Challenge   395
  Event Sponsorship 395
Public Relations Goes Beyond Publicity: An Integrated Marketing
Communications Approach 396
  Crisis Management 396
  Internal Marketing and Employee Relations 397
FOCUS ON TRENDS Ritz-Carlton's Employee Empowerment   398
International Public Relations 399
Evaluating and Monitoring Public Relations 399
Ethical Issues in Advertising and Public Relations 399
  Deceptive and Misleading Practices 399
  Public Standards 400
  The Quality of Children's Lives 401
Summary 401
Key Terms 402
Questions for Review and Critical Thinking 403

INTERNET INSIGHTS   404
ETHICS IN PRACTICE: TAKE A STAND   404
VIDEO CASE 14–1 Lee Jeans   405
CASE 14–2 TV3   406

15 Personal Selling, Sales Management,
and Sales Promotion   408

Personal Selling Defined 410
The Characteristics of Personal Selling 411
   Personal Selling Is Flexible 411
   Personal Selling Builds Relationships 411
FOCUS ON TRENDS IBM's Virtual Sales Office   412
   Some Limitations of Personal Selling 412
The Types of Personal Selling Tasks 413
   Order Taking 413
   Order Getting 414
   Sales Support and Cross-Functional Teams 414
The Creative Selling Process 415
   Step One: Locating Qualified Prospects 416
   Step Two: Preapproach Planning 417
   Step Three: The Approach 417
   Step Four: The Sales Presentation 418
   Step Five: Handling Objections 419
COMPETITIVE STRATEGY: WHAT WENT RIGHT? SOQ NOP   420
   Step Six: Closing the Sale 420
   Step Seven: The Follow-up—Building Relationships 421
FOCUS ON GLOBAL COMPETITION Selling in
        Japan—A Lengthy Process   422
Sales Management 422
   Setting Sales Objectives 422
   Organizing Sales Activity 423
FOCUS ON QUALITY James River Corp.   424
   Recruiting and Selecting the Sales Force 425
   Training the Sales Force 426
   Compensating the Sales Force 426
   Motivating the Sales Force 428
   Evaluating and Controlling the Sales Force 428
Ethical Issues in Sales and Sales Management 429
Sales Promotion 429
   Sales Promotions Geared Toward Wholesalers and Retailers 430
   Sales Promotions Aimed at Ultimate Consumers 431
COMPETITIVE STRATEGY: WHAT WENT RIGHT? Oscar Mayer   432
FOCUS ON RELATIONSHIPS McDonald's and Disney   434
Summary 435
Key Terms 436
Questions for Review and Critical Thinking 436
INTERNET INSIGHTS   437
ETHICS IN PRACTICE: TAKE A STAND   437
VIDEO CASE 15–1 Stone Hill Winery   438
Enhance Your Marketing Skills with CD-ROM 439

PART 6   PRICING STRATEGY

16 Introduction to Pricing Concepts   440

What Is Price? 442
Price as a Marketing Mix Variable 442
COMPETITIVE STRATEGY: WHAT WENT WRONG? Sprint   443
  Price Competition 443
  Price and Marketing Effectiveness 444
Price in the Economy 444
  Demand Curve 444
  Supply Curve 445
FOCUS ON RELATIONSHIPS Hyatt Hotels   446
The Fundamentals of Pricing Strategy 446
Pricing Objectives 446
  Income-Oriented Objectives 447
  Sales-Oriented Objectives 449
  Competition-Oriented Objectives 450
  Objectives Related to Social Concerns 451
Target Market Considerations 451
FOCUS ON TRENDS USA Today   452
Know Your Demand 452
  Price Elasticity of Demand 452
  Cross-Elasticity of Demand 454
Know Your Costs 455
Summary 456
Key Terms 457
Questions for Review and Critical Thinking 457
INTERNET INSIGHTS   458
ETHICS IN PRACTICE: TAKE A STAND   458
CASE 16–1 Toy Scalpers   459

17 Pricing Strategies and Tactics   462

An Overview of Pricing Strategies 464
Differential Pricing Strategies 464
  One-Price Policy versus Variable Pricing 464
  Second-Market Discounting 465
  Skimming 465
  Other Price-Reduction Strategies 466
Competitive Pricing Strategies 466
  Meeting the Competition 466
COMPETITIVE STRATEGY: WHAT WENT WRONG? Sony MiniDisc   467
  Undercutting the Competition 467
  Price Leaders and Followers 467
  Penetration Pricing 468
  Traditional Pricing 469
  Inflationary Pricing 470
Product-Line Pricing Strategies 470
  Captive Pricing 470
  Leader Pricing and Bait Pricing
  Pricing Lining 471

FOCUS ON QUALITY Parker Pen   471
Price Bundling and Multiple-Unit Pricing 472
Psychological and Image Pricing Strategies 473
Reference Pricing 473
Odd versus Even Pricing 473
Prestige Pricing 473
FOCUS ON GLOBAL COMPETITION Levi's   474
Distribution-Based Pricing Strategies and Tactics 474
F.O.B. 474
Delivered Pricing 474
Basing-Point Pricing 475
Additional Pricing Strategies and Tactics 475
Establishing the Exact Price 476
Markup on Selling Price and Markup on Cost 476
The Cost-Plus Method 477
The Average-Cost Method 477
Target Return Pricing 478
Break-Even Analysis 479
Price Adjustments 480
Cash Discounts 480
Trade Discounts 481
Quantity Discounts 481
Seasonal Discounts 481
Chain Discounts 482
Promotional Allowances 482
Pricing and the Law 483
Robinson-Patman Act 483
The Repeal of Fair Trade Acts 483
Unfair Sales Practices Acts 484
Other State Laws and Local Laws 484
Pricing and Social Responsibility 484
Summary 485
Key Terms 486
Questions for Review and Critical Thinking 487
INTERNET INSIGHTS   487
ETHICS IN PRACTICE: TAKE A STAND   488
VIDEO CASE 17–1 Pacific Paper Tube   488

APPENDIX A Careers and the Internet   491
Internet Insights 491

APPENDIX B The Marketing Audit   494

APPENDIX C Marketing Arithmetic for Business Analysis   496

The Profit and Loss Statement 496
Marketing Analysis and Performance Ratios 497
Return on Investment 499
Break-Even Calculations 500
Price Elasticity 500
Price Elasticity 500

Glossary   502
Endnotes   523
Acknowledgments   530
Photo Credits   535
Name Index   537
Company/Product Index   541
Subject Index   547

Preface

The first edition of *Effective Marketing: Creating and Keeping Customers,* was the direct result of listening to a segment of marketing professors who told us about their classroom needs for a shorter book. We are pleased that the book we wrote to satisfy these professors' needs was so well received.

Effective Marketing, Second Edition, which consists of 17 chapters, is shorter than our other book, *Marketing,* Fifth Edition, but it shares many of the same attributes. *Effective Marketing* presents a lively picture of marketing as a dynamic, competitive, and creative activity that is part of our everyday lives. This book discusses academic theory, yet it is contemporary and practical. It is also very readable. *Effective Marketing* has a straightforward and conversational prose style with balanced coverage of marketing concepts and practical examples that make marketing easy to understand.

In writing a shorter book, we have not simply pared our coverage to the essentials of marketing but have organized many topics in a unique way. The material is arranged to show that marketing activities are not independent but that they work together to achieve the organization's goals. For example, there is no separate chapter on services marketing because the marketing of services is discussed in virtually every chapter.

The subtitle of our book is "Creating and Keeping Customers" because relationship marketing is a recurring theme. The book stresses that the marketing process does not end with the sale. *Effective Marketing* discusses how marketers establish and build relationships with customers. Many examples illustrate that both large and small businesses can apply these concepts. For instance, Chapter 1 portrays Fletcher Music Centers in Clearwater, Florida, as a retailer that understands that the key to winning and keeping customers is to figure out what they need, sometimes before they figure it out themselves. Furthermore, the discussions of relationship marketing recognize that the way business is being conducted has dramatically changed in recent years.

Companies, especially those engaged in multinational marketing, often rely on collaborating organizations. Chapter 4, "The Microenvironment in an Era of Global Competition," introduces the concept of collaborators and the value chain, and the remainder of the book provides insights about managing relationships with suppliers, intermediaries, and customers.

Another overall theme of this book is how effective marketers gain and maintain competitive advantages in a global environment. International issues and global competition are carefully integrated into every chapter in the text. Chapter 4 pays special attention to the increased level of global competition and how marketing strategies, even those of domestic marketers, are influenced by international business. Placement of this chapter at this point in the textbook facilitates additional discussion of international issues when marketing mix strategies are addressed in the remaining chapters.

Integrating international issues into every subsequent chapter allows us to deal with conceptual issues of international marketing when the marketing principles being discussed have global dimensions. For example, discussions about distinctive competitive environments and whether world brands should be customized for different countries or standardized around the globe are found in Chapter 10, on product strategy. We believe this approach will give students a heightened appreciation of the pervasiveness of global issues.

Effective Marketing employs current examples about both domestic and global markets from the real world to enhance understanding of marketing concepts and strategies. For example, Chapter 1 begins with an opening vignette about Turner Field, the new home of the Atlanta Braves. This vignette illustrates how the Braves create "added value" for its fans and additional revenue for the club by providing many entertaining activities and services beyond the actual game of baseball. Chapter 3's opening scenario reveals how pagers are more popular than conventional telephones in China. The reason is that resourceful Chinese use the pager not as an accessory to the phone, but as a sort of primitive substitute for it.

Effective Marketing also stresses the logic of marketing management, relating strategy and tactics to the environmental opportunities and constraints with which managers must deal on a daily basis. The concepts of effective marketing, customer value, competitive strategy, cross-functional teams, total quality management, relationship marketing, and adapting to change in our global economy are emphasized throughout the book, so that readers are able to see the difference between intuitive decision making and sound marketing management. For example, Chapter 1 discusses how Ford Motor Company's total quality management program fits into its overall competitive strategy.

Theories and strategies that marketing managers use to create competitive advantages have a central importance in *Effective Marketing*. Theoretical concepts, such as those found in the study of buyer behavior, are presented so that students can understand their practical value for marketing managers. Competitive market strategies, such as those used for segmenting, targeting, and positioning, appear early in the book. They provide a foundation to build upon when marketing mix strategies are discussed later.

Commenting on A. Bartlett Giamatti, former president of Yale University and former commissioner of major league baseball, Whitey Herzog said: "For being book smart, he had an awful lot of street smarts." We wrote *Effective Marketing* with the goal of helping students become both book smart and street smart about marketing.

Effective Marketing was also written to be teachable. A considerable effort was made to ensure that the pedagogy meets the needs of modern marketing professors. Learning objectives and chapter summaries are coordinated to help students organize their thoughts. Color graphics experts and graphic designers assisted the editor and authors in designing a book that highlights key concepts and ideas to the benefit of the reader and the instructor. As further aids to students, various exhibits, boxes, and in-text features illustrate practical marketing activities as they occur in advertising, brand management, pricing, and every other facet of marketing. New to this edition is a home page on the Internet (http://zikmund.swcollege.com) that offers added value for both students and professors.

ORGANIZATION OF THE BOOK

Although it shares many features of our other book, *Effective Marketing* is not just a condensed version. The book's organizational structure has been designed to integrate topics that in many textbooks are often isolated in a chapter at the end of the book.

The book is organized into six parts. Part One discusses the nature of marketing, the fundamentals of marketing strategy, and the marketing environment. Chapter 1, "The Nature of Marketing," introduces the marketing concept and explains how a marketing orientation relates to total quality management. Chapter 2, "Marketing Management: Strategy and Ethical Behavior," establishes the nature of marketing strategy. It also includes extensive coverage of ethics and moral behavior to serve as a framework and a springboard for further discussions of ethical concerns in the remaining chapters. We chose this organization because students need some background in marketing principles before they can truly understand how an organization's ethical principles influence its marketing decision making. Chapter 2 also introduces the "Ethics in Practice: Take a Stand" feature as part of the end-of-chapter materials. This feature encourages students to think about ethical principles and how they affect decision making in specific situations.

Coverage of the environmental factors has undergone major revision. Chapter 3 now deals with the macroenvironment, and Chapter 4 discusses the microenvironment. Both chapters feature a world perspective. In Chapter 3 emphasis is given to the competitive environment, especially challenges from global competitors. The chapter highlights how certain aspects of the global environment influence consumers and marketing strategies.

Chapter 4, "The Microenvironment in an Era of Global Competition," is new. It introduces the 4 C's of business: Company, Customer, Collaborators, and Competitors. The discussion highlights the value chain and how organizations are gaining a competitive advantage by forming alliances, joint ventures, and other collaborations, and explains many strategic global issues within this framework. This chapter helps set the stage for a continuing discussion of the nature of competition and the need for collaborators in international marketing activity.

Part Two, "Analysis of Market and Consumer Behavior," discusses information management and consumer and market behavior. Coverage of global information systems and the Internet is greatly expanded in Chapter 5. Chapter 6 provides a model and an overview of consumer behavior. It concentrates on both the psychological dimensions of the decision-making process and the sociological and cultural factors influencing the consumer. Chapter 7, "Business Markets and Organizational Buying," discusses business-to-business marketing with a focus on buying behavior. It has been substantially revised to discuss the North American Industry Classification System (NAICS) which replaces the United States' SIC system and Canada's and Mexico's separate classification systems with one uniform system for classifying industries.

Chapter 8, "Market Segmentation, Targeting, and Positioning Strategies," applies the behavioral theories discussed in other chapters to the concept of market segmentation. It explains how segmentation and targeting strategies are part of an effective marketing strategy and shows how both large multinational firms and small domestic marketers can use these strategies. This chapter offers complete coverage of positioning strategies, placing positioning in a strategic framework that is compatible with the material on target marketing.

Part Three, "Product Strategy," deals with both goods and services. It discusses the elements of products, the product life cycle, and product strategies for new and existing products. The material on product strategy completely integrates the marketing of services into Chapters 9 and 10. The process for implementing total quality management programs is discussed at length in Chapter 10, "New Products and Product Life Cycle Strategies."

Part Four, "Distribution Strategy," has been totally revised in this edition. It now consists of two chapters that focus on the nature of distribution within the value chain. The material on physical distribution and the theory of distribution systems is now combined into an integrated discussion in Chapter 11 about how value is added throughout the entire logistical system of the firm. In Chapter 12, retailing and wholesaling strategies are presented as they apply in today's highly technological environment.

Part Five, "Integrated Marketing Communications," contains chapters introducing promotional concepts, advertising and publicity/public relations, personal selling, and sales promotions. All chapters emphasize integrated marketing communications and creative promotional strategy. Greater emphasis is given to direct marketing's new role in the promotion mix. Chapter 15, "Personal Selling, Sales Management, and Sales Promotion," highlights the importance of personal selling and relationship management. The material on sales promotion has been expanded to reflect its increased importance in many marketing mixes.

Part Six, "Pricing Strategy," consists of two chapters: "Introduction to Pricing Concepts" and "Pricing Strategies and Tactics." This material shows how price plays a role in the allocation of goods within economies and how it plays a practical role in the marketing mix. Much of the material explains the need for and nature of pricing objectives and the way pricing strategy is developed to satisfy these objectives. Our treatment remains a very pragmatic approach to this key marketing mix element.

Three appendixes end the book. "Career and the Internet" provides information to help students learn what career options are available and what preparation is required for employment in these fields. "The Marketing Audit" provides a sample outline for conducting a marketing audit. "Marketing Arithmetic for Business Analysis" explains financial concepts and many analytical ratios that marketing managers use in decision making.

Additional appendixes and other useful information appear on the Zikmund and d'Amico Web site. For example, "Organizing the Marketing Function" allows the professor to introduce this material at any point in the academic term.

SOME DISTINCTIVE FEATURES STUDENTS WILL LIKE

In every chapter, an opening vignette describes an actual situation relevant to the material in the chapter and focuses student attention on the pragmatic aspects of each chapter. For example, Chapter 2 begins by showing how Enterprise Rent-A-Car's understanding of consumer lifestyles and implementation of a strategy, completely different from that of Avis and Hertz, helped it become the biggest rent-a-car company. Chapter 5 opens with a discussion of what happened when Chee-tos product taste tests revealed its traditional cheese flavor did not appeal to Chinese consumers.

Each chapter begins with a clear statement of learning objectives to provide students with expectations about what is to come. The summary at the end of each chapter helps solidify these learning objectives.

Graphics and exhibits are designed to encourage student involvement and learning. Thought-provoking photographic exhibits include clear, understandable captions that reinforce a theory or principle explained in the text.

Interesting and relevant end-of-chapter materials such as video cases and questions for review and critical thinking reflect practical marketing problems. Many are designed to stimulate students to search for additional information about marketing.

Key terms are listed at the end of each chapter. These terms are defined in a margin glossary that runs through the text to help students learn the vocabulary of marketing. In addition, a glossary of key terms appears at the end of the book as a reference source.

Numerous real, easy-to-understand examples help students gain insight and perspective. Many examples reflect the increased competition from foreign competitors and the importance of service marketing in the world economy. Highlights of special chapter features appear below.

Competitive Strategy: What Went Right or Wrong?

Unique "Competitive Strategy: What Went Right?" and "Competitive Strategy: What Went Wrong?" boxes illustrate successes and failures in specific marketing situations. They focus on decisions made by particular organizations and the outcomes of those decisions. For example, Merry Maids manages to instill a sense of dignity and importance in low-paid people doing menial jobs. A competitive strategy box explains what went right for this service marketer. A "What Went Wrong" box explains why electronic ticketing by airlines has frustrated many business travelers.

Focus Sections

All chapters include special sections that focus on four important aspects of marketing: global competition, trends in the contemporary environment, quality strategies to offer superior customer value, and relationship marketing. Examples from actual business and nonprofit organizations show how the concepts explained in the text are implemented in practice. These company focus sections—entitled "Focus on Global Competition," "Focus on Trends," "Focus on Quality," and "Focus on Relationships"—are not isolated boxes. Each features a particular company's application of the theoretical concepts just discussed in the preceding section.

Focus on Global Competition

At home, contemporary marketers face competition from global organizations that compete in the United States. Abroad, marketers must adapt their strategies to the countries where their products are marketed. These challenges are addressed in "Focus on Global Competition" boxes, which reflect increased competition from foreign competitors at home and abroad. For example, one feature explains how the CIRRUS ATM system's inter-European switching center in Belgium helps Americans in Paris use banking services in the United States.

Focus on Trends

Contemporary trends, such as advances in telecommunications technology and a heightened concern about ecology, have had major impacts on markets. Emerging trends, such as the development of the Internet, have changed the way marketing managers do their jobs. "Focus on Trends" explores how certain companies have spotted trends and capitalized on them to serve marketing efforts. For example, one feature reveals how a study of eating patterns in America found a number of changes in eating patterns over the last decade. Among them: The number of take-out dinners has more than doubled. One marketing implication is that many of today's restaurants function as prepared-food supermarkets.

Focus on Quality

Organizations that market high-quality goods and services have an edge. Recent concerns about the quality of Japanese automobiles versus that of American automobiles offer but one example of this phenomenon. In organizations that have adopted the marketing concept, every aspect of the business must have a quality focus. "Focus on Quality" shows how organizations have implemented total quality management programs to continually improve quality. For example, one feature explains why Digital Equipment Corporation's customer satisfaction soared when it replaced its automated telephone answering system with real people. Another shows that comparative advertising promoting quality doesn't have to be scientific and dull. To illustrate its brand quality, Scotch-Brite Never Rust soap pads from 3M associates its competitor Brillo with a dinosaur.

Focus on Relationships

Several trends have focused more attention on relationship marketing. Strategic alliances are made with businesses in other countries. Distribution channels are becoming more interdependent. Organizations are downsizing and relying more on collaboration with other organizations. Many of our focus sections discuss how establishing long-term relationships benefits all parties. For example, one "Focus on Relationships" feature points out how H.O.G.—Harley owner's group—helps motorcycle owners feel special and part of the Harley-Davidson tradition.

Ethics in Practice

We discuss ethical issues in Chapter 2. An "Ethics in Practice" section at the end of each of the remaining chapters poses "Take a Stand" questions to give students the chance to think about ethical principles and how they apply in specific situations.

Internet Insights

Because information technologies are changing the way business is conducted around the world, we have added an innovative new feature to the book: Internet Insights. Each Internet Insight has Exercises and an Address Book with URL information about interesting Web sites. Exercises are an innovative new addition to the book that provides students with a hands-on means for learning how to use the Internet. Students will be guided through the World Wide Web and various search engines to gather data, to learn about careers, and to gain additional insights about marketing principles. The Address Books provide World Wide Web URLs worth knowing about.

A related feature, unique to this book, is the South-Western Publishing World Wide Web page (http://zikmund.swcollege.com) that allows both professors and students to access supplemental information about the text and its teaching materials.

SPECIAL FEATURES THE PROFESSOR WILL LIKE

A professor's job is demanding. Because every professor's job demands a lot, we expect professors to demand a lot from both the publisher and the authors of this book. Both the textbook and the instructor's materials have been developed to help instructors excel when performing their vital teaching function.

The extensive learning support package with *Effective Marketing* includes an instructor's resource manual with lecture outlines, and materials on discussion questions, cases, and "Ethics in Practice" exercises. There is a verified test bank and a computerized test bank. More than 100 full-color transparency acetates, advanced instruction modules, and PowerPoint presentation software help the professor prepare lecture and discussion materials. Furthermore, there is a comprehensive multimedia program. Videotapes and CD-ROM ancillary materials provide the means to bring the contemporary world of marketing to the classroom visually. A student learning guide and a Marketing Plan Project Manual are also available. Highlights of some of the instructor's materials appear below.

Test Bank

Special attention was given to the preparation of the test bank, because it is one of the most important ancillary materials. Joe Ballenger of Stephen F. Austin State University rewrote and supplemented the authors' multiple-choice and true/false questions. The test bank contains over 4,000 multiple-choice, true/false, and essay questions. The questions have been categorized according to Bloom's taxonomy for cognitive complexity. The questions are classified as recall, comprehension, calculation, and application. Furthermore, difficulty rankings allow the instructor to know in advance if students will find a question easy, medium, or hard.

Westest, the computerized version of the test bank, provides instructors with a convenient means of generating tests. The menu-driven testing package has many user-oriented features, including the ability to edit and add exam questions, to scramble questions within sections of the exam, and to merge questions. Westest is available for Windows. Call-in testing is also available.

Multimedia Program

Video materials bring an excitement to physical distribution, advertising, personal selling, market segmentation, and other topics in a way that nothing else can. The comprehensive video accompanying *Effective Marketing* is described later.

Principles of Marketing CD-ROM

South-Western's Principles of Marketing CD-ROM provides the student with a unique multimedia-based approach to learning introductory marketing concepts. Instead of reading text on a CD-ROM, students can experience marketing through exciting full-motion video clips, photo montages, and animated slide shows. Students can also explore and learn topics via interactive exhibits, process models, and diagrams. This CD-ROM supplement contains 32 interactive modules covering a broad range of concepts.

Video Cases

The video cases are much like regular end-of-chapter cases but with an accompanying video segment that portrays some elements of the case. For example, the Minnesota Twins baseball team allowed us to produce video case materials exclusively for this textbook. Other video cases, such as Weather or Not, Inc., focus on small business. Each of the video cases in the book is based on real businesses.

The INC. Video Lecture Support Series

A number of video tapes dealing with some of the most important and timely issues in marketing are available in the *INC. Magazine* video library. Qualified adopters may select from videos dealing with personal selling, customer service, starting a new business, and other important topics.

Supplemental Video Lecture Support Series

The supplemental video lecture series includes 14 separate video segments on international topics, total quality management, advertising, small businesses, and entrepreneurship. This exciting video tracks the people and their marketing strategies in this important industry. Marketing is not an isolated business activity. Each video segment shows marketing decisions and explores how these decisions must be integrated with other functional areas of the corporation, such as finance, human resources, operations, etc.

Instructor's Resource Manual

The instructor's resource manual, prepared by Tobin Zikmund and the authors, provides an average of 50 pages of important information for each chapter. The instructor's manual is also available on disk for instructors who prefer to work on disk. Each chapter contains the following information.

- **Chapter Scan:** a brief overview of the chapter.
- **Suggested Learning Objectives:** expanded objectives related to those presented in the student's textbook.
- **Chapter Outline:** a detailed, three-level outline of chapter material.
- **The Chapter Summarized:** an extended outline with narratives under each major point to flesh out the discussion and show alternative examples and issues to bring forward.
- **Answer Guidelines for End-of-Chapter Materials:** detailed responses to the questions for discussion, "Ethics in Practice: Take a Stand" exercises and video case questions. Answers to the "Take a Stand" questions are extensive and provide detailed ethical implications. Video case answers include video location, time, subject matter, at-a-glance overview, and complete answers to the discussion questions.

PowerPoint Presentation Software

PowerPoint is a state-of-the-art presentation graphics program for IBM-compatible computers. Prepared by Susan Peterson of Scottsdale Community College, this integrated program allows instructors to retrieve and edit any of the preloaded slides that accompany the book. Images can easily be edited, added, or deleted. Other features of the system include the following.

- The instructor can present the slides electronically in the classroom.
- Four-color prints of slides can be made from the program (a four-color printer is required).
- Student and instructor notes pages can be prepared from the slides.
- The instructor can edit and change any of the slides.
- The instructor can animate and prepare a slide show with transition effects.

Internet Web Site

The Zikmund and d'Amico marketing Web site (http://zikmund.swcollege.com) is the latest supplement from South-Western that puts the most current information in your hands as soon as it is available. Qualified adopters can log onto the Bulletin Board from their home or office and immediately gain access to the most recent information to support their lectures, including recent examples, cases, and other newsworthy items. This data can then be transferred to a word-processing program for editing, printout, and classroom use while the information is still topical.

AIM: Advanced Instructional Modules

The advanced instructional modules have been expanded in this edition to include two new modules—relationship marketing and database marketing. All eleven modules are self-contained units on current "hot" topics in marketing. The objective of each module is to provide instructors with comprehensive lectures beyond what is contained in the textbook. Along with complete lectures, each module contains student learning objectives, outlines of the lectures, transparency masters to support the lectures, and test questions covering the module's content. The modules are available as a separate printed instructor's supplement. The subjects and authors of the modules are listed below.

- "Services Marketing" by Professor Stephen J. Grove, Clemson University
- "Developing a Marketing Plan" by Professor William J. Quain, University of Central Florida
- "Marketing Ethics" by Professor Geoffrey P. Lantos, Stonehill College (Massachusetts)
- "Marketing Math" by Professor John R. Brooks, Jr., Houston Baptist University
- "Careers in Marketing" by Professor Matthew D. Shank, Northern Kentucky University
- "Total Quality Management" by Professor Barbara Dyer, Ohio University
- "International Marketing" by Professor David Andrus, Kansas State University
- "Multicultural Segmentation" by Professor Marye C. Tharp, University of Texas-Austin
- "Strategic Alliances" by Professor John R. Brooks, Jr., Houston Baptist University
- "Relationship Marketing" by Tobin Zikmund and Professor William G. Zikmund, Oklahoma State University
- "Database Marketing" by Tobin Zikmund and Professor William G. Zikmund, Oklahoma State University

Transparency Acetates

Over 100 full-color transparency acetates are provided with the book. Many of the transparencies were selected from the text, and others were prepared to supplement the text by illustrating concepts that do not appear in the text itself.

Student Learning Guide

This extended study guide was written by Ron E. LaFreniere of Shoreline Community College. For each chapter, this comprehensive guide includes a chapter summary, vocabulary-building matching exercises, vocabulary-building fill-in-the-blank exercises, true/false questions, multiple-choice questions, and experiential activities. Students will also benefit from the quizzes that reinforce each chapter objective.

PowerNotes

This unique bound supplement includes copies of the PowerPoint slides provided to instructors, printed at fifty percent of their normal size, on full sheets with space for students to take notes during lectures. Detailed outlines are also provided for each chapter of the book. This supplement can be ordered shrinkwrapped with the text at a significant discount.

INC. Reader

A readings book is available for those professors who wish to supplement text assignments with articles from *INC. Magazine*. This softcover book contains multiple selections that discuss contemporary issues and trends in marketing.

JIAN MarketingBuilder *Express*

The project manual, JIAN MarketingBuilder *Express*, was written by Erika Matulich, Texas Christian University. For instructors who assign a marketing plan to students, the project manual provides hands-on assistance by covering topics such as selecting a client, presenting information, creating a marketing plan outline, preparing a situation analysis, writing strategies, and evaluating performance.

Marketing Trivia Book

This unique instructor's supplement written by William Zikmund includes hundreds of interesting marketing facts and figures that can be used to add a lighter side to lectures and class discussions. Topics are organized according to the textbook's structure to make integration easy.

OUR COLLABORATORS ARE APPRECIATED

Several of our colleagues reviewed various drafts of the manuscript to evaluate scholarly accuracy, writing style, and pedagogy. Many aspects of this book are based on their suggestions. Several professors prepared supplementary teaching materials. We greatly acknowledge their help. They are:

Thomas L. Ainscough
University of Massachussetts-Dartmouth

Joe Ballenger
Stephen F. Austin State University

John Beisel
Pittsburgh State University

William Carner
University of Texas-Austin

Pola Gupta
University of Northern Iowa

Craig A. Kelley
University of Texas-Austin

Ron E. LaFreniere
Shoreline Community College

Lawrence J. Marks
Kent State University

Lee Meadow
Northern Illinois University

Leonard Miller
College of Eastern Utah

Susan A. Peterson
Scottsdale Community College

Kenneth Thompson
University of North Texas

Timothy W. Wright
Lakeland Community College

Our thanks also go to the individuals listed below for their earlier contributions:

Patricia Baconrind
Fort Hays State University

Todd Baker
Salt Lake City Community College

Phil Berger
Weber State College

Michael Bolin
Abilene Christian University

Wendy Bryce
Western Washington University

Barbara Dyer
Ohio University

Linda Gerber
University of Texas-Austin

Jack Gifford
Miami University

Vicki Griffis
University of South Florida

Frederick Hebein
California State University-San Bernardino

Craig Hollingshead
Marshall University

Richard Houser
Southern Methodist University

Tim Johnson
University of Tennessee-Knoxville

William Kilbourne
Milwaukee Area Technical College

Terry Kroeten
Concordia College

Rajshek Lai Javalgi
Cleveland State University

Robert Lambert
Belmont College

Timothy Longfellow
Illinois State University

Michael Mayo
Kent State University

Rusty Mitchell
Inver Hills Community College

John Porter
West Virginia University

Murphy Sewall
University of Connecticut

Frederick Stephenson
University of Georgia

Sue Umashankar
University of Arizona

Charles Vitaska
Metropolitan State College of Denver

ACKNOWLEDGMENTS

Effective Marketing was completed because of the hard work of a team of people at South-Western Publishing Company. Team Leader, John Szilagyi, offered support and encouragement throughout a demanding period of transition. Our editor,

Dries Van Landuyt, was responsible for the strategic focus of this second edition. He was sympathetic to our needs and worked with us to make the important decisions that gave a clear focus to this second edition. On top of this, it was always a pleasure to work with this ardent fan of the Chicago Cubs. We are in his debt. We greatly appreciate his help.

The efforts of Atietie O. Tonwe, developmental editor, show in the close coordination between the book and the supplementary instructor's materials. He managed the details and eliminated many of the problems of working with a large number of people. This is often a thankless task, but not to us. The wisdom and experience of Barbara Fuller Jacobsen, production editor, made a big difference. Her phone conversations always gave veteran counsel, which is greatly appreciated. The efforts of Malvine Litten of LEAP; Jeanne Busemeyer of Hyde Park Publishing Services; designer Craig LaGesse Ramsdell and art director Jennifer Mayhall, both of South-Western College Publishing, resulted in a book that is lucid in exposition and a paragon of state of the art in publishing. Jean Privett, Webmaster, deserves appreciation for creating a cool Web site. Tobin Zikmund helped with the instructor's resource manual.

Preparing the instructional materials to enhance classroom efforts required an army of people. Joe Ballenger of Stephen F. Austin State University prepared the Test Bank. Ron E. LaFreniere of Shoreline Community College prepared the Student Learning Guide. The PowerPoint Presentation package as well as the transparency acetates were prepared by Susan Peterson of Scottsdale Community College. Kevin von Gillern, media technology editor at South-Western, with the valuable assistance of Robin K. Browning, media production editor, worked closely with a team of in-house and outside professionals to ensure that the development and production of the video and other media materials met our high standards.

We would also like to thank the International Thomson Company's sales force for diligently working to ensure that the instructor and student benefit from what we hope will be a long-term relationship.

There are many long-term debts owed as well to our parents, professors, families, and friends. George Zikmund, who spent his entire life in sales and sales management, was responsible for leaving an indelible sense of the practical side of marketing to his son. Philip Cateora, as an assistant professor teaching Principles of Marketing at the University of Colorado, inspired a directionless young man to major in marketing. Phil Campagna later served as a wise marketing mentor at Remington Arms company. Learning to understand marketing, and to be both book smart and street smart, takes many years, and these long-term debts are impossible to repay. We hope this book will pass on insights from parents, teachers, and mentors to others.

William G. Zikmund
Michael F. d'Amico

PART 1

THE NATURE OF MARKETING

Chapter 1

Learning Objectives

After you have studied this chapter, you will be able to:

1. Understand how marketing affects our daily lives.
2. Define marketing and discuss marketing in its broadened sense.
3. Identify the elements of the marketing mix.
4. Understand that marketers must contend with external environmental forces.
5. Explain the marketing concept.
6. Explain total quality management (TQM).
7. Define the societal marketing concept.

A visit to Turner Field, the Atlanta Braves' $242.5 million, state-of-the-art ballpark, feels like a trip back to the future. BellSouth, one of the team's corporate sponsors, describes the stadium as "20th century tradition meets 21st century technology."

The Braves' marketing campaign reflects the charm and nostalgia of baseball's past, but it has a futuristic slogan, "Turner Field: Not just baseball. A baseball theme park."

Sure, baseball purists will love the fact they're closer to the action at Turner Field than at any other major league ballpark. It's only 45 feet from first and third base to the dugouts. On top of that, there's a Braves Museum and Hall of Fame with more than 200 artifacts. Cybernauts will find Turner Field awesome because it's a ballpark that makes them a part of the action. At the stadium, built for the 1996 summer Olympics and converted for baseball use since the Games, there are:

- Interactive games to test fans' hitting and pitching skills, as well as baseball trivia.
- Electronic kiosks with touch screens and data banks filled with scouting reports on 300 past and present Braves, along with the Braves' Internet home page.
- A dozen 27-inch television monitors mounted above the Braves' Clubhouse Store, broadcasting all the other major league games in progress.
- A video ticker-tape screen underneath, spitting out up-to-the-minute scores and stats
- A sophisticated BellSouth communications system, with 4 miles of fiber-optic cable underneath the playing field that will allow for World Series games to be simulcast around the globe, as well as special black boxes placed throughout the stadium to allow for as many as 5,500 cellular phone calls an hour.

Welcome to baseball, circa 1997—and beyond. The idea behind the marketing of Turner Field is that for many fans, it is not enough to just provide nine innings of baseball.

Turner Field's theme-park concept was the brainchild of Braves President Stan Kasten. In the early 1990s, as the Braves grew into one of the best teams in baseball, Kasten increasingly became frustrated while watching fans flock to Atlanta-Fulton County Stadium a few hours before games, with little to do but eat overcooked hotdogs and watch batting practice.

As Kasten saw it, they spent too much time milling on the club-level concourse and too little time spending money.

What if he could find a way for families to make an outing of it, bring the amenities of the city to Hank Aaron Drive, and create a neighborhood feel in a main plaza at the ballpark?

"I wanted to broaden fans' experience at the ballpark and broaden our fan base," Kasten says. "People have no problem spending money when they're getting value. We have one of the highest payrolls in baseball, and I needed to find new ways to sustain our revenues."

Turner Field's main entry plaza opens three hours before games—compared to two hours for the rest of the ballpark—and will stay open about two hours after games. On weekends, there'll be live music.

Everyone's invited—$1 "skyline seats" are available for each game—and that buck gets you anywhere, from the open-air porch at the Chop House restaurant, which specializes in barbecue, bison dogs, Moon Pies, and Tomahawk lager, to the grassy roof at Coke's Sky Field, where fans can keep cool under a mist machine.

Interactive games in Scouts Alley range from $1 to $4, and the chroma-key studios in the East and West Pavilions, where fans can have their picture inserted into a baseball card or a great moment in Braves history, cost $10–$20. The Museum is $2.

And it should come as no suprise that there are seven ATMs located throughout the ballpark.

One of the Braves' key marketing objectives is to help build a new generation of baseball fans. Its new stadium was planned so fans will find something to be loved and learned at every turn. The minute a fan's ticket is torn, that fan becomes part of the happening Turner Field. Turner Field is the result of creative marketing.

Why do people go to baseball games? What role does a winning team play in increasing the number of fans who visit the stadium? How important is the price of a ticket? What do baseball marketers and stadium managers do that motivate consumers to buy a ticket? Are all baseball teams and ball parks thought of as the same? Is being socially responsible an important concern for a marketing organization? The answers to questions like these lie in the field of marketing, the subject of this book.

MARKETING AFFECTS OUR DAILY LIVES

Perhaps you have thought of answers to the questions we asked in the introduction. After all, you have visited shopping centers, compared prices, and evaluated and purchased a wide range of products. If you think about it, we all play a part in the marketing system, so we all know something about marketing. We all recognize brand names like Nike and Nintendo 64 and their corporate and product symbols such as the Nike "Swoosh" and Super Mario. Television advertising has been both an irritant and source of pleasure to us all.

Some aspects of marketing are less widely known than others. Although most of us deal regularly with retailers and sales clerks, we less frequently encounter wholesalers, industrial sales representatives, advertising agents, and export trade companies. Indeed, there are many aspects of marketing that many people have never considered systematically. Most people do not fully understand marketing's place in society or how marketing activities should be managed. To fully understand marketing, we must first know what it is and what it includes.

MARKETING—WHAT IS IT?

As we will see, there are several ways to consider the subject of marketing, so there are a number of ways to define the term itself. Because for most people marketing has a business connotation, it is best to begin by discussing marketing from a business perspective.

Marketing, as the term implies, is focused on the marketplace. A businessperson who is asked the question, "What is marketing?" might answer that marketing is selling, or advertising, or retailing. But notice that these are marketing activities, not definitions of marketing as a whole.

Marketing activities are aimed at bringing buyers and sellers together. At the beach, the thirsty sunbather seeks the Pepsi-stand owner. The owner is, in turn, interested in selling soft drinks to satisfy the customer's thirst. Marketing activities such as locating the stand at the beach and advertising the price on a sign help bring buyer and seller together. This, of course, is a simple example. A more sophisticated situation requires more complex marketing activities.

Suppose you were the marketing vice-president of Bandai America, a company in Cerritos, California, that markets the Mighty Morphin Power Ranger toys. The company's headquarters are in Japan, and most of Bandai's toys are produced in Asia and Mexico. Thus, production—which is an important business activity but not a marketing activity—is not directly under your control. Instead, your marketing activities might be identified as product planning, determining prices, advertising, selling, distributing products to consumers, and servicing the products after sales have been made. And even this extensive list is not complete.

A full understanding of marketing requires recognition of the fact that product development activities and product modifications are planned in response to the public's changing needs and wants. A major marketing activity, then, is paying continuous attention to customers' needs, identifying and interpreting those needs before other steps, including production, are undertaken. Although most marketing activities are intended to direct the flow of goods and services from producer to consumer, the marketing process begins with customer analysis even before the product is manufactured.

Consider again Bandai's Mighty Morphin Power Ranger toys. These action figures are toy replicas of the multi-ethnic characters on television's popular Mighty Morphin Power Rangers show. The program features six teenage characters who,

armed with power derived from prehistoric animals, do battle against evil forces and robot vehicles to save the earth.[1]

Before the Power Rangers, Bandai's main business—creating toys from popular Japanese movie and television characters—had been very successful in Japan but had failed abroad. Popular Japanese toys such as Ultraman, a metallic superhero with laser-beam eyes, were "too foreign" for the U.S. market.[2] In essence, Bandai had failed to mount the marketing efforts needed to adapt its toys to American markets.

However, with the support of Japanese moviemaker Toei Company, California producer Saban Entertainment, and Fox Children's Network, Bandai was able to make the long-running Japanese Jyu Rangah (Power Ranger) television series and toys work for U.S. viewers.

Based on American needs, Bandai made some changes in the Japanese models. It toned down the violence of the television program for the U.S. audience, portraying the off-duty Rangers as normal kids who shoot baskets, mall-hop, and do aerobics when they aren't battling evil space aliens. And it added a moral at the end of each show. Bandai also "Americanized" the toys, making the unmasked characters look "American" and giving more focus to the female part of the team. It did, however, stay faithful to the toys' original technical intricacy (ensuring, for example that the index finger moves to hold a laser gun) because both Japanese and American children like such features.

By discussing the new product idea with Americans before beginning to manufacture the toys, Bandai marketers developed a better understanding of the differing needs of Japanese and American children. Thus, Bandai's American operation does not merely manufacture toys; it interprets the U.S. market's needs. Today, Power Rangers can be found adorning all sorts of products. The distinctive images of Billy the Blue Ranger, Jason the Red Ranger, Trini the Yellow Ranger, Zak the Black Ranger, Kimberly the Pink Ranger, and Tommy the Green Ranger are popping up on underwear, T-shirts, bubble bath bottles, jigsaw puzzles, stickers, coloring books, paper plates, and wastebaskets.

NOT-FOR-PROFIT ORGANIZATIONS ARE MARKETERS TOO

"Perform a death-defying act—eat less saturated fat." The American Heart Association offered this admonition in an advertisement, yet the Heart Association

A broad perspective of marketing includes not-for-profit organizations like the Brookfield Zoo in the Chicago area. Today's zoos recognize that they market both education and entertainment. The customers of not-for-profit organizations consume their services for many different reasons.

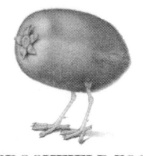

The day should never come when your kids think this is a kiwi bird.

Show them a real one. And thousands of other rare and wonderful things they've never imagined. Spend a day together at Brookfield Zoo. To find out more, call us at 708-485-0263.

BROOKFIELD ZOO
Where Imagination Runs Wild

does not seek to make a profit, nor does it charge a price for most services. Is the American Heart Association engaging in marketing? Are your university, church, and local police department marketers? If we take a broadened perspective of marketing, the answer is unquestionably "Yes."

Exchange Process
The interchange of something of value between two or more parties.

If the concept of marketing is broadened to include not-for-profit organizations, then the primary emphasis of marketing involves an **exchange process** in which two or more parties exchange, or trade, something of value.[3] An economic transfer of goods or services in exchange for a price expressed in monetary terms is the marketing exchange most frequently analyzed. Yet exchanges also occur in a politician's campaign, a zoo's fund-raising drive, or an anti-smoking group's program. When a donation is made to the American Heart Association, to a zoo, to a political campaign, or to an anti-smoking effort, something is given and something is received—even though the "something received" may be intangible, such as a feeling of goodwill or a sense of satisfaction. Whenever activities are planned to bring about an exchange, they may be viewed from a marketing perspective.[4]

A DEFINITION OF MARKETING

The Bandai example illustrates what marketing is like in a well-managed business. The American Heart Association example illustrates that not-for-profit organizations engage in marketing. Thinking about these examples should help you to understand that *effective marketing* consists of a consumer-oriented mix of business activities planned and implemented by a marketer to facilitate exchange.

Marketing
The process of planning and executing the conception, pricing, promotion, and distribution of ideas, goods, and services to create exchanges that will satisfy individual and organizational objectives.

More specifically, **marketing** is the process of planning and executing the conception, pricing, promotion, and distribution of ideas, goods, and services to create exchanges that will satisfy individual and organizational objectives.[5] Effective marketing requires the conception and development of goods, services, or ideas so they may be brought to market and purchased by buyers. Pricing, promotion, and distribution of these goods, services, or ideas facilitates the basic function of bringing marketers (suppliers) together with consumers (buyers). Each party must gain something; revenues satisfy the marketer's objectives, and products satisfy the consumer's needs.[6] Each party contributes something of value because each expects to be satisfied by the exchange. Effective marketing involves initiating and facilitating exchanges between the marketer and the customer so that both parties are satisfied.

KEEPING CUSTOMERS AND BUILDING RELATIONSHIPS

Relationship Marketing
Marketing activities aimed at building long-term relationships with parties, especially customers, that contribute to the company's success.

So far, our discussion of marketing has focused on the idea of creating exchanges. We have talked about attracting customers; but keeping customers is equally important. Marketers want customers for life. Effective marketers work to build long-term relationships with their customers. The term **relationship marketing** or **relationship management** is used to communicate the idea that a major goal of marketing is to build long-term relationships with the parties who contribute to the company's success. Once an exchange is made, effective marketing stresses managing the relationships that will bring about additional exchanges. Effective marketers view making a sale not as the end of a process but as the start of an organization's relationship with a customer. Satisfied customers will return to the company that treated them best if they need to repurchase the same product in the future. If they need a related item, satisfied customers know the first place to look.

In summary, marketers strive to initiate exchanges and build relationships. More simply, you can think about marketing as an activity involved in *getting and keep-*

ing customers. It is the marketer's job to create, interpret, and maintain the relationship between the company and the customer.[7]

WHAT IS A MARKET?

Market
A group of potential customers that may want the product offered and that has the resources, the willingness, and the ability to purchase it.

The root word in the term *marketing* is *market*.[8] A **market** is a group of potential customers for a particular product who are willing and able to spend money or exchange other resources to obtain what they value in the product offering. The term *market* can be somewhat confusing, because it has been used to designate buildings (the Fulton Fish Market), places (the Greater Houston Metropolitan Market), institutions (the stock market), and stores (the supermarket), as well as many other things. But each usage—even the name of a building in which trading is carried out—suggests people or groups with purchasing power who are willing to exchange their resources for something else. It will become clear as you read this book that the nature of the market is a primary concern of marketing decision makers.

THE MARKETING MIX

Marketing Mix
The specific combination of interrelated and interdependent marketing activities in which an organization engages to meet its objectives.

Our definition of marketing indicates that marketing includes many interrelated and interdependent activities meant to encourage exchange. The term **marketing mix** describes the result of management's efforts to creatively combine these activities.[9] Faced with a wide choice of product features, messages, prices, distribution methods, and other marketing variables, the marketing manager must select and combine ingredients to create a marketing mix that will achieve organizational objectives. The marketing mix may have many facets, but its elements can be placed in four basic categories: product, place (distribution), price, and promotion. These are commonly referred to as the **four Ps of marketing** or—because they can be influenced by managers—as the **controllable variables** of marketing.[10] The four Ps constitute a framework that can be used to develop plans for marketing efforts. Preparing a marketing strategy requires considering each major marketing mix element and making decisions about the development of substrategies within each area.

Four Ps of Marketing
The basic elements of the marketing mix: product, place (distribution), price and promotion; also called the controllable variables of marketing because they can be controlled and manipulated by the marketer.

The First Element—Product

Controllable Variables
Marketing mix elements managers use to develop plans for marketing efforts.

The term **product** refers to what the business or nonprofit organization offers to its prospective customers or clients. The offering may be a tangible good, such as a car; a service, such as an airline trip; or an intangible idea, such as the importance of parents reading to their children.

Product
A good, service, or idea that offers a bundle of tangible and intangible attributes to satisfy consumers.

Because customers often expect more from an organization than a simple, tangible product, the task of marketing management is to provide a complete product offering with customer value superior to competitive offerings. A "total product" includes not only the basic good or service but also all the "extras" that go with it. The product of a city bus line may be rides or transportation, for example, but its total product offering should include courteous service, on-time performance, and assistance in finding appropriate bus routes. Binney and Smith, marketers of Crayola Crayons, views itself as not just a crayon company, but as being in the business of providing assorted products that are fun to use and inspire creative self-expression. This effective marketer realizes what a product is and what its customers value.

A product is what is offered to customers. A rock concert by Hootie and the Blowfish is not a tangible good, but it is a product nonetheless. Developing a product, even a concert, requires that it have the characteristics and features the customer wants. Every product, whether it is a good, a service, or an idea, requires marketing. Some organizations are effective marketers who create value for their customers, and others are not.

The product the customer receives in the exchange process is the result of a number of product strategy decisions. Developing and planning a product involves making sure that it has the characteristics and features customers want. Selecting a brand name, designing a package, planning a warranty program, developing appropriate service plans, and other product decisions are also concerned with developing the "right" product.

As we will see, product strategies must take into consideration the other three elements of the marketing mix. Price, distribution, and promotion enhance the value of the product offering.

The Second Element—Place

Place (Distribution)
An element of the marketing mix involving all aspects of getting products to the consumer in the right location at the right time.

Channel of Distribution
Complete sequence of marketing organizations involved in bringing a product from producer to consumer.

Determining how goods get to the customer, how quickly, and in what condition involves **place,** or **distribution,** strategy. Transportation, storage, materials handling, and the like are physical distribution activities. The selection of wholesalers, retailers, and other types of distributors is also a place activity.

A **channel of distribution** is the complete sequence of marketing organizations involved in bringing a product from the producer to the consumer. Its purpose is to make possible transfer of ownership and/or possession of the product. Exhibit 1–1 illustrates a basic channel of distribution consisting of the manufacturer, the wholesaler, the retailer, and the ultimate consumer. Each of these four parties engages in a transaction that involves movement of the physical good and/or a transfer of title (ownership) of that product.

Some definitions are in order:

- *Manufacturer:* An organization that recognizes a consumer need and produces a product from raw materials, component parts, or labor to satisfy that need.
- *Wholesaler:* An organization that serves as an intermediary between manufacturer and retailer to facilitate the transfer of products or the exchange of title to those products, or an organization that sells to manufacturers or institutions

EXHIBIT 1–1
Who is involved in a basic
channel of distribution?

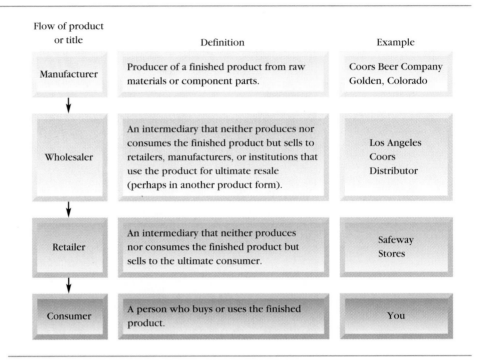

EXHIBIT 1–1
Who is involved in a basic channel of distribution?

Flow of product or title	Definition	Example
Manufacturer	Producer of a finished product from raw materials or component parts.	Coors Beer Company Golden, Colorado
Wholesaler	An intermediary that neither produces nor consumes the finished product but sells to retailers, manufacturers, or institutions that use the product for ultimate resale (perhaps in another product form).	Los Angeles Coors Distributor
Retailer	An intermediary that neither produces nor consumes the finished product but sells to the ultimate consumer.	Safeway Stores
Consumer	A person who buys or uses the finished product.	You

that resell the product (perhaps in another form). Exhibit 1–1 shows the type of wholesaler that sells to retailers. Wholesalers neither produce nor consume the finished product.

- *Retailer:* An organization that sells products it has obtained from a manufacturer or wholesaler to the ultimate consumer. Retailers neither produce nor consume the product.
- *Ultimate consumer:* An individual who buys or uses a product for personal consumption.

The actual path that a product or title takes may be simpler or much more complex than the one illustrated in Exhibit 1–1. For example, a manufacturer may sell directly to an organizational buyer. The term organizational buyer refers to an organization, such as an automobile manufacturer, that purchases a product (such as steel) that it will use to produce another good or service or a product (such as a computer) that it will use in operating its business. Various distribution systems are explained in Chapter 11.

Excluded from the channel of distribution are numerous specialists who perform specific facilitating activities for manufacturers, wholesalers, or retailers. For example, the airline or the railway that transports the product from Boston to Philadelphia and the advertising agency on Madison Avenue that creates the advertising message and selects the appropriate media perform facilitating activities. These specialists, or collaborators, are hired because they can more efficiently or more effectively perform a certain marketing activity for an organization in a basic marketing channel. However, they are not among the organizations included in our definition of channel of distribution.

It is important to realize that distribution mixes vary widely even among companies selling directly competitive products. For example, Avon and Amway use sales representatives selling directly to consumers as their primary source of distribution, while Gillette and Colgate-Palmolive, selling similar goods, deal with many wholesalers and retailers in their distribution systems.

The Third Element—Price

Price
The amount of money or other consideration—that is, something of value—given in exchange for a product.

The amount of money, or sometimes goods or services, given in exchange for something is its **price.** In other words, price is what is exchanged for the product. Just as the customer buys a product with cash, so a company "buys" the customer's cash with the product. In not-for-profit situations, price may be expressed in terms of volunteered time or effort, votes, or donations. Marketers must determine the best price for their products.

According to economists, prices are always "on trial." Pricing strategies and decisions require establishing appropriate prices and carefully monitoring the competitive marketplace. Prices are subject to rapid change, in part because—unlike the other three elements of the marketing mix—price is relatively easy to change. Of course, changes that are poorly thought out can lead to disaster.

The Fourth Element—Promotion

Promotion
The element of the marketing mix that includes all forms of marketing communications.

Marketers need to communicate with consumers. **Promotion** is the means by which marketers "talk to" existing customers and potential buyers. Promotion may convey a message about the organization, a product, or some other element of the marketing mix, such as the new low price being offered during a sale period.

To illustrate the value of promotional efforts in a marketing mix, think about Energizer batteries. You probably can envision one of the television commercials featuring a pink mechanical Energizer bunny in some hilarious situation. Perhaps you recall a tireless drum-playing bunny crossing a desert, Darth Vader's light saber failing because he did not have Energizer batteries, or, in a spoof of the movie *Twister,* a team of bunny spotters attempting to follow the pink bunny's path. However, from the marketer's point of view, the most important thing you probably remember is that the Energizer "keeps going, and going, and going." Energizer's promotion accomplishes its task; it communicates the message about its long-lasting battery to consumers.

Advertising, personal selling, publicity, and sales promotion are all forms of promotion. While each offers unique benefits, all are communications that inform, remind, or persuade. For example, advertising that tells us "Always Coca-Cola" or "Always the real thing" reminds us of our experiences with a familiar cola. An IBM sales representative presents a personal message that informs us how a computer network will help our organization and then attempts to persuade the company to purchase the product. The essence of all promotion is communication aimed at informing, reminding, or persuading potential buyers.

Different firms emphasize different forms of promotional communication. Some firms advertise heavily, for example, while others hardly advertise at all. A firm's particular combination of communication tools is its promotional mix.

MARKETING MIX ELEMENT	COMPANY OR ORGANIZATION	EXAMPLE
Product		
Product development	Procter & Gamble	Olean fat substitute
	Coca-Cola	Citra, a new citrus soft drink
Product modification	Pizza Hut	Higher quality, better tasting pepperoni pizza
	Charles Schwab	Schwab's broker service now accessed via the Internet
	Disney	DisneyWorld's Tomorrowland is remodeled and modernized
Branding	3M Company	Scotch brand cellophane tape
	National Multiple Sclerosis Society	MS—as in "Help fight MS"
Trademark	Michelin	Tire Man
Warranty	Sears	"If any Craftsman hand tool ever fails to give complete satisfaction, Sears will replace it free"
Distribution		
Channel of distribution	Hoover Vacuum	Ships directly to Wal-Mart
	U.S. Postal Service	Sells stamps by mail order, in vending machines, and at post offices
Physical distribution	South-Western College Publishing	Uses FedEx to transport rush orders
Promotion		
Advertising	Australia Office of Tourism	"Australia—come and say g'day"
	The Advertising Council	"Remember, only you can prevent forest fires"
Personal selling	Girl Scouts	Door-to-door cookie sales
	Hitachi	Sales representatives sell fiber optic communication systems to business organizations
Sales promotion	Bloomingdales	Irish heritage celebrated with exhibits of Irish homes and country cottages in 14 stores
	Metropolitan Life Insurance	Gives away "Let's Go Mets" T-shirts at New York Mets baseball games
Publicity	The Spice Girls (band)	Appear on the David Letterman show
Price		
Price strategy	Absolut Country of Sweden Vodka	Expensive
	AT&T System	"True Savings"
	Southwestern Bell	"The Works"—12 best-selling services offered together at a price 45 percent lower than what a customer would pay if the services were ordered separately

EXHIBIT 1–2
Elements of the Marketing
Mix—Creative Examples

The Art of Blending the Elements

A manager selecting a marketing mix may be likened to a chef preparing a meal. Each realizes that there is no "one best way" to mix ingredients. Different combinations may be used, and the result will still be satisfactory. In marketing, as in cooking, there is no standard formula for a successful combination of ingredients. Marketing mixes vary from company to company and from situation to situation.

Exhibit 1–2 provides examples of many marketing mix elements. The vast majority of marketers agree that the blending of these elements is a creative activity. For example, though both firms are successful at selling motorcycles, the marketing mix strategies of Honda and Harley-Davidson differ greatly. Far greater differences can be seen in marketing mixes for different products, such as a Pearl Jam concert and Steinway pianos. The field of marketing encompasses such differing approaches because the design, implementation, and revision of a marketing mix is a creative activity.

EXHIBIT 1–3
Consumer behavior and the
marketing mix are shaped
by environmental forces.

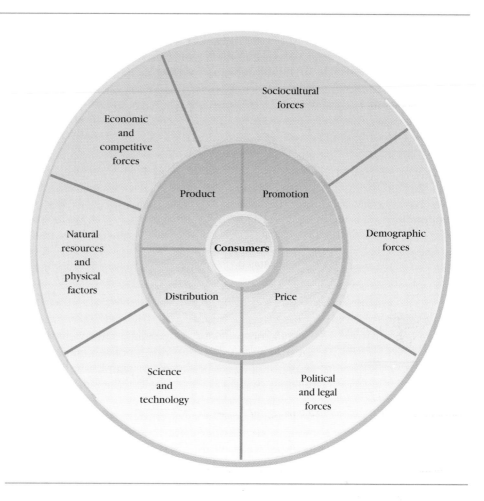

Some experts claim marketing is, or could be, a science. Certain aspects of marketing, such as the gathering of information by marketing researchers, are indeed scientific in nature. The fact remains, however, that there are no pat solutions in marketing. Even frequently encountered problems have unique aspects. This absence of certainty may annoy those who are accustomed to solving math or accounting problems and arriving at one "right" answer. But marketing is different. Its relationship to the ever-changing environment requires that it be creative and dynamic, constantly altering its approaches to the marketplace.[11] Each product's marketing mix must be altered as new problems and environmental changes develop.

THE MARKETING ENVIRONMENT—COPING WITH THE UNCONTROLLABLE

All organizations operate within environments. That is, all organizations, whether for-profit or not-for-profit, are surrounded by, and must contend with, external forces. Except in rare instances, managers cannot govern these external, or environmental, forces; therefore, the forces are called **uncontrollable variables.** Uncontrollable variables affect both consumers' behavior and organizations' development of effective marketing mixes, as shown in Exhibit 1–3.

Uncontrollable Variable
*Force or influence external
to the organization and
beyond its control.*

	FOCUS	MEANS	GOAL	ILLUSTRATIVE COMMENTS
Production Orientation	Manufacturing	Making high-quality products	Produce all that is possible	"You can have any color you want as long as it's black." "Make the best product you can and people will buy it." "I know people want my kind of product."
Sales Orientation	Selling existing products	Aggressive sales and advertising efforts	Maximize sales volume	"You don't like black? I'll throw in a set of glassware!'" "Sell this inventory no matter what it takes." "Who cares what they want? Sell what we've got."
Marketing Orientation	Fulfilling actual and potential customer needs and wants	Consumer orientation, profit orientation, and integrated marketing	Make profits through customer satisfaction	"Find out what consumers want before you make the product." "Maybe people don't want the 'best' product. Find out what they do want." "I'm going to find out what the people want."

EXHIBIT 1–4
Orientations toward
Marketing

Inflation provides an example. Organizations' reactions to high inflation rates are easy to spot in their pricing policies. Similarly, other economic forces—for example, shortages of materials or high land prices—might lead to a decline in home building. Such a decline would reduce the demand for bulldozers, concrete mixers, nails, and even work clothes.

The influence of some environmental forces, for example, social values, may be more subtle. Consider that most of our grandparents thought it a vice for children to eat between meals.[12] Today, most parents allow children to eat a series of mini-meals and snacks throughout the day. These parents differ from past generations in their beliefs about such issues as whether a 5 p.m. cookie can "spoil" their children's dinner. Many view snacks not just as a form of sustenance but as a means to buy peace. Mothers tuck lollipops in their purses to appease restless children in church. Goody bags are served on car trips of more than 30 minutes. Marketing managers must be able to accurately recognize and analyze subtle uncontrollable variables like this, so they can plan marketing mixes compatible with the environment.

Reacting and adapting to competition, economic forces, social trends, government regulations, and the many other environmental influences surrounding an organization is a major part of the marketing manager's job. On the one hand, the manager may try to change or influence the environment in some way. Although environmental forces are, for the most part, beyond the control of any individual organization or group of organizations, an organization may be able to influence some aspect of its environment through political lobbying or some other such activity. The marketing mix, on the other hand, is controlled by the organization. The marketing manager can adjust the marketing mix to reflect changes in the environment. Chapters 3 and 4 discuss environmental forces in depth.

MODERN MARKETERS USE THE MARKETING CONCEPT

An organization's marketing sophistication is often reflected in its goals and in the general principles underlying the way it conducts its activities. Marketing sophistication can be judged in terms of whether an organization is production-oriented, sales-oriented, or marketing-oriented. These orientations also describe the prevailing philosophies of certain historical eras.[13] Exhibit 1–4 illustrates the differences among the orientations.

Production Orientation—"As Long as It's Black"

Production Orientation
Organizational philosophy that emphasizes physical production and technology rather than sales or marketing.

Marketing managers operating with a **production orientation** focus their efforts on physical production and stress developments in technology. Henry Ford's famous description of the Model T—"You can have any color you want as long as it's black"—sums up the prevailing attitude of the production orientation.

Organizations with a production orientation typically do best in a seller's market, in which demand exceeds supply. Manufacturers simply produce a high-quality product and expect to sell it easily. During the 1800s, production-oriented organizations were more common than they are today. Today, few organizations in the United States can survive for long if they maintain a philosophy that gives little thought to marketing.

Sales Orientation—Changing Their Minds

Sales Orientation
Organizational philosophy that emphasizes selling existing products, whether or not they meet consumer needs, often through aggressive sales techniques and advertising.

The philosophy of an organization with a **sales orientation** is to change consumers' minds to fit the product. It is epitomized by the slogan "Push! Push! Sell! Sell!"

Organizations that subscribe to a sales orientation stress aggressive promotional campaigns to "push" their existing products. These organizations concentrate on selling what they make rather than on learning what will best satisfy consumers and then marketing those products. Sales-oriented organizations emphasize short-run increases in sales of existing products rather than long-run profits.

The sales orientation is perhaps most common during economic periods when supply exceeds demand, such as the Great Depression (1929–1933). Companies that maintain a sales orientation while competitors move on to a marketing-oriented philosophy may find themselves in difficulty.

The Marketing Concept—The Foundation of a Marketing Orientation

Marketing Concept
Organizational philosophy that stresses consumer orientation, long-range profitability, and the integration of marketing and other organizational functions. The marketing concept, which focuses on satisfying consumers' wants and needs, is the foundation of a marketing orientation.

The philosophy known as the **marketing concept** is central to all effective marketing thinking, planning, and action.[14] The marketing concept relates marketing to the organization's overall purpose—to survive and prosper by satisfying a clientele—and calls on management and employees to do three things.

1. To be consumer-oriented in all matters, from product development to honoring warranties and service contracts.
2. To stress long-run profitability rather than short-term profits or sales volume.
3. To integrate and coordinate marketing functions and other corporate functions.

Companies that subscribe to this philosophy have a *marketing orientation*.

Consumer Orientation

Consumer Orientation
First aspect of marketing concept; emphasizes the importance of consumers' needs.

Consumer orientation is the first aspect of the marketing concept. The consumer, or customer, should be seen as "the fulcrum, the pivot point about which the business moves in operating for the balanced interests of all concerned."[15] Organizations that have accepted the marketing concept try to create goods and services with the customer's needs in mind. Effective marketers recognize that they must offer products that consumers perceive to have greater value than those offered by competitors.

It follows that the first determination must be what the customer wants. The marketing concept rightly suggests that it is better to find out what the customer wants and offer that product than it is to make a product and then try to sell it. A company that subscribes to the marketing concept, then, must figure out what customers need—sometimes before customers figure it out themselves (like Fletcher Music Centers, described in the accompanying Competitive Strategy feature). In

COMPETITIVE STRATEGY: WHAT WENT RIGHT?

Fletcher Music Centers

Fletcher Music Centers in Clearwater, Florida, understands that the key to winning and keeping customers is to figure out what they need, sometimes before they figure it out themselves. A few years ago Fletcher was struggling along with other retailers in the ailing business of selling organs. "There is no natural market for organs," says Fletcher president John Riley, 42. "No one goes to a mall to shop for one." But after conducting focus groups with its main clientele, senior citizens who retire to Florida, Fletcher realized that what these people wanted wasn't so much a musical instrument as companionship.

Today Fletcher drums up business by positioning a "meet 'em and greet 'em" salesperson at the keyboard within earshot of elderly mall patrons. "What's your favorite song?" he'll ask. And to the peals of Chattanooga Choo Choo, he'll begin his line of patter: "Where ya from? You must have just moved here? Do you play the organ at all? Ever seen one like this? It's specially designed for someone just like you with no musical background. Come on inside and try it out."

Once inside, the prospect is treated to a sales pitch heavy with subtext: Buy from us because we can help enliven your retirement years. Whether the customer springs for the $500 used model or the $47,000 top of the line, free weekly group lessons—good for a lifetime—come with the package. Says Riley: "We've seen a fair share of romances develop at these lessons."

Then there are the small details that show elderly customers how much Fletcher cares about their needs: large type on the keys and oversized knobs that arthritic fingers can easily manipulate. Says Sherman Wantz, 75, who just bought his fourth Fletcher organ: "They know how to treat elderly people without making them feel like children. They appeal to a desire in older people to continue accomplishing things in their lives." Such satisfaction is music to Fletcher's ears.

many instances, the technological innovations of visionaries are the roads to customer need satisfaction.

According to most marketing thinkers, consumer orientation—the satisfaction of customer wants—is the justification for an organization's existence. Progressive companies wisely spend a great deal of time and effort learning what consumers value. Consider the following examples.

The chairman of the board of McDonald's restaurants increased his company's consciousness of the importance of consumer orientation. While visiting one of McDonald's outlets, he encountered a sign ordering customers to "MOVE TO THE NEXT POSITION." He required that such signs be removed from all McDonald's outlets and stated, "It's up to us to move to the customer."

Crisco Savory Seasonings, a new line of flavored vegetable oils patterned after more expensive gourmet cooking oils, is a good example of consumer orientation. The oils come in four all-natural flavors: Roasted Garlic, Hot & Spicy, Classic Herb, and Lemon Butter.[16] The oils fill a consumer need for quick and easy preparation. The flavored oils can be used in a wide range of cooking methods—stir-frying, sauteing, pan-frying, marinades, and dressings—either as an ingredient or a cooking medium. Savory Seasonings can be thought of as a "speed-scratch product" that helps consumers cut down on meal preparation time, yet satisfy their desire for giving meals a homemade touch.

Many organizations that have adopted the marketing concept realize that the organization must see itself not as producing goods and services but as "buying customers, as doing the things that will make people want to do business with it."[17] Unfortunately, not all firms have adopted a consumer orientation as their philosophy. To some extent, the consumerism movement and consumer activists like Ralph Nader represent a protest against firms that have not adopted a consumer orientation but have remained sales- or production-oriented.

Marketing Orientation
Organizational philosophy that focuses on consumers' wants and needs.

Companies that have superior skill in understanding and satisfying customers are said to be market-oriented, or to have a **marketing orientation.**[18] Marketing-oriented organizations embrace the idea of an organization-wide focus on learning customers' needs so they can offer superior *customer value*—that is, so they can satisfy customer needs better than their competitors. These organizations realize that the organization must see itself not as producing goods and services but as buying customers—as doing the things that will make people want to do business with it rather than with its competitors.[19]

Long-Term Profitability

Even though the marketing concept stresses consumer orientation, an organization need not meet every fleeting whim of every customer. Implicit in the marketing concept is the assumption that the organization wishes to continue to exist. Therefore, long-term profits, not only current profitability, are accented in this philosophy. Consumers would prefer that the price of a new Mercedes-Benz be under $15,000. But because the manufacturing and marketing costs associated with such a car far exceed that figure, Daimler-Benz, the Mercedes' manufacturer, and its distributors would soon be out of business if they attempted to satisfy that particular consumer desire. Not only consumer wants but also costs and profits must be taken into consideration in determining a market offering.

The profit-oriented aspect of the marketing concept argues that organizations should not seek sales volume for the sake of volume alone. Sales volume can be profitless, and a firm can actually increase its sales volume while decreasing its profits—for example, when big discounts attract more customers but result in less income. It may be possible to "buy volume" by advertising heavily, cutting prices to levels below cost, or other methods. Few marketing analysts see this as a profitable strategy, however. As most aggressive price cutters ultimately find out, the profit requirements of an operation regulate marketing activities over any but the shortest time periods.

Integrated Marketing Effort

Marketing personnel do not work in a vacuum, isolated from other company activities. The actions of people in such areas as production, credit, and research and development may affect the organization's marketing efforts. Similarly, the work of marketers affects these other departments. Problems are almost certain to evolve unless an integrated, company-wide effort is maintained.

Difficulties may arise when a focus on consumer needs is viewed as the responsibility solely of the enterprise's marketing department. Other functional areas may have goals that conflict with customer satisfaction or long-term profitability. For instance, the engineering department will want long lead times for product design, with simplicity and economy as major design goals. Marketing, however, will want short lead times and more complex designs, including optional features and custom components. Similarly, the finance department may want fixed budgets, strict spending justifications, and short-term prices that always cover costs. The marketing department, on the other hand, may seek flexible budgets, looser spending rationales, and short-term prices that may be less than costs but that allow markets to be quickly developed.

Similar differences in outlook occur between marketing and other functional areas of the organization, and these too may be sources of serious conflicts. Total quality management is a means to resolve such conflicts.

✳ TOTAL QUALITY MANAGEMENT (TQM)

Total Quality Management (TQM)

A management principle that seeks to instill the idea of customer-driven quality throughout the organization and to manage all employees so that there will be continuous improvement in quality.

The management principle known as **total quality management (TQM)** derives from a business philosophy that has much in common with the marketing concept's focus on customer satisfaction, long-run profitability, and integrated activities. Total quality management involves instilling the idea of customer-driven quality throughout the organization and managing all employees so that there will be continuous improvement in quality. Quality is no longer narrowly viewed as something the manufacturing department achieves by inspecting products for compliance with specifications and eliminating defective ones. Total quality management means everyone in all parts of the organization places top priority on continuous improvement of customer-driven quality. As you can see, the marketing concept and total quality management are closely related.

When Ford Motor Company advertises that "Quality is Job 1," the production department must make sure that every automobile that comes off the assembly line will meet customers' quality expectations. The marketing concept encourages integrating the marketing effort throughout the organization. Ford coordinates engineering, production, and marketing by using the principles of total quality management.

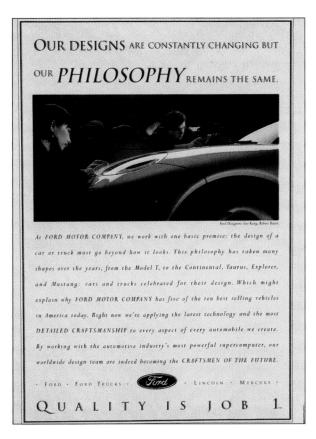

OUR DESIGNS ARE CONSTANTLY CHANGING BUT OUR **PHILOSOPHY** REMAINS THE SAME.

Ford Designers: Sav Kang, Robert Bauer.

At FORD MOTOR COMPANY, we work with one basic premise: the design of a car or truck must go beyond how it looks. This philosophy has taken many shapes over the years, from the Model T, to the Continental, Taurus, Explorer, and Mustang: cars and trucks celebrated for their design. Which might explain why FORD MOTOR COMPANY has five of the ten best selling vehicles in America today. Right now we're applying the latest technology and the most DETAILED CRAFTSMANSHIP to every aspect of every automobile we create. By working with the automotive industry's most powerful supercomputer, our worldwide design team are indeed becoming the CRAFTSMEN OF THE FUTURE.

· FORD · FORD TRUCKS · *Ford* · LINCOLN · MERCURY ·

QUALITY IS JOB 1.

In a company that practices total quality management, manufacturing's orientation toward achieving lowest-cost productivity must be compatible with marketing's commitment to offering high-quality products at an acceptable price. For example, if Ford Motor Company advertises that "Quality is Job 1," the production department must offer assurance that every automobile that comes off the assembly line will meet the quality specifications that consumers expect. The notion that "quality improvement is every employee's job" must be integrated throughout the organization so that marketing and production will be in harmony. But this focus may conflict with manufacturing's desire to increase weekly production by allowing for variations from quality standards. To avoid such problems, the firm must combine its systems for statistical quality controls with improvements in the manufacturing operation so that productivity will increase along with quality.

Total quality management will be explained further throughout this book. In particular, Chapter 2 considers total quality management as a corporate philosophy, and Chapter 10 investigates continuous quality improvement as a product strategy.

✳ MARKETING AND SOCIETY

We must look at marketing not only in terms of its role in individual organizations but also in terms of the important role it plays in society. Before we explain, a note on terminology is in order. When referring to marketing as the aggregate of marketing activities within an economy or as the marketing system within a soci-

FOCUS ON TRENDS

Marriott: Marketing-Oriented and Future-Oriented

You arrive at the hotel, pop your smart card in a doorway slot to introduce yourself, then go straight to your room, assigned earlier by computer. To enter, say your name, and the door magically opens. You hang up your coat, punch in channel 162 on the TV, and hold a videoconference with colleagues. When the meeting ends, you flip to another channel to shop for a gift, then call home on the videophone to see how the family is faring while you are on the road.

Scenes like the one above will be commonplace soon, because companies like the Marriott hotel chain are listening to their customers and hurrying to satisfy their demands with just the right combination of high and low technology.

Hotel guests frequently complain about time spent at check-in. So Marriott launched a new program called "1st 10" that virtually eliminates the front desk. Pertinent information such as time of arrival and credit card number is collected when the reservation is made, thus reducing check-in time from an average three minutes (higher at big convention hotels) to 1fi minutes. Marriott, with the help of smart-card technology, someday hopes to lower it to seconds. To make better use of the room, the chain will also roll out videophones so that guests can visually communicate with clients, colleagues, and family. In-room videoconferencing may arrive at Marriott before the new century does.

Macromarketing
The aggregate of marketing activities in an economy or the marketing system of a society, rather than the marketing activities in a single firm (micromarketing).

ety, some prefer to use the term **macromarketing.** Thus, marketing may be split in the same way as economics is split into microeconomics and macroeconomics. Our preference is simply to use the term *marketing,* making its meaning clear by the context in which it is discussed. Marketing's role in society can be illustrated by the description of marketing (or macromarketing) as "the delivery of a standard of living to society."[20] It may seem a bit grandiose to describe marketing in this way, but some reflection will bear out the truth of that statement.

When we think of the aggregate of all organizations' marketing activities, especially when we include transportation and distribution activity, we can see that the efficiency of the system for moving goods from producers to consumers may substantially affect a society's well-being. Consider marketing activities in undeveloped countries. Transportation, storage, and other facets of distribution are vital undertakings in any society; but in many undeveloped nations, marketing intermediaries, such as wholesalers, are inefficient or even nonexistent. In at least some cases, less-developed countries may be "poor" because their marketing systems are too primitive or inefficient to "deliver" an improved quality of life. To reach a higher level of economic well-being, such a country must improve its macromarketing.

THE SOCIETAL MARKETING CONCEPT

Societal Marketing Concept
Organizational philosophy that stresses the need for marketers to consider the collective needs of society as well as individual consumer's desires and organizational profits.

The recognition that marketing plays an important role in society has led a number of marketing thinkers to refine the marketing concept philosophy. The marketing concept stresses satisfying consumer needs at a profit. The **societal marketing concept,** which can be in perfect harmony with the marketing concept, requires that marketers consider the collective needs of society as well as individual consumers' desires and the organization's need for profits. For example, the Body Shop sells products bearing names like Rhassoul Mud Shampoo, Raspberry Ripple Bathing Bubbles, and Peppermint Foot Lotion. The colorful shampoos, lotions, soaps, and cosmetics all carry the same label: "Against animal testing." The Body Shop develops most of its products from natural ingredients, such as fruit and vegetable oils. The plastic bottles are returnable for a discount, and customers are supplied with biodegradable plastic bags. Part of the Body Shop's profits goes to fund environmental campaigns such as saving Amazon rain forests.

Kids really like animals and Nabisco's Barnum Animal Crackers. Nabisco Endangered Species Collection Crackers and the company's support of the World Wildlife Fund illustrate how the societal marketing concept can be good for business.

These actions reflect a marketing philosophy that recognizes that every consumer, as a member of society, has a long-term need for conservation of the Earth's resources as well as a short-term need for cosmetics. The Body Shop, then, has adopted a societal marketing philosophy that integrates the fulfillment of consumers' short-term preferences with what is best for consumers and society in the long run.

Sometimes, however, conflicts exist between customers' expressed preferences for immediate fulfillment and the organization's interpretation of what is good for society. Many McDonald's customers, especially teenagers, loved McDonald's french fries when they were cooked in beef tallow. However, McDonald's believed that the saturated fat content of some of its menu items, like french fries, was too high. It stopped frying french fries in beef tallow because it felt a responsibility to offer as healthy a menu as possible. Marketers adhering to the societal marketing concept believe that the organization must reconcile any differences between customers' expressed preferences for goods and services and the organization's interpretation of what is good for society. Marketers practicing the societal marketing concept believe that, in the long run, this extension of the marketing concept is good for business. In short, organizations that subscribe to the societal marketing concept attempt to be socially responsible. They consider the ethical consequences of how their actions might affect the interests of others. These topics are discussed more fully in Chapter 2.

WHY STUDY MARKETING?

Why study marketing? One practical reason is that marketing offers many career opportunities, including advertising, sales, product management, retail store management, and others. An appendix, Career Opportunities in Marketing, on the Internet Web page for this book, provides information to help you learn what career options are available and what preparation is required for employment in these fields (Appendix A).

You may not be planning a career in marketing. This does not mean that the study of marketing holds no importance for you. Many students will work for business organizations in some capacity and so will work with employees actively engaged in marketing. The study of marketing principles can help these students become more productive, valuable co-workers. If you are planning to own your own

VIDEO CASE 1-2

 Lawn Care of Wisconsin

It's hard to imagine anything worse befalling a business that promises customers lush, green grass than what happened to Terry Kurth's Lawn Care of Wisconsin, Inc., a few years ago. To Kurth's horror, grass of customers who had signed up for a top-of-the-line lawn-care program was mysteriously turning brown.

Kurth had begun the business, which operates Barefoot Grass Lawn Service franchises in Madison and Little Chute, Wis., nine years earlier, and it grew healthily, thanks to a reputation for quality lawn maintenance. When customers began calling to report brown areas, and competitors got wind of an epidemic of "burned" Barefoot Grass lawns, its reputation and health were in grave danger.

Sleuthing solved the brown grass mystery. The company keeps extensive records—date, employee name, products applied, etc.—on each property worked on. The affected lawns had a common denominator: All had been treated with a granular fertilizer that contained a fungicide. Kurth, who has an agronomy degree, asked a University of Wisconsin plant pathologist to inspect some of the lawns, and he said they looked like they had been damaged by atrazine.

Atrazine? It is designed to eliminate grass in cornfields, corn being one of the few plants it doesn't affect. Kurth called the furtilizer supplier, asking that someone fly in to meet with him. A representative of the supplier arrived the next day; he reported his company had already performed lab tests and had found random atrazine contamination. The supplier stopped making atrazine at the plant where the fertilizer came from, but what of the problem at hand?

The supplier agreed to pay for damage repair, but it was up to Kurth and his managers to do the repairing. They gave affected customers an information sheet—most of them before their grass started turning brown. Then, calling in outside landscaping firms to help get the job done faster, they applied activated charcoal to affected lawns. There were 325 in all, and the process was messy, staining clothing and equipment. However, the atrazine was neutralized, and lawns were renovated. Sometimes reseeding was adequate; sometimes an entire lawn was removed and replaced with sod.

"Though our customers were overwhelmingly impressed," Kurth says, "we felt they deserved an additional thank-you for their understanding." Each received a gift box containing an assortment of meats that could, over a long period, be grilled while they were out on their lawns, reminding them of how Barefoot Grass Lawn Service had taken care of them.

Questions

1. What is the product being marketed by Lawn Care of Wisconsin? What customer needs does this product satisfy?
2. Which of the philosophies/orientations toward marketing discussed in the textbook has Lawn Care of Wisconsin embraced?
3. Why did the company provide their customers with a gift of assortment of meats?

MARKETING MANAGEMENT: STRATEGY AND ETHICAL BEHAVIOR

Chapter 2

Learning Objectives

After you have studied this chapter, you will be able to:

1. Differentiate between marketing strategy and marketing tactics.
2. Discuss the role of marketing planning at the corporate level, at the strategic business unit level, and at the operational level of management.
3. Understand the concept of the organizational mission.
4. Understand the nature of a competitive advantage.
5. Understand the importance of total quality assurance strategies in the total quality management process.
6. Explain the market/product matrix.
7. Identify the stages in the strategic marketing process.
8. Explain what positioning involves.
9. Understand what marketing objectives are and how they relate to the marketing plan.
10. Understand the nature of marketing ethics and socially responsible behavior.

Suppose you were asked to name the biggest rent-a-car company. And, suppose you were told that the answer is not Hertz nor Avis, but Enterprise Rent-a-Car. Would you say you barely heard of them? It's okay; most frequent fliers have never come near an Enterprise office. And that's just fine with Enterprise. While Hertz, Avis, and lots of little companies were cutting one another's throats to win a point or two of the "suits and shorts" market from business and vacation travelers at airports, Enterprise invaded the hinterlands with a completely different strategy—one that relies heavily on doughnuts, ex-college frat house jocks, and your problems with your family car.

In the 39 years since it was founded in St. Louis, Enterprise has blown past everybody in the industry. It now owns more cars (310,000) and operates in more locations (2,800) than Hertz.

Enterprise's approach is astoundingly simple: It aims to provide a spare family car. Say your car has been hit, or has broken down, or is in for routine maintenance. Once upon a time you could have asked the missus to come get you and borrowed her car, but she's commuting to her own job now and testy about having to hitchhike. Lo and behold, even before you have time to kick the repair shop's Coke machine, a well-dressed, intelligent young Enterprise agent materializes with some paperwork and a car for you. Typically, you pay 30 percent less for an Enterprise car than for one from an airport. And your insurance or warranty usually picks up part of the tab. You sign and drive off.

Wow! How simple! So why haven't Hertz and Avis made road kill out of Enterprise? And how come Hertz's CEO, concedes he "missed a big opportunity" by letting Enterprise run away with this business? Because the replacement business is harder than it looks, and because years ago Enterprise developed a bunch of quirky but simple hiring and promotion practices that have produced a culture perfectly suited to its part of the industry.

Instead of massing 10,000 cars at a few dozen airports, Enterprise sets up inexpensive rental offices just about everywhere. As soon as one branch grows to about 150 cars, the company opens another a few miles away. Once a new office opens, employees fan out to develop chummy relationships with the service managers of every good-size auto dealership and body shop in the area. When your car is being towed, you're in no mood to figure out which local rent-a-car company to use. Enterprise knows that the recommendations of the garage service managers will carry enormous weight, so it has turned courting them into an art form. On most Wednesdays all across the country, Enterprise employees bring pizza and doughnuts to workers at the garages.

Enterprise is also betting that you, stuck, won't be in the mood to quibble about prices. Yes, it has cars for $16 a day—the amount many insurance policies pay for replacement rentals. But those are often tiny GEO Metros; about 90 percent of people pay more for a bigger car. Enterprise buys cars from a wide variety of American, Japanese, and European automakers. To reduce costs, it keeps its cars on the road up to six months longer than Hertz and Avis do. If your insurance covers a replacement rental, you can get a

Chrysler Neon in New Jersey for $21 a day from Enterprise, and a BMW 325 for $49.

Enterprise doesn't just wait for your car to break down to capture you as a customer. A huge chunk of its recent growth has come as auto dealers increasingly offer customers a free or cheap replacement while their cars are in the shop for routine maintenance. Enterprise has agreements with many dealers to provide a replacement for every car brought in for service. At major accounts, the company sets up an office on the premises, staffs it for several hours a day, and keeps cars parked outside so customers don't have to travel back to the Enterprise office to fill out paperwork.

Unusual hiring and promotion practices drive much of the company's hustle and rapid growth. Virtually every Enterprise employee is a college graduate; in a unionized, labor-intensive industry that seeks to keep wages low, that's unusual enough. But there's more. Hang around Enterprise people long enough, and you'll notice that despite their informal exteriors, most seem to have the competitive, aggressive air of an ex-athlete. It's no accident. Brainy introverts need not apply, says the company's chief operating officer. "We hire from the half of the college class that makes the upper half possible," he adds wryly. "We want athletes, fraternity types—especially fraternity presidents and social directors. People people."

The social directors make good salespeople, able to chat up service managers and calm down someone who has just been in a car wreck.

Enterprise built itself around a marketing strategy that differentiated it from its competitors. As this example illustrates, developing a marketing strategy is crucial to an organization's success. Marketing strategy is the subject of this chapter.

The chapter begins by discussing the activities of marketing managers and defining marketing strategy. Next, it discusses planning at various levels in the organization, giving special attention to the organizational mission and to planning for marketing at the strategic business unit level. It then addresses each stage in the strategic marketing process. A discussion of execution and control follows the material on marketing planning. Finally, the chapter introduces the topic of ethics and social responsibility in marketing, an important and pervasive topic that will be discussed throughout the textbook.

MARKETING MANAGEMENT

Organizations, whether charities, universities, or giant businesses like the Microsoft Corporation, must have managers. Managers develop rules, principles, and ways of thinking and acting to further the organization's goals and objectives. Corporate managers, or top managers, are the executives responsible for the entire organization. Every aspect of the organization's operations—production, finance, personnel, and marketing—depends on these executives' plans for the organization's long-term future.

Marketing managers work at the middle level of the organization. They are responsible for managing marketing efforts in the organization's business units and major departments. **Marketing management** is the process of planning, executing, and controlling marketing activities to attain marketing goals and objectives effectively and efficiently. Successful marketing rarely, if ever, occurs without good management.

Of course, the time, effort, and resources associated with introducing a new flavor of dental floss, for example, differ from the time, effort, and resources associated with introducing a new product, such as PowerDialer (a telephone redi-

Marketing Management
The process of planning, executing, and controlling marketing activities to attain marketing goals and objectives effectively and efficiently.

Parmalat is the world's largest producer of milk. In developing countries like Brazil and China, its strategy has the basic objective of convincing mothers that children need dairy products on a regular basis. The advertisements shown here show children dressed as animals with the headline "Because we are Mammals." Choosing whether children are portrayed as pandas, lambs, or other animals are tactical decisions.

aling device that continuously retries a number until it encounters either a ring-back or speech). Yet in both cases success depends on planning, execution, and control. These are the basic functions of management.

Because marketing managers must deal with change, the marketing management process is a continuous one: Planning, execution, and control are ongoing and repetitive activities.[1] A major aspect of dealing with change is the development of appropriate marketing strategies.

WHAT IS A MARKETING STRATEGY?

Marketers, like admirals and generals, must develop strategies to help them attain their objectives. The military planner's endeavors can end more disastrously than those of the businessperson. However the loss of the means to make a living, the closing of a factory, or the "defeat" of a product in the marketplace are serious matters indeed to the investors, executives, and workers involved in an unsuccessful business venture. Many executives have noticed similarities between military strategy and marketing strategy. Therefore, a number of military terms—strategy, tactics, campaigns, maneuvers, and so on—have been adopted by business-people to describe their activities.

One such term, strategy, has been defined in many different ways. For our purposes, a **marketing strategy** is a plan identifying what basic goals and objectives will be pursued and how they will be achieved in the time available. A strategy entails commitment to certain courses of action and allocation of the resources necessary to achieve the identified goals.

Marketing Strategy
A plan identifying what marketing goals and objectives will be pursued and how they will be achieved in the time available.

The armed forces describe *strategy* as what generals do and *tactics* as what lower officers, such as captains and lieutenants, do. This description rightly suggests that tactics are less comprehensive in scope than strategies. **Tactics** are specific actions intended to implement strategy. Therefore, tactics are most closely associated with the execution of plans.

Tactics
Specific actions intended to implement strategies.

McDonald's basic strategy, for example, is to have clean family-style restaurants that offer friendly service, high-quality food, and good value. Offering Happy Meals for children at reasonable prices is a tactic used to implement this strategy. It encourages consumers to bring their families to McDonald's because high-quality children's meals are a good value there. Providing pamphlets explaining that "your fork" is the only thing that is not nutritious in a Chunky Chicken Salad is another tactic that helps convey the idea that McDonald's offers high-quality foods. McDonald's uses many tactics like these to implement its "quality, service, cleanliness, and value" strategy.

✳ PLANNING—DESIGNING A FRAMEWORK FOR THE FUTURE

Planning
The process of envisioning the future, establishing goals and objectives, and designing organizational and marketing goals to be implemented in the future.

Recall that the basic functions of management are planning, execution, and control. In this part of the chapter, we focus on planning.

Planning is the process of envisioning the future, establishing goals and objectives, and designing organizational and marketing strategies and tactics to be implemented in the future. In planning, managers analyze perceived opportunities and select those courses of action that will help achieve the organization's objectives in the most efficient manner. Managers plan what activities will be implemented, when the activities will be performed, and who will be responsible for them.

The purpose of planning is to go beyond diagnosis of the present and attempt to predict the future by devising ways to adjust to an ever-changing environment before problems develop. Planning helps an organization to shape its own destiny by anticipating changes in the marketplace rather than merely reacting to them. For example, an organization that anticipates changes in the public's and legislators' attitudes toward the need for recyclable packaging may plan to convert to environmentally "friendly" packaging before laws require this action. Planning allows the manager to follow the maxim "Act! Don't react." In short, planning involves deciding in advance. Planning, including marketing planning, goes on at every level of management in the organization. For the sake of simplicity, we will say that there are three such levels: top management, middle management, and operational or first-line management. These levels are shown in Exhibit 2–1.

Strategic Planning
Long-term planning dealing with the organization's primary goals and objectives, carried out primarily by top management. Also called corporate strategic planning.

At the top level, managers engage in **strategic planning**—long-term planning dealing with an organization's primary goals and objectives. As we move from top

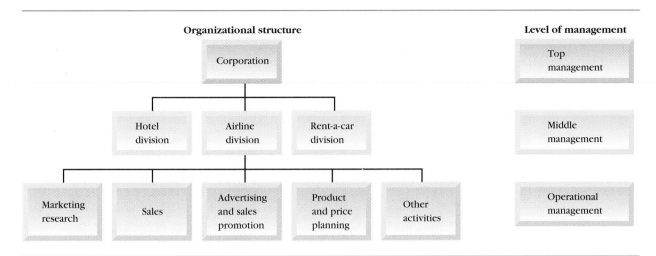

Organizational structure

Corporation

Hotel division

Airline division

Rent-a-car division

Marketing research

Sales

Advertising and sales promotion

Product and price planning

Other activities

Level of management

Top management

Middle management

Operational management

EXHIBIT 2–1
An Example of Three Levels of Management

management to middle management, determining long-term goals and planning strategies for the entire organization becomes a less time-consuming part of the job, while planning strategy and tactics for business units (such as divisions) and for specific products becomes a more important job dimension. Middle managers are responsible for planning the marketing mix strategy and coordinating the activities of operational managers. At the level of operational management, **operational planning,** which concerns day-to-day functional activities, becomes dominant. Thus, while a vice-president of marketing (a top-level manager) spends most of his or her time planning new products and strategy modifications for entire product lines, a sales manager (an operational manager) concentrates on supervising and motivating the sales force. Exhibit 2–2 (on page 32) shows how the focus of planning and basic strategic and tactical questions vary among the three major levels of the organization.

A manager's level in the organization dictates the focus of planning.

Operational Planning
Planning that focuses on day-to-day functional activities, such as supervision of the sales force.

 TOP MANAGEMENT MAKES CORPORATE STRATEGIC PLANS

As noted, corporate strategic planning is the responsibility of top management and pertains to long-term planning for the organization as a whole. It is the process of determining the organization's primary goals and developing a comprehensive organizational framework for accomplishing them. Answering questions such as "What business are we in?" and "How do we organize our business?" determines the organization's strategies for long-term growth. All organizations, not just corporations, should engage in corporate strategic planning to determine the organization's direction.

Strategic corporate goals are broad statements about what the organization wants to accomplish in its long-term future. The organization's mission statement identifies its primary strategic corporate goal.

Strategic Corporate Goals
Broad organizational goals related to the long-term future. The organization's primary strategic corporate goal is identified in its organizational mission statement.

Defining the Organizational Mission

Top managers decide the organizational or corporate mission. It is a strategic decision that influences all other marketing strategies. An **organizational mission** is a statement of company purpose. It explains why the organization exists and what it hopes to accomplish. It provides direction for the entire organization.

Organizational Mission
A statement of company purpose. It explains why the organization exists and what it hopes to accomplish.

EXHIBIT 2–2
A manager's level in the organization dictates the focus of planning.

Level of management	Focus of planning	Basic marketing questions
Top management	Corporate plans	What is our organizational mission? How do we organize our business?
Middle management	Strategic business unit (e.g., division or product)	What is our competitive strategy for growth? What is our competitive advantage?
Operational management	Operational plans for tactical execution	How can we best support the competitive strategy? What are our schedules for weekly operations?

For example, when the Ford Motor Company was founded in 1903, Henry Ford had a clear understanding that cars need not be only for the rich—that the average American family needed economical transportation in the form of a low-priced car. Ford also had the insight to know that he could use product standardization and assembly-line technology to accomplish this mission. Modern marketers should strive to have an equally clear sense of purpose for each aspect of the business.

The mission statement of The Limited, Inc., provides an example of a comprehensive mission statement:

Our commitment is to offer the best customer shopping experience, the best merchandise, the best merchandise presentation, the best customer service, the best value, the best everything that a customer sees and experiences, and to treat all the women, men and children who enter our stores with the same respect and dignity we accord to our family and friends. To achieve this goal:

We must maintain a restless, bold and daring business spirit noted for innovation and cutting-edge style;

We must be tough-minded, disciplined, demanding, self-critical and yet supportive of each other, our team, and our suppliers;

We must seek and retain Associates with an unquestioned reputation for integrity and respect for all people: customers, suppliers, shareholders and fellow Associates;

We must continue to make risk acceptable by rewarding the risk-taker who succeeds—that goes without saying—and not penalizing the one who fails;

We must utilize our capacity to set qualitative and quantitative standards for our industry.

We are determined to surpass all standards for excellence in retailing by thinking—and thinking small. By staying close to our customer and remaining agile, we will continue as a major force in retailing.[2]

Product success, industry leadership, and even the organization's survival depend on satisfying the consumer. When a company defines the broad nature of its

The Limited has a well-articulated organizational mission that provides direction for the entire organization. Its statement of company purpose explains why the organization exists and what it hopes to accomplish.

business, it must take a consumer-oriented perspective. It must avoid shortsighted, narrow-minded thinking that will lead it to define its purpose from a product/production orientation rather than from a consumer orientation. Thus, railroads should define their industry as transportation-oriented rather than railroad-oriented. People who make movies should see themselves as being in the entertainment business rather than the movie business. A firm's failure to define its purpose from a broad consumer orientation is referred to as **marketing myopia.**[3]

Marketing Myopia
Failure to define organizational purpose from a broad consumer orientation.

Establishing Strategic Business Units

The organizational mission and other strategic corporate goals, once established, provide a framework for determining what organizational structure is most appropriate to the organization's marketing efforts. For a company that markets only one product or service, the structure will be relatively simple. However, many organizations—like General Electric—operate a diverse set of businesses. General Electric's businesses range from the marketing of light bulbs to the marketing of aircraft engines. In medium-sized and large organizations that engage in diverse businesses, establishing strategic business units is another aspect of corporate-level planning.

Strategic Business Unit (SBU)
A distinct unit, such as a company, division, department, or product line, of the overall parent organization with a specific marketing focus and a manager who has the authority and responsibility for managing all unit functions.

A **strategic business unit (SBU)** is a distinct unit, such as a company, division, department, or product line, of the overall parent organization with a specific market focus and a manager who has the authority and responsibility for managing all unit functions. For example, a bank may have a real estate division, a commercial division, and a trust division, along with its retail division, which offers traditional banking services for the general public.

The logic that underlies the concept of the strategic business unit is best understood through example. Consider these statements: Procter & Gamble does not compete against Kimberly-Clark, and Dow Chemical does not compete against Union Carbide. Competition is not carried on at the corporate level but at the individual business-unit level. Thus, Procter & Gamble's Pampers compete against

Disney says it is in the business of "Using our imagination to bring happiness to millions." It understands the broad nature of its business goes beyond animation and the movies. It entertains people in movie theaters, in theme parks, and in their homes. Disney, as a marketer of happiness, is not marketing myopic.

Luvs disposable diapers, a Kimberly-Clark product. Dow might compete with Union Carbide for certain types of chemical customers but not others. Acknowledgment of this simple reality has led top managers to identify separate manageable units or autonomous profit centers within their organizations so that performance can be monitored at the level of individual business activities rather than at the overall corporate level only.

The idea is that each SBU operates as a "company within a company." The SBU is organized around a cluster of organizational offerings that share some common element, such as an industry, customer needs, target market, or technology. It has control over its own marketing strategy, and its sales revenues may be distinguished from those of other SBUs in the organization. It can thus be evaluated individually and its performance measured against that of specific external competitors.

MIDDLE MANAGERS PLAN STRATEGIES FOR SBUs

Top managers are responsible for the entire organization. They assign to middle managers the responsibility for planning business-unit strategy and marketing strategy for individual products. Corporate-level planning does, however, strongly influence the marketing planning activities of middle managers. Corporate-level strategies outline broad principles that are expected to flow down through the organization. Exhibit 2–3 depicts how corporate strategies influence marketing strategies at the business-unit level and the operational level.

Business-Unit Strategies for Competitive Advantage

Competitive Advantage
Superiority to or favorable difference from competitors along some dimension important to the market.

One of the most common business-unit goals is to establish and maintain a **competitive advantage**—to be superior or to be favorably different from competitors in a way that is important to the market. Illustrations of two basic marketing strategies (there are many others) should help you understand what a business-level strategy is and how it can establish a competitive advantage.

EXHIBIT 2–3
Corporate strategy filters
down to other levels.

Strategic corporate planning
- Define organization mission
- Establish strategic business units
- Anticipate change

Marketing planning for SBU's
- Set marketing objectives
- Develop marketing strategy
- Formalize marketing plan

Operational marketing plans

Price Leadership Strategy
Strategy in which the marketer emphasizes underpricing all competitors.

A **price leadership strategy,** or low-cost/low-price strategy, emphasizes producing a standardized product at a very low per-unit cost and underpricing all competitors.[4] For example, Papermate and Parker ballpoint pens were market leaders for many years. Then, Bic pens, capitalizing on cheaper resources in foreign countries, produced a product comparable in quality to its competitors and marketed it at a rock-bottom price.

This strategy works equally well with services. Southwest Airlines, unlike most other domestic airlines, does not have long-distance flights. It links city pairs with frequent flights, almost like a shuttle airline. It does not offer preflight seat selection, hot meals, nor baggage transfer to other airlines. Its low-cost/low-price strategy has been so successful that Western Pacific Airlines has developed a similar regional service to compete in the western United States.

Differentiation Strategy
Strategy in which the marketer offers a product that is unique in the industry, provides a distinct advantage, or is set apart from competitors' brands in some way other than price.

A **differentiation strategy** emphasizes offering a product that is unique in the industry, provides a distinct advantage, or is set apart from competitors' brands in some way other than price. The product's styling, a distinctive product feature, compelling advertising, faster delivery, or some other aspect of the marketing mix is planned to produce the perception that the product is unique—that it offers consumers value that is different from or better than what competitors offer. Consider, for example, a strategy to enter the market for scouring pads. Steel wool soap pads had been on the market for almost 80 years when 3M introduced Scotch-Brite Never Rust Wool Soap Pads made entirely of recycled beverage bottles. The pads contain phosphorus-free soap and are biodegradable. Scotch-Brite's tremendous success was a result of 3M's differentiation strategy to market soap pads which look and feel like competitive brands but do not rust or splinter.

Total Quality Management to Achieve Differentiation

In working to differentiate their products or services, many organizations use a quality assurance strategy, which makes market-driven quality a top priority. This strategy is implemented and adjusted through total quality management.

Establishing and maintaining a competitive advantage can be achieved in many ways. Western Pacific Airlines links pairs of cities through its Colorado Springs hub almost like a shuttle airline. It does not offer preflight seat selection, paper tickets, hot meals, or baggage transfer to other airlines, but it does offer low prices. Its low-cost/low-price strategy provides customer value because its service quality meets flyers' expectations.

For many years, U.S. corporations did not keep pace with the product quality strategies of a number of overseas competitors. For example, Xerox Corporation lost a substantial portion of its market share to Ricoh, Canon, and other Japanese copier manufacturers because the Japanese products offered not only lower prices but higher quality as well. Xerox scrutinized its product and its production strategies and discovered it was destroying itself with sloppiness and inefficiency. The conclusion of an internal audit was that Xerox (like many other U.S. businesses) had lost sight of "an axiom as old as business itself . . . focusing on quality that meets the customer's requirements."[5]

Total Quality Management
A differentiation strategy that promises the customer will be satisfied with product quality.

Today, Xerox and many other organizations have implemented **total quality management** programs. These programs are not the exclusive domain of marketing managers, because production quality control and other business activities are integral aspects of their implementation. However, they are market-focused in that in organizations driven by the marketing concept, the definition of quality comes from the consumer. The philosophy underlying the programs is epitomized in a statement by a Burger King executive: "The customer is the vital key to our success. We are now looking at our business through the customers' eyes and measuring our performance against their expectations, not ours."[6] A company that employs such a program must evaluate quality through the eyes of the customer. Every aspect of the business must focus on quality—for example, the company's performance appraisal system may evaluate employees in terms of the service they provide to customers. Further, the organization may establish cross-functional teams that strive for continuous improvement.

Cross-functional Teams
Individuals from various organizational departments such as engineering, production, finance, and marketing working together and sharing a common purpose.

Cross-functional teams are composed of individuals from various organizational departments such as engineering, production, finance, and marketing who share a common purpose. Current management thinking suggests that cross-functional teams help organizations focus on core business processes, such as customer service or new product development. Working in teams reduces the tendency for

COMPETITIVE STRATEGY: WHAT WENT WRONG?

Trouble-Shooter Barbie

Going into the 1995 holiday shopping season there was no must-have toy hit. Bad news for some, perhaps, but not for Mattel's Barbie. She was poised for another year of steady sales—until Thanksgiving weekend. That's when Mattel realized its Happy Holidays Barbie, a $30 collector's special bedecked in sequins and white lace, was selling out, with no way to boost production in time for Christmas.

Mattel needed lightning-quick thinking to keep pace with unprecedented consumer demand and maximize sell-through for the rest of the season. In just 10 short days, a marketing team devised and executed Mattel's first-ever certificate redemption program. Consumers who purchased the certificates and mailed them back to Mattel by a certain date were guaranteed receipt of a doll within four months.

Among the program components: a "suitable for framing" portrait of Happy Holidays Barbie signed by the doll's designer and Mattel CEO Jill Barad; a certificate for gift-givers with a cover letter from Barad. When retailers depleted their supply of dolls, they restocked shelves with certificates. Sales of redemption certificates exceeded expectations by a whopping 237 percent.

employees to focus single-mindedly on an isolated functional activity. The use of cross-functional teams to improve product quality and increase customer value is a major trend in business today.

In some situations, total quality managers determine that a marketing strategy's focus must be aimed at reducing consumption or discouraging buying. **Demarketing** is the name of a strategy designed intentionally to discourage all or some customers from buying or consuming the product on either a temporary or a permanent basis. Suppose, for example, that a manufacturing firm finds that it has a temporary shortage of finished goods available because of a scarcity of raw materials. To reduce customer demand, the firm might use demarketing strategies, such as reducing advertising, increasing prices, instituting a rationing system, or some other, more original, activity.

Demarketing
Marketing strategy designed to discourage all or some customers from buying or consuming a product on either a temporary or permanent basis.

Is demarketing different from the first-come, first-served, take-it-or-leave-it attitude a marketer of goods in short supply might take? Yes. Demarketing stresses a key aspect of marketing—consumer satisfaction. It emphasizes maintaining high quality and trying to keep customers over the long run rather than antagonizing them with a take-it-or-leave-it attitude. This is why demarketing fits into an overall total quality management strategy.

Situations that warrant demarketing strategies are encountered often. Kellogg's introduction of Kellogg's Rice Krispies Treats Cereal was flawed by a great underestimation of demand. Out-of-stock conditions quickly developed in retail outlets. Kellogg's newspaper ads read "We're sorry if you can't find our new cereal. But we're sure you'll find it worth the wait." Kellogg's was stressing that the shortages were temporary. In some situations, excess demand or overcrowding is unalterable, and demarketing is a long-lived strategy. In Washington, D.C., the Metro subway system engaged in selective demarketing by raising rates during morning and evening rush hours. The fare increase discourages tourists, shoppers, and others who could use the subway in non-rush hours from traveling during peak periods.

Increased product usage may be an objective for a market penetration strategy. Morton Salt uses a market penetration strategy to encourage existing users to increase usage of its product.

Market/Product Matrix
A matrix containing the four possible combinations of old and new products with old and new markets. The purpose of the matrix is to broadly categorize alternative opportunities in terms of basic strategies for growth.

Market Penetration
The strategy by which sales of an established product grow because of increased use of the product in existing markets.

Market Development
The strategy by which an organization attempts to draw new customers to an existing product, most commonly by introducing the product in a new geographical area.

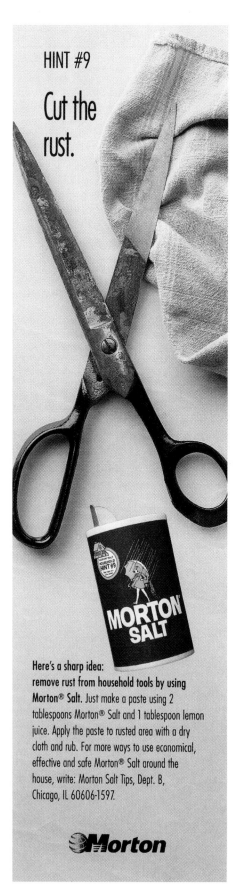

HINT #9

Cut the rust.

Here's a sharp idea: remove rust from household tools by using Morton® Salt. Just make a paste using 2 tablespoons Morton® Salt and 1 tablespoon lemon juice. Apply the paste to rusted area with a dry cloth and rub. For more ways to use economical, effective and safe Morton® Salt around the house, write: Morton Salt Tips, Dept. B, Chicago, IL 60606-1597.

Morton

MORTON SALT

Planning Business-Unit Growth Strategies

Managers responsible for strategic business units must also plan for business growth. The **market/product matrix,** which broadly categorizes alternative opportunities in terms of basic strategies for growth, serves as a planning tool. Exhibit 2–4 shows how the matrix cross-classifies market opportunities and product opportunities.

Market-Related Strategies for Existing Products

Two major strategy paths are available to an organization seeking to expand sales of existing products. One is **market penetration.** Here, sales of an established product grow because of increased use of the product in existing markets. Arm & Hammer has, with considerable success, convinced customers to purchase more baking soda by showing them new and creative ways to use the product. One suggestion, offered in advertisements and on packages, was to put an opened box of baking soda in the refrigerator to reduce food odors. Lest consumers feel that a box of baking soda must simply be thrown away once it has remained in the refrigerator for a time, the company suggested that the product then be poured down the kitchen drain to freshen the drain. This gave baking soda two new uses and gave buyers a way to dispose of the product in a useful manner. Similarly, cereal companies frequently demonstrate how cereals like Cheerios and Rice Krispies can be used to make cookies and snack foods. Consumers are encouraged to try, for example, "Cooking with Kellogg's."

A somewhat different strategy is **market development,** in which the organization attempts to draw new customers to an existing product. The most common market development strategy is to enter a new geographical area. The recent changes in Eastern Europe present a market development opportunity for many multinational organizations. The markets of Poland, Slovakia, the

Strategic Gap
The difference between where the organization wants to be and where it is.

assess its present situation. Chances are good that the desired position differs somewhat from the actual position. The difference between the two can be called the **strategic gap.** Planning occurs so that the gap may be closed, so the organization can move from a situation it doesn't want to one that it does want.

In evaluating opportunities, marketers must consider competitors' strengths and weaknesses. An assessment of marketing opportunities typically identifies competitors, reviews their marketing programs, weighs their relative capabilities and resources, and evaluates how well they are serving their customers. Although it is important to carefully examine what competitors have done in the past, it is equally important to anticipate what strategies and tactics they might implement in the future. Furthermore, marketing managers should consider the possible emergence of new competitors, perhaps foreign competitors, and their potential impact on the company's marketing opportunities.

FOCUS ON GLOBAL COMPETITION

General Electric Lighting

Effective managers analyze threatening situations and foresee problems that may result. They then adapt their strategies in hopes of turning threats into opportunities. An example comes from General Electric Lighting.

General Electric Lighting is an ancient business, begun in 1878. It is headquartered in Cleveland, Ohio, on a leafy campus of brick Georgian buildings separated by placid lawns. Like sin into Eden, the world burst through the gates in 1983, when traditional rival Westinghouse sold its lamp operations to Phillips Electronics of Holland. To John Opie, GE Lighting's chief, the memory is so vivid that he describes it in the present tense: "Suddenly we have bigger, stronger competition. They're coming to our market, but we're not in theirs. So we're on the defensive."

But it was not long until GE turned this threat into an opportunity. GE's 1990 acquisition of Hungarian lighting company Tungsram was the first big move by a Western company in Eastern Europe. Now, after buying Thorn EMI in Britain in 1991, GE has 18 percent of Europe's lighting market and is moving into Asia via a joint venture with Hitachi. As recently as 1988, GE Lighting got less than 20 percent of its sales from outside the United States. Today, more than 40 percent of sales come from abroad; by 1996, more than half will. In a few short years, General Electric Lighting's world changed utterly.

Stage 2: Analyzing Market Segments and Selecting Target Markets

Consumer Market
Market consisting of buyers who use the product to satisfy personal or household needs.

Organizational Market (Business Market)
Market consisting of buyers who use the product to help operate a business or for resale.

As discussed in Chapter 1, a market can be a group of organizations or individuals that are potential customers for the product offered for sale. There are many types of markets. The most fundamental distinction among them is drawn in terms of the buyer's use of the good or service being purchased. If the buyer is an individual who will use a product to satisfy personal or household needs, the good or service is a *consumer* product sold in the **consumer market.** When a product is purchased by an organization to help operate its business (as when wood is purchased by a furniture manufacturer) or to be resold (as when a facsimile machine is purchased by a wholesaler), that organization is buying an *organizational,* or *business,* product in the **organizational market,** or **business market.**

Market Segment
A portion of a larger market, identified according to some shared characteristic or characteristics. Dividing a heterogeneous market into segments is market segmentation.

A **market segment** is a portion of a larger market. Thus, African-Americans constitute a segment of the total U.S. market. African-Americans between the ages of 30 and 40 years are a smaller, more narrowly defined segment. Female African-Americans between the ages of 30 and 40 who use electric rather than gas stoves are yet a smaller market segment. Market segments can be defined in terms of any number of variables from race or sex to air travel behavior. **Market segmentation** is the dividing of a heterogeneous mass market into a number of segments. The segments seen by analysts as being good potential customers for the organization's product are likely to become the organization's **target markets**—that is, the specific groups toward which the organization aims its marketing plan. For example, Revlon's ColorStay long-wearing lipstick was targeted at 18–24-year-old females and not older women. Virtually all marketers agree that market segmentation is extremely useful and valuable. Identifying and choosing targets, rather than trying to reach everybody, allows the marketer to tailor marketing mixes to a group's specific needs. As the old adage states, "You can't be all things to all people." A firm selects a target market because it believes it will have a competitive advantage in that particular segment.

Target Market
A specific market segment toward which an organization aims its marketing plan.

Market segmentation is such an important topic that it will be treated more fully in Chapter 8. Suffice it to say here that identifying and evaluating marketing opportunities (the first stage in our six-stage strategic marketing process) must be followed by a decision about where marketing efforts will be directed—that is, by market segmentation and targeting—before the next step, planning a market position and developing the marketing mix, can be undertaken.

Stage 3: Planning a Market Position and Developing a Marketing Mix Strategy

Planning a market position and constructing a marketing mix comprise the third step in the strategic marketing process. After a target market has been selected, marketing managers position the brand in that market and then develop a marketing mix to accomplish the positioning objective.

Positioning
Planning the market position the company wishes to occupy. Positioning strategy is the basis for marketing mix decisions.

Positioning relates to the way consumers think about all the competitors in a market. A **market position,** or **competitive position,** represents the way consumers perceive a brand relative to its competition. Each brand appealing to a given market segment has a position in relation to the competition in the buyer's mind. Subaru Outback, for example, positions itself as the "World's First Sports Wagon"—neither a full-sized sports utility vehicle nor an ordinary station wagon. Grasshoppers by Keds positions itself as an inexpensive shoe for practical consumers ("If you feel the need to spend more on shoes, you could always buy two pair"). The object of positioning is to determine what distinct position is appropriate for the product. Positioning will be discussed more fully in Chapter 8. At this point, you should recognize that the marketing mix an organization selects depends on the organization's strategy for positioning its product.

Market Position (Competitive Position)
The way consumers perceive a product relative to its competition.

Planning a marketing mix, as mentioned in Chapter 1, requires a combination of the four Ps: product, price, promotion, and place (distribution). Much of the remainder of this book discusses how marketing managers select the appropriate marketing mix elements for a variety of circumstances.

Stage 4: Preparing a Formal Marketing Plan

Marketing Plan
A written statement of the marketing objectives and strategies to be followed and the specific courses of action to be taken when (or if) certain events occur.

The preparation of the formal marketing plan is the final planning stage of the strategic marketing process. A formal **marketing plan** is a written statement of the

College students comprise an important market segment to the marketers of credit card services. The Visa credit card positions itself as the most widely accepted credit card. The marketing objective is to communicate the message that Visa can be used in many unexpected places, even at colleges for payment of tuition.

Marketing Objective
The level of performance the organization, SBU, or operating unit intends to achieve. Objectives define results in measurable terms.

marketing objectives and strategies to be followed and the specific courses of action to be taken when (or if) certain events occur. It outlines the marketing mix, explains who is responsible for managing the specific activities in the plan, and provides a timetable indicating when those activities must be performed. Certain aspects of the plan may ultimately be scrapped or modified because of changes in the society or in other portions of the market environment.

Establishing action-oriented objectives is a key element of the marketing plan. A **marketing objective** sets the level of performance the organization, SBU, or operating unit intends to achieve. Objectives are more focused than goals because they define results in measurable terms. For example, "to increase our dollar-volume share of the Japanese market from 9 percent to 15 percent by December 31" describes the nature and amount of change (a 6 percent increase), the performance criterion (market share measured by percentage of dollar volume), and the target date for achieving the objective.

Marketing plans may be categorized by their duration: long-term (five or more years), medium-term (two to five years), and short-term (one year or less). Long-term marketing plans usually outline basic strategies for growth. Most organizations prepare an annual marketing plan because marketing activity must be coordinated with annual financial plans and other budgetary plans that follow the fiscal year.

Stage 5: Executing the Plan

Once marketing plans have been developed and approved, they must be executed, or carried out. Making a sales presentation, inspecting proofs of advertising copy, setting prices and discounts, and choosing transportation methods are all aspects of execution of a marketing plan.

Execution
Carrying out plans, also called implementation.

Execution, or implementation, requires organizing and coordinating people, resources, and activities. Staffing, directing, developing, and leading subordinates are major activities used to implement plans. Clearly, the best marketing plans can fail if not properly executed. Speakers at sales meetings are fond of describing the salesperson who read every book on planning for success, who spent every waking hour developing approaches to customers and getting all aspects of his sales career in perfect order, but was fired. Why? He never got out of the house to sell anything! Planning is extremely important, but it means little without execution.

An important aspect of the middle-level marketing manager's job is to supervise the execution of the marketing plan. Translating the plan into action is a task delegated to operational managers and their staffs. Operational managers, such as a district sales manager or a manager of the jewelry department in a department store, plan activities that will support the business-level marketing strategy. They make specific plans that clearly set out the marketing tactics to be executed. For example, if the organization's marketing plan presents a 25 percent increase in sales volume as an objective, the regional sales manager may plan to employ two additional sales representatives during the next month. Then the manager implements the necessary marketing activities, such as hiring and training the new employees and directing their selling efforts, so the objectives may be met.

Mistakes of execution may be made in the completion of any task. Great caution is needed to avoid such errors, some minor, some perhaps unavoidable; but all of them damaging to some degree. For example:

> *Instructions on the front of Lite Way brand salad dressing packages read, "Just mix with water and cider vinegar." On the reverse side of the package, the instructions read, "Mix with low-fat milk and cider vinegar."*
>
> *Joseph A. Banks Clothier, Inc., wished to shorten the company name in the yellow-page ads. A corporate executive told the people at the phone company to drop "Incorporated" so the name would be shorter. The name that actually appeared in the Atlanta phone book was "Drop Inc."*[10]

Most plans are properly executed, but it is important to remember that "the best-laid plans of mice and men" may go astray. Proper execution should never be taken for granted (as the accompanying Competitive Strategy feature illustrates).

Stage 6: Controlling Efforts and Evaluating Results

Control
The process by which managers ensure that planned activities are completely and properly executed.

The purpose of managerial **control** is to ensure that planned activities are completely and properly executed. The first aspect of control is to establish acceptable performance standards. Control also requires investigation and evaluation. Investigation involves "checking up" to determine whether the activities necessary to the execution of the marketing plan are in fact being performed. Actual performance must then be assessed to determine whether organizational objectives have been met. Performance may be evaluated, for example, in terms of the number of sales calls made or new accounts developed. Sales and financial figures may also be judged to appraise individual or organizational successes.

Control activities provide feedback to alert managers because they indicate whether to continue with plans and activities or to change them and take corrective action. Marketing executives may discover, by means of the control activity, that the actions and results that were part of the marketing plan are not being matched "in the field." When this happens, either the marketing plan must be corrected to reflect environmental realities or the employees responsible for carrying out the plan must be more strongly motivated to achieve organizational goals.

Marketing Audit
A comprehensive review and appraisal of the total marketing operation; often performed by outside consultants or other unbiased personnel.

The **marketing audit** is a comprehensive review and appraisal of the total marketing operation. It requires a systematic and impartial review of an organization's recent and current operations and its marketing environment. The audit examines the company's strengths and weaknesses in light of the problems and opportunities it faces. Because the marketing audit evaluates the effectiveness of marketing activities, it is often best performed by outside consultants or otherwise unbiased personnel. Appendix B discusses how to conduct a marketing audit.

COMPETITIVE STRATEGY: WHAT WENT WRONG?

Play 'n Learn

A wrong number in a computer manual has caused headaches and a huge phone bill for a small educational toy distributor. Compaq Computer Corp., the world's biggest personal computer maker, printed the toll-free number for Play 'n Learn Sales Inc. in manuals as the help line for a WordPerfect program that is installed on its Presario 7100 machines.

As a result, dozens of calls a day come into the family-run Play 'n Learn, sometimes through the night, from people who have a question about the program WordPerfect Works. Some callers turn angry when they realize the tiny firm can't help.

"On top of the nuisance of it, we're losing business because our lines get tied up and our customers can't get through," said owner Kathleen Henn.

She filed suit against Compaq, seeking payment for the more than $6,000 in erroneous calls to her company's toll-free line.

The problem first began in January 1995 when operators for Novell Inc., which then owned WordPerfect, occasionally gave people the wrong number. It snowballed last fall when the Compaq manuals were distributed with the wrong number.

The help line for the software is not a toll-free number. It has the area code 801, which is the area code for Utah where Novell and WordPerfect are based.

Play 'n Learn's 1-800 number is the same as the software help line's 1-801 number. Novell runs the help line even though it sold Word Perfect to Corel Inc. earlier this year. Henn said her attempts to get any of the companies to fix the problem have produced no concrete response. "It's impossible to get hold of anybody at Compaq, WordPerfect, or Novell," she said. The lawsuit she filed in state court against Compaq alleges negligence, invasion of privacy and emotional harm. Yvonne Donaldson, a spokeswoman for Compaq, declined comment on the lawsuit, saying she was unfamiliar with the mix-up.

Play 'n Learn represents about 30 manufacturers and sells wholesale to about 1,400 stores, specializing in science and nature toys. Three rooms in Henn's home have been converted to offices and three friends and her daughter work at the company. Henn has ordered a new toll-free number, but she doesn't want to drop her old one because some customers still use it and it's listed in lots of flyers and trade catalogs.

"The worst thing you can do is change your 800 number," she said. "I'm going to be answering WordPerfect's calls forever." Her attorney, Lee Atkinson, said he suggested that Compaq put out a message on its Internet home page, or send out new manuals. "They have not been very responsive," Atkinson said. "Their basic response was 'Change your 800 number,' as if her business wasn't as important to her as their business is to them."

PLANNING, EXECUTION, AND CONTROL ARE INTERRELATED

Planning, execution, and control are closely interrelated. A consideration of the marketing environment leads to the formulation of marketing plans. These in turn must be executed. Execution of the plans must then be controlled through investigation and evaluation. The results generated during the control phase serve as new inputs for both planning and execution, providing a basis for judging both the marketing plans and their execution. Thus, a series of logical steps is maintained, as shown in Exhibit 2–7.

Planning, execution, and control of marketing strategy and tactics also are interrelated because they share ethical dimensions. Understanding the nature of marketing ethics is essential for any student who plans to be a manager. The remainder of this chapter addresses this issue.

EXHIBIT 2–7
Planning, execution, and
control are interrelated.

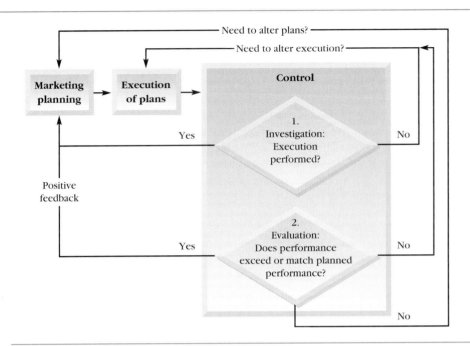

EXHIBIT 2–7
Planning, execution, and
control are interrelated.

MANAGERIAL ETHICS AND SOCIALLY RESPONSIBLE BEHAVIOR

In recent years, many highly publicized stories have appeared in the media about organizations, and individuals in organizations, that did not act according to high ethical standards. For example, there was a barrage of criticism about the high price charged for AZT, the first drug approved to fight AIDS. And marketers of batteries received so much criticism about the mercury, cadmium, and other toxic metals in batteries that Energizer virtually eliminated mercury from its Green Power batteries. (Other battery marketers began to package toxic batteries in packages that could be returned to the manufacturer for recycling.)

Society clearly expects marketers to obey the law, but a socially responsible organization has a responsibility broader than its legal responsibility. **Social responsibility** refers to the ethical consequences of a person's or an organization's acts as they might affect the interests of others.[11] Every marketing manager makes decisions with ethical implications.

Ethics involves values about right and wrong conduct. **Marketing ethics** involves the principles that guide an organization's conduct and the values it expects to express in certain situations.[12] **Moral behavior** in the marketing context reflects how well an individual's or an organization's marketing activity exhibits these ethical values.

Ethical principles reflect the cultural values and norms of a society. **Norms** suggest what ought to be done under given circumstances. They indicate approval or disapproval, what is good or bad. Many norms in Western society are based in the Judeo-Christian ethic. Being truthful is good. Being fair—"doing unto others as you would have them do unto you"—meets with approval. Other norms have a utilitarian base.[13] They may arise from a concern about the consequences of one's ac-

Social Responsibility
The ethical consequences of a person's or an organization's acts as they might affect the interests of others.

Marketing Ethics
The principles that guide an organization's conduct and the values it expects to express in certain situations.

Moral Behavior
In regard to marketers, how well an individual's or organization's marketing activity exhibits the ethical values to which the individual or organization subscribes.

Norm
A social principle identifying what action is right or wrong in a given situation.

tions: "You ought to obey product safety laws, or you may go to jail." They may also arise from expectations about how society should function: "A company's shareholders should receive its profits, because profits are the shareholders' reward for investment and risk taking."

Some ethical principles for personal conduct dictated by broad norms have direct counterparts in marketing actions. Being truthful, a societal norm, and avoiding deceptive, untruthful advertising are closely linked. Where such clear-cut links exist, the expected moral behavior is relatively clear. But though morally accepted behavior may be clear-cut in many circumstances, in others, determining what is ethical is a complicated matter open to debate.

Ethical Dilemma

A predicament in which a marketer must resolve whether an action that benefits the organization, the individual decision maker, or both, may be considered unethical.

An **ethical dilemma** for a marketer is a predicament in which the marketer must resolve whether an action that benefits the organization, the individual decision maker, or both, may be considered unethical.[14] An ethical dilemma may arise when two principles or values are in conflict. For example, a corporation's president may value both high profits and a pollution-free environment. When one of these values or preferences in any way inhibits the achieving of the other, the president is faced with an ethical dilemma. Problems also arise when others do not share the principles or values that guide a marketer's actions. Consider these questions: Is it wrong to pay a bribe in a foreign country where bribery is a standard business practice? Should MTV avoid airing a Madonna video if its sexual overtones offend certain viewers? Answering these questions involves resolving ethical dilemmas.

In many situations, individuals agree on principles or values but have no fixed measure by which to judge actions. An engineer can calculate how strong a steel girder is, and a chemist can offer the formulation of chemicals necessary to perform a task, but the business executive often cannot be so precise. Even where specific laws seem to guide action, the laws and their application may be subject to debate. Although marketers and other businesspeople often pride themselves on their rational problem-solving abilities, the lack of permanent, objective ethical standards for all situations continues to trouble the person seeking an ethical course of action in business.

Thus, there rarely is an absolute consensus when ethical behavior is discussed. Different people, and even a single person, can evaluate a question from several different perspectives. For example, the belief that smoking harms health has led to regulations restricting smoking in airplanes and other public places and barring cigarette commercials from radio and television. Yet to some this is a controversial matter. Of course, good health is important, but what about the smoker's freedom of choice?

In general, when marketing decision makers encounter ethical dilemmas, they consider the impact of the organization's actions and attempt to operate in a way that balances the organization's short-term profit needs with society's long-term needs. For example, a cookie marketer, such as Keebler, knows that people buy cookies because they taste good. It also knows certain inexpensive cooking oils enhance taste but are not as low in cholesterol as other, more expensive ingredients. The company may conduct research to reformulate the cookies by changing to healthier ingredients while maintaining good taste.

More specifically, marketers must ask what is ethical in a particular situation. Marketers must establish the facts in the situation and determine if their plans are compatible with the organization's ethical values. They must determine at what point certain marketing practices become ethically questionable. Is it ethical for a sales representative to pay for a purchasing agent's lunch? To give the purchasing agent a birthday gift? To arrange for an expense-free vacation for the agent if the sales representative's company gets a big contract?

To help marketers act in a socially responsible manner, President John F. Kennedy outlined the consumer's basic rights: the right to be informed, the right to safety, the right to choose, and the right to be heard. Since Kennedy's pronouncement, others have argued that consumers have additional rights, such as the right to privacy and the right to a clean and healthy environment. Arguments have been made that children have special rights because they have not developed mature reasoning powers. Rights like these are embodied in organizations' and associations' codes of conduct. A **code of conduct** establishes guidelines for a company or professional organization with regard to its ethical principles and what behavior it considers proper. Following a code of conduct helps resolve some ethical dilemmas but not others. Many ethical dilemmas involve issues that are not black and white, and individuals often have to resolve such dilemmas using judgments based on their own ethical values. The checklist that follows offers some good general advice about considering ethical dilemmas.[15]

Code of Conduct

A statement establishing a company's or a professional organization's guidelines with regard to ethical principles and acceptable behavior.

1. Recognize and clarify the dilemma.
2. Get all possible facts.
3. List the options—all of them.
4. Test each option by asking: "Is it legal? Is it right? Is it beneficial?"
5. Make your decision.
6. Double-check your decision by asking, "How would I feel if my family found out about this? How would I feel if my decision were printed in the local newspaper?" Do you still feel you made the correct decision?
7. Take the action if warranted.

It should be clear by now that ethical values influence many aspects of marketing strategy. Throughout this book, we will see that ethical considerations, and laws based on these considerations, can affect every aspect of the marketing mix. Similarly, ethical considerations can play a part in the development and implementation of that mix. Exhibit 2–8 presents some ethical questions concerning each of the four major portions of the marketing mix. In considering them, remember that ethical issues are philosophical in nature and that parties may disagree about answers to ethical dilemmas.[16] However, there has been an undeniable trend toward broadening the social responsibility of marketing organizations beyond the limitations of their traditional role as economic forces.

EXHIBIT 2–8
Selected Ethical Questions Related to the Marketing Mix

Product
- Who must accept responsibility for an injury caused by a product that was used improperly?
- Is the package a source of unnecessary environmental pollution?
- Just how much does eating cookies made with tropical oils contribute to a person's risk of heart disease?

Promotion
- Can advertising persuade us to purchase products that we don't really want?
- What effect does advertising have on children?

Price
- Should pricing laws protect consumers or protect small business?
- Do the poor really pay more?

Distribution
- Should modern shopping malls be built in low-income areas?
- If a retailer wishes to carry only one of a manufactuer's products, should the manufacturer be able to force the retailer to carry all of its products?

eas seeking to enjoy a blend of country and city living. Growth in suburban areas has caused the populations of metropolitan areas to remain stable and even to rise. Indeed, the most dramatic growth of the past decade was in the suburbs.

Growth in the Sunbelt

The states of the southern and western United States, sometimes called the Sunbelt, grew most rapidly in the two decades between the last censuses. Between 1980 and 1990, almost all (87 percent) of the net gain in the U.S. population was in the South and West. Between 1990 and 1995, more than 4 million people immigrated to the United States from other countries, and more than half of these people (54 percent) went to California, Texas, and Florida. As a result, 37 percent of the nation's population growth in this period occurred in these three states.[6] In 1990, California, the most populous state, held the rank of fifth fastest-growing state, but dropped to nineteenth during the 1990–1994 period. In recent years California has had heavy out-migration—that is, many Californians have moved to other states. In fact, California lost more from out-migration than it gained from migration of people from other states into California.[7] Texas grew by 9 percent and New York grew by 1 percent. As a result, Texas overtook New York as the second most populous state. In recent years Nevada and Arizona have showed the highest rates of population growth. However, the *rate* of population growth can be somewhat misleading; Nevada, for example, has always been, and continues to be, small in terms of population despite high growth rates.

It is important to remember that long-term trends reflect the past and not necessarily the future. For example, as suggested earlier, it appears that the vast migration of people from other states to California is over. For the year ending July 1, 1993, California grew more slowly than the nation as a whole for the first time in two decades. And as noted, California recently has been losing more population to other states than it has been gaining from them. Exhibit 3–3 shows projected state population change between the years 2000 and 2025.

Age

When the very first U.S. census was taken in 1790, the median age of the population was only 16 years. Today, the median age is 32.6 years. That means that half the population is older and half younger than 32.6.

A consumer's age category—or, as demographers say, *age cohort*—has a major impact on his or her spending behavior. Teenagers spend a great deal of money on soft drinks and fast foods, for example. Many senior citizens spend a lot on travel and prescription drugs. Understanding the age distribution of the population helps marketers anticipate future trends. Exhibit 3–4 shows U.S. generations by age distribution for 1995.

The U.S. population has been growing older in recent decades, and this trend is expected to continue. The trend has occurred for two reasons. One is a lowering of the death rate, and the other is aging of the "baby boomers."

The lowering of the death rate means that more people are living longer. The average life expectancy in the United States has increased to 76 years; people over 65 years of age constitute a growing segment of the population. Many senior citizens do not fit the stereotype of an oldster sitting on a rocking chair waiting for a social security check. They are healthy and active, with sufficient finances to enjoy sports, entertainment, international travel, and other products they may have denied themselves while raising families. Some estimates indicate that nearly half of all savings account interest is earned by people over 65. This has particular significance to bank marketers but should be considered by all other marketers as well. The "graying of America" has been as potent an influence on U.S. marketing as was the baby boom of years past.[8]

EXHIBIT 3–3
State Population—Projected Percent Change, 2000–2025, and Other Demographic Facts

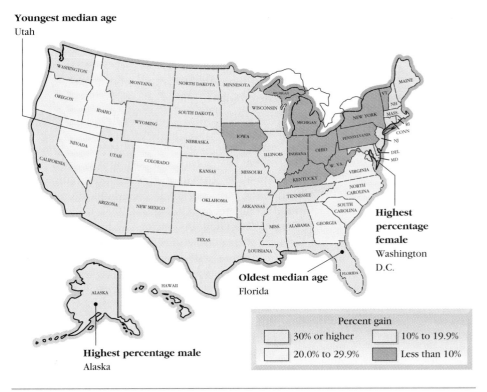

Youngest median age
Utah

Highest percentage female
Washington D.C.

Oldest median age
Florida

Highest percentage male
Alaska

Percent gain	
30% or higher	10% to 19.9%
20.0% to 29.9%	Less than 10%

SOURCE: U.S. Census Bureau. Projections' percentage change of the total population of state: 2000 to 2025 Series A.

The baby boom is the tremendous increase in births during the 20 years following World War II. Four out of every ten adults are baby boomers. The impact of the baby boom age cohort on U.S. society has been far-reaching, and as these consumers age, they should continue to be a major influence in marketing strategies for decades. For example, by 2000 all baby boomers will be over 35 years old and many will be in their mid-50s. These are the peak earning and spending years. Baby boomers becoming middle aged will have a major impact on the marketers of investment plans for retirement, health care services, and products such as Centrum Silver vitamins.

Seniors and baby boomers have received a great deal of attention, but other groups should not be overlooked. The generation of Americans born between 1965 and 1976 is often called **Generation X.** Generation X is smaller than the baby boom generation. Nevertheless, the 45 million adults between 21 and 32 years old make up the second-largest group of young adults in U.S. history. It is estimated that more than 40 percent of Generation X is unmarried and living with parents. However, as Generation X consumers age into their 30s during the late 1990s, its members will get better paying jobs, buy homes, and start families.[9] Generation X represents $125 billion in annual purchasing power. By the year 2000, it is expected to overtake baby boomers as a primary market for most product categories. Generation X has been stereotyped as an angry, resentful, cynical generation. We will have more to say about this group throughout the textbook.

Another group came into being in the 1980s, when adult baby boomers who had postponed starting families began having children, creating a "baby boomlet." In this "echo" of the baby boom there were about a half million more births annually in the 1980s than in the late 1970s. By 1990, there were 19 million children under five years of age, compared with 16 million in 1980. Approximately 20.4

Generation X
Americans born between 1965 and 1976.

EXHIBIT 3–4
Generations by Age in
United States—1995

GENERATION	AGE	PERCENT OF POPULATION	SIZE (IN MILLIONS)
Kids and teens	Under 18	26%	68
Generation X	18 to 29	17	45
Baby boomers	30 to 49	31	81
Mature market	50 and older	26	68

million babies were born between January 1990 and December 1994. This was more than in any five-year period since the last five years of the baby boom (1960–1964).[10]

Already the effects of the boomlet are being felt. After years of decline, America's elementary school enrollment began rising in 1985 and continues to do so today. Think of the implications for the marketers of scissors, construction paper, and school glue.

The growth in preteen and teenage groups has tremendous implications for the economy. This age group represents a sizable pool of people who will, in 10 or 15 years, be forming households and having and raising children. They will constitute prime markets for homes, furniture, appliances, and other durable products.

Profile of the "Average American Consumer"

What is the "average American consumer" like? Because of the many variables involved, there is no true "average" American. But it is intriguing to try to paint a picture of one. First, there are more women than men in the United States, so the average American is female. And as we mentioned earlier, the median age of Americans is 32.6. The median number of years of schooling is 12.7. Thus, the "average" American is a woman about 32 years old with a high school education and perhaps a year of college.

The Changing American Household

A household is a dwelling unit occupied by a group of related people, a single person, or several unrelated people who share living quarters. What is the typical U.S. household like? Father, mother, and two children? Wrong! Fewer than 10 percent of all households include husband, wife, and exactly two children. Married couples with children account for only one-fourth of all households. Single-parent households and households composed of unmarried individuals have proliferated in the past 20 years. In 1997, there were almost 100 million U.S. households—up from 81 million in 1980. The average household declined in membership from 3.14 persons in 1970 and 2.76 persons in 1980 to 2.63 persons in 1990.

Single-Person and Single-Parent Households. People living alone comprise *single-person households*. These households account for one of every four households, but they constitute only 9 percent of the population. The fact that single-person households exist at all demonstrates that although many people think a household is the same as a family, it need not be. Today, according to the Census Bureau, nonfamily households account for 30 percent of all households.

There are several reasons for increases in single-person households. More people than ever before have never married, and young singles are remaining single longer. A high percentage of marriages end in divorce. The longer life expectancy of women over men means that widows constitute a sizable population segment. Households maintained by women with no husband present doubled between 1980 and 1990 (from 5.5 million to 10.7 million). An aging mother (or father) living alone

Demographers find that more babies are born in August and September than in any other months. This does not occur because parents plan it that way but apparently just the opposite. Married women who wish their babies to be born in the spring stop taking birth control pills nine or ten months before they would like the baby to arrive. Many find that becoming pregnant takes several months longer than anticipated, however. So the marketers of cribs, baby bottles, and other baby products plan to sell more products as greater numbers of babies arrive in late summer.

may require shopping help from others or may prefer to live in a retirement apartment that provides meal services and other assistance.

There are 9.7 million *single-parent households*. Many of these are headed by women who are divorced or who have never married. (Approximately one-third of all U.S. births are to unmarried women.) But the number of single-parent households headed by men is growing 2.5 times as fast as the number headed by women. Buying behavior in a single-parent household may be different from that in the two-parent household. For example, a teenager may do the shopping and have the primary responsibility for preparing meals.

Working Women. The advent of the modern career-oriented woman is a major change in the American family. With increasing career orientation have come changes in the age at which women have children, whether they have children at all, and even whether they choose to live as single parents.

The number of people in the work force grew rapidly in the past decade and will continue to do so. The labor force will grow from 128 million workers in 1993 to at least 137 million people (if growth is slow) or as many as 144 million (if growth is rapid), by the year 2000, according to recent Bureau of Labor Statistics projections. Women will account for almost two-thirds of the growth and will represent 47 percent of the labor force by 2000. Almost 60 percent of children under the age of six have mothers who work outside the home, up from about 18 percent in 1960. Forecasters predict that in 2000, the "traditional" husband-wife household with only one partner employed outside the home will account for less than 20 percent of all households.

Obvious changes in the marketplace reflect these developments: Many stores are open weekends to permit working people to shop, and it is the rare store that is not open late at least one or two nights per week. Internet, on-line, and catalog shopping sell large volumes of merchandise. Easily prepared microwave dinners are now commonplace. Take-out food, whether from a restaurant or from the prepared-foods section of a supermarket, has gained great popularity.

FOCUS ON TRENDS

American Eating Patterns

The Eating Patterns in America report, based on an annual survey of 2,000 households, found a number of changes in eating patterns over the last decade. Among them:

Today only 55 percent of dinners include one homemade dish. Ten years ago, the figure was 64 percent. The number of ingredients is also at an all-time low.

Dishes such as potatoes, bread, and salad are served less often. Vegetables, once in more than half of all dinners, are now served at only 43 percent.

When they do cook, more people make extra portions, planning leftovers for future meals—a practice that's up 30 percent.

The number of take-out dinners has more than doubled. Many restaurants function as prepared-food supermarkets.

The National Restaurant Association, which conducts its own survey each year, says Americans also are eating out more. Restaurant sales may reach a record $300 billion in 1997. The group's data shows that the average number of times Americans eat out has increased to 4.1 times weekly.

In the 1990s, many families are composed of two working adults, and time is a very valuable commodity. Americans' need for convenience is shaping their eating patterns.

Family and Household Income[11]

The United States Census Bureau defines a family as a group of two or more persons related by birth, marriage, or adoption and residing together. The annual median family income in the United States was $36,959 in 1993, up from $21,023 in 1980 and $9,867 in 1970.

In 1993, approximately 30 percent of U.S. households had incomes above $50,000, and 24 percent had incomes below $15,000. Only 6 percent had incomes above $100,000. More than two-thirds of all households earning more than $100,000 are headed by college graduates. The average annual income of college graduates is about double that of high school graduates who did not graduate from college.

In the early 1990s, the wealthiest 20 percent of households earned more than the 60 percent of households in the middle classes.[12] Trends in household income (including the income of single-person households) show that there has been a decline in the percentage of middle-income households.

The upper-income group has expanded, in part due to an increase in the number of affluent two-income married couples. Working wives contribute about 40 percent of family income. There are approximately 10 million two-income families earning more than $50,000. This affluent group has considerable discretionary income, and it has an impact on the market for luxury goods.

A Multicultural Population

The United States has a *multicultural population*—that is, a population made up of many different ethnic and racial groups. One out of every five U.S. residents is African-American, Hispanic, Asian, Native American Indian, Eskimo, or a member of another minority group.[13] In 1995, African-Americans represented about 12 percent of the U.S. population, Hispanic-Americans about 10 percent, and Asian-Americans about 3.4 percent. These three minorities respectively account for approximately 31 million, 26 million, and 9 million people. (See Exhibit 3–5.) Native Americans account for less than 1 percent of the population.

The trend is clearly toward increased diversity. In the 1960s, nine out of ten Americans were white. Today, about three out of four Americans are non-Hispanic

RACE	POPULATION IN MILLIONS	PERCENT OF TOTAL	MEDIAN AGE	PERCENT CHANGE 1990–95	PERCENT OF 1990–95 GROWTH
All persons	262	100.0%	34	5.6%	100%
White, non-Hispanic	193	73.8	36	2.8	38
Black, non-Hispanic	31	12.0	29	7.8	16
Asian, non-Hispanic	9	3.4	30	24.8	15
Hispanic	26	10.0	27	18.8	30
American Indian, Eskimo, and Aleut, non-Hispanic	2	0.7	27	7.0	1

Note: Hispanics may be of any race. Numbers may not add to total due to rounding.

EXHIBIT 3–5
Minority Markets—1995

SOURCE: Adapted from Peter Francese, "America at Mid-Decade," *American Demographics,* February 1995, p. 28. © 1995 *American Demographics Magazine.* Adapted with permission. For subscription information, please call 800/828-1133. Data from Census Bureau surveys.

whites. Only a small percentage of immigrants are of European origin. Immigrants, along with Hispanic-Americans and African-Americans, tend to have more children than the non-Hispanic white population. If these immigration and birth-rate trends continue, the United States will continue to become increasingly diverse.

In recent years, many demographers have predicted that Hispanic-Americans will replace African-Americans (and other blacks) as the largest U.S. minority group by the year 2010. Data from the 1990 census and other censuses show that although the populace of Hispanic origin increased rapidly in the 1980s (53 percent versus 13 percent for blacks) and between 1990 and 1995 (18.8 percent versus 7.8 percent), there is still a gap of about 5 million people between the two groups. Projections generally assume that present trends will continue. Although the Hispanic population's size has continued to increase in recent years, its growth rate has been on the decline. It may be that even by the year 2010 African-Americans will still outnumber Hispanics.

The census bureau revealed other trends in the United States population's multicultural component. Perhaps the most significant trend for the entire country was that the number of Asians and Pacific Islanders living in the United States doubled between 1980 and 1990 and increased by almost one-quarter between 1990 and 1995.

The trend toward diversity and a multicultural society has had its greatest impact on certain regions of the country. For example, most of the growth in the Asian-American population has been in California, and most of the Hispanic growth has been in Florida, Texas, and California. The non-Hispanic white population in certain cities in these states, such as San Diego, accounts for less than 50 percent of the population.

World Population

The world population exceeds 6 billion people. Because markets consist of people willing and able to exchange something of value for goods and services, this total is of great marketing significance. However, the exponential growth of population, particularly in less-developed countries, puts a heavy burden on marketing. The distribution of food, for instance, is a marketing problem that may prove crucial to the survival of the planet. The world population is expected to grow by at least 140 million per year. (See Exhibit 3–6.) That's about 16,000 new people per hour.

Although the bulk of this section has dealt with the demography of the U.S. market, it is important to remember that the future of both developed and devel-

EXHIBIT 3–6
World Population Growth

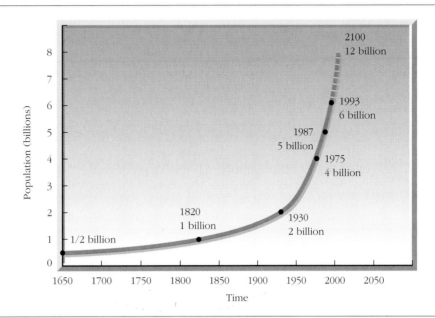

oping economies is well served by vigorous international trade. This trade cannot be effectively implemented and maintained unless marketers concern themselves deeply with what is going on in "the rest of the world."

Three areas of the world—North America, Europe, and the Pacific Rim countries surrounding Japan—are economically important areas where global competition can be intense. They will receive special attention in our discussions throughout this textbook.

ECONOMIC AND COMPETITIVE FORCES

Economic and competitive forces strongly influence marketing activity at all levels. In this section, we discuss macromarketing concerns—economic systems and general economic conditions. In Chapter 4, when we discuss the microenvironment, we consider how competitive forces influence an individual firm's activities.

Economic Systems

Economic System
The system through which a society allocates its scarce resources.

A society's **economic system** determines how it will allocate its scarce resources. Traditionally, capitalism, socialism, and communism have been considered the world's major economic systems. In general, the Western world's economies can be classified as modified capitalist systems. Under such systems, competition, both foreign and domestic, influences the interaction of supply and demand. Competition is often discussed in this context in terms of competitive market structures. The competitive market structure describes the number of competing firms in some segment of an economy and the proportion of the market held by each competitor. The market structure in which a firm operates strongly influences its pricing strategies. Pure competition, monopolistic competition, oligopoly, and monopoly are the four basic types of competitive market structures.

Pure Competition
A market structure characterized by free entry, a homogeneous product, and many sellers and buyers, none of whom controls price.

Pure competition exists when there are no barriers to competition. The market consists of many small, competing firms and many buyers. This means that there is a steady supply of the product and a steady demand for it. Therefore, the price cannot be controlled by either the buyers or the sellers. The product itself is homogeneous—that is, one seller's offering is identical to the others. The markets for basic food commodities, such as rice and mushrooms, approximate pure competition.

Monopolistic Competition
A market structure characterized by a large number of sellers offering slightly differentiated products and exerting some control over their own prices.

The principal characteristic of **monopolistic competition** is product differentiation—a large number of sellers offering similar products differentiated only by minor changes in, for example, product design, style, or technology. Firms engaged in monopolistic competition have enough influence on the marketplace to exert some control over their own prices. The fast-food industry is a good example of monopolistic competition.

Oligopoly
A market structure characterized by a small number of sellers who control the market.

Oligopoly, the third type of market structure, exists where a small number of sellers dominate the market. Oligopoly is exemplified by the commercial aircraft industry, which is controlled by a few large firms: Boeing, McDonnell Douglas, and Airbus Industrie. Getting established in an oligopoly like the commercial aircraft industry often requires a huge capital investment, which presents a barrier to new firms wishing to enter the industry. The distinguishing characteristic of an oligopoly, however, is not the size of the company measured by assets or sales volume but its control over the marketplace measured by market share. Each of the companies in an oligopoly has a strong influence on product offering, price, and market structure within the industry. The companies do not, however, generally compete on price.

Monopoly
A market structure characterized by a single seller in a market in which there are no suitable substitute products.

Finally, markets with only one seller, such as a local telephone company or electric utility, are called monopolies. A **monopoly** exists in a market in which there are no suitable substitute products. Antitrust legislation strictly controls monopolies in the United States.

Economic Conditions

Gross Domestic Product (GDP)
The total value of all the goods and services produced by capital and workers in a country.

Economic conditions are of obvious interest to marketers. Two common measures of the health of a country's economy are **gross domestic product (GDP)** and **gross national product (GNP).** GDP measures the value of all the goods and services produced by workers and capital in the United States. GNP measures the value of all the goods and services produced by United States residents or corporations regardless of location. Thus, revenues on overseas operations of American companies are included in the GNP, but not in GDP. Revenues that foreign companies make in the United States are included in GDP, but not in GNP. Both GDP and GNP provide economic yardsticks of business output. The difference between these two measures has to do with whether we wish to know what is produced inside our borders or what is produced by Americans around the world.[14]

Gross National Product (GNP)
The total value of all the goods and services produced by a nation's residents or corporations, regardless of location.

In the United States, per capita GDP was approximately $27,500 and the inflation rate was 2.5 percent in 1995. Exhibit 3–7 shows per capita GDP and inflation rates for several countries in 1995. Notice how greatly economic conditions differ around the world.

Business Cycle
Recurrent fluctuations in general economic activity. The four phases of the business cycle are prosperity, recession, depression, and recovery.

The **business cycle** reflects recurrent fluctuations in general economic activity. The various booms and busts in the health of an economy influence unemployment, inflation, and consumer spending and savings patterns, which in turn influence marketing activity. The four phases of the business cycle are as follows:

- *Prosperity:* The phase in which the economy is operating at or near full employment, and both consumer spending and business output are high.
- *Recession:* The downward phase, in which consumer spending, business output, and employment are decreasing.
- *Depression:* The low phase of a business cycle, in which unemployment is highest. Consumer spending is low, and business output has declined drastically.

EXHIBIT 3–7
Per Capita GDP and
Inflation Rates for Selected
Countries

COUNTRY	1995 PER CAPITA GROSS DOMESTIC PRODUCT (U.S. DOLLARS)	1995 ANNUAL CONSUMER PRICE INFLATION (PERCENT)
Argentina	$ 8,100	1.7%
Belgium	19,500	1.6
Brazil	6,100	23.0
China	2,900	10.1
Czech-Republic	10,200	9.1
Egypt	2,760	9.4
France	20,200	1.7
Greece	9,500	8.1
India	1,500	9.0
Israel	15,500	10.1
Italy	18,700	5.4
Mexico	7,700	52.0
Nigeria	1,300	57.0
Poland	5,800	21.6
Portugal	11,000	4.6
Taiwan	13,500	4.0
Zimbabwe	1,600	25.8

SOURCE: *The World Fact Book: 1996* (Central Intelligence Agency Web page: http://www.odi.gov/cia/publications).

- *Recovery:* The upward phase, when employment, consumer spending, and business output are rising.

Marketing strategies in a period of prosperity differ substantially from strategies in a period of depression. For example, products with "frills and extras" sell better during periods of prosperity than in periods when the economy is stagnant or declining. During periods of depression or recession, when consumers have less spending power, lower price becomes a more prominent consideration in spending decisions.

Because marketing activity is strongly influenced by the business cycle, the economic environment is closely watched by marketing managers. Unfortunately, the business cycle is not always easy to forecast. The phases of the cycle need not be equal in intensity or duration, and the contractions and expansions of the economy do not always follow a predictable pattern. Furthermore, not all economies of the world are in the same stage of the business cycle. So a single global forecast may not accurately predict activity in all countries.

 SCIENCE AND TECHNOLOGY

Science
The accumulation of knowledge about humans and the environment.

Technology
The application of science to practical purposes.

Although the two terms are sometimes used interchangeably, **science** is the accumulation of knowledge about human beings and the environment, while **technology** is the application of such knowledge to practical purposes. Thus, the discovery that certain diseases might be prevented by immunization is scientific, but how and when immunization is administered is technical. Like other changes in the environment of marketing, scientific and technological advances can either revolutionize or destroy an industry. The popular allergy medicine Seldane exemplifies how quickly such changes can occur. When the Federal Trade Commission concluded that the benefits of Seldane no longer outweighed the risks of potentially fatal cardiac side effects, the market share of the allergy medicine fell to almost nothing within three months.

Changing technologies in our digital age have had a major impact on the use of copyrighted material. This advertisement for IBM points out that it is easy to share images with millions on the Internet and that it is possible for someone to download them commercially without permission. So, IBM used its technology to develop a digital watermark. The digital watermark protects images without obscuring them—much like the watermarks on rare manuscripts, such as the one pictured in its advertisement.

Scientific and technological forces have a pervasive influence on the marketing of most goods and services. The discovery that sunburn can cause skin cancer certainly affected suntan-lotion marketers. Similarly, the knowledge that moderate use of red wine and aspirin may help reduce the risk of heart attack has led to changes in the advertising messages and package labels of existing products.

Space science and technology offer examples of advances that have been seized on by marketers. Besides Tang, freeze-dried ice cream, and some other food products, the space program has yielded CAT scan equipment, solar calculators, and the microchips that are found in word processors and personal computer games. In addition, space technology has found industrial applications: A firefighter in a lightweight fire-fighting suit can now communicate with others through a built-in communication system. The nonfogging face protector the firefighter wears to improve visibility is also a product of space technology.

Information technology has reshaped the way business is conducted around the world. The Internet has been of particular significance because it has influenced so many organizations. The Internet is a worldwide network of computers that gives users access to information and documents from distant sources. Using the Internet has become routine for millions of individuals and organizations. The Internet is described in more detail in Chapter 5.

The Internet, along with satellite communications systems, modems, fax machines, and other advances in information technology, have made communication with suppliers, distributors, and customers in other countries much more efficient and in many cases instantaneous.[15] Global information systems (discussed further in Chapter 5) have been instrumental in the growth of global business. Indeed, many business analysts believe the key to success in the global economy lies in effective use of information technology.

Because of global information systems, the location of a business enterprise has become less important than its ability to keep in touch with other company divisions or other companies via computers and telecommunications. A company in, say, Boise, Idaho, can keep in touch with world financial markets and global customers as easily as a company in Los Angeles or New York.

In the future, integration of computers, television, and telephones will further change the way business is conducted. In the not-too-distant future, for example, television viewers will be able to watch an automobile commercial and, with the press of a button, instantly summon up additional information to be delivered on screen or to a printer near the TV set.[16] Also with the press of a button, the viewer will be able to request a test-drive, and within an hour, a local dealer will telephone and schedule a convenient time to stop by with a car. Interactive television with programs on request, home shopping, and travel reservations is now being tested in selected areas.

Numerous examples of organizations that suffered because they did not adapt to changing science and technology can be found. For instance, Atari and several other marketers of video games fell victim to competitors such as Sega and Nintendo that switched to more technologically advanced, higher-performance microprocessors. Because changes in science and technology can have a major impact, organizations of all types must monitor these changes and adjust their marketing mixes to meet them.

FOCUS ON TRENDS

High-Tech Packaging

Rarely since the advent of cellophane in 1923 has the packaging industry come up with so many new materials and designs. Today's high-tech packages can look better than traditional bottles, boxes, and cans. And when the packaging's work is done and the stuff goes the way of all wrappers, it takes up less space in the local landfill. Some high-tech packages even facilitate correct cooking of the products they contain.

Printpack of Atlanta used film coated with metal strips, called susceptors, to line the pouch it created for Rudolph's Bacon Snaps pork rind nuggets. When the package is placed in a microwave, some of the susceptors heat up to make the nuggets brown and crispy, while others reflect energy from the nuggets to promote more even cooking. Other packaging manufacturers such as Cryovac ... and Ever-Fresh ... make films that keep fruits and vegetables fresh by reducing the concentration of gases like oxygen and ethylene that aid ripening.

The packages of the future will be even more versatile. Temperature-sensitive labels will indicate whether products have gotten too hot or too cold during shipping. Microwave films for TV dinners will deep-fry some parts of the meal, like chicken, while keeping others, such as applesauce, cool. Some day, when peaches are covered with protein film and peas come in a bag that dissolves as they cook, we may even be able to eat the packages themselves.

POLITICS AND LAWS

Political Environment
The practices and policies of governments.

Legal Environment
Laws and regulations and their interpretation.

The **political environment** (the practices and policies of governments) and the **legal environment** (laws and regulations and their interpretation) affect marketing activity in several ways. First, they can limit the actions marketers are allowed to take—for example, by restricting the percentage of foreign ownership of a company operating in another country or by barring certain U.S. goods from leaving the country (as when Congress passed the Export Administration Act prohibiting the export of strategic high-technology products to nations such as Libya). Second, some actions may be required. For example, cookies called "chocolate chip cookies" are required to contain chips made of real chocolate; and cigarette makers are required to print the surgeon general's warning on all cigarette packages. Last, certain actions can be prohibited, including the sale of products such as opium, heroin, and nuclear weapons, except under the strictest of controls.

Political processes in other countries may have dramatic impacts on international marketers. For example, the former Soviet Union's initiation of *perestroika* (economic restructuring) and *glasnost* (openness about public and political events) ultimately led to the dissolution of the union. These historic political actions opened new markets in Asia and Europe. Today, U.S. marketers in independent states, such as Russia, Lithuania, and Ukraine, find the business climate totally different from the climate that existed only ten years ago.

The civil war in Rwanda in the mid-1990s illustrates the uncertainty of political forces and how swiftly political situations change. After the movie *Gorillas in the Mist,* thousands of international tourists traveled to Rwanda to pay $170 per hour to observe the mountain gorillas in the Varunga Volcanoes. However, soon after the war in Rwanda began, virtually all international tourism stopped.

Of course, not all political and legal influences involve dramatic changes like those in the former Soviet Union and Rwanda. Laws, in particular, tend to have a stable long-term influence on marketing strategy.

FOCUS ON GLOBAL COMPETITION

Pepsi

Political forces were clearly at play when Pepsi-Cola International was preparing to introduce Pepsi products into India. Just when Pepsi's cola, orange, and lemon soft drinks were a few weeks away from introduction to the Indian market, the new nationalist administration in India came up with a costly requisite, all in the name of patriotism. Pepsi had to change the name of its soft drinks from "Pepsi Era" to "Lehar Pepsi" (*Lehar* means wave in Hindi)—a move that cost the company a maharajah's ransom in design and packaging changes. After years of political pressure, the name changing was just one final, expensive concession Pepsi was willing to make in order to boost its international market share. It was a struggle to enter this huge market, but Pepsi-Cola International kept fighting to get into a country that had locked out its chief rival, the Coca-Cola Co. Pepsi's marketing efforts had been plagued by government inquiries, but the administration was not its only opponent. Parle Exports Ltd. of Bombay, which dominates India's soft-drink market, threw up hurdles of another kind.

Parle played up patriotism in an aggressive campaign of propaganda, bad press, and image advertising. After the elections in which a nationalistic government defeated the reform-minded Rajiv Gandhi, Parle managing director Ramesh Chauhan decided to launch a marketing war against Pepsi.

"The government should help Indian companies along," Chauhan said. "We are the ones in the fortress. Pepsi is the one trying to break in." Parle used every means at its disposal to keep Pepsi out of the market—which included scheming with nationalist government forces and issuing threats. Chauhan is part of a large and influential segment of Indian business that harbors a deep-seated fear of multinationals. Chauhan's bare-knuckles style works well in India, where knowing people in high places is key to business success.

When Pepsi began negotiations to set up operations in India several years earlier, no one anticipated it would become the center of one of the most publicized marketing struggles in India's history. However, after working for years to market soda and snacks in India, it now seems that Lehar Pepsi has overcome all the obstacles resulting from the political environment.

in general economic activity. The various booms and busts in the economy influence unemployment, inflation, and consumer spending and savings patterns, which in turn influence marketing activity.

Learning Objective 5

Understand the three levels of U.S. law and the growing need to know the laws of other nations.

Federal laws control many business activities, such as pricing and advertising by manufacturers, wholesalers, and retailers. The FTC, in particular, affects almost all marketers. State laws also deal with many areas, including foods, manufactured goods, lending, real estate, banking, and insurance. Local laws affect zoning and licensing, among other things. Laws that govern the marketing of products in foreign countries and in multinational marketing groups are subject to tremendous variation and will affect any organization that engages in international marketing.

KEY TERMS

Domestic environment (p. 58)	Demography (p. 62)	Business cycle (p. 70)
Foreign environment (p. 58)	Generation X (p. 64)	Science (p. 71)
Macroenvironment (p. 58)	Economic system (p. 69)	Technology (p. 71)
Microenvironment (p. 58)	Pure competition (p. 69)	Political environment (p. 73)
Physical environment (p. 58)	Monopolistic competition (p. 70)	Legal environment (p. 73)
Green marketing (p. 59)	Oligopoly (p. 70)	Antitrust legislation (p. 75)
Culture (p. 59)	Monopoly (p. 70)	Federal Trade Commission (FTC) (p. 75)
Social value (p. 60)	Gross domestic product (GDP) (p. 70)	Multinational marketing group (p. 78)
Belief (p. 60)	Gross national product (GNP) (p. 70)	

QUESTIONS FOR REVIEW AND CRITICAL THINKING

1. What domestic and foreign environmental factors might have the greatest influence on each of the following firms?
   a. General Motors
   b. McDonald's
   c. Starbuck's Coffee
   d. Humana Hospitals

2. What impact would the development of efficient solar energy have on each of the following industries?
   a. housing industry
   b. automobile industry
   c. other industry of interest to you

3. Evaluate society's continuing concern for physical fitness from the point of view of each of the following.
   a. manufacturer of packaged foods
   b. leasing agent for an office building
   c. maker of athletic shoes and clothing

4. World population is rising much more quickly than the U.S. population. What opportunities does this present to U.S. marketers? What constraints?

5. What is a household? What do you predict will be the nature of households in the year 2010?

6. What businesses would be influenced if a fire destroyed a telephone switching station and it took two weeks to get local service working?

7. What U.S. states seem to be bellwether states—that is, states predicting future environmental trends throughout the rest of the country?

8. Are economic forces the most important environmental influences on marketing activities?

9. What laws are unique to your state?

10. How much can marketers control political and legal influences on the marketing mix?

11. Form small groups as directed by your instructor. As a group, come to a consensus on the five environmental factors that will most strongly influence an industry designated by your instructor. Discuss as a class the groups' conclusions and how each group arrived at a consensus.

INTERNET INSIGHTS

Exercise

1. Go to *http://census.gov* and navigate to the POP-CLOCK to find the Census Bureau's estimate of the U.S. population on today's date.

2. *USA Today*'s Interactive edition is a good place to keep track of environmental changes. Go to

    http://www.usatoday.com

    and write a short report on trends affecting marketing activity.

3. The Australian National University maintains a Web page that keeps track of leading demographic information facilities worldwide. Go to

http://coombs.anu.edu/ResFacilities/
DemographyPage.html

to find more than 150 interesting Web pages.

Address Book

American Demographics
http://www.marketingtools.com/publications/AD/index.htm

Popular Science Magazine
http://www.popsci.com

Home of Mister Economy
http://amos.bus.okstate.edu

Federal Trade Commission
http://www.ftc.gov

ETHICS IN PRACTICE: TAKE A STAND

1. Do you agree that products containing hydrocarbons should not be sold in the United States?

2. Should products containing high sodium levels, such as fast-food hamburgers and breakfast sausage, be advertised on children's television?

3. Should English be made the national language? Should all products have labels in English only?

4. Tokyo-based Ito-Yokado owns a 70 percent share of the 7-Eleven convenience store chain. Should this fact be stated on a decal on store windows?

VIDEO CASE 3-1

LION Coffee

James Delano is president of The Woolson Spice Co., a Hawaiian firm that roasts coffee and sells it at wholesale and retail. Delano unexpectedly was faced with regulatory action [in 1991] that could cripple the business.

The Woolson Spice Co.'s annual permit to import green coffee beans was expiring in two weeks. Now the state's Department of Agriculture notified Woolson, which does business as LION Coffee, of impending catastrophe: The permit might not be renewed because of a provision in an old state law that had not been applied to LION before.

Under the law, coffee beans may not be imported by roasters on Hawaiian islands where coffee is grown. At one time this law affected only the state's biggest island, Hawaii, where coffee is grown on the Kona coast. But today, coffee is also grown on other islands, including Oahu, where Woolson is located.

LION produces blends almost exclusively. Without imported beans, its coffee-roasting facility would have to shut down. It was the biggest challenge since Delano had bought a dormant Woolson Spice in 1979 and, with two employees, started roasting and packaging coffee in downtown Honolulu.

Action was required, and fast.

Questions
1. How uncontrollable is the legal environment in the Hawaiian Islands? What actions should LION take to get the annual permit reissued?
2. What other environmental forces, other than legal action, might shape LION's marketing mix?

CASE 3–2

 Thirty Years of Freshman

Once upon a time boys and girls went to college to learn the meaning of life. They ruminated on Kierkegaard and Kant, dealt with existential dilemmas, argued over war, the Bomb and whether to protest or not to protest. "Thirty years ago," recalls Alexander Astin, a professor of education at the University of California, Los Angeles, "students were preoccupied with questions such as 'What is life all about?' and 'Who is God?' "

Once upon a time is over. A study released [in 1997] by UCLA and the American Council on Education compares the attitudes of 9 million freshmen who have answered questionnaires on 1,500 campuses over the past three decades. In 1967, 82% of entering students said it was "essential" or "very important" to "develop a meaningful philosophy of life"—making that the top goal of college freshmen. Today that objective ranks sixth, endorsed by only 42% of students. Conversely, in 1967 less than half of freshmen said that to be "very well off financially" was "essential" or "very important." Today it is their top goal, endorsed by 74%. Idealism and materialism, says Astin, who has directed the surveys since their creation, "have basically traded places."

Today there is a convergence in the goals of men and women. Three decades ago, less than half of female freshmen planned to get a graduate degree. Now nearly 68% of women plan to get higher degrees, vs. 65% of males. Thirty years ago, men were nine times more likely to want to be lawyers. Today there is less than half a percent difference. Among freshmen who want to be doctors and dentists, females outnumber males.

Feminist values are now entrenched. "It is hard to believe that in 1967 fully two-thirds of men agreed with the statement 'The activities of married women are best confined to the home and family,' " Astin remarks. Today that has dropped to 31%. But a gender gap persists: only 19%

of female freshmen agree. University of South Carolina professor John Gardner, head of the National Resource Center for the Freshman Year Experience, laments that the survey also confirms how "women have taken on some of our worst habits. They smoke and drink more—binge drinking has become their problem too." Thirty years ago, male freshmen were nearly 50% more likely to be frequent smokers. Today more females than males smoke frequently—about 16%, vs. 13%. A point of divergence: only 31.9% of women, vs. 53.8% of men, agree that "if two people really like each other, it's all right for them to have sex, even if they've known each other only a very short time."

Freshmen who reported feeling "overwhelmed" nearly doubled, from 16% in 1985 to nearly 30% in 1996. As a result of such anxieties, says Gardner, "students today are practical and grade grubbing." Many scholars blame economic insecurity for the change. Says James Spring, associate admissions director at the State University of New York at Binghamton: "As a student in the '60s, I could think about my philosophy of life because I didn't worry about getting a job." Indeed, those who report a "major concern" that they will lack funds to complete college jumped from less than 9% three decades ago to 18% now. Still, there are positives. Today's freshmen, says Gardner, "hold down jobs after school and volunteer in community service as much as ever. We don't recognize their fine qualities enough."

Questions

1. Analyze the findings presented in the case. What are the most significant environmental changes that occurred between 1966 and 1996?
2. How should your college or university adapt its marketing strategy based on these environmental trends?

THE MICROENVIRONMENT IN AN ERA OF GLOBAL COMPETITION

Chapter 4

Learning Objectives

After you have studied this chapter, you will be able to:

1. Understand how the microenvironment affects a company's marketing activities.
2. Identify the four Cs of marketing.
3. Recognize how marketing creates economic utility for customers.
4. Identify the various types of competitors and understand how marketers anticipate and react to competitors' strategies to gain competitive advantages.
5. Describe the value chain and explain why it must be managed.
6. Understand the importance of global competition in today's economy.
7. Apply the four Cs in a global business context.

Whirlpool, based in Benton Harbor, Michigan, manufactures and markets washing machines, refrigerators, and other appliances and has more than $7 billion in annual revenues. The company has concentrated on expanding its business globally, investing heavily in Europe and Asia. Whirlpool has manufacturing facilities in 12 countries.

Whirlpool exports some of its appliances to Taiwan and the Republic of China and is taking steps that eventually will allow it to produce washers, refrigerators, and other products in either or both of those countries. If successful, the new manufacturing operations would bring the export business to an end.

Whirlpool and Teco Electric & Machinery Co., Ltd., of Taiwan are forming a joint venture to market and distribute home appliances—including Whirlpool's—in Taiwan. Until recently, the distribution of those appliances was handled by Teco, which had been Whirlpool's largest international customer. After agreeing to collaborate, Whirlpool also became involved in distribution and sales, and the two companies are working together to benefit from manufacturing opportunities both in Taiwan and in China.

Some of the steel-, aluminum-, and plastic-intensive appliances that Whirlpool currently sells in Taiwan and China are made in North America of materials from North American suppliers, and some are built in Europe. The company's principal domestic steel suppliers are Inland Steel Co., Chicago; LTV Steel Co., Cleveland; U.S. Steel Group, Pittsburgh; and Dofasco, Inc., Hamilton, Ontario.

Appliance industry executives regard China as the biggest potential market for home appliances—particularly clothes washers, refrigerators and ranges—in the world. According to David R. Whitwam, chairman and chief executive officer of Whirlpool, in order to succeed in the Far East and to "create value within the Asian home appliance market, Whirlpool must participate as a true insider."

Whirlpool is typical of companies striving to be competitive in this age of global competition. It is customer-driven. It sees the world as its market. And it works with collaborators to gain competitive advantage.

The macroenvironment, those broad societal forces that affect every business and nonprofit marketer, were discussed in Chapter 3. Marketers, however, are more directly influenced by their individual microenvironments. A microenvironment consists of a company, its customers, and other economic institutions that regularly influence its marketing practices. This chapter discusses the nature of the microenvironment and the ways in which the microenvironmental forces shape marketing strategy.

THE MICROENVIRONMENT—THE FOUR Cs

To explain the dramatic impact of the microenvironment, it is useful to organize all microenvironmental forces into four basic categories: company, customers, competitors, and collaborators. We will call these the **four Cs.** Each C represents a participant that performs essential business activities.[1]

Company

Four Cs
An acronym for the microenvironmental participants who perform essential business activities: company, customers, competitors, and collaborators.

Company
The business or organization itself.

The term **company** refers to the business or organization itself. Marketing, although exceedingly important, is only one functional activity of the organization. Every marketer must work with people in the organization who perform nonmarketing tasks. For example, in a large manufacturing company, manufacturing, engineering, purchasing, accounting, finance, and personnel are all part of the internal company environment. These functional activities, the level of technology, and the people who perform them have an impact on marketing. Marketers, for example, work within the framework of the corporate mission set by top managers, who are responsible for the company's operations. Furthermore, companies like 3M and Disney have several divisions and market many different products. The way one of a company's products is marketed often affects the marketing of other company products.

In today's companies, owners and managers must strive to be flexible to keep up with dynamically changing business environments. In doing so, they often take an entrepreneurial approach to running the business.

Entrepreneur
A risk-taking individual who sees an opportunity and is willing to undertake a venture to create a new product or service.

An **entrepreneur** is someone willing to undertake a venture to create something new. The traditional view of an entrepreneur is one of a single individual who sees an opportunity and is willing to work long and hard to turn an idea into a business. Entrepreneurs are typically creative, optimistic, and hard-working individuals who risk their own money to start small companies to make something happen.[2] The story of the entrepreneurial development of the personal computer is well known. Starting out in a garage, two risk-taking individuals with a vision built the first personal computers and then developed Apple Computer into a multinational corporation. Entrepreneurs throughout the world who assume all the risks associated with their innovative ideas have always been at the cutting edge of new product development.

The top managers of many large organizations try to instill an entrepreneurial spirit in their companies. To avoid confusion with the traditional definition of entrepreneur, we say a large **intrapreneurial organization** encourages individuals to take risks and gives them the autonomy to develop new products as they see fit.

Intrapreneurial Organization
An organization that encourages individuals to take risks and gives them the autonomy to develop new products as they see fit.

Intrapreneurial companies try to create company cultures that encourage employees to be proactive. These companies favor organizational structures that allow employees to initiate marketing action swiftly rather than forcing them to follow rigid bureaucratic procedures before taking action. For example, at Sara Lee—global marketers of Hanes, Playtex, Coach leatherwear, and Sara Lee brands—the chief executive officer says this about intrapreneurship in large corporations:

> *Decentralized management is our point of difference. Why do you think big businesses are imploding all over America? They cannot match the creativity that can come out of individual, highly motivated small businesses. We operate about 100 discrete profit centers, each with a chief officer and a management team.[3]*

Customers

Customer
Buyer of goods or services.

Customers are the lifeblood of every company. A company that does not satisfy its customers' needs will not stay in business over the long run. It is difficult to think of a more direct influence on marketing than gaining or losing customers.

Economic Utility

The ability of an organization marketing a product to satisfy a consumer's wants or needs; includes form utility, place utility, time utility, and possession utility.

Form Utility

Utility created by conversion of raw materials into finished goods or service processes that meet consumer needs.

Place Utility

Utility created by making goods and services available where consumers want them.

Time Utility

Utility created by making goods and services available when consumers want them.

Possession Utility

Utility created by transfer of physical possession and ownership of a product to a consumer.

Competitor

One of two or more rival companies engaged in the same business.

Product Category

A subset of a product class containing products of a certain type.

Product Class

A broad group of products that differ somewhat but perform similar functions or provide similar benefits.

Brand

A name or some other identifying feature that distinguishes one marketer's product; much competition is among brands.

Historically, consumer needs have been discussed in terms of economic utility. **Economic utility** is the ability of an organization marketing a good or service to satisfy some aspect of a consumer's wants or needs. There are four specific types of economic utility: form utility, place utility, time utility, and possession utility.

In converting raw materials into finished goods, an organization's production department alters the materials' forms. It creates **form utility.** However, transforming a sheet of leather and thread into a purse does not create form utility unless the new shape is designed to satisfy a consumer need. Marketing helps production create form utility by communicating consumer needs for products of various configurations and formulations to production planners.

Products available at the right place—that is, where buyers want them—have **place utility.** A bottle of Pepsi-Cola at a bottling plant far from a consumer's hometown has considerably less place utility than does a Pepsi in the refrigerator.

Storing products so they are available when needed by consumers creates **time utility.** A bank may close at 5:00 p.m., but by maintaining a 24-hour automatic teller machine, it produces additional time utility for its customers.

Homeowners enjoy greater freedom to alter their homes, such as the right to paint walls bright orange, than do renters. They have possession utility. **Possession utility** satisfies the consumer's need to own the product and to have control over its use or consumption. It is created at the conclusion of a sale when the transfer of ownership occurs. These economic utilities serve as the underlying bases of competition, which we discuss in the following section.

Competitors

Competitors are rival companies engaged in the same business. They are interested in selling their products and services to another company's customers and potential customers. Residence Inn and Holiday Inn are competitors. So are two plumbing companies in your neighborhood.

Product categories are subsets of product types contained within a **product class.** In the household cleaner example, the cleaners, taken together, constitute the product class, but the subdivisions liquids, powders, and sprays are product categories. Consider another product class—beer. There are a number of product categories within that class, including light beer, regular beer, microbrewery beer, imported beer, and so on.

To complete their view of competition, marketing managers must consider the matter of brand. **Brands** identify and distinguish one marketer's product from its competitors'. All of us are familiar with hundreds of brands of products. For example, the light beer category is made up of brands such as Miller Lite, Coors Light, Bud Light, and many others.

All three groupings—product class, product category, and brand distinctions—must be considered in answering the question "Who is the competition?" A liquid cleaner like Top Job can be used to clean floors. So can a powdered cleaner like Spic and Span. Liquid Lysol can do anything that spray Lysol can do, except provide the convenience of the spray can itself.

In a sense, any cleaner, beer, or hotel can compete against any other member of its product class. However, brands of products compete primarily within product categories. While the entire class of goods or services should be kept in mind, it is the product category that contains the major competitors, because the category reflects a specific consumer's wants, needs, and desires.

The Four Types of Competition

There are four general types of competition: price, quality, time, and location. These types of competition are related to the utilities described earlier.

In today's information age, organizations must have the ability to anticipate, adjust, and react. Time is a competitive weapon in our global economy. State Farm Insurance's claims representatives once used ballpoint pens, paper and stacks of huge construction manuals in their offices to estimate damage from fires and other disasters. Today, they use IBM ThinkPad computers to review building data, and calculate and print estimates at the loss site. Using modern information technology has reduced processing time for claims from weeks to hours.

Price Competition
Competition based on price; associated with possession utility.

Quality-Based Competition
Competition based on product quality; associated with form utility.

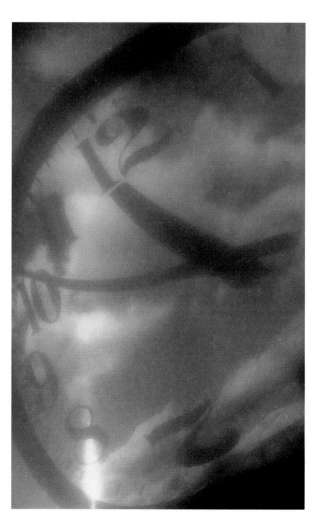

To obtain possession utility, consumers must pay a price. That is, they must exchange something of value, which we call a price, for the good or service they desire. Economists have spent a great deal of time investigating **price competition.** In general, a price that is lower than competitors' prices will attract customers to the lower-priced product.[4]

Form utility increases as product quality improves. Many businesses choose to compete on the basis of product quality rather than on the basis of price. **Quality-based competition** is more complex than price competition because consumers define quality in many different ways. Durability and reliability are traditionally associated with quality. So are design, color, style, and many other attributes that determine the physical nature of products. Prompt, polite, and friendly service are also associated with consumers' perceptions of quality. All other things, including price, being equal, the higher the perceived quality, the more likely consumers are to buy a product.

Time-Based Competition
Competition based on providing time utility by delivering the product when the consumer wants it.

Time-based competition is directly associated with time utility. In the simplest sense, buyers prefer to take possession of their goods exactly when they need them, which is often as soon as possible. Time-based competition is exceedingly important in many industries, especially those in which most competing products are seen as being virtually identical. Moreover, time as a competitive weapon is becoming more important in a world of ever-faster global communications. A marketing manager in today's competitive environment "has to think like a fighter pilot. When things move so fast, you can't always make the right decision—so you have to learn to adjust to correct more quickly."[5]

Location-Based Competition
Competition based on providing place utility by delivering the product where the consumer wants it.

Location-based competition is based on providing more place utility than competitors do. Location is extremely important for retail businesses. The 7-Eleven conveniently located at a high-traffic intersection will sell more milk and soft drinks than a grocery store located on a little-traveled road. A small store inside a shopping mall has many drop-in customers who come to the mall to shop at the large department stores.

Competitive Advantage

Competitive Advantage
Superiority over competitors in terms of price, quality, or location.

In Chapter 2, we mentioned that a company strives to obtain an edge, or competitive advantage over industry competitors. To establish and maintain a **com-**

petitive advantage means to be superior to or different from competitors in some way. More specifically, it means to be superior in terms of price, quality, time, or location. A company may achieve superiority by operating a more efficient factory, selling at a lower price, designing better-quality products, being the first on the market with an innovation, or satisfying customers in other ways. In other words, market-oriented organizations can use many alternative strategies to outperform competitors in terms of price, quality, time, or location.

Collaborators

Collaborator
Person or company that works with a marketing company. Collaborators help the company run its business without actually being part of the company.

Buying materials and supplies, hiring an advertising agency, or getting a loan from a bank requires that one company work with another company. These companies are collaborators. A **collaborator** is a person or a company that works with your company. Collaborators help the company run its business without actually being part of the company. They are often specialists who provide particular services or supply raw materials, component parts, or production equipment. Collaborators that provide materials, equipment, and the like are called **suppliers.**

The notion of the virtual organization is based on working closely with collaborators. Automobile companies operate factories in which everything from carburetors to windshield wipers are outsourced. Suppliers design the parts as well as make them. They distribute the appropriate quantity of parts to an automaker's assembly plant exactly when they are needed. Collaboration with suppliers frees up automakers' resources so they may concentrate on what they do best. Having every organization in the value chain focus on core competencies results in lower cost and better-designed products.

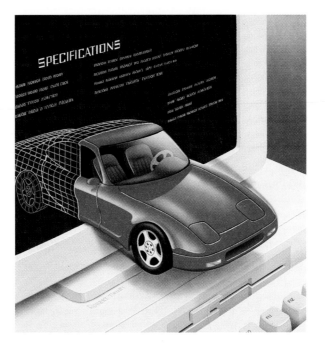

Many terms—including *alliances, networks,* and *informal partnerships*—have been used to describe the kinds of relationships just mentioned. However, the term collaborators works well because it implies that a company and another party are engaged in an ongoing relationship. In today's business climate, companies must be flexible and able to change quickly. Working with collaborators helps companies enhance their flexibility, especially in global marketing activities.

The number of collaborative relationships has grown significantly in recent years, and organizational collaborations are expected to be increasingly important in the 21st century. Contemporary organizations no longer believe they have to perform all business activities internally. Managers recognize that organizational collaborators may have special competencies that allow them to excel at certain tasks. Companies today believe that there is value in making joint commitments and sharing resources.

Supplier
An organization that provides raw materials, component parts, equipment, services, or other resources to a marketing organization; also called a vendor.

Some companies' marketing strategies are highly dependent on collaborations. In fact, business thinkers have created a name for organizations that use collaboration extensively: *virtual corporations.* The name virtual is derived from terminology used in the early days of the computer industry. The term *virtual memory* described a way of making a computer act as if it had more storage capacity than it really possessed.[6] Thus, the so-called virtual corporation, which appears to be a single enterprise with vast capabilities, is the result of numerous collaborations whose resources are garnered only when they are needed.

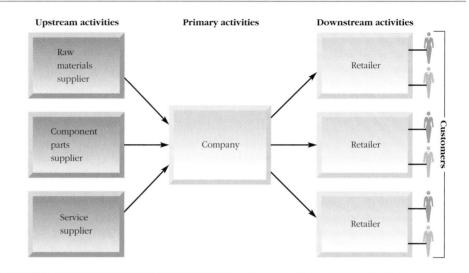

EXHIBIT 4–1
The Value Chain

Upstream activities   Primary activities   Downstream activities

Raw materials supplier

Component parts supplier

Service supplier

Company

Retailer

Retailer

Retailer

Customers

 ## THE VALUE CHAIN

Value Chain

Chain of activities by which a company brings in materials, creates a good or service, markets it, and provides service after a sale is made. Each step creates more value for the consumer.

Exhibit 4–1 shows what we can call the **value chain.**[7] The activities portrayed in the exhibit illustrate how operating a business involves a system of activities and relationships. Each part of the system—each link in the chain—adds value to the product customers ultimately buy.

The exhibit illustrates the relationships between a company, its customers, and some of its collaborators by dividing activities into *primary, upstream,* and *downstream* activities. Notice that before the company engages in its primary operations, such as production, accounting, and pricing, it engages in upstream activities, such as purchasing equipment and materials from suppliers. Downstream activities, performed after the product has been produced, require dealing with other collaborators, such as transportation companies and retailers. These upstream and downstream activities are called *supportive activities.* They provide the support necessary for carrying out primary activities or for concluding the sale of goods or services to the final buyer.

Collaborators in the value chain create new value together.[8] These companies link themselves together to achieve a common purpose. Each company values the skills that its partners bring to the collaboration. By linking their companies' capabilities, the collaborators can increase the value that the ultimate customer obtains.

CORE COMPETENCIES

Core Competency

A proficiency in a critical functional activity—such as technical know-how or a particular business specialization—that helps provide a company's unique competitive advantage.

Before an organization decides how much it will work with collaborators, its managers should ascertain the company's core competencies.[9] A **core competency** is a proficiency in a critical functional activity—such as technical know-how or a particular business specialization—that helps provide a company's unique competitive advantage. The company may be able to do something its competitors cannot do at all or that they find difficult to do even poorly.[10] Simply put, core competencies are what the organization does best.

A company enhances its effectiveness by concentrating its resources on a set of core competencies that will allow it to achieve competitive superiority and pro-

Collaboration in the value chain involves creating new value together. Companies link themselves together to achieve a common purpose. Each company values the skills that its partner brings to the collaboration. All of Nike's shoe production is outsourced. Research and development for product design and marketing are among Nike's core competencies.

vide unique or differentiated value for customers. For example, Nike manufactures only key technical components of its "Nike Air" system. All of its shoe production is performed by Asian collaborators. Research and development for product design and marketing are Nike's core competencies, not production.

An understanding of core competencies helps managers determine what value-creating activities can be outsourced. **Outsourcing** means having these activities performed by collaborators—outside sources. Outsourced activities, such as the production of major parts or subassemblies by suppliers, may be integral to the company's operations. Consider that for Chrysler's Eagle Vision and its other LH series cars, there are ten distinct sections. Chrysler makes the engine, transmission, and metal exterior.[11] The remaining seven sections are made by contract manufacturers like Textron, which produces and delivers a fully assembled instrument panel containing a speedometer, radio, glove-box door, and air-conditioner louvers. For the 1998 models, Textron became responsible for detailed design and engineering tasks.

Outsourcing
Buying or hiring from outside suppliers.

The major reason for outsourcing is that, simply put, few companies possess adequate resources and capabilities to perform all primary activities, upstream activities, and downstream activities themselves. In today's era of intense global competition, it would be almost impossible for any organization to have all the necessary competencies that would allow it to excel at every activity in its value chain. Companies that recognize this fact carefully plan their collaborations with other companies so they can combine complementary strengths to increase customer value.

Companies often have problems when they stray too far from their core competencies. Burger King, for example, expanded its menu with Snickers ice cream bars, chef's salads, and Breakfast Buddy and bagel sandwiches. It offered a special dinner service, which included fried shrimp and trays brought to tables by staff.[12] After several years of broadening its offerings, the company realized it had veered too far from its core competencies. Burger King retrenched. It decided to concentrate on the business it knew best—the burger, fries, and drink business. The company again stresses flame broiling, taste, and value.

Businesses in the United States have passed through a transition from a domestic economy to a global economy. Today, marketing managers conduct business around the globe. A trip to Asia is second nature to many executives in multinational corporations.

RELATIONSHIP MANAGEMENT

Effective executives stress managing the relationships that make the value chain productive. These managers work to build long-term relationships with suppliers, resellers, and, ultimately, customers who buy the product for consumption. The term **relationship management** is used to communicate the idea that a major goal of business is to build long-term relationships with the parties that contribute to the company's success.

Relationship Management
The building and maintaining of long-term relationships with the parties that contribute to the organization's success.

Companies strive to initiate collaborations and build loyalties. It is the manager's job to create, interpret, and maintain the relationships between the company and its collaborators.

MICROENVIRONMENTS AND THE FOUR Cs IN A GLOBAL ECONOMY

"On a political map, the boundaries between countries are as clear as ever. But on a competitive map, a map showing the real flows of financial and industrial activity, those boundaries have largely disappeared."[13] The world has become a global economy in which corporations market their products in many areas outside their home countries. In consumer electronics, for instance, Japanese marketers like Sony and Panasonic have high market shares in the United States and compete effectively throughout the world. Not only marketing but also manufacturing has taken on an international character for some organizations. Honda lawn mowers, for example, are manufactured in Swepsonville, North Carolina. Is this an American product or a Japanese product?

An organization that sells its products beyond its home nation's boundaries engages in **international marketing.** International marketing involves the adoption of a marketing strategy that views the world market rather than a domestic market as the basis for marketing operations.

International Marketing
The adoption of a marketing strategy that views the world market rather than a domestic market as the basis for marketing operations.

Many U.S. companies are thoroughly involved in multinational marketing. Gillette, Coca-Cola, and Johnson & Johnson earn well over 50 percent of their prof-

A McDonald's restaurant located in New Delhi, India, is the only in the world with no beef on the menu. Some 80 percent of Indians are Hindu, a religion whose adherents don't eat beef and believe cows are a sacred symbol. Instead of the Big Mac, the Indian menu features the Maharaja Mac— "two all-mutton patties, special sauce, lettuce, cheese, pickles, onions on a sesame-seed bun." For the strictest Hindus, who eat no meat at all, there are rice-based patties flavored with peas, carrots, red pepper, beans, coriander and other spices. The vegetable burgers are deep fried, emerging from their oil bath as crisp as the Middle Eastern chickpea snack known as falafel and tasting vaguely spicy.

McDonald's, which has restaurants in more than 95 countries, adapts its menu to local tastes around in the world. Thai customers can sample Samurai Pork Burgers topped with a sweet barbecue sauce, and burgers in Japan are garnished with a fried egg.

its overseas. The U.S. government encourages U.S. companies to expand their international marketing efforts. The United States is, in fact, a major exporting country in terms of absolute dollar volume.

The United States has passed through a transition period from a domestic orientation to a global orientation. At one time, an American marketer could be content to ignore world trade and compete with other domestic marketers for business in the growing U.S. economy. Today, however, with multinational organizations employing global marketing strategies, a domestic marketer must be aware of foreign competitors' influences not only in international markets but in its own domestic market. Competition is global, and the future of marketing is global. Companies must therefore analyze microenvironments in various parts of the world.[14] For that reason, it is useful to consider global marketing within the framework of the four Cs. We begin by looking at the global consumer.

Customers—The Era of the Global Consumer

International marketers, like domestic marketers, focus on satisfying customer needs. These needs often vary by country and culture. For example, Campbell's Soup Company has found that most Americans cringe at the thought of a bowl of pumpkin soup; but in Australia, cream of pumpkin soup is a national favorite. Pumpkin soup to Australians is very much what tomato soup is to Americans. Such differences often result from differences in countries' cultural environments.

Sometimes differences are the results of laws shaped by cultural values. For example, in Iran, foreign brands are not allowed to advertise on Iran's two television channels because of their perceived detrimental Western influence.[15] Global marketers should recognize similarities and differences among customers in different areas of the world and incorporate this knowledge into their marketing strategies.

Multinational Economic Community

A collaboration among countries to increase international trade by reducing trade restrictions. Typically, a group of countries forms a unified market within which there are minimal trade and tariff barriers; the European Union is an example.

Marketers often view global customers from a regional perspective, reflecting a trend toward formation of multinational economic communities. A **multinational economic community** is a collaboration among countries to increase international trade by reducing trade restrictions. The formation of economic communities not

EXHIBIT 4–2
The European Union

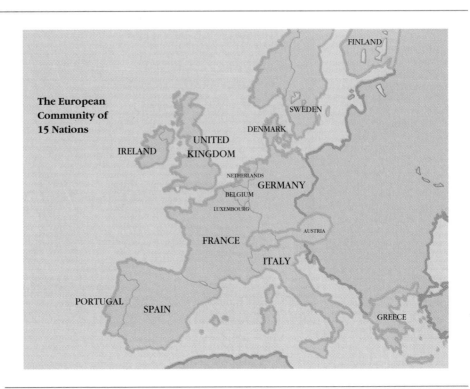

only makes it easier for member nations to trade with each other but also makes it easier for outsiders to trade with member nations.

Perhaps the best-known economic community is the European Union, also known as the European Community or Common Market. As shown in Exhibit 4–2, it consists of Portugal, France, Ireland, the United Kingdom, Spain, Denmark, Germany, the Netherlands, Belgium, Luxembourg, Italy, Greece, Austria, Finland, and Sweden. Although Europeans have been working on a "borderless" economy for more than 30 years, 1992 marked the date that finally eliminated national trade barriers, differences in tax laws, conflicting product standards, and other restrictions that had kept the member nations from being a single market. Trade within this union almost parallels trade among U.S. states—minimal significance for borders and no customs controls.

The European Union presents a single market with more than 323 million consumers—an enormous marketing opportunity. It has been estimated that since 1992, the European Union has been the largest single market in the world. Today, market spending exceeds $50 trillion. Each year, U.S. companies sell more than $500 billion of goods and services in the European Union. Furthermore, by the year 2000, this group of economic partners may encompass most of the continent. Austria, Finland, and Sweden joined in 1992 and Iceland, Norway, and Switzerland approved a pact that over time will integrate these countries with the European Union. Three former Eastern bloc countries—the Czech Republic, Hungary, and Poland—are seeking associate-member status with the European Union, and they may become full members by the turn of the century. Some marketing analysts estimate that in the year 2000, the European Union's trading area will include 450 million people.

In North America, the stage has been set for the development of a single trading market of more than 350 million people. NAFTA, the North American Free Trade Agreement, was passed by the United States Congress in 1993. This agreement allows for increased trade between Mexico, Canada, and the United States.

COMPETITIVE STRATEGY: WHAT WENT WRONG?

Gestures Speak Louder Than Words

"I knew I'd committed a monumental goof. But I just couldn't imagine how."

A young computer salesman from New Jersey is remembering his first overseas sales pitch. The scene was his company's offices in Rio, and it had gone like a Sunday preacher's favorite sermon. As he looked around the table, he knew he had clinched the sale. Triumphantly, he raised his hand to his Latin customers and flashed the classic American okay sign—thumb and forefinger forming a circle, other fingers pointing up.

The sunny Brazilian atmosphere suddenly felt like a deep freeze. Stony silence. Icy stares. Plus embarrassed smirks from his colleagues.

Calling for a break, they took him outside the conference room and explained. Our hero had just treated everyone to a gesture with roughly the same meaning over there as the notorious third-finger sign conveys so vividly here. Apologies saved the sale, but he still turns as pink as a Brazilian sunset when retelling the tale. It is only natural when you find yourself at sea in the local language to use gestures to bail yourself out. . . . Gestures pack the power to punctuate, to dramatize, to speak a more colorful language than mere words. Yet, like the computer salesman, you may discover that those innocent winks and well-meaning nods are anything but universal.

It will have a major impact on production location, imports, exports, and unemployment in selected industries.

In 1994, NAFTA meant that the United States canceled tariffs on 60 percent of Mexican goods that had been subjected to taxes. **Tariffs** are taxes imposed by a nation on selected imported goods brought into that nation to make those goods more costly in the marketplace. Other tariffs are being phased out over a 15-year period. Exports from the United States grew by more than 20 percent in the first nine months NAFTA was in effect.[16] Mexican consumers bought U.S. products whose production requires technology that Mexico does not yet possess. U.S. consumers have increased purchases of Mexican agricultural products and other goods produced by operations that are labor-intensive. We will continue to discuss global customers and their unique needs throughout this book.

Tariff
A tax imposed by a government on an imported product.

Competitors in a Worldwide Arena

We have already mentioned that marketers in the United States and throughout the world are confronted with global competition. Intensified global competition can stimulate and improve domestic competition in an industry. For example, consumers complained for years that American automobile manufacturers were unconcerned about quality and inattentive to market needs. When Japanese and European cars gained a large share of the U.S. auto market, American producers began to remedy these deficiencies. Such improvements in domestic competition spur improvements in living standards as well as general economic well-being.

International marketers hope they can compete on a "level playing field," where no one has an "unfair" advantage. However, this is not the case for all products or all markets. Sometimes competitors headquartered in foreign countries enjoy government subsidies or benefit from legislation that grants them other economic advantages in their home markets.

The Japanese practice of *keiretsu* provides a good example of a fundamental difference in the way U.S. and Japanese companies conduct business in Japan. Keiretsu are groups of companies that form "corporate families." Bound together

The federal government's declaring a tariff on imported motorcycles with large engines had a dramatic impact on the Harley-Davidson company.

by mutual shareholdings or other financial ties, members of the keiretsu engage in cooperative business strategies. For example, because Toyota's keiretsu includes Koito Manufacturing, an automobile parts company, Koito has special privileges when supplying parts to Toyota. Outside companies find it difficult to market competitive products to Toyota in the same way as competitors who are members of Toyota's keiretsu.[17]

Governments often protect certain domestic industries by imposing tariffs to restrict the activity of foreign companies. Tariffs can have a dramatic impact on foreign competitors. Because the imported product is higher priced (as a result of the tariff), domestic production may be encouraged or consumption of the imported product may be discouraged. For example, at one time, the United States imposed a high tariff (50 percent) on imported motorcycles with engines larger than 700cc. Harley-Davidson, the only American-owned motorcycle manufacturer, made no motorcycles with engines smaller than 1000cc and did not care about small-engined motorcycles. Clearly, the existence of high restrictive tariffs in a country can discourage competitors of another nation from marketing in that country.

Import Quota

A limit set by a government on how much of a certain type of product can be imported into a country.

Import quotas, or government-imposed limits on a type of imported good, are another restrictive factor. Countries trying to promote domestic production or discourage domestic consumption may impose quotas on certain imported products. Some quotas set absolute limits, and goods can be imported only until the set level is reached. After that, no further imports are allowed. Other quotas are established with tariffs in such a way that an extremely high tariff is levied on goods imported beyond the quota limit. The ultimate form of restriction is the **embargo,** in which a government may completely shut down trade with a particular country or restrict trade for a particular product class.

Embargo

A government prohibition of trade, especially for a particular product.

The automotive industry in the United States illustrates the use of quotas. Faced with increased competition from imported cars and increased pressure from automotive labor unions in the United States, the auto industry and the U.S. government have worked to get Japan to agree to a limit on the number of cars Japanese companies export to the United States. Such a restriction is clearly a form of import quota. Honda and Toyota, as well as Volkswagen and other foreign automobile markers, have established production facilities in the United States partly in response to these pressures.

Governments may impose a variety of other restrictive controls to discourage foreign companies from doing business in their markets. Sometimes countries require that all trade with other nations be approved by some form of central ministry. This allows for the establishment of various types of quotas and controls over goods brought into the country. Still other nations establish boycotts or other barriers by using restrictive criteria set up to eliminate the importing of certain products. A local government may, for instance, establish buying criteria for food products so that food products may not be shipped in from certain countries.

Even when there is a level playing field without government restrictions, an exporter may face disadvantages relative to domestic competitors. Procter & Gamble's Pampers, for example, could not beat stiff competition in the Australian and New Zealand markets. Pampers were imported, rather than manufactured locally, and high transportation costs and currency fluctuations meant they had to be priced higher than the competition.[18]

The Company as an International Marketer

In spite of the global nature of today's business environment, not all U.S.-based companies choose to market their products outside the United States. A bagel bakery may limit its marketing to New York City, for instance. The organization's resources or market demand may justify this strategy. Large corporations, of course, are more likely to find it advantageous to spend considerable time and effort marketing beyond their national boundaries. However, not all large corporations engage in international marketing. Southwest Airlines, for example, chooses to market its services only inside the United States. The same fundamental marketing concepts that apply in domestic marketing apply in international marketing. Uncontrollable environmental factors must be analyzed, and target markets must be determined. Competitive market positions must be considered, and marketing mix strategies must be planned and executed to appeal to these target markets.

Political stability, tariffs, and exchange rates are some of the factors a company must take into account when it is making the decision to market in another country. The factors that affect a company's decision to enter a certain market are discussed in Chapter 8, "Market Segmentation, Targeting, and Positioning Strategies."

After a company decides it will do business in a certain market, it must make decisions about what degree of ownership and management involvement it will pursue. Market potential, the organization's experience in international marketing, the organization's willingness to subject itself to risks, and host country policies often influence these decisions. These factors may cause a multinational marketer to be involved at different levels in different countries.

The basic types of involvement are direct investment, exporting, and joint venturing. We examine direct investment and exporting next. With joint venturing, we move into the area of collaborations. Exhibit 4–3 outlines these strategies.

Direct Foreign Investment
Investment of capital in production and marketing operations located in a host foreign country.

If foreign market demand is great, a company may directly invest in manufacturing and marketing operations in a host foreign country. This is called **direct foreign investment.** Coca-Cola owns a bottling plant in Guangzhow (Canton) China, for example. Several Japanese automobile manufacturers have built automobile plants in the United States. This enables the automakers to minimize the shipping expenses and political pressures associated with selling foreign-made cars in the U.S. market. In other instances, an organization may directly invest in plant operations in developing countries to take advantage of low-cost labor. Whatever the reason, direct investment in manufacturing facilities and marketing operations reflects a long-term, high-level commitment to international marketing.

STRATEGY	LOCATION OF PRODUCTION FACILITY	FOREIGN COMPANY'S PRIMARY INVOLVEMENT	OWNERSHIP OF FOREIGN OPERATION	CAPITAL OUTLAY REQUIRED
Direct				
Direct Investment	Foreign country	Native sales force may be used; sometimes foreign intermediaries used	Complete domestic ownership	High
Direct Exporting	Domestic	None	None	Low
Global Collaborators				
Indirect Exporting	Domestic	Intermediary ensures foreign distribution and sales	Foreign ownership of intermediaries	Low
Licensing/ Franchising	Foreign country	Owns right to manufacture/ service and use product name; local marketing	Joint according to contract	Low
Contract Manufacturing	Foreign country	Production according to specifications	Foreign ownership of production facility	Low
Joint Ownership	Foreign country	Partner	Partner	Moderate to high

EXHIBIT 4–3
Summary of International Involvement

Many risks are associated with a long-term direct investment strategy. For example, Iraq's invasion of Kuwait had a major impact on Exxon, Aramco, and other oil companies that had oil-exploration facilities destroyed or damaged during the Gulf War. In some countries, a change in governments may lead to nationalization of foreign companies' assets, that is, a transfer of the assets to the new government. If the risk of nationalization of a multinational's operations is high, direct investment becomes less attractive.

Exporting
Selling domestically produced products in foreign markets.

In contrast to direct investment, **exporting** is a relatively low-level commitment to international marketing. Exporters, manufacturing or harvesting in their home countries, sell some or all of their products in foreign markets. Such distribution may be accomplished either directly, through the company's sales force, or indirectly, through intermediaries. (Thus, exporting may or may not involve collaborators.) There is no investment in overseas plant or equipment in either case.

With *indirect exporting,* a domestic company does not deal directly with overseas customers. Instead, it sells a portion of its inventory to some intermediary that conducts business (usually buying) in the company's home country. The intermediary then distributes the product in foreign markets. The major strength of the intermediary is its accessibility to foreign customers. Some companies exporting indirectly do not routinely engage in this activity, viewing the international marketplace simply as a place to get rid of surplus inventory or unwanted products. Others choose to export on a more continuous and systematically planned basis. Whatever the degree of indirect exporting, the company uses its domestic sales force to sell its products to the intermediaries.

Direct exporting may be used when a firm wants greater control over the foreign sales of its product. Direct exporting can take several forms. Some companies use their own traveling salespeople, who make occasional visits to overseas markets to try to sell the product there. These salespeople may meet with limited success unless they can cultivate the right prospects and understand what is required to conduct business in another culture. Other companies establish a domestic-based export department or division. The scope of this unit is determined in part by the degree of commitment the company feels toward international marketing.

Because the perspective of these two approaches to direct exporting is often domestic-based, they do not always meet with success. Therefore, some companies choose to establish overseas sales offices, branches, or distributors to maintain a continued presence in the host country or overseas market. Such organizations can develop a better understanding of the differences in foreign markets than salespeople making occasional visits.

Global Collaborations

Collaborations on a global scale have increased as a result of the globalization of the marketplace. Using export management companies, engaging in joint ventures, and outsourcing from companies operating outside the United States have allowed U.S. companies to marshal more resources for international marketing. In our discussion of exporting, we mentioned that indirect exporting requires the use of intermediaries. Companies often develop collaborative relationships with **export management companies,** intermediaries that specialize in buying from sellers in one country and marketing the products in other countries. Export management companies, which assume ownership of the goods, reduce the risk of multinational marketing for companies without a great deal of exporting experience. Like other wholesalers, export management companies perform many distribution functions for sellers. However, in most cases, selling and taking responsibility for foreign credit are their primary functions. Other intermediaries that represent companies in overseas selling activities include various types of export agents who do not take title to the goods.

In **joint venturing,** domestic and host companies join to set up production and marketing facilities in an overseas market. Unlike exporting, joint venturing involves some agreement for production of the product on foreign soil. The Whirlpool example at the beginning of this chapter discussed a joint-venturing agreement for operations in the Far East.

There are several forms of joint venturing. One simple method is **licensing,** in which a company (the *licensor*) wanting to do business in a particular overseas market enters into a licensing agreement with an overseas company (the *licensee*) that permits the licensee to use the licensor's manufacturing processes, patents, trademarks, trade secrets, and so on in exchange for payment of a fee or royalty.

Licensing provides a means to conduct business in a country whose laws discourage foreign ownership. One disadvantage of licensing is loss of managerial control. The foreign company makes key decisions without input from the licensor. On the positive side, a licensee may provide a greater understanding of the local culture, experience with the local distribution system, and the marketing skill required to succeed in the foreign market.

International franchising is a form of licensing in which a company establishes overseas franchises in much the same way it establishes franchises in its own country. Because many franchisors desire consistency, franchising agreements are most often found in markets where conditions are similar to those in the domestic market. A potential disadvantage of international franchising is the possibility that this type of operation will foster future competitors. Sometimes, after gaining enough training and experience, franchisees start their own rival companies.

Some companies believe that the risks of licensing are too great and prefer to maintain greater marketing control. These companies use **contract manufacturing,** under which a company agrees to permit an overseas manufacturer to produce its product. The domestic company supplies the product specifications and the brand name, and the foreign company produces the product under that label for the domestic company. Overseas sales of the product are typically handled and controlled by the domestic company. In Mexico and Spain, for instance, Sears may establish its own stores; but rather than filling these stores with imported products, it often uses

Export Management Company
A company that specializes in buying from sellers in one country and marketing the products in other countries. Such companies typically take title to the products.

Joint Venturing
In international marketing, an arrangement between a domestic company and a foreign host company to set up production and marketing facilities in a foreign market.

Licensing
In international marketing, an agreement by which a company (the licensor) permits a foreign company (the licensee) to set up a business in the foreign market using the licensor's manufacturing processes, patents, trademarks, trade secrets, and so on in exchange for payment of a fee or royalty.

International Franchising
A form of licensing in which a company establishes foreign franchises. Franchising involves a contractual agreement between a franchisor, often a manufacturer or wholesaler, and a franchisee, typically an independent retailer, by which the franchisee distributes the franchisor's product.

Contract Manufacturing
In international marketing, an agreement by which a company allows a foreign producer to manufacture its product according to its specifications; typically, the company then handles foreign sales of the product.

local manufacturers to produce Sears-label products to specifications. In many foreign markets, contract manufacturing also offers the opportunity to use labor that is less expensive, thus yielding lower product prices or greater savings to the company.

Joint Ownership Venture
In international marketing, a joint venture in which domestic and foreign partners invest capital and share ownership and control.

A final form of joint venturing is the **joint ownership venture.** Under this arrangement, the domestic and foreign partners invest capital and share ownership and control of the partnership in some agreed-on proportion. Ownership is not always equal. AT&T has a joint venture agreement with PTT Telecom of the Netherlands and Ukraine's State Committee of Communications to modernize phone service in Ukraine, which currently routes long-distance calls through Moscow on poor-quality lines. The venture, which will allow Ukrainians to direct-dial to foreign countries, is owned 39 percent by AT&T, 10 percent by PTT Telecom, and 51 percent by the government of Ukraine. A common reason for entering into a joint venture is that some countries that restrict foreign ownership of investments require such an arrangement. Mexico bars total foreign ownership of Mexican advertising agencies, for example. International agencies such as J. Walter Thompson, Inc., must therefore be involved in joint ventures if they wish to operate in Mexico. In other countries, the government may require that the local company maintain a majority interest in the venture, keeping foreign control in the company under 50 percent.

Another reason for joint ownership ventures is financial. A U.S. company may wish to set up European operations but may find it economically difficult. A joint ownership venture with a European firm may be the solution.

A key to the success of a joint ownership venture, as with any type of partnership, is finding and keeping the right mix of companies. Overseas and American firms do not always have the same views. Europeans tend to be engineering-oriented, for instance. The term *marketing* may simply mean "sales" to them. American companies, in contrast, often put marketing first. Management becomes difficult when the partners disagree on fundamental components of the business. Finding the right partner reduces these differences.

Whatever form global collaborations take, technology plays a central role. Satellite communications systems, modems, fax machines, and other advances in information technology have made collaboration with companies in other countries much more efficient. In many cases, instantaneous communication is possible. Global information systems, which are discussed in Chapter 5, have been instrumental in the growth of global business and international collaborations. Many business analysts believe the key to success in the global economy lies in effective use of information technology.

FOCUS ON RELATIONSHIPS

Nike

Nike buys the rubber for its shoes from companies in Asia whose main business is manufacturing rubber. Nike works with its advertising agency, Wieden & Kennedy, and basketball stars Charles Barkley and Michael Jordan to create exciting television commercials. It uses Roadway Express and Federal Express to transport its shoes to Athlete's Foot stores, where personalized customer service is given.

Nike also works with Sports Specialties Corporation, a specialist in professional sports licensing, which involves paying sports teams for the use of their names and logos. Through Sports Specialties, Nike collaborates with top-ranked college football and basketball teams and provides them with everything from pants and jerseys to warm-up jackets. These apparel lines are also for sale in retail stores.

Nike thus works with many collaborators who provide special services or contribute unique talents that strengthen and support Nike as a business.

SUMMARY

It is useful to organize all microenvironmental forces into four basic categories: company, customers, competitors, and collaborators. These are called the four Cs of marketing.

Learning Objective 1

Understand how the microenvironment affects a company's marketing activities.

The microenvironment consists of the company, its customers, and other economic institutions that shape its marketing practices. Thus, the effect of the microenvironment is regular and direct.

Learning Objective 2

Identify the four Cs of marketing.

The four Cs are company, customers, competitors, and collaborators. Each represents a participant that performs essential business activities. The term *company* refers to the business or organization itself. *Customers* are the lifeblood of every company; a company that does not satisfy customers' needs will not stay in business. *Competitors* are rival companies engaged in the same business. *Collaborators* are persons or companies that work with another company.

Learning Objective 3

Recognize how marketing creates economic utility for customers.

Marketing includes designing, distributing, storing, and scheduling the sale of products and informing buyers about them. It thus helps to create form utility and creates place, time, and possession utility. Together, these constitute economic utility.

Learning Objective 4

Identify the various types of competitors and understand how marketers anticipate and react to competitors' strategies to gain competitive advantages.

Competitors are rival companies interested in selling their products and services to a company's customers and potential customers. There are four general types of competition: price, quality, time, and location. To establish and maintain a competitive advantage means to be superior to or different from competitors in one of these four areas. This may be accomplished by operating a more efficient factory, by selling at a lower price, by designing better-quality products, or by satisfying customers in other ways.

Learning Objective 5

Describe the value chain and explain why it must be managed.

The value chain portrays the system of collaborative activities and relationships involved in operating a business. Each link in the chain adds value to the product customers ultimately buy. Having every organization in the value chain focus on core competencies results in lower-cost, better-designed products.

Learning Objective 6

Understand the importance of global competition in today's economy.

The United States—indeed, the world—has passed through a transition period from a domestic orientation to a global orientation. Today, a domestic marketer must be aware of foreign competitors' influence not only in international markets but also in its own domestic market. Markets have been internationalized; competition is global; and the future of marketing is global.

Learning Objective 7

Apply the four Cs in a global business context.

Because competition is global, companies must analyze microenvironments in various parts of the world. International companies must focus on satisfying customer needs by working with collaborators to gain competitive advantage. The four Cs often vary by country and culture.

KEY TERMS

Four Cs (p. 84)
Company (p. 84)
Entrepreneur (p. 84)
Intrapreneurial organization (p. 84)
Customer (p. 84)
Economic utility (p. 85)
Form utility (p. 85)
Place utility (p. 85)

Time utility (p. 85)
Possession utility (p. 85)
Competitor (p. 85)
Product category (p. 85)
Product class (p. 85)
Brand (p. 85)
Price competition (p. 86)
Quality-based competition (p. 86)

Time-based competition (p. 86)
Location-based competition (p. 86)
Competitive advantage (p. 86)
Collaborator (p. 87)
Supplier (p. 87)
Value chain (p. 88)
Core competency (p. 88)
Outsourcing (p. 89)

Relationship management (p. 90)
International marketing (p. 90)
Multinational economic community
    (p. 91)
Tariff (p. 93)

Import quota (p. 94)
Embargo (p. 94)
Direct foreign investment (p. 95)
Exporting (p. 96)
Export management company (p. 97)

Joint venturing (p. 97)
Licensing (p. 97)
International franchising (p. 97)
Contract manufacturing (p. 97)
Joint ownership venture (p. 98)

QUESTIONS FOR REVIEW AND CRITICAL THINKING

1. Tell what the four Cs of marketing stand for and give an example for each C.

2. What are the core competencies of the following organizations?
   a. Levi Strauss
   b. Southwest Airlines
   c. Chicago Bulls
   d. AT&T

3. Identify the participants in a value chain that brings automobiles to the ultimate consumer.

4. Identify the competitive advantages of the following products.
   a. Microsoft
   b. Scribner bookstores
   c. DeBeers diamonds
   d. Visa credit cards
   e. TCI Cablevision

5. Why is global collaboration growing in importance?

6. Explain how global competition affects a small business in your college town.

7. What factors affect a company's ability to compete in international markets?

8. Japan has manufactured automobiles in the United States for more than two decades. What impact has this had on the world automobile market?

9. Compare and contrast direct foreign investments with joint ownership ventures.

10. Suppose you are the marketing manager of a company that outsources key components of the product it manufactures. What are the job titles of the people in the supplier company with whom you would expect to work? As a customer, should your company maintain total control, or should you try to work as a team with your collaborator in a joint effort?

INTERNET INSIGHTS

Exercise

1. Go to the Yahoo search engine

        http://www.yahoo.com

   and enter European Union as a search phrase. What type of information is available?

2. Use the Internet to learn what you can about Indonesia.
   a. Use your Web browser to go to

            http://www.indonesiatoday.com

   b. Visit the CIA factbook

            http://www.odic.gov/cia

       Then navigate to Indonesia. What type of information is available?

   c. Use InfoSeek and type in Indonesia as a search word. How much information is available?

3. If your college or university has an account (identification number and password) with Stat-USA, use the Internet to learn what types of reports are available from the NTDB (National Trade Data Base).

Address Book

Financial data finder
http://www.cob.ohio-state.edu/dept/fin/osudata.htm

Free Trade Zone—Trade News
http://www.tradehere.com/news/news.htm

ETHICS IN PRACTICE: TAKE A STAND

1. Is it ethical for a company to engage in international trade and work with collaborators in the People's Republic of China, a communist country that has been accused of human rights violations?

2. Often, when a company enters into a collaborative relationship with a single supplier, other suppliers are locked out of doing business with that company for several years. Is this consistent with our free enterprise system?

3. A multinational food company markets powdered milk around the world. Critics say many Third World mothers do not understand that mixing the powder with impure water is unsafe. Because many mothers are incapable of using the product properly, these critics believe the product should be distributed only through physicians and hospitals. Do you agree that this collaboration is necessary?

VIDEO CASE 4-1

Sonic Drive-Ins

Sonic Corp., of Oklahoma City, Okla., has a history of more than 40 years as a fast-food drive-in franchise chain.

The company has seen growth, decline, and then stronger growth since its start in 1953 in Shawnee, Okla., where founder Troy Smith put covered stalls in his hamburger-stand parking lot, each with a speaker system. Customers ordered a hamburger and a drink from their cars, and a carhop would bring the orders.

By 1958 Smith and a partner had four drive-in hamburger stands. Their slogan was "Service with the speed of sound."

Sonic drive-ins spread across Oklahoma and into neighboring Kansas and Texas. Each drive-in operator was also a part owner. These owner-managers did not contribute to advertising, enjoyed no territorial rights, and paid a one-cent royalty per sandwich bag.

In the late 1960s and early '70s, as the number of drive-ins grew to more than 150, the company was reorganized several times. A group of franchisees bought Sonic's name, slogan, trademark, logos, and supply division. They offered other operators the option to buy stock, and Sonic Industries became a publicly traded company.

By 1978 there were 800 drive-ins in more than a dozen states. But field support was lagging, and some locations did not follow established operating standards. Sonic's sales began to decline. By 1981, 300 drive-ins had closed.

In 1983 C. Stephen Lynn, an experienced franchising and fast food executive, was brought in as president to turn the company around. He worked to build unity within the owner-operated chain.

To begin, he focused on 17 key markets. He persuaded operators of 200 drive-ins there to commit to purchase and advertise together for one year, promising the arrangement would increase same-store sales 15 percent and cut food costs 3 percent.

Performance was as good as Lynn said it would be. Today 95 percent of the chain, linked in advertising co-ops, spends more than $20 million a year on advertising, and 99 percent of the chain buys food and other supplies together.

Working capital to set up and administer the co-operative programs, and to provide field support, was produced when Lynn orchestrated a $10 million leveraged buyout of the company in 1986. In 1991 a public offering raised $52 million with which Sonic bought out venture capital investors, paid off debt, and added to working capital.

Today there are more than 1,400 Sonic drive-ins in 25 sun-belt states, and sales have been increasing at a 14.4 percent annual compounded rate. The decline under way in the early 1980s has been replaced by something of a Sonic boom.

Questions

1. Describe Sonic's microenvironment using the four Cs perspective.
2. What were the key elements of Sonic's competitive strategy?
3. What aspects of the macroenvironment are most likely to affect the company's competitive strategy?
4. Why do you think Sonic was able to turn the company around?

VIDEO CASE 4-2

 Gaston's White River Resort

Gaston's White River Resort, a 10-cottage trout-fishing camp at the end of a country road near Lakeview in northern Arkansas, was having trouble staying afloat in 1965. Revenues were insufficient, and the bank was moving toward foreclosure. Jim Gaston, the resort's young owner, had some ideas about saving it, though, and the bank listened to him. Instead of foreclosing, it granted him a new $15,000 loan.

Gaston was thinking big. In 1965 at an Arkansas fishing resort you rented a room with carpetless, linoleum floors for $7.50 a day. If you wanted TV it was $1 extra, and the same for air conditioning. Gaston began charging $10 a night for a room with carpeting, air conditioning, and TV. The local competition thought he had lost his mind, but a growing clientele supplied evidence that he hadn't.

Actually, Gaston felt the challenge was to compete with much more than the fishing camp down the road. He was after a world market, competing with the fishing experience in New York, or Canada, or Wisconsin, or Alaska.

To help make his resort world-class, he hired his own fishing guides, whom he describes as the best on the White River. He says other fishing camps rely on a pool of guides, and their best customers may not get the best service. His customers do, he says.

He required all his employees—today, there are 75 year-round and 47 more in the summer—to pay particular attention to customer satisfaction. You will never find resort employees more helpful than those at Gaston's, he boasts. The resort has a high rate of repeat guests.

Gaston learned to maintain contact with members of the outdoors press—writers for such publications as *Field and Stream* or *Fly Fisherman*—and to promote his resort as a place where corporate types could get away from it all. He installed a landing strip.

He also learned to market to a clientele that changes with the seasons: Arkansans in late winter, Texans and other out-of-staters in the summer; couples in the off season, families with kids in the peak season. Gaston keeps track of customer patterns by computer, to the point where he says he almost knows too much. Operation modes, he says, must change about four times a year to match the crowd.

In that crowd, which is bringing Gaston's White River Resort $5 million in annual sales and has required an increase in the number of its cottages to 73, are faces familiar to many Americans. TV's Phil Donahue, for example, settles in once a year with a group of friends from his college days at Notre Dame. Jim Gaston says he considers it a great compliment that a man who could charter a cruise ship comes back again and again to stay in one of his cottages, eat in his restaurant, and fish for trout in one of his 20-foot john boats.

Questions

1. Use the four Cs concept to outline Gaston's marketing microenvironment.
2. How has Gaston's established a competitive advantage?
3. How important is relationship management to Gaston's success? Identify several ways for Gaston's to build strong relationships with its customers and collaborators.

ENHANCE YOUR MARKETING SKILLS WITH CD-ROM

1. How do other functional activities within an organization, such as production and finance, influence marketing activities?

STRATEGY MODULE
THE ORGANIZATIONAL CONTEXT OF MARKETING*

2. If you were to give an award to companies that have excellent total quality management programs, what criteria would you use to evaluate quality?

STRATEGY MODULE
MANAGING FOR QUALITY AS A STRATEGY

3. What are the factors that influence ethical decision making in marketing?

MACROMARKETING MODULE
ETHICS

*You will find each exercise on the CD-ROM developed for use with this textbook. Each exercise has a name and is located within a module. For example, this exercise can be found in the Strategy Module by clicking on The Organizational Context of Marketing.

PART 2

GLOBAL INFORMATION SYSTEMS AND MARKETING RESEARCH

Chapter 5

Learning Objectives

After you have studied this chapter, you will be able to:

1. Explain why information is essential to effective marketing decision making.
2. Explain the importance of global information systems and the Internet.
3. Describe the nature of decision support systems and intranets.
4. Explain the contribution of marketing research to effective decision making.
5. Describe the stages in the marketing research process.
6. Explain how exploratory research relates to specific marketing management problems.
7. Understand why secondary data are valuable sources of information.
8. Understand the uses of surveys, observation, and experiments.
9. Demonstrate your knowledge of the purposes of sales forecasting.
10. Evaluate the advantages and disadvantages of the various forecasting methods.

Chee-tos, the cheesy corn puffs, were introduced in the United States almost 50 years ago. Recently, Frito-Lay's Chee-tos became the first major brand of snack food to be made and marketed in China. Frito-Lay's research established that per-capita expenditure on snack food in China—nearly zero—was small compared to the $35 per capita expenditure in the Netherlands and the $52 per person in the United States. Yet, the large number of people in China indicated a vast market potential if the company could successfully introduce its brand into the market.

Marketing research also discovered that cheese and other dairy products are not regular items in the Chinese diet. In addition, product taste tests revealed traditional cheese flavored Chee-tos did not appeal to Chinese consumers.

Rather than be discouraged by these findings, Chee-tos' marketing managers decided that additional marketing research was needed to investigate how the company could creatively adapt its product for the Chinese market. The company conducted consumer research with 600 different flavors to learn what favors would be most appealing. Among the flavors tested and disliked by Chinese consumers were: ranch dressing, nacho, Italian pizza, Hawaiian barbecue, peanut satay, North Sea crab, chili prawn, coconut milk curry, smoked octopus, caramel and cuttlefish. Research did show some flavors consumers liked. So, when Chee-tos were introduced to China they came in two flavors: Savory American Cream and Zesty Japanese Steak.

While cheese-less Chee-tos may seem like a contradiction in terms, it mattered little in the Chinese market. After six months Chee-tos were a such a big hit that processing plants had trouble keeping Chinese retailers' shelves stocked.

The brand name Chee-tos corresponds to the Chinese characters *qi duo* translated as "new surprise." The name is fortunate for the marketers at Frito-Lay. However, Frito-Lay did not count on good fortune to achieve success in the Chinese market. The company spent considerable effort researching flavors and learning how the Chinese would react to Chester Cheetah as a spokestoon in advertising because the company did not want a surprise like the one it got in the United Kingdom.

In 1990 Chee-tos were introduced to the United Kingdom with little, if any, consumer research. The London managers boldly stormed ahead using the American flavors and positioning strategy. The product bombed. The company had not worked diligently to understand the United Kingdom's snacking behaviors and adapt the product characteristics to local tastes.

Although many factors have contributed to Chee-tos success in China, marketing research was a major influence. Frito-Lay understands the importance of information to modern marketing managers in the United States and around the globe. This chapter focuses on how marketing managers use marketing information, especially marketing research.

The chapter begins with a discussion of the role information plays in the marketing decision-making process and goes on to discuss global information systems and decision support systems. The stages in the marketing research process are then described in detail. The chapter ends with an explanation of the importance of accurate sales forecasting.

INFORMATION—THE BASIS OF EFFECTIVE MARKETING

Marketing managers spend much of their time making decisions.[1] An integral aspect of decision making is the analysis and evaluation of information about the organization's customers, environment, and marketing activities. To be effective, the marketer needs to gather enough information to understand past events, to identify what is occurring now, and to predict what might occur in the future. Good, timely marketing information is an extremely valuable management tool because it reduces uncertainty and the risks associated with decision making. Marketing information can lead the marketing manager to new products, to improvement of existing products, and to changes in price, promotion, or distribution strategies and tactics. Information can also help define problems or identify opportunities. Once a marketing problem or opportunity is identified, systematically gathering further pertinent information helps the marketing manager deal objectively with the situation.

GLOBAL INFORMATION SYSTEMS IN THE 21st CENTURY

The well-being of business organizations planning to prosper in the 21st century depends on information about the world economy and global competition. Contemporary marketers require timely and accurate information from around the globe to maintain competitive advantages. In today's world, managers find that much information can be made instantaneously available. This has changed the nature of marketing decision making.

Global Information System (GIS)
An organized collection of telecommunications equipment, computer hardware and software, data, and personnel designed to capture, store, update, manipulate, analyze, and immediately display information about worldwide business activity.

As a result of increased global competition and technological advances, global information systems have developed. A **global information system (GIS)** is an organized collection of telecommunications equipment, computer hardware and software, data, and personnel designed to capture, store, update, manipulate, analyze, and immediately display information about worldwide business activity.[2]

Consider a simple example. At any moment, on any day, United Parcel Service (UPS) can track the status of its shipments around the world. UPS drivers use handheld electronic clipboards, called delivery information acquisition devices (DIAD), to record data about each pickup or delivery. The data is then entered into the company's main computer for record keeping and analysis. Then, using a satellite telecommunications system, UPS can track any shipment for its customers.

Consider how global information systems are changing the nature of business. If executives at Motorola must make pricing decisions about their European markets for cellular phones, they can get immediate information about international currency and exchange rates without leaving their desks. If a salesperson needs information about a corporation's executives, he can access a full report on the corporation from a remote location using a personal communication device. If a marketing manager requires a bibliography on a particular subject, she can generate hundreds of abstracts with a few simple keystrokes.

Global information systems are the result of satellite communication, high-speed microcomputers, electronic data interchanges, fiber optics, CD-ROM data storage,

FAX machines, and other technological advances involving interactive media. The age of global information has begun. Yet, as amazing as today's technology is, it will seem primitive in the 21st century.

DATA AND INFORMATION

We have been discussing information in a general sense. Before we go on, we must define the difference between information and data. **Data** are simply facts, recorded measures of certain phenomena, whereas **information** is a body of facts in a format suitable for use in decision making.

The proper collection of data is the cornerstone of any information system.

Data
Facts and recorded measures of phenomena.

Information
Data in a format useful to decision makers.

The data collected should be pertinent, timely, and accurate. There are two types of data: primary data and secondary data. **Primary data** are data gathered and assembled specifically for the project at hand. For example, a company that designs an original questionnaire and conducts a survey to learn about its customers' characteristics is collecting primary data. **Secondary data** are data previously collected and assembled for some purpose other than the project at hand. Secondary data come from both internal sources, such as accounting records, and sources external to the organization, such as the U.S. Bureau of the Census. Generating information may require collecting secondary data, primary data, or both. The Internet is a vast source of secondary data.

Primary Data
Data gathered and assembled specifically for the project at hand.

Secondary Data
Data previously collected and assembled for some purpose other than the one at hand.

THE INTERNET—A NEW MEANS OF GLOBAL COMMUNICATION

Internet
A worldwide network of computers that gives individuals access to electronic mail and vast amounts of information and documents from distant sources.

As we have already mentioned, the **Internet** is a worldwide network of computers that gives individuals access to information and documents from distant sources. An estimated more than 5 million computers and 50 million users are linked across the Internet. The number of users doubles annually, making it the fastest-growing communications medium in history.[3]

In essence, the Internet is a combination of a worldwide communications system and the world's largest public library. The Internet also can be used for e-mail (electronic mail) to send messages and ask questions of experts or individuals who share similar interests.[4] The Internet also can be used to find information "published" by both noncommercial and commercial organizations. A wealth of data is

Every evening, Wal-Mart transmits millions of characters of data about the day's sales to its apparel suppliers. Wrangler, a supplier of blue jeans, for example, shares the data and a model that interprets the data. It also shares software applications that act to replenish stocks in Wal-Mart stores. This decision support system determines when to send specific quantities of specific sizes and colors of jeans to specific stores from specific warehouses. The result is a learning loop that lowers inventory costs and leads to fewer stock outs.

available. For example, the United States Library of Congress provides the full text of all versions of House and Senate legislation and the full text of the Congressional Record. South-Western College Publishing has an on-line directory that allows college professors to access information about the company and its textbooks.

The Internet began in 1969 as an experimental hookup between computers at Stanford University, the University of California at Santa Barbara, UCLA, and the University of Utah in conjunction with the Department of Defense.[5] The Defense Department was involved because it wanted a research and development communications network that could survive severe battlefield conditions. The Internet gradually grew into a nationwide network and now is a worldwide network often referred to as the "information superhighway." The Internet has no central computer; instead each message sent bears an address code that lets any computer in the Net forward it toward its destination.[6] The primary benefit of the Internet arises because it is a collection of thousands of small networks, both domestic and overseas, rather than a single computer operation. These many small networks contain millions of databases accessible to Internet users, mostly without fees.

The Internet consists of host computers that access servers to get to data. A *host* is a computer through which smaller computers connected to it can access network services. For example, university professors and students often have accounts on a campus mainframe computer tied into the Internet. The mainframe acts as a host for the faculty and students, allowing them to access other Internet hosts and servers through computer terminals or personal computers. A *server* is a computer that provides services on the Internet. For example, a file server contains documents and programs that can be accessed and downloaded via the host to a user's own computer; a list server permits subscribers to a mailing list to communicate with one another around the globe; and a user discussion server permits multiple users to communicate in real time with one another. Note that a host may also be a server. For instance, the same university mainframe that provides Internet access for faculty and students may also act as a server, providing Internet users with a collection of publicly accessible files.

In its early years, the Internet was not as easily accessible. Today, however, any individual with a computer and a modem can access the Internet by subscribing to a commercial on-line service such as America Online or Microsoft Explorer. At one time, an individual had to follow complex procedures to conduct Internet searches, but today the Internet is very user-friendly with point-and-click graphics that resemble the familiar Windows or Macintosh interfaces. Netscape and Microsoft Explorer are menu-based software systems called *Web browsers* that are so simple that even a novice on the Internet can search for information with little instruction.

A Web browser lets people get the information they want via a system of links called the *World Wide Web (WWW)*. Using a mouse, the user points to an icon or a keyword in the description and then clicks the mouse button to go immediately to the file, regardless of what server it may be stored on, and either reads or downloads the material. By clicking on "U.S. Government Information Servers" in one electronic document, for example, a Netscape user can connect to a computer with more information in Washington, D.C. A few more clicks, and the user can go to Web sites managed by the United States Census or the Small Business Administration.

Most Web browsers also allow the user to enter a *Uniform Resource Locator,* or *URL,* into the Web program. The URL is really just an address of a Web site. For example, *http://www.sbaonline.sba.gov* is the URL for the small business administration. The "gov" indicates the Web site is a government institution. Educational sites end in "edu" and commercial sites end in "com." Most nonprofit organizations sites end in "org."

A *search engine* is a computerized directory that allows anyone to search the World Wide Web (WWW) for information indexed in a particular way—some search titles or headers of documents, others search the documents themselves, and still others search other indexes or directories. For example, *Yahoo, Excite, AltaVista, Open Text Index* and *InfoSeek* are among the Internet's most comprehensive and accurate WWW search engines. All a researcher has to do is type the search term in plain English or just point and click to key words and phrases. *Yahoo* is a search engine that lists broad topics, such as Art, Business, Entertainment, and Government. Clicking on one of these topics leads to other subdirectories or home pages. *Open Text Index* is a search engine that searches every word of every Web page the company has indexed.

Most Web sites allow any user or visitor to access the site without previous approval. However, many commercial sites require that the user have a valid account and password before access is granted. The *Wall Street Journal Interactive* is a valuable Internet resource for subscribers who pay a fee. Exhibit 5–1 provides a listing of some popular Internet sites along with their addresses.

DECISION SUPPORT SYSTEMS AND INTRANETS

Decision Support System
A computer system that stores and transforms data into accessible information.

To store data and to transform data into accessible information, companies use computer systems called **decision support systems.**[7] Such systems serve specific business units within a company. A business unit's decision support system is not independent of the corporation's global information system. Indeed, a large organization may have several decision support systems operating within the context of the global information system.

The purpose of a decision support system is to allow decision makers to answer questions through direct interaction with databases. As Exhibit 5–2 shows, the system consists of databases and software.

Database
Collection of data arranged in a logical manner and organized in a form to be stored and processed by a computer.

A **database** is a collection of data arranged in a logical manner and organized in a form that can be stored and processed by a computer. For example, customer names, addresses, zip codes, and previous purchases may be contained in a company's internal database. Another database may record population and income data by state, county, and zip code.

NAME	DESCRIPTION	WEB ADDRESS
Search Engines		
YAHOO	Allows searches by words, phrases, or category.	*http://www.yahoo.com*
HOTBOT	Searches more than 54 million documents in its databases.	*http://www.hotbot.com*
EXCITE	Usenet search engine providing access to news, travel, and reference information.	*http://www.excite.com*
ALTAVISTA	Searches Usenet and the entire Web.	*http://www.altavista.digital.com*
INFOSEEK	General-purpose search engine.	*http://www.infoseek.com*
Sources for Marketing Information		
CENSUS BUREAU	Demographic information from US Census	*http://www.census.gov/*
STAT-USA/Internet	A comprehensive source of United States Government Information that focuses on economic, financial, and trade data.	*http://www.stat.usa.gov/inqsample.html*
ADVERTISING AGE	*Advertising Age* magazine provides marketing, media, advertising, and public relations content.	*http://www.adage.com*
WHOWHERE?	WhoWhere? is a comprehensive, easy to use White Pages service for locating e-mail addresses of people and organizations on the Internet.	*http://www.whowhere.com*
ZIKMUND AND D'AMICO HOME PAGE at South-Western College Publishing		*http://zikmund.swcollege.com*

EXHIBIT 5–1
Popular Internet Addresses

Many commercial organizations assemble and market computerized databases, which may be accessed through telecommunications links. America Online, Prodigy, CompuServe, Dialog Information Service, ABI/Inform, Dow Jones News/Retrieval, and many other database services make economics statistics, industry news, journal articles, and other data accessible instantaneously to an organization's computers.

Internal records and company reports provide a wealth of information related to costs, shipments, sales, and so on. For example, the database collected by accounting and other personnel can be used to generate a number of reports that managers use to improve performance. A typical product manager can ask the computer for weekly (or daily) sales by product line, inventory reports, back-order reports, and other performance measures.

The software portion of a decision support system consists of various types of programs that tell computers, printers, and other hardware what to do. Advances in spreadsheet and statistical software have revolutionized the analysis of marketing data. A decision support system's software allows managers to combine and restructure databases, diagnose relationships, estimate variables, and otherwise analyze the various databases.

Most of today's software is so user-friendly that it is easy for nonexperts to maintain direct control over the computer's tasks and outcomes. A manager can sit at a computer terminal and instantaneously retrieve data files and request spe-

EXHIBIT 5–2
The Decision Support
System

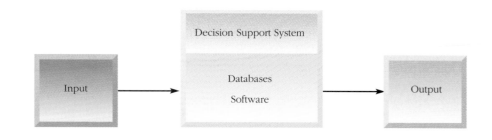

cial, creative analyses to refine, modify, or generate information in a tailor-made format. At Kmart, a computerized point-of-sale checkout system and a satellite communications system linked to a marketing decision support system allow managers at headquarters to retrieve and analyze up-to-the-minute sales data on all merchandise for the company's 2,400 stores.

Intranet
A company's private decision support system that uses Internet standards and technology.

If a company's decision support system is a private data network that uses Internet standards and technology, it is called an **intranet.**[8] The information on an intranet (data, graphics, even video and voice) is available only inside the organization. Thus, a key difference between the Internet and an intranet is that "firewalls" or security software programs are installed to limit access to only those employees authorized to enter the system.[9]

A company's intranet uses Internet features, such as electronic mail, Web pages and browsers to build a communications and data resource at a specific company.[10] Company information is accessible using the same point and click technology found on the Internet. Managers and employees use *links* to get complete up-to-date information. An intranet lets authorized personnel—some of whom previously were isolated on departmental local area networks—look at product drawings, employee newsletters, sales and other kinds of company information. Managers and employees using an intranet do not have to worry about the format of the information. Whether the information originated as a spreadsheet or a word processing document is not an issue.

In short, setting up an intranet involves adding Web-like functionality to an organization's existing global information system.

FOCUS ON TRENDS

Silicon Graphics

For a glimpse of the future, consider Silicon Graphics. This maker of high-end graphics workstations began using the Web internally almost as soon as Mosaic, the original Web browser, was introduced. The company started out publishing information electronically and making it available to employees at the company's headquarters near San Francisco and around the world. Today, says Frank Dietrich, corporate Web systems manager at Silicon Graphics Inc., "there's barely a piece of information that's not on-line."

Silicon Graphics has continued its forward march. Using

its intranet, called Silicon Junction, the company has made accessible more than two dozen corporate databases that employees can tap into by clicking on brightly colored hyperlinks. Prior to this, to get the same information, an employee had to submit a request to a staff of specially trained experts who then would extract the requested data from the company's databases—a time-consuming route. On top of this, the company also regularly sends video and audio feeds to employees around the world on the Net.

DATA-BASED MARKETING

Data-Based Marketing
The practice of maintaining customer databases with the customers' names, addresses, phone numbers, past purchases, responses to previous offers, and demographic characteristics.

Many organizations create databases containing huge amounts of data about individual customers and potential customers. Marketers use this information for computer-generated mailing lists and individualized promotional messages. The practice of maintaining customer databases with customers' names, addresses, phone numbers, past purchases, responses to previous offers, and demographic characteristics is referred to as **data-based marketing.** Data-based marketing has implications for many aspects of marketing strategy, and this topic will be discussed throughout the textbook.

FOCUS ON RELATIONSHIPS

Manhattan East Suite Hotels

Manhattan East Suite Hotels compiles a detailed database on the guests at its nine luxurious New York City properties, which include the Beckman Tower Hotel and the Shelburne-Murray Hill. Doormen greet arriving guests by name, and reservation agents know without asking whether a guest prefers a room facing northeast, say, or requires a nonsmoking room. Manhattan East has been logging occupancy rates of almost 20 percent higher than the citywide average for hotels.

WHAT IS MARKETING RESEARCH?

Marketing research allows managers to make decisions based on objective, systematically gathered data, rather than on intuition. What is the distinction between marketing research and other forms of marketing information? With or without a formal research program, a manager will have some information about what is going on in the world. He or she may discover that a competitor has announced a new product, that the inflation rate is stabilizing, or that a new highway will be built and a shopping mall erected north of town simply by reading the newspaper or watching TV. All of these things may affect the marketer's business, and this information is certainly handy to have, but is it the result of marketing research?

Marketing Research
The systematic and objective process of generating information for use in marketing decision making.

The answer to this question is no. **Marketing research** is the systematic and objective process of generating information for use in making marketing decisions. This process includes defining the problem and identifying what information is required to solve the problem, designing the method for collecting information, managing and implementing the collection of data, analyzing the results, and communicating the findings and their implications.[11] This definition suggests that marketing research is an organized effort rather than a haphazard attempt at gathering information. Thus, glancing at a newsmagazine on an airplane or overhearing a rumor is not marketing research. Even if a rumor or a fact casually overheard becomes the foundation of a marketing strategy, it is not a product of marketing research because it was not systematically and objectively gathered and recorded. The term "marketing research" suggests a specific, serious effort to generate new information. The term research suggests a patient, objective, and accurate search.

Although marketing managers may perform the research task themselves, they often use the help of specialists known as marketing researchers. The researcher's role requires detachment from the question under study. If researchers lack this impersonal quality, they may try to prove something rather than to generate objective data. If bias of any type enters into the investigation, the value of the findings must be questioned. Yet this can happen relatively easily. For example, a developer who owned a large parcel of land wanted to build a high-priced, high-prestige shopping center and conducted a study to demonstrate to prospective mall occupants that there was an attractive market for such a center. By conducting the survey only in elite neighborhoods, she generated "proof" that area residents wanted a high-prestige shopping center. Misleading "research" of this kind must be avoided. Unfortunately, businesspeople with no knowledge of proper marketing research methods may inadvertently conduct poorly designed, biased studies or may be sold such work by disreputable marketing research firms. Businesspeople should understand marketing research well enough to avoid these mistakes.

STAGES IN THE RESEARCH PROCESS

Marketing is not an exact science like physics but that does not mean that marketers and marketing researchers should not try to approach their jobs in a scientific manner. Marketing research is a systematic inquiry into the happenings of the marketplace, just as astronomy is a systematic investigation of the stars and planets. Both use step-by-step approaches to gaining knowledge.

The steps in these processes are highly interrelated, and one step leads to the next. The stages in the research process often overlap. Disappointments encountered at one stage may mean returning to previous stages, or even starting over. Thus, it is something of an oversimplification to present a neatly ordered sequence of activities. Still, the stages of marketing research often follow a generalized pattern of seven stages. These stages are: (1) defining the problem, (2) planning the research design, (3) selecting a sample, (4) collecting data, (5) analyzing data, (6) drawing conclusions and preparing a report, and (7) following up.

Again, these stages overlap and affect one another. In some cases, the "later" stages may be completed before the "early" ones. For example, the research objectives outlined as part of the problem definition stage will have an impact on the sample selection and data collection stages. A decision to sample people of low educational levels will affect the wording of the questions posed to these people. The research process, in fact, often becomes cyclical and ongoing, with the conclusions of one study generating new ideas and suggesting problems requiring further investigation.

Within each stage of the research process, the researcher faces a number of alternative methods, or paths, from which one must be chosen. In this regard, the research process can be compared to a journey.[12] On any map, some paths are more clearly charted than others. Some roads are direct, and others are roundabout. Some paths are free and clear; others require a toll. The point to remember is that there is no "right" or "best" path. The road taken depends on where the traveler wants to go and how much time, money, ability, and so forth are available for the trip.

Although there is no "right" path, the researcher must choose an appropriate one—that is, one that best suits the problem at hand. In some situations, where time is short, the quickest path is best. In other circumstances, where money, time, and personnel are plentiful, the chosen path may be long and demanding.

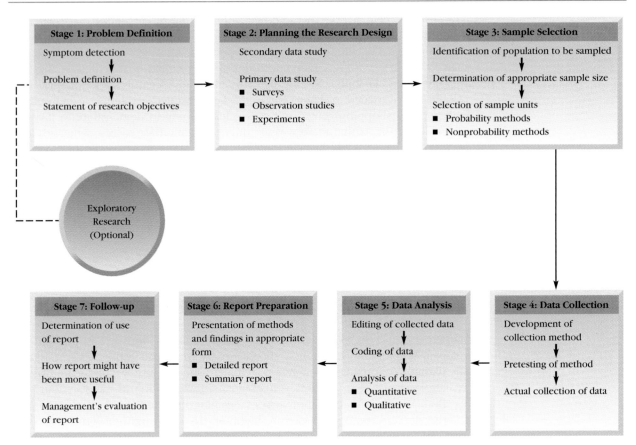

Dotted line indicates the path the research takes when problem definition requires exploratory research to analyze the situation.

Exploring the various paths marketing researchers encounter is the main purpose of this section, which describes the seven stages of the research process. Exhibit 5–3 illustrates some choices researchers face at each stage.

Stage One: Defining the Problem

Problem Definition
The crucial first stage in the marketing research process. It consists of determining the problem to be solved and the objectives of the research.

The idea that **problem definition** is central to the marketing research process is so obvious that its importance is easily overlooked. Albert Einstein noted that "the formation of a problem is often more essential than its solution."[13] This is valuable advice for marketing managers and researchers, who, in their haste to find the right answers, may fail to ask the right questions. Too often, data are collected before the nature of the problem has been carefully established. Except in cases of coincidence or good luck, such data will not help resolve the marketer's difficulties. The old adage "a problem well-defined is a problem half-solved" puts all of this into perspective.

Problems Can Be Opportunities

On many occasions, the research process is focused not on a problem but on an opportunity. In this happier circumstance, for example, a toy maker who has developed a fabulous new item might face the "problem" of determining what age groups will most likely want the toy or which advertising media are the best to use. In cases such as these, the problem definition stage of the research might well be called the opportunity definition stage. The point is that the problems addressed by marketing research are frequently "good" problems, not always disasters.

Don't Confuse Symptoms with the Real Problem

There is a difference between a problem and the symptoms of that problem. Pain, for example, is the symptom of a problem. The cause of the pain, perhaps a broken leg, is the problem. In marketing, falling sales are a symptom that some aspect of the marketing mix is not working properly. Sales may be falling because price competition has intensified or because buyer preferences have changed. Defining the general nature of the problem provides a direction for the research.

Consider the case of Ha-Psu-Shu-Tse (the Pawnee word for "red corn") brand fried Indian bread mix. The owner of the company thought that his product, one of the few Native American food products sold in the United States, was selling poorly because it was not advertised heavily. His feeling about this led him to hire a management consulting group to research new advertising themes. The consultants suggested, instead, that the product's brand name (Ha-Psu-Shu-Tse) might be the main problem. They proposed that consumer attitudes toward the name and product should be the starting point for the research. In effect, the consultants were reluctant to choose advertising, one component of the marketing mix, as the area of concern without checking for more basic causes of the firm's difficulties. The researchers did not confuse symptoms with the real problem.

Exhibit 5–4 shows that the problem definition stage is likely to begin with the discovery that some problem exists because symptoms have been detected. If managers are uncertain about the exact nature of the problem, they may spend time analyzing and learning about the situation. For example, they may discuss the situation with others, such as sales representatives who are close to the customers.

A small-scale exploratory investigation may be conducted to ensure that Stage 2, planning the research design, will not begin with an inadequate understanding of exactly what information needs to be collected. Exploratory research is optional and is not used in all research projects.

Finally, as Exhibit 5–4 shows, the problem is defined, and a series of research objectives related to the problem are stated. No decisions about the remaining stages of the marketing research process should be made until managers and researchers clearly understand the objectives of the research about to be undertaken.

Exploratory Research

Exploratory Research
Research to clarify the nature of a marketing problem.

Exploratory research, as noted, is sometimes needed to clarify the nature of the marketing problem. Management may know from noting a symptom such as declining sales, that some kind of problem is "out there." Exploratory research may

---

EXHIBIT 5–4
Stage 1, defining the problem, results in clear-cut research objectives. Dotted lines indicate the path the research takes when problem definition requires exploratory research to analyze the situation.

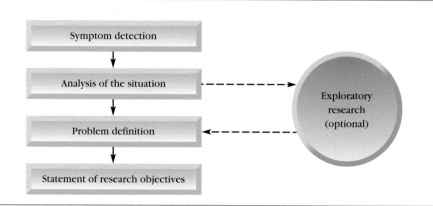

be used to try to identify the problem. Or management may know what the problem is but not how big or how far-reaching it is. Here too, managers may need research to help them analyze the situation. Providing conclusions is not the purpose of exploratory research. Its purpose is simply to investigate and explore. Usually, exploratory research is undertaken with the expectation that other types of research will follow and that the subsequent research will be directed at finding possible solutions. In any research situation, it is generally best to check available secondary data before beginning extensive data collection. Some work at a library, on the Internet, or with an internal database may result in saving time and money.

However, there isn't any set formula prescribing exactly how to analyze a situation. Sometimes checking secondary sources may not be the appropriate first step. A short series of interviews with a few customers may be in order. If a fast-food restaurant were considering adding a low-fat menu or a line of tacos to its standard hamburger fare, marketing managers might begin their research by conducting some unstructured interviews with customers. Customers might surprise management with negative comments on the proposed additions. Exploratory research in this case could serve to identify problem areas or point to a need for additional information.

Although there are many techniques for exploratory research, our discussion highlights one popular method—the **focus group interview**—to illustrate the nature of exploratory techniques. (Another type of exploratory research is described in the accompanying Competitive Strategy feature.) Focus group interviews are loosely structured interviews with groups of six to ten people who "focus" on a product or some aspect of buying behavior. During a group session, individuals give their comments and reactions to new product ideas or explain why they buy (or do not buy) certain products. Researchers later analyze those comments for meaningful and useful ideas, such as that a product is "too high-priced" or "looks like it would break easily." Focus group research is extremely flexible and may be used for many purposes—for example, to learn what problems consumers have with products. During one of Rubbermaid Inc.'s focus groups on housewares, a

Focus Group Interview
A loosely structured interview in which a group of 6 to 10 people discusses a product or focuses on some aspect of buying behavior.

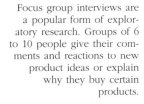

Focus group interviews are a popular form of exploratory research. Groups of 6 to 10 people give their comments and reactions to new product ideas or explain why they buy certain products.

COMPETITIVE STRATEGY: WHAT WENT RIGHT?

Fisher-Price's Play Laboratory

Seated in a darkened room behind a row of one-way mirrors, designers and marketing researchers observe children who are trying out new toys in Fisher-Price's Play Laboratory. "Somehow there's some magic in a successful toy that catches children's interest, and we have to figure out what that is," Kathleen Alfano tells me as we peer out from our hiding place. She is the company's manager of the child research department, which includes not only the on-site Play Laboratory but also extensive in-home testing around the country. The waiting list of children for the free 12-session program can stretch up to two years. On the other side of the mirrors from us, a group of toddlers is hard at work, toy testing. One very small boy swings a pink plastic iron by its cord and bashes a toy ironing board with it, looking up to watch the other children as he does so. The lab is a large nursery with bins, shelves, and cupboards overflowing with toys: stuffed animals, plastic dinosaurs, dollhouses, toy vacuum cleaners. The tip-off that this is more than an exceptionally well-stocked day-care center is the pair of professional-looking microphones dangling from the ceiling between a set of fish mobiles.

"It's easy to say what doesn't work," Alfano comments, "but finding out what makes a toy work is harder because children put a little of themselves into it." That all-important feature—play value—isn't some ingredient contained in a toy, she explains; play value arises from the way a child decides to interact with a toy, for whatever reason.

Just beyond the mirrors, a two-year-old girl in a blue tank top has stepped up to one of Fisher-Price's hits of Christmas past, a two-burner kitchen stove with a plastic telephone mounted on the side. The child moves a pot from one burner to the other, then, satisfied, picks up the phone. She punches a few push buttons without looking at the numbers. Then, cocking her head to one side and throwing out a hip, she smiles and says, "Hi ya, Mom!" into the receiver. This is play value. If only it could be bottled. Obviously, the more expensive a toy is, the more guaranteed fun a parent expects it to deliver. If a $1.59 wooden top holds a child's interest for 20 minutes, that might be well worth the money. A $250–300 battery-powered, rechargeable, sit-down, two-seater automobile, such as Fisher-Price's new sports car, had better do more than that. During my visit to the play Laboratory, the company's research and development (R&D) staff is watching closely to see how its little guinea pigs take to an advance fleet of the jeeplike vehicles.

In a small parking lot next to the R&D building, five four-year-olds, three boys and two girls, are motoring about in fast curves and figure eights, fast being about five miles per hour. "They all have them set on high," says Bernie Schaub, the project engineer. "Kids don't want to go slow." This propensity does not, however, mean that a dashboard switch offering a slower speed will be dropped from the final version. "The competition provides two speeds," says Schaub, referring to a toy called Power Wheels. "We have to be equal or better." In other words, some of the features on a toy are not really aimed at the child at all, but at the parents who will pay for it.

Fisher-Price's marketing research efforts in the Play Laboratory provide information to help the company evaluate both its own toys and the competition's toys. Research helps take the guesswork out of the design and marketing of fun.

---

woman accused the industry of sexism.[14] "Why do companies continue to treat brooms and mops like they were 'women's tools?'" she complained. "They're poorly designed and second-class to hammers and saws, which are balanced and molded to fit men's hands. Brooms and mops make housework more miserable, not easier." Rubbermaid did not make cleaning products, but the woman's remarks eventually convinced the company that there was an opportunity to be had. After five years of research and development, Rubbermaid introduced a line of about 50 cleaning products and brushes designed to make cleaning easier, with handles that fit comfortably in consumers' hands and bristles angled to reach tight spaces.

What Is a "Good" Research Objective?

Marketers contemplating a research project must decide exactly what they are looking for. For example, research objectives for a local Big Brothers and Sisters

EXHIBIT 5–5
Secondary Data Sources

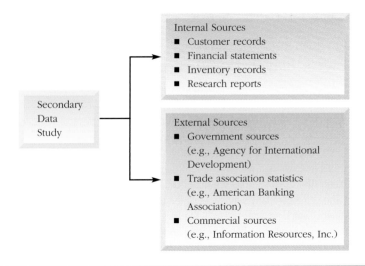

organization might be

- To determine males' awareness of the Big Brothers and Sisters organization
- To determine males' awareness of the organization's need for volunteers
- To determine males' willingness to volunteer as big brothers
- To determine a demographic profile of those most likely to volunteer.

A formal statement of the problem(s) and the research objective(s) must be the culmination of Stage 1 of the research process. These provide the framework for the study.

Stage Two: Planning the Research Design

Research Design
A master plan that specifically identifies what techniques and procedures will be used to collect and analyze data relevant to the research problem.

After the researcher has clearly identified the research problem and formulated research objectives, the next step is to develop a formal research design. The **research design** is a master plan that specifically identifies the techniques and procedures that will be used to collect and analyze data relevant to the research problem. The research design must be carefully compared against the objectives developed in Stage 1 to assure that the sources of data, the data collected, the scheduling and costs involved, and so on, are consistent with the researcher's main goals.

At the outset, the researchers should determine if the data needed has already been generated by others or if primary research is required. In other words, as suggested in Exhibit 5–3, researchers planning a research design must first choose between using secondary data and primary data.

Research Designs—Secondary Data

As we have mentioned, data already in the researcher's decision support system or in the library may be adequate to begin a formal research effort. For example, a marketer of mobile homes might know that sales of this product rise as building permits issued for traditional homes decline. Using government figures showing building permits issued and trends in home building, the mobile home seller can develop a quantitative model to predict market behavior, basing the research design entirely on the analysis of secondary data. Meaningful secondary data may come from internal sources, such as company databases, or external sources, such as government agencies, trade associations, and companies that specialize in supplying specific types of data. Exhibit 5–5 shows some examples of the types of secondary data that are available.

The primary advantages of secondary data are: (1) they almost always are less expensive to collect than primary data, and (2) they can be obtained rapidly. Secondary sources must be used with care, however, as they have certain disadvantages:

- Secondary data may be "old" and possibly outdated. Some data are collected only periodically. For example, the population census is taken only once a decade. Comparatively up-to-date estimates are often available in such cases, however.
- Data may not have been collected in the form preferred. Sales figures for a county may be available, but not for a particular town within that county.
- Users of secondary data may not be able to assess its accuracy. For example, previous researchers may have altered the data to "prove" some point or theory.

In general, the inherent disadvantage of secondary data is that they were not designed specifically to meet the researcher's needs. The manager's task is to determine if the secondary data are pertinent and accurate.

FOCUS ON TRENDS

Information Resources

Information Resources, Inc., is an innovative organization leading the trend toward use of new technologies in marketing research. The organization specializes in providing data about brand and product sales known as *scanner data*. Optical scanners in supermarkets read and record the universal product code (UPC) of each product sold. The UPC contains product identification information, such as package size, flavor, price, and so on. Information Resources organizes the scanner data into an appropriate format for competitive analysis. Marketers who use the company's reports can analyze them to determine which package sizes sell best, what price is most effective, and how their brands are doing in relation to the competition. Modern computer and scanner technology makes data from any store available on a weekly, or even daily, basis.

Research Designs—Primary Data

Researchers who do not find appropriate secondary data can choose from three basic designs for collecting primary data: surveys, observation studies, and experiments.

Surveys. Primary data are commonly generated by survey research. Survey results on one topic or another are reported almost daily by the news media. Most adult Americans have been stopped by interviewers at shopping centers or voting places or have received mailings or phone calls from survey takers. In general, a **survey** is any research effort in which data are gathered systematically from a sample of people by means of a questionnaire. Researchers using surveys may collect data using telephone interviews, mailed questionnaires, or personal interviews, either door-to-door or in shopping malls, or other communication method, such as fax or Internet.

Survey research has several advantages. How better to provide buyers with what they want than to first ask them what they want? For example, U.S. automobile makers operate style research clinics to appraise consumer reactions to car designs. First, mock-ups of proposed designs are constructed; then consumers, or respondents, are recruited by means of short telephone interviews. These respondents are brought in secret to a showroom and shown a car mock-up and competitive autos from around the world. As the "buyers" look over the cars, profes-

Survey
Any research effort in which data are gathered systematically from a sample of people by means of a questionnaire. Surveys are conducted through face-to-face interviews, telephone interviews, and mailed questionnaires.

sional interviewers ask for their reactions to virtually every detail. The survey results are then fed back to designers in Detroit.

When surveys are properly planned and executed, they can prove to be quick, efficient, and accurate means of gathering data. Survey research can involve problems, however. Careless researchers may design or conduct surveys improperly and produce incorrect and worthless results—that is, results marked by **systematic bias.** The survey questions might be poorly worded, respondents might be reluctant to provide truthful answers, the sample may not be representative, or mistakes might be made entering data into the computer. The specific advantages and disadvantages of surveys are best discussed in reference to the form of data collection used. These are outlined in Exhibit 5–6. You can see from this exhibit that choosing one method over another involves trade-offs. For instance, a low-cost mail survey takes more time and is less versatile than a higher-cost personal interview at the consumer's doorstep.

Systematic Bias
A research shortcoming caused by flaws in the design or execution of a research study.

How does the researcher choose the appropriate survey technique? The marketing problem itself generally suggests which technique is most appropriate. An advertiser placing a message on a popular television program like the Super Bowl or the World Series might contact viewers in their homes via telephone to gather reactions to its commercial. A manufacturer of industrial equipment might choose a mail survey because the executives it wishes to question are hard to reach on the phone. A political party might prefer to employ a door-to-door personal survey so that voters can, after some guidance by interviewers, formulate and voice their opinions on current issues. In these examples, the cost, time, and perhaps accuracy involved vary. It is the researcher's job to weigh the advantages and disadvantages involved and find the most appropriate way to collect the needed data.[15]

Wording survey questions is a skill that can be learned. Avoiding complexity and using simple, accurate, conversational language that does not confuse or bias the respondent is the goal of the questionnaire writer. The wording of questions should be simple and unambiguous so that the questions are readily understandable to all respondents.

Consider, for example, the following question:

The Limited should continue its excellent gift-wrapping program.
    (a) Yes
    (b) No

The gift-wrapping program may not be excellent at all. By answering "yes," a respondent is implying that things are just fine as they are. But by answering "no," she implies that The Limited should discontinue the gift wrapping. Questions should be worded so the respondent is not put in this sort of bind. Many respondents are susceptible to leading questions such as "You do agree that U.S. automobiles are a better value than Japanese automobiles, don't you?" Leading questions should be avoided.

Sometimes rating scales are used to measure consumers' attitudes. Two of the most common attitude scales are the Likert scale and the semantic differential. A Likert scale asks respondents to indicate the degree of agreement with a statement, as in the following example:

Timberland boots are expensive.
Strongly agree   Agree   Undecided   Disagree   Strongly disagree

A semantic differential identifies a company, store, brand, or the like and asks the respondent to place a check mark on a bipolar rating scale, as in the following example:

Timberland boots
Expensive —:—:—:—:—:— Inexpensive

	PERSONAL INTERVIEWING		MAIL	TELEPHONE
	Door-to-door	*Shopping mall*		
Speed of data collection	Moderate to fast	Fast	Researcher has no control over return of questionnaire	Very fast
Respondent cooperation	Good	Moderate	Moderate—poorly designed questionnaire will have low response rate	Good
Flexibility of questioning	Very flexible	Very flexible	Highly standardized format	Moderately flexible
Questionnaire length	Long	Moderate to long	Varies depending on incentive	Moderate
Possibility for respondent misunderstanding	Low	Low	Highest—no interviewer to clarify	Average
Influence of interviewer on answers	High	High	None	Moderate
Cost	Highest	Moderate to high	Lowest	Low to moderate

EXHIBIT 5–6
Typical Characteristics of
Four Survey Methods

Observation Research
The systematic recording of behavior, objects, or events as they are witnessed.

Observation. If the purpose of a research effort is to note actions that are mechanically or visually recordable, observation techniques can form the basis of that effort. **Observation research** involves the systematic recording of behavior, objects, or events as they are witnessed.

Companies that sell space on outdoor billboards are interested in traffic patterns—specifically, the numbers of cars and people passing the billboard installations each day. Mass transit organizations may want to know how many people ride each bus and at what stops most of them get on or off. In both cases, the information could be recorded either by human observers stationed on street corners or in buses or by mechanized counters.

Investigations of individuals as they consume or shop are common observation studies. Researchers for Nissan North America put video cameras and tape recorders in some Nissan cars to learn more about how people behave when they are driving. Among the things they have learned are: (1) Drivers want to feel in touch with the road, while passengers want to be insulated from it; and (2) Cars need more individual storage space because people always look uncomfortable when they want to put something away.

"Mystery shoppers" can be used to check on the courtesy or product knowledge of retail salespeople. Researchers "disguised" as customers, store employees, or product demonstrators might subtly observe consumer reactions to prices, products, package designs, or display cases. The consumers are unaware their behavior is being observed.

The greatest strength of observation is that it permits the recording of what actually occurs in a particular situation. Its biggest weakness is that the observer cannot be sure why the observed behavior occurred. Still, in some cases, it is enough to know that something happened. Nielsen Media Research, for example, uses mechanical observation to rate television shows in sample homes where the people agree to participate. Its peoplemeter, a recording device attached to a family's television, uses a microprocessor (called a "people meter") to identify which family members are viewing and what station is being watched. The questions of why a show is popular and why the ratings of old movies beat those of the president's State of the Union address are often left to the critics.

Experiment
A research method in which the researcher changes one variable and observes the effects of that change on another variable.

Experiments. **Experiments** have long been used by scientists attempting to discover cause-and-effect relationships. Almost every day we encounter news stories about an experimental group of white mice that were exposed to some substance and then developed more cancers than mice in a group not so exposed. The assumption, of course, is that the substance involved increased the chance of cancer. A properly run experiment allows the investigator to change one variable, such as price, while observing the effects of those changes on another variable, such as sales. Ideally, the experimenter holds all factors steady except the ones being manipulated, thus showing that changes can be caused by the factors being studied.

Marketing researchers use experimental techniques both in the marketplace, or field, and in controlled, or laboratory, atmospheres. For example, McDonald's conducted experiments in the marketplace to determine if it should add a single-slice McPizza to its menu. The company sold the product in test markets—cities where a test product is sold just as it would be if it were marketed nationwide. Test markets provide a trial run to determine consumers' reactions and actual sales volume. For McDonald's, sales of the pizza slices were disappointing, and the company discontinued its plans to market pizza.

Laboratory Experiment
An experiment in a highly controlled environment.

In contrast, advertisers often use laboratory settings to test advertising copy. One group of subjects is shown a television program that includes one version of the advertisement. A second group views the same program with a different advertisement. Researchers compare the groups' responses. Research like this is conducted in a controlled setting, rather than a natural setting, to increase researchers' control of environmental variables. Such an experiment is known as a **laboratory experiment.**

Selecting the Research Design

After considering the many research alternatives, the marketing researcher must pick the one that will be used. Because there are many alternative ways to tackle a problem, there is no one "best" research design. Certain techniques are simply more appropriate than others.

For example, which technique should the Chicago Museum of Science and Industry use to determine which of its exhibits is the most popular? A survey? (Could you really expect visitors to remember and rate all the museum's exhibits?) Experimentation? (Would you close off the exhibits one at a time and count the complaints associated with each closing?) Secondary data? (That might tell you what exhibits are most popular at other museums.) The Chicago museum's researcher actually suggested the simple and inexpensive observation technique of keeping track of the frequency with which the floor tiles had to be replaced in front of each exhibit—indicating which exhibit drew the heaviest traffic. Of course, had the museum been in a hurry for information, another method would have been more proper, but the floor tile approach gave museum operators a good measurement over time at a low cost. (Incidentally, the chick-hatching exhibit was the most popular.)

Stage Three: Selecting a Sample

Sampling
Any procedure in which a small part of the whole is used as the basis for conclusions regarding the whole. The small part is called the sample; and the whole, the population.

Once the researcher has determined which research design to use, the next step is to select a sample of people, organizations, or whatever is of interest. The methods for selecting the sample are important for the accuracy of the study. Though sampling is a highly developed statistical science, we apply its basic concepts in daily life. For example, the first taste (or sample) of a bowl of soup may indicate that the soup needs salt, is too salty, or is "just right." **Sampling,** then, is any pro-

COMPETITIVE STRATEGY: WHAT WENT WRONG?

The Fiasco of 1936

A famous example of sample selection error is the *1936 Literary Digest* fiasco. The magazine conducted a survey and predicted that Republican candidate Alf Landon would win over Democrat Franklin Roosevelt by a landslide. History tells us this was an error due to sample selection. The post-mortems showed that *Literary Digest* had sampled telephone and magazine subscribers. In 1936, this was not a representative cross-section of voters but one that was heavily loaded with Republican voters, who, naturally, favored Landon.

cedure in which a small part of the whole is used as the basis for conclusions regarding the whole.

Sample

Portion, or subset, of larger population.

Population

In marketing research, any complete group of entities sharing some common set of characteristics; the group from which a sample is taken.

Census

A survey of all the members of a group (an entire population).

Target Population

The population of interest in a marketing research study; the population from which samples are to be drawn.

A **sample** is simply a portion, or subset, of a larger **population.** It makes sense that a sample can provide a good representation of the whole. A well-chosen sample of lawyers in California should be representative of all California lawyers. Such a sample can be surveyed, and conclusions can be drawn about California lawyers, making surveying all of them unnecessary. A survey of all the members of a group is called a **census.** For a small group—say, a group comprising the presidents of all colleges and universities in Nebraska—sampling is not needed. All the presidents can be easily identified and contacted. Sampling essentially involves answering these three questions.

1. Who is to be sampled? Specifying the **target population,** or the total group of interest, is the first aspect of sampling. The manager must make sure the population to be sampled accurately reflects the population of interest. Suppose a department store manager who wants to analyze the store's image in the community at large uses current credit-card records to develop a survey mailing list. Who will be surveyed? Only current credit-card customers, not noncredit customers, and certainly not noncustomers, though these groups may be important parts of "the community at large."

   Population lists from which a sample will be taken may be based on lists of customers, telephone directories, membership lists, lists of automobile registrations, and many other sources. Selecting a list is a crucial aspect of sampling. If the lists are inaccurate, the sample results may not be representative.

2. How big should the sample be? The traditional tongue-in-cheek response to this question—"big enough"—suggests the true answer. The sample must be big enough to properly represent the target population. In general, bigger samples are better than smaller samples. Nevertheless, if appropriate sampling techniques are used, a small proportion of the total population will give a reliable measure of the whole. For instance, the Nielsen TV ratings survey, which appears to be highly accurate, involves only a few thousand of the 96 million U.S. households. The keys here are that most families' TV viewing habits are similar and that the "Nielsen families" are selected with meticulous care to assure the representativeness of the sample.

Probability Sample

A sample selected by statistical means in such a way that all members of the sampled population had a known, nonzero chance of being selected.

3. How should the sample be selected? The way sampling units are selected is a major determinant of the accuracy of marketing research. There are two major sampling methods: probability sampling and nonprobability sampling.

When the sampling procedures are such that the laws of probability influence the selection of the sample, the result is a **probability sample.** For example, a *simple random sample* consists of individuals' names drawn according to chance selection procedures from a complete list of all people in a population. All these people have the same chance of being selected. The procedure is called simple because there is only one stage in the sampling process.

When sample units are selected on the basis of convenience or personal judgment (for example, if Portland is selected as a sample city because it appears to be typical), the result is a **nonprobability sample.** In one type of nonprobability sample, a *convenience sample,* data are collected from the people who are most conveniently available. A professor or graduate student who administers a questionnaire to a class is using a convenience sample. It is easy and economical to collect the sample data this way; but unfortunately, it often produces unrepresentative samples. Another nonprobability sample, the *quota sample,* is often utilized by interviewers intercepting consumers at shopping malls. Here, people are chosen because they appear to the interviewers to be of the appropriate age, sex, race, or the like. The Competitive Strategy feature "The Fiasco of 1936" describes a nonprobability sample that was far from representative.

Nonprobability Sample
A sample chosen on the basis of convenience or personal judgment.

Stage Four: Collecting Data

The problem has been defined, the research techniques chosen, and the sample to be analyzed selected. Now the researcher must actually collect the needed data. Whatever collection method is chosen, it is the researcher's task to minimize errors in the process—and errors are easy to make. Interviewers who have not been carefully selected and trained, for example, may not phrase their questions properly or may fail to record respondents' comments accurately.

Generally, the actual collection of the desired data is preceded by **pretesting** the collection method. A proposed questionnaire or interview script might be tried out on a small sample of respondents in an effort to assure that the instructions and questions are clear and comprehensible. It may develop that the survey instrument is too long, causing respondents to lose interest, or too short, yielding inadequate information. The pretest provides the researcher with a limited amount of data that will give an idea of what can be expected from the upcoming full-scale study. In some cases, these data will show that the study is not answering the researcher's questions. The study may then have to be redesigned. After pretesting shows the questionnaire to be sound, the data are collected using the appropriate method.

Pretesting
Conducting limited trials of a questionnaire or other aspect of a study to determine its suitability for the planned research project.

Stage Five: Analyzing the Data

Once the researcher has completed what is called the "fieldwork" by gathering the data germane to solving the research problem, that data must be manipulated, or processed. The purpose is to place the data in a form that will answer the marketing manager's questions.

Processing requires entering the data into the computer. Data processing ordinarily begins with a job called **editing,** in which surveys or other data collection instruments are checked for omissions, incomplete or otherwise unusable responses, illegibility, and obvious inconsistencies. The editing process may result in certain collection instruments being discarded. In research reports it is common to encounter phrases like this: "One thousand people were interviewed, yielding 856 usable responses." The process may also uncover correctable errors, such as the recording of a usable response on the wrong line of a questionnaire.

Once the data collection forms have been edited, the data undergoes **coding.** That is, meaningful categories are established so that responses can be grouped

Editing
Checking questionnaires or other data collection forms for omissions, incomplete or otherwise unusable responses, illegibility, and obvious inconsistencies.

Coding
Establishing meaningful categories for responses collected by means of surveys or other data collection forms so that the responses can be grouped into usable classifications.

into usable classifications for computer analysis. For example, with a survey focusing on response differences between men and women, a gender code, such as 1 = male and 2 = female, might be used.

Data Analysis

Statistical and/or qualitative consideration of data gathered by research.

After editing and coding, the researcher is ready to undertake the process of analysis. **Data analysis** may involve statistical analysis, qualitative analysis, or both. The type of analysis to be used should be based on the information requirements faced by management, the research objectives, the design of the research itself, and the nature of the data collected.

A review of the many statistical tools that can be used in marketing research is beyond the scope of this text. It should be noted, however, that they can range from simple comparisons of numbers and percentages ("100 people, or 25 percent of the sample, agreed") to complex mathematical computations requiring a computer. Statistical tools such as the *t*-test of two means, the Chi-square test, and correlation analysis are popular standbys used to analyze data. It may be surprising, in light of the availability of these and many other techniques, that a great number of studies use statistics no more sophisticated than averages and percentages.

Stage Six: Drawing Conclusions and Preparing the Report

Remember that the purpose of marketing research is to aid in the development of effective marketing decisions. The researcher's role is to answer the question "What does this mean to marketing managers?" Therefore, the culmination of the research process must be a report that usefully communicates research findings to management. Typically, management is not interested in how the findings came about. Except in special cases, management is likely to want only a summary of the findings. Presenting these clearly, using graphs, charts, and other forms of art work, is a creative challenge to the researcher and any others involved in the preparation of the final report. If the researcher's findings are not properly communicated to and understood by marketing managers, the research process has been, in effect, a total waste.

Stage Seven: Following Up

After the researcher submits the report to management, he or she should follow up to try to determine if and how management responded to the report. The researcher should ask how the report could have been improved and made more useful. This is not to say that the report's conclusions or suggested courses of action must be followed by management. Deciding such things is, after all, the role of management, not of researchers. Marketing management, for its part, should let researchers know how reports can be improved or how future reports might be of better use.

MARKETING RESEARCH IS A GLOBAL ACTIVITY

Marketing research, like all business activity, has become increasingly global. Many companies have far-reaching international marketing research operations. For example, Upjohn conducts marketing research in 160 different countries.

Companies conducting business in foreign lands must understand the nature of customers in these markets. For example, although the 15 nations of the European community now share a single market, research shows they do not share identical tastes. Marketing researchers have learned that there is no such thing as a typical European consumer; the nations of the European Union are divided by language, religion, climate, and centuries of tradition. For example, Scantel Research, a British firm that advises companies on color preferences, found inexplicable differences in the way Europeans take their medicine. The French like to pop purple pills, while the English and Dutch prefer white ones. Consumers in all three countries dislike bright red capsules, which are big sellers in the United States. This example illustrates that companies doing business in Europe must learn whether adapting to local customs and buying habits is necessary.[16]

Decisions about international strategies and tactics should be based on sound market information. But in many foreign nations, U.S. marketing researchers encounter circumstances far different from those they are accustomed to. To begin with, there is rarely a wealth of available secondary data. (American researchers are lucky; there are volumes of data about the people and markets in the United States.) In some countries, no census has ever been taken. Some developing nations seem to take the view that anyone wanting to pry into another person's life must have less than honorable motives. Often, too, lack of data and unfamiliar social patterns make it difficult for a researcher to use all the tools available. Carefully planned samples may be impossible to develop. Telephone directories do not include the entire population and may be woefully out of date. Street maps are unavailable in many cities in South America, Central America, and Asia. In fact, in some large metropolitan areas of the Near East and Asia, streets are unnamed and the houses on them are unnumbered.

In spite of these hardships, marketing research does take place around the globe. A. C. Nielsen, the television ratings company, is the world's largest marketing research company. More than 60 percent of its business comes from outside the United States.[17] Although the nature of marketing research can change around the globe, the need for marketing research and accurate information is universal.

FOCUS ON GLOBAL COMPETITION

Domino's

Domino's uses marketing research both at home and abroad to help its managers make decisions about its pizza and its delivery service.

When Domino's investigated marketing pizza in Japan, the marketing research findings suggested that home delivery of pizza wouldn't work there. Japanese diets emphasize such foods as raw fish, rice, and seaweed, and consumers are known to dislike both tomatoes and cheese (which they think looks and tastes like soap). Pizza is considered a snack food rather than a meal, which makes it difficult to justify the high prices necessary to make the home-delivery business profitable. The consumers who like pizza the most are teenage girls, the market segment with the least disposable income. Further, the research showed that because Japanese families typically live in tiny apartments, those who are more likely to pay a premium price for a meal prefer to go out to a more spacious restaurant. Finally, Domino's guarantee of speedy delivery was perceived to be impossible in traffic-congested Tokyo.

Rather than being discouraged by what they learned, the Japanese entrepreneurs made three creative changes in the product strategy. The pizzas were made smaller: the sizes of 12 and 16 inches, common in the United States, were reduced to 10 and 14 inches. Two optional toppings, corn and tuna (toppings that Americans might consider stomach-curdling) were added to make pizza more harmonious with the Japanese diet. And to overcome drivers' problems with Tokyo's narrow streets and heavy traffic, Domino's used souped-up, streamlined motor scooters rather than cars to deliver the pizzas. A few months after the first Domino's opened, the number of scooters doubled, then tripled. Shortly thereafter, additional outlets were opened, and it was clear Domino's had scored a big success.

Although many factors determined Domino's success, its use of marketing research to understand the Japanese perspective, and its willingness to adapt based on what it learned, exerted a major influence.

SALES FORECASTING—RESEARCH ABOUT THE FUTURE

Marketing managers need information about the future to make today's decisions. They need to ask: "What will be the size of the market next year?" "How large a share of the market will we have in five years?" "What changes in the market can we anticipate?" Sales forecasting involves applying research techniques to answering questions like these.

Sales forecasting is the process of predicting sales totals over some specific future period. An accurate sales forecast is one of the most useful pieces of information a marketing manager can have because the forecast influences so many plans and activities. A good forecast helps in the planning and control of production, distribution, and promotion activity. Forecasting may suggest that price structures need adjusting or that budgeting or inventory holdings should be changed. Because operational planning greatly depends on the sales forecast, ensuring its accuracy is important. Mistakes in forecasting can lead to serious errors in other areas of the organization's management. For example, an overestimate of sales can lead to an overstocking of raw materials, while an underestimate can mean losing sales because of material shortages.

The sales forecast provides information for the control function by establishing an evaluation standard. Management uses it for gauging the organization's marketing successes and failures. Without a standard, there is no way to measure the success or failure of any endeavor.

Break-Down and Build-Up Forecasting

Sales forecasts are focused on company sales, but they may be based on forecasts of general economic conditions, industry sales, and market size. A bank, for example, may use the Wharton forecast of the U.S. economy to develop its own forecast for the banking industry. Based on that forecast, bank management will try to estimate the demand for loans at its various branch locations. This approach—that is, starting with something big, like the U.S. gross domestic product, and working down to an industry forecast, and then a company forecast, and even a product forecast—is called the **break-down method** of forecasting.

The **build-up method** starts with the individual purchaser and then aggregates estimates of sales potential into progressively larger groups. For example, a tool manufacturer might estimate that 10 percent of all electrical contractors in Georgia will buy a drill, 15 percent of all carpenters in Georgia will buy a drill, and so on. Adding subtotals for each state leads to a buildup forecast.

The Three Levels of Forecasting

Market potential, sales potential, and sales forecast are the three levels of forecasting.

- **Market potential** refers to the upper limit of industry demand, or the expected sales volume for all brands of a particular product type during a given period. Market potential is usually defined for a given geographical area or market segment under certain assumed business conditions.
- **Sales potential** is an estimate of an individual company's maximum share of the market, or the company's maximum sales volume for a particular product, during a given period. Sales potential reflects what demand would be if maximum sales-generating activities were executed in a given period under certain business conditions.
- The **sales forecast,** or expected actual sales volume, is usually lower than sales potential because the organization is constrained by resources or because the

Sales Forecasting
The process of estimating sales volume for a product, an organizational unit, or an entire organization over a specific future time period.

Break-Down Method
Forecasting starts with large-scale estimates (for example, an estimate of GDP) and works down to industrywide, company, and product estimates.

Build-Up Method
Forecasting starts with smaller-scale estimates and works up to larger-scale ones.

Market Potential
The upper limit of industry demand. That is, the expected sales volume for all brands of a particular product during a given period.

Sales Potential
The maximum share of the market an individual organization can expect during a given period.

Sales Forecast
The actual sales volume an organization expects during a given period.

managerial emphasis is on the highest profits rather than the largest sales volume.

Conditional Forecasting—"What If?"

Forecasters often assume the upcoming time period will resemble the past. However, marketing is carried on in a dynamic environment. An efficient forecaster is one who recognizes that the forecast will be accurate only if the assumptions are accurate. Therefore, organizations often create three variants on each forecast: one based on optimistic assumptions, one based on pessimistic assumptions, and one based on conditions thought to be "most likely." The most likely forecast is not always halfway between the other two. In bad times, "most likely" might be awfully close to disaster. The advantage of this threefold forecasting approach is that the forecaster clearly distinguishes between what is actually predicted and what is possible.

Forecasting by Time Periods

A good forecast specifies the time frame during which the forecasted goal is to be met. Managers frequently use expressions like short term, long term, and intermediate term to describe these time periods. Such expressions can mean almost anything, depending on the marketing problem under discussion. For novelty items such as toy action figures based on a movie, the difference between the short and the long term may be very short, indeed. Such products may have a life of only a few months and then disappear from the market. However established products like Honda motorcycles and Lawn Boy lawn mowers may survive for years or even decades.

Though situations vary, there is general agreement that a short-term forecast covers a period of a year or less and that long-term forecasts cover periods of 5 to 10 years. The intermediate term is anywhere in between.

Generally, forecasting time frames do not exceed 10 years. For some products, such as automobile tires, it should be safe to assume that a market will exist 10, 20, or even 50 years into the future. It is not safe to assume that any product will be around "forever." Some forecasters do make such long-range forecasts. The problem is that the longer the time period, the greater the uncertainty and risk involved. The level of uncertainty increases immensely for each year of the forecast. As time frames are lengthened, what was once thought to be a forecast can become a fantasy. The history of business is littered with stories of managers who encountered disastrous failure because they made such assumptions. Marketing's dynamic environment does not offer the safety long-term planners would like to have. Thus, many forecasters revise sales forecasts quarterly, monthly, or weekly, as the situation warrants.

Forecasting Options

There is no best way to forecast sales. This does not mean that the marketing manager faces total chaos. It does mean that there are many different methods, ranging from simple to complex, for forecasting. These methods include executive opinion, sales force composite, customer expectations, projection of trends, and analysis of market factors.

Executive Opinion

Top-level executives with years of experience in an industry are generally well informed. Surveying executives to obtain estimates of market potential, sales potential, or the direction of demand may be a convenient and inexpensive way to forecast. It is not a scientific technique, however, because executives may, consciously or unconsciously, be biased and thus either overly pessimistic or overly optimistic. Used in isolation executive opinion has many pitfalls. But when used in conjunction with one or more of the other methods, the seasoned opinion of industry executives may be a useful supplement.

Sales Force Composite

Asking sales representatives to project their own sales for the upcoming period and then combining all these projections is the sales force composite method of forecasting. The logic of this technique suggests that the sales representative is the person most familiar with the local market area, especially competitive activity, and therefore is in the best position to predict local behavior. However, this method may yield subjective predictions and forecasting from a perspective that is too limited.

Survey of Customers

Asking customers how many units they intend to buy is the logic underlying the survey of consumer expectations. This method is best for established products. For a new product concept, however, customers' expectations may not indicate their actual behavior.

Projection of Trends

Identifying trends and extrapolating past performance into the future is a relatively uncomplicated forecasting technique. Time series data are identified and plotted on a graph, and the historical pattern is projected for the upcoming period. Thus, if sales have increased by 10 percent every year for the last five years, a 10 percent increase is forecast for next year. This common method of forecasting can work well in mature markets that do not experience dynamic changes. The underlying assumption is that the future will be somewhat like the past. However, if environmental change is radical, or if new competitors are entering the market, blindly projecting trends may be less useful and may even be detrimental. An advantage of projecting past sales trends is that data can usually be found in the company's decision support system.

Analysis of Market Factors

Market Factor
A variable associated with sales that is analyzed in forecasting sales.

Market Factor Index
A number of variables that in a combined index are associated with sales.

The **market factor** method is used when there is an association between sales and another variable, called a factor. For example, population is a general market factor that will help determine whether sales potential for Coca-Cola is higher in Albany, New York, or Boise, Idaho. New housing starts may be a factor that predicts lumber sales. When a number of factors are combined into an index, they are referred to as a multiple **market factor index.** Correlation methods or regression methods are mathematical techniques that may identify the degree of association between sales and the market factor.

SUMMARY

Effective marketing management relies on accurate, pertinent, and timely information, supplied in appropriate form by a well-designed decision support system.

Learning Objective 1

Explain why information is essential to effective marketing decision making.

The marketing manager needs timely, systematically gathered information about the organization's customers, environment, and marketing activities. Without it, the marketing manager has no accurate basis on which to make decisions. Information reduces uncertainty and helps to define problems and identify opportunities.

Learning Objective 2

Explain the importance of global information systems and the Internet.

A global information system (GIS) is an organized collection of telecommunications equipment, computer hardware and software, data, and personnel designed to capture, store, update, manipulate, analyze, and immediately display information about worldwide business activity. The well-being of business organizations planning to prosper in the 21st century depends on such information. The Internet is a worldwide network of computers that gives individuals access to electronic mail and vast amounts of information and documents from distant sources. It can be described as a combination of a worldwide communication system and the world's largest public library. Web browsers and search engines make accessing information much easier than in the past.

Learning Objective 3

Describe the nature of decision support systems and intranets.

The decision support system includes: (1) databases that provide logically organized data; and (2) software systems for analysis of data. If a company's decision support system is a private data network that uses Internet standards and technology, it is called an intranet.

Learning Objective 4

Explain the contribution of marketing research to effective decision making.

Marketing research is intended to provide objective information about marketing phenomena to reduce uncertainty and lead to more rational and effective decisions.

Learning Objective 5

Describe the stages in the marketing research process.

Marketing research studies generally follow seven major steps: (1) defining the problem, (2) planning the research design, (3) selecting the sample, (4) collecting data, (5) analyzing data, (6) drawing conclusions and preparing the report, and (7) following up.

Learning Objective 6

Explain how exploratory research relates to specific marketing management problems.

Exploratory research clarifies the nature of problems that are not clearly understood so that further research can be conducted.

Learning Objective 7

Understand why secondary data are valuable sources of information.

Secondary data have been previously collected and assembled. They may be obtained quickly and inexpensively.

Learning Objective 8

Understand the uses of surveys, observation, and experiments.

Primary data are collected by surveys, observation, and experiments. Surveys are used to study large groups of subjects by mail, telephone, or personal interview. Observation is used to record actual behavior. Experiments are tightly controlled research designs that manipulate an experimental variable and measure its effect under controlled conditions.

Learning Objective 9

Demonstrate your knowledge of the purposes of sales forecasting.

Sales forecasting is the prediction of an organization's anticipated sales over a specific time period. The forecast is used to plan such activities as production schedules, distribution, and promotion and to measure the success of these activities. Good forecasting improves planning and control.

Learning Objective 10

Evaluate the advantages and disadvantages of the various forecasting methods.

Forecasting methods such as executive opinion, sales force composites, and surveys of customers use the opinions of experienced individuals. Personal biases or lack of knowledge may, however, affect the results. Trend analysis is appropriate in some situations but assumes that the future will be like the past. Market factor analysis and published indexes are useful where sales are affected by certain external variables.

KEY TERMS

Global information system (GIS) (p. 106)
Data (p. 107)
Information (p. 107)
Primary data (p. 107)
Secondary data (p. 107)

Internet (p. 107)
Decision support system (p. 109)
Database (p. 109)
Intranet (p. 111)
Data-based marketing (p. 112)
Marketing research (p. 112)

Problem definition (p. 114)
Exploratory research (p. 115)
Focus group interview (p. 116)
Research design (p. 118)
Survey (p. 119)
Systematic bias (p. 120)

Observation research (p. 121)
Experiment (p. 122)
Laboratory experiment (p. 122)
Sampling (p. 122)
Sample (p. 123)
Population (p. 123)
Census (p. 123)
Target population (p. 123)

Probability sample (p. 123)
Nonprobability sample (p. 124)
Pretesting (p. 124)
Editing (p. 124)
Coding (p. 124)
Data analysis (p. 125)
Sales forecasting (p. 127)
Break-down method (p. 127)

Build-up method (p. 127)
Market potential (p. 127)
Sales potential (p. 127)
Sales forecast (p. 127)
Market factor (p. 129)
Market factor index (p. 129)

QUESTIONS FOR REVIEW AND CRITICAL THINKING

1. What role does marketing research play in the development of marketing strategies and the implementation of the marketing concept?

2. Define or describe, in your own words, each of the following:
   a. Global information system
   b. Internet
   c. Decision support system
   d. Intranet
   e. Marketing research
   g. Data-based marketing

3. How can the Internet be used to help managers obtain marketing information?

4. What does marketing research do for the manager? What does it not do?

5. What is exploratory research? Give an example of its proper application.

6. What are the stages in a formal research project? Which is the most important?

7. Why would a marketing manager choose to investigate secondary data rather than primary data?

8. What are the strengths and weaknesses of the following marketing research methods?
   a. Mail surveys
   b. Telephone surveys
   c. Observation studies
   d. Experiments

9. What are the primary considerations in the selection of a sample?

10. Give some examples of population lists from which samples may be drawn.

11. What is the difference between market potential, sales potential, and the sales forecast?

12. What market factors might help predict market potential for the following products?
    a. Forklift trucks
    b. Chain saws
    c. Soft drinks
    d. Playground equipment

13. What forecasting method would be best for each of the following products?
    a. Cigars
    b. New flavor of Pete's Wicked Ale
    c. Baseball attendance at your college or university

14. What do the executive opinion and sales force composite methods have in common?

15. Form small groups as directed by your instructor. Select a local retailer or a campus organization. Define a marketing problem/opportunity and design a questionnaire that will yield valuable information to help the organization.

INTERNET INSIGHTS

Exercises

1. The Spider's Apprentice is a Web site that provides many useful tips about using search engines. Go to

   http://www.monash.com/spidap.html

   to learn the ins and outs of search engines.

2. Marketers scan the environment for changes in social values and beliefs. Go to the Gallup Organization's home page at

   http://www.gallup.com/

   Select the option Gallup Poll Monthly Newsletter Archives. Read the results of a recent survey. What are the implications for marketers of the societal attitudes the survey reports? Make a list of five businesses that would be affected by the results of the survey you accessed. Go back and select the option Take a Gallup Poll. Complete one of the Gallup Polls before you exit.

Address Book

NPD Group Inc.
http://www.npd.com

Advertising Research Foundations
http://www.arfsite.org

New York Public Library
http://nypl.org

Penn Library Business Reference Desk
http://www.library.upenn.edu.resources/business/busref.html

ETHICS IN PRACTICE: TAKE A STAND

1. A retailer asks customers for their phone numbers, which are entered (via the cash register system) into a computer file. The retailer then sells its customer list, which includes both names and phone numbers, to other marketers. Is this ethical?

2. Should an individual's answers to a survey be confidential?

3. Is telephoning someone at 8:30 p.m. and asking him or her to participate in a survey ethical?

4. In its telephone sales solicitation for cemetery plots, a company begins the call by saying it is conducting a survey. Is this ethical?

CASE 5–1

 Space Wheyfers

Space Wheyfers are new crispy snacks in the shapes of missiles, flying saucers, and rocket ships. They are made from whey. Whey is what is left over from cheese manufacturing. In the past, small cheese producers often dumped this waste from cheese making into streams, where it polluted the water by inducing algae growth.

Space Wheyfers were developed as a snack food to compete with potato chips, pretzels, and other empty-calorie foods. Space Wheyfers have fewer calories and less fat than the snack foods currently being marketed. Because they are made from protein-potent whey, Space Wheyfers contain about 15 percent protein, substantially more than most potato chips.

The Blue Lake Cheese Corporation developed this product because it was a natural for the company. Blue Lake believed that its dairy scientists' development—a yeast process to convert whey into solid protein for the Space Wheyfers—was a major breakthrough for the company.

Because teenagers often eat too much junk food, management believes that teenagers should be the prime market for Space Wheyfers. The space and galactic themes have been very popular since the movie Star Wars launched the space-cowboy era.

One of the best things about Space Wheyfers is that they can be given any appealing color or taste. The flavor of the food and the texture of the Wheyfers, however, need to be investigated in a taste test.

Questions
1. What is the marketing problem facing management at Blue Lake Cheese Company?
2. Do you agree that the taste test should be the very first marketing research project?
3. What additional information would be useful to help in the marketing of this product?
4. How can the company forecast sales?

CASE 5-2

First Bank Systems of Minneapolis

First Bank Systems (FBS) of Minneapolis engages in three core business areas: retail and community banking, commercial banking, and the trust and investment group. Retail and community banking includes consumer and small business banking, residential mortgage lending, and consumer and corporate credit card and payment systems processing. Commercial banking provides lending, cash management, and other financial services to midsized and large corporate and mortgage banking companies. The trust and investment group includes corporate, personal, and institutional trust services; investment management services; and a full-service brokerage company. In March 1994, the company's assets exceeded $26 billion.

FBS's mission statement says, "We will be one of the top-performing banks, measured in terms of market share and long-term profitability." A major goal is to obtain the leading market share in the markets that FBS serves. This goal is pursued, in part, through acquisition.

FBS's growth strategy seeks to aggressively expand in a number of financial services. For example, Duluth-based St. Louis Bank for Savings—the fifth largest thrift in the state—was acquired by FBS in 1994. The acquisition makes sense because it gives FBS a stronger presence in Duluth and falls in line with the company's strategy of trying to beef up its position in major cities and regional trade centers.

When FBS purchases a financial institution, it has determined many strategic, geographic, and logistic reasons why the institution is a good fit. One very important reason is the organization's customers. And retaining 100 percent of the acquired institution's customers is one of the most critical goals during acquisition and integration. Julie Cornelius, vice president of acquisitions integration, says, "We want customers of the acquired organization to be disrupted as little as possible. We want them to have confidence that with the new organization, they'll receive more value for their banking relationships through new products and services. If we have to take something away, we hope we're adding benefits someplace else."

Questions

1. Who are a bank's retail and community customers? What problems do these consumers have with banks? How can a marketing orientation improve the marketing of bank services?
2. When FBS makes an acquisition, what should it have as objectives to accomplish the integration of new customers?
3. In what way can the bank's information system be used to accomplish the integration of new customers?
4. How might a bank like FBS use marketing research in its retail and community banking operations?
5. What environmental factors are most likely to influence a bank's operations and its service to its customers? How can a bank obtain information about these factors?

CONSUMER BEHAVIOR: DECISION-MAKING PROCESSES AND SOCIOCULTURAL FORCES

Chapter 6

Learning Objectives

After you have studied this chapter, you will be able to:

1. Understand the basic model of consumer behavior.
2. Describe the consumer decision-making process and understand factors, such as consumer involvement, that influence it.
3. Appreciate the importance of perceived risk, choice criteria, purchase satisfaction, and cognitive dissonance.
4. Recognize the influence of individual factors, such as motives, perception, learning, attitude, and personality, on consumer behavior.
5. Explain the nature of culture and subculture in terms of social values, norms, and roles.
6. Characterize social class in the United States.
7. Explain the influence of reference groups on individual buyers.
8. Examine the roles in the joint decision-making process.

Gabriella Sahlman dressed to the nines this past holiday season: a $250 red velvet dress, $15 white stockings, $55 patent leather flats. Her everyday wear was more casual: sweater, turtleneck, leggings, all told about $120 per outfit. She has six. Sahlman sleeps on a $750 antiqued wooden bed. Her wicker bureau ran to $2,000 at a Madison Avenue boutique. No, Gabriella is no yuppie, not yet. On Feb. 6 she turned 21 months.

The consumer society neglects no potential markets, and so infant wear and other items for infants, toddlers and preschoolers, once the domain of hand-me-downs, is now a $23 billion business. While not entirely new, the idea of dressing little kids as if they were dolls has spawned a growth industry. The market is up by a third since 1987, according to the Port Washington, N.Y., NPD Group, which tracks consumer spending. That compares with 25 percent in women's wear.

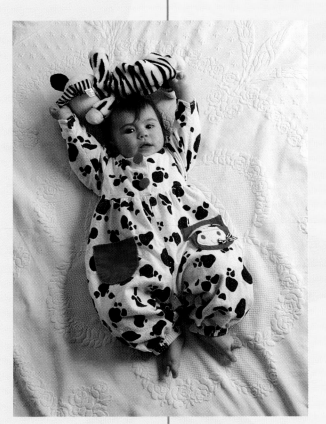

"Babies are the BMWs of the Nineties," says Stanley Fridstein. That makes Fridstein happy. Sniffing the trend, he founded The Right Start catalog and retail operation, which specializes in children's products to make life easier for mom and dad.

Baby as status symbol. "It's 'Look at my child and see who this family is,'" explains James McNeal, a marketing professor at Texas A & M University who has been studying family spending habits for more than 30 years. McNeal notes that as far back as the 1930s, parents tended to reach for status by spending money on soapflakes to put clean clothes on the kids. It was okay if the fit was a bit loose and if a couple of generations of cousins had already used the stuff. It was enough that it was neat. The baby business has demographics going for it as well as status. The U.S. population of kids under age 5 is at 23.6 million, up from 19.6 million in 1980. These babies are increasingly being born to dual-career couples who are waiting longer to have children and are thus able to spend more money on them once they arrive. The number of women who are 30 or older when their first child is born has more than quadrupled since 1970; the number of first children born to women over 40 more than doubled between 1984 and 1990, according to the National Center for Health Statistics.

And families have gotten smaller, making it easier to pamper the children, while working mom assuages some of her guilt by lavishing money on the child. "The girls' clothes just melt your heart. Since she's been born, I've hardly bought myself anything. I'd rather spend on her," says Texan Tracy Wolfe, a 34-year-old accountant and mother of 30-month-old Kelsey.

"I went nuts on layettes," says New Yorker Debra Kolitz, the mother of a 4-year-old and a 2-year-old. "Hundred-dollar blankets, $60 playsuits. My budget the first year? Not counting furniture? Between $5,000 and $10,000," says Kolitz.

In many ways Kolitz speaks for her generation of mothers: "It sounds sort of shocking, but it's true. You could probably do with a quarter of it, but it's so bloody appealing. I had my first child at 32. By the time they have that child, people like me are so caught up. These babies are so coveted that nothing is good enough."

Extravagant spending on babies' clothing, furniture, and accessories illustrates how consumers influence the marketing mix. It also shows how fascinating, yet baffling, consumer behavior can be.

This chapter begins our explanation of why people buy. The chapter opens by developing a model that gives an overview of consumer behavior. It then explains the consumer decision-making process and the psychological factors that influence this process. Finally, it describes sociocultural factors in consumer behavior.

WHAT IS CONSUMER BEHAVIOR?

Effective marketing must begin with careful evaluation of the problems potential customers face. This is because, according to the marketing concept, marketing efforts must focus on consumers' needs and provide answers to buyers' problems. A key to understanding consumers' needs and problems lies in the study of consumer behavior. A knowledge of consumer behavior gives the marketing manager information he or she can use to increase the chance of success in the marketplace.

Consumer Behavior
The activities people engage in when selecting, purchasing, and using products so as to satisfy needs and desires.

Consumer behavior consists of the activities people engage in when selecting, purchasing, and using products so as to satisfy needs and desires. Such activities involve mental and emotional processes, in addition to physical actions.[1] Consumer behavior includes both the behavior of ultimate consumers and the business behavior of organizational purchasers. However, many marketers prefer the term buyer behavior when discussing organizational purchasers.

A SIMPLE START: SOME BEHAVIORAL FUNDAMENTALS

Our discussion of consumer behavior starts with a basic building block: Human behavior of any kind (B) is a function (f) of the interaction between the person (P) and the environment (E)—that is, $B = f(P,E)$. Simple though it is, this formula says it all.[2] Human behavior results when a person interacts with the environment. Whether behaviors are simple or complex, they flow from the person's interaction with environmental variables. Exhibit 6–1 expands the basic formula for behavior, $B = f(P,E)$, into a more elaborate model of consumer decision making.[3] The model presents a decision-making process influenced by numerous interdependent forces rather than by any single factor. Activities of marketers, such as television advertising, are environmental forces, as are social forces such as culture and family. The characteristics of the individual, such as attitudes and personality, may also influence the decision-making process at a particular moment in time.

THE DECISION-MAKING PROCESS

Marketers who study consumer behavior are ultimately interested in one central question: How are consumer choices made? One important determinant is the situation in which a decision is made. In regard to situation, there are three categories of consumer decision-making behavior: routinized response behavior, limited problem solving, and extensive problem solving.

Routinized Response Behavior
The least complex type of decision making in which the consumer bases choices on past behavior and needs no other information.

Routinized response behavior is the least complex type of decision making because the consumer has considerable past experience in dealing with the situation at hand and thus needs no additional information to make a choice. To a cola

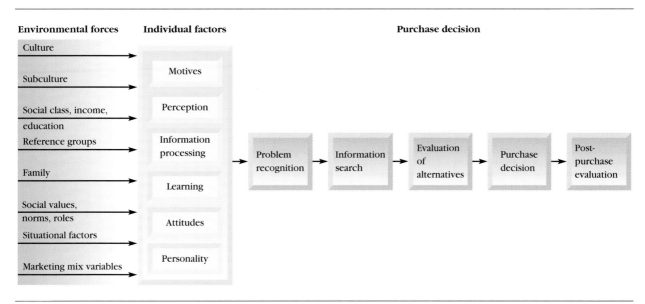

Environmental forces	Individual factors	Purchase decision
Culture	Motives	
Subculture	Perception	
Social class, income, education	Information processing	Problem recognition → Information search → Evaluation of alternatives → Purchase decision → Post-purchase evaluation
Reference groups		
Family	Learning	
Social values, norms, roles	Attitudes	
Situational factors		
Marketing mix variables	Personality	

EXHIBIT 6–1
Consumer Behavior Model of How the Decision-Making Process Works and What Influences It

Extensive Problem Solving
In-depth search for and evaluation of alternative solutions to a problem.

Limited Problem Solving
An intermediate level of decision making between routinized and extensive problem solving in which the consumer has some purchasing experience but is unfamiliar with stores, brands, or price options.

Consumer Involvement
The extent to which an individual attaches interest and importance to a product and is willing to expend energy in making a decision about purchasing the product.

The decision-making process is often shaped by the level of consumer involvement. For most people, chewing gum is a low-involvement product that is routinely purchased. This advertisement for Wrigley's Spearmint gum attempts to get the reader to be more involved with the advertisement and to think more about the product.

drinker, purchasing a particular brand in a matter of seconds is a routine matter. The purchase of a new house by a consumer or a fleet of trucks by an organization, however, usually requires **extensive problem solving.** The process may take months to complete, with a series of identifiable decisions made at different points. **Limited problem solving** is an intermediate level of decision making in which the consumer has some previous purchasing experience but is unfamiliar with stores, brands, or price options.

PURE CHEWING SATISFACTION?

WRIGLEY'S SPEARMINT CHEWING GUM

(Draw your own conclusions.)
It all connects. The cool, refreshing taste. . .the mouth-pleasing feeling. . . the enjoyment that goes on and on. Try some and you'll see that Pure Chewing Satisfaction is as easy as. . .Wrigley's Spearmint Gum.

Wrigley's Spearmint Gum.   Pure Chewing Satisfaction.

The seeming "snap judgment" and the more extensive processes are more closely related than it may seem. The routine decision is likely to have been preceded by a series of trials and errors in which the consumer tested different brands of cola before becoming able to make a routine choice. Both the routine choice and the more extensive problem-solving procedures may involve the same series of steps completed at different speeds.

Related to these problem-solving situations is the consumer's involvement in the purchase. **Consumer involvement** has to do with the importance an individual attaches to a product and the level of energy he or

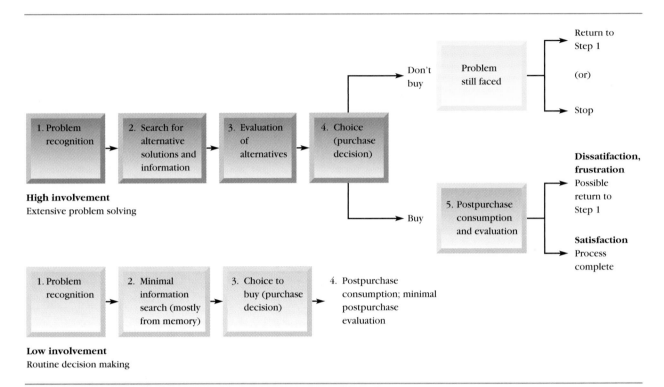

she directs toward making a decision. High involvement occurs when the decision to be made involves a high-interest product that is pertinent and relevant to the individual. The product's price may also be a factor. Involvement may include both thoughts and feelings, so high involvement can mean thinking more strongly or feeling more strongly.[4] A person who is highly involved with a product will exert more energy in decision making than a person whose involvement is low. A new mother may be highly involved in the selection of a pediatrician but far less involved in the purchase of talcum powder.

Exhibit 6–2 illustrates the steps in a high-involvement situation, a situation involving extensive problem solving. It also shows a low-involvement situation, which usually requires only a limited information search and no evaluation.

Let us look more closely at these steps, focusing primarily on situations in which extensive problem solving takes place. Remember, however, that (1) different consumers may pass through these steps at different rates of speed and (2) the five-step process need not be completed, even if it is begun. Frequently, buyers take a long time to reach the purchase stage, if only because of a money shortage. Others do not reach the purchase stage at all because they evaluate alternatives and determine that no available alternatives are satisfactory.

Step 1: Problem Recognition

Problem Recognition

The awareness that there is a discrepancy between an actual and a desired condition.

A tire blows out on a car being driven on an interstate highway. This is a case of instantaneous problem recognition. Problem recognition also can be a more complex, long-term process. A person whose car occasionally "dies" and isn't very shiny or attractive anymore may start to recognize a problem in the making. Perhaps when the new automobile models become available, she becomes aware her needs are not completely satisfied. **Problem recognition** is this awareness that there is a discrepancy between an actual and a desired condition.

The person who has become aware that a new car is in order may take a bit of time getting one. However, a smoker who realizes that he is lighting his last cigarette is likely to make a purchase decision very rapidly, passing through Steps 2 and 3 of the decision-making process so rapidly as to appear to have skipped them. For all practical purposes, these stages have been skipped, because the necessary information is stored in the consumer's memory. Marketers know that buyer behavior as routinized as this is difficult to alter. A buyer who devotes some time and consideration to decision making opens up more opportunities for effective marketers to appeal to him and to offer a product that may satisfy his need. Of course, marketers of the most popular brands of cigarettes, gum, and candy are happy that their regular customers have developed a routinized approach to solving problems.

Step 2: Search for Alternative Solutions and Information

Even the habitual buyer of Snickers candy bars is very likely to consider, however briefly, some other choices before selecting Snickers as usual. However, where highly involved buyers are purchasing a product for the first time or making a purchase that could have major financial, social, or other consequences, the search for alternatives and information about those alternatives is most easily observed.[5]

Perceived Risk
Consumers' uncertainty about the consequences of their future actions. The perception on the part of a consumer that a product may not do what it is expected to do.

That buyers in such positions behave as they do is explained by the theory of **perceived risk**—the perception that there is a chance the product may not do what it is expected to do. Consumers perceive that their actions may produce unpleasant consequences that cannot be anticipated with anything approaching certainty.

Several types of risk are encountered when expensive clothing is purchased, for example: Is the clothing too expensive? Will it be durable? What will my friends say when they see this suit? Will I look good in this? Exhibit 6–3 identifies several types of risks that may concern potential buyers. The accompanying Competitive Strategy feature describes how one marketer solved a problem of perceived risk. Buyers seek to reduce feelings of uncertainty by acquiring information. They may read advertisements. They may take family members or friends shopping with them.

Information Search
An internal or external search for information carried out by the consumer to reduce uncertainty and provide a basis for evaluating alternatives.

They may want the salesperson or tailor or some other expert to tell them that the product is well made and that it looks good. In other words, consumers engage in **information search** to acquire information that will reduce uncertainty and provide the basis for evaluation of alternatives. Information search may be internal or external.

EXHIBIT 6–3
The Types of Risk That Concern Potential Buyers

TYPE OF RISK	TYPICAL CONCERN
Performance risk	The brand may not perform its function well; it may not work; it may break down.
Financial risk	The buyer may lose money; pay too much; miss buying something else.
Physical risk	The product may be harmful or unhealthy; it may cause injury.
Social risk	Friends, relatives, or significant others may not approve of the purchase.
Time-loss risk	Maintenance time or time required to return the product to the place of purchase may be excessive.

COMPETITIVE STRATEGY: WHAT WENT RIGHT?

You'll Be Brilliant

Armstrong World Industries, a company that markets sheet-vinyl floor coverings to do-it-yourselfers, learned that women were the catalysts in the residential floor-covering purchase decision but men did the actual installation. Through its marketing research, Armstrong discovered that a high perceived risk—a fear of the first cut—was associated with the purchase. When interviewers asked people who examined but walked away from an in-store display why they did not buy the product, nearly 60 percent said they feared botching the job.

Armstrong developed a marketing strategy to combat this fear. A "Trim and Fit" kit was introduced and promoted with the message "Go on, cut. You'll be brilliant." When retailers were slow to push the kit because of its small retail markup, Armstrong added a sure-fire risk reducer—a "fail safe" guarantee. If the do-it-yourselfer made a mistake, the company would replace the floor covering at no cost. The biggest barrier to the purchase had been substantially removed. The strategy was a giant success.

Internal Search

Internal search is the mental activity associated with retrieval of information from memory. After an individual has recognized a problem, the first step in solving it is to scan memory for pertinent information. Information stored in memory may have come from prior purchase behavior, advertising, conversations with friends, or other experiences. When the buying situation facing the consumer differs from past situations, internal search may not provide enough information.

External Search

External search, the gathering of information from sources other than memory, may require time, effort, and money. External search is most likely in high-involvement situations and tends to be quite limited in low-involvement situations. Consumers gather external information from experience (such as shopping), personal sources (such as friends), public media (such as newspaper articles and the Internet), and marketer-dominated sources (such as magazine advertisements).

Marketers provide numerous sources of information to satisfy the consumer's need to reduce risk. Guarantees, a liberal return policy, store displays or advertisements that show that a product actually delivers what is promised, and a pledge that "We service what we sell" may reduce the consumer's uncertainty about perceived risk. These are not "tricks." To reduce our chances of injury, damage, or loss, all of us prefer to deal with companies that give us such assurances.

In low-involvement situations, in which external search is almost nonexistent (and even internal search is minimal), it is extremely important for the company's brand name to be prominent in the customer's memory. Thus, assuming consumers spend little time making decisions about soft drink choices, an effective marketing strategy is to make the name Coca-Cola prominent in consumers' minds. Often, in such situations, the objective of advertising is to create awareness and familiarity through repetition. Such messages should remain simple, because the consumer is not highly involved. However, in high-involvement situations, consumers may be more receptive to more complex messages, and the advertising may emphasize information about comparative features of competitive brands, stressing unique benefits of the advertiser's brand.

Step 3: Evaluation of Alternatives

Evaluation of alternatives begins when an information search has clarified or identified a number of potential solutions to the consumer's problem. Often the alternative solutions are directly competitive products. An alternative to a Vermont skiing vacation may be a skiing vacation in Squaw Valley or St. Moritz, for example. Other times, however, the alternative to a skiing vacation in Vermont is a new station wagon. The outcome of the process is usually the ranking of alternatives, the selection of a preferred alternative, or the decision that there is no acceptable alternative and that the search should continue.

Choice Criteria

The critical attributes a consumer uses to evaluate product alternatives.

In analyzing possible purchases, the prospective buyer considers the appropriate choice criteria. **Choice criteria** are the critical attributes the consumer uses to evaluate alternatives. For an automobile tire, product features (such as mileage, warranty, and brand name) and price might be the typical choice criteria. Which choice criteria are used depends on the consumer and the situation. For example, some people who need automobile tires may buy them at the neighborhood service station even if prices there are higher than at other places. They may feel that the time saved is worth the extra dollars spent. They may know the local station owner and want to "give him some business." They may be trying to keep on the station owner's good side in case they ever need emergency help. They may want to deal with a local seller so they can complain if something goes wrong.

Many buyers appear not to want to evaluate too many factors when choosing among alternatives. The average person looking for a new car does not want (or cannot understand) the kinds of facts and figures mechanical engineers might be able to provide. The typical car buyer wants very simple facts: The car "looks good"; the car dealer is a "good guy." The buyer does not want an analysis of the car's aerodynamics or an art expert's opinion of its looks. In fact, Honda's "We make it simple" promotions are based on the finding that many consumers are confused about optional accessories and mechanical details. Offering only cars with "standard options" simplifies the choice criteria and the buying situation.

Step 4: Choice: Purchase Decisions and the Act of Buying

Sooner or later the prospective buyer must make a purchase decision or choose not to buy any of the alternatives available. Assuming that the decision maker has decided which brand to purchase, the mechanics of the purchase must be worked out. The actual purchase behavior may be simple, especially if the buyer has either a credit card or a checkbook with a sufficient balance. The decision to buy can bring with it a few other related decisions: Should the buyer get new valve stems too? How about a lifetime wheel-balancing agreement with the seller?

Step 5: Postpurchase Consumption and Evaluation

Purchase Satisfaction

The feeling on the part of the consumer that the decision to buy was appropriate.

Consumption, naturally, follows purchase. If the decision maker is also the user, the matter of **purchase satisfaction** (or dissatisfaction) remains. In some cases, satisfaction is immediate, as when the buyer chews the just-bought gum or feels pleased that the decision-making process is over. Frequently, after making a purchase, we think to ourselves or tell others, "Well, I bought a great set of tires today." This patting ourselves on the back is an attempt to assure satisfaction. We are telling ourselves that we are pleased with the purchase. In this case, marketing has achieved its goal of consumer satisfaction.[6]

However, the opposite can occur—we can feel uneasy over the purchase. Are the tires good on snow? Has someone acted surprised that we bought this brand instead of that one? Second thoughts about things can create an uneasy feeling, a sensation that the decision-making process may have yielded the wrong decision. These feelings of uncertainty can be analyzed in terms of the theory of cognitive dissonance.

Cognitive Dissonance
In consumer behavior, the negative feelings that may occur after a commitment to purchase has been made. It describes the tension that results from holding two conflicting ideas or beliefs at the same time.

In the context of consumer behavior, **cognitive dissonance** is a psychologically uncomfortable postpurchase feeling. More specifically, it refers to the negative feelings that can follow a commitment to purchase. It results from the fact that people do not like to hold two or more conflicting beliefs or ideas at the same time. Suppose the car owner has bought the tires and has left the shop; there's no turning back now. Should he or she have bought Michelin tires instead, even though the price was a bit higher? Dissonance theory describes such feelings as a sense of psychic tension, a tension that the individual will seek to relieve. Each alternative has some advantages and some disadvantages. Buyers reduce cognitive dissonance by focusing on the advantages of the purchase—by carrying out postpurchase evaluation in a way that supports the choice made. Buyers may seek reinforcement from friends or from the seller. They may mentally downgrade the unselected alternatives and play up the advantages of the selected brand to convince themselves that they made the right choice.

Effective marketers don't want dissatisfied customers. When marketers understand that any choice can create cognitive dissonance, they can seek to support their customer's choice. Promising good service, telling the buyer to come right back if there's any trouble, and giving a toll-free "hotline" number are good business.

FOCUS ON QUALITY

Packard Bell

The decision to purchase a multimedia personal computer is a high-involvement decision for most first-time buyers. And before consumption can follow the purchase, the consumer must install and connect the component parts. Packard Bell uses a KISS—Keep It Simple, Stupid—philosophy and a color-coding system to avoid frustrating consumers. The personal computer buyer connects the keyboard to the PC by inserting a purple plug into a purple socket. Next, he or she connects the teal mouse cord into the teal socket and the orange cord for the monitor into the orange slot on the computer. After that, the beige cord is plugged into the electrical outlet. When the computer is turned on, the computer user finds more than 25 software programs preloaded on the computer.

INDIVIDUAL FACTORS THAT SHAPE THE DECISION-MAKING PROCESS

Taking a decision-making perspective helps us understand a great deal about consumers' problem-solving behavior. But consumer behavior is complex, and there is much more to learn. Now that we have presented an overview of decision-making processes, we can explore the psychological variables that activate and influence them.

Motivation

Marketers wish to know the underlying causes of buying behavior. They wish to know how consumer behavior gets started, is directed toward certain products, and is stopped. Psychologists explain such behavior in terms of motivation.

Orthodontists may increase their patients' satisfaction by giving cards like this one after braces have been removed. This also decreases the cognitive dissonance of the parents, who have been paying for the dental service for several years, and increases the likelihood that they will choose the same orthodontist for their other children.

Motivation and Needs Defined

Motivation

An activated state that causes a person to initiate goal-directed behavior.

Motivation is an activated state within a consumer that causes the consumer to initiate goal-directed behavior. Accordingly, a **motive** is an aroused need that serves to energize behavior and direct it toward a goal. A **need** reflects the lack of something that would benefit the person—a gap between the consumer's actual and desired state. The larger the gap between the consumer's actual and desired state, the more motivated the consumer is to solve the problem. Notice that this definition is consistent with our description of the problem definition step of the decision-making process. Problem recognition is, in effect, the creation of a consumer need state. Needs are always within us, but they may not be strong enough to cause us to act. When, by whatever means, a need is activated, it becomes a motive. Thus, jogging may stimulate the basic thirst need that is always with us. Our motive to find and drink a beverage to satisfy our thirst is an aroused need. An **incentive** (in this case, water or Gatorade) can be any object, person, or situation that we believe will satisfy a particular motive.

Motive

An aroused need that energizes behavior and directs it toward a goal.

Need

The gap between actual and desired states.

Incentive

Something believed capable of satisfying a particular motive.

What is it that arouses motives? What gets us going? In general, it is either an internal force or an external stimulus. For example, when we are hungry, internal biological mechanisms (grumbling stomach, empty feeling) arouse behaviors aimed at satisfying that hunger. We can satisfy the motive of alleviating hunger by following the steps in Exhibit 6–4 (on page 144), a simple model of motivated behavior. In this example, the unfulfilled motive pushes us toward an incentive that will satisfy the motive. We may respond by reaching for a candy bar on the desk, strolling to the refrigerator, or making an automobile trip to a store or restaurant.

Classifying Needs and Motives

Physiological Need

Need based on biological functioning, like the needs for food, water, and air.

Social and Psychological Need

Need stemming from people's interactions with the social environment.

Many psychologists have attempted to classify needs and motives. There is little agreement among these classifications. In fact, the only area of commonality is the general agreement that two basic groups of needs exist. The first group is made up of **physiological needs,** or needs stemming from biological mechanisms. The second group consists of **social and psychological needs,** or needs resulting from our interaction with the social environment. An example of marketers who deal with both sorts of needs are food marketers. Humans need food to live (a physi-

EXHIBIT 6–4
Simple Model of Motivated
Behavior

ological need), but the social environment creates other needs. For example, some Americans patronize elegant restaurants to show they are more successful than the Joneses next door (a social need).

Maslow's Hierarchy of Needs

Abraham Maslow, a psychologist, believed that even though each individual is unique, all humans have certain common needs. Maslow identified these needs and ordered them from the most basic to the highest-level need. His needs hierarchy provides the basis for many theories of motivation. The five classes identified by Maslow, which are also shown in Exhibit 6–5, are as follows:[7]

1. Physiological needs (food, water, air, sex, control of body temperature).
2. Safety needs (protection and security from threats).
3. Love and social needs (affection and feelings of belonging).
4. Self-esteem needs (feelings of self-worth, achievement, respect of others, prestige).
5. Self-actualization needs (self-fulfillment, becoming increasingly like what one is capable of becoming).

Maslow believed that individuals try to fill the most basic needs first. He suggested that a largely satisfied need is no longer a motivator of behavior. (It is not necessary that the need be totally satisfied.) People move on to try to satisfy higher-level needs as lower levels are met. It follows from this that, for example, the need for food does not motivate people whose hunger is satisfied regularly in the same way it motivates people who are regularly concerned about the availability of food. In countries where hunger and even starvation are major problems, food is marketed almost entirely through simple distribution. No inducement other than availability is required. But U.S. marketers of food know that they must appeal to higher-level needs. Thus, Rice-a-Roni is "the San Francisco treat" and Weight Watchers Chocolate Dessert Sensations offer "Total indulgence. Zero guilt." Dining as San Franciscans do or indulging oneself is not basic to human life, but it may be appealing to consumers seeking affection or self-esteem.

Finally, consumers may seek to meet lower-level and higher-level needs at the same time. The person who is installing a home burglar or fire alarm system to satisfy a need for safety may also be seeking social acceptance and self-esteem by exercising, eating healthy foods, and dressing well to gain the respect of others.

Motivation and Emotion

Emotions are states involving subjectively experienced feelings of attraction or repulsion. There is a complex interrelationship between motivation and emotion. Romantic love, joy, fear, and anger are some of the emotions that may be associated with a motivated state.

Emotion
State involving subjectively experienced feelings of attraction or repulsion.

EXHIBIT 6–5
Maslow's Hierarchy of
Needs

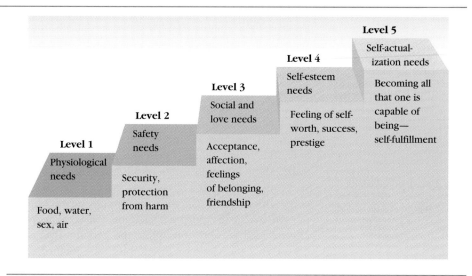

EXHIBIT 6–5
Maslow's Hierarchy of Needs

Have you ever gone shopping because you were bored or made an impulsive purchase because you needed a little variety in your life? Most people answer "yes" to this question. The experiential perspective on consumer behavior suggests that consumers shop or buy certain products to have fun, to enjoy the process of shopping, and to achieve increased levels of arousal. These are motivations influenced by emotion.

Early categorizations of motives by marketers used classifications meant to describe the role emotions play in motivation. Therefore, motives were incorrectly grouped into two separate and distinct categories: "emotional" versus "rational". While this distinction is inappropriate, dichotomies of this sort are still in use. They persist because they serve to remind marketers that consumers, and even organizational buyers, are not strictly rational.

Perception

Although the idea of "reality" may at first seem straightforward, individuals differ in how they perceive reality. For example, no two people will perceive a product, store, or advertisement in exactly the same way. Perception takes place through the senses. To perceive is to see, hear, taste, feel, or smell some object, person, or event and assign meaning in the process.

Products offered by marketers provide many examples of this phenomenon. A three-year-old car may appear to be just a used automobile to some, but a teenager may be thrilled to have it as a first car. The teenager's parents may see the car in a different light. The used-car dealer may view it in still another. Their images of the automobile—their perceptions—are very different.

Perception

The process of interpreting sensations and giving meaning to stimuli.

Perception, then, is the process of interpreting sensations and giving meaning to stimuli. This process occurs because people constantly strive to make sense of the world and, when faced with new sensations or data, seek patterns or concepts that may relate new bits of information to each other and to past experience. Perception is the interpretation of reality, and each of us views reality from a different perspective.

What Is Selective Perception?

Individuals receive information, or stimuli, by hearing, seeing, touching, tasting, and smelling. How they organize and interpret these stimuli with regard to the decision-making process depends on their involvement in the decision-making process, their abilities to experience sensations, the context in which they encounter the stimuli, their intelligence and thought processes, and even their moods. These factors combine to create a mental phenomenon known as **selective perception**— that is, the tendency of each individual to screen out certain stimuli and to color or interpret other stimuli with meanings drawn from personal backgrounds.

Selective Perception
The screening out of certain stimuli and the interpretation of other stimuli according to personal experience, attitudes, or the like.

The *Time* magazine advertisement in Exhibit 6–6 shows one way in which we add meaning and interpretations to stimuli. The picture actually contains these elements: T, stamps, M, and E. yet we read "TIME" because of our tendency to mentally "fill things in" or "finish things off." This aspect of perception is called **closure.** Many advertisements make use of this concept by not showing the product, showing only part of it, or showing only its shadow. The viewer supposedly becomes more involved with the advertisement through the process of closure. A person who can't perceive closure will be annoyed by the advertisement, so the closure idea is used only when the product is very well known and the advertiser is sure that the viewer can complete the picture. Selective perception may involve selective exposure, selective attention, or selective interpretation.

Closure
An element of perception by which an observer mentally completes an incomplete stimulus.

Individuals actively and selectively seek to be exposed to certain stimuli about products they intend to buy. In other circumstances, consumers avoid stimuli by simply avoiding exposure to them. For example, many cable TV subscribers choose to block out the reception of certain channels to avoid exposure to certain programs and advertisements. This is **selective exposure.**

Selective Exposure
The principle describing the fact that individuals selectively determine whether or not they will be exposed to certain stimuli.

Even if individuals are exposed to information, they may not want to receive certain messages, so they screen these stimuli out of their experience. They pay no attention—at least, no conscious attention—to the stimuli. This is **selective attention.** For example, a person who has just purchased a new Sony TV does not want to hear an advertisement announcing that Sony's prices have just been cut in half. The person may not pay attention to such advertisements.

Selective Attention
A perceptual screening device whereby a person does not attend to a particular stimulus.

Finally, even a person who pays attention may distort a newly encountered message that is incompatible with his or her established values or attitudes. This is **selective interpretation.** The owner of a Ford pick-up truck is likely to distort information detailing why Dodge Rams are better trucks than Fords, for example. Looking carefully at perception teaches the truth of the old adage, "It's not what you (the marketer) say, it's what they (consumers) hear."

Selective Interpretation
A perceptual screening device whereby a person distorts a stimulus that is incompatible with his or her values or attitudes.

There is not much the marketer can do to overcome selective exposure other than to carefully plan the placement of advertisements so that the target customer will be reached. Selective attention may be overcome with attention-getting messages. The size of an advertisement, the colors used, the novelty of pictures included, and many other **stimulus factors** have been shown to have considerable effects on the amount of attention a viewer will give an advertisement.

Stimulus Factor
A characteristic of a stimulus—for example, the size, colors, or novelty of a print advertisement—that affects perception.

More subtly, an advertisement may gain increased attention by featuring aspects that speak to the viewer's needs, background, or hopes, because perception is also influenced by **individual factors.** Generally a full-page color advertisement will attract more attention than a quarter-page advertisement in black and white. However, a black-and-white advertisement offering the hope of "a better appearance" to balding men is likely to attract a lot of attention among its target group, balding men, because they are highly involved. Similarly, advertisements promising aid for losing weight will be noticed by people who need this help, even if others think the advertisements lack attention-getting features. Many rules of advertising (use color, don't be wordy) are profitably broken when the target consumers are willing to devote attention to a problem that means something to them. This illustrates a basic fact about the perception of advertising: Consumers pay attention to advertisements when the products featured interest them.

Individual Factor
With reference to perception, a characteristic of a person that affects how the person perceives a stimulus.

EXHIBIT 6–6
Example of Closure in the Selective Perception Process

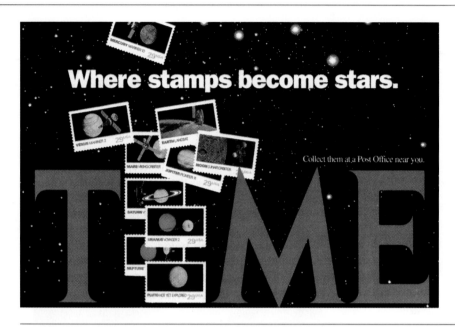

Perception and Brand Image Marketing

Product distinctions often exist in the minds of consumers and not in the products themselves. The symbolic meaning associated with brand distinctions, developed as a result of selective perception, is known as brand image. A **brand image** is a complex of symbols and meanings associated with a brand. Over the years, for example, General Mills has established a strong image for its Betty Crocker brand. The image is one of dependability and honesty—valuable images for a food product. There never was a real Betty Crocker, but the General Mills products are good and reliable, just like Betty's image. Research has shown that brand image can be the key factor in a buying decision.

Brand Image
The complex of symbols and meanings associated with a brand.

That *perception* of reality is extremely important in brand image marketing is demonstrated in the various "taste test" ads we see on television. Diet Pepsi, for example, shows us that Ray Charles cannot be tricked into drinking Diet Coke even though he cannot read the label. In fact, it has been shown in formal research that for a number of products—among them cola and beer—consumers cannot distinguish among the various brands once the labels have been removed.[8]

Subliminal Perception

Can advertisers send us messages of which we are not consciously aware? In the 1950s, there was considerable controversy about the possibility of this so-called subliminal advertising. In a movie theater "experiment," the phrases "eat popcorn" and "drink Coca-Cola" were flashed on the screen so rapidly that people were unaware of them. Sales in the movie theater were reported to have increased 58 percent for popcorn and 18 percent for Coca-Cola. Psychologists, alarmed at this result, seriously studied the "experiment" and concluded that it had lacked scientific rigor. Subsequent investigations of *subliminal perception* (perception of stimuli at a subconscious level) suggested that advertisers trying to achieve "perception without awareness" would face technical problems so great that the public need not be apprehensive about the possibility. Subliminal stimuli are simply too weak to be effective. For example, only very short messages can be communicated, and the influence of selective perception tends to be stronger than the weak stimulus factors.[9]

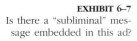

EXHIBIT 6–7
Is there a "subliminal" message embedded in this ad?

It is interesting to note that the public frequently misuses the word subliminal. Symbolism is not subliminal, nor are embedded messages "hidden" in pictures. Neither symbolism nor embedded messages are perceived at an unconscious level—that is, without the individual's knowledge of their existence. The picture shown in Exhibit 6–7 allegedly hides an embedded "subliminal" message. Can you see it? If you can, of course, you have not perceived it subliminally.

FOCUS ON GLOBAL COMPETITION

Copying in Korea

A package of gum sold in South Korea has a bright yellow wrapper, bold black lettering, and a small red design at one end. It may look like Juicy Fruit gum, but it isn't. Most likely it's Juicy & Fresh gum from Lotte Confectionery Company. Or it could be Tong Yang, which has a very similar package. Then again, it could be Hearty Juicy, which mimics all three in hopes that consumers will perceive it to be similar to the other brands. In South Korea, goods copying American brands are everywhere. Even some of the biggest compa-

nies imitate the world's best products in hope that consumers will perceive the copycat brands as similar to the originals. In supermarkets, Tie laundry detergent is packaged in orange boxes with a whirlpool design that differs little from Tide's. This brand is produced by Lucky Goldstar Group, one of South Korea's largest companies. Because of widespread copying like this, protecting intellectual property worldwide is a major problem for global marketers.

Learning

If you were asked to identify a brand of light bulbs, what brand would you name? Would you say General Electric? If so, you'd be agreeing with 86 percent of consumers asked this question. Furthermore, 55 percent of consumers said they would pick GE the next time they bought a light bulb. Most consumers have learned to be brand-loyal to GE light bulbs. How does such learning take place?

How Learning Occurs

Learning occurs as a result of experience or of mental activity associated with experience. Thus, the expression "older and wiser" is not far from the mark, because older people have had the opportunity to learn from many experiences. Experiences related to product usage, shopping, and exposure to advertisements and other aspects of marketing add to consumers' banks of knowledge and influence their habits.

Learning is defined as any change in behavior or cognition resulting from experience or an interpretation of experience. Suppose a package or display—say, for a crayon that can be cleaned away with soap and water—attracts the attention of a shopper, and the shopper gives the product a try. If the crayon works to the customer's satisfaction, she has learned through experience that the new product is acceptable. If it does not, she learns that fact instead. This knowledge becomes information in the consumer's memory. **Memory** is the information-processing function that allows people to store and retrieve information.

A type of learning called *social learning* can occur by observation of the consequences of others' behavior. For example, a younger child observes an older sibling's punishment and learns to avoid that punishment by avoiding the situation that brought it about. Similarly, buyers often purchase products that were recommended by other people who have used these products. Much television advertising is based on the idea that social learning occurs when we watch others and model their behavior. We observe the satisfaction that others, perhaps role models like Michael Jordan, derive from a product; as we do, we learn by interpreting their experiences.

Learning
Any change in behavior or cognition that results from experience or an interpretation of experience.

Memory
The information-processing function involving the storage and retrieval of information.

Consumer behavior is learned. A person who is rewarded with a unique experience when they first purchase a scuba diving vacation is likely to repeat this behavior. Operant conditioning theory suggests that repeated satisfaction creates buying habits and loyal consumers.

Operant Conditioning
The process by which reinforcement of a behavior results in repetition of that behavior.

Reinforcement
Reward; reinforcement strengthens a stimulus-response relationship.

Many theories attempt to explain exactly how learning occurs. All of the widely accepted theories acknowledge the great importance of experience. One important viewpoint focuses on **operant conditioning,** a form of learning believed to occur when a response, such as a purchase, is followed by a **reinforcement,** or reward. Exhibit 6–8 illustrates the consumer learning process according to this theory. Here, some aspect of the product provides the stimulus, and the purchase is the consumer's response to the stimulus. If the product proves to be satisfactory, the consumer receives a reward—a reinforcement. The fact is that the purchase is made in the hope that satisfaction will follow. When it does, the effect is to strengthen (reinforce) the stimulus-response process. Learning takes place as this phenomenon occurs over and over.

Some theories of learning stress the importance of repetition in the development of habits. For example, the more you are exposed to a television commercial such as Toyota's claim "I love what you do for me," the more likely it is that you have learned the content of the sales message. Repeatedly rewarding a behavior strengthens the stimulus-response relationship. More simply, repeated satisfaction creates buying habits and loyal customers.

Learning Theories and Marketing

Most learning theories are compatible with marketing activities and marketing's key philosophy, the marketing concept. The theories tell us that positive rewards or experiences lead to repeated behaviors. The marketing concept stresses consumer satisfaction, which leads to repeat purchases and long-term profitability for the organization.

Attitudes

Attitude
An individual's general affective, cognitive, and intentional responses toward a given object, issue, or person.

An **attitude** comprises an individual's general affective, cognitive, and intentional responses toward a given object, issue, or person.[10] People learn attitudes. In terms of marketing, they learn to respond in a consistently favorable or unfavor-

EXHIBIT 6–8
Effects of Reinforcement on Consumer Behavior: First Trial and Repeat Purchase Situations

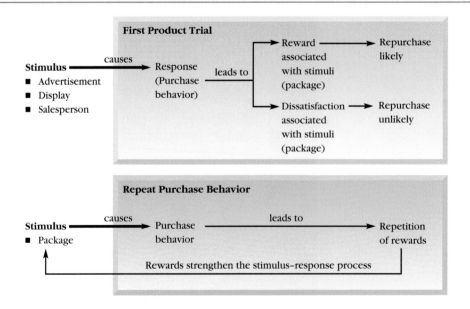

able manner with respect to products, stores, advertising, and people. Because attitudes are learned it is possible to change them. This is a goal of much promotional activity.

The ABC Model: A Three-Part Theory of Attitudes

The ABC model is the traditional way to view attitudes. In this view, an attitude has three parts. The A component is the affective, or emotional, component. It reflects a person's feelings toward the object. Is the brand good or bad? Is it desirable? Likable? The B component is the behavioral component, which reflects intended and actual behaviors toward the object. This component is a predisposition to action. The C component is the cognitive component. It involves all the consumer's beliefs, knowledge, and thoughts about the object—the consumer's perception of the product's attributes or characteristics. Is it durable? Expensive? Suitable as a gift for Aunt Mary?

How Do Attitudes Influence Buying Behavior?

Let's examine a consumer's attitude toward the Canon Photura camera. The consumer may hold several beliefs about the product: that it takes clear pictures and that its features make it easy to use, for example. She may have certain feelings about the camera as well—for example, she may feel that Canon is a good brand or that the Photura is desirable because it is the "official camera" of the Olympics. Her beliefs and feelings may create a predisposition to consider buying the product. Note that the consumer's attitude serves as a general indicator of behavior toward the attitudinal object. That is, the consumer will consider buying the product—she will not necessarily buy it. A favorable attitude toward a particular brand may not result in purchase of that brand. After all, consumers have attitudes toward competing brands as well. Furthermore, attitudes are not the sole determinant of behavior. Situational, financial, and motivational forces, as well as attitudes, influence behavior.

Because attitudes are situational, their effects are controlled by circumstances. Most Americans have very favorable attitudes toward Rolls Royce and Mercedes automobiles, yet not many own one of these cars. Many people admire—that is, have attitudes that favor—mansions surrounded by well-tended formal gardens. Few people live in such places, however. Attitudes may also be affected by other attitudes. People who don't like winter weather will probably not like snow skiing, or buy a snowmobile, or plan to live out their days in Minnesota.

Thus, it is difficult to predict a specific behavior from an attitude toward a single object. Nevertheless, in many situations there is consistency between attitudes and behavior. For example, we may think that the personnel in our favorite department store are friendly. We may also think that the store is clean and the prices are reasonable. Our purchasing behavior at this store may be consistent with our attitudes. Much managerial strategy is based on the assumption that, "all other things being equal," a positive attitude toward a store or brand will predispose the consumer to shop at the store or use the brand.

Personality and Self-Concept

We have been discussing several individual differences in consumer behavior. Where do such differences come from? Many individual differences in human behavior are related to personality and self-concept.

What Is Personality?

Like many psychological terms, the word personality is used in nontechnical ways in our everyday vocabularies. When Bill says, "Mike gets along well with others

Personality
The fundamental disposition of an individual; the distinctive patterns of thought, emotion, and behavior that characterize an individual's response to the situations of his or her life.

because he has a pleasing personality," the word is not used technically. In consumer behavior theory, **personality** is the fundamental disposition of an individual and the distinctive patterns of thought, emotion, and behavior that characterize each individual's response to the situations of his or her life. Personality refers especially to the most dominant characteristics, or traits, of a person, such as introversion and extroversion. Many personality traits—such as dominance, gregariousness, self-confidence, masculinity, conservativeness, prestige-consciousness, and independence—have been identified. We might expect traits to affect behavior. Introverts might be expected to purchase different types of automobiles than extroverts, for example.

Self-Concept: How We See Ourselves

Self-Concept
The individual's perception and appraisal of himself or herself.

The term **self-concept** refers to the individual's perception and appraisal of himself or herself. Of course, the appraisal of others plays a part in this. Ultimately, though, the self-concept is the person's own picture of who he or she is (the real self) and who he or she would like to be or is in the process of becoming (the ideal self). According to self-concept theory, consumers shop at stores and purchase goods and services that reflect and enhance their self-concepts.

Personality Theory Evaluated

The hypothesized relationship of personality (including self-concept) to buying and other aspects of consumer behavior has been studied extensively. The results indicate that the predictive power of personality to explain why one brand is chosen over another is inconsequential and that marketing managers can make only scant use of personality in formulating their marketing strategies. That is, investigating personality in isolation from other factors, such as demographic characteristics, is not an effective method of predicting specific consumer behavior. Nevertheless, the intuitive appeal of a relationship between personality and consumer behavior leads some marketing practitioners to base strategy on notions associated with personality theory.

Problems with the practical application of personality research led to the development of psychographic profiles of consumers, discussed in Chapter 8. The focus of personality theory in psychology is on the person as a person, whereas consumer behavior theory focuses on the person as a consumer, emphasizing traits related closely to day-to-day consumer activities. This seems to be a more appropriate way for marketing managers to implement ideas about individual differences in consumers.

INTERPERSONAL INFLUENCES ON THE DECISION-MAKING PROCESS

We have examined many individual factors that influence the decision-making process. But, as Exhibit 6–1 showed, environmental influences also exert an effect. In this section, we focus on sociocultural aspects of the environment. The lives of consumers are subject to countless sociocultural forces, including those created by the culture, the subculture, and various groups. Sociologists refer to these forces as *interpersonal influences*.

Social Values, Norms, and Roles

People hold certain social values, follow certain norms, and fill certain roles. As we will see, values, norms, and roles have various sources, from the overall culture to much smaller social groups.

Social Values

Chapter 3 defined social values as the goals that a society views as important. As such, they reflect the moral order of a society and give meaning to social life. For example, winning is a value considered important by our sports-oriented society.

Norms

Norms are rules of conduct to be followed in particular circumstances. Behavior appropriate to one situation may be inappropriate to another; thus, norms are "situation specific." In the United States, the general norm is for pedestrians to avoid touching each other. Jostling and crowding together are to be avoided in most circumstances; persons not following this norm are rewarded with angry stares or comments. At a parade, however, crowding and pushing are more acceptable. The norm changes with the situation.

Norms, like values, strongly affect our lifestyles and our day-to-day behavior patterns, including consumer behavior. The increasingly commonplace norm of not smoking in certain public places influences the planning of service providers such as restaurants, airports, and shopping malls. Another example of a norm is the custom of buying a diamond engagement ring. Many couples would not even consider choosing between, for example, a ruby ring and an emerald ring.

Norms vary among cultures. The Japanese attending the Tokyo Disneyland are far more restrained than Americans attending Disneyland in this country. For example, passengers on the rides in Japan do not raise their hands in the air and scream as do their American counterparts. It is not the accepted norm.

FOCUS ON GLOBAL COMPETITION

Children in China

Xiang Yinchao, a 10-year-old boy, waits quietly in a crowded Shanghai department store while his mother asks a saleswoman a barrage of questions about the VTech alphabet desk, a $70 computer keyboard that helps teach Mandarin-speaking children English. Yinchao's mother knows it's expensive, but she says, "Chinese parents want their kids to speak English. It's the international language."

Limited to one child by government regulations and determined to see their kids get ahead, Chinese parents—along with grandparents, great-grandparents, aunts, and uncles—are spoiling, fussing over, and doting on their children as never before.

Known in China as Little Emperors, Chinese kids are being showered with everything from candy to computer games. With at least 300 million people in China under the age of 15, according to government statistics, a huge market is emerging that caters to China's kiddie dynasty.

Business is driven by the "six-pocket syndrome," a phrase referring to the fact that as many as six adults may be indulging the whims of each child. The president of Walt Disney's Asian-Pacific consumer products division says, "When you look at the combined spending power of those grown-ups, the Chinese child probably has more spent on him than a child in the West."

Roles

Role
A cluster of behavior patterns considered appropriate for a position in a social setting.

Any social institution, from the smallest group to the largest organization, creates and defines roles for its members. These, like norms, are customary ways of doing things. **Roles** define appropriate behavior patterns in reference to other roles. Thus, the role of son or daughter includes expected behavior patterns that differ from the behavior patterns expected of someone in a parental role. The role of a wage earner and that of a student also require different behaviors. Furthermore, some students may dress in jeans and T-shirts to demonstrate their status as students. However, during a job interview, students of business administration may dress more formally and carry attaché cases to act out their roles as prospective businesspeople.

Roles obviously carry over into purchasing situations. There are consumer roles and seller roles. The shopper expects to have certain rights and expects the store employee to fulfill certain obligations.[11] An employee in an expensive fur salon is expected to behave differently from a check-out clerk at Kmart.

Culture

Many of our values, norms, and roles come from our overall culture. Recall that a culture consists of values, beliefs, and customary behaviors learned and shared by the members of a particular society. Essential to the concept of culture is the notion that culture is learned rather than innate. Thus, that children are born is "natural," but how the mating process is conducted and how the children are treated is "cultural."

It is important for marketers to understand the many aspects of culture. Culture obviously varies from place to place around the globe and affects the success of marketing worldwide. What seems like a normal idea, or even a great idea, to marketers in one country may be seen as unacceptable or even laughable to citizens of other lands. Campbell's Soup offered their red-and-white-labeled cans of soup in Brazil but found cultural obstacles there too difficult to overcome. Brazilian housewives apparently felt guilty using the prepared soups that Americans take for granted. They believed that they would not be fulfilling their roles as homemakers if they served their families a soup they could not call their own. Faced with this difficulty, Campbell's withdrew the product. However, Campbell's discovered that Brazilian women felt comfortable using a dehydrated "soup starter," to which they could add their own special ingredients and flair. A different situation exists in Japan. There, the marketer must realize that soup is regarded as a breakfast drink rather than a dish served for lunch or dinner.

Subcultures: Cultures within Cultures

Within a society there is a dominant culture. However, there are also cultural differences. Language differences are an example. Some countries have two (Canada and Belgium) or more (Switzerland has four) official languages. In China, five major and many minor languages are spoken. In the United States, several language groups can be identified. Spanish is now spoken by almost 20 percent of the U.S. population.

Subculture

A group within a dominant culture that is distinct from the culture. A subculture will typically display some values or norms that differ from those of the overall culture.

A **subculture** is a group within a dominant culture that is distinct because it differs from the dominant culture in one or more of a number of important ways—language, demographic variables such as ethnic or racial background, or geographical region, for example. The subculture will also differ from the overall culture in some values, norms, and beliefs. Within the U.S. culture there are many subcultures. Subcultures made up of particular racial or ethnic groups (such as the African-American, Hispanic, and Jewish subcultures) are easiest to identify, but the marketer must recognize the many other subcultural differences in the U.S. culture. These may be as simple as regional differences in food preferences.[12] In the Northeastern states, people often eat lamb chops, but in west Texas, beef is the sta-

In our diverse society, there are many subcultures based on color, language, religion, and geography. Consumption of foods, preferences for music, and forms of socializing can be strongly influenced by values, norms, and roles prescribed by the subculture.

Social Class

A group of people with similar levels of prestige, power, and wealth who also share a set of related beliefs, attitudes, and values in their thinking and behavior.

ple, and lamb chops are not as popular. Subcultural differences provide marketers with challenges and with segmentation possibilities that are rich in potential.

Social Classes

Within every culture there are social classes. A **social class** is a group of people with similar levels of prestige, power, and wealth who also share a set of related beliefs, attitudes, and values in their thinking and behavior. Exhibit 6–9, which summarizes one view of U.S. social classes, shows five discrete groups. Class structure is actually more like an escalator, however, because it runs from bottom to top without any major plateaus.

Social class explains many differences in behavior patterns and lifestyles. Social class may have a major impact on shopping patterns or products purchased. An advertisement for Lucchese boots, which are exquisitely tooled and made from the finest leathers, states that the boots are "available only at finer stores." This simple phrase may stop some readers from further consideration of these boots. Why? One of the classic studies in consumer behavior explains that the lower-status woman believes that if she goes into a high-status department store, the clerks will snub or insult her in various subtle ways, making it clear that she does not "belong." Members of different social classes know which stores and products are appropriate for people of their class.

The impact of social class on consumer behavior is often indirect. For example, most people prefer to live in neighborhoods made up of people from their own class. Thus, small-membership groups within the neighborhoods that may directly affect purchases have been touched by the influence of social class.

In the upper-middle class, the *nouveaux riches* (or "new rich") are most likely to purchase furs or yachts because these products signify achievement. The expensive car, the bigger house, private college for the kids, a summer home, a boat, and frequent vacations are all symbolic expressions of success. This kind of buying behavior was well described by the turn-of-the-century American economist Thornstein Veblen, who coined the term **conspicuous consumption.** Veblen, in criticizing persons who buy products simply to visibly consume or openly display them, hit on a fact of human nature. Consumption of certain items is a means to express one's social-class status. Even if we snicker with Veblen at this behavior, the desire to express one's feelings (or show off) may be real and quite important

Conspicuous Consumption

Consumption for the sake of enhancing social prestige.

CLASS (AND PERCENTAGE OF POPULATION)	INCOME (1994 DOLLARS)	PROPERTY	OCCUPATION	EDUCATION
Upper class (1–3%)	Very high income (over $675,000)	Great wealth, old wealth	Investors, heirs, capitalists, corporate executives, high civil and military leaders	Liberal arts education at elite schools
Upper-middle class (10–15%)	High income ($65,000 or more)	Accumulation of property through savings	Upper managers, professionals, successful small business owners	College, often with graduate training
Middle class (30–34%)	Moderate income (average almost $40,000)	Some savings	Small businesspeople, lower managers, farmers, semiprofessionals, nonretail sales and clerical workers	Some college, high school
Working class (40–45%)	Low income (about $25,000)	Some savings	Skilled labor, unskilled labor, retail sales operatives	Some high school, grade school
Lower class (20–25%)	Poverty income (below $18,750)	No savings	Working poor, unemployed, welfare recipients	Grade school or illiterate

EXHIBIT 6–9
The American Class System in the Twentieth Century

SOURCE: Adapted from Dennis Gilbert and Joseph Kahl, *The American Class Structure* (Homewood, IL: Dorsey Press, 1982); and from Daniel W. Rossides, *Social Stratification: The American Class System in Comparative Perspective,* © 1990, pp. 406–408, adapted by permission of Prentice Hall, Upper Saddle River, New Jersey.

to an individual who aspires to or has achieved membership in a higher social class. Marketers should not ignore this.

Reference Groups

Each individual belongs to many groups. From a marketing perspective, the most important are reference groups. A **reference group** is a group that influences an individual because that individual is a member or aspires to be a member of the group. The reference group is used as a point of comparison for self-evaluation.[13]

The **membership group** is a group of which the individual is actually a part. Examples include clubs, the freshman class, and UCLA alumni. Such groups strongly influence members' behavior—including consumer behavior—by exerting pressure to conform. This is known as *peer pressure.* In a **voluntary membership group,** such as a group of college peers or a political party, the individual is free to join or withdraw from the group. Sometimes, however, the individual has little or no choice as to group membership. People approaching middle age may not like that fact, but they nevertheless make changes in their lives as a result of the influence of their middle-aged peers.

A second major type of reference group is the **aspirational group.** Individuals may try to behave or look like the people whose group they hope to join. Thus, a little brother may try to act like a big brother and his buddies, or a little sister may try to act like a big sister's teenage friends. Similarly, the young business manager may choose to "dress for success." This usually means dressing like the women or men the manager hopes to join one day in the organization's higher ranks.

Reference groups influence the use of some products more than others. Examples include clothing, cars, and beer consumed publicly. The use of other products is subject to almost no group pressure. These products are so mundane or so lacking in visibility that no one uses them to express self-concept. The risks of using the "wrong" brand in private are small. One rarely hears comments about

Reference Group
A group that influences an individual because that individual is a member or aspires to be a member of the group.

Membership Group
In reference to an individual, a group to which the individual belongs.

Voluntary Membership Group
Membership group to which an individual has chosen to belong.

Aspirational Group
In reference to an individual, a group to which the individual would like to belong.

someone's eating Libby's canned peaches instead of Del Monte's. Note that some product categories can be subject to reference group influences without regard to brand name or design: "Why don't you break down and get an air conditioner, Harry?" "You mean you use instant coffee? No, thank you!" Reference groups, then, may influence the types of products consumed, the brand purchased, or both.

FOCUS ON RELATIONSHIPS

Harley-Davidson

Owners of Harley-Davidson motorcycles strongly identify with the membership group of Harley owners. They often fancy Harley riders as cowboys, desperadoes, or knights in shining armor. Marketers at Harley-Davidson exert considerable effort to make Harley owners feel special and part of the Harley-Davidson tradition. The company endorses a club—Harley Owners Group or HOG, a newsletter—Hog Tales, and many special events. For example, ZZ Top has played at HOG-members-only shows sponsored by Harley-Davidson.

Opinion Leaders

Opinion Leader
A group member who, because of some quality or characteristic, is likely to lead other group members in particular matters.

Groups frequently include individuals known as **opinion leaders.** Opinion leaders might be friends who are looked up to because of their intelligence, athletic abilities, appearance, or special abilities, such as skill in cooking, mechanics, or languages.[14] With respect to buying behavior, the role of opinion leader in any group moves from member to member, depending on the product involved. If someone is planning to buy a car, that person may seek the opinion or guidance of a friend or family member who is thought to know about cars. The same person might seek a different "expert" when he or she is buying stereo equipment, good wines, or investment plans.

In certain situations, the most powerful determinant of buying behavior is the attitude of people the individual respects. Thus, word-of-mouth recommendations may be an important buying influence. One reason marketers try to satisfy customers is their hope that the customers will recommend the product or organization to members of their social groups. The best thing a homeowner can hear when hiring a house painter, for example, is that the painter did a good job on a neighbor's or friend's house.

The Family

Family
A group of two or more persons related by birth, marriage, or adoption and residing together.

Socialization Process
The process by which a society transmits its values, norms, and roles to its members.

The United States Census Bureau defines **family** as a group of two or more persons related by birth, marriage, or adoption and residing together. An individual's family is an important reference group. The family is characterized by frequent face-to-face interaction among family members, who respond to each other on the basis of their total personalities rather than on the basis of particular roles. It is not surprising that values, self-concepts, and the products we buy are influenced by our families. That influence may continue to be strong throughout our lives.

The family is the group primarily responsible for the **socialization process—** that is, the passing down of social values, norms, and roles. Socialization includes the learning of buying behavior. Children observe how their parents evaluate and select products in stores.[15] They see how the exchange process takes place at the cash register and quickly learn that money or a credit card changes hands there. That is how children learn the buying role. When children receive money as gifts or allowances and are permitted to spend it, they act out the buying role, thus learning an activity they will perform throughout their lives.

Social Situations

Another environmental influence on the decision-making process is the social situation. Consider the gasoline-buying consumer who is late for an appointment and notices the tank is nearly empty. The situational pressure may increase the importance of convenient location as a choice criterion and decrease the importance of other attributes. It would be impossible to list all the social situational influences on buyer behavior. However, it is important to appreciate that one brand may be purchased in one social situation and another in a different social situation.

JOINT DECISION MAKING

Joint Decision Making

Decision making shared by all or some members of a group. Often, one decision maker dominates the process.

Some consumer choices are made not by individuals but by groups of two or more people. This is referred to as **joint decision making** (or household decision making). Families may, for example, choose a car or a house together. Or parents may sit down together to talk over insurance purchases, furniture purchases, or retirement plans.

Despite this image of togetherness, most purchases are dominated by one group member. In the case of the family group, the parents, rather than the grade-school kids, dominate. Older children may have greater influence—as when the teenage son who "knows all about cars" advises his parents on the selection of a new auto. The dominant role in group decision making is commonly taken by different group members for different purchases. Even though changing sex roles are influencing traditional roles in family decision making, in most households the husband usually dominates decisions relating to purchases of insurance, while decisions regarding clothing for the children, food purchases, and household furnishings are most often wife-dominated.[16] This reflects our society's norms and traditional role expectations. Decisions made by husband and wife together are common when entertainment, housing, and vacation choices are being made. However, changes taking place in our society are making the process of identifying the major decision-influencer more difficult.

To simplify the discussion, we have not mentioned the distinctions among consumers' roles during the buying effort. However, there are several roles to be played in any buying decision. These roles are: (1) the *buyer*, who, narrowly defined, is the person who goes to the store and actually purchases the product; (2) the *user*, who, narrowly viewed, is the person who actually consumes or uses the product; and (3) the *decision maker*, who decides which product or brand to buy. Think about it for a while. Each role could be played by a different person, or all could be played by the same person, or the roles could be played by any combination of people.

The purchase of baby food is the classic example of different people playing the roles. The baby eats the food but is denied any comment on it. The buyer could be an older child sent to the store by Mom. Mom is the decision maker who, by means of experience, the influence of advertisements, or her own mother's suggestions, has determined which brand of baby food to buy. The purchase of gum or a haircut, however, may involve only one person performing all three roles.

In more complex buying decisions, such as the purchase of a new home or a family automobile, a family member may also play the role of influencer or gatekeeper. The **influencer** expresses an opinion about the product or service to persuade the decision maker. ("Dad, we need to sell the station wagon and buy a car that won't embarrass me.") The **gatekeeper** controls the flow of information ("I won't tell Bob about the house on Rockwood Drive because I liked the one on Hazel Boulevard better.") The focus of marketing changes with the role structure of the buying decision. When only one person is involved, marketing can be more concentrated than when several people in different roles are involved. In the baby food example, whom should the marketer attempt to reach? The decision maker—the person with the real "say" in the matter—should be the target. Thus, baby food advertisements appear in publications and on TV and radio programs that reach mothers. These advertisements stress the concerns of mothers, such as nutrition. These are matters that neither the baby nor the older sibling sent to the store really care about.

Influencer
A group member who attempts to persuade the decision maker.

Gatekeeper
A group member who controls the flow of information to the decision maker.

SUMMARY

Understanding consumer behavior helps the marketer bring about satisfying exchanges in the marketplace. Consumer behavior is affected by a variety of individual and interpersonal (or sociocultural) factors, which influence the decision-making process. They must be taken into account by marketers.

Learning Objective 1
Understand the basic model of consumer behavior.
Consumer behavior results from the interaction of person and environment, $B = f(P,E)$. Consumer behavior theorists have expanded and explained this basic model with many theories.

Learning Objective 2
Describe the consumer decision-making process and understand factors, such as consumer involvement, that influence it.
The decision-making process varies depending on how routine the consumer perceives the situation to be. For decisions involving extensive problem solving, consumers follow a multi-step process: (1) recognizing the problem, (2) searching for alternative solutions, (3) evaluating those alternatives, (4) deciding whether to buy, and (5) if a purchase is made, evaluating the product purchased. Many internal and environmental factors affect this process, including consumer involvement and situational influences.

Learning Objective 3
Appreciate the importance of perceived risk, choice criteria, purchase satisfaction, and cognitive dissonance.
Perceived risk is the consumer's uncertainty about whether a product will do what it is intended to do. Choice criteria are those critical attributes the consumer uses to evaluate a product alternative. Purchase satisfaction on the consumer's part means that marketing has achieved its goal. However, the consumer may instead experience cognitive dissonance—a sense of tension and uncertainty after deciding to make a purchase. Marketers must address all these issues if satisfactory exchanges are to take place.

Learning Objective 4
Recognize the influence of individual factors, such as motives, perception, learning, attitude, and personality, on consumer behavior.
Motivation theory attempts to explain the causes of goal-directed behavior in terms of needs, motives, incentives, and drives. Needs can be classified in many ways. Maslow's needs hierarchy ranks human needs from the most basic (physiological) to the highest (self-actualization). As the lower needs are satisfied, the higher needs become more important. Perception is the process of interpreting sensations and stimuli. Each person's perceptions differ at least slightly from every-

one else's. Selective perception is the process of screening out or interpreting stimuli—including marketing stimuli. Learning is important to marketing because consumers learn to favor certain products and brands and to dislike others. Consumers also learn to have certain attitudes, which have affective, behavioral, and cognitive components. Personality reflects the individual's consistent ways of responding to his or her environment. It is generally agreed that the influence of personality on consumer behavior should be studied only along with other factors, such as attitudes and demographic characteristics, to predict specific behaviors.

Learning Objective 5
Explain the nature of culture and subculture in terms of social values, norms, and roles.
Marketers look at culture as the values, beliefs, and customary behaviors learned and shared by the members of a society. Insofar as consumers in a society share a culture, they will think and act in similar ways. A subculture is a group within a dominant culture that has values and distinctive characteristics not shared with the larger culture. Cultures and subcultures prescribe certain values, norms, and roles for their members.

Learning Objective 6
Characterize social class in the United States.
A social class is a group of people with similar levels of prestige, power, and wealth. According to one view, U.S. society may be roughly divided into five social classes determined by wealth, education, occupation, and other measures of prestige. Social classes differ in lifestyle, purchase preferences, and shopping and consumption patterns.

Learning Objective 7
Explain the influence of reference groups on individual buyers.
Groups strongly influence individuals' behavior. Reference groups, including membership and aspirational groups, provide points of comparison by which the individual evaluates himself or herself. These groups have many direct and indirect influences on purchasing behaviors.

Learning Objective 8
Examine the roles in the joint decision-making process.
The joint decision-making process includes the roles of buyer, user, and decision maker, as well as influencer and gatekeeper in more complex decisions. In general, the decision maker should be the focus of marketing efforts.

KEY TERMS

Consumer behavior (p. 136)
Routinized response behavior (p. 136)
Extensive problem solving (p. 137)
Limited problem solving (p. 137)
Consumer involvement (p. 137)
Problem recognition (p. 138)
Perceived risk (p. 139)
Information search (p. 139)
Choice criteria (p. 141)
Purchase satisfaction (p. 141)
Cognitive dissonance (p. 142)
Motivation (p. 143)
Motive (p. 143)
Need (p. 143)
Incentive (p. 143)
Physiological need (p. 143)

Social and psychological need (p. 143)
Emotion (p. 144)
Perception (p. 145)
Selective perception (p. 146)
Closure (p. 146)
Selective exposure (p. 146)
Selective attention (p. 146)
Selective interpretation (p. 146)
Stimulus factor (p. 146)
Individual factor (p. 146)
Brand image (p. 147)
Learning (p. 149)
Memory (p. 149)
Operant conditioning (p. 150)
Reinforcement (p. 150)
Attitude (p. 150)

Personality (p. 152)
Self-concept (p. 152)
Role (p. 153)
Subculture (p. 154)
Social class (p. 155)
Conspicuous consumption (p. 155)
Reference group (p. 156)
Membership group (p. 156)
Voluntary membership group (p. 156)
Aspirational group (p. 156)
Opinion leader (p. 157)
Family (p. 157)
Socialization process (p. 157)
Joint decision making (p. 158)
Influencer (p. 159)
Gatekeeper (p. 159)

QUESTIONS FOR REVIEW AND CRITICAL THINKING

1. Use the consumer behavior model shown in Exhibit 6–2 to explain how an individual might arrive at a decision to:
   a. Buy a package of Doublemint chewing gum.
   b. Not buy a BMW convertible.
   c. Buy a new house.
   d. Not take a group of three children to the Ice Capades.

2. Using examples from your own experience, explain how the following have affected your purchasing behavior.
   a. Extensive problem solving
   b. Perceived risk
   c. Choice criteria
   d. Cognitive dissonance

3. What might a marketer do to reduce cognitive dissonance in the following situations?
   a. A consumer purchases an automobile.
   b. A wholesaler agrees to carry an industrial product line.
   c. A parent purchases an expensive video game for her children.
   d. A man purchases a magazine subscription on a "to be billed later" basis.

4. Tell how the last major purchase you made can be linked to a perceived risk and information search behavior.

5. Name the five levels in Maslow's need hierarchy. Which group of needs is the most powerful?

6. What is selective perception? How does it influence behavior?

7. Use learning theory to explain why products are repurchased.

8. Do unfavorable attitudes lead to behaviors that are undesirable? Why or why not?

9. What purchases might be particularly influenced by the buyer's personality and self-image? Name some products and explain your choices.

10. Distinguish between norms and values.

11. How might the marketers of McDonald's be influenced by cultural forces in U.S. marketing? In international marketing?

12. How likely it is that the following people would purchase a ticket to the ballet, to a professional baseball game, and to Disneyland?
    a. 34-year-old steelworker who graduated from high school
    b. 44-year-old college professor
    c. 21-year-old executive secretary
    d. 21-year-old counter helper at Burger King

13. Is social class useful in marketing planning? Name three products whose purchase might be influenced by the buyer's social class.

14. Is a reference group likely to influence the purchase of the following brands or products?
    a. Laundry detergent
    b. Shampoo
    c. Polo sports shirt
    d. Wristwatch
    e. Athletic club membership
    f. Milk

15. How much husband-wife joint decision making would you expect for the following purchases?
    a. Life insurance
    b. Steam iron
    c. Trip to Europe
    d. Box of candy

16. In a family consisting of a father, a mother, and an 11-year-old daughter, what roles might be played, and by whom, in the purchase of a new home?

17. Think of a recent purchase you have made. Identify all the social forces that may have influenced your purchase.

INTERNET INSIGHTS

Exercises

1. Go to the SRI International home page at:

   http://future.sri.com

Select the Values and Lifestyles (VALS) program option and read some of the background information on the VALS system. Select Discover Your iVALS Type or another available option to complete a VALS survey on-line. When you have completed your questionnaire, select the Submit button to submit your completed questionnaire. Wait for the analysis. (Your answers will be analyzed in less than a minute.)

What is your primary VALS type? What is your secondary VALS type?

Address Book

Association for Consumer Research
http://www.the-shack.webpage.com:8080:/acr/

Society for Consumer Psychology
http://www.cob.ohio-state.edu/scp/

Yankelovich Partners Monitor
http://www.yankelovich.com/monitor.monitor.htm

ETHICS IN PRACTICE: TAKE A STAND

1. After a winter storm, your car is covered with ice. There is an old spray can of deicer in the basement. You read the ingredients and discover it contains chlorofluorocarbons. Do you use the spray?

2. You purchase a new copy of a Lotus 1-2-3 spreadsheet program at a computer store. Several weeks later a friend says he would like to have a copy of Lotus 1-2-3 and asks you to make a copy for him. Do you make the copy?

3. Is using embedded stimuli in advertisements immoral?

4. You pick up a friend, and she is wearing a fur coat. Do you tell her she shouldn't wear the coat because of the harm to animals?

5. After 76 years in the Southwest Athletic Conference, the University of Arkansas switched to the Southeast Conference to obtain higher television revenues. Did the university violate any norms?

6. Some pawnshops are now marketing themselves as "lending institutions for the working poor." Does this service raise any ethical concerns?

VIDEO CASE 6-1

The Minnesota Twins (B)

Clay Tucker and his wife Carol are in their late 30s. They have two children, a son age 9 and a daughter age 7. The Tuckers own their own home in Edina, Minnesota, a suburb of Minneapolis. Both Clay and Carol are college graduates. Clay attended college on a track scholarship. Today, he works for a bank in a middle-management position. He drives a four-wheel-drive Ford Explorer. Carol was an art major in college, and she teaches art in high school. She drives a Mazda sedan.

One Monday morning in June, Clay read in the newspaper that the New York Yankees were coming to town for a four-day series beginning on Thursday. His thoughts went back to his high school days in Chicago. He remembered when he and a group of his teenage pals would go to Comiskey Park to root for the White Sox against the arch-rival Yankees. It was always great fun.

The Twins play in the Metrodome, so Clay knew there was no chance for a rain-out. He said to himself, "Why not take the family out to the ball park on Saturday?" The price of a general admission ticket would be about $6, he thought.

Grandstand reserve might be about $10, and a box seat would probably be less than $15. They could drive to the stadium around 6 p.m., find parking nearby, and buy some hot dogs for dinner.

Questions

1. Outline the decision-making process for the Tucker family's purchase of tickets to a Twins game.
2. What choice criteria are used to make this decision about family entertainment?
3. Suppose the Tuckers do go to the game. What other purchase decisions will be made? Identify whether these are routine or problem-solving decisions.
4. For each member of the Tucker family, what factors will contribute to consumer satisfaction?
5. What role does learning play in becoming a loyal Twins fan?
6. Describe the sociocultural forces that make a baseball game at the Metrodome a likeable product.

BUSINESS MARKETS AND ORGANIZATIONAL BUYING

Chapter 7

Learning Objectives

After you have studied this chapter, you will be able to:

1. Identify the types of organizations that make up the business, or organizational, market.

2. Know the steps involved in an organizational buying decision.

3. Characterize the three basic organizational buying situations: the straight rebuy, the modified rebuy, and the new task purchase.

4. Explain why the buying center concept is important to business-to-business marketing.

5. Appreciate the needs of organizational buyers and explain how marketers can react to those needs.

6. Describe the NAICS system and analyze its usefulness to marketers.

Forming strategic alliances with other companies is fast becoming a necessity for small businesses trying to stay competitive.

From biotechnology to retailing, small firms are forming partnerships to achieve goals that would be too costly, time-consuming, or difficult to accomplish on their own. They're also pursuing alliances to encourage product innovation, bring stability to cyclical businesses, expand product portfolios, and forge new kinds of supplier relationships.

New Pig Corporation wanted to make itself a world-class competitor, but having merely good supplier relationships wasn't enough to bring about the dramatic changes necessary to achieve that goal.

The 300-employee company has grown rapidly as a leader in the manufacture of contained absorbents—sock-like bundles of absorbent materials used to soak up industrial spills. New Pig set down a whole host of goals it deemed necessary to propel the company forward.

Because New Pig sells 3,000 products through its catalog and depends on its suppliers for some element of every item, the firm's management decided to focus on improving the firm's purchasing operation.

The company's goals included reducing the time it takes to introduce products, improving product quality, bringing about joint problem solving with suppliers and joint adjustments to market conditions, and involving suppliers early in product development.

To meet those goals, management decided, the firm had to go beyond traditional relationships with its key suppliers and develop strategic alliances with them. New Pig wanted to establish a level of communication with suppliers that fostered continuous improvement and problem solving.

As a starting point, the company began measuring suppliers' performance and, in turn, asked its 30 largest-volume suppliers to evaluate New Pig as a customer.

For these evaluations, absolute candor was the company's guiding principle. "It was quite shocking," says Doug Evans, New Pig's director of strategic purchasing. "We didn't have as close a relationship with suppliers as we thought we did."

His team discovered, for example, why a long-time vendor consistently failed to come up with the innovative approaches that New Pig sought. "We found out that [our people] always faulted them for making mistakes, so they never offered us anything that wasn't time-tested and perfect," says Evans. "Without even knowing it, we were discouraging them from bringing us new ideas."

As such problems began to be addressed, relationships began to improve. In the 18 months since the program has been in place, several joint projects with suppliers have led to improved processes and reduced costs; one change in a shipping method, for instance, produced savings of hundreds of thousands of dollars.

"What's different about this approach is the depth of the relationship," says Evans. "With the usual customer-supplier relationship, you're talking about a phone call as your only contact. With our strategic partners, we have tons of communications, we sit down with product-development teams, and we go out and look at [their] tooling."

The effort that goes into these relationships explains why only 20 to 50 of New Pig's 800 suppliers will be strategic partners. "Like peeling back an onion, you learn things about each other's operation," says Evans. "We've developed a synergy and are moving forward together to cut costs, be more efficient, and increase profits. There's a ton of opportunity out there if you talk."

New Pig markets to business organizations, not to ultimate consumers. But, as we have just seen, understanding the buyer-seller relationship is just as important in the business market as in the consumer market. This chapter investigates how organizational buying behavior differs from ultimate consumers' behavior.

The chapter begins by defining business-to-business marketing and organizational buying behavior. Then it explains the different types of organizational buying decisions and the role of the buying center. Finally, it discusses the nature of industrial demand and the characteristics of business markets.

ORGANIZATIONAL BUYING BEHAVIOR

Business-to-Business Marketing
Marketing aimed at bringing about an exchange in which a product or service is sold for any use other than personal consumption. The buyer may be a manufacturer, a reseller, a government body, a not-for-profit institution, or any other organization. The transaction occurs so an organization may conduct its business.

A business marketing transaction takes place whenever a good or service is sold for any use other than personal consumption. In other words, any sale to an industrial user, wholesaler, retailer, or organization other than the ultimate consumer is sold in the business market. Such sales involve **business-to-business marketing.**

All products other than consumer products are organizational products. They are sold in the business market and are used to help operate an organization's business. The term *organizational* is broader than the terms *business* or *industrial,* but both of the latter terms remain in common use. In fact, the term *business market,* which narrowly defined would only refer to manufacturers, service marketers, wholesalers, and retailers, is broadly used by most marketing writers to include organizational buyers such as governments, churches, and other nonprofit entities.

Faced with indecision as to whether a product is a consumer product or an organizational product, ask these two questions:

1. Who bought it?
2. Why did they buy it?

Notice that it is not necessary to ask the question "What did they buy?" For example, airline travel may be a consumer or an organizational product, depending on who bought it and why it was purchased. The fact that it is an airline ticket is not relevant to its classification in this regard.

What, then, do organizations buy? Manufacturers require raw materials, equipment, component parts, supplies, and services. Producers of nonmanufactured goods require many of these same products. Wholesalers and retailers purchase products for resale, as well as equipment such as trucks, shelving, and computers. Hospitals, zoos, and other nonprofit organizations use many goods and services to facilitate the performance of their business functions, as do federal, state, and local governments. In fact, the federal government is the largest single buyer of organizational products. In participating in business-to-business exchanges, all these organizations display **organizational buying behavior.** Exhibit 7–1 illustrates some of these behaviors.

Organizational Buying Behavior
The decision-making activities of organizational buyers that lead to purchase of products.

SEGMENT OF ORGANIZATIONAL MARKET	TYPICAL BUYING SITUATION
Agriculture	A farmer purchases a tractor from a farm equipment dealer.
Mining, forestry, fishing	Reading and Bates purchases offshore drilling equipment from the manufacturer.
Construction	A home construction company hires a CPA firm.
Manufacturers of consumer goods	The Smucker Co. supplies fruit filling for Kellogg's Pop Tarts.
Manufacturers of industrial goods	Boeing purchases steel as a raw material from USX.
Wholesalers and retailers (resale market)	Bloomingdale's purchases towels from a wholesaler.
Information	TCI Cablevision must make a decision whether to offer WGN as part of its programming.
Service industries	Walker Marketing Research Company purchases computer paper from an industrial distributor.
Nonprofit organizations	The San Diego Zoo hires an advertising agency to produce TV commercials.
Government	The federal government asks for competitive bids on solar panels for a space telescope.

EXHIBIT 7–1
Examples of Organizational Buying Behavior

Buying is a necessary activity for all business and not-for-profit organizations. In organizational buying situations, the process for purchasing goods and services, such as semiconductors and accounting services, may be complex. Purchasing agents and other organizational members determine the need to purchase goods and services, engage in information-seeking activities, evaluate alternative purchasing actions, and negotiate the necessary arrangements with suppliers.[1]

Placing an order with a supplier is generally not a simple act. Organizational buying takes place over time, involves communications among several organizational members, and entails financial relationships with suppliers.

CHARACTERISTICS OF THE BUSINESS MARKET

The agricultural, financial, and manufacturing industries are quite different from one another, yet they share some basic characteristics that are typical of the business market. First, particular business markets often contain relatively few customers. Often these customers are geographically concentrated. Even though some American automakers have moved production facilities to the Sun Belt, for example, their headquarters remain mostly in their traditional center in Detroit.

A second characteristic of business markets is that the demand for goods and services is derived. A reduction in consumer demand for housing has a tremendous and obvious impact on the building supply products industry. Similarly, downturns in the economy may cause people to cut back on their use of airlines, which in turn reduces the need for airplane fuel and the parts and tools used in airplane maintenance. Ultimately, even the demand for such mundane items as the brooms used to sweep out airline hangars will decline as airline usage declines. All of these examples demonstrate a basic truth: All organizational demand depends ultimately on consumer demand. It is **derived demand**—that is, derived from consumer demand.[2]

Derived Demand
Demand for a product that depends on demand for another product.

The effects of derived demand on marketing efforts is important to business-to-business marketers, and not just because those effects are potentially devastat-

The Internet and electronic commerce are dramatically changing business-to-business marketing. The Internet puts product specifications and other information at the fingertips of organizational buyers. For example, General Electric does $1 billion of business on its Trading Process Network Web site.

ing. Derived demand presents certain opportunities. Under some circumstances, the business-to-business marketer can stimulate the demand for the consumer product on which demand for the organizational product depends. For example, advertisements suggesting that milk is better in unbreakable plastic jugs may be sponsored by the producers of plastic jugs or the manufacturers of machines that make plastic jugs. Recognizing a trend of declining per capita beef consumption, the Beef Industry Council targeted advertisements to consumers in an attempt to reverse the trend. Pork producers and lamb producers have done much the same thing, even though all these organizations represent farmers and ranchers who are several steps removed from the consumer in the channels of distribution.

A third characteristic of organizational buyers is their preference for buying directly from the manufacturer or producer. This preference may come from the desire to buy in large quantities or to avoid intermediaries in an effort to obtain a better price. It may also be a function of the technical complexity of many of the products these buyers use and the fact that many such products are made to order. (Consider how the U.S. government purchases weapon systems, for example.) For all of these reasons, the desire to deal directly with producers is understandable.

A fourth characteristic of organizational purchasers is their comparative expertise in buying. They buy, almost always, in a scientific way, basing decisions on close analyses of the product being offered and careful comparisons with competing products. Moreover, terms of sale, service, guarantees, and other such factors are likely to be carefully weighed. If a product is a highly technical one, the buyer may assign properly trained engineers or scientists to participate in the purchase decision. For a major purchase decision, a committee will likely be formed to evaluate certain factors such as the business-to-business marketer's product, technical abilities, and position vis-a-vis competitors. Here again, strategic alliances may be formed to work out technological problems. For example, Fujitsu's engineers shared technologies and worked closely with product developers at Sun Microsystems to jointly develop a new microchip for Sun's workstations.

A fifth characteristic of the business market involves the importance of repeated market transactions. The focus of much business-to-business marketing has shifted from the single transaction to the overall buyer-seller relationship—a focus known

Strategic Alliance
An informal partnership or collaboration between a marketer and an organizational buyer.

as *relationship marketing.* By establishing strong working relationships, suppliers and customers can work together to improve distribution processes and other joint activities. In fact, many business-to-business marketers form **strategic alliances,** or informal partnerships, with their customers. For example, Sherwin-Williams, the paint producer, let Sears executives help select the people who would service the Sears account. Its logic was that the two companies had joint sales goals, so it made sense to jointly select the people responsible for achieving these goals.[3]

We have already discussed the sixth characteristic of the business market, but it is worth repeating. Business-to-business marketing has become a global activity. Global competition can be intense, and taking a world perspective is essential. In many instances, a business-to-business marketer's main competition does not come from its home country. Indeed, it may have no domestic competitors. Taking a global perspective is important to marketers selling in consumer markets, of course, but in business markets it is so crucial that it may involve the survival of the marketer's business. Managers in business-to-business marketing organizations often find that their decisions about international strategy are the most vital decisions they make.

The characteristics of organizational customers mentioned here do not relate to every organizational buyer. Furthermore, they by no means constitute an exhaustive list of such factors. But they do give some indications of how marketers deal with these special buyers. The fact that there are often relatively few buyers, who may be geographically concentrated and who prefer to deal directly with suppliers, encourages—indeed, often mandates—the extensive use of personal selling. The technical nature of many of the products and the expertise of the persons engaged in making purchase decisions demand a well-trained sales force with an extensive knowledge of the products they sell. Representing a maker of nuclear power plants is quite different from selling Legos or Loc Blocs to Christmas-shopping grandparents. The various characteristics of business markets often combine to permit the marketer to identify almost all potential customers. This capability can make personal selling, which is usually expensive, a cost-efficient marketing tool.

THREE KINDS OF BUYING

The buyer of organizational goods and services, whether chemicals, machinery, or maintenance services, may go through a decision-making process similar to, but more complex than, the consumer decision-making process discussed in Chapter 6. As shown in Exhibit 7–2, organizational buying behavior may be viewed as a multistage decision-making process. However, the amount of time and effort devoted to each of the stages, or **buy phases,** depends on the number of factors such as the nature of the product, the costs involved, and the experience of the organization in buying the needed goods or services. Consider these three situations:[4]

Buy Phase
One of the stages of the multistage process by which organizations make purchase decisions.

Straight Rebuy
A type of organizational buying characterized by automatic and regular purchase of familiar products from regular suppliers.

- An organization buys goods and services on a regular basis from the same suppliers. Careful attention may have been given to selection of the suppliers at some earlier time, but the organization is well satisfied with them and with the products they offer. The organization buys from these suppliers virtually automatically. This is the **straight rebuy** situation. Everything from pencils to legal advice to equipment may be bought this way if the buyer is satisfied with the supplier's past performance.

Modified Rebuy
An organizational buying situation in which a buyer is not completely satisfied with current suppliers or products and is "shopping around" rather than rebuying automatically.

- An organization is discontented with current suppliers or suspects that "shopping around" may be in its best interest. It knows what products are needed and who the likely suppliers are. This is the **modified rebuy** situation. Here, too, any type of good or service may be involved.
- An organization is facing a new problem or need and is not certain what products or what suppliers will fill the need. If the purchase is expected to be very

EXHIBIT 7–2
Buy Phases: Steps in an
Organizational Buying
Decision

1. Anticipation or recognition of a problem (need)
2. Determination of the characteristics of the product and the quantity needed
3. Description of precise product specifications and critical needs
4. Search for and qualification of potential sources
5. Acquisition and analysis of proposals
6. Evaluation of proposals and selection of suppliers
7. Selection of an order routine
8. Performance feedback and evaluation

SOURCE: Based on Michael D. Hutt and Thomas W. Speh, *Business Marketing Management* (Hinsdale, IL: Dryden Press, 1995), p. 71.

New Task Buying
An organizational buying situation in which a buyer is seeking to fill a need never before addressed. Uncertainty and lack of information about products and suppliers characterize this situation.

expensive, the sense of concern and uncertainty is heightened. This is **new task buying.** In each situation, the length of the decision-making process as a whole may vary among purchases, as may the time spent on each individual buying phase.

Understanding the types of buying situations and behavior to be found in organizations is extremely important for organizational marketers, just as consumer behavior patterns are important for marketers of consumer products. Each buying situation suggests a different marketing mix—an adjustment of the four major elements to fit particular circumstances.

A marketing manager facing a new task buying situation, for example, understands that the target customer is uncertain what steps should be taken to satisfy his or her organization's needs. Such a buyer probably will require a good deal of information about the supplier, its products, and its abilities to deliver and service the products. This suggests a marketing mix that stresses promotion, especially communication of information that will help the customer to evaluate alternatives and to understand why the marketing company is the one to choose.

A buyer in a modified rebuy mode might require information of another type. This buyer knows something of what is needed and who likely suppliers are. In such a case, communications built around very specific problem areas might be appropriate. If the target buyer is searching for new suppliers, the marketer must find out why. Have deliveries been spotty? Have there been product failures? Are prices perceived as too high? The marketer must come up with responses to these problems that can show the target buyer why dealing with this supplier can answer those problems.[5]

In the case of the straight rebuy, the marketer may be in the strong position of being the supplier benefiting from the rebuy situation. In such circumstances, the marketer seeks to assure that the target customer does not become discontented but continues to make purchases on a regular basis. Maintaining the relationship is the key marketing objective.

THE CROSS-FUNCTIONAL BUYING CENTER

Buying Center
An informal, cross-departmental decision unit for which the primary objective is the acquisition, dissemination, and processing of relevant purchasing-related information.

As mentioned earlier, many persons may be involved in an organizational buying decision. How do marketers manage to consider all these persons, their motives, and their special needs? It is a complicated and difficult task. However, the concept of the buying center helps marketers to visualize the buying process and to organize their thinking as the marketing mix is developed.[6] The **buying center** in any organization is an informal, cross-departmental decision unit in which

In many small businesses, the roles of user (the person who actually uses the product), decider (the person who actually makes the decision), and buyer (the person with the formal authority to make the decision) are played by the same person.

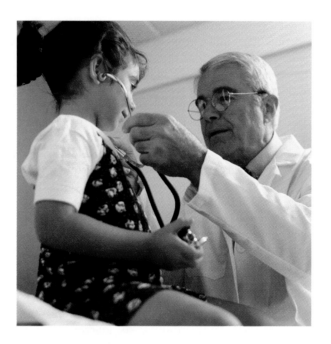

the primary objective is the acquisition, dissemination, and processing of relevant purchasing-related information. In somewhat simpler terms, the buying center includes all the people and groups that have roles in the decision-making processes of purchasing. Because all these people and groups take part, they are seen as having common goals and as sharing in the risks associated with the ultimate decision. Membership in the buying center and the size of the center vary from organization to organization and from case to case. In smaller organizations, almost everyone may have some input; in larger organizations, a more restricted group may be identifiable. The buying center may range in size from a few people to perhaps 20.

When thinking in terms of a buying center, one must realize that the center is not identified on any organization chart. A committee officially created to decide on a purchase is likely to be but one part of the buying center. Other members have unofficial but important roles to play. Indeed, membership in the buying center may actually change as the decision-making process progresses. As the purchasing task moves from step to step, individuals with expertise in certain areas are likely to lose their membership while others are added. It must be repeated that this membership is informal, so no announcements are likely to be made of who has been dropped and who has been added.

Buying centers, then, include a wide variety of individuals who work in different functional areas of the organization. In other words, buying centers are cross-functional. Consider the example of buying air compressors for manufacturing plants. The following individuals and groups were all found to be involved in some part of the purchasing decision: president, vice president of engineering, vice president of manufacturing, plant facilities manager, maintenance supervisor, chief electrician, and purchasing department personnel.[7] Each member of a buying center has an official place in the organizational structure as well as an unofficial one in the buying center. Official organizational roles may influence those played within the buying center. For example, the formal organization of a hospital might require that all marketers of hospital equipment be screened by the purchasing department, even though the physicians, surgeons, and hospital executives actually have more influence over the decision-making process.

Furthermore, roles generally vary with the complexity of the product under consideration. As complexity increases, engineers and technicians may have a greater say in purchasing decisions. If the product is not complex, or if a regular pattern of purchase has been developed and agreed on, a purchasing agent or some other formally identified buyer is likely to have buying responsibility.

In spite of its apparent complexity, buying behavior in buying centers is somewhat like buying behavior in households, discussed in Chapter 6. There, different members of the household may play certain roles in the purchase decision. We can identify five similar roles in organizational buying behavior: *users, gatekeepers, influencers, deciders, and buyers.*

Users are employees or managers who will actually use the products. A retail sales clerk may be the user of a computerized cash register, but he or she may have little influence on the decision to buy the product.

The **buyer** has the formal authority to purchase the product. This may include choosing a supplier and negotiating the terms of the purchase. The purchasing agent may fill this role. Alternatively, a purchasing agent may gather information, such as product specifications and prices, while engineers or others within the organization make the buying decision. The role of collecting and passing on information—or withholding it—is known as the **gatekeeper** function. In some cases, the "gate" may be opened or closed by someone having very little else to do with the process. For example, suppose a secretary requests new word processing software. The office manager who supervises the secretary may act as gatekeeper by simply passing along (or failing to pass along) the request to higher management. Perhaps, though, the office manager has the ultimate responsibility to decide whether the secretary will get the new software. In that case, the office manager is also the **decider**—the person who makes the actual purchase decision. In any case, marketers must direct much of their effort toward gatekeepers because they control the flow of information related to the purchase.

The **influencer** affects the purchase decision by supplying advice or information. In the software purchase, a consultant may supply technical information. (Note here that an outsider can play a role in the buying center.) A secretary in another department may relate past experiences with a particular product. Influence can also take the form of information about what course of action is preferred by persons of high position in the organization.

Remember that a person in a particular position may play several roles and that a particular role may be played by persons in several types of positions. Note also that the importance of a particular role varies from decision to decision. We can see that the buying center is often loosely constructed and somewhat difficult to identify clearly. Nevertheless, because of its potent influence, the marketer should devote time and effort to investigating its effects in the marketing situation at hand.

User
The buying-center role played by the organizational member who will actually use the product.

Buyer
The buying-center role played by the organizational member with the formal authority to purchase the product.

Gatekeeper
The buying-center role played by the organizational member who controls the flow of information related to the purchase.

Decider
The buying-center role played by the organizational member who makes the actual purchase decision.

Influencer
The buying-center role played by organizational members (or outsiders) who affect the purchase decision by supplying advice or information.

 ## WHY DO ORGANIZATIONS BUY?

Do rational buying criteria dominate organizational buying behavior, or do emotional motives come into play? Reasonable observers must acknowledge that good sales skills and effective advertisements often appeal to an organizational buyer's emotional need to buy "the best" or to take pride in the products purchased. One compelling argument may lead students of organizational buying to believe that, while emotional buying motives may be identified, they are not always the most important ones. The argument is that no organizational buyer would put his or her job and reputation on the line by purchasing a product simply because a friendly salesperson satisfies some emotional need of that buyer. When a sale goes to the sales representative who entertains the prospect and satisfies certain needs for affiliation, that salesperson's product almost certainly met all the rational criteria by which the purchaser was expected to judge the product. That is, the emotional reasons to buy are almost always supplemental buying criteria.

COMPETITIVE STRATEGY: WHAT WENT WRONG?

Electronic Ticketing by Airlines

When a ticket for a flight on an airline is purchased by a businessperson for a business trip, it is an organizational product. These business travelers have needs quite different from from people who fly for pleasure.

After two years of electronic ticketing by airlines, it is clear that flights without tickets aren't flights without hassles. Herbert Slezinger is one of a growing number of travelers who can attest to that. Having used electronic ticketing to schedule a recent flight from San Diego to San Francisco, Mr. Slezinger thought he could avoid airport tie-ups; instead, he had to stand in a long line for a boarding pass—as his business companion, old-fashioned ticket in hand, hopped aboard the plane. "I thought I could just breeze right on through" says the 53-year-old executive for a San Diego mortgage company.

When major U.S. airlines began introducing electronic-ticketing programs, they made grand promises: no more fears of lost tickets; no piles of paperwork for ticket changes; and no more waiting in long check-in lines. Some of these promises have been kept—but have created other problems. For example, while ticketless passengers don't lose tickets—airlines sometimes lose passengers' reservations.

Among other drawbacks, electronic tickets, also called e-tickets, lack some of the conveniences of a paper ticket. Business travelers complain that receipts come days or even weeks after a trip, ruffling feathers in some corporate expense-accounting departments. And while airlines have traditionally honored each other's tickets as cash, there is currently no way to transfer electronic tickets between airlines.

This became clear to Randy Petersen, editor of *InsideFlyer* of Colorado, when he decided to take an earlier flight than the one he had booked—electronically—out of Newark International Airport. To change flights, which also involved changing airlines, Mr. Petersen says he had to go to the United Airlines terminal to get a paper ticket and then take a shuttle to the Continental Airlines terminal. "I had to leave for the airport 45 minutes earlier," he says. "It was really frustrating."

Airlines have the incentive of cost savings to correct electronic-ticket problems. Excluding commissions to travel agents, United says it costs about $8 to administer a paper ticket, compared with about $1 to process an e-ticket. And those e-tickets booked directly through the airline—as most are—entail no travel-agent commission. In addition, a paper ticket at United gets handled 15 times after it is given to a customer service agent, while processing an e-ticket requires only one step. "The big cost savings is administrative, the handling of the ticket," says United spokesman Tony Molinaro.

With that in mind, the airlines train their reservation agents to offer e-tickets first, and travel agents' computer reservation systems automatically default to electronic ticketing.

Many customers insist on paper. Cynthia Perper, director of corporate travel services for Colgate-Palmolive Co. in New York, says she sees no real incentive to go with ticketless travel. "The real detriment to it now is that there can be no accounting trail," she says.

The ticketless revolution might catch on faster if corporations are given an incentive to sign on. So far, the airlines have not lowered prices for corporations that use electronic tickets.

There are many rational reasons for buying. The importance of each factor varies from situation to situation, and some may not come into play in a given purchase decision. Our discussion here focuses on a few of the most influential purchasing criteria.

Product Quality

Product quality can be an extremely important purchasing criterion. Organizations may make certain purchases without carefully analyzing the products they are buying simply because the costs and risks involved in making a bad choice are not very great. All paper clips and thumbtacks are pretty much alike, for example, and are often bought without close scrutiny. However, most goods and services bought by organizations are not like that, and organizational buyers are usually careful. In fact, many products are made according to the buyer's own specifications, indicating that the buyer closely considers exactly what quality is required to perform a given task. In many industries, such as aerospace and defense, the reliability of the component part is the most important criterion.

Many organizations have adopted total quality management (TQM) programs that directly impact on the organizational buying decision. A manufacturer who grants its customers an assurance of defect-free products will not tolerate parts suppliers who do not adopt TQM programs of their own. Thus, product quality must not only conform to customer requirements, it may have to exceed the expectations of organizational buyers. High quality, as the customer defines it, is a major reason for buying in the 1990s.

FOCUS ON GLOBAL COMPETITION

ISO 9000 and ISO 14000

What is ISO 9000—dial-a-horoscope? A foreign sports car? A new galaxy? No, try again: ISO 9000 is a standard of quality management, hugely popular in Europe. In the early 1990s ISO, which stands for the International Standards Organization, was primarily considered a requirement for U.S. firms wanting to do business in Europe, but the series of international quality-control standards is rapidly taking hold in the United States—and around the globe.

Du Pont, General Electric, Eastman Kodak, British Telecom, and Philips Electronics are among the big-name companies that are urging—or even coercing—suppliers to adopt ISO 9000. GE's plastics business, for instance, commanded 340 vendors to meet the standard. Declares John Yates, general manager of global sourcing: "There is absolutely no negotiation. If you want to work with us, you have to get it."

"It" is a certificate, awarded by one of many independent auditors, attesting that a company's factory, laboratory, or office has met quality management requirements determined by the International Organization for Standardization. The ISO 9000 standards do not tell a manufacturer how to design a more efficient earth mover or build a more reliable industrial robot. But they do provide a framework for showing customers how a company tests products, trains employees, keeps records, and fixes defects. Think of ISO 9000 not as another variant of total quality management but as a set of generally accepted accounting principles for documenting quality procedures. With certificates issued worldwide estimated at more than 30,000, the standard is rapidly becoming a internationally recognized system, comprehensible to buyers and sellers.

In addition the International Standards Organization has published ISO 14000, which is a guide for environmental standards that relate to product design.

Related Services

Service is an important variable in organizational purchasing. Before the sale is consummated, the marketer may have to demonstrate the ability to provide rapid delivery, repair service, or technical support. After the sale, the supplier had better be able to deliver the promised services, because "downtime" costs money and may be a great source of frustration for the buyer of, for example, an office photocopier, a computer, or an assembly line conveyor system.

In business-to-business marketing, relationship marketing often means effectively being part of a collaborator's organization. Red Star Specialty Products, a Universal Foods Company, is the largest North American producer of yeast-based flavor enhancers. It offers clients applications support, technical seminars, prototype products, and a technically trained staff of field representatives.[8] Maintaining

FOCUS ON QUALITY

Digital Equipment Corp.

Digital Equipment Corp. is replacing computers with humans. Digital has hired 90 people to do something computers do badly: answer the phone. The company unplugged its automated system in Littleton, Massachusetts, where potential customers inquire about products and services. DEC is not going warm and fuzzy on us. The company made the change for the same reason it installed the automated system in the first place: to improve efficiency. "By firing the computer and bringing in live people to handle customer calls, [the company] dramatically increased both customer satisfaction and sales and marketing performance."

Customer satisfaction, as measured by reaching the right person, shot up from 73% to 97%. The rate of misdirected calls has fallen to just 1%. And each caller who is misdirected now receives an apology—yes, a personal one—from the person who did the misdirecting.

and enhancing relationships with its customers by providing "extra services" is a vital aspect of its marketing efforts.

Prices

Price can be the single most important factor determining many organizational buying decisions. There is an old adage that says: "Farmers are price takers, not price makers." It suggests that farmers (who are organizational marketers) face keen competition in a marketplace where the products sold are more or less the same. Not all organizational marketers are quite so much at the mercy of market forces as farmers, but many organizational goods and services face strong competition from products that are close substitutes. In such situations, price is likely to be the key to completing a sale. Organizational buyers often gather competitive bids from suppliers, further heightening the effects of competition on price.

Organizational buyers can be expected to analyze price carefully, examining not just the list price but also any discounts, terms of sale, and credit opportunities that accompany a purchase agreement. Further, some buyers make a distinction between first cost (initial price) and operating cost (price over a specific time period). Coupled with a thorough knowledge of the product, such cost analysis allows buyers to make detailed comparisons of value, increasing the potency of price as a buying criterion.

Reliable Delivery and Inventory Management: Opportunities for Organizational Collaboration

For many organizations, the assurance of reliable delivery of purchases is essential. A related concern, inventory management, may also be an important buying criterion. As business becomes more global and as information technology advances, organizational buyers are increasingly concerned with collaborative efforts and with building strategic alliances with other organizations. Strategic alliances related to inventory management may take the form of single-sourcing.

Single-Sourcing
Purchasing a product on a regular basis from a single vendor.

Single-sourcing occurs when an organization buys from a single vendor. In such situations the organizational marketer usually works closely with the buyer to coordinate delivery of inventory items just as the buyer's inventory is being depleted. The seller may, for example, ship high-quality tires needed for production so that they arrive exactly when needed in the quantity needed. The degree of cooperation may be so great that buyer and seller share information technologies and a common database reflecting the customer's current inventory. Single-sourcing such as this involves electronic data interchanges between companies.

The Bottom Line

The relative importance of each of the major organizational buying criteria—product quality, service, price, and delivery—may vary with the buyer, the situation, or the product. For example, at Copperweld Robotics, a producer of industrial robots, research showed that customers wanted answers to three questions in the following order: (1) Will it do the job? (2) What service is available? (3) What is the price? Copperweld knows that for the industrial robot, industry service is absolutely the number one criterion for creating and maintaining customer relationships. If one component of the robot doesn't work, the customer's whole production line shuts down.

In general, in any organizational buying decision, the criteria interact. Each contributes to the final decision, and each affects the importance of the others. Yet they often boil down to one overriding factor: the need to operate a profitable organization. General Motors' truck and coach division emphasizes issues like corrosion resistance and low fuel consumption in its advertising. The strategy is based on the belief that GM customers don't buy trucks because they like them, but because they need them to earn a profit.

THE NORTH AMERICAN INDUSTRY CLASSIFICATION SYSTEM

A wide variety of profit and not-for-profit institutions make up the business market. Knowing how many of each kind of organization are in operation, where they are located, their size, and so on can help marketers implement research activities and plan marketing strategies. Fortunately, there is a great deal of data available on business markets. Although much of this information is gathered by private companies, governmental agencies are also important sources.

North American Industry Classification System
A numeric coding system developed by the North American Free Trade Agreement partners and widely employed to classify organizations in terms of the economic activities in which they are engaged.

A new tool for use in researching the organizational marketplace is the **North American Industry Classification System (NAICS).** The NAICS system is a numerical coding scheme developed by the North American Free Trade Agreement partners' governments and used to classify a broad range of organizations in terms of the type of economic activity in which they are engaged.

As of 1997, the North American Industry Classification System (NAICS) replaces the separate classification systems of the United States, Canada, and Mexico with one uniform system for classifying industries.[9] In the United States, NAICS replaces the Standard Industrial Classification, a system used since the 1930s. The North American Industry Classification System will allow marketers to better compare economic and financial statistics and ensure that such statistics keep pace with the changing global economy.

In a marked change from the old SIC system, NAICS reflects the enormous changes in technology and in the growth and diversification of services that have marked recent decades.

	TWO-DIGIT CODE
Agriculture, forestry, fishing, and hunting	11
Mining	21
Utilities	22
Construction	23
Manufacturing	31–33
Wholesale Trade	42
Retail Trade	44–45
Transportation and Warehousing	48–49
Information	51
Financial and Insurance	52
Real Estate and Rental Leasing	53
Professional, Scientific, and Technical Services	54
Management of Companies and Enterprises	55
Administrative and Support, Waste Management and Remediation Services	56
Educational Services	61
Health Care and Social Assistance	62
Arts, Entertainment and Recreation	71
Accommodation and Food Services	72
Other Services (except Public Administration)	81
Public Administration	92

New NAICS sectors include:

1. The Information Sector, which covers industries that create, distribute, or provide access to information, including: satellite, cellular, and pager communications; on-line services; software and database publishing; motion picture; video, and sound recording; and radio, television, and cable broadcasting.
2. The Health Care and Social Assistance Sector, which organizes those industries by intensity of care and recognizes new industries, such as HMO medical centers, outpatient mental health care, and elderly continuing care.
3. The Professional, Scientific, and Technical Services Sector, which recognizes industries that rely primarily on human capital, including legal, architectural, engineering, interior design, and advertising services.

The major divisions used in the system are shown in Exhibit 7–3. The two-digit codes shown in the exhibit can be extended to three digits, four digits, or more to identify finer and finer gradations of differences within any particular area. Consider Information as an example. The two-digit code is 51. Publishing Industries (511), Motion Picture and Video Industries (512), and Broadcasting and Telecommunications (513) are examples of three-digit codes. A four-digit code within the Broadcasting and Telecommunications group includes Telecommunications (5133) and a five-digit code for Wireless Telecommunications Carriers (except Satellite) is 51332.

The new North American Industry Classification System and the old Standard Industrial Classification System are important to marketers because they are a guide to vast amounts of information published by the federal government. The Census of Retail Trade, the Census of Manufacturing, County Business Patterns, and many other useful government publications are based on these systems. Furthermore, because the system is so heavily employed in government statistics, these systems are used by most private companies that generate marketing research data.

SUMMARY

The behavior of organizational buyers often differs significantly from that of ultimate consumers. Marketing managers must understand the special characteristics of this unique market.

Learning Objective 1

Identify the types of organizations that make up the business, or organizational, market.

The business or organizational market is composed of businesses, nonprofit groups, charitable and religious organizations, governmental units, and other nonconsumers.

Learning Objective 2

Know the steps involved in an organizational buying decision.

Organizational buying takes place over time, involves communications among several organizational members, and demands financial relationships with suppliers. An organizational buying decision is the result of a multistage process that includes: (1) anticipating or recognizing a problem, (2) determining the characteristics and quantity of the product needed, (3) describing product specifications and critical needs, (4) searching for and qualifying potential sources, (5) acquiring and analyzing proposals, (6) evaluating proposals and selecting suppliers, (7) selecting an order routine, and (8) using feedback to evaluate performance.

Learning Objective 3

Characterize the three basic organizational buying situations: the straight rebuy, the modified rebuy, and the new task purchase.

The straight rebuy requires no review of products or suppliers; materials are reordered automatically when the need arises. The modified rebuy occurs when buyers are discontented with current products or supplier performance and investigate alternative sources. The new task purchase involves evaluating product specifications and reviewing possible vendors in a purchase situation new to the organization.

Learning Objective 4

Explain why the buying center concept is important to business-to-business marketing.

The buying center is an informal network of people who have various roles in the purchasing decision process. The people and their roles vary over time. Roles include users, gatekeepers, influencers, deciders, and buyers. Marketers must identify members of the buying center and evaluate their importance at various stages of the process in order to target marketing efforts most effectively.

Learning Objective 5

Appreciate the needs of organizational buyers and explain how marketers can react to those needs.

Needs of organizational buyers include product quality, related services, low price, and reliable delivery (perhaps including enhanced inventory management). The relative importance of these factors may vary with the buyer, the situation, or the product. The marketer must first determine what these needs are and then react to them through appropriate adjustments in the marketing mix.

Learning Objective 6

Describe the NAICS system and analyze its usefulness to marketers.

The NAICS system, a coding method used to classify many organizations in the United States, Canada, and Mexico, can be used to identify products, individual manufacturers, purchasers of various products, and other useful facts. Governments, trade associations, and other sources use these codes to categorize information. Marketers who understand the system have access to vast amounts of published data and can use the codes to determine market potentials and gain other insights into the structure of markets.

KEY TERMS

Business-to-business marketing (p. 166)
Organizational buying behavior (p. 166)
Derived demand (p. 167)
Strategic alliance (p. 169)
Buy phase (p. 169)
Straight rebuy (p. 169)

Modified rebuy (p. 169)
New task buying (p. 170)
Buying center (p. 170)
User (p. 172)
Buyer (p. 172)
Gatekeeper (p. 172)

Decider (p. 172)
Influencer (p. 172)
Single-sourcing (p. 175)
North American Industry Classification
    System (p. 176)

QUESTIONS FOR REVIEW AND CRITICAL THINKING

1. In what ways does business-to-business marketing differ from consumer marketing?

2. Compare and contrast the consumer's decision-making process and the organization's decision-making process.

3. For the following products, indicate whether the organization's buying task will be straight rebuy, modified rebuy, or new task buying. Briefly explain your answers.
   a. Lawn maintenance for the Mercedes-Benz regional headquarters building in suburban New Jersey
   b. Roller bearings as a component part for Snapper lawn mowers
   c. An industrial robot to perform a function currently done manually
   d. Personal computers for top-level managers

4. What difficulties for sellers are suggested by the buying center concept?

5. What variables might be used to estimate demand for the following products?
   a. Paper clips
   b. Staplers
   c. Lubricants for industrial-quality drill presses
   d. Forklift trucks

6. Define derived demand and give an example of its effect on the sale of packaging materials.

7. Is a business-to-business marketer more likely to stress personal selling or advertising in promoting a product? Why?

8. Form small groups as directed by your instructor. Pick a local business organization and identify at least four job titles held by the owner and employees. Discuss who will influence the company's buying decisions for straight rebuys, modified rebuys, and new task buying.

INTERNET INSIGHTS

Exercises

1. You will find the entire North American Industry Classification System at

   http://www.census.gov/epcd/www/naics.txt

   Explore information for one of the industries mentioned in Exhibit 7–3. Identify three products based on codes of at least four digits.

Address Book

International Organization for Standardization
http://www.iso.ch/

About ISO 9000—Dun & Bradstreet
http://www.dnb.com/dbis/purchase/hpurcha2.htm

Quality Standards—ISO 9000
http://www.mep.nist.gov/centers/resources/standards/iso9000/iso9000.html

ETHICS IN PRACTICE: TAKE A STAND

1. A purchasing agent likes to work with Company A, whose prices are rarely the lowest. The purchasing agent solicits competitive bids from Company A and two other companies that are known for exceedingly high quality and extremely high prices. Two other companies whose quality meets the organization's specifications and whose prices are generally the lowest in the industry are not invited to submit bids. Company A, whose product meets minimum quality specifications, wins the contract. Is this ethical?

2. A purchasing agent attends a lewd party sponsored by a company that wants to do business with the agent's company. Should the purchasing agent have attended?

3. A company gives preferential treatment to minority-owned raw materials suppliers. Is this a good policy?

VIDEO CASE 7-1

 Weather Or Not, Inc.

Sara Croke was known for her accuracy as a TV weather forecaster, she says, but that didn't cut any ice when a contract with a Kansas City station ran out and she set up shop as a private forecaster under the name Weather Or Not, Inc. Potential clients kept saying no.

Construction companies and other outdoor businesses insisted they could get what weather information they needed from TV or radio, even though she frequently heard lamentations like: "They said it was going to rain yesterday, so I sent my guys home. Then the sun came out, and now the general contractor's all over me for losing a day."

It wasn't until she went to a small business development center that the cloud over her sales efforts began to lift. The center, at Rockhurst College in Kansas City, Mo., helped her find her initial market—those already spending money on forecasts.

Walked through her first government bid, she got a six-month contract with KCI Airport. It paid $230 a month which, she says, "I supplemented with unemployment checks."

A business writer, sent her way by the center, wrote about accurate rainout forecasts she had given the groundskeeper at Royals Stadium (the writer didn't know the forecasts were gratis), and that led to her first construction-firm contract. Unlike similar firms Croke had approached, this one already had a private forecaster but was dissatisfied.

Next Croke added marketing training to the meteorological training she already had. A sales consultant provided a play-by-play of how to make cold calls, design proposals and marketing packets, and—most important—close sales.

"The No. 1 factor became relating bad weather to bad profits," Croke says. "Instead of 'I know all about weather,' it became 'I know you guys got caught last week with that surprise rain. Weather Or Not's clients had several hours' warning before the rain started. They prepared and didn't lose a dime.'"

Also, Croke would point out that weather broadcasts gave information for an area up to 100 miles wide, while she could find out each morning where clients' projects would be, pinpoint information, and call clients if there were changes. Construction supervisors or tournament-running golf pros had other things to do besides sit and watch the weather all day, she would note. Now they could have "someone baby-sitting the weather for them."

Today Weather Or Not, which started out nine years ago in Croke's one-bedroom apartment, is in two sites in Westwood, Kans., near Kansas City, Kans. It is staffed by an office manager; four forecasters, including a chief meteorologist; and Croke who pulls a 4-9 A.M. forecasting shift and then concentrates on sales.

Clients have increased along with personnel. They include company CEOs who, for example, change travel plans when warned that ice will glaze over a corporate jet's destination. Thanks in part to satellite technology, Weather Or Not can retrieve the time and place of lightning strikes anywhere in the U.S.—a one-phone-call time-saver of value to insurance companies and lawyers. The same technology makes it possible to warn people running a golf tournament hundreds of miles away that lightning is approaching their area.

Croke sees much growth ahead in these areas, and in mail-order sale of radios that sound an alarm at any hour when severe weather threatens. Dollars that a business spends with her firm in a year can be made back, she says, in minutes.

Questions

1. What is the broad industry classification for a company like Weather Or Not, Inc.?
2. The text identifies several characteristics (e.g., derived demand) that are typical of the business market. How well does Weather Or Not match those characteristics that are typical of business-to-business marketers?
3. Identify what type of organizational buying situation faced by most of Weather Or Not's customers.

VIDEO CASE 7-2

Nypro

Nypro of Clinton, Massachusetts, is a privately owned company engaged in the manufacture of injection-molded plastics, a business that some consider a commodity business.

Started 40 years ago with one machine in a garage in Clinton, Nypro today is 70 percent owned by President Gordon B. Lankton. About 100 employees own the remaining 30 percent. The company has a long-standing profit-sharing policy that covers all employees. Under this plan, $20 million has been distributed since 1964.

Nypro makes mostly penny items, with many ranging from 3 cents to 5 cents, for its customers. These products vary from simple plastic items such as toothbrush handles to intricate plastic structures like diagnostic units, which Nypro makes for practically all the major health care products companies. Nypro also churns out small containers and wire fasteners, women's shavers (30 million in 1993), cellular telephone components, computer parts, three-color ink jet printer cartridges, and components for pagers.

Nypro is a major producer of floppy disks for computers. Another low-cost, large-volume item is contact lens molds. Nypro makes toothbrushes for Johnson & Johnson, fasteners for Avery Dennison, and cellular phone components for Motorola. The health care market is Nypro's most important, accounting for more than 50 percent of its sales. It used to represent two-thirds of Nypro's overall business; but while the health care products business grew in 1994, the segment's overall share of revenues was reduced by design, because Nypro did not want to become wholly dependent on one market segment.

Nypro used to be the fifth-largest injection molder but dropped to ninth place after a number of large molders in Detroit merged and surpassed it. These companies are mostly geared to the automotive industry. Nypro also does some work for that market, but it is not a major business.

Nypro's marketing strategy involves seeking to do business only with the best customers. The strategy stems from the belief that having too many customers may cause quality problems if each customer has its own quality system, its own way of communicating specifications, and so on.

Nypro wants to build relationships with customers that will be desirable partners. Nypro is proud of its high standards for customers. If a customer can't meet its criteria, it might as well go elsewhere, because Nypro won't do business. Nypro hasn't pursued many contracts with automakers, for instance, because they're driven by unit price and cronyism rather than quality and supplier partnerships.

Nypro's criteria for doing business relate directly to the customer's purchasing philosophy and strategy. "If they like to play hardball by dividing up the business and playing one supplier against the other in terms of price, we're not interested," says Brian Jones, vice president of quality. "If they're used to short-term commitments, if their supplier relationships are driven by fear and intimidation rather than improvement and collaboration, or if the only way they know how to evaluate a supplier's performance is on price and delivery, we don't want them."

Nypro prefers customers that are open to a certain amount of training on how to source. They also must be interested in a close involvement with their suppliers.

"We have engineers who are living full-time in our customers' operations and are helping in yield and manufacturing improvements," Jones says. "We want to share technologies and help our customers set more vigorous standards than their market requires."

Nypro customers must be interested in a collaborative, not autocratic, arrangement.

"Most purchasers like to tell their suppliers what their latest market-driven requirements are—whether it be JIT, EDI, or TQM—and then turn on the heat to make them comply," Jones says.

"We prefer a shared movement forward, where the purchaser listens as well as speaks."

Nypro's commitment to quality is illustrated by its 1989 decision to "shoot for the moon." The industry standard at the time was 10,000 defects per million, yet Nypro chose to adopt the so-called six sigma standard (3.4 defects per million). That meant firing, in effect, about 90 percent of the company's 800 customers and focusing on about 30 (such as Baxter International and Gillette) sophisticated enough to appreciate Nypro's extreme quality commitment.

Questions

1. How important is strategic planning to Nypro? Overall, how would you characterize Nypro's marketing strategy?
2. Is reducing the number of customers a wise marketing strategy? Why would Nypro want fewer rather than more customers?
3. How important is technology to a company like Nypro?
4. Identify what type of organizational buying situations face most of Nypro's customers.
5. Is Nypro following the marketing concept?

MARKET SEGMENTATION, TARGETING, AND POSITIONING STRATEGIES

C h a p t e r 8

Learning Objectives

After you have studied this chapter, you will be able to:

1. Define the term *market*.
2. Explain the concept of market segmentation.
3. Relate the identification of meaningful target markets to the development of effective marketing mixes.
4. Distinguish among undifferentiated, concentrated, differentiated, and custom marketing strategies.
5. Demonstrate the effect of the 80/20 rule and the majority fallacy on marketing strategy.
6. List the market segmentation variables available to marketing managers and explain how marketers identify which ones are appropriate.
7. Explain what a positioning strategy does.

Japanese marketers are racing to keep pace with a progressive new cultural evolution involving women.

While some marketers still picture the stereotypical housewife in ads for cleaning products and the like, a new breed of working woman is being addressed in advertisements for products as diverse as frozen vegetables, cigarettes, and no-smear lipstick.

More than half of Japan's married women now hold full- or part-time jobs, according to the government's Management & Coordination Agency, and women comprise 40.5 percent of Japan's 64.5 million workers. The agency said that even during the height of the recession in 1993, there were 26.1 million working women in Japan, up from 23.7 million in 1985.

The change in attitude toward working women was a slow process. Unlike the United States, which was swept by women's liberation in the 1970s, Japan experienced the women's rights movement as an evolutionary, not a revolutionary, process. And much progress still needs to be made. A survey by the Labor Ministry, for example, reported that 60.1 percent of young women on a career track felt they were "treated unfairly in hiring, promotions, and job responsibility." And a private survey showed that women have become presidents of only 5 percent of Japan's one million companies.

But while Japanese women haven't become as liberated as Western women, they have become as busy. Working women are increasingly looking for products that are convenient and time-saving. Because of their unique needs, they are an attractive target market.

For example, the rise of working women in Japan has given birth to a fad one can't kiss off easily: long-lasting, no-smear lipstick. Targeted at fast-moving Japanese businesswomen, the products, which didn't even exist three years ago, are now a booming $45 million business monthly.

The long-lasting lipsticks give women the power to pucker up without compunction. The country's largest cosmetic marketer, Shiseido, touts this in commercials for Reciente Perfect Rouge long-lasting lipstick brand, telling women they can "dine, chat, kiss, and change [their] dress without leaving smudges." The commercials feature Ryo, a popular 21-year-old model, racing through her day wearing no-smear lipstick.

This freedom doesn't come cheaply. The lipsticks come in a variety of colors and are priced at $30 for a 3.6 gram tube. A cleansing agent to remove the lipstick costs $10.

The popularity of no-smear lipstick is attributed to the 50 percent of Japanese women who work outside the home and prefer brands that eliminate time-consuming applications. No-smear lipstick also solves a sticky yet common problem in crowded Japan. A Shiseido survey found that 40 percent of all male commuters have been smeared by lipstick in Tokyo's infamous jam-packed trains and subways. Lipstick smudges, of course, have caused more than one of these men to have problems at home.

Reciente Perfect Rouge sold 2.3 million units in the first two months of introduction, more than double the company's normal lipstick sales of one million units during an average two-month period in the Japanese market.

This chapter considers in greater depth the definitions of the terms *market* and *market segmentation*. It discusses how marketers determine which target marketing strategy will best serve their objectives. Then it examines the many variables used to segment consumer and organizational markets. Finally, it considers how marketers develop positioning strategies.

WHAT IS A MARKET? WHAT IS MARKET SEGMENTATION?

We have already defined market, but let us revisit that definition. A market is a group of actual or potential customers for a particular product. More precisely, a market is a group of individuals or organizations who may want the good or service being offered for sale and who possess these three additional characteristics:

1. The purchasing power to be able to buy the products being offered.
2. The willingness to spend money or exchange other resources to obtain the product.
3. The authority to make such expenditures.

Economics textbooks often give the impression that all consumers are alike. As long as they have a willingness and an ability to buy, economists frequently draw no distinctions among different types of buyers. Young and old buyers, men and women, people who drink 12 beers a day and those who drink one beer on New Year's Eve are all lumped together. Experience tells us, however, that in many cases, buyers differ from one another even though they may be buying the same products. Marketers try to identify groups and subgroups within total markets— that is, they try to segment the market.

Recall that market segmentation consists of dividing a heterogeneous market into a number of smaller, more homogeneous submarkets. Almost any variable— age, sex, product usage, lifestyle, expected benefit—may be used as a segmenting variable, but the logic of the strategy is always the same.

Not All Buyers Are Alike

Subgroups of people with similar behavior, values, or backgrounds may be identified. The subgroups will be smaller and more homogeneous than the market as a whole. It should be easier to deal with smaller groups of similar customers than with large groups of dissimilar customers.

Usually, marketers are able to cluster similar customers into specific market segments with different, and sometimes unique, demands. For example, the computer software market can be divided into two segments: the domestic market and the foreign market. The domestic market can be segmented further into business users and at-home users. The at-home user segment can be further subdivided into sophisticated personal computer users, people who hate but use personal computers, people who use computers only for games, and so on. The number of market segments within the total market depends largely on the strategist's creativity in identifying those segments. Needless to say, a single company is unlikely to pursue all possible market segments. In fact, the idea behind market segmentation is for an organization to choose one or a few meaningful segments and concentrate its efforts on satisfying those selected parts of the market. Focusing its efforts in this way enables the organization to allocate its marketing resources effectively.

As mentioned in Chapter 2, the market segment, or group of buyers, toward which the organization decides to direct its marketing plan is called the *target mar-*

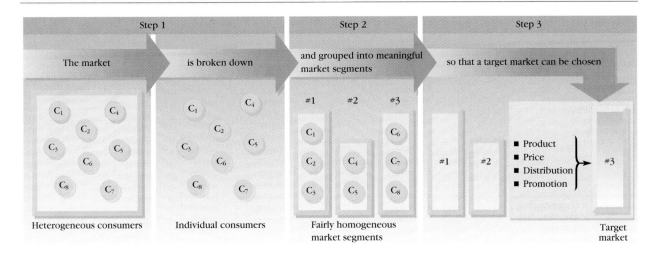

EXHIBIT 8–1
The Major Steps in Market Segmentation and Selection of Target Markets

ket. The target market for Shower Shaver, for example, is that subgroup of women who shave their legs in the shower. Because it is possible to segment markets in so many ways, target marketing opportunities abound. For example, there are "left-hander" shops specializing in products for left-handed people, tobacco shops catering to wealthy pipe smokers, and dress shops such as the 5-7-9 Shops that target women who wear certain clothing sizes. As you can see, the process of segmentation provides hints on how to market to the targeted segments identified.

Selection of the target market or markets (in some cases, more than one may be selected) is a three-step process, as shown in Exhibit 8–1. First, the total market, consisting of many different customers, is studied and broken down into its component parts—that is, individual customers, families, organizations, or other units. The customers are then regrouped by the marketing strategist into market segments on the basis of one or several characteristics that segment members have in common. Then the strategist must select the segments to which the organization will appeal. When that is done, the strategist has answered the question "What are our target markets?"

Choosing Meaningful Market Segments

Target marketing rests on the assumption that differences among buyers are related to meaningful differences in market behavior. The identification of market segments that are not meaningful has little value. The following five criteria make a segment meaningful:

1. The market segment has a characteristic or characteristics that distinguish it from the overall market. This characteristic should be stable over time.
2. The market segment has a market potential of significant size—that is, large enough to be profitable.
3. The market segment is accessible through distribution efforts or reachable through promotional efforts.
4. The market segment has a unique market need, and the likelihood that the market segment will favorably respond to a marketing mix tailored to this specialized need is high.
5. The segment's market potential should be measurable. Ease of measurement facilitates effective target marketing by helping to identify and quantify group purchasing power and to indicate the differences among market segments. Although ease of measurement is desirable, it is not mandatory.

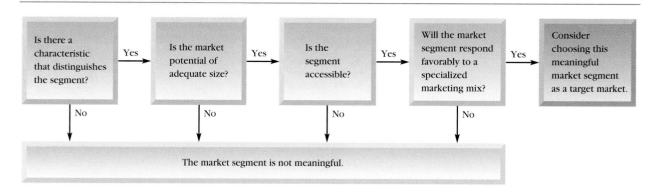

EXHIBIT 8–2
Determining Whether a
Market Segment Is
Meaningful

Exhibit 8–2 outlines these criteria. Marketing effectiveness depends on how well marketers use the criteria to identify target markets. Selecting a group that is not easily distinguishable or accessible, or appealing to a segment that is too small to generate adequate sales volume, or selecting a group that the company will have difficulty attracting is not effective market segmentation.

Consider the following example. Cuban citizens born on September 10 form a possible market segment. This is a large group. But even assuming it has unique market demands (which is probably not the case), this segment is not meaningful. The U.S. government has placed an embargo on Cuba and these restrictions have completely shut down trade with this island. The market segment of Cubans born on September 10 does not meet the criterion of accessibility.

A product that successfully appealed to a meaningful market segment was the First Alert Traveling Smoke and Fire Detector. The product was designed for the sizable number of frequent travelers who worry about hotel fires. Marketers can reach frequent travelers through specific promotional efforts (for example, advertising in inflight magazines). Offering a high-quality portable smoke alarm at a fair price by mail is a marketing mix that may appeal to the specialized needs of this market segment. Thus, First Alert met the criteria for meaningfulness. Another market segmentation example is presented in the accompanying focus on trends feature.

FOCUS ON TRENDS

National Basketball Association—The NBA

Watch sports on television, and the commercials you see are for beer, razor blades, and trucks—men's stuff.

Those commercials are missing the most important emerging sector of the sports consumer market—girls and women, according to a group of sports marketing executives who met recently in Lake Buena Vista, Florida.

"The total growth of all major (spectator) sports for the remainder of this decade will come from women," Nye Lavalle, chairman of the Sports Marketing Group, said.

Some companies are already targeting women. The National Basketball Association created a women's marketing department last year. Research showed that girls and women account for 44 percent of total NBA merchandise sales, said Michele Brown, director of women's marketing for the league. One out of every five teenage girls in the United States owns or has bought a piece of NBA clothing, Brown said, and those are clothes designed for men.

To broaden its appeal to women, the league plans to begin producing a line of women's wear. "The NBA views women as an untapped market," Brown said.

EXHIBIT 8–3
Cross-Classification Used by
a New York City Tennis
Shop to Identify Market
Segments

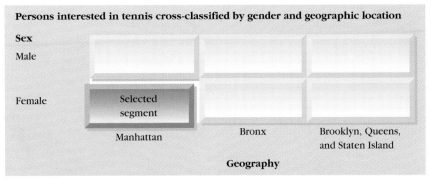

Persons interested in tennis cross-classified by gender and geographic location

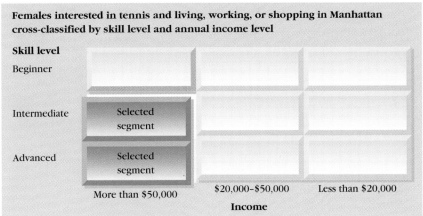

Females interested in tennis and living, working, or shopping in Manhattan cross-classified by skill level and annual income level

The Market Segment Cross-Classification Matrix

Effective marketers segment the markets they address and then select attractive target markets. Some do this almost unintentionally, even unwittingly, as did the owner of a small grocery store in Seattle. The store serves only a small portion of the Seattle market, perhaps an area of a few blocks. In a sense, by choosing the store's location, the store's owner has "segmented" and "targeted" the market geographically. However, proper market segmentation and target marketing generally involve serious consideration of a total market, the variables that can be used to identify meaningful segments in that market, and the creation of marketing mixes aimed at satisfying chosen target segments.

Cross-Classification Matrix
A grid that helps isolate variables of interest in the market. For example, a geographic variable might be cross-classified with some other variable of interest, such as income.

One way marketers can identify target markets involves the use of a **cross-classification matrix,** a grid that helps to isolate variables of interest in the market. Exhibit 8–3 shows cross-classifications the owners of a tennis shop in New York City might use to segment the retail tennis equipment market. First, the total group of people interested in tennis is cross-classified by use of a geographic variable and the variable of sex. Then the chosen segment is cross-classified with income and level of tennis skill. It appears from Exhibit 8–3 that our tennis shop's selected target market is the group of females interested in tennis who have access to shopping in Manhattan, are intermediate or advanced players, and have annual income levels more than $50,000.

The variables used to segment the tennis market could be portrayed on a single, three-dimensional figure, as in Exhibit 8–4. However, portrayal becomes increasingly difficult when more than three variables are employed. Thus, the cross-classified matrix concept is better understood when only two dimensions are shown, as in Exhibit 8–3.

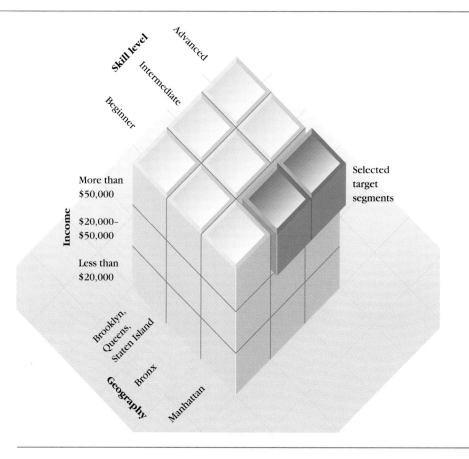

Matching the Mix to the Target Market

Having determined that its target segment will be intermediate and advanced female tennis players with incomes in excess of $50,000, the tennis shop owners must develop a marketing mix aimed at satisfying that group of consumers. This process can be very difficult, even risky. Yet the segmentation effort itself simplifies some of the choices to be made.

1. What brands should be stocked? Those that appeal to female players who are not beginners. Names such as Prince Vortex and Wimbledon Dynamic Super Lite appeal to this segment.
2. Should credit cards be accepted? Probably so, because the shop is dealing with women who have high incomes and, therefore, good credit.
3. What newspapers should be used to advertise the store? The best choice is, likely, the *New York Times,* which appeals to well-off readers, rather than the *Daily News* or *New York Post,* which appeal to downscale readers.

This example shows how market segmentation and target marketing can help not only in identifying whom to target but also in suggesting how to make the appeal.

FOUR STRATEGIES FOR TARGET MARKETING

The idea of zeroing in on a given market segment suggests analogies with rifles and shotguns. The shotgun approach spreads marketing efforts widely, while the

EXHIBIT 8–5
The Undifferentiated
Marketing Approach

rifle approach allows for greater precision by focusing on one target market. We can develop this analogy by examining four target marketing strategies.

Undifferentiated Marketing: Everyone Is a Customer

Sometimes marketers determine that there is little diversity among market segments. A firm selling hacksaw blades, brass or silver polish, or garbage cans to consumers may find it more efficient not to distinguish between market segments. This absence of segmentation, illustrated in Exhibit 8–5, is called **undifferentiated marketing.**

Undifferentiated Marketing
A marketing effort not targeted at a specific market segment but designed to appeal to a broad range of customers. The approach is appropriate in a market that lacks diversity of interest.

In some situations, undifferentiated marketing may result in savings in production and marketing costs, which can be passed on to consumers in the form of lower prices. After all, it should be cheaper to make and sell only one car model in one color, as Henry Ford did with the Model T, than to produce and sell dozens of models in many colors and with various options, as General Motors does today. However, the attempt to appeal to everyone may make an organization extremely vulnerable to competition. Even producers of a common, unexciting product like salt have found this out. Products like No-Salt, Lite Salt, sea salt, popcorn salt, flavored salts, and noniodized salt may chip away at a marketer of a single common salt. Similarly, facial tissues may all be pretty much alike, but a product marketed in a Scooby-Doo package may appeal to buyers with small children. While "everyone" buys salt and tissues, buyers' secondary desires (for example, to please a child with the Scooby-Doo package) may provide the basis for segmentation. The undifferentiated brand cannot offer the same specialized benefits.

Undifferentiated marketing can succeed. A small grocery store in a small, isolated town seeks all the people in that town as its customers. The store operator must construct one well-prepared marketing mix to please all, or at least most, customers.

Concentrated Marketing: Zeroing in on a Single Target

Suppose a chain saw manufacturer identified three major market segments: the casual or occasional user (such as the suburban homeowner), the farm user, and the professional lumberjack. Each of these users has special needs; each will use the chain saws in different ways; each reads different magazines and watches different television programs. If the chain saw marketer selects just one of these segments (say, the farm user), develops an appropriate marketing mix, and directs its marketing efforts and resources toward that segment exclusively, it is engaged in **concentrated marketing.** Exhibit 8–6 illustrates this strategy.

Concentrated Marketing
Developing a marketing mix and directing marketing efforts and resources to appeal to a single market segment.

A firm might concentrate on a single segment because management believes the company has a competitive advantage in dealing with the segment. For example, chain saws sold to the farm and professional segments are generally gaso-

EXHIBIT 8–6
The Concentrated Marketing
Approach

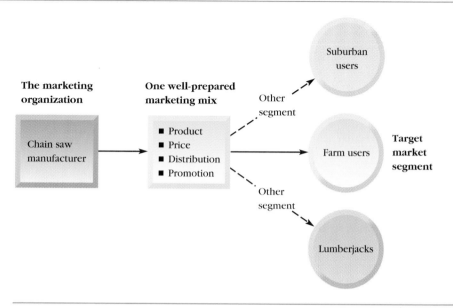

line-powered. However, the casual-user segment, with less demanding performance standards and far fewer acres to cover, may be content with less powerful electrical saws. Thus, a manufacturer of gasoline-powered lawn mowers may decide to produce gas-powered chain saws. A maker of electrical tools might find that its existing production facilities are compatible with the production of electrical chain saws. Each can select market segments that provide a match-up between company goals and abilities and customer needs. Concentrated marketing strategies can be employed by both firms.

Concentrated marketing is not risk free. If an organization specializes its efforts, it lacks diversity and has the problem of "putting all its eggs in one basket." If the market segment is too narrow or if growth in the market segment slows, major financial problems arise.

Concentrating on one market segment is often more attractive when the marketer knows that a small percentage of all users of a product accounts for a great portion of that product's sales. The **80/20 principle** is the name given to this phenomenon because, typically, 20 percent of the customers buy 80 percent of the product sold. This 20 percent (which may really be 25 percent or some similar percentage) may be called "heavy users" or "major customers." The 80/20 situation is found in both consumer and organizational markets.

Concentrating on the largest or heaviest user segment may not always be the best course of action. Some organizations mistakenly aim at such a segment just because it is so obviously attractive. These organizations have fallen—hook, line, and sinker—for the majority fallacy. The **majority fallacy** is the name given to the blind pursuit of the largest, or most easily identified, or most accessible market segment. Why is it a fallacy? Simply because that segment is the one that everybody knows is the biggest or "best" segment. Therefore, it is the segment that probably attracts the most intense competition and may actually prove less profitable to firms competing for its attention. For example, Procter and Gamble's Prell and Pert are aimed at broader markets than its dandruff-fighting Head and Shoulders, but Head and Shoulders sells more than the other two brands combined. Clearly, the point made by the majority fallacy idea is that it may be better for a marketer to go after a small, seemingly less attractive market segment than to pursue the same customers everyone else is after.

80/20 Principle
In marketing, a principle describing the situation in which a relatively small percentage of customers accounts for a disproportionately large share of the sales of a product.

Majority Fallacy
The error caused by a marketing effort that blindly pursues the largest, or most easily identified, or most accessible market segment. The error lies in ignorance of the fact that other marketers will be pursuing the same segments.

Differentiated Marketing: Different Buyers, Different Strategies

Of course, it is possible for an organization to target more than one market segment. Once the various segments likely to exist in a total market have been identified, specific marketing mixes can be developed to appeal to all or some of the submarkets. When an organization chooses more than one target market segment and prepares a marketing mix for each one, it is practicing **differentiated marketing,** or **multiple market segmentation.** For example, Marriott Corporation markets its hotel/motel service in many different price ranges. Residence Inns, Marriott Courtyard, Fairfield Inns, Marriott Hotels, and Marriott Resort Hotels appeal to different buyers attempting to satisfy different needs. Marriott thus practices differentiated marketing.

A differentiated marketing strategy exploits the differences between market segments by tailoring a specific marketing mix for each segment. For instance, the chain saw manufacturer, instead of concentrating on only one of three market segments, could have attempted to appeal to each segment of the chain saw market. This would have meant a greater investment of money and effort, because each segment would require its own specially tailored product, price, distribution, and promotion.

Of course, some markets are much more diverse than our chain saw illustration. A good example of an industry facing a wide diversity of customers is the hair-coloring industry. Some customers want to change hair color, some want to cover traces of gray, and some want to highlight or brighten hair. Within these large customer groups, additional segments can be found. Exhibit 8–7 illustrates how Clairol segments the hair-coloring market. In this case, identifying the segments is not particularly difficult. The real work and expense come in creating the marketing mixes that satisfy each segment.

Custom Marketing and Data-Based Marketing: To Each His Own

Sometimes the market facing a given marketing manager is so diverse, its members so different from one another, that no meaningful groups of customers can be identified. When this kind of diversity exists, a special kind of marketing effort is necessary. This situation requires **custom marketing,** the attempt to satisfy each customer's unique set of needs. In this case, the marketer must develop a marketing mix for each customer. A manufacturer of industrial robots faces such a prospect. Industrial robots are usually custom-designed to fit the buyer's special manufacturing problems. Each buyer demands a unique product, with special size and strength characteristics that depend on the job to be done. Each will probably require delivery and installation, thus somewhat altering the marketer's distribution system. In addition, individual customers may have difficult technical questions, requiring salespeople with broad technical knowledge. The salesperson, who is the key element in promotional efforts, may be required to alter the pricing variable to fit the custom-designed product's cost. In all, for our robot maker, each prospect may be considered a market segment, as seen in Exhibit 8–8.

Custom marketing strategies are often used by marketers of services, such as architects, tailors, and lawyers. The nature of these services requires that each customer be treated in a unique way.

Data-Based Marketing to Customize Promotional Materials

In Chapter 5, we introduced the topic of data-based marketing. Companies such as Lexus create databases containing large amounts of information about individ-

Differentiated Marketing
A marketing effort in which the marketer selects more than one target market and then develops a separate marketing mix for each. Also called multiple market segmentation.

Custom Marketing
A marketing effort in which the marketer seeks to satisfy each customer's unique set of needs. In effect, each customer is an individual market segment.

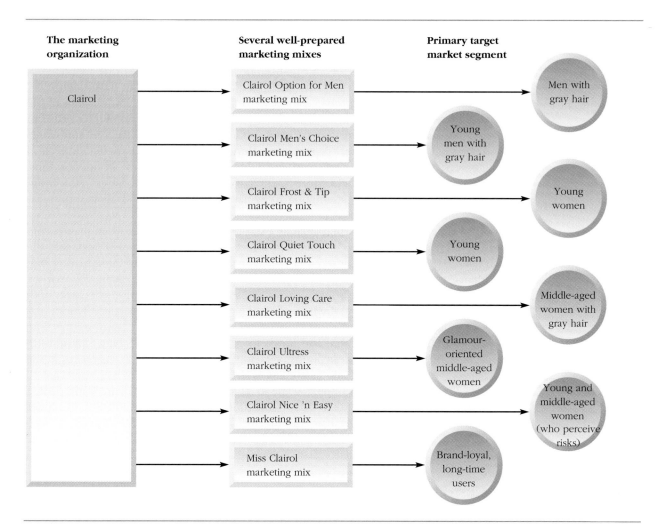

| The marketing organization | Several well-prepared marketing mixes | Primary target market segment |

EXHIBIT 8–7
The Differentiated Marketing
Approach

ual customers and potential customers. Many marketers use such information for computer-generated mailing lists and individualized promotional messages. In other words, computer technology has made it possible for a marketer to adapt a custom marketing strategy with individualized promotional messages.

Mass Customization

New technologies are changing the face of traditional custom marketing in other ways as well. Today, for example, marketers offer tennis shoes, basketball shoes, walking shoes, running shoes, aerobics shoes, and many other shoes for specific activities. Bicycling shoe marketers offer specialized models for off-road use, for specific road and track conditions, for both racing and riding purposes, and with each pair matched to one or more pedal-and-shoe locking systems.[1] This wide variety of shoes is possible because of mass customization rather than traditional mass production.

A mass production process results in low-cost, standard goods and services. **Mass customization** is a strategy that mobilizes the power of mass production technologies combined with computers to make varied, customized products for small market segments. In fact, in many situations, such as personalized greeting card kiosks, products are customized for one or a very few customers.

Mass Customization
A strategy that combines mass production with computers to produce customized products for small market segments.

EXHIBIT 8–8
The Custom Marketing
Approach

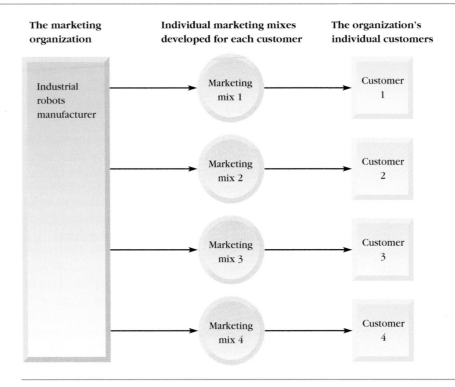

The marketing organization	Individual marketing mixes developed for each customer	The organization's individual customers

Marketers can offer mass customization to very small and specialized market segments because of technological advances in manufacturing that allow for the coordination of relatively autonomous process or task modules. Flexible manufacturing systems are replacing mass production with mass customization because more flexible, computerized production technologies are making it possible to make products, like bicycle shoes, both in large volume and in great variety. These manufacturing systems also allow changes in design or style to be made rapidly. For example, Panasonic consumer electronic products are replaced with modified models approximately every 90 days.

Mass customization calls for flexibility and quick responsiveness to give customers exactly what they want. USSA uses a mass customization strategy to target its financial services to events in a customer's life, such as buying a house or car, getting married, or having a baby.[2] First, a sales representative inputs customer information into its

Walt Disney World appeals to many diverse groups. Its Internet page allows prospective visitors to click on an icon that best describes their market segment. Those who click on "Families traveling with children under 6" tour of Walt Disney World features different attractions than the tour for those who click on "Young couples traveling without children."

COMPETITIVE STRATEGY: WHAT WENT RIGHT?

Lexus

Lexus would like consumers to feel that ownership of an exclusive car entitles them to membership in an exclusive club—the Lexus Club.

The luxury car division of Toyota Motor Sales USA takes pains to include existing customers in all of its integrated marketing plans. When the division introduces a new model, it makes sure current Lexus owners, as well as prospective buyers, know about it. Lexus believes people who have already purchased a Lexus are an important target market.

Lexus keeps in steady contact with current owners and prospective buyers through data-based marketing. For example, before the first pre-launch ads for its new GS 300 mid-luxury model appeared, all Lexus owners received a letter alerting them to "the new Lexus," the same positioning line used later in traditional media ads. The letter even included an offer for a free videotape on the new car.

Lexus also mailed the letters and videotapes to key prospects, primarily owners of competitive models such as the Infiniti J30, the BMW 535i, and the Mercedes-Benz 300E. At the same time, Lexus has built a dossier on its buyers. The four-year-old division has logged every new Lexus owner into a database now totaling more than 300,000 names. "We like to think that by going into the database and analyzing the characteristics of the existing Lexus owners, we can extend those characteristics to a broader mar-

ket," says Fred Arnow, Lexus national marketing development manager.

Lexus faces a problem common to all luxury car marketers: The buyer group is small. Only about 9 percent of all cars sold are luxury vehicles, with near-luxury cars representing an additional 3.8 percent, according to Automotive News. This makes mass media, such as network TV or general magazines, inherently wasteful. So in addition to direct mailings to its customers, Lexus engages in the promotion of special events, sports sponsorships, and media advertising under the "relentless pursuit of perfection" theme.

The thinking behind this strategy is simple: Lexus owners report higher satisfaction than owners of any other company's cars, so they also become the best promoters of the brand through another proven tool, word-of-mouth. That's why Lexus strives to keep its customer base excited about what the automaker is doing.

Lexus marketing executives see data-based marketing and special promotions as a means to build relationships. The company's relationship marketing, when done correctly, can keep a customer in the fold while at the same time further identifying common denominators among customers. Because Lexus sees its owner base as a significant source of word-of-mouth endorsements, it attempts to keep this target market excited about the Lexus brand.

---

customer database. Then, specialized software programs analyze the customer's needs and instantly provide customized suggestions for personalized marketing action. Database marketing and mass customization help an organization to better meet customers' needs. This often allows marketers to charge a higher price for their mass-customized products.

Exhibit 8–9 summarizes the typical characteristics of the four basic market segmentation strategies.

IDENTIFYING MARKET DIFFERENCES

Marketing is a creative activity, and many marketing success stories are the results of the creative identification of market segments with unsatisfied needs. The essence of market segmentation strategy is looking for differences within total markets on which to base the development of successful marketing mixes. Marketers ask, "What variables are associated with meaningful differences?" Unfortunately, there is not a simple, irrefutable answer to this question, because the bases for differentiating market segments are virtually unlimited. For example, Mercedes-Benz automobiles are sold to the prestige auto segment. No More Tangles creme rinse and shampoo is aimed at mothers who recognize their children's need for "tangle-free hair with-

	UNDIFFERENTIATED MARKETING	CONCENTRATED MARKETING	DIFFERENTIATED MARKETING	CUSTOM MARKETING
Market Segment	Everyone	One select segment	Multiple segments	Complete segmentation
Typical Market Characteristics	Little diversity	Special needs in targeted segment	Wide diversity of customers	Each customer unique
Company Objectives	Production savings	Competitive advantage of specialization; match one well-prepared marketing mix with special segment needs	Exploit differences between market segments; maximum market share	Satisfy each customer's unique needs
Major Disadvantages	Competitors may identify segments	Lack of diversity; market segment may be too narrow; intense competition for majority segment	Extensive resources required	High marketing costs
Example of an Organization (or Brand) Utilizing This Strategy	Chicago Museum of Science and Industry	Maternity shop or "oldies" radio station	Eastman Kodak cameras	Hitachi industrial robots

EXHIBIT 8–9
Summary of the Typical Characteristics of the Basic Market Segmentation Strategies

out tears" (and find a personal need to get through bath time without a lot of crying and fussing). Purina Puppy Chow is for puppy owners, and Dog Chow is for owners of grown dogs. Purina Fit and Trim is for owners of fat dogs.

Two things make the task of dealing with the almost limitless bases for market segmentation easier to handle. One is that the variables can be categorized into major groups, making them somewhat simpler to use and to remember. Exhibit 8–10 shows just such an arrangement for segmenting consumer markets. The other simplifying factor is that, although the possible segmenting variables are numerous, a far smaller number of variables are, in fact, the ones most commonly used. We look next at variables commonly used in segmenting consumer markets. Then we discuss segmentation in organizational markets.

Geographic Segmentation

Simple geography can be an important basis for market segmentation. The demand for suntan lotion is far greater in Florida, for example, than in Saskatchewan. In some cases, a geographic variable might indicate to a marketer that there is absolutely no demand for a certain product in a certain area, such as for snow shovels in Puerto Rico.

Geographic market segmentation often begins with the broad distinction between domestic and foreign markets. Organizations that market their products outside their own countries are engaged in **international,** or **multinational marketing.** International marketers recognize that people in different nations may have different needs. In Argentina, for example, most Coca-Cola is consumed with food, but in many Asian countries it is rarely served with meals. Not all U.S.-based firms choose to market their products outside the United States. An organization's resources or market demand may justify this strategy. However, many firms find it advantageous to spend considerable time and effort marketing beyond their national boundaries.

International Marketing
Marketing across national boundaries. Also called multinational marketing.

EXHIBIT 8–10
Typical Bases for
Segmentation of Consumer
Markets

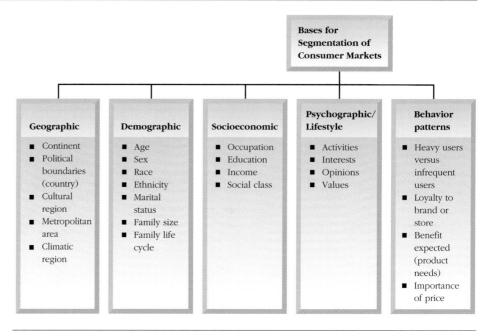

Geographic segmentation also includes distinctions based on continents, cultural regions, and climate. Another basis for geographic segmentation is political boundaries such as state and city lines. However, populations are not always adequately described by these political boundaries. Marketers are most concerned with the population map—where the people are—rather than with such matters as the "line" that "separates" Billings Heights, Montana, from Billings, Montana. Expressions— "Greater New York," "the Dallas-Fort Worth Metro-Plex," and "the Bay Area"— indicate there is no distinct political boundary line for certain market segments.

Demographic Segmentation

Demographic characteristics, such as sex, age, marital status, family size, and ethnicity, are segmentation variables that are easily understood. Their relationship to different product needs has been well established. Measurement of demographic

FOCUS ON GLOBAL COMPETITION

Barbie

Mattel pursues a differentiated international marketing strategy with its Barbie dolls. In Japan and other parts of Asia, for example, Barbie is Asian, with proportions quite different from those of American Barbie. When the political climate in Eastern Europe changed, Mattel identified a new market and began marketing Friendship Barbie. The new doll, wearing a pink cocktail dress with iridescent trim, made her debut in Hungary, The Czech Republic, and other Central European countries. With a $5 price tag, Friendship Barbie won't mean big profits for Mattel immediately. However, the company's product introduction into this new geographic market segment is part of a long-run strategy for international expansion. The company knows from its experience in the United States that the over-35 Barbie doll (introduced in 1959) means a lot to young girls. In the United States, the average owner has five Barbie dolls.

characteristics and of their relationships to purchasing behavior is not difficult. Further, information about the demographic composition of markets is widely available from a variety of sources. For these reasons, demographic characteristics are among the most commonly used segmentation variables.

Chapter 3 discussed several demographic trends. In this section, we illustrate how a few demographic variables have been used as bases for segmentation.

Age

Infants and toddlers, young children, teenagers, adults, and senior citizens are typical age-based market segments. Classifying consumers into age groups like these is useful when people of different ages have different purchasing behaviors. Changing age distributions may dramatically affect a company targeting an age-based market. The heaviest consumption of soft drinks, for example, occurs among teenagers. A decline of four million persons in the 13 to 24 age group, the heaviest users of soft drinks, would represent an annual consumption loss of 3.3 billion cans of soft drinks.

Many marketers targeted their efforts toward the 45 million Americans, born between 1965 and 1976, known as Generation X. Consumers in this first "latchkey"

Generation X is an important market segment consisting of people born between 1965 and 1976. The television show "Friends" reflects their lifestyle. They're big entertainment consumers, but of all their luxuries they prefer eating out most of all.

generation are in their 20s or early 30s. They are heavy consumers of flannel shirts, baggy jeans, Teva sandals, Timberland Boots, and baseball caps, which they wear backwards. Xers can be reached in magazines such as *Spin, Sassy,* and *Enter-tainment Weekly* and on MTV. Mountain Dew advertising appeals to this group, which feels they live on the edge, with com-mercials that show wild, daredevil activities known as extreme sports.

At the beginning of this century, only one person in 25 was over 65. When the next century dawns, one person in 5 will be over 65. With the growth in the number of older consumers, more firms will be targeting this market segment with products—such as appliances with large letters and big knobs—that reflect the needs of older people.

Family Life Cycle

A marketer of trash compactors, refrigerators, or credit cards might concentrate efforts on households or families rather than on individual consumers. To such marketers, knowing the composition of households is important.

When the word family is mentioned, most people think first of parents and their children. However, families are diverse, in part because they change over time. The **family life cycle,** a series of traditional stages through which most families pass, helps describe how diverse families may be. Exhibit 8–11 shows that people marry, raise children, and live together after the children go out on their

Family Life Cycle
A series of stages through which most families pass.

Almost 90% of Lego System's toys are bought for boys. The company knows that if it could find a way to sell as many of those little building blocks to girls, it would increase its business substantially. The company's marketing research showed that if children were playing with Lego bricks and identical pieces were put in front of boys and girls, the boys would build cars and girls would build walls and structures to live in. This research finding, along with other research information, led to the introduction of Paradisa. This product line highlighted colors such as lavender and pink and was targeted directly at girls. It allowed girls to build homes, swimming pools, stables, and other socially oriented structures.

own. Individuals may pass through these stages at different rates of speed, and the process may be disrupted by divorce or death of a spouse. It is difficult to say exactly what is a "normal" family.

Family responsibilities and the presence of children may have a much stronger influence on spending behavior than age, income, or other demographic variables. Therefore marketing managers may use the family life cycle as a basis for segmentation for entertainment, household furniture, appliances, and many other product categories. Consider several people in their twenties: one may be single, one may be married without children, and one may be married with two children ages 1 and 3. In regard to spending behavior, these consumers are likely to have little in common.

Exhibit 8–12 lists some products more likely to be used during certain life-cycle stages than during others. The accompanying Competitive Strategy feature describes what happened to one marketer who targeted the wrong life-cycle group.

Socioeconomic Bases of Segmentation

Socioeconomic variables are special demographic characteristics that reflect an individual's social position or economic standing in society. A professor may have a low economic position but a respectable social standing. A surgeon usually rates high in both areas. An unskilled laborer may rate low in both. Socioeconomic factors such as occupation and income are often combined with other demographic variables to describe consumers (for example, white, male, professional, aged 35 to 40, making $75,000 or more).

Social class is one socioeconomic variable that can be used to distinguish groups of customers. Although Americans, perhaps disliking the term class, tend to speak of rich and poor people rather than high- and low-class people, class distinctions do exist. There is a considerable difference between a married couple with high-school educations making a combined annual income of $50,000 as toll collectors on the New Jersey Turnpike and a couple who are both graduates of the Harvard Medical School earning a combined income of $400,000 a year practicing in Beverly Hills, California. And the difference is not just the money they make. The doctors may have attended preparatory schools and prestigious private colleges, inherited

In the tea example, positioning was based on certain product characteristics. Consumers view competitive offerings from many other perspectives as well. For example, a brand or product may be viewed relative to offerings in another product class—low-saturated-fat olive oil relative to high-saturated-fat butter, for example—or according to purchase situation or usage occasion—an ordinary table wine versus a wine for a celebration. A marketer planning positioning strategy must take these considerations into account.

When marketing managers are confident that they understand how consumers see their brand's position in relation to the competition, they must decide if they wish to maintain that position or reposition the brand. We have already seen how Ben-Gay was repositioned as a sports warm-up cream. Similarly, Ethan Allen introduced a new Country Colors collection, a reasonably priced natural color furniture line, and advertised it on "Friends" because it wanted to reposition as a furniture maker having something for everyone rather than a company that makes expensive furniture for older consumers.[5] **Repositioning** may require rethinking the benefits offered to consumers through the marketing mix. Jello, which for years has stressed its appeal as a dessert, has been repositioned as a snack food. Its Jiggler recipe and Jiggler forms allow kids to eat Jello with their hands.

Repositioning
Changing the market position of a product.

The target market strategy and the positioning strategy provide the framework for the development of the marketing mix. Target marketing, positioning, and the marketing mix are highly interdependent. More will be said about each of these topics in later chapters.

SUMMARY

Market segmentation is one of marketing's most powerful tools. Whatever variables they use, effective marketers try to identify meaningful target segments so they can develop customer-satisfying marketing mixes.

Learning Objective 1
Define the term market.
A market is composed of individuals or organizations with the ability, willingness, and authority to exchange their purchasing power for the product offered.

Learning Objective 2
Explain the concept of market segmentation.
In order to identify homogeneous segments (subgroups) of heterogeneous markets, marketing managers research an entire market, break it down into parts, and regroup the parts into market segments according to one or more characteristics, such as geography, buying patterns, demography, or psychographic variables.

Learning Objective 3
Relate the identification of meaningful target markets to the development of effective marketing mixes.
Marketing mixes are effective only if they satisfy the needs of meaningful target markets. A meaningful target market is distinguishable from the overall market, has a market potential of significant size (and, ideally, a measurable market potential), is accessible through distribution or promotional efforts, has a unique market need, and is highly likely to respond to a marketing mix tailored to this need.

Learning Objective 4
Distinguish among undifferentiated, concentrated, differentiated, and custom marketing strategies.
The undifferentiated marketing strategy is used if no meaningful segment is identified. If one meaningful segment is the target of an organization's marketing mix, the concentrated marketing strategy is used. If several market segments are targeted, the differentiated marketing strategy is employed. When markets are so diverse that each customer requires a special marketing mix, the custom marketing strategy is appropriate.

Learning Objective 5
Demonstrate the effect of the 80/20 rule and the majority fallacy on marketing strategy.
According to the 80/20 principle, a small percentage of buyers account for the majority of a product's sales. These users constitute an attractive target market; however, competitors often target this market as well. Failure to take this into account is the majority fallacy.

Learning Objective 6

List the market segmentation variables available to marketing managers and explain how marketers identify which ones are appropriate.

In consumer markets, segmentation variables include geographic, demographic, socioeconomic, and psychographic factors, as well as behavior and usage patterns and geodemographic variables. In business markets, geographical areas, organizational characteristics, purchase behavior and usage patterns, and organizational predispositions or policies are used as segmentation variables. The marketing manager must deter- mine which variables will isolate a meaningful target market.

Learning Objective 7

Explain what a positioning strategy does.

Each product or brand appealing to a given market segment has a position in the consumer's mind. The gist of a positioning strategy is to identify a product's or brand's competitive advantage and to stress salient product characteristics or consumer benefits that dif- ferentiate the product or brand from those of com- petitors.

KEY TERMS

Cross-classification matrix (p. 187)
Undifferentiated marketing (p. 189)
Concentrated marketing (p. 189)
80/20 principle (p. 190)
Majority fallacy (p. 190)
Differentiated marketing or multiple market segmentation (p. 191)

Custom marketing (p. 191)
Mass customization (p. 192)
International marketing or multinational marketing (p. 195)
Family life cycle (p. 197)
Lifestyle (p. 199)
Psychographics (p. 199)

Benefit segmentation (p. 202)
Geodemographic segmentation (p. 202)
Head-to-head competition (p. 203)
Repositioning (p. 205)

QUESTIONS FOR REVIEW AND CRITICAL THINKING

1. Why do organizations practice market segmenta- tion?

2. Think of some creative ways the following orga- nizations might segment the market:
   a. Rent-a-car company
   b. Zoo
   c. Personal computer manufacturer
   d. Science magazine

3. What are some unusual ways markets have been segmented?

4. Identify and evaluate the target market for the fol- lowing:
   a. *The Wall Street Journal*
   b. The Chicago Cubs
   c. SnackWell cookies
   d. Perrier bottled water
   e. Butterfinger candy bars
   f. *Wired* magazine

5. What questions should a marketer ask to deter- mine if a market segment is meaningful?

6. Think of examples of companies that use undif- ferentiated marketing, concentrated marketing, dif- ferentiated marketing, and custom marketing. What is the strategy appropriate in each instance?

7. Should firms always aim at the largest market seg- ment?

8. What is the relationship between data-based mar- keting and mass customization?

9. How might Levi's segment the men's clothing mar- ket? How might Anheuser-Busch segment the mar- ket for beer?

10. What variable do you think is best for segmenting a market?

11. What variables might a business-to-business mar- keter use to segment a market?

12. What is positioning? Provide some examples.

13. Identify the positioning strategy for the following brands:
    a. 7-Up
    b. American Airlines
    c. AT&T long distance service
    d. Gateway 2000 computers

14. Form small groups of four or five students. Assume your group has been hired by a rental car company as a consultant. Research and identify a market segmentation strategy and a positioning strategy for the company.

INTERNET INSIGHTS

Exercise

1. Abott Wool's Market Segment Resource Locator provides numerous links to information and Web sites related to market segmentation. Go to

    http://www.amic.com.awool/

    and answer the following questions.
    a. What type of information can be obtained about the African-American market, the Asian-American market, and the Hispanic-American market?
    b. Select the disabled segment. How large is this market? Summarize the characteristics of this market segment.

2. Go to the Census Bureau's home page (http://www.census.gov). What three states are forecasted to increase the most in population between 1995 and 2020? What is the expected growth of the Asian-American market? The Hispanic-American market?

Address Book

Statistics Canada
http://statcan.ca/start.html

Pampers Total Baby Care
http://www.totalbabycare.com

iGolf
http://www.igolf.com

NYNEX interactive yellow pages
http://www.niyp.com

ETHICS IN PRACTICE: TAKE A STAND

1. The cigarette named Uptown was carefully researched to be targeted to African-Americans, a group that had a higher-than-average number of heavy smokers. Is segmentation based on race ethical in this case?

2. There are many people who watch TV evangelists and consider themselves "born again." Is it ethical for a consumer products marketer to sell products to consumers on the basis of religion?

3. Is the marketing of sugar-coated cereals on Saturday morning television programs good for society?

CASE 8-1

VALS™ 2

The VALS (Values And Lifestyles) system is a popular psychographic classification scheme. The VALS 2 typology, developed by SRI International, segments U.S. adults based on psychological attributes that drive consumer buying behavior. VALS 2 classifies consumers based on their answers to 35 attitudinal statements and 4 demographic questions.

Using the VALS national database of products, media, and services, manufacturers and advertisers identify the consumer groups who are most naturally attracted to their products and services. This enables them to select an appropriate consumer target. Marketers design their advertising messages for the target by using words and images that appeal to their target. They then put the advertising in media that the target actually uses. (VALS tracks the television, magazine, and radio preferences of each of the eight consumer groups annually.)

Consumer data by VALS-type is provided by linkages with Simmons' annual *Survey of the American Household*, SRI's retail financial services survey, MacroMonitor, and other databases.

Marketers also apply VALS to direct marketing using GeoVALS™ to identify ZIP codes and block groups that have large concentrations of their target consumers in them. Other products include iVALS, which measures and represents consumer preferences in on-line environments, and Japan VALS™, which segments Japanese consumers based on their psychographic profiles.

CASE EXHIBIT 8–1
VALS™ 2 Segmentation
System

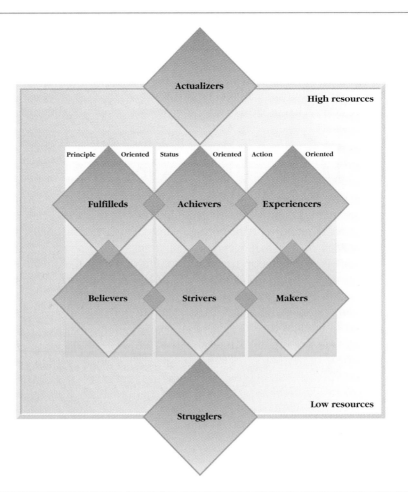

CONSUMER TYPE	PERCENT OF POPULATION	MEDIAN AGE	DISTINCTIVE PURCHASE BEHAVIORS
Actualizers	10%	42	Possessions reflect a cultivated taste for finer things in life
Fulfilleds	10	55	Desire product functionability, value, and durability
Believers	17	58	Favor American products and established brands
Achievers	14	39	Prefer products that demonstrate success to peers
Strivers	14	36	Emulate those with impressive possessions
Experiencers	13	24	Avid consumers of clothing, fast food, music, movies, and videos
Makers	11	35	Unimpressed by material possessions (except those with a practical purpose)
Strugglers	10	67	Modest resources limit purchases to urgent needs

CASE EXHIBIT 8–2
Characteristics of VALS™ 2
Market Segments

SOURCE: Updated by SRI in April 1995 from VALS2/Simmons Study of Media and Markets database. Used with permission from SRI International, Menlo Park, Calif.

VALS is built on two key concepts—self-orientation and resources. Self-orientation determines what in particular about the self or the world is the meaningful core that governs a person's activities in life. According to VALS, consumers are motivated by principle, status, or action. Principle-oriented consumers are guided in their choices by abstract, idealized criteria rather than by feelings, events, or desire for approval and opinions of others. Status-oriented consumers look for products and services that demonstrate their success to their peers. Action-oriented consumers are guided by a desire for social or physical activity, variety, and risk taking.

Resources include the full range of psychological, physical, demographic, and material means and capacities consumers have to draw upon. It encompasses education, income, self-confidence, health, eagerness to buy, and energy level. Resources run on a continuum from minimal to abundant.

Based on these dimensions, VALS 2 defines eight segments of adult consumers, as illustrated in Case Exhibits 8–1 and 8–2. Actualizers and Strugglers represent the upper and lower ends of the resource dimension. The other six groups—Fulfilleds, Believers, Achievers, Strivers, Experiencers, and Makers—represent combinations of self-orientation and resource availability.

For example, both Achievers and Strivers are status-oriented consumers, but Achievers have more resources. Achievers are successful career and work-oriented people who value structure, predictability, and stability over risk, intimacy, and self-discovery. They are deeply committed to their work and families, and their social lives are structured around family, church, and business. As consumers, they favor established products and services that demonstrate their success to their peers. Strivers seek motivation, self-definition and approval from the world around them. They are striving to find a secure place in life. Unsure of themselves and low on economic, social, and psychological resources, they are deeply concerned about the opinions and approval of others. They may try to emulate people who own more impressive possessions, but what they wish to obtain is often beyond their reach.

Questions

1. Evaluate VALS 2 as the basis for a market segmentation strategy.
2. What types of products are most likely to benefit from segmentation based on VALS 2?

CASE 8-2

The Point—105.7

With his Pauly Shore laugh and a penchant for broadcasting naughty words, Tim Virgin, a weeknight disc jockey for 105.7, The Point, likes to play bands that sound as angry as their names: Rage Against the Machine, Bad Religion, Social Distortion, Rancid. He occasionally taunts callers on the air.

But Virgin's main mission is to give listeners exactly what they want. Before he can have his pudding of punk, he must chew his broccoli—a computer-generated playlist of adolescent confessions from Alanis Morissette and cheery frat anthems from the Dave Matthews Band; self-loathing from the Smashing Pumpkins and jingle-jangle from the Gin Blossoms.

"Hey, could you play (Dishwalla's) 'Counting Blue Cars'," requests one caller.

Virgin rolls his eyes and offers a lame, "I'll see what I can do."

"Yeah, just what you wanted to hear again—Dishwalla," he mutters.

That ability to dance between alternative rage/angst and mainstream Midwestern sensibilities has taken The Point a long way—from its first broadcast $3\frac{1}{2}$ years ago to one of the top-rated alternative rock stations in the nation.

The Point's 300,000 weekly listeners are more loyal and tune in more often than any modern rock audience in the nation, according to Arbitron, the company that compiles radio ratings. KPNT-FM recently tied venerable rock station KSHE for fifth in the overall ratings, which track the 12-and-up age group from 6 a.m. to midnight over a full week. (The Point ranks lower in some important, more narrowly defined categories.)

"They had a mission to make alternative work and they have succeeded so against the odds," said Sky Daniels, who reports on alternative radio for Radio and Records, an industry magazine. "The station is being recognized as very successful. Record labels know they need to get The Point on a record."

After The Point introduced its alternative format, early results were mixed. Intrigued by the new sound, listeners gave the station a chance, but quickly returned to rock and pop formats they were used to.

"There was this great buzz when we went on air," said Greg Berg, one of the original jocks. "At first it looked like they were going to live up to it." But Berg said The Point maybe took the format too far by playing unfamiliar tunes and avoiding repetition of the favorites. "The general populace just didn't get it," he said. "We thought it was great,

but the more we did it, the more the ratings went down."

So The Point went about recasting its sound in a decidedly unalternative way. It used market research.

According to Berg, pollsters phoned potential Point listeners and asked them what they thought of a variety of songs. The response: shelve oldies by acts like Elvis Costello and The Replacements, stay away from dance grooves by New Order and Erasure, and go easy on British pop like The Smiths and Cocteau Twins. What's left? Soundgarden, Pearl Jam, The Red Hot Chili Peppers—rock-rooted material with an edge.

"I was overly optimistic. I figured once alternative came to town, people would learn and want to hear a variety of music, but they all call and say, 'Dude, you haven't played Garbage in 10 minutes and I want to hear it again,'" Berg said.

Berg was fired for straying from the playlist. He and other alternative purists may miss the station's original underground sensibility. But a wider audience of local listeners and music business bigwigs have taken notice.

You can chalk up some of The Point's success to timing. "Alternative" is no longer the private purview of college art students and teen-aged malcontents. Morissette's "Jagged Little Pill" is on its way to selling 12 million copies and Pearl Jam's "No Code" debuted on the Billboard album chart at No. 1.

Alternative music can be heard on rock, pop and sometimes adult contemporary stations. So what is "alternative" then? Well, it's like pornography—impossible to define precisely, but you know it when you see it—or in this case, hear it. It may be easier to define the genre by what it's not: Mariah Carey is too mawkish to be alternative, John Mellencamp is too earnest, Aerosmith's Steve Tyler uses too much hairspray.

To The Point's marketing and sales team, who listens to alternative music is the relevant question. The short answer: Adults between ages 19 and 34 with a lot of disposable cash. The Scarborough Report, which tracks demographic trends for different radio formats, reports that modern rock listeners are more likely than the general population to favor Dr. Pepper and Mountain Dew, foreign sports cars, imported beer and in-line skating. And contrary to their slacker image as coffeehouse employees with full goatees and empty wallets, modern rock listeners are working professionals with good paychecks.

"The revenues have tripled since I've been here. It's been

tremendous," says John Kijowski, general sales manager for The Point and its sister station, 101 The River (WVRV-FM, 101.1).

"Here's the difference. It's not mom and pop and the three kids who are listening. It's not the teen station. Our listeners are single or they are married with one or no children. So-called Generation Xers have one of the highest incomes in St. Louis and they are the most educated. They have money to spend. They don't read papers and are very selective when it comes to TV. Radio is the best way to reach them."

The Point has become a role model for other modern rock stations. There are about 200 such stations in the nation that reach, on average, about 4.4 percent of their respective markets. Talk, country, adult contemporary, Top-40, album-oriented rock, urban, Spanish and oldie stations—in that order—all are more popular nationwide than modern rock stations.

In St. Louis, the Point reaches about 5.7 percent of the local audience, Arbitron reports. Loony D.J.'s, free trips and a monopoly on the modern-rock market account somewhat for the edge, but Daniels says station programmer Alex Luke, along with Virgin and assistant programming director Eric Schmidt, deserves most of the credit.

Whereas Virgin comes off as a punk and Schmidt is the boy-next-door with bleached blond hair and a few earrings, Luke looks more like an extra from an Annette and Frankie beach flick.

He was studying chemical engineering at Texas A&M when he decided to make a profession out his passion for music. He owns about 20,000 discs and rare LPs and just started his own record label.

Luke came here from Dallas more than two years ago, working under Jim McGuinn, then programming director. McGuinn helped reverse the station's trend of sagging ratings by recognizing one simple truth about the Gateway City: St. Louisans like rock. Luke, who loves disco and ABBA, is following in McGuinn's direction.

"There are no rules or formula for programming. You have to do what's right for the city that you're in, and St. Louis is a rock town," said Luke.

With one ear tuned to latest alternative releases and the other ear to listener requests, Virgin, Schmidt and Luke decide every Monday afternoon what fans will and will not hear when they tune in 105.7. Playlists from MTV and other alternative stations, plus pressure from label executives, color their decisions. But what rules are their instincts and market research.

Songs get thrown onto the playlist that none of them likes, but all acknowledge will hit big with listeners. Likewise, they forgo playing a lot of what they consider great music.

Take the case of The Afghan's Whigs, a modern rock band from Cincinnati and one of Schmidt's favorites. He fought to get the band's single "Honkey's Ladder" on the playlist last spring. Virgin and Luke agreed, but after a few weeks, market researchers—armed with survey results—came back with a thumbs down.

"We played 'Honkey's Ladder' 270 times and still thought we didn't give it a long enough life," Schmidt said. "Do we have an obligation to educate? Yes. But the average Point listener only tunes in for 15 minutes a day, and in that time we have to get their attention and let them know what we're all about."

Still, insists Virgin, "We break more bands than any other station. If somebody hears the Cranberries on 104.1 (WKBQ, a top-40 station), they will realize they heard it first here and they will stick around. We play the stuff people say is cheesy so we can play the really deep stuff."

Questions

1. How did The Point develop its market segmentation strategy?
2. What is The Point's target market? Do you agree with their decision?

PART 3

BASIC CONCEPTS ABOUT GOODS, SERVICES, AND IDEAS

Chapter 9

Learning Objectives

After you have studied this chapter, you will be able to:

1. Define product and explain why the concept of the total product is important to effective marketing.
2. Differentiate among convenience products, shopping products, and specialty products.
3. Categorize organizational products.
4. Explain the difference between product lines and product mixes.
5. Understand brand-related terminology, including brand, brand name, brand mark, trademark, manufacturer brand, distributor brand, and family brand.
6. Discuss the characteristics of effective brand names.
7. Analyze the importance of packaging in the development of an effective product strategy.
8. Discuss the role of customer service in product strategy.
9. Discuss the nature of a service product and explain the four basic characteristics of services.
10. Discuss product strategies for services.

The crash scene at the intersection of 40th Street and 26th Avenue in Tampa is chaotic and tense. The two cars are bent and battered. Their drivers and passengers are not bleeding, but they are shaken up and scared. Just minutes after the collision, a young man dressed in a polo shirt, khakis, and wingtips arrives on the scene to assume command. Bearing a clipboard, a camera, a cassette recorder, and an air of competence, Lance Edgy, 26, calms the victims and advises them on medical care, repair shops, police reports, and legal procedures. Edgy is not a cop or a lawyer or a good Samaritan. He is a senior claims representative for Progressive Corp., an insurance company that specializes in high-risk drivers, high-octane profits—and exceptional service. Edgy

invites William McAllister, Progressive's policyholder, into an air-conditioned van equipped with comfortable chairs, a desk, and two cellular phones. Even before the tow trucks have cleared away the wreckage, Edgy is offering this client a settlement for the market value of his totaled 1988 Mercury Topaz. McAllister, who does not appear to have been at fault in this accident, is amazed by Progressive's alacrity: "This is great—someone coming right out here and taking charge. I didn't expect it at all." Welcome to the front line of the new American economy, where service—bold, fast, unexpected, innovative, and customized—is the ultimate strategic imperative, a business challenge that has profound implications for the way we manage companies, hire employees, develop careers, and craft policies.

It matters not whether a company creates something you can touch, such as a computer, a toaster, or a machine tool, or something you can only experience, such as insurance coverage, an airplane ride, or a telephone call. What counts most is the service built into that something—the way the product is designed and delivered, billed and bundled, explained and installed, repaired and renewed.

This is the first of two chapters dealing with product issues for both goods and services. It begins by explaining how marketers view products and product strategy. It then categorizes products using several different classification schemes and goes on to discuss the nature of product lines and product mixes. Next, it discusses the nature of branding, packaging, warranties, and customer service. The chapter ends with a consideration of the special issues involved in marketing services.

WHAT IS A PRODUCT?

The product an organization offers to its market is not simply a bar of soap, a rental car, or a charitable cause. As with so many other marketing elements, there is more to the product than meets the eye. A product may be a thing, in the nuts-and-bolts sense, but it does not have to be something tangible. It can be a reward offered to those willing to pay for it: a mowed lawn is the payoff for someone who buys a lawn mower. To an organization, a product is a bundle of benefits. This customer-oriented definition stresses what the buyer gets, not what the seller is selling. For example, a

DisneyWorld resort hotel provides more than a place to stay. It offers sun and fun, relaxation and entertainment, and a sense of pride about being a good parent. Defining the product in terms of benefits allows anything from tangible items to services to ideas to be identified as products. Whether an organization's offering is largely tangible (a ship), intangible (financial counseling), or even more intangible (the idea of world peace), its offering is a product.

The Total Product

Total Product
The wide range of tangible and intangible benefits that a buyer might gain from a product after purchasing it.

Primary Characteristic
A basic feature or essential aspect of a product.

Auxiliary Dimension
An aspect of a product that provides supplementary benefits, such as special features, aesthetics, package, warranty, repair service contract, reputation, brand name, or instructions.

Because a product can have so many aspects and benefits, marketers think in terms of the **total product**—the broad spectrum of tangible and intangible benefits that a buyer might gain from a product once it has been purchased. Marketers view total products as having characteristics and benefits at two levels. **Primary characteristics** are basic features and aspects of the core product. These characteristics provide the essential benefits common to most competitive offerings. Here, consumers expect a basic level of performance.[1] A quarter-inch drill, for example, is expected to provide quarter-inch holes. **Auxiliary dimensions** of a product provide supplementary benefits and include special features, aesthetics, package, warranty, instructions for use, repair service contract, reputation, brand name, and so on. Each auxiliary dimension is part of the augmented product. Together, these two groups of features fulfill the buyer's needs. Any one of many benefits may be important to a particular buyer. Effective marketers build strategies emphasizing those benefits that are most meaningful to the target markets.

Exhibit 9–1 uses Close-Up toothpaste to illustrate the nature of a core product and the associated auxiliary dimensions. The essential benefits of any toothpaste are cleaning teeth and preventing tooth decay. Close-Up's package (a tube with a flip-cap) also benefits the consumer by making the product convenient to store, easy to use, and easy to reuse. The brand name Close-Up suggests social confidence and romance. The manufacturer's name, country of origin, and telephone hotline number printed on the package provide a safety benefit. Each auxiliary dimension adds a benefit that may be important to a buyer.

Product Strategy and the Product Concept

Product Strategy
The planning and development of a mix of the primary and auxiliary dimensions of a product's attributes.

Product Concept
The marketing strategist's selection and blending of a product's primary and auxiliary dimensions into a basic idea emphasizing a particular set of consumer benefits. Also called the product positioning concept.

Product strategy involves planning the product concept and developing a unified mix of product attributes. Successful product strategy requires that all aspects of the product be analyzed and managed in light of competitive offerings. Deciding on which product features and which consumer benefits to stress is the creative dimension of product strategy.

The **product concept** (also called the product positioning concept) defines the essence or core idea underlying the product features and benefits that appeal to the target market. The product concept reflects the marketing strategist's selection and blending of a product's primary characteristics and auxiliary dimensions into a basic idea or unifying concept. In short, it provides a reason for buying the product. The product concept often is described in the same terms used to characterize the competitive market position that the product is expected to occupy in consumers' minds. For example, Ritz Air Crisps's product concept stresses that Air Crisps are a new generation of cracker—lighter, air-filled crackers to be eaten by the handful rather that with a slice of cheese. Some widely used product concepts are: "Our product has the most advanced technology"; "We build the highest-quality product"; "Our product is made in the USA"; and "Ours is a basic, no-frills product—it's the best value."

THE PRODUCT LINE AND THE PRODUCT MIX

Product Item
A specific version of a specific good or service.

In discussing consumer and organizational products, we have treated each product type separately, as if a given organization offered just one **product item**—that is, one specific version of a specific good or service. In reality, most organizations market more than one product. Even an industrial cleaning company, whose product would appear to be simply "cleaning," offers an array of services. Does the client want a daily cleanup or a weekly one? Did the client hire the company to do a once-a-year major cleaning or to clean up after some remodeling work? Does the customer want the windows washed? What the cleaning firm has to offer is, in fact, a product line.

Product Line
A group of products that are fairly closely related.

Depth of Product Line
The number of different items in a product line.

From a marketing perspective, then, a firm's **product line** is a group of products that are fairly closely related. The term **depth of product line** describes the number of different product items offered in a product line. For example, Louis Rich's food product line has grown to include several variations: turkey franks, turkey bologna, turkey pastrami, and several other lunch meats made of turkey. All these items are closely related because they are all in the same product category. A line such as this has considerable depth.

The products that constitute a product line may be related to one another in several ways. They may be similar only in a broad sense, such as belonging to the same product class. Procter & Gamble, for example, has a food products line, a paper products line, a cleaning products line, and a cosmetic products line. Products in a line may perform some particular function. Clairol's hair-coloring product line is somewhat different from its shampoo and conditioner line and certainly different from its line of hair dryers, curlers, and other appliances. A product line may also be identified as a group of products that are sold to the same customer groups. For example, Black & Decker, a company that dominates the mass market for power tools sold in stores like Kmart, was losing ground at residential construction sites where the more profitable high end, durable tools are sold. So Black & Decker introduced its DeWalt professional and industrial power-tool line which consists of 30 drills, saws, and sanders to appeal to this market.[6]

A product line may be identified by price or quality. A&P divides its private label products into lines based on price. Its cheaper brand products are distinct from its more expensive Ann Page brands.

Product Mix
All the product offerings of an organization, no matter how unrelated.

Width of Product Mix
The number of product lines within a product mix. A wide mix has a high diversity of product types; a narrow mix has little diversity.

A marketing organization may offer several product classes and define its various product lines in many ways. The term **product mix** encompasses all offerings of the organization, no matter how unrelated they may be. General Motors Corporation manufactures and sells large-, medium-, and small-sized cars, buses, army tanks, locomotive engines, and a wide range of parts and other products. Other organizations are similarly diversified. The term **width of product mix** is used to identify the extent of the product lines associated with one firm, no matter how diverse or narrow they may be. Frequently, we are surprised to discover just how varied the product mix of a firm like Chesebrough-Ponds, Beatrice Foods, or Procter & Gamble really is.

THE MARKETER'S PRODUCT PORTFOLIO

Just as the investor or financial advisor seeks to assemble a group of stocks or other investments so that the total package is considered sound, so the marketing manager can view the product mix as a collection of items to be balanced as a group. A balanced product mix might contain some good old standby products, some new products that have already shown promise, and products in research

COMPETITIVE STRATEGY: WHAT WENT RIGHT?

Quidel Corp.

Walk into an Osco drugstore, and on a shelf near the ovulation testing kits you'll find Conceive brand pregnancy tests. A cherubic infant smiles at you from the pink box. Price: $9.99.

A little farther down the aisle, near the condoms, you'll find another pregnancy test, called RapidVue. The package features no smiling baby, just brick-red lettering against a mauve background. Price: $6.99.

Both tests are products of San Diego-based Quidel

Corp—and they are identical except for the brand name and the packaging. What's different is the market. "The market definitely divides between the women who want babies and those who don't," explains Quidel Chief Executive Steven Frankel. He explains why the smiling baby sells for more than the plain-wrapper product: "It's like what Charles Revson said about cosmetics: People buy hope. In our case, they pay more for hope than for possible relief."

Product Portfolio
A collection of products to be balanced as a group.

Product Portfolio Analysis
The interrelationships of products within a product mix. The performance of the mix is emphasized rather than the performance of individual products.

and development that may be a bit risky but have a high payoff potential. The marketing manager considers the interrelationships and cash flows for the complete mix of products rather than concentrating on isolated problems of the individual members of that mix. Evaluation of a company's or strategic business unit's product mix is called **product portfolio analysis.**

Product portfolio analysis, as envisioned by the Boston Consulting Group, is illustrated in Exhibit 9–5. The horizontal scale depicts the relative market shares as high and low. On the vertical scale, the same words refer to market growth rate. The combinations of these variables yield four quadrants:

High-market-share product in a high-growth market.
High-market-share product in a low-growth market.
Low-market-share product in a high-growth market.
Low-market-share product in a low-growth market.

Star
High-market-share product in a high-growth market.

Cash Cow
High-market-share product in a low-growth market.

Problem Child
Low-market-share product in a high-growth market.

Dog
Low-market-share product in a low-growth market.

To put this in perspective, let's assign some picturesque names and familiar products to each of the matrix cells. The market for DVD players is high growth, and Sony has a high market share. It is a **star.** The canned-meat market is low growth, and Spam has a high market share. It is a **cash cow.** The home video recorder market is growing rapidly, and Sanyo has a low market share. Products in high-growth markets that seem to be having trouble picking up market share are, for their marketers, **problem children,** or question marks. The face soap market is low growth, and Palmolive has a low market share. It is a **dog.** Clearly, every company would like to market a star. But cash cows also have their value. Although Spam may not be involved in an exciting and growing market, for example, it does make a lot of money for Hormel. This product and other cash cows are likely to have a long-standing record of popularity and to generate cash flow. Excess monies generated by the cows can be used to finance the growth of products the organization hopes will become stars or to overcome obstacles confronting a problem child. Some marketing experts believe organizations should get rid of dogs so they may concentrate on more profitable projects, but such an approach cannot work for every organization. Not every product can be a star, and dogs do have some attractions. They might be profitable in the sense that they contribute to meeting overhead and administrative expenses. Furthermore, products with low shares of low-growth markets may continue to appeal to customers who have special needs or who buy primarily on the basis of price. Many brewers, for example, maintain low-priced brands that appeal to bargain hunters. The investment made in mar-

EXHIBIT 9–5
The Product Portfolio

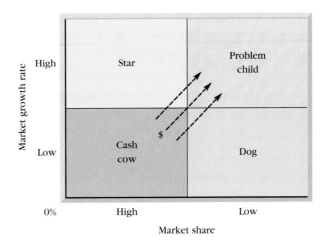

keting these products is small. Because there may be no advertising and no expenses incurred in improving the product, the brand that is simply placed on the shelf for sale may be profitable. A dog product may occupy a safe and secure market niche in which there are few challenges from competitors.

The product portfolio concept does have limitations. The first is that it may give the inexperienced student of marketing an unjustified feeling of security. Simply placing the names of products in the appropriate boxes is not the purpose of the portfolio; that merely helps to describe the problem. When the matrix is formed, the marketing manager's difficult decisions are only beginning. If we have a star, is competition desperately trying to knock it down? Probably. So what steps come next? If we have a cash cow, how vulnerable is it to competition? Wouldn't the competitors like to have a cash cow of their own? They certainly would. How about the dogs? Should we sell them off? Who would buy them? Should we keep them? How can that be done to maximize the cash flow? Should we hold on to them for a longer period because no competitor seems to be addressing their limited target markets? How much are we willing to spend trying to turn the problem child into a star?

A second overriding problem that the portfolio concept only begins to address is the reality of the marketplace and of human nature. On the surface, the portfolio suggests that the marketing manager should work hard either to turn problem children into stars or to develop stars in some other way. However, keeping up a steady flow of stars is difficult, to say the least. The Etch A Sketch has been the staple of Ohio Art's toy line for more than 30 years. Yet although Ohio Art has a cash cow, the company has not been very successful in developing additional items in the star category, and profits have been declining in recent years. Many organizations and their marketing managers are tempted to build up the cash cows to make sure they retain a high market share. Often, however, competition or other environmental forces may block the development of stars with cow money.

BRANDING—WHAT'S IN A NAME?

According to legend, the practice of branding products originated when an ancient ruler decided that goods should bear some sort of symbol so that, if something should go wrong, buyers and the authorities would know who to blame. Forced to identify their products with themselves, the story goes, producers began to take greater pride in their products and to make them better than those of their competitors, thus reversing the negative intent of the king's order. Whether the story is true or not, it makes the point that branding serves many purposes, both for the buyer and for the seller.

Branding helps buyers determine which manufacturers' products are to be avoided and which are to be sought. Without branding, a buyer would have difficulty recognizing products that proved satisfactory in the past. Many consumers are not able to analyze competing items strictly on the basis of physical characteristics. They rely, therefore, on a brand's or firm's reputation as an assurance that the product being purchased meets certain standards.

Branding helps sellers to develop loyal customers and to show that the firm stands behind what it offers. A brand that has earned a reputation for high quality may pave the way for the introduction of new products. Part of the attraction of Fat-Free Miracle Whip, for example, is its connection with the original Miracle Whip, a branded product with a long record of public acceptance.

In large measure, the free enterprise system, with its accent on letting the market decide which firms will succeed and which will fail, depends on branding. Even societies that have tried to do away with branding, such as China, have found that citizens somehow determine which products are good and which are bad, even if they have to use product serial numbers or other bits of information to differentiate products.

Brands and Trademarks

Despite the common practice of speaking of brands, brand names, and trademarks as if all these terms mean the same thing, some technical differences among them should be noted.

Brands

Brand
Any name, term, symbol, sign, design, or unifying combination of these.

Brand Name
The verbal part of the brand—the part that can be spoken or written.

Brand Mark
A unique symbol that is part of a brand.

Logo
A brand name or company name written in a distinctive way; short for logotype.

Trademark
A legally protected brand name or brand mark. Its owner has exclusive rights to its use. Trademarks are registered with the U.S. Patent and Trademark Office.

Earlier, we defined brand as an identifying feature that distinguishes one product from another. More specifically, a **brand** is any name, term, symbol, sign, design, or unifying combination of these. A **brand name** is the verbal part of the brand. For example, Sega, Cover Girl, and WordPerfect are brands. When these words are spoken or written, they are brand names. Many branded goods and services rely heavily on some symbol for identification. Merrill Lynch, a stockbroker, makes considerable use of an image of a bull, and Microsoft Windows is represented by a window that has "materialized" out of an expanding pattern of rectangles floating to its left. Such unique symbols are referred to as **brand marks.** When a brand name or company name is written in a distinctive way—as when Coca-Cola is written in white script letters on a red background—this is called a **logo,** short for logotype.

Trademarks

A brand or brand name can be almost anything a marketer wants it to be, but it does not have any legal status. A **trademark,** on the other hand, is a legally protected brand name or brand mark. The owners of trademarks have exclusive rights to their use. Thus, the word trademark is a legally defined term. A brand name is either a registered trademark or it is not. The registered trademark gives a marketer proprietary rights to a symbol or name. The NBC peacock is a registered trademark. So is the name Coca-Cola, the script style in which it is written, and the product's distinctive bottle design. Since the holder of a trademark has ex-

COMPETITIVE STRATEGY: WHAT WENT WRONG?

Toyota

Shortly after the Czech Republic gained independence and initiated a market economy, Marek Nemec decided to sell sewing machines. His company would be the first Czech company to specialize in sewing machines. He considered several brand names for his Chinese-made product, including Visa, Royal, and Toyota. Eventually, he chose Toyota and, after two years of operation, registered it as a trademark.

Czech law requires the Office of Industrial Properties to register a trademark to the first person who applies for it. The Japanese Corporation Toyota is fighting in the Czech courts to protect its name. However, in the meantime, Nemec has received more than 30 trademarks and has at least 50 applications pending.

clusive rights to use the trademarked name or symbol, a certain amount of protection is provided to the trademark holder. The name Ball Park Frankfurters is a registered trademark, so no other franks with that name are likely to appear on the market. There is even some protection against similar names, if a legal authority can be induced to agree that the similarity is great enough to constitute an infringement of the original trademark. A company selling Ball Game Frankfurters is thus very likely to hear from lawyers representing Ball Park Frankfurters.

Service Marks

Service Mark
A symbol that identifies services. It distinguishes a service in the way a trademark identifies a good.

Service marks provide the same identifying function for services that trademarks provide for goods. Like brands, they can be legally protected by registration. The NBC chimes and GM's Mr. Goodwrench are thus legally protected. Service marks may also include slogans like "Fly the Friendly Skies of United."

Generic Names

Generic Name
A brand name so commonly used that it is part of the language and is used to describe a product class rather than a particular manufacturer's product.

Some words are so obviously part of our everyday language that no one should be permitted to use them exclusively. These **generic names** describe products or items in terms that are part of our standard vocabulary—for example, flower and cat food. Other words and terms, such as nylon, kerosene, escalator, cellophane, and formica, were originally invented to name particular products but have become legally generic through common usage. Therefore, the 3M Company can call its tape Scotch Brand cellophane tape but can no longer claim that it is the one and only cellophane tape. In many instances, a brand name becomes a generic term when a judge determines that a word, such as formica, is in such common usage that the original formulator of the word can no longer hold the right to it.

It is because valuable brand names can and do become legally generic that Muzak advertisements stress that there is only one Muzak, with a capital M. Rollerblade advertisements call attention to the fact that Rollerblade is a brand name and it is technically incorrect to use "rollerblading" as a verb. Coca-Cola exerts every effort to make certain that you do not get a Pepsi when you ask a waiter for a Coke. Vaseline, Kleenex, Frisbee, and other commonly used names—names that are in fact employed to mean a generic product class—may one day be legally declared generic.

FOCUS ON QUALITY

Minnesota Moose

The Minnesota Moose may play minor league hockey but when it comes to creating a brand mark to identify and symbolically represent the team, they are major league. It sold more than $1 million in team paraphernalia, from shirts, hats and jackets to foam antlers in the first year of the club's first season. Its purple, green, and brown logo portrays a goofy moose wearing a hockey helmet and holding a hockey stick. This success didn't occur by accident. The organization sponsored a write-in contest when it was planning a team name and mascot that would create excitement and not yawns. After the moose was selected by the fans, Minnesota's marketers named it Mick E. Moose. The initial design was that of a natural, tough looking moose, but the design evolved into a cartoonish moose that seems to appeal to women and children as well as men.

A "Good" Brand Name?

What constitutes a good brand name? Instant Ocean, a synthetic sea salt for use in aquariums, has a good brand name. It is easy to remember. It is easy to say. It has a positive connotation. And it suggests what the product is supposed to do. Irish Spring deodorant soap, Orange Crush soda, and QuickSnap cameras from Fuji are also excellent names in that they associate the product with an image that is meaningful to consumers. Brand names also are often useful in reinforcing an overall product concept. Brands like Land O' Lakes butter, L'Eggs, Duracell, Moist and Easy, and Nature Made may communicate product attributes far better than any other variable in the marketing mix.

Notice that brand names and symbols say something about the product. Jiffy cake mix is quick. Ocean Freeze fish are fresh-frozen. Toast 'Em Pop-Ups' name tells both what they are and how to cook them. Spic and Span, Dustbuster, and Beautyrest tell what to expect from these products. But brand names also say something about the buyers for whom the products are intended. Narragansett is a beer for New Englanders. Lone Star is a beer for Texans. Eve and Virginia Slims are cigarette brand names that appeal to certain types of women.

A good brand name has a mnemonic quality, something that makes it distinctive and easily remembered. It has something that sticks in buyers' minds. To achieve this quality, most brand names are short, easy to pronounce, and unique. Exxon and Citgo, words coined by petroleum companies, are good brand names. In contrast, Exxon's failed office systems division offered products called Qwip, Qyz, and Vydec—names that were unique but also something of a problem to pronounce. Toys 'Я' Us employs backward Rs to conjure an image of children, as well as to make the name unique. When the sign appeared on the first store, opened in 1954, many customers informed the manager that the R on the sign was backward. That told the founder of the firm he had hit on a name that people noticed and remembered. In fact, the Я had been used instead of the word Are simply to shorten the store's name so that bigger letters could be used on the first outlet's sign. Local ordinances prohibited enlarging the sign itself.

Inventors of brand names must be aware of linguistic traps. For instance, a vitamin product was introduced into the South American market under the name Fundavit, an English modification of terms suggesting that the product satisfied all the fundamental vitamin requirements. The name had to be changed because it was too close to a Spanish term used to refer to a part of the female anatomy. Exhibit 9–6 summarizes some of the characteristics of good brand names.

EXHIBIT 9–6
Characteristics of Good
Brand Names

- Is easy to remember
- Is easy to pronounce
- Has mnemonic quality; is short and distinctive
- Invokes positive association, positive connotation
- Suggests a positive image
- Reinforces product concept
- Communicates product benefits
- Says something about user
- Avoids linguistic traps

Manufacturer Brands versus Distributor Brands

Manufacturer Brand
A brand owned by the maker of the product. Also called a national *brand.*

Many of the most familiar brand names are owned and advertised by the firms that actually manufacture the products. Black & Decker tools, for example, are made by the company of the same name. These brands are called **manufacturer brands,** or **national brands,** though in an era of global competition the latter name is less accurate.

World Brand
A product that is widely distributed around the world with a single brand name common to all countries and recognized in all its markets.

A product that is widely distributed throughout the world with a single individual brand name that is common to all countries and recognized in all of its markets is known as a **world brand.** Levi's, Marlboro, and Coca-Cola are some of the most widely known world brands. Adopting a single brand name around the globe, without translation to other languages, can facilitate the marketing of a standardized product and the management of a worldwide image.

Distributor Brand
A brand owned by a retailer, wholesaler, or other distributor rather than by the manufacturer of the product. Also called a private *brand.*

We also frequently encounter products whose names are owned by retailers or other intermediaries. The Sears line of Craftsman tools is a good example. Brands owned by Sears, Kmart, Safeway, and other retailers are called **distributor brands,** or **private brands.** (Here, the name distributor brand is more descriptive.) Brands owned by wholesalers, such as IGA, are also called distributor brands.

Why are there sometimes two types of brands of the same product, especially when Whirlpool, as a case in point, is likely to be the actual manufacturer of the Sears Kenmore line of appliances? Each brand serves a different purpose. The manufacturer brand is intended to create customer loyalty toward the products of a particular manufacturer. Beyond this, it gives the manufacturer a means to control its own products. The products bear its name and are promoted in ways it deems appropriate; furthermore, the flow of profit is directed toward the firm. In contrast, the distributor brand is intended to build loyalty for a retailer or wholesaler. The retailer, having control over the brand, can advertise it, change its price, label it, and so forth, in any way necessary to please its own customers. Traditionally, distributor brands provide the retailer with a higher margin than do manufacturer brands. To retailers and other distributors supplying retailers, this is an attractive feature.

Why should Whirlpool or any other manufacturer supply a retailer with products to be sold under the distributor's brand rather than the manufacturer's? One reason is that the goods may be sold to the retailer on a fairly mechanical basis. The specifications are met, the dealer takes possession of the goods, and the manufacturer's job is finished. There is a certain appeal in letting the distributor handle the pricing, advertising, selling, and guaranteeing of these products. The manufacturer may also be able to smooth out production runs or make better use of assets by producing both distributor brands and its own manufacturer brand. Manufacturers who provide retailers and wholesalers with goods of this type refer to the products as contract merchandise, because the products are made to order according to contract. Because a contract is involved, the manufacturer also gets the benefit of a guaranteed sale. Another reason exists for a manufacturer to provide a distributor-labeled product that will be sold, more cheaply, right next to its own nationally branded one: If, say, Libby's doesn't want to provide the product, Del Monte probably does.

FOCUS ON GLOBAL COMPETITION

Sony

When Akio Morita began to expand his company, Tokyo Tsushin Kogyo Kabushiki Kaisha, he wisely chose to give it the brand name of his popular transistor radio, Sony. He considered its friendly-sounding name (from the Latin sonus, for "sound") to be more appealing to world markets than the firm's original name. Today, the four letters, rendered since 1957 in simple, easy-to-read block type, communicate the company's standards with boldness and simplicity to consumers around the world. As Morita had anticipated, it's a name that is musical—and pronounceable—in any language.

Generic Brands

Generic Product
A product that carries neither a manufacturer nor a distributor brand. The goods are plainly packaged with stark lettering that simply lists the contents. Also called a generic brand.

It is possible for a product to carry neither a manufacturer nor a distributor brand. These products, known as **generic products,** or **generic brands,** feature a plain package (usually white) with stark, typically black lettering that simply lists the contents. These "no-name" brands offer no guarantees of high quality and are produced and distributed inexpensively. Some portion of the cost savings is passed on to consumers. The concept of generic brands is not new. Many years ago, shoppers bought most food products from bins and barrels. These were truly generic goods. During periods when increasing cost-of-living pressure is put on household budgets, many no-frills products make gains in supermarket sales, particularly in such product categories as fabric softeners, canned green beans, and facial tissues. Even among some products where brand identity is a major factor influencing purchases, such as cosmetics and beer, generics have had a modest success. Many of the same factors that encourage manufacturers to supply distributors with private brands encourage them to produce generic goods.

Family Brands and Individual Brands

Family Branding
The practice of using a single brand name to identify different items of a product line.

Family branding involves using a single brand name, like Hunt's, Del Monte, or Campbell's, over a whole line of fairly closely related items. The idea of family branding is to take advantage of a brand's reputation and the goodwill associated with the name. Introduction of a new product, such as Milky Way Lite, is made easier because of Milky Way's strong brand recognition. Similarly, family branding is used by Levi Strauss, General Electric, Volkswagen, and a host of other corporations. Use of a family branding strategy does not guarantee success in the marketplace. In what was a relatively rare occurrence, a Campbell's product failed despite the Campbell's name. The product was Campbell's Very Own Special Sauce, a prepared spaghetti sauce. Although many reasons can be offered to account for its failure, the fact that Campbell's name is strongly associated with prepared "American" foods, such as franks and beans, probably was a factor. Most prepared spaghetti sauces on the market bear names like Mama Rosa's and Prego.

Although the failure of its "special" sauce did no serious damage to Campbell's reputation, a product that proves dangerous or of poor quality can hurt an organization's overall image. A company's other brands may suffer greatly because of problems with other brands of the same name. This is one reason why some firms use individual brand names rather than family brand names. An **individual brand** is not shared by other products in that line. Besides the motive just mentioned, marketers adopt the individual branding strategy for several other reasons. For one, the products produced by a company might differ substantially from one another. Kraft Foods markets Maxwell House regular and instant coffees, as well as Sanka caffeine-free coffee. An organization may feel its products are different enough that not much can be gained by identifying the products with one another. Some organizations practice the individual branding approach because they wish to market several products that appeal to different market segments. There are, for example, many individual brands of detergents within the detergent lines of Procter & Gamble, Lever Brothers, and Colgate-Palmolive. Some contain bleaching crystals; some have fabric softeners; some have extra whitening power; some have extra strength; some have low suds; and so on.

Often, the reason a firm markets many individual brands in a product category is the belief that it is better to lose business to another of its own brands than to lose business to another company's brand. The Mars Company, for example, offers Snickers, Milky Way, Three Musketeers, M&M's, and many other candies. The matter of shelf space comes into play here. A retailer may have room to display only 25 individual brands of candy bars. If 15 of them are Mars brands, the chances of a customer selecting a Mars product are obviously much improved.

Marketers sometimes use a combination of family branding and individual branding strategies. The Kellogg's name is featured on Apple Jacks, Frosted Mini Wheats, Rice Krispies, and many other cereals whose brand names differ. The Willy Wonka name and brand mark appear on packages of candies with more exotic names, including Everlasting Gobstopper, Oompas, Dinasour Eggs, Mix-ups, and Volcano Rocks.

Co-Branding

Co-branding is the use of two individual brands on a single product. For example, Subway and Nabisco's Grey Poupon Dijon Mustard co-branded a Turkey and Ham Dijon sandwich that was offered for a limited time. In credit card marketing, Master-Card does almost 30 percent of its business with co-branded cards. Co-

Individual Brand
A brand assigned to a product within a product line that is not shared by other products in that line.

Popular characters from the "Dilbert" comic strip have brand equity. Licensing agreements with other firms allow Dilbert, Dogbert, and other characters to appear on products such as neckties.

Co-Branding
The use of two brands on a single product.

branding "partners" should be carefully evaluated to make sure their effect will be synergistic and not negative.

Licensing

As we have already indicated, a product's greatest strength may be an intangible quality or the symbols associated with it. Binney and Smith, for example, has learned that its brand name Crayola and the Crayola logo are valuable assets that other companies may want to use. When a brand name like Crayola, Harley-Davidson, or Disney adds value to a product, it is said to have brand equity. **Brand equity** means that market share or profit margins are greater because of the goodwill associated with the brand.

Brand equity may be a company's strongest asset. High brand equity often indicates that the brand can be effectively used on other products. Thus, the company may enter a licensing agreement with another firm so that the second firm may use the company's trademark. The proliferation of Coca-Cola, Garfield, and other trademarks from movies and television programs are the results of licensing.

Brand Equity
The value associated with a brand. Where there is brand equity, market share or profit margins are greater because of the goodwill associated with the brand.

PACKAGING AND PACKING

A package is basically an extension of the product offered for sale. In fact, the package is often more important than the product it contains. The Glue Stic and the hanging dispenser for Shower Mate are more than simple containers. They offer considerable consumer benefits.

Packages perform many functions. They contain a product and protect that product until it is ready for use. Beyond this, packages facilitate the storage and use of products. (Think again about the Glue Stic container.) Thus, packages should be designed for ease of handling.

Consumers often identify products by their packages. Because distinctive packages on a shelf can attract attention, they can play a major part in promotional strategy. For example, the Good Stuff company markets oval pieces of cedar that help keep moths away from woolen clothing in closets and drawers. The wood chunks are called Sweater Eggs and are packaged in egg cartons. The packaging lends charm to the product and reinforces the brand name. A package on the retailer's shelf may be surrounded by 10 or more other packages competing for consumers' attention. In these days of self-service, every package design must attract attention and convey an easily identifiable image. The package must have shelf impact. It must tell consumers what the product is and why they should buy it.

Marketers selling to wholesalers, retailers, or other organizational buyers who purchase in bulk must designate the size and type of packing boxes or other forms of containers that best meet their customers' needs. In addition marketing managers making packing decisions consider the need to facilitate transportation and storage and to protect the product from damage caused by rough handling, moisture, spoilage, and other occurrences during the transportation process. Packing and containerization decisions are particularly important when goods are exported by air or over water to many different countries far from the company's domestic operation.

Today, environmental considerations may also strongly influence packaging and packing decisions. Packaging waste is piling up, and many industries, such as the fast-food industry, try to make all packaging biodegradable or easy to recycle.

In summary, **packaging** provides a containment function, a protection-in-transit function, a storage function, a usage facilitation function, a promotion function, and an ecological function. Packaging thus involves making many decisions, including decisions about labels, inserts, instructions for use, graphic design, and

Packaging
An auxiliary product dimension that includes labels, inserts, instructions, graphic design, shipping cartons, and sizes and types of containers.

shipping cartons, as well as decisions about the sizes and types of physical containers for individual product items within the outer package.

Labeling—Telling about the Product

Label

The paper or plastic sticker attached to a container to carry product information. As packaging technology improves, labels become incorporated into the protective aspects of the package rather than simply being affixed to the package.

The paper or plastic sticker attached to a can of peas or a mustard jar is technically called a **label.** But as packaging technology improves and cans and bottles become less prominent, labels become incorporated into the protective aspects of the package. In the case of a box of frozen broccoli, for example, a good portion of the vegetable's protection comes from the label, which is more properly called, in this case, the wrapper.

Whether the label is a separate entity affixed to a package or is, in effect, the package itself, it must perform certain tasks. It carries the brand name and information concerning the contents of the package, such as cooking instructions and information relating to safe and proper use of the product. A label may also carry instructions on the proper disposal of the product and its package, or at least the plea that littering be avoided. The label must contain any specific nutritional information, warnings, or legal restrictions required by law. Some labels, such as those of Procter & Gamble, also give an 800 telephone number for customers' ideas and complaints. Consumers' calls are a major source of Procter & Gamble's product improvement ideas.

Universal Product Code (UPC)

The array of black bars, readable by optical scanners, found on many products. The UPC permits computerization of tasks such as checkout and compilation of sales volume information.

Most consumer goods are labeled with an appropriate **Universal Product Code (UPC),** an array of black bars readable by optical scanners. The advantages of the UPC—including computerized checkouts and computer-generated sales volume information—have become clear to distributors, retailers, and consumers in recent years.

Different countries' labeling laws differ dramatically. For example, some countries (e.g., Venezuela), require prices to be printed on the labels, but in Chile and several other countries this practice is against the law.

Legal Guidelines for Packaging

Package designers are relatively free to develop package designs. However, some legal guidelines and requirements must be followed. Packages intentionally designed to mislead consumers, labels that bear false or misleading information, or packages that do not provide required warnings soon draw the attention of the Federal Trade Commission, some other official body, or consumer groups. Designers must follow state and local laws, such as those requiring that soft drink bottles be clearly labeled as returnable.

PRODUCT WARRANTIES

Product Warranty

A written guarantee of a product's integrity and the manufacturer's responsibility for repairing or replacing defective parts.

A **product warranty** communicates a written guarantee of a product's integrity and outlines the manufacturer's responsibility for repairing or replacing defective parts. It may substantially reduce the risks the buyer perceives to be associated with the purchase.

Unfortunately, consumers often find that warranties are difficult-to-understand documents written in legal jargon. Several manufacturers have made use of this fact by offering warranties advertised as simple, short, "plain English" documents. Marketers who have not taken this approach may not realize that terms like fully guaranteed, unconditionally guaranteed, and lifetime guarantee don't mean much to many buyers, especially buyers who have been disappointed with the service received on other "guaranteed" goods.

Magnuson-Moss Warranty Act

Federal law requiring that guarantees provided by sellers be made available to buyers before purchase and that they specify who the warrantor is, what products or parts of products are covered, what the warrantor must do if the product is defective, how long the warranty applies, and the obligations of the buyer.

Some of the difficulties associated with warranties have been mitigated by the **Magnuson-Moss Warranty Act** of 1975. This law requires that any guarantees provided by sellers be made available to buyers prior to purchase of the product. It also grants power to the Federal Trade Commission to specify the manner and form in which guarantees may be used in promotional material. Further, the act stipulates that the warranty must use simple language and disclose precisely who the warrantor is. The warranty must indicate clearly what products or parts of products are covered by the terms of the warranty and which are excluded. The act also specifies what the warrantor is obliged to do in the event of a product defect, how long the warranty applies, and what obligations the buyer has.

The warranty is part of the total product; the seller should not view it as a nuisance. Effective marketers, such as Curtis Mathes television, use the warranty as an opportunity to create satisfied customers and to offer an intangible product attribute desired by many buyers.

CUSTOMER SERVICE

Our earlier discussion identified customer service as one element of the product mix. Effective marketers, knowing that marketing does not end with the sale of goods, may create a competitive advantage by emphasizing the amount and quality of customer services. For example, every Thanksgiving the Butterball Turkey Talk-Line's telephone hotline staff of experts receives thousands of calls and provides cooking advice as a service to help prepare, and often salvage, consumers' turkey dinners.

Delivery services, gift wrapping, repair, and other customer services all help marketers compete. These services, as auxiliary dimensions of the product, create and maintain goodwill. They provide an opportunity to enhance consumer satisfaction with the total product. The following section provides a complete discussion of the product strategies for pure services and for tangible goods with a high service component.

SERVICES ARE PRODUCTS TOO!

At the beginning of this chapter, we defined a product as a bundle of satisfactions. This definition holds as well for services as for tangible goods. Recall that services are tasks or activities performed for buyers or intangibles that cannot be handled or examined before purchase.

Services differ in their nature and in the reason consumers purchase them. Consumers purchase *instrumental services*—typically, work performed by others—to achieve a goal without direct involvement in the task. For example, a lawn care company provides an instrumental service. In contrast, a store that rents videotapes of movies provides a *consummatory service;* here, the consumer is directly involved and immediately gratified by use of the service. Taking a skiing lesson may be both instrumental and consummatory. The ski instructor performs an instructional task for the student, and the student receives gratification as the service is consumed.

Characteristics of Services

Both instrumental and consummatory services have the following characteristics: (1) intangibility, (2) perishability, (3) inseparability, and (4) heterogeneity. Marketing strategies associated with each of these service characteristics are discussed next.

Intangibility

Services are intangible, even though the production of a service may be linked to a tangible product. (The transportation service an airline provides is tied to its fleet of airplanes, renting a videotaped movie is tied to the temporary use of the video-cassette, and so on.) The element of intangibility makes the marketing of services different from the marketing of tangible goods. **Intangibility** means that buyers normally cannot see, feel, smell, hear, or taste a service before they conclude an exchange agreement with a seller. Because of this intangibility, consumers may misunderstand the exact nature of a service. For most of us, something intangible is harder to grasp than something tangible, and evaluating the quality of something intangible is difficult. To help consumers understand and evaluate the nature of their services, marketers often employ a marketing strategy to make the intangible tangible.

It can be argued that because of a service's intangibility, customers purchasing a service purchase promises of satisfaction.[7] Thus, implementing a strategy to make a service tangible requires stressing symbolic clues or providing supplemental tangible evidence to indicate that promises about a service's quality will be kept. This can be done in a number of ways. It may be as simple as polishing the brass railings to symbolically enhance a restaurant's atmosphere. Prominently displaying a brand name and logo on the organization's letterhead, facilities, and equipment or highlighting them in advertising and sales promotion efforts are other subtle ways to associate a tangible symbol with a service. Celebrity spokespersons are sometimes used to create confidence that the service marketer is committed to the promise of satisfaction. Promotional messages also often portray the people who provide the service to make the service more tangible. Allstate's slogan "You're in good hands with Allstate" promotes the idea that the people and the company are reliable. You can see for yourself that these are good people, the ads imply; if they promise something, you can rely on the promise being fulfilled. And as the Mr. Goodwrench campaign for GM's service illustrates, an entire marketing program may be developed to provide tangible symbols that the promise of good service will be kept. Effectively marketing intangibles, then, relies on developing a symbolic appearance of competency and credibility. Consumers should believe that what is promised will be delivered.

The strategy of creating tangibility through symbols is typically implemented with branding and through the promotion mix. However, service marketers often tie physical goods to their services to provide additional tangible evidence of the promised service. A health club membership comes with a membership card, for example, and a dentist's gift of a toothbrush is evidence that a dental service has been performed.

Perishability

Leo Burnett, the founder of a major advertising agency, said, "All our assets go down the elevator every evening." He was referring to the fact that services are perishable; services provided by humans cannot be stored. Thus, if the ability to produce a service exists, but this productive capacity goes unused because demand for the service is low, units of the intangible offering "perish." Consider, for example, an airplane flying from Atlanta to Charleston with half its seats empty. Every minute the plane is in the air, it produces a transport service, which is consumed by the passengers on board. The airline cannot store the service equivalent of the empty seats on that particular flight for later sale. Similarly, no-shows at a dentist's office, empty seats in a movie theater, and a slow night at a restaurant represent cases where all or part of a service supplier's productive capacity has been lost because of **perishability.**

Intangibility
A characteristic of services referring to the customer's inability to see, hear, smell, feel, or taste the service product.

Perishability
A service characteristic that determines if the service product will be long-lasting or impermanent.

**Demand Management
Strategy**
*A strategy used by service
marketers and aimed at
accurate forecasting of the
need for services so that service supply is in line with
service demand. Also called*
capacity management
strategy.

Since perishable services cannot be inventoried, service marketers plan and implement **demand management strategies** also called **capacity management
strategies.** Demand management involves managing a service's supply to be in
line with demand. For example, restaurants often hire extra part-time employees
to work during peak times and offer price reductions during slow times to even
out demand. Effective demand management, then, requires the accurate forecasting of the need for services. Because service marketers can't store their products
for sale at some other time, they must pay special attention to price adjustments.
When prices fall, a dentist's services cannot be warehoused until prices rise again.
A hotel owner in Florida cannot suspend operations without considerable cost
while waiting for customers to return during the winter season. The service marketer must keep busy and, unlike the marketer of goods, cannot keep busy by
building inventory. Pricing strategy provides an important tool for leveling the service marketer's demand.

To adjust for losses from perishability, service marketers often implement two-
part pricing. The user or subscriber of the service pays a fixed fee (for example,
membership initiation) plus a variable usage fee (for example, tennis court time).
Many hotels, restaurants, and airlines sell their services in advance or require reservations to avoid problems associated with perishability. Airlines are known for over-
booking flights, because not all travelers are on time for their flights. When everyone does show up, the airlines offer free tickets or a monetary incentive to
individuals willing to take a different flight.

Pricing is only part of a demand management strategy. Additional aspects of
demand management are discussed in the following Focus on Global Competition
featuring British Airways.

FOCUS ON GLOBAL COMPETITION

British Airways

By looking beyond its core service, air transportation, British
Airways redefined its view of what an airline does. British
Airways recast its first-class transatlantic service to emphasize what happens on the ground as much as the service in the air. Most airlines want to turn New York-to-
London flights in the front of the cabin into overnight
fantasies; passengers simply want to sleep. Responding to
them in an insightful way, British Airways gives premium
fliers the option of dinner on the ground in the first-class
lounge. Once they get on board, they can slip into BA pajamas (!) if they wish, put their heads on real pillows, curl up
under a duvet, and then enjoy an interruption-free flight. On
arrival, this presumably rested bunch can have breakfast,
use comfortable dressing rooms and shower stalls, and even
have their clothes pressed before they set off for business.

Inseparability

In marketing tangible goods, the producers (for example, industrial engineers or
assembly line workers) need not come in direct contact with those who buy the
goods. Because it is possible to separate production from consumption in exchanges
involving tangible products, distinct selling and marketing departments evolved naturally to handle the activities aimed at consummating these exchanges. This type
of separation is often impossible in marketing intangible services. In many cases,

EXHIBIT 9–7
The Effect of Inseparability
on the Exchange Process

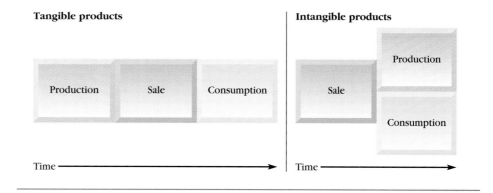

Inseparability
A characteristic of services referring to the fact that production often is not distinct from consumption of a service.

services are inseparable from their producers. **Inseparability** means that producer and consumer must be present in the same place at the same time for the service transaction to occur.

Inseparability changes the sequence of events usually involved in a marketing exchange. In goods marketing, the product is first produced, then sold, and then consumed. Usually, then, producers of tangibles can produce and show or display their offerings. Suppose however, that a patient is to be operated on by a surgeon. Delivering the promised service requires the simultaneous presence of both surgeon and patient. If either is absent, the other is likely to suffer. If the surgeon does not appear, the patient's problem may have to continue for a time, or an unfamiliar surgeon may have to perform the operation. If the patient fails to show up, the surgeon is left with unproductive time and therefore may lose some income. Exhibit 9–7 portrays the different orders for typical goods exchanges and typical service exchanges.

Essentially, inseparability constrains service suppliers' flexibility in designing their offerings, because the amount of service they can produce depends largely on the amount of time they have available. Neither a surgeon nor a hairdresser nor a rock singer can squeeze more than a certain number of operations, haircuts, or live concerts into a given day or month. Inseparability, because it often demands personal contact between buyer and seller, also can cause many distribution problems. Thus, most channels of distribution for services are direct channels in which the service provider markets the product directly to the consumer or organizational user. An accountant, for example, deals directly with a client. (However, it is possible to have intermediaries in the distribution of a service. We discuss such intermediaries in Chapters 11 and 12.)

Because of inseparability, service organizations have been extremely production-oriented in their approach to distribution. For instance, hospitals were once located at a certain place, and their clients were expected to visit the "factory." Today, under more competitive conditions, hospitals realize the need for convenient, multiple locations, emergency care centers, and ambulatory care centers that supplement the main hospital. Similarly, universities traditionally were located in small rural towns, and students could come to the service facility to purchase the service. Today, however, universities offer extension programs, telecommunication programs, and classes in urban business centers.

This production orientation means service providers tend to see themselves more as creators or producers of an offering than as marketers. They tend to accent the pride, technical difficulties, and other elements involved in production instead of understanding the need to satisfy consumers. In other words, many service providers are production-oriented rather than customer-oriented. Overcoming this orientation problem leads to a strategy in which the production process is considered a marketing activity. Thus, managing personnel becomes a marketing activity, because the standards for personnel effectiveness and efficiency must be based on consumers' perceptions, not assembly line standards.

Service Encounter
A period during which a consumer interacts with a service provider.

This leads us to a consideration of the **service encounter**—the period of time during which a consumer interacts with a service provider. A consumer's evaluation of a service offering often depends on evaluation of the physical surroundings and the behavior of the front-line employees during the service encounter. This is true even though production of the service often requires a great deal of time beyond the service encounter. For example, accountants may spend 10 times as many hours working on a tax return as they do interacting with the client. But an accountant who accurately computes a client's taxes, after having smoked a cigarette during the service encounter with the nonsmoking client, may find the client does not return the next year. The tax work was acceptable, but the smoking was not.

Most services are delivered by people. The quality of contact between customers and front-line staff provides the competitive edge, so employees are the key to success. The service marketer must therefore consider employees part of the service offering. The doctor's bedside manner and the lawyer's receptionist's personality are part of the product offered to consumers. Competent employees must be hired and then trained so that they perform the service properly. They need to know the organization's marketing goals and be trained to serve well and respond to any complaints.

Heterogeneity

Heterogeneity
The degree of variability among services provided.

Because many intangible offerings are closely tied to the supplier's personal performance, there can be great variability, or **heterogeneity,** among the services provided. Standardizing services—that is, reducing service heterogeneity—is difficult. It is not possible to deliver equal "smiling" by all employees at a service outlet, medical care of equal quality by several doctors at the same time, or even care of equal quality by the same doctor all the time. When a service is bought—say, in the form of an airline ticket—the customer can know only in a very general way what to expect from the pilot and flight attendants. Knowing precisely what to expect ahead of time is difficult, and often impossible. Heterogeneity leads service marketers to choose one of two alternative strategies: standardization or customization.

The Strategy of Standardization. Because of the heterogeneous nature of services, mass marketers may expend a great deal of effort to standardize the services they offer. For example, although a hotel room at the Hyatt Regency in San Francisco may be slightly different from a hotel room in the San Antonio Hyatt Regency, the company has made a great attempt to standardize its services. At McDonald's restaurants, all customers receive nearly the same courteous treatment.

In selected situations, it is possible to standardize services by using machines. Thus, automated car washes and electronic funds transfer systems ensure that service quality does not vary.

In general, standardization strategies require strict quality control. Standardization emphasizes careful personnel selection and extensive personnel training. It also emphasizes marketing research to discover if service falls below established standards.

The Strategy of Customization. In contrast to standardization, a customization strategy requires modifying, or customizing, a service for each individual customer. A yacht may be chartered to visit any destination chosen by the customer, for example. A health club's fitness program may be customized to suit the customer's desires and individual physical condition.

4. A doctor's bedside manner is part of the service offered to patients. Discuss this product strategy from an ethical perspective.

5. A restaurant customer asks the waiter if the fish on the menu is fresh. Although the fish was frozen, the waiter answers yes, because he knows it tastes great and the customer will love the chef's sauce. Take a stand.

6. Not-for-profit organizations that expect to bring about social change, like the National Rifle Association, have no business trying to change everyone's opinion to their point of view. Take a stand.

7. A small percentage of people suffer allergies, asthma, or sensitivity to perfumes or other chemicals. Even a whiff of some chemicals can cause respiratory problems, memory loss, or dizziness. Should there be perfume-free sections in restaurants and other service establishments?

8. The French government insists that the names of attractions—such as Fantasyland and Pirates of the Caribbean—in Euro Disneyland be translated into French. Disney officials refuse to do so. Who has the right to decide?

VIDEO CASE 9-1

 Yawgoo Valley Ski Area

Looking out over the modest slopes of Yawgoo Valley, the small ski resort near Exeter, R.I., that he had bought in 1980, Max de Wardener knew it was time to take bold action or accept loss of his investment.

What was he doing with a ski resort in Rhode Island anyway, when everybody knew the real mountains were farther north in New England? The Yawgoo Valley Ski Area had only three small slopes with 245 feet of vertical drop, an antiquated chair lift, two old rope tows, and a neglected physical plant.

Fickle winter weather, high capital requirements, and skier demand for increased services were making business more difficult every year. Yawgoo was one of only four ski areas in tiny Rhode Island and the other three were closing or about to close.

De Wardener developed a plan. He would reinforce Yawgoo's strongest point, its ski school; upgrade its physical plant; and, rather than rely solely on the short and unpredictable ski season, develop a variety of new services to bring in revenues during other seasons.

He bought more and better rental equipment. He enlarged and upgraded the school. He installed a new chair lift and state-of-the-art snowmaking equipment. He built a snow board park and added a snow board division to the ski school. He added a snow tubing area, which was open to families and to less competition-minded skiers and snow boarders.

For warm weather he installed a water slide and a park; they could use the existing lifts and slopes. He developed parks and trails and promoted the area's natural beauty to attract corporate picnics and other summer outings.

As he upgraded the buildings he put in a new nonsmoking pub (he called it The Max), for summer guests' use. He started publishing a folksy newsletter to spread a sort of hometown feeling among Yawgoo's visitors and prospective visitors.

Questions
1. Identify and evaluate the product (service) mix of the Yawgoo Valley Ski Area.
2. How has Yawgoo Valley positioned itself in the ski market?
3. How can service quality be evaluated at Yawgoo Valley Ski Area?
4. Do you think Yawgoo Valley's marketing strategy will be successful?

CASE 9-2

 Dirty Potato Chips

The product is made by Chickasaw Foods. The foil package is bright red with yellow lettering. On the front, at the top, the package says BARBEQUE FLAVOR. Then, in lettering reminiscent of the opening of Star Wars, it goes on:

> *We don't wash*
> *off the natural*
> *potato juices,*
> *so these are*
> *crisper, potatoier*
> *potato chips*
> *called "Dirty"*
> *Potato Chips.*

After that, a yellow background features red lettering that says "Cooked in 100% Peanut Oil" and "Read all about the legend of the Dirty Potato Chip on the back. Here is the Legend of 'Dirty' Potato Chips:"

Once upon a time, all potato chips tasted good. Very good. They were very crisp. And they tasted like real potatoes. Then, good ol' American mass production ingenuity took over. Bags of potato chips had to be produced by the millions. Every day. And that was a very sticky problem.

Because when you slice a potato, you know, the juice makes the slices stick together. Well, that was a real bugaboo for potato chip makers who had to cook 'em by the millions. If the slices stuck together you couldn't send them down a lickety-split production line. So, the potato chip mak-

ing geniuses solved the problem. "We'll wash off those juices," one said, "and then they won't stick together."

Problem is, when you wash off the juices two things happen. Both bad. You lose a whole lot of the crispness. And you wash off that natural potato flavor.

So, now you know our secret. We don't wash off the natural potato juices. It means we have to hand-cook our chips one batch at a time. Stirring them so they don't stick together.

Are they really "dirty"? No. We just said that because we don't wash off the juices. And it makes it easy to remember the name of the good one. We promise we don't drop any of them on the floor. And if you show the wisdom of a true potato chip lover you'll tuck this bag on the top of your shopping cart. And you'll never again endure one of those other, squeaky clean chips that taste like. . . . well, they don't taste like much of anything.

Questions

1. In your opinion, what is the product concept behind Dirty Potato Chips?
2. Should this name be registered as a trademark? Is it a good brand name?
3. What makes Dirty Potato Chips different from its competitors? Is this difference enough to make the product a success?

NEW PRODUCTS AND PRODUCT LIFE CYCLE STRATEGIES

Chapter 10

Learning Objectives

After you have studied this chapter, you will be able to:

1. Define product newness, and explain the chances of success and failure for new products.
2. Identify general product characteristics of successful new products.
3. Characterize the stages of new product development.
4. Identify some of the most common reasons for new product failures.
5. Describe the product life cycle, and characterize the stages of the product life cycle.
6. Describe the new product diffusion process, and list the groups of adopters to whom marketers must direct their appeals.
7. Identify strategies for modifying existing products.
8. Explain the total quality management process for goods and services.
9. Understand how marketers manage product lines.
10. Identify some ethical questions associated with product strategy.

Anyone who has had a routine physical knows getting a blood test is a pain—and not just because of the needle. First you pray that the technician finds your vein quickly. You watch (or look away squeamishly) as he fills two or three entire test tubes with your precious bodily fluid. Next you wait at least a day for results from the lab.

All that may change with the advent of the Piccolo Point-of-Care Whole Blood Analyzer, a desktop machine that provides blood test results in about 12 minutes. This innovative new product from Abaxis Corporation requires only a finger prick's worth of blood.

The Piccolo uses standard test chemicals that Abaxis freeze-dries in tiny beads. It seals these in chambers along the rim of a molded plastic disk, or rotor. The technician deposits the blood sample in a well at the rotor's center and pops the disk into the Piccolo, which spins it at about 4,000 rpm. Centrifugal force separates plasma from blood cells and forces precise quantities of it through thin tubes to the chambers. As the plasma and chemicals react, a spectrophotometer reads changes in color and the machine prints out results. Getting data right away lets the doctor prescribe medicine with no need for a follow-up visit or call to discuss the test.

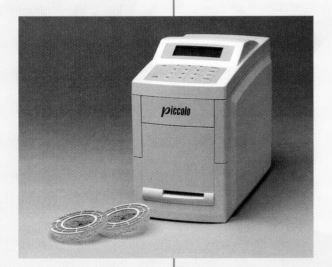

The Food and Drug Administration has approved the Piccolo and a version of the rotor containing five tests. Abaxis plans to offer combinations of about 50 tests; it will charge $8,000 for the analyzer and $8 to $20 for each disposable rotor, making Piccolo testing about as expensive as that done by a large lab. Piccolo is based on U.S. space program efforts to design a blood analyzer for astronauts to use in space. Funding ran out after the Challenger disaster in 1986, and Abaxis founders Gary Stroy and Vladimir Ostoich snapped up exclusive rights in 1988.

The Piccolo weighs just 15 pounds, takes up as much room as an oversize toaster, and can operate on a 12-volt battery, making blood tests possible in ambulances, field hospitals, and primitive countries. Nor has Abaxis forgotten space: France's space agency hopes to test the analyzer on a NASA shuttle flight in the near future.

This chapter begins by addressing the nature of new products and the characteristics associated with new product successes. It goes on to depict the new product development process and address the fact that most new products fail. Then the focus shifts to the product life cycle, an extremely influential concept in the planning of products from their births to their deaths. The adoption and diffusion processes, discussed next, help explain products' acceptance over the course of product life cycles. The chapter then addresses issues related to the marketing of products that have been on the market for some time and discusses strategies for expanding product lines and withdrawing or eliminating goods or services that no longer enjoy adequate market demand. Finally, it addresses ethical issues associated with product strategy.

WHAT IS A NEW PRODUCT?

The Piccolo Point-of-Care Whole Blood Analyzer certainly appears to be a new product. Before reading further, however, pause for a second to decide in your own mind what a **new product** is. Think of an example or two, and try to identify what makes them new. Is the video game "Super Mario 64," designed for the new Nintendo 64-bit game system, really a new product? Is a computer workstation that can be linked to other computers with invisible infrared light signals truly different from the first microcomputers? Does the ingenious, and highly practical, telephone with voice-activated dialing qualify as really new?

To some marketers, a new product may be a major technological innovation. For example, the first electronic computers were introduced in the 1940s. Though primitive by today's standards, they were at that time altogether new to the market. At one time or other, so were microwave ovens, radial tires, and automatic teller machines. To other marketers, new products might be simple additions to an otherwise unchanged product line, such as new shades of lipstick or hair coloring introduced by Revlon or Clairol. Even a "me, too" item, developed in imitation of a competitor's successful product, is a new product to the imitating company. A product also may be new because it offers some benefit that similar product offerings do not. For example, lemon juice in dishwashing liquid makes a product different from the one that was merely lemon-scented. The marketing concept, after all, tells us to consider the product as a bundle of tangible and intangible benefits. If the bundle of benefits offered by a product differs from the bundle already available, then the product can be said to be new.

From the buyer's point of view, a product may be new if it is something never before purchased, even if it has been on the market for years. In international marketing, old products may become "new" again, especially when a manufacturer's established product is being offered to people in a less-developed country. There are, for example, places in the world where videocassette recorders and cable television are new to most people.

It is clear, then, that the term *new* and the related term *novel* are used in a relative sense. They are influenced by our perceptions, whether we are marketing managers or consumers. Let's begin by taking the manager's perspective.

MANAGEMENT'S PERSPECTIVE ON NEW PRODUCTS

Managers may classify new products as new to the market or simply new to the company.[1] Here, we discuss new-to-the-world products, product category extensions, product line extensions, and product modifications. Companies have considerable experience marketing product modifications but far less with the first three categories.

- *New-to-the-world products* are inventions that create an entirely new market. These are the highest-risk products because they are new both to the company and to the market. The technology for producing these products, which is itself new to the company, is often the result of a large investment in research and development.
- *Product category extensions* are new products that, for the first time, allow a company to diversify and enter an established market for an existing product category. These products are not entirely new to the market, but the company has had no previous technological or marketing experience with them. If these products imitate competitive products with identical features, the term "me, too" products provides a good description.

EXHIBIT 10–1
The Newness Continuum

- *Product line extensions* are additions to existing product lines that supplement the basic items in an established line. Line extensions include enhanced models, low-price economy models, and variations in color, flavor, design, and so on. These new products may be family branded or marketed under a new brand name, perhaps a private label that appeals to a different market segment.
- *Product modifications* include product improvements, cost reductions, and repositionings. "New and improved" versions replace existing products by providing improved performance, enhanced features, or greater perceived value. Cost reductions replace existing products by providing similar performance at a lower cost. Repositionings are modifications of existing products targeted to new market segments or positioned as offering a new benefit or a different competitive position. The marketing task for these products often is to communicate the benefits of product modifications to consumers who do not see the products as unique or strikingly different from past offerings.

THE CONSUMER'S PERSPECTIVE ON NEWNESS

From a consumer perspective, new products also vary with respect to degree of newness. There are three types of innovations: discontinuous, dynamically continuous, and continuous, as shown in Exhibit 10–1.

Discontinuous Innovation

Discontinuous Innovation
A product so new that no previous product performed an equivalent function. Such a product requires the development of new consumption or usage patterns.

Discontinuous innovations are pioneering products, so new no previous product performed an equivalent function. As a result of this near-complete newness, new consumption or usage patterns must be established. The lithium battery pacemaker implanted in heart patients was a discontinuous innovation. The fax machine is another. These products did things no products before them had done, and using them properly necessitated extensive behavior changes. Artificial hearts and a drug to cure AIDS are still in developmental stages, but once perfected and made available, they, too, will be discontinuous innovations.

Dynamically Continuous Innovation

Dynamically Continuous Innovation
A product that is different from previously available products but that does not strikingly change buying or usage patterns.

In the newness continuum, somewhere between the breakthrough of the perfected artificial heart and the nearly commonplace newness of the "new and improved" consumer product is the **dynamically continuous innovation.** New products in this middle range represent changes and improvements that do not strikingly change buying and usage patterns.

The electric car is an example of a dynamically continuous innovation. The buying habits of those purchasing cars and fuel may be altered by successful and appealing electric automobiles, but virtually all driving behavior will remain much as it is. Compare this with the way the Model-T Ford affected society. Similarly, the electronic word processor had a genuine newness about it, but its effect on buyers and users was nothing like the effect of the first typewriter. Today, Sony's DataDiskman, an electronic book, is in the dynamically continuous category.

Continuous Innovation

Continuous Innovation
A new product characterized by minor alterations or improvements to existing products and little change in consumption patterns.

A **continuous innovation** is an ongoing, commonplace change such as a minor alteration of a product or the introduction of an imitative product. The introduction of the Microsoft Natural Keyboard is an example of a continuous innovation. The keyboard has a palm rest and curves upward, slightly parting and angling the left-hand and right-hand keys so that the hands are turned slightly toward each other, which allows the wrist and shoulder to maintain a natural position while typing. It is an improvement over the conventional keyboard. Marketers constantly strive to improve products, because even minor improvements, such as fewer calories or less salt, can provide a competitive advantage. Although this may be viewed as fine-tuning the product, the new products are innovations of a sort.

THE SLIM CHANCES OF SUCCESS

Product success is both difficult to define and difficult to achieve. It is very difficult to determine the number of new product successes and failures because, like newness, success is hard to define. How successful must a new product be before it is truly a success? It is a widely accepted belief that relatively few new product ideas become commercial successes. But because most organizations would rather not talk about their failures, much of this belief is based on estimates. Moreover, some product ideas wither in their developmental stages, and so complete documentation of ideas suggested but not implemented is not likely to be found. For our purpose, failure occurs when a product does not achieve the organization's expectations.

Several estimates of new product failure rates are available. Some of these suggest that 80 percent of new product ideas do not become commercial successes.[2] One consulting organization, after considerable study, has suggested that only one successful product is generated for every 40 new product ideas. Once a new product has actually appeared on the market, the success rate is much higher because of the research, planning, and effort that has gone into its introduction. It is estimated that there is a one-in-three failure rate among new product introductions.

Failure and success rates vary from organization to organization. In general, the failure rate is higher for consumer products than for organizational goods. In the consumer package-goods market, for instance, the failure rate is likely to be far higher than in the organizational electrical components field. Causes include the dynamic nature of the consumer marketplace and the fact that consumers often cannot tell marketers exactly what new products will satisfy them. In contrast, the organizational buyers of electrical components are able to give detailed information to component manufacturers.

THE CHARACTERISTICS OF SUCCESS

Five characteristics influence a new product's chances for success in the marketplace: relative advantage, compatibility with existing consumption patterns, trialability, observability, and simplicity.[3] When a product lacks one or more of these characteristics, the others might be used effectively to make up for the deficiency. Furthermore, nonproduct elements of the marketing mix—price, promotion, and distribution—must be developed with these same characteristics in mind.

Relative Advantage

Relative Advantage
The characteristic by which a product offers clear-cut advantages over competing offerings.

Products that offer buyers clear-cut advantages over competing offerings are said to have **relative advantage.** In organizational markets, relative advantage often arises when new products perform exactly the same functions less expensively or faster than existing products. Experience and improved technology, for example, have made possible the replacement of many metal parts with cheaper and lighter plastic ones. Similarly, computer systems that use spoken words as input have obvious advantages over earlier generations of the same systems that require typed input.

Compatibility with Existing Consumption Patterns

Everything else being equal, a new product that is compatible with existing patterns of consumption behavior stands a better chance of market acceptance than one that is incompatible. This is true even when the newer item has some relative advantage. Consider, for example, the B.A.D. Pack U-Lock, a bicycle antitheft device that features two steel strips to further reinforce the conventional U-lock design and make it impossible to insert a jack or hacksaw. It is completely compatible with cyclists' existing behavior; and because it has a relative advantage, it should achieve rapid market acceptance. On the other hand, it will take time for the market to accept the Handwriter for Windows, a digital pad that lets the user enter words or drawings into a personal computer with a pen. Although it converts handwritten characters into computerized text and gives the pen mouselike pointing capabilities with Windows programs, the thin pad is quite different from a keyboard or mouse and represents a departure from existing usage patterns.

Trialability—The Opportunity for Buyer Testing

Trialability
The characteristic by which a product can be tested by possible future users with little risk or effort.

A new product—such as Soupsations, a microwaveable bowl containing a single-serving soup mix complete with a flavor-boosting liquid stock packet—has **trialability** when it can be tested by possible future users with little risk or effort. This is true of Electrasol Tabs, a new automatic dishwasher detergent in tablet form, because it is inexpensive and does not require the buyer to invest in special equipment to use it. New shampoos and laundry products are made available to shoppers in small, inexpensive packages to encourage trial at little monetary risk. When companies give away free samples to possible buyers, bringing trialability to perhaps its highest level, the process is termed **trial sampling.**

Trial Sampling
The distribution of newly marketed products to enhance trialability and familiarity; giving away free samples.

Effective marketing management demands careful consideration of steps that may contribute to buyer sampling of a new product. For example, items intended to be sold in cases or six-packs, like juices, sodas, and other drinks, might first be offered in single-drink packages or be given away by the cupful in shopping malls. Customers may be reluctant to buy 12 of a given product but may be willing to try just one. Trialability is more appropriately referred to as a product's **divisibility** when it refers to the opportunity to try a small amount.

Divisibility
The characteristic by which a product provides the opportunity for consumers to sample small amounts.

Observability—The Chance to See the Newness

Some new products enter the marketplace with attributes or characteristics that are visible to the customer. Rockwell International's PathMaster satellite navigation system uses satellites to provide drivers with precise directions when they enter queries about a particular destination, such as a hotel. PathMaster also allows drivers to search for the nearest restaurant or select one based on descriptions of cuisine or ratings.[4] By providing precise directions from a traveler's present position, PathMaster has a relative advantage over maps and guide books. Best of all for Rockwell, the advantage is easy to see. It is a product with **observability.**

Observability
The characteristic by which a product's advantages over existing products are easily seen or understood by consumers.

Other products possess definite relative advantages that are not observable or so easily grasped. A new brand of allergy tablets with an advanced formula that relieves allergy symptoms without causing drowsiness has an advantage that may not be observable by most buyers. Advertisements for products with hidden qualities frequently feature experts or credible users who attest to the products' worth, making hidden qualities observable.

Simplicity versus Complexity

A complex product, or one that requires complex procedures for use or storage, starts out with a disadvantage. Polaroid Land cameras, at their introduction, were viewed by consumers as minor miracles. Therefore, the cameras themselves were designed for easy operation. The **simplicity of usage** offset the complexity of the product itself. Compact disc digital recordings were similarly surprising to consumers, who found it difficult to grasp the system by which these recordings were played. Makers of early CD players carefully trained salespeople to explain the new system and arranged for newspaper and magazine columnists to try it so that they could explain it to their readers.

Simplicity of Usage
Ease of operation; a product benefit that can offset the complexity of the product itself.

NEW PRODUCT DEVELOPMENT

What is the source of product innovations? How are new product ideas generated? There is no one answer to these questions. Some innovations are discovered by accident or luck, such as the vulcanization of rubber (discovered when a rubbery mixture was spilled on a hot stove) and Ivory's floating soap (first made when a mechanical mixer was left on overnight and whipped raw soap materials into a lightweight cleanser). Necessity, it seems, was the mother of invention for the ice cream seller in St. Louis who ran out of paper cups and rolled pancakes into serving cones—the first ice cream cones. On occasion, the amateur inventor working in a basement comes up with an innovation that goes on to great success. However, these days, when innovations require sizable financial investments and other resources for support and commercialization, most innovations come from serious research and development efforts undertaken with the support of formal organizations.[5]

The new product development process can be quick, the result of a sudden flash of insight. But in many cases, such as in the development of space satellites and other highly technical products, the process can take years. The development process may be lengthy not so much because of technical problems but because it takes time to research and understand potential market resistance to a new product. Even when a new product has a technological advantage, customers may not accept it.

Exhibit 10–2 shows the five general stages in the development process of new products: idea generation, screening, business analysis, development, and commercialization. Products pass through these stages at varying rates. A product may stall for a time in one, for example, and pass through another so quickly that it appears to have skipped it entirely.[6]

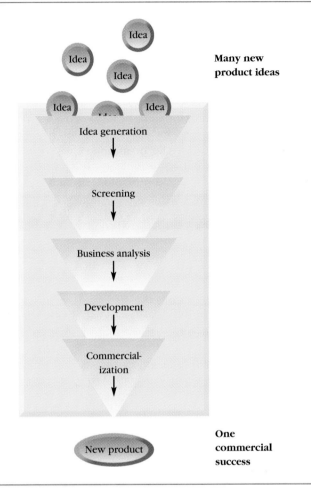

SOURCE: Adapted from Roger A. Bengston, "Nine New Product Strategies: Each Requires Different Resources, Talent, Research Methods," *Marketing News,* March 19, 1982, p. 7. Reprinted by permission of the American Marketing Association.

Idea Generation

Idea Generation Stage
The stage in new product development in which the marketer engages in a continuing search for product ideas consistent with target market needs and the organization's objectives.

In marketing-oriented organizations operating in dynamic environments, **idea generation**—the exploration stage of new product development—is less a period of time than an ongoing process. Thus, the idea generation stage involves a continuing search for product ideas that are consistent with target market needs and with the organization's objectives.

In many organizations, particularly those in industries with complex technology, generating ideas and searching for technological breakthroughs are likely to be the tasks of the research and development (R & D) department. R & D personnel may focus creative thinking on transferring a technology from an existing product category to a new product, on miniaturization, or on basic research to create new-to-the-world products. For example, Eastman Kodak's digital camera came from a technology-driven idea. This filmless camera allows a customer to store digital images, display them on a television or computer, exchange photographs on the Internet, and print as many copies as they desire. R & D engineers creatively applied consumer electronics technology from the personal computer industry to generate the idea for this product.

Although a large proportion of new product ideas flow from research departments, other sources should not be ignored. New product suggestions may come from customers. Sales representatives may uncover, or be told about, new product opportunities. Marketing research can yield new product suggestions. An employee, a supplier, or a distributor may come up with a good—or even brilliant—idea.

Companies can stimulate idea generation by encouraging employees to think about new products that could address consumer complaints, make a task easier, add benefits to existing products, or provide new uses for existing products. Many organizations have instituted reward systems to encourage employee suggestions. The focus at this stage is on encouraging creativity rather than on evaluating suggestions. The organization wishes to generate ideas, not kill them.

FOCUS ON GLOBAL COMPETITION

Yamaha

Insights into possibilities for new products that are fundamentally different—that is, new-to-the-world products—may be garnered in ways that go beyond traditional modes of marketing research.

Toshiba has a Lifestyle Research Institute; Sony explores "human science" with the same passion with which it pursues the leading edge of audiovisual technology. The insights gained allow these firms to answer two crucial questions: What range of benefits will customers value in tomorrow's products, and how might we, through innovation, preempt competitors in delivering those benefits to the marketplace?

Yamaha gained insights into the unarticulated needs of musicians when it established a "listening post" in London,

chock-full of the latest gee-whiz music technology. The facility offered some of Europe's most talented musicians a chance to experiment with the future of music making. The feedback helped Yamaha continually push out the boundaries of the competitive space it had staked out in the music business.

Yamaha's experience illustrates an important point: To push out the boundaries of current product concepts, it is necessary to put the most advanced technology possible directly into the hands of the world's most sophisticated and demanding customers. Thus arose Yamaha's London market laboratory: Japan is still not the center of the world's pop music industry.

Screening

The screening stage of the product development process involves analyzing new ideas to determine which are reasonable, pertinent to the organization's goals, and appropriate to the organization's target markets. This step is extremely important, because the underlying assumption of the entire product development process is that risky alternatives—possibilities that do not offer as much promise for success as others—should be eliminated from consideration. Resources can then be concentrated on the best prospects so that market failures can be avoided.

Screening Stage
The stage in new product development in which the marketer analyzes ideas to determine their appropriateness and reasonableness in relation to the organization's goals and objectives.

The **screening stage** also is important because it is the first stage at which alternative ideas are sorted. New ideas may now be rejected. From time to time, of course, any management team is likely to reject some ideas that they later wish they had accepted. Because mistakes will be made, managers must conduct screening with caution. In fact, because an idea rejected at this stage is eliminated from further consideration, some companies prefer to allow a marginal idea to progress further rather than to risk rejecting it too early in the process. However, at later stages, the costs of analysis and evaluation are substantially higher. Balancing the costs of additional investigation against the loss of a viable product idea is one of management's most delicate tasks.

Business Analysis

Business Analysis Stage
The stage in new product development in which the new product is reviewed from all organizational perspectives to determine performance criteria and likely profitability.

A product idea that survives the screening process enters the **business analysis stage,** where it is expanded into a concrete business recommendation. This recommendation includes such specifics as a listing of product features, information on resources needed to produce the product, and a basic marketing plan. Creativity and analysis come together at this stage. Although qualitative evaluations of the product and its likely success are still important, business analysis requires quantitative facts and figures. The new product idea is evaluated with increasingly detailed quantitative data on market demand, cost projections, investment requirements, and competitive activity. Formal buyer research studies, sales and market forecasts, break-even analyses, and similar research efforts are undertaken. In short, the business analysis is a review of the new product from all significant organizational perspectives. It emphasizes performance criteria and chances for success in the marketplace.

Development

Development Stage
The stage in new product development in which a new product concept is transformed into a prototype. The basic marketing strategy also develops at this time.

A new product idea that survives the preliminary evaluative stages is ready for the fourth stage, development. In the **development stage,** the proposed new product idea is transformed from a product concept to a product prototype. The basic positioning and target marketing strategy is developed. Decisions about the product's physical characteristics, package design, and brand name are made. Specific tactics within the product strategy are also researched during this stage.

In the development stage, paper-and-pencil concepts become demonstrable products. Research and development or production engineers give marketers a product that can be tested in customer usage studies, sold in test markets, or investigated in other limited ways. This is not to say that the product is in final form. For example, soft drink marketers may taste-test a new formulation on a panel of consumers. If the product is not well accepted, it might be reformulated or its package might be changed. The product can be retested until the proper set of characteristics has been discovered. We discuss two popular forms of testing here.

Concept Testing

Concept Testing
Research procedures used to learn consumers' reactions to new product ideas. Consumers presented with an idea are asked if they like it, would use it, would buy it, and so on.

Concept testing is a general term for many different research procedures used to learn consumers' reactions to a new product idea. Typically, consumers are presented with the idea as a pictorial or written description, and asked if they would use it, if they like it, if they would buy it, and so on. Concept testing helps to ensure that product concepts are developed with the needs of the consumer or user in mind. For example, General Electric's design engineers are sent out to talk with dealers and customers about new product concepts to ensure that market feedback goes where it can do the most good—to the engineers who design the products. GE describes the process in this way: "Engineers working at the drawing board are getting their directions from customers. The whole business is oriented toward bringing the technology and the consumer demand together."[7]

Test Marketing

Test Marketing
A controlled experimental procedure in which a new product is tested under realistic market conditions in a limited geographical area.

Test marketing is an experimental procedure in which marketers test a new product under realistic market conditions in order to obtain a measure of its potential sales in national distribution. Test markets are cities or other small geographical areas in which the new product is distributed and sold in typical marketplace settings to actual consumers. No other form of research can beat the real world when it comes to testing actual purchasing behavior and consumer acceptance of a product. Note that test marketing involves scientific testing and controlled experimentation, not just trying something out in the marketplace. Simply introducing a product in a small geographical area before introducing it nationally is not test marketing.

Test marketing serves two important functions for management. First, it provides an opportunity to estimate the outcomes of alternative courses of action. Managers can estimate the sales effect of a specific marketing variable—such as package design, price, or couponing—and then select the best alternative action with regard to that variable. Second, test market experimentation allows management to identify and correct any weaknesses in either the product or its marketing plan before making the commitment to a national sales launch, by which time it is normally too late to make changes.

In selecting test markets, the marketer must choose cities that are representative of the population—of all cities and towns—throughout the United States. Test market cities should be representative in terms of competitive situation, media usage patterns, product usage, and other relevant factors. Of course, no one ideal test market is a perfect miniature of the entire United States. Nevertheless, it is important to avoid selecting areas with atypical climates, unusual ethnic composition, or uncommon lifestyles, any of which may have a dramatic impact on the acceptance of a new product. Some of the most popular test markets are mid-sized cities where costs won't be prohibitive, such as Tulsa, Charlotte, Green Bay, Nashville, Omaha, and Spokane.

Test marketing is expensive. Developing local distribution, arranging media coverage, and monitoring sales results take considerable effort. The cost of test marketing a consumer product can exceed several million. However, if a firm must commit a substantial amount of money to investments in plant and equipment to manufacture a new product, the cost of test marketing may appear minimal compared with the cost of a possible product failure. The marketer, then, must balance the cost of test marketing against the risk of not test marketing. McDonald's marketers were glad they choose to test market McPizza, a single serving of pizza, because consumers didn't find the idea of pizza at McDonald's appealing.

Commercialization

Commercialization
The stage in new product development in which the decision is made to launch a new product's full-scale production and distribution.

After passing through the filtering stages in the development process, the new product is ready for the final stage. It is **commercialization,** the decision to launch full-scale production and distribution. The decision entails risking a great deal of money, because this stage involves a serious commitment of resources and managerial effort. It is the last chance to stop the project if managers think the risks are too high. Many successful marketing firms, such as Procter & Gamble, remain willing to stop a project right to the last moment. Although a lot of money may have been spent in reaching the commercialization stage, any amount is small compared with the sums that full commercialization will demand.

Even when great caution is employed, product failures still occur. It is not difficult to find products that should have been killed before commercialization. For example, the Dow Chemical Company developed a compound of resins and methanol to be sprayed on car tires to increase their ability to maintain traction on ice. The product, Liquid Tire Chain, truly did work, as proved by in-use testing. Not surprisingly, however, buyers stored the pressurized cans of the product in their cars' trunks. When the aerosol containers froze in winter weather, the material within them solidified, making the product useless. The in-use tests Dow had undertaken somehow missed this factor. The product failed, unfortunately for Dow, after commercialization. Had testing been more complete, this could have been avoided.

WHY DO NEW PRODUCTS FAIL?

New product failures and near-failures occur with some regularity. As we pointed out earlier, it is estimated that one in three new product introductions fail. Consider that Pillsbury's Oven Lovin', a cookie dough loaded with Hershey's chocolate chips, Reese's Pieces, and Brach's candies in a resealable tub, failed after millions of dollars had been spent in the new product development process. After researching the Oven Lovin' concept by surveying consumers, the company in a cost-saving effort skipped test marketing and launched the product nationally. Unfortunately for Pillsbury, consumers, based on limited experience during the survey, said they liked the Oven Lovin' resealable tubs. At home, however, many shoppers found they ended up baking the entire package at once—or gobbling up leftover dough raw instead of saving it—eliminating the need for the pricier packaging. The product failed within two years of its introduction.

Cajun Cola tried to compete regionally against Pepsi and Coke at a time when the two cola giants were engaged in an intensive cola war, with reduced prices and increased advertising. Cajun Cola didn't have the resources to compete.

General Mills introduced Benefit, a high-soluble-fiber cereal made with psyllium, and stressed its ability to reduce cholesterol levels. When sales did not meet expectations, the company learned that although consumers understood the role of oat bran in reducing cholesterol levels, they were confused about the term soluble fiber. The death knell for the product rang when a barrage of publicity questioned whether Benefit with psyllium was a drug or a cereal.

What are the most common reasons for product failures? Here, briefly stated, are several:

- *Inadequate product superiority or uniqueness.* If a "me, too" product is merely an imitation of products that are already on the market, if it does not offer the consumer a relative advantage, the product may be doomed from the start. Gift Mates, brightly colored batteries designed to coordinate with Christmas gift wrappings, failed to generate much interest. This new product lasted only two holiday seasons.
- *Inadequate or inferior planning.* Many product failures stem from failure to conduct proper marketing research about consumers' needs and failure to develop realistic forecasts of market demand and accurate estimates of the acceptance of new products.[8] Overly optimistic managers may underestimate the strength of existing competition. They fail to anticipate future competitive reactions and the need for sizable promotional budgets. Too often, the enthusiastic developer of a new product is surprised to find that it takes more time and effort than expected to launch a new product successfully. Fab 1 Shot, the single-packet washer-to-dryer detergent with fabric softener, provides a perfect example. Procter & Gamble and Clorox were test-marketing similar products when Colgate-Palmolive, anxious to beat its rivals to market, commercialized Fab 1 Shot. Initially, the product, which was supported with coupons and rebates, sold well. But when the company began pricing to make a profit, it quickly learned that although people found the product convenient, it was not cost-effective for large families. The lesson Colgate-Palmolive learned in the marketplace was learned in test markets by its competitors, who spent more time planning.
- *Poor execution.* No matter how good the plans, adequate resources must be allocated so that strategies can be properly executed. Many new products fail because managers who think the product is so good it will sell itself do not provide adequate resources for tactical execution. For example, Pillsbury failed

with AppleEasy because at the last minute, it reduced the amount of apples in its recipe in response to increasing apple prices. In addition, sometimes a new product requires production or marketing activities for which the organization lacks expertise, and the product fails for that reason.

- *Technical problems.* Problems may stem from the product itself—failures in production or design. Hot Scoops, a microwavable hot fudge sundae, caused consumers problems. If the microwave timer wasn't set exactly right, the consumer ended up with a mess rather than a sundae.
- *Poor timing.* The market may have changed before the new product was introduced, or the company may have entered the market too early or too late in the product life cycle. For instance, if a new luxury product is introduced just as a downturn in the economy occurs, the product's chances for success are substantially reduced.

All managers planning new product introductions have one thing in common: They must attempt to predict the future. The product designed in 1998 but commercialized in 2000 may meet an environment somewhat different from the one that existed when the product was being designed. Hence, marketing plans may not work as well as expected. New product marketing deals with forecasting. As the wry old adage goes, "Forecasts are dangerous, particularly those about the future."

THE ROLE OF THE ENTREPRENEUR

Entrepreneur
A risk-taking individual who sees an opportunity and is willing to undertake a venture to create a new product or service.

An **entrepreneur** is someone willing to undertake a venture to create something new. He or she is an individual who sees an opportunity and is willing to work long and hard to turn an idea into a business. The story of the entrepreneurial development of the personal computer is well known. Starting out in a garage, two risk-taking individuals with a vision built the first personal computer and then developed Apple Computer into a multinational corporation. Entrepreneurs throughout the world who assume all the risks associated with their innovative ideas have always been at the cutting edge of new product development. We should not underestimate the potential of creative, optimistic, and hard-working individuals who risk their own money and work in their garages to make something happen.[9]

We have already said that most new product ideas fail. We have also said that most innovations today come from organizational research and development. However, a creative person taking a proactive stance to develop a novel idea with a low chance for success can succeed—not often, but it does happen—and sometimes success can be great.

Often, the entrepreneur's vision becomes a product without formal marketing research or any activity that resembles the new product development process discussed earlier in this chapter. It is beyond the entrepreneur's power to do anything else. Simply put, entrepreneurs don't have enough money to launch their ideas the way they would like to. Because they are on their own, however, and because the rewards can be enormous, they find ways to get the job done.

Entrepreneurs may bend some of the rules discussed in this chapter. That does not mean that these principles do not serve as good guidelines for effective marketing; it means that success can come by other means. The many stories about entrepreneurs who refused to fail, who sacrificed their personal lives, and who ultimately were successful suggest that creativity, an understanding of unmet consumer needs, and hard work can pay off with new product successes.

Intrapreneurial
A term describing an organization that encourages individuals to take risks and gives them the autonomy to develop new products as they see fit.

Many large organizations try to instill an entrepreneurial spirit in their new product development process. A large organization is **intrapreneurial** when it encourages individuals to take risks and gives them the autonomy to develop new products as they see fit.

EXHIBIT 10–3
The Product Life Cycle:
Introduction, Growth,
Maturity, and Decline

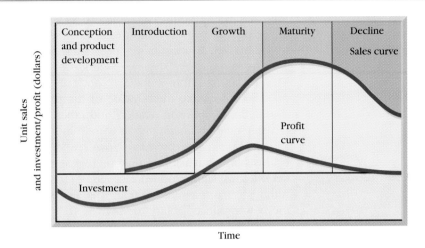

THE PRODUCT LIFE CYCLE

Product Life Cycle
A marketing management concept providing a graphic description of a product's sales history. The cycle is depicted as having four stages: introduction, growth, maturity, and decline.

The **product life cycle** is a graphic depiction of a product's sales history from its *birth*, or marketing beginning, to its *death*, or withdrawal from the market. Generally, a product begins its life with its first sale, rises to some peak level of sales, and then declines until its sales volume and contribution to profits are insufficient to justify its presence in the market. This general pattern does vary from product to product, however. Products such as salt and mustard have been used for thousands of years. Arm & Hammer baking soda has been used for more than 150 years. Cellular phones and fax machines are mere youngsters by comparison. Some products, such as Topp's Talking Baseball Cards, fail at the very start of their lives. But whether a product has a very short, short, long, or very long life, the pattern of that life may be portrayed by a charting of sales volume.

Traditionally, the product life cycle has been thought of as reflecting the life of a product class or product category as a whole—for example, the life cycle of handheld video games as a group, without regard to model or brand. However, marketing managers also use the product life cycle idea in evaluating specific brands of products, because most brands, as well as most products, have limited market lives.

The product life cycle is portrayed in Exhibit 10–3. A product's life, as suggested earlier, typically flows through several distinct stages as sales volume is plotted over time. These stages are introduction, growth, maturity, and decline. Both sales volume and industry profit change over the course of the life cycle. The exhibit also shows the period of product development, which precedes the introductory stage. During this period there are no sales, but investments are being made in the belief that future profitable sales will justify them. The product life cycle, while useful for visualizing the stages of market acceptance, has its greatest practical use as a planning tool. Many successful marketing companies build their strategies around this concept, graph financial and market data against product life cycles, and develop long- and short-range plans that complement each stage.

Introduction Stage
The stage in the product life cycle during which the new product is attempting to gain a foothold in the market.

The Introduction Stage

During the **introduction stage,** the new product attempts to gain a foothold in the market. Sales are likely to be slow at the start of the period because the product is, by definition, new and untried. It takes time to gain acceptance. Sales volume and sales revenues are still low relative to the high expenses associated with developing the product and the marketing mix necessary to introduce the product to the market. In most cases, profits are negative.

The introductory stage is a period of attempting to gain market acceptance. The marketing effort is focused not only on finding first-time buyers and using promotion to make them aware of the product but also on creating channels of distribution—attracting retailers and other intermediaries to handle the product. It is also a time for attempting to recoup most of the research and development costs associated with the product. However, during this period, product alterations or changes in manufacturing may be required to "iron the bugs out" of the new market offering. The introduction stage is, then, typically a high-cost/low-profit period. Although it is an exciting time, it is also a time of uncertainty and anxiety about the new products' ability to survive.

Selecting strategies appropriate to the introductory stage is an important matter, yet organizations differ widely in their choices. Some companies believe that being a pioneer and risk taker is the best approach—the greater the risk, the greater the reward. Thus, in many industries, such as tires and aircraft, the same companies are the leaders in new product development over and over again. Other companies quickly follow the pioneer's lead and jump into the market during the introductory stage. Still others hold back and wait to see whether the new product will actually take off into a growth period. Each approach has obvious advantages and risks that management must weigh.

The length of the introductory stage varies dramatically. Personal computers and home video games gained market acceptance rapidly. Laser disks, on the other hand, took years to reach a modest amount of popularity and experienced rapid decline as soon as CD-ROMs became a mature product. Another product category, concentrated laundry detergent, presents a further example of slow market acceptance. The first serious effort to introduce a product that cleans a whole washload with only a quarter-cup of powder was made in 1976, when Colgate-Palmolive introduced Fresh Start, a powder in a plastic bottle. But rapid sales growth for the category did not occur until 1990, when two other brands, Ultra Tide and Fab Ultra, were successfully introduced. Their marketers succeeded, in part, by stressing the environmental advantage of small packages.

Most skiing equipment is in the mature stage of the product life cycle. However, snowboards, whose sales have doubled in the past five years, are in the growth stage of their product life cycle. The snowboarder shown here has spent quite a bit for equipment.

The Growth Stage

If the product earns market acceptance, it should

Growth Stage

The stage in the product life cycle during which sales increase at an accelerating rate.

at some point enter a period of comparatively rapid growth. The classic product life cycle portrays this **growth stage** as sales increasing at an increasing rate. In other words, sales grow slowly at first but increase at a faster rate later on.

When the product enters its growth stage, profit margins can be expected to be small. As sales continue to increase during this stage, profits can be expected to increase, partly because sales are increasing but also because the start-up expenses encountered earlier can be expected to diminish. As a rule, profits peak late in the growth period.

A product that has entered the growth stage has shown that it may have a future in the marketplace. As a result, the number of competitors and the level of marketing activity can be expected to increase. Pioneering firms are often required to alter their products because competitors, having had the advantage of learning from the pioneer's mistakes and the time to study the market, may have improved on the original. More and more companies that prefer to follow rather than lead recognize an untapped potential market. Competing firms seem to feel that there is enough profit to go around and that they may be able to grab a sizable market share without focusing resources to take away business from each other (as is the case during the maturity stage).

Products still in their growth stages include cellular phones, zip drives, digital cameras, and computerized information and interactive shopping services. During their growth stages, the profits associated with these products will rise (although not for every company), peaking at the end of the period. Distribution costs will be brought under control as channels become more organized and able to perform their tasks routinely. Product quality will be stressed and improved. Persuasive efforts to create brand preference will become the emphasis of promotion. Promotion expenses will be adjusted as rising sales and profits indicate the product's potential.

The Maturity Stage

Maturity Stage

The stage in the product life cycle during which sales increase at a decreasing rate.

As the product approaches the end of its growth period, sales begin to level off. A change in the growth rate—indicated by sales increasing at a decreasing rate—heralds the end of the growth period and the beginning of the **maturity stage.** As Exhibit 10–3 showed, profits level off and then fall in the maturity stage. This is to be expected as competing firms try to operate within a static or slow-growth market. When the growth rate slows down, the product requires marketing strategies and tactics appropriate for the maturity stage. Later in this stage, for reasons such as diminished popularity, product obsolescence, or market saturation (which occurs when most target customers own the product), the product begins to lose market acceptance. Most products on the market are in the maturity phase. During this stage, competition is likely to be intense. After all, one of the goals of effective marketing is to achieve brand maturity and to maintain it for as long as the market supports the product. Further, because a product in the maturity stage has achieved wide market acceptance, the primary means for any one company to increase its market share is to take market share away from competitors. For example, in the mature automotive business, strategies to maintain market share and defend against inroads from foreign competition are common.

One strategy to increase market share is to produce private brands for distributors. Thus, private labels emerge in the maturity stage. An organization selling a mature product may pick up new business in the price-conscious segment of the market as other, less competitive companies withdraw. Persuading existing users to use more of the product may also be a major objective for marketers of mature brands. Many food products advertise recipes that require their product as an ingredient to foster increased usage.

Organizations in mature markets have solved most of the technological problems encountered early in the product life cycle. The products require little tech-

This M&M's advertisement plays off the idea that gray is not one of the chocolate candy's new hues. M&M's candy is in the mature stage of the product life cycle.

nological improvement, and changes become largely a matter of style. For example, in 1996 M&M's introduced 24 new hues—including navy blue, light purple, and teal green. (Incidentally, the classic five-color combination packages sell for $2.79 a pound but the new colors, which will be sold only in specialty stores, are priced at $5–$7 a pound.) Fashionable designs and model variations become important during the product's maturity.

Although Exhibit 10–3 showed that industry profits generally peak near the end of the growth stage, many individual firms in mature market situations are very profitable. A major reason for this is the experience gained during the earlier stages. Development of economies of scale also play a part. Organizations in mature markets whose brands are profitable typically use the funds these brands generate to support other items in the product mix. The laundry detergent industry is certainly in its mature stage, but industry leader Procter & Gamble uses the sizable profits generated by Tide and Cheer to pay for the development and introduction of new product items and lines.

Successful marketing managers, recognizing the onset of maturity, investigate the causes of that maturity. The marketer may find that a product is in the mature stage because it has become, and remains, widely used (like roofing supplies or tires) and that sales volume remains stable. In contrast, sales may have peaked because an alternative product or brand has become popular owing to some environmental change. The effective marketer needs to know why a product is in its maturity stage, not just that it is there. With this knowledge and careful planning to improve or change product features, the marketer may be able to extend the length of the maturity stage.

The Decline Stage

Decline Stage

The stage in the product life cycle during which the product loses market acceptance because of such factors as diminished popularity, obsolescence, and market saturation.

The **decline stage** in the product life cycle is marked by falling sales and falling profits. A shakeout in the number of firms in the industry is likely as managers become aware that the product has entered the decline stage. Survivor firms compete within an ever-smaller market, driving profit margins lower still. Ironically, the last surviving firm or firms may, as individual organizations, enjoy high profits at this point. This is because most competitors have withdrawn from the market, leaving what is left to one or two suppliers. Makers of parts for Edsel and

De Lorean automobiles are neither large nor numerous, yet they can survive by catering to car collectors. Brylcreem, Ovaltine, Good & Plenty, and blacksmiths are not as common as they once were, but they still survive. Nevertheless, profits for the industry will be low, because only one or two producers are left. Eventually, the decline stage ends with the disappearance of the product from the market.

FOCUS ON TRENDS

The Recording Industry

The humble black phonograph record, a mainstay of the music industry for nearly a century, is a virtually extinct species. Because of consumer preferences for audiocassettes and compact discs, conventional record albums now account for just a tiny portion of U.S. recorded-music sales (down from 30 percent of the market in 1985). Faced with this drastic decline, music marketers now are thinking about what was once the unthinkable: the prospect of a recording industry that doesn't sell records. Vinyl records are at the end of their life cycle. In contrast, since the compact disc player's introduction in 1983, CD sales have grown rapidly and now exceed the sales of audiocassettes. For more than a decade CDs were in the growth stage. Today compact disc players are in the mature stage of their product life cycle. Digital versatile disks (DVD), an alternative to the CD, are brand new. If they receive the support of recording studios, compact discs will move into the decline stage of the product life cycle.

Do All Products Follow a Product Life Cycle?

All products follow a product life cycle. All products are introduced, and most eventually disappear. But the shapes of the product life cycles, the rates of change in sales and profits, and the lengths and heights of the cycles vary greatly. As Exhibit 10–4 shows, some products, like peanut butter, seem to be firmly preserved in the maturity stage forever, whereas others, such as novelty items like talking baseball cards, have very short life cycles.

Indeed, when we look at the life cycles of specific brands, we find that marketers may expect their brands to have short lives. Cereals, snack foods, and toys, for example, may gain considerable profits as fad items. Teenage Mutant Ninja Turtles and Batman cereals were expected to be only short-term successes. Similarly,

EXHIBIT 10–4
Long and Short of Product Life Cycles

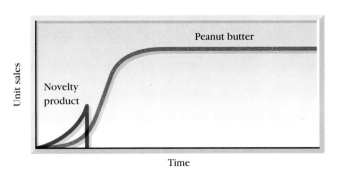

Most movies have very short product life cycles. The Trilogy of Star Wars movies and videos, however, has followed a much different life cycle pattern. Creative marketing efforts to enhance the film have extended the product's life cycle.

General Foods used carbonated confection technology to produce several fad bubble gum and candy items, including Increda Bubble, Pop Rocks, and Space Dust. These fad candies, as well as some more familiar products, are marketed on a cyclical basis that reflects a belief that their faddish nature does not justify year-round marketing expenditures. Other products are brought back in essentially unchanged form once a new generation of buyers has replaced the old. Many stories in Walt Disney comic books and movies on videotape are republished once an age cohort of readers has been replaced by a younger group. These sorts of products have short lives. Marketers aware of this can develop strategies appropriate for short product life cycles.

Is There Life after Decline?

Occasionally a product life cycle changes slope, reversing the downward trend associated with the late maturity and decline stages. Some products and brands approach extinction only to suddenly achieve new-found popularity. Such a turn of events may be due to nostalgia or to the sudden realization that an old, familiar brand or product was really pretty good after all. A change in the marketing environment may bring this about. In the last decade, for example, considerable medical attention has been given to proper nutrition and exercise as a means of maintaining good health. Fiber in the diet has been an important issue. Some new products appeared in response to this and other nutrition-related concerns, and certain old products were suddenly more in demand. Granola, soups, and natural sweeteners such as honey were among these products, and they are marketed accordingly. Similarly, the concern with physical fitness helped the sales of jogging shoes, jump ropes, bicycles, and exercise machines.[10]

Another social change has helped Erector sets, popular in the 1950s, to experience a revival in the 1990s. After a 10-year absence, Erector sets returned to the U.S. market for Christmas 1991. By Christmas 1993, Santa Claus was finding Erector sets on the wish lists of both boys and girls. In fact, that December, five 11-year old girls won Erector building contests. Erector sets are part of a "crossover" trend; marketers now realize that toys once thought appropriate only for boys are popular with girls, too.[11]

THE ADOPTION AND DIFFUSION PROCESSES

At all stages of the product life cycle, but especially during the introduction stage, organizations are concerned with who will actually buy, use, or in some other way adopt the product. Marketers who understand why and when customers accept new products are able to effectively manage product strategy over the course of a product's life cycle. This understanding involves the related processes of adoption and diffusion.

When someone purchases a product never before tried, that person may ultimately become an adopter. The mental and behavioral stages through which an individual consumer passes before actually making a purchase or placing an order constitute the **adoption process.** These stages are *awareness, interest, evaluation, trial,* and finally, *adoption.*

Not all potential buyers go through the stages of the adoption process at the same rate of speed. Some pass through them very quickly and are the first to adopt the new product. Others take longer to become aware of the product and to make up their minds to purchase it. Still others take a very long time to accept and adopt the product. This spread of the new product through society is called the **diffusion process.** The stages in the diffusion process can be charted, as shown in Exhibit 10–5. As the exhibit shows, these stages are closely related to the product life cycle.

To clarify the difference between the adoption process and the diffusion process, remember that individuals psychologically go through the various stages of adoption, but the new product as it is purchased by the various groups of adopters is diffused through the social system.[12]

Adoption Process
The mental and behavioral stages through which an individual passes before making a purchase or placing an order. The stages are awareness, interest, evaluation, trial, and adoption.

Diffusion Process
The spread of a new product through society.

EXHIBIT 10–5
The Diffusion Process Occurs over the Course of the Product Life Cycle

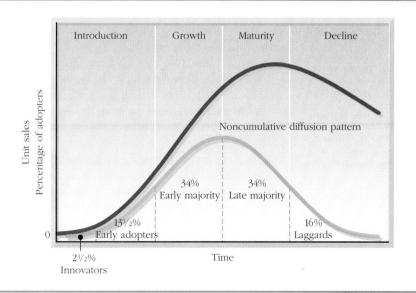

Innovators—Being Venturesome

Innovators—the consumers most likely to try something new—are the first to buy a new product. These people are venturesome, willing to be daring and different. They are the customers most confident in thinking for themselves and most likely to deviate from their local community's established way of doing things. Because they are eager to try new ideas, innovators are extremely important in getting a new product accepted in the market. As Exhibit 10–5 shows, this venturesome group's membership is small in number. As might be expected, members of this group are likely to be younger and better educated than the average consumer. They are generally higher-income buyers or financially stable individuals who can afford to take a chance on something new.

Early Adopters—Following the Lead

A larger group, but a somewhat less adventurous one than the innovators, is the **early adopter** group. Many characteristics of the innovator group also are found among the early adopters, because being an early adopter often requires the income, self-confidence, and education to use a product that has still not gained wide acceptance. A major difference, however, is that innovators adopt the product during the introduction stage of the product life cycle, while most early adopters buy the product during the growth stage.

Early adopters read more magazines than average and have high usage rates in the product category in which the innovation falls. Although members of this group follow the lead of the innovators, they are more integrated into their local communities. Early adopters are conceived of as opinion leaders who help to determine which new products later adopters will find acceptable. Early adopters can be expected to influence their friends and coworkers and thus to contribute mightily to a new product's progress. Developers of new products therefore spend considerable time and resources in identifying and reaching this group. They are a significant target for advertisements and other promotions aimed at creating a market where none existed before.

Early and Late Majorities—Riding the Bandwagon

The **early** and **late majorities,** taken together, constitute approximately 68 percent of the overall group that adopts a new product (see Exhibit 10–5). They make up the mass market on which many products depend. The two halves of this market are seen as having similar characteristics in differing degrees.

The early majority is usually made up of solid, middle-class consumers who are more deliberate and cautious in making purchasing decisions than are early adopters. Once this group adopts a new product, late in the growth stage, the product's acceptance and its diffusion throughout the social system are well established. In general, members of the early majority are of average socioeconomic status. Slightly less educated and financially stable are those in the late majority, who also are identified as older, more conservative, and more traditional. As time goes by and more and more consumers adopt an innovation, it is perceived to be less risky. At this time, the product has reached maturity, and the late majority adopts the innovation. Members of the late majority are skeptical about new product ideas and adopt innovations only reluctantly when the products no longer carry the risk associated with newness. Social pressure also may force late adopters to purchase a product.

Laggards—Bringing Up the Rear

Laggards, or final adopters, make up the last group to adopt a product. These people can make use of the product but for economic, social, or educational reasons have been slow to accept it. Innovations are not welcome with this older group, which is lowest in socioeconomic status. Laggards resist challenges to past fashion and traditions. The laggard group is especially easily identified when the product in question is clothing. Frequently, a new clothing design is adopted by innovators, early adopters, and members of the majority groups and then dropped by them as the laggard group begins to wear the style.

Nonadopters—Holding Out

No matter what the innovation, there are always some individuals who never buy the new product or adopt the new style. These people are termed **nonadopters.**

Use of the Adopter Categories

Planners about to introduce a new product should give close consideration to the diffusion process and the various adoption categories. Characteristics of the various adopter groups may provide the basis for market segmentation efforts. As we have seen, youth, economic resources, adventurousness, and other possible segmenting variables are usually not spread evenly among the adopter groups. Thought and research intended to discover the characteristics of adopters can help the new product on its way and will surely pay off for marketing managers. As the target marketing and positioning focus shifts from early adopters to the early majority and late majority, promotional and other marketing plans, including changes in prices and distribution, should be changed. Indeed, even the product strategy should be modified.

STRATEGIES FOR MODIFYING EXISTING PRODUCTS

New products should be carefully designed to appeal to carefully selected target markets. However, most products and brands enjoy limited lives because of the dynamic nature of competition within those markets. Effective product strategy does not fulfill its obligation merely by contributing to the design of the product; its role is ongoing. Dynamic markets must be monitored and researched so that appropriate strategies—designed to keep old customers, to attract new ones, and to extend the product life cycle—can be devised. Developing strategies for modifying existing products and managing the product mix is an important aspect of product management.

As has been stressed time and time again, no single facet of the marketing mix stands alone. Each facet must be viewed in light of what it contributes to the total mix, and each must be consistent with, and supportive of, the other variables. Despite these strong interrelationships, a series of marketing strategies closely allied with the marketing mix variable of product have been developed. It is to these that we now turn our attention.

The marketer's decision about **product modification**—that is, the altering or adjusting of the product mix—is typically influenced by the competitive nature of the market (such as design changes made by competitors) and by changes in the external environment (such as the discovery of a new technology). For example, in 1994, a fashion designer convinced the Hush Puppies company to dye its classic suede loafers to match his fall collection.[13] When the fashion press gave rave reviews, Hush Puppies decided that modifying its product and marketing the loafers in many funky colors would appeal to a younger target market. Sales skyrocketed.

Most product modification decisions attempt to create a competitive advantage, such as product differentiation or reduced costs. We will discuss three general strategies for modifying existing products: cost reduction, repositioning, and total quality management strategies.

Cost Reduction Strategies

Cost Reduction Strategy
A product strategy that involves redesigning a product to lower production costs.

As new competitors, perhaps global competitors with factories in newly industrialized countries, enter the market, profits may be squeezed. The company with a product in the maturity or decline stage may choose to introduce a **cost reduction strategy.** This product strategy requires redesigning the product and working in harmony with production experts to lower factory or sevice delivery costs.

Implementing a cost reduction strategy may require moving production to another country. Stanley Works, a company that 30 years ago produced all its tools in New England, now operates a factory in Puebla, Mexico, to make sledgehammers and wrecking bars. Low-cost labor was essential to compete with inexpensive imports from China.

Often, a company elects to produce a stripped-down version of the initial product made with less expensive materials to target price-conscious market segments. However, the cost reduction strategy does not always mean that quality suffers.

Repositioning Strategies

A repositioning strategy changes the product design, formulation, brand image, or brand name so as to alter the product's competitive position. Reformulating a soft drink to use NutraSweet instead of sugar, for example, may be intended to change the product's major benefit (a sweet treat) to a new benefit (weight control). Repositioning strategies typically include a corresponding change in promotion strategy. A change in the market environment or an initial mistake in brand name selection may mean that a name or symbol has to be changed to reposition the brand. The original brand name may have been a bad choice that grew worse over time. This was the case with Heartwise cereal, whose name was changed to Fiberwise after the Food and Drug Administration argued there was no evidence that the cereal was good for the heart. In other instances, a brand name or trademark symbol may serve long and well but become inappropriate as the brand ages and times change. For example, Betty Crocker's looks have changed over the years to reflect current clothing and hairstyles.

Around the world, organizations are repositioning themselves to indicate changes resulting from merger, diversification, or international interests. As international trade becomes ever more important, companies are adding words like International and Worldwide to their official names. However, each name change, especially when the original name is well established, involves many risks. Goodwill may be lost if clients fail to realize that the new company is the same as the old one.

Total Quality Management Strategies

Total Quality Management Strategy
A product strategy that emphasizes market-driven quality. Also called quality assurance strategy.

Total quality management strategies, or **quality assurance strategies,** emphasize market-driven quality as a top priority. In Chapter 2, we indicated that for many years, some U.S. corporations did not keep pace with the product quality offered by a number of overseas competitors. Today, with intense levels of global

COMPETITIVE STRATEGY: WHAT WENT RIGHT?

Silicon Graphics, Inc., Cultivates Its Most Demanding Customers

If you're running a highly successful company, the vast majority of your customers are apt to be satisfied with your products. Terrific. Maybe too terrific. How do you push your company to maintain the pace of innovation that will ensure its continuing prosperity? You seek out the customers most difficult to satisfy.

Ed McCracken, chairman of Silicon Graphics, Inc., has established a practice of actively cultivating customers who want to do things that just can't be done with the company's products—or anyone else's, for that matter. Silicon Graphics then works closely with these cutting-edge customers to design the next generation of its computers. The customers' dreams and unmet demands drive the design of the new system, pushing Silicon Graphics' engineers.

In the early 1980s, the military was Silicon Graphics' most demanding customer, the one that was willing and able to spend whatever it took to achieve the impossible. That stopped with the defense cutbacks following the end of the Cold War. Now that leadership role has been taken on by Hollywood's entertainment industry, which is entranced by high tech. Silicon Graphics has been developing the latest version of its most powerful and expensive product, the Onyx graphics supercomputer (priced at $200,000 to $1 million), specifically to meet the demands of Walt Disney's Imagineering group, which creates attractions for the famous theme parks.

Disney's version is a virtual-reality ride based on its movie Aladdin. Tourists will strap on special headgear with visual displays that give them the illusion of flying on a magic carpet through Aladdin's home base, the desert town of Agrabah. Disney engineers had backed away from attempting a virtual-reality attraction because, with earlier systems, the new medium's quality was still discouragingly spotty. Not only did the graphics lack truly realistic detail, but the motion sometimes seemed jerky or subtly out of sync—enough to make the viewer nauseated. The Disney people insisted on a computer graphics system that would closely re-create the look of the movie without compromises. Driven by this criterion, Silicon Graphics has been redesigning the Onyx, which it will sell to other corporate customers as well. Disney opened the Aladdin ride in Orlando, Florida, in 1995.

---

competition, most companies must adopt a total quality management philosophy. Total quality management involves properly implementing and adjusting the product mix and processes within the entire organization to ensure customers' satisfaction with product quality. It is a strategy based on the conviction that if an organization wishes to prosper, every employee must work for continuous quality improvement.

What is quality? Organizations once defined quality by engineering standards. Most marketers today don't see quality that way. Some marketers say that quality means that their good or service conforms to the consumers' requirements—that the product is acceptable. Effective marketers subscribing to a total quality management philosophy, however, believe that the product's quality must go beyond acceptability for a given price range. Rather than having consumers pleased that nothing went wrong, consumers should experience some delightful surprises or reap some unexpected benefits. In other words, quality assurance is more than just meeting minimum standards. Total quality management requires continuous improvement of product quality, enhancement of products with additional features as the products age, or both.

Managers continuously improve product quality to keep their brands competitive. Obviously, a Bentley from Rolls-Royce does not compete with a Geo Storm from General Motors. Buyers of these automobiles are in different market segments, and their expectations of quality differ widely. Nevertheless, marketers at both Rolls-Royce and General Motors try to establish what quality level their target market expects and then attempt to market goods and services that continually surpass

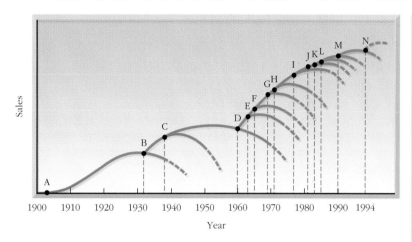

Blade	Year Introduced
A. Original Gillette blade	1903
B. Blue blade	1932
C. Thin blade	1938
D. Super blue blade	1960
E. Stainless steel blade	1963
F. Super stainless steel blade	1965
G. Platinum-plus blade	1969
H. Trac II	1971
I. ATRA	1977
J. Good News	1981
K. Good News Pivot	1983
L. ATRA Plus	1985
M. Sensor	1990
N. Sensor Excel	1994

EXHIBIT 10–6
Gillette Razor Blades'
Product Life Cycle

Product Enhancement
*The introduction of a new
and improved version of an
existing product, intended to
extend the product's life
cycle by keeping it in the
growth stage.*

expectations. Marketers expect **product enhancement**—the introduction of a new and improved version of an existing brand—to extend a product's life cycle by keeping it in the growth stage. A master at this strategy is the Gillette Company. Exhibit 10–6 depicts the product life cycle for Gillette razors. Notice how the company has managed to keep its basic product alive by steadily improving blades and razors. Gillette's strategy heavily emphasizes improving product performance— how well the razors shave. Product performance, however, is only one aspect of quality. Other dimensions are described in Exhibit 10–7.

Many of the dimensions of quality in Exhibit 10–7 are influenced by the quality of raw materials, production technology, and quality control at the factory. Middle-level marketing managers, while they do have some influence on these areas, do not have the primary decision-making responsibility for these activities. To ensure production quality, therefore, top management must communicate the consumers' needs to those who have production authority.

FOCUS ON QUALITY

Jeep

Chrysler Corporation, Jeep's parent company, asked the approximately 380 paint line workers who wash, wipe, and prepare Jeep Cherokees and Comanches for painting to stop using antiperspirants. Total quality management is the reason why. Chrysler's investigation showed that antiperspirants worn by workers flaked and fell onto the new paint. Antiperspirants contain chemicals, such as zinc zirconium, that can damage paint. The paint flows away from the fallen flake, causing a depression about the size of a baby's fingertip. "Who would've known that spraying that . . . under your arms would hurt the finish?" asked Freddie Robinson, a plant worker for eight years.

Chrysler looked into the matter after its quality control system reported that every vehicle coming off the line had up to 50 imperfections on the roof and hood. Such damage can be enough for an inspector to send a car back for thousands of dollars in repairs.

Jeep workers are not banned from wearing antiperspirants, but they are being educated about the problem. An awareness program that employees helped develop includes a training session that shows some of the common causes of paint flaws. "You do what you got to do," said one paint line worker. "We want to turn out the best Jeeps. If antiperspirants are causing problems, you got to give them up."

critics reacted. Critics, who contend the new genes that go into these tomatoes may be medically and environmentally unsafe, want genetically engineered tomatoes to be labeled. They want the **right to be informed.**[17]

Right to Be Informed
The consumer's right to have access to the information required to make an intelligent choice from among the available products.

Most people agree that the consumer should not be exposed to grossly misleading information, deceptive advertising, fraudulent labeling, or other deceitful practices. The consumer has the right to be given the facts needed to make an informed choice. Requirements relating to truth-in-lending and package design also point out the importance of this right. The right to be informed is also reflected in laws and practices involving the labeling of such things as nutritional content, product content, country of origin, and quality.

Quality of Life and Ecology

As the United States, Canada, and certain other nations have become more affluent, the values of their citizens have changed. People are increasingly concerned with **quality of life.** This term, although difficult to define precisely, reflects a lessening concern with being economically well-off and an increasing concern with well-being.

Quality of Life
The sense of well-being perceived by people in a society.

In the business community, this shift translates into a feeling that organizations should be expected to be more than economically efficient. Customers call on business organizations to be economically efficient, to preserve the environment, and to conserve natural resources—all at the same time.

Quality of life issues spring from the idea that citizens have certain rights that no organization can be permitted to violate. Meeting quality-of-life expectations while fulfilling other missions has caused organizations many problems. Yet if the demands of consumers—most of whom are interested in both quality-of-life issues and the demands of the law—are to be met, organizations must address these problems.

A major quality-of-life issue involves ecology and the protection of the environment. Many people believe that organizations, as important members of society, have a responsibility not to tamper with or damage the environment. However,

Around the world there is a growing ecological concern. Many consumers will use only products that do not harm the environment.

this issue is complex, because people want other things as well. Environmental issues are loaded with trade-offs such as these:

- Marketers of electric power are told that nuclear plants are disruptive to ecosystems and very dangerous. Yet people want low-priced electricity and do not want to burn coal, which causes both air pollution and disfigurement of the earth through mining.
- Nonreturnable cans and bottles create litter problems and damage the environment in other ways. But people do not like the bother and expense associated with returnables and often just throw them away.
- People want and enjoy convenience in fast-food packaging but complain that wrappers cause litter problems.

The fact that marketing has a social responsibility to our environment is obvious. What is not obvious is how that responsibility will be met. Who will pay—in dollars and inconvenience—for a cleaner environment? Is society willing to pay a higher price for products that reduce pollution? Does society place a higher value on lower-priced automobiles or on clean air?

Perhaps a cleaner environment can be partially achieved by recycling waste products to make "new" products. The recycling process can reduce trash and litter and conserve natural resources.

Product Obsolescence

Product Obsolescence
The condition in which an existing product becomes out of date because of the introduction of a new product.

Physical Obsolescence
Breakdown of a product due to wear and tear.

Planned Obsolescence
The practice of consciously attempting to make existing products out of date by frequently introducing new products at planned intervals.

Right to Choose
The consumer's right to have viable alternatives from which to choose.

The issue of **product obsolescence,** which occurs when an existing product becomes out of date because of the introduction of a new product, is another ethical concern. Some critics have said it is inappropriate for marketers to strive to make existing products obsolete, or out of date—especially when the obsolescence is related to a change in fashion rather than technology.

To be sure, no product lasts forever. When a product breaks down because of wear and tear, as when a lawn mower breaks down after six years, **physical obsolescence** occurs. **Planned obsolescence** is more controversial. Because new products yield the greatest profits, marketers may plan product obsolescence to help maintain an adequate profit level and ensure corporate survival. Many products, then, are designed not to last a long time. Although it may sound paradoxical, this is generally an attempt to satisfy consumer needs. For most consumers, purchasing a $450 lawn mower that lasts for six summers is preferable to spending $1,400 for one that lasts thirty years. Furthermore, individuals in our culture find new styles of apparel, extra gadgets on appliances, and the latest automobile models more attractive. Although these style changes may not improve the performance of a product, they satisfy a number of psychological and social needs.

Product obsolescence is part of a broader issue that has been called the **consumers' right to choose** within a free enterprise system. Some argue that planned obsolescence violates consumers' rights to have alternatives from which to choose; they suggest that consumers are being manipulated. Others argue that although the macromarketing system has occasionally failed to observe consumers' right to choose, if a poor product is offered or if a product unnecessarily becomes obsolete, competitors usually take advantage of the situation by offering those products demanded by consumers.

Our free enterprise system, with rare exception, does serve the consumer's right to choose, and serves it well. This right is interrelated with the need for competition. The Sherman Act, the Clayton Act, the Federal Trade Commission Act, the Robinson-Patman Act, the Wheeler-Lea Act, and the Celler amendment to the Clayton Act all protect consumer choice. Each of these acts is discussed elsewhere in this book.

SUMMARY

Products differ in their degree of newness and in their chance of succeeding in the marketplace. Marketers must understand what is involved in developing and introducing new products. They must also understand the product life cycle and plan strategies to enable their products to succeed throughout the life cycle.

Learning Objective 1
Define product newness, and explain the chances of success and failure for new products.
Managers and consumers view newness differently. Managers classify new products on the basis of newness to the company and newness to the market. Consumers distinguish products on a newness continuum that includes discontinuous innovations, dynamically continuous innovations, and continuous innovations. A new product's chances for commercial success are generally low, especially for consumer products.

Learning Objective 2
Identify general product characteristics of successful new products.
Five product characteristics influence a new product's chances for success in the marketplace: (1) relative advantage, a clear-cut improvement over existing products; (2) compatibility with existing consumption and usage patterns; (3) trialability, which permits buyers to test the new product with little effort or risk; (4) observability, which allows the buyer to see and understand the product's advantages over existing products; and (5) product simplicity, which allows the consumer to understand and operate the product.

Learning Objective 3
Characterize the stages of new product development.
New product development involves five processes: (1) idea generation, the search for a new idea; (2) screening, the evaluation of an idea's suitability to the organization and target markets; (3) business analysis, the detailed study and testing of the new idea; (4) development, the construction and testing of the actual product; and (5) commercialization, the full-scale production and marketing of the new product.

Learning Objective 4
Identify some of the most common reasons for new product failures.
Some of the most common reasons for new product failures are inadequate product superiority, inferior or

inadequate planning, poor execution, technical problems, and poor timing.

Learning Objective 5
Describe the product life cycle, and characterize the stages of the product life cycle.
The product life cycle charts the sales history of a product from introduction to withdrawal. The life cycle stages are introduction, growth, maturity, and decline. The introduction stage is characterized by large expenditures, an intensive marketing effort, and low profits. In this stage, the marketer must generate product awareness and create channels of distribution. The growth stage involves large expenditures and increasing competition, as well as rapid sales growth. The marketer must create brand preferences and promote differential features. During the maturity stage, sales growth decreases, reflecting intense competition. The goal is to maintain or expand market share. Decreasing profits and decreasing expenditures mark the decline stage. Introducing a new and improved product may reverse declines in sales, but termination is typically the final phase.

Learning Objective 6
Describe the new product diffusion process, and list the groups of adopters to whom marketers must direct their appeals.
Not all buyers adopt a new product at the same time. The path is blazed by innovators, followed by early adopters, members of the early and late majorities, and finally laggards. Members of the first groups tend to be younger, more adventurous, better educated, and wealthier than members of later groups. Each group has characteristics and concerns that the marketer must address.

Learning Objective 7
Identify strategies for modifying existing products.
Developing strategies for modifying existing products is an important aspect of product management. These strategies include cost reduction, repositioning, and total quality management. Decisions to modify products are typically influenced by the degree of competition in the marketplace and by changes in the external environment.

Learning Objective 8
Explain the total quality management process for goods and services.

Total quality management programs measure quality from the customer's perspective and adjust product strategies accordingly. Implementing a total quality management strategy involves discovering what customers want, establishing quantitative measures to serve as benchmarks, establishing the quality improvement process within the organization, measuring customer satisfaction with the improvements, and so on in a continuous process of quality improvement.

Learning Objective 9
Understand how marketers manage product lines.
The product line strategy, which attempts to match product items to markets, is influenced by the diversity of the market and the resources available to the company. Marketers must ask themselves how many variations of a product can be offered before the extra customer satisfaction achieved is no longer worth the expense to the company.

Learning Objective 10
Identify some ethical questions associated with product strategy.
Ethical issues associated with product strategy include those involving the right to safety, the right to be informed, and the quality of life. The issue of whether product obsolescence, and especially planned obsolescence, is ethical is part of a broader issue dealing with the consumers' right to choose.

KEY TERMS

New product (p. 248)
Discontinuous innovation (p. 249)
Dynamically continuous innovation (p. 249)
Continuous innovation (p. 250)
Relative advantage (p. 251)
Trialability (p. 251)
Trial sampling (p. 251)
Divisibility (p. 251)
Observability (p. 252)
Simplicity of usage (p. 252)
Idea generation stage (p. 253)
Screening stage (p. 254)
Business analysis stage (p. 255)
Development stage (p. 255)
Concept testing (p. 255)
Test marketing (p. 255)
Commercialization (p. 256)
Entrepreneur (p. 258)
Intrapreneurial (p. 258)

Product life cycle (p. 259)
Introduction stage (p. 259)
Growth stage (p. 261)
Maturity stage (p. 261)
Decline stage (p. 262)
Adoption process (p. 265)
Diffusion process (p. 265)
Innovator (p. 266)
Early adopter (p. 266)
Early majority (p. 266)
Late majority (p. 266)
Laggard (p. 267)
Nonadopter (p. 267)
Product modification (p. 267)
Cost reduction strategy (p. 268)
Total quality management strategy, or quality assurance strategy (p. 268)
Product enhancement (p. 270)
Product design (p. 271)

Style (p. 272)
Fashion (p. 272)
Fad (p. 272)
Product line strategy (p. 273)
Full-line, or deep-line, strategy (p. 273)
Limited-line strategy (p. 273)
Single-product strategy (p. 273)
Product line extension (p. 274)
Product category extension (p. 274)
Brand extension (p. 274)
Cannibalization (p. 275)
Globalization strategy (p. 275)
Customization strategy (p. 275)
Right to safety (p. 276)
Right to be informed (p. 277)
Quality of life (p. 277)
Product obsolescence (p. 278)
Physical obsolescence (p. 278)
Planned obsolescence (p. 278)
Right to choose (p. 278)

QUESTIONS FOR REVIEW AND CRITICAL THINKING

1. What is your definition of a new product?

2. Classify the type of innovation used in each of the following products.
   a. A personal communications device that combines a cellular phone, a pager, keys, and credit cards
   b. An identity checker that verifies, in seconds, people's identity for banks and classified areas by use of magnetically coded cards and electronic sensors to check hand geometry
   c. A new, aerodynamically designed motorcycle with low wind resistance

3. For the products in Question 2, identify product features that might speed acceptance.

4. Identify the steps in the new product development process. What takes place in each?

5. What are the main reasons why new products fail?

6. What are the benefits and limitations of test marketing?

7. At what stage of the product life cycle would you place each of the following products?
   a. Cigars
   b. Coffee
   c. Pen-based (stylus-activated) personal computers
   d. Theme amusement parks
   e. Tennis balls
   f. Slide rules

8. Try to trace the product life cycle for a particular brand, such as the Sony compact disc player.

9. Identify some typical marketing mix strategies used during each stage of the product life cycle.

10. Does marketing grow in importance as a product matures and moves from the introductory stage through the growth stage and into the maturity stage? Explain.

11. What are the most prominent characteristics of each adopter group in the diffusion process?

12. What guidelines would you suggest for rejuvenating old brands in the mature stage of the product life cycle?

13. How important is product quality to being competitive around the world?

14. What companies have recently implemented cost reduction strategies? Are such strategies always incompatible with product quality strategies?

15. How important is brand equity to a line extension strategy?

16. What are the pitfalls of a brand extension strategy that, for example, extends a name from a hair spray product to a facial cream?

17. Some homes are now being marketed with cable setups so that computer terminals may be installed. What product strategy does this reflect?

18. SNOT (Super Nauseating Obnoxious Treat), Wurmz n Dirt, and Bubble Tongue are names of some recently introduced novelty candy items. Form groups as directed by your instructor. Step 1: You have 10 minutes after the instructions "Begin brainstorming" to generate new product ideas for novelty candies. Do not evaluate the ideas, just generate as many as you can. Step 2: In the next 10-minute period, evaluate the ideas and decide which products should be considered for business analysis. Step 3: Discuss as a class how each group's ideas emerged and how the group did or did not come to a consensus about which products were best.

INTERNET INSIGHTS

Exercises

1. Go to

   http://www.nabisco.ca/Nabisco/NewProducts.html

   and learn what new products are being offered by Nabisco Canada. Then go to

   http://www.nabisco.com

   to see what's new in the United States. Write a short statement comparing the differences.

2. Go to

   http://www.mmm.com/quiz

   and take the 3M Innovation Quiz for long-term business strategy. How well did you score?

Address Book

New Product News
http://www.newproductnews.com

Inc Magazine's Guide to Business Technology
http://www.inc.com/technology

ETHICS IN PRACTICE: TAKE A STAND

1. Coffee is a product in the mature stage of its life cycle. It has been served for hundreds of years. A few years ago, an Albuquerque woman bought a 49-cent cup of coffee at the drive-in window of a McDonald's and, while removing the lid to add cream and sugar, spilled it, causing third-degree burns of the groin, inner thighs and buttocks. She was in the hospital for more than a week. Later, she sued McDonald's. Her lawsuit claimed the coffee was "defective" because it was so hot. A jury awarded the woman $2.9 million. If this case were being appealed, what stand would you take? If you owned a fast-food franchise, at what temperature would you serve coffee?

2. What arguments are given by critics who say that it is inappropriate for marketers to strive to make perfectly good products obsolete?

3. Pet owners complain that a new flea and tick spray is making their dogs sick. Should the company take the product off the market?

4. A pajama manufacturer develops a new fire-resistant chemical that will not wash out of children's pajamas until they have been washed more than 100 times. Should this product be marketed as fire resistant?

5. In the United States, packaged goods meant to be ingested by consumers must be approved by the Food and Drug Administration before they can be marketed. A multinational company, which has conducted its own laboratory test on a new over-the-counter drug, has not received approval from the FDA to market the drug in the United States. It plans to market the drug in several Asian countries where there are no requirements for government approval. Is this socially responsible?

6. Is it ethical to initiate a cost reduction strategy that requires closing a U.S. factory and opening a factory in a third-world nation?

CASE 10–1

 Water Joe—Johnny Beverages Inc.

First there was water. Then there was coffee.

Now, two of the hottest products in the beverage industry have been merged. The result is called caffeinated water.

Water Joe, bottled in Crivitz, Wis., by Nicolet Forest Bottling Co., went on the market . . . in Milwaukee, Madison, Wis., and Chicago.

The product, which tastes like water, sells for 89 to 99 cents per half-liter bottle. The amount of caffeine in the water equals that in one cup of coffee.

"It's really meeting all of our expectations," says Rick Nap, a representative for Nicolet in Wisconsin. "The key thing we want consumers to realize is it's a caffeine alternative in a healthier format."

David Marcheschi, now a 29-year-old real estate broker in Chicago, came up with the idea of putting caffeine in water when he was trying to stay awake while studying at Arizona State University. He found a chemist who created the proper formula, and Mr. Marcheschi then created a company, Johnny Beverages Inc., to market the concept.

Chris Connor, a 34-year-old furniture company owner, joined Mr. Marcheschi to help sell the idea. They spent a year promoting the concept before Nicolet Forest joined the project. The 8-year-old company helps finance Water Joe's production and distribution, but neither side will disclose the investment.

Water Joe's target market consists of working people and students, both of whom need a shot of caffeine at times.

The drink doesn't have the bitter taste and staining attributed to coffee, Mr. Marcheschi says.

His challenge is to distinguish Water Joe from the 50 or so bottled water labels that already crowd supermarket shelves. His solution: Put the drink closer to coffee items on their store shelves.

That kind of talk gives pause to people in the coffee industry. "What?" asked Robert Nelson, president of the National Coffee Association of America, when told about the product. He couldn't recall a drink quite like it, then added that it seemed "twisted." "People don't just drink coffee for the caffeine," he said. "They drink it for the overall experience of coffee, which includes aroma and taste."

Questions

1. In your opinion what type of new product, if at all, is Water Joe?
2. What marketing objectives should Water Joe have at this moment in time?
3. Evaluate the brand name Water Joe?
4. Describe the product strategy for Water Joe as it is described in this case? Can the strategy be enhanced?

VIDEO CASE 10-2

Spanier & Bourne Sailmakers

A pleasure sail from New Zealand to the New Hebrides Islands in 1978 came to an abrupt end for young Geoff Bourne and Barry Spanier. Their boat, a 38-foot one-master that Spanier had built, was destroyed in a violent storm, and they were shipwrecked on a small island in New Zealand waters occupied only by two caretakers. It took 22 days to get transport off the island. In a way, the misfortune made the fortunes of two men who, after getting out of college in California, had wandered from job to job—most connected with sailing—while taking lots of time off.

Today they own a Hawaii firm that has successfully applied new technology to an old craft, sailmaking. Spanier & Bourne Sailmakers, Inc., located in Kahului on the island of Maui and known widely as Maui Sails, has earned international recognition and growing revenues, primarily from designing windsurfing sails and equipment for a Hong Kong manufacturer. The firm also does custom manufacturing—of sails for boats as well as sailboards—and runs a wholesale/retail business.

Barry Spanier and Geoff Bourne had been enjoying a vagabond existence in 1978, but the shipwreck left Spanier broke and Bourne with no plans. It seemed a time to reenter the world of employment.

From a visit to Maui, Spanier knew there were many charter sailboats there, but no sailmakers. With $10,000 of starting capital—Bourne's savings—the friends rented a loft and went into business. They had sailmaking experience and talent, and they soon had numerous customers in Maui's charter fleet.

In 1980 a monster storm hit Maui, wrecking many boats. Maui Sails' customer base was wiped out. For some time to come, the charter skippers wouldn't be sailing or buying sails, just salvaging what they could.

Luckily, some California windsurfers, sailing in Maui's Hookipa area, brought in sails for repairs. "We had tons of high grade material for yacht sails and suggested that we could improve on the design and construction of their rigs," Spanier says. The firm became so popular with windsurfers that international sailboard brands asked for its services as

a designer. Two years later it became the exclusive research and development facility for Neil Pryde, owner of Neil Pryde Ltd., of Hong Kong, a major manufacturer of sailboards and other windsurfing equipment. Maui Sails, which had two employees, hired more—it has 11 now—and invested in tools and material.

Things went swimmingly until, in 1986, Pryde lost his largest customer to bankruptcy. As one step to save his business, he cut Maui Sails' royalties. Unsure of the future, the firm concentrated on increasing its custom sail output—and on something new.

Spanier and Bourne applied the computer to sailmaking. With the aid of a skilled programmer, Sandy Warrick, and financial backing from Pryde, who worked his company back to profitability, they developed a computerized system of designing windsurfing sails. The system cut costs and spurred sales by speeding design changes.

In the past few years defense spending cutbacks have propelled talented people into work for competitors of Maui Sails. There has been a technological explosion as light but strong aerospace materials have been used in sailing.

But storm survivors Spanier and Bourne, who began using aerospace materials in 1983, believe they have the answer to sophisticated competition. Maui Sails, which now has $1.2 million in annual revenues, will be taking the next steps first, they say. Their competitors will have to run just to keep up.

Questions

1. Discuss the general nature of the product life cycle for sails.
2. Spanier & Bourne is a small business. How does its new product development process differ from that of a large corporation?
3. How important are technology and the production process in the development of Spanier & Bourne's products?
4. What steps would be necessary for Spanier & Bourne to implement a total quality management program?

PART 4

THE NATURE OF THE VALUE CHAIN AND DISTRIBUTION

Chapter 11

Learning Objectives

After you have studied this chapter, you will be able to:

1. Explain the general purpose of distribution and logistics in the marketing system.
2. Evaluate the role of logistics and physical distribution in the marketing mix.
3. Show how distribution managers can make physical distribution provide maximum satisfaction to buyers while reducing costs.
4. Explain the total cost approach to physical distribution.
5. Understand that all marketers—even not-for-profit and service organizations—engage in distribution.
6. Characterize the functions of channel intermediaries.
7. Identify the major channels of distribution used by marketers.
8. Describe the major vertical marketing systems.
9. Explain how distribution interacts with other elements of the marketing mix.
10. Differentiate among channel cooperation, channel conflict, and channel power.

Greens and fairways at the nation's 14,000 golf courses take a daily beating from golf carts and divot diggers. Keeping the grounds up to par can be tough for maintenance crews, so for help many rely on Lesco's "store on wheels." The company's fleet of 59 tractor-trailers delivers a full stock of Lesco fertilizers, pesticides, and equipment—just about any landscaping product a greenskeeper might need. They bring the store to the clubhouse door at nearly half the courses in the United States, including such gems as Grand Cypress and Augusta National.

The manufacturing company, in Rocky River, Ohio, has three plants where it makes more than 17,000 lawn care products for the professional land-

scaping market. It sells such tools of the trade as mowers and seed spreaders and their replacement parts. Lesco's other main products are fertilizers and turf-protection mixes, many of which it makes specifically for different regions of the country. In Florida, for example, it markets a special fertilizer to replenish the nutrients in sandy soil.

Although the stores on wheels have traveled to golf courses since 1976, the majority of Lesco's sales today occur at its 121 service centers, scattered mainly through the South, Northeast, and Midwest. The company plans to open more service centers, where most of the sales staff are trained as agronomists and able to consult with customers on the latest products.

In 1993, Lesco entered the consumer market, and now it distributes its products through 103 Home Depot stores. Lesco executives see an opportunity for growth in the consumer products category, but the company is cautious because it doesn't want to risk losing focus on its efforts in the professional market.

Of course, Lesco's products set the company apart from most others, but Lesco relies on a distribution strategy that utilizes a number of channels of distribution. Much of Lesco's success can be traced to effective performance of its distribution function.

This chapter provides an overview of the purpose of the distribution element of the marketing mix. It defines logistics, physical distribution, and channels of distribution. It explores the functions intermediaries perform and the many alternative channels of distribution for goods and services. Next, it addresses the major decisions managers make in planning a distribution strategy. It discusses how the implementation of a distribution strategy may create channel conflict and, finally, describes some of the legal and ethical issues related to channels of distribution.

DISTRIBUTION DELIVERS A STANDARD OF LIVING TO SOCIETY

The major purpose of marketing is to satisfy human needs by delivering products to buyers when and where they want them and at a reasonable cost. A key element in this statement of marketing's mission is delivery—the movement of product from the point of production to the point of consumption. In many ways, all marketing effort is meaningless unless products are placed in the hands of those who need them. Thus, distribution is of overwhelming importance in any discussion of marketing functions. Distribution is estimated to account for about one-quarter of the price of the consumer goods we buy. Most would agree that this is a cost well worth bearing. Distribution creates time utility and place utility.

Distribution of products among the members of a society becomes necessary because the idea develops that efficiency can be gained—even in a primitive economy—if one person specializes in, say, hunting and another person specializes in fishing or farming. In a primitive economy, distribution is fairly straightforward; but in today's global economy it is far more complex. For example, products shipped into Baltimore may ultimately be sold in Oregon, and Washington state apples may be consumed in Florida. The basic function of distribution, however, remains the same. In one way or another, the distance between the grower or producer of a product and the final user of that product must be bridged. The distance to be covered can be quite long, as when Mexican oil ends up in Australia. It can also be quite short, as when a farmer at a roadside stand sells the watermelon that grew just a few yards away. Whatever the distance, society relies on the marketing function of distribution to do the job—to provide products in the right place at the right time.

LOGISTICS AND PHYSICAL DISTRIBUTION DEFINED

Logistics
The activities involved in moving raw materials and parts into the firm, in-process inventory through the firm, and finished goods out of the firm.

Materials Management
The activities involved in bringing raw materials and supplies to the point of production and moving in-process inventory through the firm.

Physical Distribution
The activities involved in the efficient movement of finished products from the end of the production line to the consumer.

Logistics describes the entire process of moving raw materials and component parts into the firm, in-process inventory through the firm, and finished goods out of the firm.[1] Logistics management thus involves planning, implementing, and controlling the efficient flow of both inbound materials and outbound finished products.

The term *logistics* is broad in scope. As shown in Exhibit 11–1, the logistics process can be divided into two parts: materials management and physical distribution. **Materials management** is concerned with bringing raw materials and supplies to the point of production and moving in-process inventory through the firm. **Physical distribution** describes the broad range of activities concerned with efficient movement of finished products from the end of the production line to the consumer.

Physical distribution consists of several identifiable concerns and activities:

1. *Inventory management.* For example, a retailer determines how many Phoenix Suns baseball caps is an adequate number and when to order.
2. *Order processing.* Customers' orders are received by sales office personnel, who then arrange for the requested merchandise to be shipped and for the customer to be billed.
3. *Warehousing and storage.* Producers of seasonal goods, such as air conditioners, bathing suits, and mittens, hold products in storage for distribution as needed through the seasons.
4. *Materials handling.* Forklifts, conveyor belts, and other means are used to move merchandise into and within warehouses, retail stores, and wholesaler's facilities.

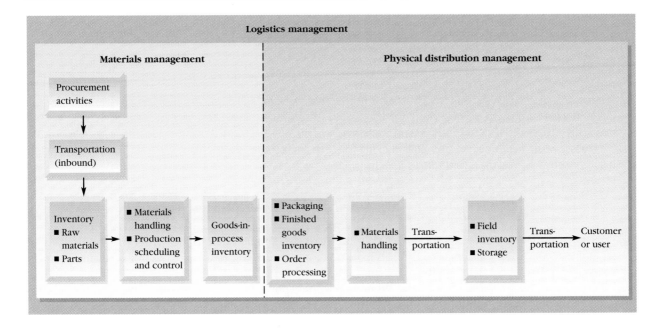

EXHIBIT 11–1
Logistics Management and
the Organization's Flow of
Materials

5. *Protective packaging and containerization.* For example, sheets of paper for photocopiers are bound into packs of 500 sheets, placed in cardboard boxes containing 10 packs, and placed on pallets.

6. *Outbound transportation.* For example, automobiles made in Japan are loaded on ships sailing to America and then transported by rail and/or truck to dealers around the United States.

Physical distribution, then, deals with the flow of products from producers to consumers. Its major focus is the physical aspects of that flow rather than the institutional activities involving changing title, facilitating exchanges, and negotiating with intermediaries. (These topics, which involve activities within channels of distribution, are discussed later in this chapter.) As part of the "place" portion of the overall marketing mix, physical distribution activities contribute time and place utility. The physical aspect of distributing ice cream is the subject of the accompanying Competitive Strategy feature.

Logistics deals with the "big picture" of an organization's supply and distribution processes. Therefore, it relies heavily on demand estimation or sales forecasting to achieve its goal of smoothly controlling the physical flow of goods through the organization and its distribution channels. Forecasting enables managers concerned with logistics to synchronize the activities that make up the distribution effort.

THE OBJECTIVES OF PHYSICAL DISTRIBUTION

Physical distribution has many objectives. All of them can be condensed into one overall statement of purpose—to minimize cost while maximizing customer service. This goal is the statement of an ideal. Unfortunately, the lowest total cost and the highest levels of service seldom go together. For example, achieving high-level customer service suggests that an appliance marketer should operate many warehouses, each carrying a large inventory so that local customers' orders can be filled

COMPETITIVE STRATEGY: WHAT WENT WRONG?

A Triple Treat?

The physical distribution system for McDonald's Triple Ripple, a three-flavored ice-cream product, was the major reason the product was dropped. Experiments indicated that the product would freeze, defrost, and refreeze in the distribution system. Solving the problem would have required each McDonald's city to have an ice-cream plant with special equipment to roll the three flavors into one. As this example shows, physical distribution has a dramatic influence on a product's success.

rapidly. In lieu of that, the marketer should have a fleet of jet transports ready at all times to fly merchandise to customers within a few hours of receiving their orders. Both approaches to maximizing customer service are likely to prove inconsistent with the other half of the physical distribution objective, which calls for minimizing cost. Minimizing cost generally suggests few warehouses, low inventories, and slow, inexpensive means of transportation.

The twin goals of maximum service and lowest cost, while not necessarily contradictory, can both rarely be met. Some compromise usually is necessary. Thus, physical distribution managers, while striving for the ideal, must work toward realistic objectives, performing a sort of balancing act in the process.

In many cases, organizations can establish competitive advantages over rivals through more effective physical distribution. This is especially true in industries where the products of one organization are essentially the same as those of competitors, as in the coal and the steel industries. Marketers experience difficulty in establishing competitive advantages through price differentials or product superiority in such industries, but physical distribution offers an avenue to develop an advantage. Providing more reliable delivery or faster delivery, avoiding errors in order processing, and delivering undamaged goods are all potential areas of competitive advantage.

Manufacturers selling directly to consumers perform the physical distribution function on their own. However, many physical distribution functions are carried out by intermediaries within a channel of distribution.

CHANNEL OF DISTRIBUTION—DEFINED

We briefly discussed channels of distribution in Chapter 1. The term *channel of distribution* has its origins in the French word for canal. This suggests a path that goods take as they flow from producers to consumers. In this sense, the channel of distribution is defined by the organizations or individuals along the route from producer to consumer. Because the beginning and ending points of the route must be included, both producer and consumer are always members of the channel of distribution. In addition, there may be intermediate stops along the way. Several marketing institutions have developed to facilitate the flow of the physical product, or title to the product, from the producer to the consumer. These marketing intermediaries specialize in distribution rather than production. They include wholesalers, which sell to retailers or other organizations that resell the product, and retailers, which sell to ultimate consumers. When intermediaries join with a manufacturer in a loose coalition to engage in exploiting joint opportunities, a channel of distribution is formed.[2]

Channel of Distribution
The complete sequence of marketing organizations involved in bringing a product from the producer to the ultimate consumer or organizational user.

A **channel of distribution** consists of producer, consumer, and sometimes intermediary organizations aligned to provide a vehicle that makes possible the passage of title or possession of a product from producer to consumer.[3] (For many products, the term "consumer" refers to an organizational user, not the "ultimate" consumer.) Thus, a channel of distribution is the complete sequence of marketing organizations involved in bringing a product from the producer to the consumer or organizational user. The channel of distribution also can be seen as a system of interdependency within a set of organizations, a system that facilitates the exchange process.

All discussions of distribution channels concern a product that has taken on its final form. The channel of distribution for an automobile begins after the product has become a finished automobile. It does not include the paths of raw materials (such as steel) or component parts (such as tires) to the automobile manufacturer. These products have their own channels, which end with the organizational user, the auto manufacturer.

It also should be emphasized that the channel's purpose in moving products to buyers is more than a simple matter of transportation. The channel of distribution must accomplish the task of transferring the title to the product as well as facilitating the physical movement of the goods to their ultimate destination. Although title transfer and the exchange of physical possession (transportation) generally follow the same channel of distribution, they do not necessarily need to follow the same path.

Merchant Intermediary
A channel intermediary, such as a wholesaler or a retailer, that takes title to the product.

Agent Intermediary
A channel intermediary that does not take title to the product. Agent intermediaries bring buyers and sellers together or otherwise help to consummate a transaction.

All but the shortest of channels include one or more intermediaries. (In the past, intermediaries were called middlemen.) A distinction may be made between **merchant intermediaries,** which take title to the product, and **agent intermediaries,** which do not take title to the product. Although agent intermediaries never own the goods, they perform a number of marketing functions, such as selling, that facilitate further transactions in the exchange process.

Most intermediaries are independent organizations tied only by mutual agreements to the producers with whom they deal. Some intermediaries are owned by producers, such as the company-owned sales branches and sales offices that sell NCR office equipment. However, these company-owned sales offices and branches are easily identified as being separate from the production facilities operated by NCR.

In service marketing, it sometimes appears that there is no channel of distribution. When a beautician delivers a product, such as a haircut, he or she deals directly with the customer. But even in these shortest of distribution channels, where no intermediaries are involved, marketing functions are being performed. The required activities are simply performed by the provider of the service (or, in a self-service environment, by the ultimate consumer).

When identifiable intermediaries are present, the channel members form a coalition intended to act on joint opportunities in the marketplace. Each channel member, from producer to retailer, must be rewarded or see some opportunity for continued participation in the channel.

Conventional Channel of Distribution
A channel of distribution characterized by loosely aligned, relatively autonomous marketing organizations that carry out a trade relationship.

The coalition between channel members may be a loose one resulting from negotiation or it may be a formal set of contractual arrangements identifying each party's role in the distribution process. The **conventional channel of distribution** is characterized by loosely aligned, relatively autonomous marketing organizations that have developed a system to carry out a trade relationship. In contrast, a formal vertical marketing system is a more tightly organized system in which channel members are either owned by a manufacturer or a distributor, linked by contracts or other legal agreements such as franchises, or informally managed and coordinated as an integrated system through a strategic alliance. Vertical marketing systems are discussed in greater detail later in this chapter.

Excluded from the channel of distribution are transportation companies, financial institutions, and other functional specialists. They are collaborators who are

The main business of the Hollywood movie studios once was simply making films—that is, production. Today, the crucial factor determining a studio's profitability is film distribution. Major U.S. film studios produce only about half the movies they distribute. They purchase many films from independent studios. The large studios concentrate on distribution and other marketing functions and are compensated for these efforts through a fee system, usually 25 to 30 percent of a film's rentals. Film distribution itself also has changed in recent years. Supplying films to theaters is no longer enough. Home Box Office, Showtime, and other cable systems, as well as TV networks, independent stations, and videocassette marketers, are now critical in the film marketing process. Distribution is the name of the game in Hollywood.

hired because they can more efficiently or more effectively perform a certain marketing activity for an organization in a basic marketing channel.

MARKETING FUNCTIONS PERFORMED BY INTERMEDIARIES

Perhaps the most neglected, most misunderstood, and most maligned segment of the economy is the distribution segment. Retailers are seen by some as the principal cause of high consumer prices simply because consumers have more contact with retailers than with other channel members. Retailers collect money from consumers, so even though much of that money is passed to other distributors or to manufacturers, retailers often bear the brunt of customers' complaints. Wholesalers also are thought to cause high prices, perhaps because most of their activities are outside the view of consumers.

In either case, "cutting out the middleman" often is suggested as a means to lower the prices of consumer goods. This kind of sentiment goes back thousands of years. The activities of those who perform the distribution function have long been misunderstood, and so it continues today. But students of marketing should understand that an efficient distribution system must somehow be financed. Most of the time, "eliminating the middleman" will not reduce prices, because the dollars that go to intermediaries compensate them for performing tasks that must be accomplished regardless of the economic system in effect.

HOW INTERMEDIARIES FIT IN CHANNELS

In Chapter 1, we discussed a conventional channel of distribution consisting of a manufacturer, a wholesaler, a retailer, and the ultimate consumer. Not all channels include all of these marketing institutions. In some cases, a unit of product may pass directly from manufacturer to consumer. In others, it may be handled by not just one but two or more wholesalers.

Consider this conventional channel of distribution:

Manufacturer ⟶ Retailer ⟶ Ultimate consumer

It is possible to have a channel of distribution that does not include a separate wholesaler. A manufacturer may choose to sell directly to retailers, in effect eliminating the wholesaler. However, the marketing functions performed by wholesalers must then be shifted to one of the other parties in the channel—the retailer or the manufacturer. If the manufacturer assumes some or all of these functions, they are said to have been shifted backward in the channel. If the retailer assumes them, they are said to have been shifted forward in the channel. For example, the manufacturer may decide to perform the function of breaking bulk—sending comparatively small orders to individual retail customers. With the wholesaler out of the picture, the manufacturer may have to create a sales force to call on numerous retailers. On the other hand, the retailer may be willing to accept truckload lots of the product, store large quantities of it, and perform the activity of breaking down these larger quantities into smaller quantities. In any case, the functions once performed by the eliminated wholesaler do not disappear; they are simply shifted to another channel member. The channel member assuming these functions expects to be compensated in some way. The retailer may expect lower prices and higher margins. The manufacturer may expect larger purchase orders, more aggressive retail promotion, or more control over the distribution process.

The key to setting the structure of a channel of distribution is to determine how the necessary marketing functions can be carried out most efficiently and effectively. Certain variables, such as price, the complexity of the product, and the number of customers to be served, can serve as guides to the appropriate channel structures. However, the functions to be performed should be the primary consideration in the marketing manager's distribution plans. Let us consider some of the major functions performed by intermediaries: physical distribution, communication, and facilitating functions.

PHYSICAL DISTRIBUTION FUNCTIONS

Physical distribution functions include breaking bulk, accumulating bulk, creating assortments, reducing transactions, transporting, and storing.

Breaking Bulk

Bulk-Breaking Function
An activity performed by marketing intermediaries, consisting of buying products in relatively large quantities and selling in smaller quantities.

Most intermediaries perform a bulk-breaking function. The **bulk-breaking function** consists of buying in relatively large quantities and then selling in smaller quantities, passing the lesser amounts of merchandise on to retailers, organizational buyers, wholesalers, or other customers. By accumulating large quantities of goods and then breaking them into smaller amounts suitable for many buyers, intermediaries can reduce the cost of distribution for both manufacturers and consumers. Consumers need not buy and store great amounts of merchandise. They benefit by lowering their own storage costs and avoiding such risks as spoilage, fire, and theft. Manufacturers are spared the necessity of dividing their outputs into the small-order sizes retailers or consumers might prefer.

Accumulating Bulk

Although the intermediary generally breaks bulk, an intermediary may also create bulk, buying units of the same product from many small producers and offering

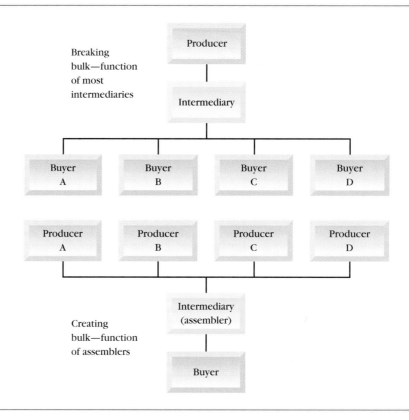

**Bulk-Accumulating
Function**
*An activity performed by
marketing intermediaries,
consisting of buying small
quantities of a particular
product from many small
producers and then selling
the assembled larger
quantities.*

Assembler
*A marketing intermediary
that performs a bulk-
accumulating function.*

Sorting Function
*An activity performed by
marketing intermediaries in
which accumulated products
are classified as to grade
and size, then grouped
accordingly.*

Assorting Function
*An activity performed by
marketing intermediaries,
consisting of combining
products purchased from
several manufacturers to
create assortments.*

the larger amount to buyers that prefer to purchase in large quantities. These intermediaries are performing a **bulk-accumulating function.** An intermediary performing this function is called, not surprisingly, an **assembler.** The classic examples of assemblers are encountered in the agriculture and fishing businesses. A maker of applesauce, such as Mott's, or a fish canner, such as Bumble Bee, would probably not want to have to deal with many comparatively small farming businesses or independent owners of fishing boats. Assemblers gather large quantities of apples or tuna or other products attractive to large buyers. Exhibit 11–2 contrasts the operation of the assembler with that of other intermediaries.

After accumulating bulk, marketers of agricultural products and raw materials typically perform a **sorting function,** which involves identifying differences in quality and breaking down the product into grade or size categories. For example, eggs are sorted into jumbo grade AA, large grade AA, and so on.

Creating Assortments

Another function intermediaries perform is the creation of assortments of merchandise that would otherwise not be available. This **assorting function** resolves the economic discrepancy resulting from the factory operator's natural inclination to produce a large quantity of a single product or a line of similar products and the consumer's desire to select from a wide variety of choices. Wholesalers that purchase many different products from different manufacturers can offer retailers a greater assortment of items than an individual manufacturer is able to provide.

Consider how intermediaries are used by magazine publishers and retailers to solve a very big assorting problem. There are tens of thousands of different magazine titles available from American publishers. No newsstand operator or other retailer carries anything like that number; a series of intermediaries is used to sort these many titles into appropriate groupings for individual stores.

National wholesalers, such as Hearst, ICD and Select Magazines, move the thousands of titles to approximately 500 local wholesalers. Their reward for fulfilling this gargantuan task is about 6 percent of the magazines' retail prices, out of which they must pay all expenses involved.

The local distributors continue the task of breaking bulk, moving the magazines to countless supermarkets, newsstands, drugstores, and other retail spots. But there is more to the local wholesaler's task than simply breaking bulk and making delivery. The local wholesaler must select, from among the more than 30,000 available titles, magazines appropriate for the individual retailer's operation. Then, this assortment of titles is assembled in the proper numbers for each retailer. The local wholesaler is paid about 20 percent of the cover prices.

Reducing Transactions

There is one underlying reason why intermediaries can economically accumulate bulk, break bulk, and create assortments: The presence of intermediaries in the distribution system actually reduces the number of transactions necessary to accomplish the exchanges that keep the economy moving and consumers satisfied.

As Exhibit 11–3 indicates, even if only four suppliers of grocery items attempt to transact business with just four supermarket buying headquarters, the number of interrelationships necessary is far greater than the number needed once an intermediary, such as a food wholesaler, is added to the system. Channel intermediaries, in their dual roles as buying agents for their customers and selling agents for the manufacturers with which they deal, simplify the necessary transaction

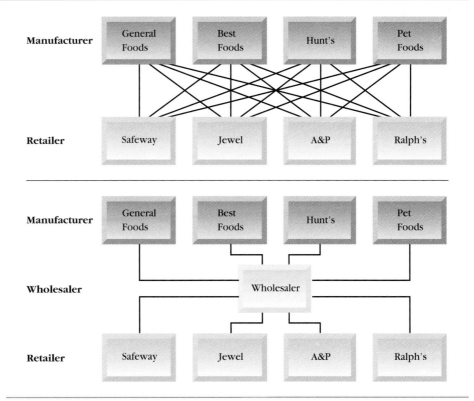

EXHIBIT 11–3
How an Intermediary
Reduces Transactions

process considerably. (Of course, channels of distribution can become too long. Such channels are common in Japan.)

Intermediaries not only reduce the number of transactions but also reduce the geographic distances that buyers and sellers must travel to complete exchanges and spare manufacturers the trouble of locating and contacting individual potential customers. These are some of the reasons why the presence of wholesalers and retailers can reduce costs. If manufacturers and consumers had to perform all these activities themselves, they would have to bear the costs involved.

Transportation and Storage

Intermediaries, in most cases, perform, manage, or collaborate with two other physical distribution functions: transportation and storage. Merchandise must be physically moved from points of production to points of consumption. Storage of inventory at various locations along the way often is necessary.

Transportation

Transportation *In relation to physical distribution, the physical movement or shipment of products to locations in the distribution channel.*

Transportation decisions involve selecting the specific mode that will be used to physically move products from a manufacturer, grower, wholesaler, or other seller to the receiving facilities of the buyer. The major alternative modes of transportation include railroad, motor carrier, air freight, water transportation, and pipeline.

There are several cost trade-offs to consider when selecting modes of transportation. The first consideration is always the needs of the buyer. If it is extraordinarily difficult or expensive to satisfy a need (e.g., urgent delivery), the seller should investigate the buyer's willingness to bear the extra costs involved. Transportation considerations include the nature of the product (bulk, perishability, weight, fragility), the necessary speed and dependability of delivery, and the cost and availability of transportation methods and storage space. Alternative modes of transportation may be evaluated in terms of these variables.

Each mode of transportation has advantages and disadvantages. For example, the primary advantages of air freight are its speed and distance capabilities, but it is expensive. As a rule, water transportation offers a very low-cost means of moving products. It is most appropriate for bulky, low-value, nonperishable goods such as grain and coal. Railroads demonstrate their comparative advantage over other transportation modes when the freight to be hauled consists of heavy and bulky items to be transported over land. However, railroads do not go everywhere. Motor vehicles are more accessible and more flexible than railroads, and trucks are most efficient at moving comparatively small shipments over short distances. A general comparison of transportation alternatives appears in Exhibit 11–4.

Railroad. Railroads demonstrate their comparative advantage over other transportation modes when the freight to be hauled consists of heavy and bulky items. These can be moved by rail over long distances at low cost. Shippers may find that unit costs of transporting smaller shipments are lower if the goods are shipped by truck. However, as shipment size increases, the economies of rail transport come to equal, and then exceed, those of truck shipment.

The major disadvantages of rail shipment are that it is relatively slow and that it can be used only where tracks are located. In addition, the industry has both a reputation for damage in transit and an unreliable delivery record. However, in recent years, some rail lines have attempted to modernize operations and have become more competitive with other means of transportation. For example, some lines provide diversion-in-transit privileges, which permit a shipper to direct the shipment to a destination that was not specified at the start of the trip. A fruit and vegetable shipper may send California oranges or artichokes to the East Coast and

LOW COST	SPEED	RELIABILITY OF DELIVERY	ABILITY TO DELIVER TO MANY GEOGRAPHICAL AREAS	REPUTATION FOR DELIVERING UNDAMAGED GOODS
(1) Pipeline	(1) Air	(1) Pipeline	(1) Motor	(1) Pipeline
(2) Water	(2) Motor	(2) Air	(2) Rail	(2) Water
(3) Rail	(3) Rail	(3) Motor	(3) Air	(3) Air
(4) Motor	(4) Pipeleine	(4) Rail	(4) Water	(4) Motor
(5) Air	(5) Water	(5) Water	(5) Pipeline	(5) Rail

NOTE: These comparisons are of a very general nature intended only to show the trade-offs involved when cost of use is compared with other attributes of transportation modes.

EXHIBIT 11–4
General Comparison of
Attributes of Various
Transportation Modes

then, when the products are approaching that part of the country, divert them to the particular eastern city where prices are highest or demand greatest. This and other services and special rates have been introduced by railroads in an attempt to offset some of the advantages offered by their competitors, especially truckers.

Motor Carrier. Motor carriers include trucks as well as far less important operations like Greyhound's package service, which uses buses as carriers. Motor carriers are preferred over rail shipment—especially by marketers of consumer products in boxed cartons—despite the fact that trains can move greater quantities of products at lower prices. One reason is that damage in transit is less likely than when rail freight is used. Furthermore, trucks are more accessible and more flexible than railroads, and they are generally more reliable in terms of delivery deadlines. Although they are most efficient at moving comparatively small shipments over short distances, they also are effective for long distances.

Air Freight. The primary advantages of air freight are its speed and distance capabilities. For many shippers, these advantages compensate for the high costs associated with air transportation. There are other advantages as well. Fast transportation permits inventory reductions and savings in warehousing costs. Air freight has a record for seldom damaging goods in transit. In remote areas inaccessible by truck or railroad, it may be the only transportation choice available. Traditionally, air transportation has been used primarily to move goods of high unit value, perishable goods, and emergency orders. The growth of international trade has contributed to a dramatic increase in the use of air transport during the past two decades, however. Today, manufacturers, especially producers of high-technology products, often choose to ship goods on demand via air freight rather than incur the costs of carrying inventory. Indeed, the use of air freight, electronic interchanges, and strategic alliances is causing a shift away from use of regional warehouses and trucks to an instant or "just-in-time" supply cycle.

Water Transportation. As a rule, water transportation offers a very low-cost means of moving products. It is most appropriate for bulky, low-value, nonperishable goods such as grain and coal. It is also appropriate for some fairly expensive items, such as automobiles from Germany or Japan being sent to U.S. or Canadian markets, if they can be properly protected from damage during transit. Transport by water takes place on inland bodies of water, such as the Great Lakes and the Mississippi River, as well as on oceans. Considerable problems, such as the closing of some routes and ports by ice during winter, may arise in these waterways. Water is also the slowest mode of transportation. However, when time constraints

Intermodal transportation involves transporting loaded containers by one transportation method, such as ship, and then by another, such as rail or truck.

are not great or when bulk and low unit value will not justify faster, more expensive transportation, water transportation is employed extensively.

Pipeline. Pipelines are the most specialized transportation means because they are designed to carry only one or two products. They are used mainly to transport natural gas and crude petroleum, moving these products from wells to storage or treatment facilities. Most pipelines are owned by the companies that use them, such as gas and oil producers. Pipeline shipping is generally less expensive than rail but more expensive than waterway transportation. A big part of the expense results from construction of the pipeline itself. Once in place, however, pipelines are a low-cost and reliable method of transportation.

Intermodal Transportation. In many instances, an intermodal service, which combines two or more modes of transportation, provides advantages. Many such services involve transporting loaded truck trailers or other large containers to some location from which they can be moved to local destinations by trucks. For example, railroad flatcars may carry the containers to the first location, then the containers are transferred onto trucks. This intermodal service combines the long-distance hauling attractions of the railroad with the local delivery flexibility of trucks. Similar intermodal methods involve transporting loaded containers first by ship, barge, or airplane and then by truck.

Storage and Inventory Control

Storage

The holding and housing of goods in inventory for a certain period of time.

Storage consists of holding and housing goods in inventory for a certain time period. It is necessary because of the almost inevitable discrepancies between production and consumption cycles. Consider this extreme example: The materials needed to operate Midwestern steel mills come from the northern Great Lakes via ship or barge. But shipment is impossible in the winter because the lakes freeze. Therefore, the materials must be stored at accessible locations. Such storage diminishes the effects that an uneven production cycle caused by a cyclical supply of raw materials would have on the steel business. In other cases, marketers have more goods than they can sell at one time. Products of a seasonal nature, such as air conditioners, class rings, skis, and wedding gowns, can be manufactured throughout the year, but there is a seasonal demand. Storage in buildings known as **warehouses** permits the makers of these items to operate a steady production stream.

The need for storage is one of the primary reasons for using intermediaries. Intermediaries of all types, including retailers, frequently store goods until they are demanded by customers further along in the channel of distribution. Hence, a fundamental concern of intermediaries is control of inventory levels. **Inventory control** involves decisions concerning the size of inventories. It weighs the benefits of overstocking inventory against the dangers of costly stock-outs—which means that the product desired by the customer is not on hand. The ideal inventory level is one that provides adequate service to customers while keeping suppliers' costs as low as possible. The presence of these twin goals, set at cross-purposes, complicates inventory decisions.

Valuable guidance on questions of inventory control can be found in sales forecasts. Also useful are facts such as how much inventory was needed in past planning periods, how much was "left over" at the ends of past periods, the inventory turnover rates of the individual warehouses, the value of the inventories, and the inventory carrying costs.

Integration of the Physical Distribution Functions

Breaking physical distribution down into components permits us to concentrate on individual aspects of a complex subject. However, this approach is somewhat misleading because it suggests that the parts operate separately, without interacting. It is important to understand that the components operate as a system. The **systems concept**—the idea that elements may be strongly interrelated and may interact toward achieving one goal—is of special value in distribution. Even the casual observer can see that a warehouse is of no meaningful use unless it fills and empties as part of a system intended to achieve some distribution goal. No shipment of merchandise via railroad or plane is of real value unless it is taken from the carrier and moved to where it is actually needed. In seeking to satisfy customer service demands at reasonable cost, marketing managers can use each part of a distribution system to help attain that goal, but only within the context of the system.

The key ideas inherent in the systems approach to physical distribution have contributed to the development of the **total cost concept.** Marketing managers who have adopted this concept see the answer to the distribution problem as a system—a system aimed at reducing total physical distribution cost.

Let's consider the case of an organizational good, a file cabinet, produced in California and intended for sale in New Hampshire. A relatively slow means of transportation from West Coast to East Coast, such as ship or train, would reduce the cost of the transcontinental shipment. But if the purchaser of the file cabinet could not wait for a slow shipment, the distributor would have a problem. A large inventory might be warehoused on the East Coast. This would involve high costs for paperwork, inventory handling, and local taxes, but the cost in terms of lost sales could be even greater if the inventory was not available. Could the problem be solved simply by using a more expensive means of transportation directly from the West Coast, eliminating the need for an East Coast warehouse? Using air freight likely would reduce problems of storage and handling at both ends of the trans-

---

Warehouse
A building or other repository for the storage of goods between the time they are produced and the time an order is shipped to the buyer.

Inventory Control
The activities involved in decisions relating to inventory size, placement, and delivery.

Systems Concept
The idea that elements may be strongly interrelated and may interact toward achieving a goal.

Total Cost Concept
In relation to physical distribution, a focus on the entire range of costs associated with a particular distribution method.

action and would probably lessen the total cost. Inexpensive transportation, then, could prove more costly in the long run.

Minimizing the costs associated with only one or two steps of a multistep process can result in increasing the cost of the whole process. Systems-oriented managers make trade-offs, increasing the cost of some parts of the system to produce even greater cost reductions in other parts of the system, thus reducing the total cost.

Total cost is an important measure that was not always appreciated. At one time, shippers selected their transportation modes in a one-dimensional way. If management thought a product required quick delivery, the fastest mode of transportation was chosen. If quick delivery was thought not to be a major concern, the cheapest means of transportation, within reason, was selected. Looking back, we may wonder why transportation experts frequently did not attempt to determine whether it was possible to lower the total cost of distribution, even if that meant using a more expensive means of transportation; but this approach was uncommon until relatively recently.

Sometimes the customer's satisfaction may be more important than a dollars-and-cents cost reduction. One possible payoff of increasing some system costs may come in the form of greater buyer satisfaction. Unfortunately, it is easy for distribution managers to become so concerned with dollars that customer costs and payoffs are neglected.

COMMUNICATION FUNCTIONS

Communication Function
Buying and selling functions whose ultimate purpose is ownership transfer.

Intermediaries perform a **communication function,** which includes buying and selling functions. The ultimate purpose of the communication link between the manufacturer and the retailer or the wholesaler and the retailer is to transfer ownership—that is, consummate an exchange of title.

Selling Function
Activities associated with communicating ideas and making a sale, thus effecting the transfer of ownership of a product.

In order to sell the product, wholesalers and retailers may perform important promotional activities for manufacturers. Most frequently, the **selling function** is carried out by a sales force. However, intermediaries also use advertising and such sales promotion tools as retail displays.

The logic for this is simple. An intermediary is closer to its own customers. It is in the ideal position to use promotional activities to build and maintain a mutually productive relationship. In other words, an intermediary's position in the channel allows it to communicate to a particular level of customers more efficiently than the manufacturer. The wholesaler's sales force may communicate how the retailer would benefit from carrying the product. Retailers may use newspaper advertising to communicate product features to the ultimate consumer. The selling function, using a variety of promotional tools, is perfomed at each level of the channel of distribution.

Buying Function
Activities associated with making a purchase and thus effecting the transfer of ownership of a product.

The wholesaler provides a **buying function** for retailers, organizational users, and other customers. A wholesaler's contact with numerous manufacturers allows it to evaluate the product quality standards of wide assortments of goods from competing manufacturers. Thus, the retailer or other customer is free to specialize in the retailing or merchandising of products. Intermediaries further serve as channels of communication in such ways as informing buyers how products are to be sold, used, repaired, or guaranteed. Because intermediaries typically deal with a number of manufacturers or other suppliers of goods, they are in unique positions to serve as conduits of information. Intermediaries, being "in the middle," are uniquely placed not only to pass information from producers to other channel members but also to collect information from channel members or retail shoppers and return it to producers. For example, retailers may be faced with serious consumer complaints about a product or some product-related issue such as repair service. The retailers should pass this information backward in the channel to the wholesalers, who can bring the matter to the attention of the producer. *Should* is the key word here. Too often, whether because of apathy or the fear of somehow being blamed for a problem, intermediaries fail to perform this potentially valuable service. Marketers at all levels should encourage communication throughout channels of distribution, because the satisfaction of all channel members—including the consumer—is at stake.

FACILITATING FUNCTIONS

Many intermediaries perform other functions to help facilitate channel operations. The tasks of a channel intermediary can be so varied that it is nearly impossible to list all the facilitating functions a channel member might perform. However, most involve providing "extra" services or risk taking.

"Extra" services include a range of activities that increases the efficiency and effectiveness of the channel. In providing these activities, intermediaries perform a **service function.** For many products, the availability of a post-sale repair service is an absolute necessity. Office photocopiers always seem to need either routine maintenance or minor or major overhauls, for example. Wholesalers and retailers of such machines usually offer repair services on a contract or "emergency" basis. Honoring manufacturers' guarantees can be another responsibility of intermediaries.

Management services also can be provided by channel intermediaries. In the food industry, for example, wholesalers offer a variety of management services, including computerized accounting systems, inventory planning, store site selection, store layout planning, and management training programs. The extra services offered are good business for the wholesalers in that (1) they attract customers to the wholesalers offering the service and (2) they help to keep food retailer customers in business and successful.

Most intermediaries also perform a **credit function** by offering credit service of one kind or another. Some wholesalers and retailers operate exclusively on a cash-and-carry basis, promising to pass related savings on to their customers, but these make up a relatively small proportion of the millions of intermediaries operating in the United States. Wholesalers in many fields routinely offer 30, 60, or more days to pay for merchandise ordered. Often the days do not start "counting" until the goods are delivered to the buyer's place of business. In effect, such a service permits the buyer to make some money on a product before having to pay for it.

In almost everything they do, channel intermediaries perform a **risk-taking function.** When purchasing a product from a manufacturer or supplier of any type, intermediaries run the risk of getting stuck with an item that falls out of favor with the buying public because of fashion shifts or quickly dying fads. It is also possible for the product to spoil while in storage or be lost through fire or some other disaster. Intermediaries bear these risks in addition to risks in offering credit to individuals and organizations to whom they sell. They take legal risks in that intermediaries, not just manufacturers, can be held responsible for problems caused by faulty products or misleading claims.

Service Function
Activities performed by channel members that increase the efficiency and effectiveness of the exchange process. Repair services and management services provided by intermediaries are examples.

Credit Function
Provision of credit to another member of a distribution channel.

Risk-Taking Function
Assumption of the responsibility for losses when the future is uncertain.

FOCUS ON GLOBAL COMPETITION

ATM Services

In the distribution of services, the extra services provided by intermediaries are extremely important. Consider how important "extra services" are in the following account of the distribution of currency from an automatic teller machine (ATM).

I'm in Paris, it's late evening, and I need money, quickly. The bank I go to is closed, of course, but outside sits an ATM, an automated teller machine—and look what can be made to happen, thanks to computers and high-speed telecommunications. I insert my ATM card from my bank in Washington, D.C., and punch in my identification number and the amount of 1,500 francs, roughly equivalent to $300.

The French bank's computers detect that it's not their card, so my request goes to the CIRRUS system's inter-European switching center in Belgium, which detects that it's not a European card. The electronic message is then transmitted to the global switching center in Detroit, which recognizes that it's from my bank in Washington. The request goes there, and my bank verifies that there's more than $300 in my account and deducts $300 plus a fee of $1.50. Then it's back to Detroit, to Belgium, and to the Paris bank and its ATM—and out comes $300 in French francs. Total elapsed time: 16 seconds.

TYPICAL CHANNELS OF DISTRIBUTION

As we have discussed, the variety of distribution channels is extensive. That is because marketers are constantly seeking new ways to perform the distribution function. Both manufacturers and intermediaries have contributed to this effort and have developed all sorts of variations on the basic theme of distribution. Each variation was developed in an effort to better perform the distribution function and thereby attract business.

Channels may be distinguished by the number of intermediaries they include; the more intermediaries, the longer the channel. Some organizations choose to sell their products directly to the consumer or organizational user; others use long channels that include numbers of wholesalers, agents, and retailers to reach buyers.[4] Our discussion focuses on the most common of the numerous channels of distribution available. Exhibit 11–5 shows the primary channels for consumer and organizational products.

Channels of Distribution for Consumer Goods and Services

The middle panel of Exhibit 11–5 gives examples of typical channels for the distribution of consumer goods and services.

Direct Channel for Consumer Goods and Services

A good example of the direct channel is the neighborhood bakery, which converts flour, water, and other raw materials into baked goods and then retails these products, providing any other functions that might be necessary to complete the transaction. The direct channel also is familiar as the distribution method used by many marketers of services and not-for-profit groups that solicit donations.

Marketers of consumer goods and services that promote their products through mail-order catalogs, telemarketing (telephone sales), and 800 numbers listed in advertisements and that distribute directly to consumers through the mail or a delivery service are also classified as using direct channels. The strategies of these direct marketers, who do not use retail outlets or contact customers in person, rely

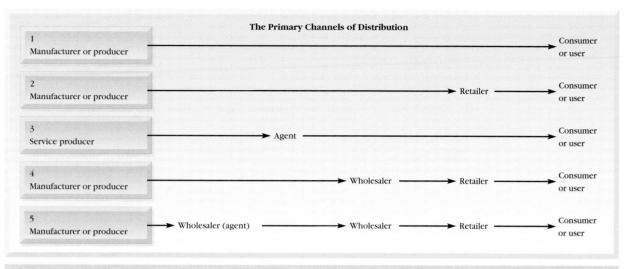

The Primary Channels of Distribution

1 Manufacturer or producer → Consumer or user

2 Manufacturer or producer → Retailer → Consumer or user

3 Service producer → Agent → Consumer or user

4 Manufacturer or producer → Wholesaler → Retailer → Consumer or user

5 Manufacturer or producer → Wholesaler (agent) → Wholesaler → Retailer → Consumer or user

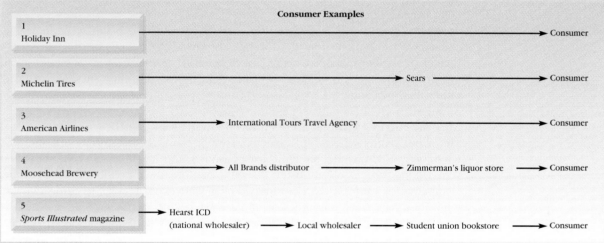

Consumer Examples

1 Holiday Inn → Consumer

2 Michelin Tires → Sears → Consumer

3 American Airlines → International Tours Travel Agency → Consumer

4 Moosehead Brewery → All Brands distributor → Zimmerman's liquor store → Consumer

5 *Sports Illustrated* magazine → Hearst ICD (national wholesaler) → Local wholesaler → Student union bookstore → Consumer

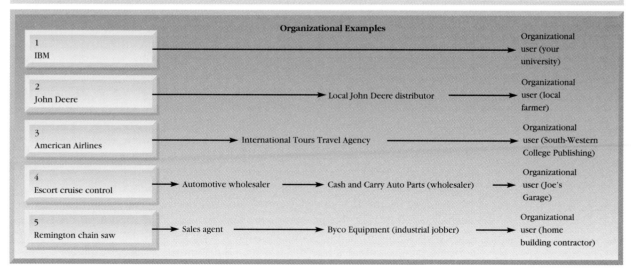

Organizational Examples

1 IBM → Organizational user (your university)

2 John Deere → Local John Deere distributor → Organizational user (local farmer)

3 American Airlines → International Tours Travel Agency → Organizational user (South-Western College Publishing)

4 Escort cruise control → Automotive wholesaler → Cash and Carry Auto Parts (wholesaler) → Organizational user (Joe's Garage)

5 Remington chain saw → Sales agent → Byco Equipment (industrial jobber) → Organizational user (home building contractor)

EXHIBIT 11–5
Typical Channels of
Distribution

largely on database management and certain direct-response promotional strategies. We discuss direct marketing further in Chapters 14 and 15.

Manufacturer (Producer)-Retailer-Consumer Channel

The manufacturer-retailer-consumer channel commonly is employed when the retailer involved is a sizable organization, such as a discount chain like Wal-Mart. This type of retail marketing organization may prefer to deal directly with manufacturers to be able to order specially made merchandise or obtain discounts or other benefits. Generally, the benefits must be important enough to make the retailer willing to perform many wholesaling functions. However, in an effort to please large retailer customers, the manufacturer may agree to perform wholesaler functions. Efficiencies that accrue to a manufacturer because of the large orders placed by Sears or Wal-Mart can more than offset the wholesaling costs the manufacturer may have to absorb.

Service producers also use this channel of distribution. For example, HBO Visitor Information Network (VIN) is a tourism channel that provides continuous programming for hotel rooms, highlighting local attractions, dining, and shopping.[5] The channel of distribution for this service is VIN-hotel-consumer or producer-retailer-consumer.

Many other service marketers use a producer-retailer-consumer channel when consumers can benefit from the location, product information, or other services a retailer offers. For example, many dry cleaners have their customers' suede clothing dry-cleaned by companies specializing in the dry cleaning process for suede rather than retailing.

Manufacturer-Wholesaler-Retailer-Consumer Channel

The manufacturer-wholesaler-retailer-consumer channel of distribution is the most commonly used channel structure for consumer goods. This is because most consumer goods are so widely used. It would be virtually impossible for the Wrigley Company, for example, to deal individually with every retailer stocking chewing gum, let alone every consumer of gum. Thus, a long channel, using at least two intermediaries, is needed to distribute the product. Wholesalers also can be used in the distribution of services.

Channels That Include Agents

A familiar type of agent is the real estate agent. Consumers marketing their homes (or other used goods) often lack time and marketing skills, so they hire agents. Manufacturers, especially those lacking expertise in marketing a particular product line, may choose to permit manufacturers' agents or selling agents to handle the marketing of their products. Such agents do not take title to the goods they sell and usually earn commissions rather than a salary.

In marketing channels for consumer goods, agents may, depending on circumstances and the product they offer, sell to retailers or wholesalers. The manufacturer-agent-wholesaler-retailer-consumer channel is widely used in the marketing of consumer products, especially convenience goods.

It might seem that travel agents function as retailers of airline services. Technically, however, this is a channel using an agent. The service producer-agent channel is common in marketing consumer services. Ticketmaster provides such services for sports teams like the Chicago Bulls and the Chicago Cubs.

Channels of Distribution for Business-to-Business Marketing

Business-to-business marketers use channels similar to those used by the marketers of consumer products. The primary channels are illustrated in the bottom panel of Exhibit 11–5.

The travel agent is the traditional intermediary in the purchase of airline tickets. However, a growing number of travelers are using the Internet to purchase tickets directly from the airline service provider.

Direct Channel in Business-to-Business Marketing

The name "business-to-business" suggests the importance of the direct channel in the marketing of organizational products. Indeed, the direct channel is the one most commonly found in the marketing of organizational goods. Direct organizational sales of industrial machinery such as escalators, power-generating machinery such as turbine engines, metals such as titanium, and many other products require well-informed salespeople and perhaps engineers, who can help the buyer fit the product into the organizational facility or manufacturing process. Otis Elevator, for example, is a business-to-business marketer that uses a direct channel.

Manufacturer-Wholesaler-Organizational User Channel

Because, by definition, retailers deal with consumers, there is no distribution channel for organizational goods that directly parallels the manufacturer-retailer channel. However, there is a trade channel for organizational goods that relies on just one wholesale intermediary, which performs a function much like that of a retailer. This is the manufacturer-distributor-organizational user channel. The names for this type of wholesaler vary from industry to industry; among the most common terms used is **jobber.**

Jobber
A wholesale intermediary in a channel of distribution for an organizational good.

Snap-On Tools, maker of socket wrenches and other hand tools, uses distributors who, working out of well stocked vans, call directly on Snap-On's customers—professional mechanics. Distributors selling to organizational users also may operate store-like facilities that buyers, such as electricians or plumbers, may patronize. In either format, organizational distributors perform storage and communications functions. They may, as in the Snap-On example, provide delivery and also supply credit or perform other functions. The organizational distributor is classified as a merchant intermediary, because this distributor takes title to the goods. Channels of distribution for organizational goods sometimes include more than one merchant wholesaler. This is most common in international marketing.

Agents in Business-to-Business Marketing

The manufacturer-agent-organizational user channel commonly is used in business-to-business marketing by small manufacturers that market only one product to many users. The wide range of customers to which agents sell suggests their main attraction to manufacturers—flexibility. One type of agent intermediary, the **broker,** can be used on an occasional basis as needed. No continuing relationship—

Broker
An agent intermediary whose major role is placing buyers and sellers in touch with one another and assisting in contractual arrangements.

and therefore no continuing financial or other obligation—is necessary. Similarly, manufacturers' agents operate on a commission basis within fixed geographic territories. Therefore, they appeal to small organizations with limited financial resources that have difficulty funding their own sales forces. Manufacturer's agents also are attractive because they can be employed in "thin" market areas or in foreign countries where potential sales do not seem to justify a manufacturer's deployment of its own sales force.

VERTICAL MARKETING SYSTEMS

In many industries, such as the fast-food restaurant industry, the dominant distribution structure is the vertical marketing system. The concept of a vertical marketing system emerged along with the need to manage or administer the functions performed by intermediaries at two or more levels of the channel of distribution.

Vertical Marketing System
Networks of vertically aligned establishments that are professionally managed as centrally administered distribution systems.

Vertical marketing systems, or vertically integrated marketing systems, consist of networks of vertically aligned establishments that are professionally managed as centrally administered distribution systems. Central administration achieves technological, managerial, and promotional economies of scale through the integration, coordination, and synchronization of transactions and marketing activities necessary to the distribution function. There are three types of vertical marketing systems: corporate, administered, and contractual.

Corporate Systems—Total Ownership

Corporate Vertical Marketing System
A vertical marketing system in which two or more channel members are connected through ownership.

The **corporate vertical marketing system** connects two or more channel members through ownership. It is exemplified by a retailer, such as Sears, that integrates backward into manufacturing to assure quality control over production and corporate control over the distribution system. A manufacturer may obtain complete control of the successive stages of distribution by vertically integrating through ownership. Sherwin-Williams administers a corporate vertical marketing system by owning more than 2,000 retail paint outlets.

Administered Strategic Alliances—Strong Leadership

Administered Strategic Alliance
A vertical marketing system in which a strong channel leader coordinates marketing activities at all levels in the channel through planning and management of a mutually beneficial program.

In an **administered strategic alliance,** a strong position of leadership, rather than outright ownership, is the source of influence over channel activities. The "administrator" may be any channel member that has the size or market clout required to dominate the others. Alternately, a strategic alliance may be built on a commitment to establish a long-term relationship based on collaborative efforts.

Administered systems generally are constructed around a line of merchandise rather than the complete manufacturing, wholesaling, or retailing operation. For example, suppose a manufacturer wishes to ensure that wholesalers and retailers follow its comprehensive program of marketing activities. Using an administered vertical marketing system, the manufacturer could coordinate marketing activities through planning and management of a program made attractive (for example, through sizable discounts or financial assistance) to all parties. Examples of strong channel leadership and administered marketing systems may be found in companies such as O. M. Scott and Sons Company (a producer of lawn products) and Ralph Lauren (a designer and producer of men's apparel). This position of strength can be held by a wholesaler or a retailer as well as by a manufacturer.

FOCUS ON RELATIONSHIPS

Caterpillar

Caterpillar, Inc., a leader in the global machinery and engines market, wants to move mountains for its dealers. The dealerships are all independently owned, but Caterpillar considers its dealers to be partners, not agents or intermediaries. Caterpillar is as concerned about dealers' performance as the dealers are, because the machinery and engine maker's enormous and loyal dealer network is one of its major competitive advantages.

Because of its strong focus on collaborating with dealers, Caterpillar offers a range of support and consulting services aimed at helping dealers boost their profitability. "When you buy the iron you get the company," Caterpillar literature says.

One Caterpillar service ensures that dealers' inventories are at the right level. An electronic data interchange linking all dealers to the computer at Caterpillar's Indianapolis distribution center enables dealers to order any part they need for delivery the next day. The company will buy back parts the dealers do not sell. And it tries to pace its introduction of new products according to dealers' capabilities. Caterpillar even has a subsidiary, Caterpillar Logistic Services, that distributes Caterpillar parts directly to its dealers' customers.

Caterpillar's dealerships have become diversified companies in their own right. With the strong encouragement of Caterpillar, many have established related businesses, such as refurbishing tractor parts and rebuilding diesel engines. Caterpillar loses some new-parts business this way,

but it gains in the long run, because its equipment becomes more economical for the customer.

In 1992, Caterpillar introduced "customer sensitivity training" programs for its 2,400 dealer salespeople in the United States, all of whom work for independently owned dealerships. The business operations manager for Caterpillar's North American commercial division says, "We want the entire distribution network to focus on the customer first. We train our sales force to understand why customers buy our products, what their needs are, the importance of follow-up, the need to let a customer vent his anger, and how to help a customer resolve problems without passing the responsibility on to someone else in the company."

Caterpillar's focus on dealer relationships is not limited to the United States. It has dealers around the world. In 1993, it positioned itself to take advantage of business opportunities in eastern Europe as Russia and many other countries attempted to establish capitalistic economies. In 1994, it entered a joint venture with a Russian company, Amo-Zil, Russia's leading truck manufacturer, to produce parts for Caterpillar equipment. It also is developing a network of dealers and support organizations in these countries to provide support for products powered by Caterpillar engines.

Perhaps the most significant indicator that Caterpillar believes in long-term relationships with its dealers is the fact that the company conducts a course at its headquarters to encourage dealers' children to remain in the business.

Contractual Systems—Legal Relationships

Contractual Vertical Marketing System
A vertical marketing system in which channel coordination and leadership are laid out in a contractual agreement.

Retailer Cooperative Organization
A group of independent retailers that combine resources and expertise to control their wholesaling needs, as through a centralized wholesale buying center.

In a **contractual vertical marketing system** channel leadership is assigned not by ownership or by less formal leadership but by agreement in contractual form. In such a channel, relationships are spelled out so that there is no question about distribution coordination. The relationship between McDonald's franchise holders and McDonald's headquarters is a contractual one wherein the rights and responsibilities of both parties are identified clearly. The idea behind such an approach to distribution is that if all parties live up to their sides of the agreement, the system will work smoothly and well. There are three subtypes of contractual systems: retailer cooperative organizations, wholesaler-sponsored voluntary chains, and franchises.

A **retailer cooperative organization** is a group of independent retailers, such as Certified Grocers, that have combined their financial resources and their expertise to more effectively control wholesaling needs. By capitalizing on economies of scale, they lower wholesaling costs by maintaining a centralized buying center. Yet these retailers are able to maintain their independence.

Voluntary Chain
A vertical marketing system initiated by a wholesaler so that a group of independent retailers participate in a relationship linked to the wholesale supplier.

The **voluntary chain** is similar to the cooperative organization except that the wholesaler initiates the combining of services. The independent retailers served agree to utilize only this one wholesaler, while the wholesaler agrees to service all the organized retailers. Ace Hardware and Coast-to-Coast stores are examples of voluntary chains.

Franchise
A contractual agreement between a franchisor and a franchisee by which the franchisee distributes the franchisor's product.

A **franchise** is a contractual agreement between a franchisor, typically a manufacturer or service provider, and a number of independent retailers, or franchisees. The franchise agreement often gives the franchisor much discretion in controlling the operations of the small retailers. In exchange for fees, royalties, and a share of the profits, the franchisor offers assistance and often supplies. Franchise assistance may take the form of marketing research information or strategic marketing planning aids (for example, new product planning) from franchisor experts. The franchisee is usually responsible for paying for insurance, property taxes, labor, and supplies.

The franchise has been quite popular and often successful in the fast-food industry (Subway, Wendy's, Domino's), lodging industry (Holiday Inn and Red Roof Inn), and repair service industry (Midas and AAMCO). One of its main advantages is that it offers a brand identity and a nationally recognizable storefront for a retail outlet. The person driving down the highway thus has a very clear conception of what products or services will be found within the franchise outlet.

 # MANAGING THE CHANNEL OF DISTRIBUTION

Distribution strategy requires two major decisions. The first concerns determining the structure of the channel of distribution. The second concerns deciding on the number of intermediaries, or the extent of distribution.

Determining the Structure of the Channel

What determines whether a channel of distribution will be short or long? The selection criteria are influenced by the other elements of the marketing mix strategy, by organizational resources, and by a number of external environmental factors.

The Marketing Mix Strategy

In selecting the channel of distribution, the organization must consider other elements of the marketing mix. For example, an organization's long-term strategic pricing plan may determine whether it will distribute a product through high-margin outlets or through high-volume outlets appealing to price-conscious consumers. The product's characteristics, especially its tangible characteristics, may also play an important role in channel selection. For instance, if live Maine lobsters are to be sold in Tokyo, the channel of distribution will be largely dictated by the perishability of the product. Many products require after-sale service; hence, an intermediary's technical repair service often is an important consideration in selecting a channel of distribution. The size, bulk, and weight of a product will determine whether short channels are necessary to reduce transportation and handling costs. Other product considerations, such as the technical complexity, the replacement rate, the gross margin, and the image of the product, also influence the type of channel selected.

Organizational Resources

Arm & Hammer Heavy Duty Detergent is marketed by Church & Dwight, a small company compared with Procter & Gamble and Colgate, its competitors. Church

& Dwight works with 80 food brokers to market its product in supermarkets, whereas Procter & Gamble has the luxury of its own sales organization. Utilizing one or more marketing intermediaries, as Church & Dwight does, disperses the responsibility for the performance of the distribution function. Thus, an organization unwilling to devote financial resources to supporting its own sales force, storing and holding a large inventory, or providing other distribution functions may use wholesalers or retailers to provide the resources or managerial expertise to handle these activities.

A company's existing channels of distribution for its other products are tremendous resources—they may be the main determinant in the selection of a channel of distribution. Wow Lays, a new Frito Lay snack food, was marketed through the same channel as Doritos and other Frito Lay snacks. Relationships within this channel already had been established. Carrying several items may lead to certain economies of scale.

External Environmental Criteria

Many elements of the external environment can affect channel selection. We will discuss market characteristics, consumer preferences and behavior, the nature and availability of intermediaries, and several other factors.

Market Characteristics. The number of customers and the amount of the average purchase influence the length of the channel of distribution selected. If the market consists of a few large purchasers, channels are likely to be short. Conversely, if there are many small customers, channels are likely to be long.

Consumer Preferences and Behavior. Customers' past behavior and preferences as to purchase location are major selection criteria. Perhaps ultimate consumers prefer to buy a certain product in a wholesale club, such as Sam's. If Sam's prefers to purchase directly from manufacturers rather than through wholesalers, this preference has a dramatic impact on channel selection. At each market level, customer preferences must be considered. Furthermore, if a manufacturer finds that some of its buyers prefer to purchase its product in drugstores and others prefer to buy the product in discount stores, multiple channels of distribution may be necessary.

Nature and Availability of Intermediaries. In many cases, capable intermediaries either are unavailable or unwilling to handle a product. When the Levi Strauss Company tried to market Tailored Classic men's suits, a high-quality, medium-priced product, the company found retailers resistant to handling the wool and wool-blend line because of Levi's traditional association with more casual clothing. Retailers insisted on displaying the Levi's suit and sport-coat line next to low-priced clothing and demanded price reductions. Other retailers would not carry the line because their store images contrasted with the image of the traditional Levi product line.

When the preferred intermediary is unavailable, a manufacturer may alter its channel of distribution. Often the manufacturer eliminates a wholesaler and goes directly to the ultimate consumer in a certain territory.

Other Environmental Factors. Any of the environmental forces discussed in Chapter 3 or Chapter 4 may have an impact on the channel of distribution. For example, the wholesaling and retailing structure in Japan is strongly influenced by political and legal factors. An organization must carefully consider all possible environmental forces before making the channel of distribution decision.

COMPETITIVE STRATEGY: WHAT WENT RIGHT?

American Greetings

The big three card companies—led by Hallmark, with American Greetings right behind, and $546 million Gibson Greetings a distant third—favor different channels of distribution to reach card buyers. Hallmark is number one in specialty stores, American Greetings is the leader in mass retail chains, and Gibson heads up deep-discount stores. This works out well for American Greetings, since there's no doubt that mass retail chains are now the place to be. For years, most women, 90 percent of card purchasers, bought their cards from specialty card shops. These days, however, 64 percent of cards are bought in mass retail out-lets, while card purchases in specialty stores like Hallmark's have declined 36 percent since 1980.

American Greetings will be in good shape if it continues to grow with mass retail outlets like Wal-Mart and Target, whose sales are increasing 20 percent a year. If American Greetings continues to build its market share in these chains, it will likely take the leadership slot away from Hallmark within the next five to 10 years, even though both companies' annual sales growth has been about 8 percent over the past few years.

The Extent of Distribution: How Many Outlets?

Once the structure of the distribution channel has been determined, the manufacturer is faced with the problem of deciding on the intensity of distribution. Determining the number of wholesalers and the number of retail outlets is an important decision that will determine where potential customers can expect to find the product. The degrees of distribution intensity are: (1) intensive, (2) selective, and (3) exclusive. The degree of distribution intensity must be determined for each level in the channel. For example, a manufacturer like Coca-Cola may execute an intensive distribution strategy at the retail level and a strategy of exclusive distribution at the wholesale level.

Intensive Distribution

Intensive Distribution
A distribution strategy aimed at obtaining maximum exposure for the product at the retail or wholesale level.

The strategy of **intensive distribution** seeks to obtain maximum product exposure at the retail level. When consumers will not go out of their way to purchase a product or will readily accept substitutes when the brand is not available, the appropriate strategy is to saturate every suitable retail outlet with the brand. Gasoline, chewing gum, and other convenience goods normally receive intensive distribution. Intensive distribution at the wholesale level allows almost all appropriate wholesalers to carry the product. Products intensively distributed may be presold with mass media advertising or by other means. Pennzoil, for example, needs little personal selling. Pennzoil intensively distributes its motor oil in service stations, as well as in Kmarts, Target stores, and other mass-merchandising outlets, where more than half of U.S. car motor oil is sold. Furthermore, to increase the intensity of its distribution, Pennzoil purchased a large share of Jiffy-Lube International, the leading oil-change-while-you-wait franchise.

Selective Distribution

Selective Distribution
A distribution strategy in which the product is sold in a limited number of outlets.

At the retail level, a strategy of **selective distribution** restricts the sale of the product to a limited number of outlets. The manufacturer of Tommy Hilfiger shirts, for example, focuses its marketing efforts on certain selected outlets with the desired store image. Each store selected must meet the company's performance standards while appealing to a select target market. As distribution becomes more selective, the manufacturer may expect a greater effort on the part of the retailer (for example, a willingness to hold a larger inventory). Because retailers benefit from limits on the number of competitors, they are expected to be more willing to accept the manufacturer's suggestions and controls on the marketing strategy—for example, by supporting the list price. As you might expect, selective distribution is more commonly used for specialty and shopping goods than for convenience goods.

Exclusive Distribution

Exclusive Distribution
A distribution strategy in which only one outlet in a given area is allowed to sell a product.

When a product requires aggressive personal selling, a complete inventory of the product line, repair service, or other special effort, an intermediary may be granted an exclusive area. Generally, a manufacturer or wholesaler that grants a retailer **exclusive distribution** expects a maximum sales effort or other benefit from the prestige or efficiency of the retail outlet. Exclusive distribution agreements often involve contractual arrangements. Suppliers often have written agreements with exclusive distributors stipulating certain responsibilities that are too important to be left to a mutual understanding. Contracts are signed, outlining tenure of appointment, trading area, sale conditions, warranty considerations, and extent of product line coverage. However, exclusive dealing may not be legal if it tends to lessen competition in the exclusive geographical area.

Caterpillar Tractor Company relies on a strong network of exclusive dealers. Its president and chairman made this statement: "We have a tremendous regard for our dealers. We do not bypass or undercut them. Some of our competitors do and their dealers quit. Caterpillar dealers don't quit, they die rich."[6] This statement illustrates the cooperation and loyalty that can exist in an exclusive distribution system.

CHANNELS OF DISTRIBUTION: A SYSTEM OF INTERDEPENDENCY

Channel Interdependency
The interdependent relationships among the members of a channel of distribution.

Now that we have described some channels of distribution, we should emphasize that any such channel is a system of interdependency among its members. If all participants recognize this **channel interdependency,** the channel operates properly and smoothly.

When a manufacturer seeks the help of an intermediary in distributing products, it relinquishes some measure of control over its own products. However, the manufacturer gains the benefit of not having to finance or manage the relinquished activities. It is thus free to concentrate on its core competencies—the activities it can best perform. Some manufacturers, realizing that production is the activity they can best handle, surrender virtually all marketing activities to intermediaries. Thus, the use of channel intermediaries is a manifestation of specialization of labor—or, in this case, specialization of management.

The efficiency of the distribution system is affected by channel interdependency because the actions of one channel member can greatly affect the performance of another or of the channel as a whole. Although the survival of intermediaries is in grave jeopardy if the manufacturer's operation fails, the manufacturer may also be driven out of business by the mistakes and failures of distributors. Channel success is thus rooted in a community of mutual interest and functional interdependency.

Because the actions of one channel member may greatly influence the performance of another channel member, the relations among channel members are of considerable interest. The retailer relies on the manufacturer to create an adequate sales potential through advertising, product development, and other marketing strategies. An exclusive dealer's welfare is in jeopardy if a manufacturer's marketing strategy is not successful. A manufacturer may depend on the successful performance of a small group of wholesalers, which cannot be left to sink or swim on their own merits. In the following sections, we examine several issues concerning the interdependency among channel members.

Channel Cooperation

The objectives and marketing strategies of two channel members—for example, a manufacturer and a retailer—may be in total harmony. Both parties may recognize that their tasks are linked and that by working together they can jointly exploit a marketing opportunity. The manufacturer promptly delivers a high-quality product with a good reputation; the retailer prices the product as expected and carries an inventory of the full product line. **Channel cooperation** is a situation in which the marketing objectives and strategies of two channel members are harmonious.

Channel Cooperation
A situation in which the marketing objectives and strategies of distribution channel members are harmonious.

Channel Conflict

Channel conflict is a situation in which channel members have disagreements; their relationship is antagonistic. Disagreements may relate to the channel's common purpose or the responsibility for certain activities. The behavior of one channel member may be seen as inhibiting the attainment of another channel member's goals.[7]

Consider the following instance of channel conflict. In 1992, Goodyear began selling its products to Sears—something it had not done before. In fact, for more than 60 years, Goodyear tires could be purchased only on new cars or from the company's exclusive network of independent dealers. In 1993, Goodyear started selling replacement tires to Discount Tire Co., a big independent tire retailer. These new alignments with Sears and Discount caused considerable channel conflict. Goodyear's independent dealers expressed anger and feelings of betrayal. They protested that Goodyear's actions had eroded their competitive positions. Many dealers retaliated by taking on competing brands, especially private brands.

Channel conflict also arises when a wholesaler is frustrated because a manufacturer bypasses it and sells directly to the larger accounts. Another typical situation occurs when a dealer believes its investment in inventory should be minimized, but its distributor's promise of speedy delivery cannot be relied on because the distributor does not maintain the proper inventory level.

Other issues of conflict relate to manufacturers', wholesalers', or retailers' opinions that they are not making enough money on the product line because another channel member's actions are inadequate.

Channel Conflict
A situation in which antagonism exists between distribution channel members.

Channel Power

An organization in the channel of distribution that is able to exert power and influence over other channel members is referred to as the **channel leader,** or **channel captain.**[8] For instance, Home Box Office is the channel captain for the distribution of movies on pay TV. HBO virtually dictates how much it will pay for a film. Furthermore, HBO may finance film production. In recent years, it has become a major source of financing for independent movie producers. Similarly, a large retailer such as Wal-Mart may be able to exert so much channel power, by the size of its purchases, that it can dictate marketing strategy to less powerful channel members. In placing an order for a private-label brand, Wal-Mart may insist on certain product specifications, prices, or delivery dates. A small manufacturer may be so dependent on the Wal-Mart order that it changes the specifications on its own brand so it can produce a product that meets Wal-Mart specifications.

Channel Power
The extent to which a channel member is able to influence the behavior of another channel member.

Channel Leader
A distribution channel member that is able to exert power and influence over other channel members. Also called channel captain.

REVERSE DISTRIBUTION

Backward Channel
A channel of distribution for recycling in which the customary flow from producer to ultimate user is reversed.

In recent decades, the recycling of waste has become an important ecological goal. The major problem with recycling is determining who is responsible for the "reverse distribution" process it involves. The macromarketing task is to establish a **backward channel** of distribution, one in which the ultimate consumer who seeks to recycle waste materials must undergo a role change.[9]

By recycling your old newspapers or metal cans, you become a "producer" of a usable product that has some economic utility. Thus, in this backward channel, the consumer has become the first link in a distribution process rather than the last. Realistically, the backward channel is likely to be run by traditional manufacturers of paper or cans. Yet the flow of goods is the reverse of what most descriptions of marketing operations suggest.

ETHICAL, POLITICAL, AND LEGAL FORCES IN DISTRIBUTION MANAGEMENT

We might think of recycling as involving certain ethical issues as well as issues of distribution. Indeed, several ethical issues arise in connection with distribution and its macromarketing role. One of the most controversial issues is discussed below.

Does Distribution Cost Too Much?

As mentioned earlier, a commonly heard cry is "eliminate the middleman!" But as we have explained, eliminating intermediaries does not eliminate the functions they perform. Thus, a manufacturer that eliminates wholesalers will have to perform the wholesaling function itself. This may cost more than using independent wholesalers, because the wholesalers were better at their job than the manufacturer would or could be.

A critic might note that some individual aspects of the distribution system are nonessential. Yet it has been shown over and over again that "nonessentials" such as convenience are important to consumers. The success of 7-Eleven, Quick-Trip, and similar stores proves that consumers want, and will pay for, convenient location and quick service. The customers decide the trade-offs in this case, paying a little more money to avoid paying with their time. People can quickly and profoundly influence the distribution system simply by where they shop. It is arguable that distribution is the aspect of marketing that is most responsive to consumer demands.

SUMMARY

Distribution is a necessary but often misunderstood marketing function. The common desire to "eliminate the middleman" shows that the general public has little appreciation for the role played by the channels of distribution.

Learning Objective 1
Explain the general purpose of distribution and logistics in the marketing system.
A channel of distribution makes it possible for title or possession of a product to pass from producer to con-

sumer. Distribution provides time and place utility to buyers by delivering the right products at the right time in the right place. Logistics helps bridge the gap between manufacturers and final users.

Learning Objective 2
Evaluate the role of logistics and physical distribution in the marketing mix.
Logistics describes the entire process by which materials, in-process inventory, and finished goods move into, through, and out of the firm. Logistics manage-

ment involves planning, implementing, and controlling the efficient flow of both inbound materials and outbound finished products. Physical distribution, one aspect of logistics, provides time and place utility by moving products from producer to consumer or organizational user in a timely and efficient manner.

Learning Objective 3
Show how distribution managers can make physical distribution provide maximum satisfaction to buyers while reducing costs.
The central objective of physical distribution is to keep costs down while keeping the level of service up. Yet improved service raises costs, and reduced costs lower levels of service. Distribution managers must balance these two elements. The marketing concept suggests that managers should determine what level of service will fit buyers' needs and what prices are acceptable to them.

Learning Objective 4
Explain the total cost approach to physical distribution.
The total cost concept takes a systems approach to physical distribution. By placing the emphasis on controlling total cost, the manager focuses on how the parts of the distribution system can be used to keep total costs down. Raising expenditures in one part of the system may reduce total costs; lowering expenditures in one part of the system might raise total costs.

Learning Objective 5
Understand that all marketers—even not-for-profit and service organizations—engage in distribution.
All marketers, including not-for-profit, service, and for-profit concerns, engage in some form of distribution because there is always some gap between the marketer and the customer that must be bridged.

Learning Objective 6
Characterize the functions of channel intermediaries.
Channel intermediaries perform a variety of functions, including breaking bulk, accumulating bulk, sorting, creating assortments, reducing transactions, transportation, storage, communication (selling and buying), financing, management services, and other facilitating functions.

Learning Objective 7
Identify the major channels of distribution used by marketers.
The major distribution channels for consumer goods are: (1) producer to consumer; (2) producer to retailer to consumer; (3) producer to wholesaler to retailer to consumer (the most commonly used consumer goods channel); and (4) producer to wholesaler (agent) to wholesaler to retailer to consumer. The major organizational products channels are: (1) producer to user; (2) producer to wholesaler to user; and (3) producer to agent (wholesaler) to user. There are many variations on these basic channel models, many of which involve specialized intermediaries.

Learning Objective 8
Describe the major vertical marketing systems.
In the corporate vertical marketing system, the members are owned outright by the controlling organization to ensure cooperation and increase effectiveness. An administered strategic alliance is made up of organizations that collaborate or follow the lead of the dominant member of the system. In a contractual vertical marketing system, the members are linked to the channel leader by formal contract. In all cases, the purpose of the vertical marketing system is to ensure cooperation among channel members, and the goal is increased effectiveness of the channel.

Learning Objective 9
Explain how distribution interacts with other elements of the marketing mix.
Marketing mix elements are interdependent. For example, an organization's pricing plan may determine its distribution outlets, and many product characteristics—such as perishability, technical complexity, and image—affect the channels of distribution used.

Learning Objective 10
Differentiate among channel cooperation, channel conflict, and channel power.
Channel cooperation occurs when channel members share harmonious marketing objectives and strategies. Channel conflict characterizes channels of distribution in which there is some disharmony. Conflict should not go unmanaged. Channel power is the ability of one organization in a channel of distribution to exert influence over other channel members. The most powerful organization is the channel leader.

KEY TERMS

Logistics (p. 288)
Materials management (p.288)
Physical distribution (p. 288)
Channel of distribution (p. 291)
Merchant intermediary (p. 291)
Agent intermediary (p. 291)
Conventional channel of distribution
   (p. 291)
Bulk-breaking function (p. 293)
Bulk-accumulating function (p. 294)
Assembler (p. 294)
Sorting function (p. 294)
Assorting function (p. 294)
Transportation (p. 296)
Storage (p. 298)
Warehouse (p. 299)

Inventory control (p. 299)
Systems concept (p. 299)
Total cost concept (p. 299)
Communication function (p. 300)
Selling function (p. 300)
Buying function (p. 300)
Service function (p. 301)
Credit function (p. 301)
Risk-taking function (p. 301)
Jobber (p. 305)
Broker (p. 305)
Vertical marketing system (p. 306)
Corporate vertical marketing system
   (p. 306)
Administered strategic alliance
   (p. 306)

Contractual vertical marketing system
   (p. 307)
Retailer cooperative organization
   (p. 307)
Voluntary chain (p. 308)
Franchise (p. 308)
Intensive distribution (p. 310)
Selective distribution (p. 310)
Exclusive distribution (p. 311)
Channel interdependency (p. 311)
Channel cooperation (p. 312)
Channel conflict (p. 312)
Channel power (p. 312)
Channel leader, or channel captain
   (p. 312)
Backward channel (p. 313)

QUESTIONS FOR REVIEW AND CRITICAL THINKING

1. Define logistics. What are its components?

2. Indicate what is meant by the systems concept in physical distribution. In what ways does the use of this concept benefit marketers?

3. What are the major ways in which an organization can use physical distribution as a means of establishing a competitive advantage?

4. What type of physical distribution system would you use for the following products?
   a. Bird of Paradise plants from Hawaii
   b. Kiwi fruit and avocados from California
   c. Barbie dolls

5. What might happen if we eliminated wholesaler intermediaries for the following brands?
   a. Hathaway shirts
   b. Cutty Sark scotch whisky
   c. Weyerhauser lumber

6. Outline the macromarketing functions performed by wholesalers and retailers.

7. At a national bottlers' meeting, the vice-president of marketing for the Dr Pepper Company said: "No matter how good a job we do, [consumers] can't get Dr Pepper unless you [bottlers] have made the sale to retailers." Why would the vice-president say this?

8. A few years ago, Airwick professional products division, which sells a variety of disinfectants, cleaning agents, insecticides, and environmental sanitation products, sold its products through a network of 65 distributors and 10 branch sales offices. The company decided to drop its sales branches. What circumstances might lead to such a change in channel strategy?

9. Only recently have medical professionals started to realize that they, like manufacturers, must give thought to their distribution systems. What distribution decisions might hospitals, dentists, and pediatricians have to make?

10. How will the purchase decisions of Sam's Wholesale Club, Price Club, and similar stores affect Procter & Gamble's distribution system?

11. If you were a manufacturer of the following products, what channels of distribution would you select?
   a. Fax machines
   b. Automobile mufflers
   c. Personal computers
   d. Telephones
   e. Toy dolls

12. Outline the channel of distribution for the following:
    a. Airline
    b. Japanese automobile
    c. Pizza restaurant

13. What advantages do vertical marketing systems have over conventional marketing systems?

14. Would you use exclusive, selective, or intensive distribution for the following products? Why?
    a. Dr Pepper
    b. Lexus automobiles
    c. Ethan Allen furniture
    d. Fieldcrest Mills towels
    e. Michelin tires

15. Identify some possible sources of conflict in a channel of distribution.

16. What macromarketing functions do intermediaries perform for society at large?

17. Form groups of six with two students representing a supermarket retailer, two students representing a grocery wholesaler, and two students representing a manufacturer of packaged foods. Identify at least three issues over which channel conflicts might arise. Each channel member team should state its position on these issues.

INTERNET INSIGHTS

Exercises

1. Traditionally travel agents have played a key role in the distribution system for travel services. As use of the Internet continues to expand, however, radical changes are taking place in the travel services distribution system. Go to a search engine such as Yahoo (http://www.yahoo.com) or HotBot (http://www.hotbot.com). Then enter Airlines—Reservation Systems as a subject. Select a document. Read the document for information about using the Internet to purchase airline tickets. Then answer the following questions on a sheet of paper. Bring your answers to class for discussion.
    a. What are the best ways to make airline reservations using the Internet?
    b. Who is most likely to use the Internet as the distribution system for airline tickets?
    c. Who will be unserved by this distribution system? What alternative channel will best reach the unserved group?
    d. Is there potential for channel conflict? Explain your answer.
    e. What is the future of this distribution system for airline tickets? For other travel services? Why?

2. RIC, Inc. is a speciality food broker. Go to
    http://www.ricbrokers.com
    and describe RIC's service. Read the selection on "Why use a food broker?" and summarize the main points.

3. The Rainforest company is both a manufacturer and wholesaler. Go to:
    http://www.the-rainforest.com.forest1
    What type of products do they distribute? Why do they have information about rain forests on their home page?

Address Book

Logistics Business Magazine
http://www.ibclogistics.demon.co.uk/

U.S. Council for International Business
http://www.imex.com/uscib

ETHICS IN PRACTICE: TAKE A STAND

1. A liquor wholesaler wishes to purchase five cases of a small California winery's vintage cabernet sauvignon (a red wine) which has received favorable reviews. The winery says this wine is in short supply and it ships five-case orders only to wholesalers that also purchase five cases of its chablis

(a white wine). The chablis is rated as a very ordinary wine, and the wholesaler sells many comparable brands. What should the wholesaler do?

2. A supermarket sells many products packaged in aluminum cans and glass bottles. It does not offer any recycling facility or service. Is this responsible?

3. Wal-Mart notifies manufacturers that it no longer will deal with intermediaries. Its intentions are to deal directly with manufacturers. The move squeezes independent wholesalers and brokers out of the picture. Is this right?

VIDEO CASE 11-1

StockPot Soups

StockPot Soups is a manufacturer of fresh, homemade-style soup concentrates. The Fortun brothers founded StockPot Soups after 20 years in the food business. The company has 100 employees. Its products include homemade-style soups, such as lobster bisque, chicken-flavored vegetable gumbo, cream of broccoli, and clam chowder. Production is labor intensive, which drives up the cost. Grocery wholesalers and retailers often stock five or six competing brands. Most competitors offer national brands. Like many small start-up companies in their early years, StockPot faces the daunting challenge of convincing distributors to carry its products. Wholesalers that supply grocers simply do not want to carry another soup. This is also true of wholesalers that supply food services and institutional customers.

Questions
1. Describe StockPot's distribution channel(s).
2. What strategy can StockPot use to gain distribution?
3. Are there any innovative channels of distribution that StockPot can tap?

VIDEO CASE 11-2

Aquathin Corporation

"Be humble." "It's not what happens during the day—it's how you handle it." "The customer is always right—within reason." "Profit is not a dirty word—if you earn it."

Those maxims are on a list of 23 "Aquathin axioms" disseminated by Aquathin Corp., a Pompano Beach, Florida, maker of water purification systems. It calls them "principles under which the company operates." If Aquathin's founders have difficulty observing the first one, it is understandable. Alfred Lipshultz and his father, Mitchell, have every right to take great pride in their company's success.

The company began operations in 1980, with the Lipshultzes and a partner putting up $14,000 as start-up capital for making a sink-top purifier. The partner was to handle manufacturing and the Lipshultzes marketing. But things didn't go well.

Revenues, $70,000 the first year, fell to $30,000 the next. There were problems with assembling the product and financial disagreements with physicians' clinics that were selling it. The Lipshultzes bought out their partner and shifted sales from the clinics to a dealer network.

Now Aquathin's revenues top that second-year figure every three days. It has 57 water purification products and three patents, including one for a reverse osmosis/deionization system that cleanses tap water of salts, heavy metals, disease-causing microorganisms, industrial pollutants, and pesticides.

Aquathin's purifiers are used in homes, businesses, and laboratories. When the company realized that problems existed abroad with drinking water supplies and inferior filters, the company saw opportunities for international marketing.

Questions
1. What is the nature of Aquathin's markets?
2. In your opinion, what type of distribution system would work best for Aquathin?
3. What tactics would be necessary to implement the distribution system you suggested?
4. In your opinion, what type of distribution would be necessary for international marketing?

RETAILING AND WHOLESALING OF GOODS AND SERVICES

Chapter 12

Learning Objectives

After you have studied this chapter, you will be able to:

1. Describe the nature of retailing and wholesaling.
2. Categorize the various types of retailers by ownership and prominent strategy.
3. Discuss the growth of direct marketing as a retail strategy.
4. Explain the major premise of the wheel of retailing theory.
5. Understand the nature of retailers' marketing mixes.
6. Distinguish between merchant wholesalers and agents and describe their functions in the distribution system.
7. Show how full-service and limited-service merchant wholesalers contribute to the marketing system.
8. Identify the marketing contributions of agent intermediaries, such as brokers, auction companies, and selling agents.
9. Understand the key elements of wholesalers' strategies.
10. Describe some of the legal concerns associated with the development and management of channels of distribution.

Supermarket-sized health foods stores are springing up in selected markets around the country, and produce is one of the keys to their growth.

Natural foods chains, such as Whole Foods Market, Wild Oats, and Fresh Fields, are setting the pace in a trend toward big stores. With selling floors that range from 20,000 square feet to 30,000 square feet, these operators can offer the variety that consumers normally associate only with traditional supermarkets. Since natural foods stores traditionally have been small, ranging from 2,000 square feet to 5,000 square feet, the big stores represent just what supermarket operators might be expected to dread: yet another alternative type of food retailer.

The big health foods stores can knock smaller health foods operations in the same market for a loop. And while they pose less of a challenge to the supermarket industry, they tend to put upscale operators on red alert.

Natural foods chains are riding on the back of a long-running trend: consumers' increased attention to, and knowledge of, nutrition. However, it's not all milk and honey for the big natural foods retailers, as the experience of Fresh Fields in Richmond, Virginia, demonstrates. The chain, based in Rockville, Maryland, opened a 30,000-square-foot "healthy foods supermarket" in Richmond in February 1993 and closed it eight months later because of flat sales. What went wrong?

Competitive reaction from Ukrop's Super Markets, the market leader, was one aspect of the problem for Fresh Fields. Six months before Fresh Fields opened, dozens of Ukrop's employees made as many as 50 to 60 visits to Fresh Fields stores in Charlottesville and northern Virginia to check out the competitor. Ukrop's expanded its offerings of organic produce and put into circulation a new advertising slogan: "Taste the freshness." Another tactic Ukrop's employed to protect market share was to run promotions in partnership with Good Foods Grocery, a local health foods retailer with stores near two of Ukrop's units.

Another factor in Fresh Fields' failure was that it operated only one store in the market. More than one store was needed to offset overhead. Pricing may also have been a factor because, although Fresh Fields' prices on many items were competitive, the store didn't have the lowest prices.

Retailers like Fresh Fields, Whole Foods Market, and Ukrop's are vital components in the channel of distribution. This chapter begins by addressing the importance of retailing and classifying retailers according to several criteria. It then describes a theory proposed to explain the historical patterns of change in retail institutions. Next, it discusses retail management strategies, focusing on merchandise assortment, location, atmospherics, and customer services. It then turns to wholesaling, examining types of wholesalers, their importance to the U.S. economy, and the strategies they use to market goods and services.

RETAILING AND ITS IMPORTANCE

Retailing
All business activities concerned with the sale of products to the ultimate users of those products.

Retailing consists of all business activities concerning the sale of goods and services to ultimate consumers. Retailing involves a retailer, traditionally a store or a service establishment, dealing with consumers who are acquiring goods or services for their own use rather than for resale. Of course, Wal-Mart, The Gap, Best Buy, and other familiar organizations offering products for sale to consumers are retailers. However, the definition of retailing includes some less-than-obvious service marketers, such as hotels, movie theaters, restaurants, and ice-cream truck operators. And even if an intermediary calls itself a "factory outlet," a "wholesale club," or a "shopping channel," it is a retailer if its purpose is to sell to the ultimate consumer.[1]

Viewed in the context of the channel of distribution, retailers are the important "final link" in the process that brings goods from manufacturers to consumers. Poor marketing on the part of retailers can negate all the planning and preparation that has gone into other marketing activities.

In the United States, there are more than 2.6 million retailing institutions accounting for well over $1.9 trillion in sales.[2] About 14 percent of U.S. workers are employed in retailing, and retailers' sales account for approximately 97 percent of the sizable chunk of the gross national product known as personal income.

RETAILING INSTITUTIONS—TOWARD A SYSTEM OF CLASSIFICATIONS

Retailers are a diverse group of businesses. In the distribution of food there are supermarkets, convenience stores, restaurants, and various specialty outlets. Merchandise retailers may be department stores, apparel stores, consumer electronics stores, home improvement stores, pet shops, or various types of retailing systems for home shopping. Service retailers, such as movie theaters and banks, are as diverse as the types of services they offer for sale.

Retailing is dynamic, and retail institutions evolve constantly. For example, institutions such as "mom and pop" grocery stores are at the end of their life cycle. Individual companies like Sears, which began this century as a mail-order retailer of watches, are constantly evolving into new types of retailers. Warehouse clubs and interactive shopping at home with personal computers are but two retailing innovations developed in recent decades. In the next 20 years, we can expect retailers to adjust to their changing environments by making further transformations.

In light of this constant change, and of the very large number of retailers in the United States, how can we classify retail institutions into more easily analyzed groups? Two commonly used methods classify retailers on the basis of ownership and prominent strategy.

Classifying Retailers by Ownership

Independent Retailer
Retail establishment that is not owned or controlled by any other organization.

Leased Department Retailer
Independent retailer that owns the merchandise stocked but leases floor space from another retailer and usually operates under that retailer's name.

One method of categorizing retailers is by ownership. Most retailers are **independent retailers,** operating as single-unit entities. Independent operations may be proprietorships, partnerships, or corporations, but they are usually owned by one operator, a family, or a small number of individuals. They are not generally integrated into a larger corporation. These retailers are often thought of as small, but some are quite sizable. Taken together, they are an important part of the American retailing scene.

An independent retailer that owns the merchandise stocked but leases floor space from another retailer is a **leased department retailer.** A leased department—for example, a jewelry, camera, or pharmaceutical department—operates independently from the lessor retailer, although it often operates under the lessor's name. The lessor grants leased department retailers this degree of independence because they have special expertise in handling the particular product line, will increase total store traffic, or are necessary to the lessor because consumers expect to find the departments' merchandise in the store.

If a retail establishment is not independent, it is classified into one of two basic groups: chains or ownership groups. The most familiar of these classifications is the **chain store**—one of a group of shops bearing the same name and having roughly the same store image. Chain-store systems consist of two or more stores of a similar type that are centrally owned and operated.

Chain Store
One of a group of two or more stores of a similar type, centrally owned and operated.

Chains have been successful for a number of reasons, but one of the most important is the opportunity they have to take advantage of economies of scale in buying and selling goods. Conducting centralized buying for several stores permits chains to obtain the lower prices associated with large purchases. They can then maintain their prices, thus increasing their margins; or they can cut prices and attract greater sales volume. Unlike small independents with lesser financial means, they can also take advantage of promotional tools, such as television advertising, by spreading the expense among many member stores, thus "stretching their promotional budget." Other expenses, such as costs for computerized inventory control systems, may also be shared by all stores.

Chains vary in size. Dean & DeLuca, with two gourmet food stores; Hansen Galleries, with six art gallery outlets; and Kmart, with more than 2,500 stores, are all chain stores. The number of stores in a chain can make a big difference in the way the business operates.

Corporate Chain
Chain with 11 or more stores.

According to the U.S. Department of Commerce, the term **corporate chain** is used for chains with 11 or more stores. Typically, as the number of units in a chain increases, management becomes more centralized, and each store manager has less autonomy for determining the overall marketing strategy. Although corporate chains possess many advantages over independents, some analysts say independents and smaller chains are more flexible. They may be better able to apply such marketing techniques as segmentation than bigger operations, whose appeal must be more general.

Retail franchise operations are a special type of chain. Although the broad marketing strategy is centrally planned, the retail outlets are independently owned and operated. Franchises provide an excellent example of how chains fit the American culture. Midas Muffler Shops, Arby's, and other nationwide franchise chains can be found in nearly every population center. Thus, as our mobile citizenry moves from place to place, a familiar Midas shop or Arby's is "waiting" for them when they arrive. Each new franchise benefits from the company's experience, reputation, and shared resources.

Ownership Group
Organization made up of stores or small chains, each having a separate name, identity, and image but all operating under the control of a central owner.

The other type of retailing organization is the **ownership group**—an organization made up of various stores or small chains, each having a separate name, identity, and image but all operating under the ultimate control of a central owner. Typically, the members of such groups are former corporate chains bought out by the much larger ownership groups. Dayton-Hudson, Federated Department Stores, and B.A.T. Industries are ownership groups that operate stores with different names. For example, Dayton-Hudson operates Target stores, Scribner's, Mervyn's, and others. Bloomingdale's, Lazarus, Burdines, Rich's, Jordan Marsh, The Bon Marché, Abraham & Straus, and Stern's are owned by the Federated ownership group.

Classifying Retailers by Prominent Strategy

We can also classify retailers based on their most prominent retail strategies. The decision to market products and services with an in-store retailing strategy or a direct marketing (nonstore) retailing strategy is such a discriminating factor that we

MAJOR GROUP	RETAILER CLASSIFICATION	BRIEF DESCRIPTION
In-store	Specialty store	Narrow variety, deep selection within a product class, personalized service; makes up large bulk of all retailing operations
	Department store	Generally chain operations, wide variety, full range of services
	Supermarket	Wide variety of food and nonfood products, large departmentalized operation featuring self-service aisles and centralized checkouts
	Convenience store	Little variety, shallow selection, fast service
	General mass merchandiser	Wide variety, shallow selection of high-turnover products, low prices, few customer services
	Catalog showroom	General mass merchandiser using a catalog to promote items
	Warehouse club	General mass merchandiser that requires membership to allow shopping, goods stored warehouse-style
	Specialty mass merchandiser	Less variety but greater depth than general mass merchandiser, low prices, few customer services
	Off-price retailer	Specialty mass merchandiser selling a limited line of nationally known brand names
	Category discounter	Specialty mass merchandiser offering deep discounts and extensive assortment and depth in a specific product category
Direct marketing	Mail-Order/Direct response	Generally low operating costs; emphasis on convenience; often uses computerized data bases; includes mail order, television home shopping, and telephone sales
	Door-to-door selling	High labor cost, image problems; decreasing in the U.S., increasing in less-developed countries
	Computer-interactive retailing	Consumer initiates contact with retailer via interactive computer system
	Vending machines	High-turnover products, low prices

EXHIBIT 12–1
Some Retailers Classified by
Prominent Strategy

will break our discussion into these two major groupings. Exhibit 12–1 shows these groupings and their subcategories.

In-Store Retailing

Many fundamental strategies differentiate in-store retailers. The variety of products they sell, store size, price level relative to competitors, degree of self-service, location, and other variables can be used to categorize retailers by strategy. Each has its particular advantages and disadvantages, and each fits particular markets and situations. Try to envision the following store classes for what they represent—responses to particular marketing opportunities.

Specialty Store
Retail establishment that sells a single product or a few related lines.

Specialty Stores. **Specialty stores,** also called *single-line retailers* and *limited-line retailers,* are differentiated from other retailers by their degree of specialization—that is, the narrowness of their product mixes and the depth of their product lines. These traditional retailers specialize within a particular product category, selling only items targeted to a narrow market segment or items requiring a particular selling expertise, such as children's shoes, automobile mufflers, or clocks. Service establishments, such as restaurants and banks, are often classified as specialty retailers. These retailers do not try to be all things to all people.

General stores dominated American retailing until after the Civil War because, except in large cities, too few people could be found to justify specialty retailers. Specialty stores have enjoyed remarkable success in recent years, however, illustrat-

Department store buyers often manage product lines such as housewares. College graduates often find buyer positions lead to executive-level jobs in retailing.

ing the importance of effective market segmentation and target marketing. The major reason for their success is the development of considerable expertise in their particular product lines. Wallpapers to Go, for example, offers free wallpapering lessons to instruct consumers on what wallpapering techniques to use and what to buy.

Department Store
Departmentalized retail outlet, often large, offering a wide variety of products and generally providing a full range of customer services.

Department Stores. **Department stores** are typically larger than specialty stores. They carry a wide selection of products, including furniture, clothing, home appliances, housewares, and, depending on the size of the operation, a good many other products. These stores are "departmentalized" both physically and organizationally. Each department is operated largely as a separate entity headed by a buyer, who has considerable independence and authority in buying and selling products and who is responsible for the department's profits. Independent department stores do exist, but most department stores are members of chains or ownership groups.

Most department stores are characterized by a full range of services, including credit plans, delivery, generous return policies, restaurants and coffee shops, and a host of other extras such as fashion clinics, closed-door sales for established customers only, and even etiquette classes for customers' children. Such services, as well as the need to carry a wide variety of merchandise and maintain a large building, increase store operating costs and necessitate higher prices than those at mass merchandise discount stores. Some consumers seek the service and atmosphere of the department store but then make actual purchases at a discount store or by calling a catalog retailer's 800 number or visiting their Internet site. In short, discounters and other types of store operators are formidable competitors for traditional department stores.

Supermarkets and Convenience Stores. The modern supermarket differs greatly from the "grocery store" from which it evolved. The grocery operator of the early 1900s knew most customers, personally filled customers' orders, and was likely to offer both delivery service and credit. With the advent of the telephone, the grocer accepted phone orders and offered delivery service to the customer's home. When the Great Atlantic and Pacific Tea Company discontinued its delivery service in 1912, A&P began the transformation process from grocery to supermarket.

In 1933, King Kullen Stores (Jamaica, New York) placed its cans, packages, and produce on crates and pine boards and introduced self-service. The evolution of the supermarket continues today.

Supermarket
Any large, self-service, departmentalized retail establishment but especially one that primarily sells food items.

Today's **supermarket** is a large departmentalized retail establishment selling a variety of products, mostly food items but also health and beauty aids, housewares, magazines, and much more. The dominant features of the supermarket marketing strategy are large in-store inventories on self-service aisles and centralized checkout lines. Often, low prices resulting from self-service are stressed.

Scrambled Merchandising
Offering of products for sale in a retail establishment not traditionally associated with those products.

The inclusion of nonfood items on supermarket shelves was once novel in that it represented the stocking of items that did not traditionally belong in the supermarket's group of offerings. The name given to this practice is **scrambled merchandising.** Scrambled merchandising permits the supermarket (as well as other types of retailing institutions) to sell items that carry a higher margin than most food items; thus, it provides a means to increase profitability. Across the board, however, supermarket profit margins are slim—only 1 to 2 percent of total sales. Supermarkets rely on high levels of inventory turnover to attain their return on investment goals.

Supermarkets were among the first retailers to stress *discount strategies.* Using such strategies, large self-service retail establishments sell a variety of high-turnover products at low prices. A good part of a retailer's ability to hold prices down stems from the practice of offering few services. Other than the costs of the goods they sell, most retailers find that personnel costs are their largest financial outlay. Thus, by eliminating most of the sales help, having no delivery staff, and hiring employees who are stock clerks and cash-register operators rather than true salespeople, discounters are able to take a big step toward reducing their prices. Buying in large volume also reduces the cost of goods sold.

Convenience Store
Small grocery store stressing convenient location and quick service and typically charging higher prices than other retailers selling similar products.

Convenience stores are, in essence, small supermarkets. They have developed rapidly as a major threat to their larger cousins. 7-Elevens, Quick-Trips, and other imitative convenience stores have sprung up and multiplied across America. These stores carry a carefully selected variety of high-turnover consumer products. As their names generally imply, the major benefit to consumers is convenience—convenience of location and convenience of time. By choosing handy locations and staying open 15, 18, or 24 hours a day, seven days a week, convenience stores add "extra" time and place utility. Consumers must pay for these conveniences and seem quite willing to do so.[3] Managers of these stores price most of their "convenience goods" at levels higher than supermarkets to provide high profit margins. Convenience stores are unusual among retailers because they have both a high margin and a high inventory turnover.

Mass Merchandise Retailer
Retailer that sells products at discount prices to achieve high sales volume. Also called a mass merchandise discount store.

Mass Merchandisers. **Mass merchandise retailers** (or mass merchandise discount stores) sell at discount prices to achieve high sales volume. Mass merchandisers cut back on their stores' interior design and on customer service in their efforts to reduce costs and maintain low prices.

Supermarkets were the forerunners of mass merchandisers. In fact, the term *supermarket retailing* has been used to describe Target, Venture, and many other stores that have adopted the supermarket strategy, incorporating large inventories, self-service, centralized checkouts, and discount prices. Using supermarket-style discount strategies helps mass merchandisers to offer prices lower than those at traditional stores.

General Mass Merchandisers
Mass merchandisers that carry a wide variety of merchandise cutting across product categories.

We can classify mass merchandisers as general or specialty. **General mass merchandisers,** such as Wal-Mart, carry a wide variety of merchandise that cuts across product categories. They may carry everything from drug and cosmetic items to electrical appliances, clothing, and toys. The wide variety of goods general mass merchandisers carry at low prices means that they usually cannot afford to carry a deep selection of goods in any product line. Retailers usually carry either a wide variety or a deep selection, but not both. The expense associated with having many kinds of goods and many choices of each kind make the two possibilities largely mutually exclusive. (Indeed, small retailers often can compete with giant mass merchandisers on the basis of selection.)

In contrast with general mass merchandisers, **specialty mass merchandisers** carry a product selection that is limited to one or a few product categories. For example, some specialty mass merchandisers sell only clothing.

We will discuss two types of general mass merchandisers, catalog showrooms and warehouse clubs, and two types of specialty mass merchandisers, category discounters and off-price retailers. **Catalog showrooms,** like Service Merchandise, publish large catalogs identifying products for sale in the store. Typically, these are high-margin items. The catalog, or an accompanying price list, shows the "normal" retail price of the items and the catalog discounter's much lower price. Often, the discounter's price is printed without a dollar sign in the form of an easily decipherable "code" to let the buyer know that a special deal—not available to just anyone—is being offered. Catalog discounters, like other discounters, lack customer conveniences and salesperson assistance. Service is slowed by the need to wait for purchased products to be delivered from a storage place. However, this formula permits lower prices.

Some discounters operate a special sort of store called a **warehouse club,** or closed-door house. At Sam's Wholesale Club and Price Club, customers are asked to be "members" and are issued cards that permit entry to the store. Some closed-door houses require that customers already be members of some specific group, such as a labor union or the civil service. While these operations may run the risk of being seen as discriminating against persons not in the target customer group, the membership idea has been found by some retailers to be effective in building store loyalty. Moreover, if membership involves developing an actual list of customers, direct-mail advertisements can be sent to these people, eliminating, to a large extent, other forms of advertising with their large proportions of waste circulation.

Warehouse clubs combine wholesaling and retailing functions. For these marketers, the showroom facility doubles as a storage place, or warehouse, holding the retailer's stock in amounts far greater than traditional retailers retain. Furthermore, when they sell to wholesale or business members, such as restaurants, schools, and day-care centers, the clubs are actually wholesalers. However, many members who purchase as small-business customers also use these stores for personal shopping, and these are retail sales.

Warehouse clubs focus on sales volume and often sell in bulk. This requires that manufacturers change their packaging strategy. For example, Kellogg, which initially refused to package in bulk, now provides dual packages of its cereals and Pop-Tarts for warehouse clubs.

Off-price retailers are specialty mass merchandisers that aggressively promote a limited line of nationally known brand names at low prices. Dress Barn and Burlington Coat Factory stores are typical examples. Off-price retailers can purchase brand name goods such as apparel or footwear at below-wholesale prices (even below prices paid by traditional mass merchandisers) because they typically do not ask for promotional allowances, return privileges, extended payment terms, or the highest-quality merchandise. Off-price stores have evolved because many name-brand manufacturers that once sold exclusively to retailers such as Sak's Fifth Avenue, Neiman Marcus, and Bloomingdale's are now more willing to sell seconds, overruns, discontinued items, or out-of-season merchandise to large volume retailers, even when retail prices are below suggested levels. When a manufacturer owns and operates an off-price store, the retailer is called a *factory outlet.*

Specialty Mass Merchandisers
Mass merchandisers that carry a product selection limited to one or a few product categories.

Catalog Showroom
General mass merchandise outlet in which customers select goods from a catalog and store employees retrieve the selected items from storage.

Warehouse Club
General mass merchandise outlet in which only "members" are allowed to shop. Also called a closed-door *house.*

Off-Price Retailer
Specialty mass merchandise outlet offering a limited line of nationally known brand names.

Category Discounter
Specialty mass merchandise outlet offering extensive assortment and depth in a specific product category. Also called a category killer.

Toys 'Я' Us, Builder's Supply, and Sportsmart are specialty mass merchandisers that apply the supermarket format to the marketing of toys, building supplies, and sporting goods. A mass merchandise discounter specializing in a certain product category is called a **category discounter,** or *category killer.* Sportsmart, which sells 100,000 different items, provides an example. It is radically different from the typical independent sports store because it stocks virtually all competitive offerings of soccer balls, baseball gloves, sports team jackets, and the like, rather than carrying a single brand, as most sports stores do. Category discounters apply a deep discount strategy, with prices even lower than those of general mass merchandisers, and offer the most extensive assortment and greatest depth in the product lines they carry. This retailing strategy is expected to attain most of the local business for the product category and eliminate (or "kill") the competition.

Direct Marketing

Direct Marketing
Marketing in which advertising, telephone sales, or other communications are used to elicit a direct response, such as an order by mail or phone. In a retailing context, also called direct-response retailing.

Direct marketing involves the use of advertising, telephone sales, or other communications to elicit a direct response from consumers. Direct marketing in a retailing context also has been called *nonstore retailing, direct-response retailing,* and *interactive marketing.* The many means of direct marketing include mail-order, direct-response advertising, television home shopping, telemarketing, door-to-door selling, computer interactive retailing, Internet retailing, and vending machines.

What most attracts consumers to the various forms of direct marketing is convenience. Shopping at home, especially at such harried times of the year as the Christmas holidays, provides an undeniable attraction. So does the fact that many direct marketers will ship gift-wrapped orders directly to the person for whom the merchandise was bought, thus freeing the customer from wrapping and delivery chores.

Direct marketing may attract retailers because it offers many opportunities to reduce operating costs. No in-store salespeople need be hired, trained, or paid. Database marketing techniques can customize promotional messages to be targeted to an individual's needs. Often businesses may be headquartered in low-rent areas that ordinary retailers would eschew. Indeed, many corners can be cut by the retailer who conducts business out of the consumer's view.

On the other hand, direct marketing retailers face certain special expenses. The catalog retailer incurs considerable expense in the preparation and mailing of catalogs, for example. Direct marketing retailers also must expedite shipments of goods so that customers receive their orders quickly and in good condition. In part to overcome the sense of unease some feel about buying merchandise they cannot examine, many direct retailers offer liberal return policies.

Whether direct marketing uses catalogs, letters, television, telephone or online services to reach consumers, it always calls for a direct response, generally an order by mail or telephone.

Mail-Order Catalogs. Mail-order retailing through catalogs is one of the oldest forms of direct marketing. Sears, Roebuck and Company began in the mail-order business and moved on to other types of marketing. Today, the famous Sears "wish book" catalog no longer exists. However, companies such as Banana Republic and Sharper Image still combine catalog advertising with both mail-order and in-store retailing. Others, like Sundance, are exclusively committed to direct marketing operations.[4]

Catalog retailers and some other mail-order marketers make extensive use of data-based marketing, discussed in Chapter 4. They compile or buy computer-generated mailing lists from companies that specialize in developing them. The lists can be narrowly focused on selected interest groups, age groups, homeowners, renters, and so on.

EXHIBIT 12–3
Elements of the Retail
Marketing Mix

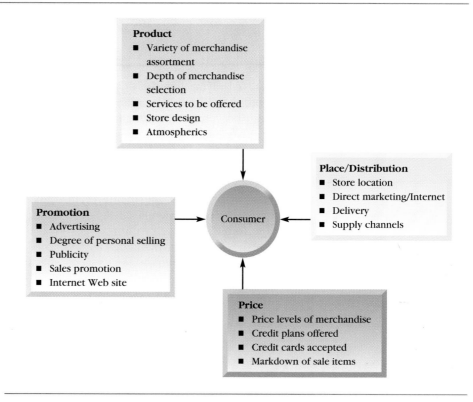

shows some of the decision elements retail marketers face in developing a retail marketing mix.

This chapter will address five areas of special importance to retail strategy. These are merchandise assortment, location, atmosphere, customer service, and database management.

Merchandise Assortment

One image that comes immediately to mind when the word *store* is mentioned is a physical place where merchandise for sale has been assembled. One of a retailer's prime functions is to provide a product assortment for customers. Retailers, then, perform an assorting function—they build desired assortments of varied goods so that manufacturers and customers need not. It is clearly in the interests of both consumers and producers to allow retailers to perform this service and to reward them for it. From the individual customer's perspective, a major advantage of one retailer over a competitor is merchandise assortment. Other things are important, of course, but no shopper will patronize a store unless he or she feels that there is some chance that the merchandise sought will be found there.

How does a retail marketer decide what merchandise assortment to carry? Information and suggestions are available from manufacturers and from intermediaries. Trade magazines and newspapers may offer useful insights. But most importantly, the retailer must carefully consider the target market's needs and wants and match the merchandise selection with those desires. This truth is elemental in effective retail marketing. Yet retailers frequently make "buying mistakes," the costs of which must be absorbed through markdowns or other means. Buying errors cannot be totally avoided, but careful planning can minimize their occurrence. The matter of aligning merchandise offerings with customer desires cannot be detailed here, but it is important to note that marketing—not guesswork—must be the basis of all decisions in this area.

Location, Location, and Location

There is an old saying that the three most important factors in successful retailing are location, location, and location. This is not absolutely true; an out-of-the-way location can be compensated for by other means, especially huge selections and low prices. Nonetheless, the adage makes a point. Retailers are justifiably concerned about locating in the right part of the right town. They must monitor changes that may affect the suitability of an existing location or make another site more attractive. Sometimes they must change an overall location strategy when they move into new areas, as the accompanying Competitive Strategy feature describes.

The right location depends on the type of business and the target customer, not on any formula or rule of thumb. As with merchandise assortment questions, the answer lies in careful planning. Experience dictates certain guidelines, however. Toys 'Я' Us, for example, has several specific guidelines for store location. Its outlets must be in metropolitan areas with populations of at least a quarter-million people, of which an established percentage must be children. Ideally, the selected market should be large enough to support four stores, each of which can be located in an unattached, or free-standing, building near a major mall.

Retail site selection experts note that an important attribute of any intended site is the other types of outlets around it.[5] Obviously, Toys 'Я' Us expects major shopping malls to generate traffic near its toy store locations. More specifically, many retailers seek what are called complementary businesses. Placing a diner near a gas station makes more sense than locating a dress shop there. The nature of the retailer's business operations may affect whether the number or the nature of nearby businesses is important, however. Catalog discounters, for example, can rely on their customers to do some preshopping using the catalogs. This, plus lower prices and the immediate gratification of being able to take items home from the store, reduces the need to locate stores in expensive, high-traffic areas. On the other hand, the traffic generated by a shopping center is far more important to a Docktor Pet Center, a Sharper Image electronics store, or an Orange Julius shop.

Shopping centers are, in fact, important locations for many retailers. As you are well aware, there are several kinds of shopping centers. Older versions are often built as long strings of stores set in a parking area. This design is called a *strip*. A design that features stores built around a central area intended for strolling is called a *mall*.

Shopping centers come in different sizes, essentially small, medium, and large. The official designations are *neighborhood, community,* and *regional*. The neighborhood shopping center is likely to be a small strip containing such shops as a druggist, a dry cleaner, and a supermarket. The community center is larger, with perhaps a variety store, clothing store, or small furniture dealer. The regional center is the largest, with 100 or even 200 stores, serving a large population and drawing customers from a wide geographic area.

The downtown area is, or at least used to be, a shopping center. For any number of reasons, including parking, crime, and a lack of public transportation, *downtowns,* or *central business districts,* have declined greatly in retailing importance since the post-World War II exodus of population to the suburbs. Some city governments have successfully revitalized downtown areas with "downtown malls" built to rekindle interest in downtown-based activities. Inner-city shopping malls such as those located in Boston's Faneuil Hall marketplace and Chicago's Watertower Plaza are thriving.

COMPETITIVE STRATEGY: WHAT WENT RIGHT?

McDonald's International

McDonald's top managers in the United States learned much about efficiency from their colleagues abroad. Whereas the company built its American business in the suburbs, outside the United States it moves first to city centers, where space tends to be expensive and tight. "We had to become very flexible," says James Cantalupo, who oversees McDonald's International in 66 countries.

McDonald's has crammed restaurants into some tight spots—among them, a 13th-century building in Shrewsbury, England, and an 870-square-foot space in Tokyo's Ginza. (The traditional McDonald's occupies 4,500 square feet.)

Menus have also become flexible abroad. In Tokyo, McDonald's offers Teriyaki Burgers (sausage patties with teriyaki sauce) and Chicken Tatsuta (chicken breast in a tempura batter on a bed of sprouts with soy sauce and ginger).

Some overseas McDonald's restaurants, the Euro-195 models, are assembled on-site from five factory-built modules. They have inspired a U.S. counterpart, the Series 2000, named for its square footage. These models have enabled the company to drop its golden arches in towns once deemed too small, such as Holdredge, Nebraska (pop. 5,670).

McDonald's is eyeing more unusual locations. In the past, PepsiCo, which owns Pizza Hut and Kentucky Fried Chicken in addition to Taco Bell, has led the way in offbeat sites, such as mobile carts in airports. But now McDonald's runs restaurants inside 30 Wal-Marts and two Sears stores. It is negotiating to open more such eateries in Home Depots. McDonald's is adding two new restaurants per day worldwide, giving it a count surpassing 14,000.

Atmospherics

Atmospherics
Physical characteristics of a store's environment, such as appearance, layout, and displays.

Retail strategy includes managing every aspect of the store property and its physical characteristics to create an atmosphere conducive to buying. **Atmospherics** are physical characteristics of the environment, such as the store's exterior and interior appearance, layout, and displays, which contribute to the shopper's mental impression of what the store is. Store atmosphere may influence store image, increase store traffic, influence the amount of time shoppers spend in the store, or encourage shoppers to make impulse purchases.[6]

Exterior atmospherics can exert a strong influence on new customers' willingness to enter a store. The building's architecture, parking facilities, storefront, and other outside features may either encourage or discourage patronage by communicating a certain message. The architectural motif of a Taco Bell, for example, makes an impression on the consumer and communicates a message about the restaurant's product line. Planning the interior design and layout to influence the movement and mood of the customer is a primary concern of retailers. Atmospherics, such as lighting, music, colors, and the perception of uncrowded space, are used to foster favorable customer attitudes. Disney stores' layouts are designed to communicate the fun and excitement of Disney theme parks and characters.[7] They are also designed to get customers to walk to the back wall; a large video screen at the back of every store shows animated features as familiar songs are played. The chances are good that customers will walk back to the front by a different route and see additional merchandise.

Customer Service

The customer service a retailer offers may be as important as the merchandise offered for sale—sometimes more important. The courteous personal service and

Retail marketers create and maintain atmospherics as part of their marketing strategies. In the Nike Store on Michigan Avenue in Chicago, life-sized models of cyclists hanging from the ceiling give shoppers the feeling that Nike knows about sports. The store has an art gallery atmosphere that portrays a fun, high-tech, and sports-active image.

information provided by a salesperson may make the difference between success and failure in a retail setting. Services such as maintaining convenient store hours, providing parking facilities, and offering product information are essential to the operation of many retail operations. Other services, such as delivery, alterations, repair, credit, return privileges, and gift wrapping, supplement the retailer's merchandise offerings. In some cases, such as Domino's Pizza, the service offering (in-home delivery) is the primary reason for selecting one retailer over another.

Service Level
Extent of extra services provided to customers; often related to price.

Development of the retailer's marketing mix thus requires decisions about the **service level,** or the extent of extra service that will be provided to consumers. Service-level strategies are often interrelated with pricing strategies. An organization that desires to be competitive in price will typically match competitors' service levels. Retailers that emphasize nonprice competition may provide extra service to create a competitive advantage. Consumers' expectations also are a major determinant of service level. Many retailers regularly survey consumers to determine the amount and quality of service expected.

Database Management

Retailers, as the final link in the distribution channel, have always had direct contact with their customers and in many cases one-on-one relationships with individual customers. The local butcher knew when a customer walked in the shop how she wanted her steaks and chops trimmed. The jewelry store salesperson often sent a note to male customers just before their wife's birthday. So it should come as no surprise that retailers, especially direct marketers, have recognized that customer databases can be used to better serve customers and to develop customer loyalty.

Retailers are in the ideal situation to build proprietary databases. A consumer makes a purchase and it can be automatically entered into and stored on the store's or direct marketer's computer. When that purchase can be linked to the customer's name (phone number or other piece of information that can be linked to customer name), demographic information, and other purchases, it can provide extremely useful information. For example, Helzberg Diamonds, which has 191 stores and operates in 28 states, uses its database to identify customers who responded to special sales promotions in the past. The company then mails letters and brochures encouraging customers to visit the store when similar promotions are taking place.

Supermarkets have learned from their databases that men who purchase diapers between 6 P.M. and 8 P.M. are also likely to purchase beer. Data like these about past purchases and frequency of purchases have immense consequences for retailers. Database marketing is an important part of contemporary retailers' marketing efforts.

WHOLESALING

Wholesaler
Organization or individual that serves as a marketing intermediary by facilitating transfer of products and title to them. Wholesalers do not produce the product, consume it, or sell it to ultimate consumers.

A wholesaler neither produces nor consumes the finished product. A **wholesaler** is a marketing intermediary that buys products and resells them to retailers, other wholesalers, or organizations that use the products in the production of other goods or services. A wholesaler's primary function is facilitating either the transportation of or the transfer of title to the products.

Wholesalers have much in common with retailers. Both act as selling agents for their suppliers and as buying agents for their customers. Both are creators of time and place utility. Both must carefully evaluate the needs of their customers and deliver an appropriate total product of goods and services if they are to succeed. And both have developed ways of performing marketing functions that specially suit market conditions.

CLASSIFYING WHOLESALERS

We discussed the functions of all intermediaries, including wholesalers, in Chapter 11. This section describes the different types of wholesaling establishments and institutions in the United States.

Intermediaries performing wholesaling functions are traditionally divided into two groups—merchants and agents. The only distinction between these categories is whether their members take title to the goods they sell. *Merchant intermediaries* take title; *agent intermediaries* do not. This has nothing at all to do with possession of goods. Some merchants take possession of merchandise and others do not. Some agents take possession of the goods they sell, but most do not. By taking title to goods, the merchant intermediary owns that merchandise and must be prepared to handle any risks associated with ownership—including getting stuck with merchandise that, for whatever reason, turns out to be unsalable.

A recent Census of Wholesale Trade reported that there were approximately 495,000 wholesale trade establishments in the United States.[8] About 415,000 of these were merchant wholesalers. There were more than 41,000 manufacturer's sales branches and more than 36,000 agents and brokers.

Merchant Wholesalers

Merchant Wholesaler
Independently owned wholesaling concern that takes title to goods it distributes.

Merchant wholesalers are independently owned concerns that take title to the goods they distribute. Merchant wholesalers account for over 57 percent of all wholesale transactions.[9] They represent about 84 percent of all wholesaling concerns in the United States. Many of these operations are fairly small, and most of the small wholesalers restrict their business to a limited geographical area. Many merchant wholesalers cover only single cities or areas stretching 100 to 200 miles from the main office. This allows them to replace retailers' inventory quickly. It also reduces or eliminates the need for overnight trips by trucks or sales personnel and so holds down expenses. Merchant wholesalers may be classified in terms of the numbers and types of services they provide to their customers. In this regard, they are perfect examples of how marketing firms adjust their total product offerings of goods and services to reflect the demands of particular situations and market segments.

Full-Service Merchant Wholesalers

Full-Service Merchant Wholesaler

Merchant wholesaler that provides a complete array of services, such as delivery, credit, marketing information and advice, and managerial assistance. Also called a full-function *wholesaler.*

As their name suggests, **full-service merchant wholesalers** provide their customers with a complete array of services in addition to the merchandise they offer. Such services include delivery, credit, marketing information and advice, and possibly even such managerial assistance as accounting or other nonmarketing aids. Full-service wholesalers are also called *full-function wholesalers.*

Within this category, three subsets of wholesalers are identifiable by lines of goods offered: **general merchandise wholesalers,** which sell a large number of different product types; **general line wholesalers,** which limit their offerings to a full array of products within one product line; and **specialty wholesalers,** which reduce their lines still further. A coffee and tea wholesaler or a spice wholesaler exemplifies this last class. Wholesalers determine how wide or narrow a line to carry by carefully considering the customers they serve and the industry in which they operate. When the target customers are operators of general stores, the decision to be a general merchandise wholesaler is logical. In some industries, however, traditional marketing practices may require some degree of specialization. Occasionally, the specialization is required by law, as in the case of beer wholesalers, which in many states are not permitted to deal in any other alcoholic beverage.

General Merchandise Wholesaler

Full-service merchant wholesaler that sells a large number of different product lines.

General Line Wholesaler

Full-service merchant wholesaler that sells a full selection of products in one product line.

Specialty Wholesaler

Full-service merchant wholesaler that sells a very narrow selection of products.

Limited-Service Merchant Wholesalers

Limited-Service Merchant Wholesaler

Merchant wholesaler that offers less than full service and charges lower prices than a full-service merchant wholesaler. Also called a limited-function *wholesaler.*

Regardless of the product line carried, full-service merchant wholesalers provide an essentially complete line of extra services. However, some customers may not want, or may not want to pay for, some of those services. They may prefer to sacrifice services to get lower prices. Thus, a group of **limited-service merchant wholesalers,** or limited-function wholesalers, has developed.

Cash-and-Carry Wholesaler

Limited-service wholesaler that does not offer delivery or credit.

Cash-and-Carry Wholesalers. Buyers not willing to pay for and not needing certain wholesaler services, such as delivery and credit, may choose to patronize **cash-and-carry wholesalers.** Such intermediaries eliminate the delivery and credit functions associated with a full-service wholesaler and permit buyers to come to the warehouse or other point of distribution to pick up their merchandise and to pay cash. Resultant savings are passed on to buyers, who are, after all, performing several functions normally associated with wholesalers.

Truck Wholesaler

Limited-service wholesaler that sells a limited line of items (often perishable goods) from a truck, thus providing immediate delivery. Also called a truck jobber.

Truck Wholesalers. **Truck wholesalers,** also called *truck jobbers,* typically sell a limited line of items to comparatively small buyers. Most of these merchant wholesalers sell perishable items. Their mode of operation, selling from a truckful of merchandise, can be justified by the increased freshness immediate delivery offers. Some truck wholesalers sell items that are not particularly perishable but that face keen competition. They might, for example, sell snack items to tavern owners. Although truck jobbing is an expensive means of distributing relatively small amounts of merchandise, it is an aggressive form of sales and provides instant delivery to buyers.

Direct-Marketing Wholesaler

Limited-service wholesaler that uses catalogs, mail or telephone ordering, and mail delivery.

Direct Marketing Wholesalers. **Direct-marketing wholesalers** operate in much the same way as mail-order catalog retailers and other direct marketers. They use catalogs, direct mail, and the Internet, take phone and fax orders, and then forward merchandise to buyers via mail or a parcel delivery service. Traditionally, these wholesalers have been most important in reaching remote rural locations where market potential is low. However, in recent years, many types of wholesalers, such as office supply wholesalers, have made strategic decisions to focus on direct marketing.

Drop Shipper
Limited-service wholesaler, often dealing in bulky products, that takes customer orders and arranges for shipment of merchandise from the producer directly to the customer. Also called a desk jobber.

Drop Shippers. **Drop shippers** are merchant wholesalers that take title to goods but do not take possession of the goods or handle them in any way. Drop shippers accept a buyer's order and pass it on to a producer or supplier of the desired commodity, which then ships the product directly to the buyer.

The big advantage of this system is that the product escapes double handling—that is, it need not be loaded and unloaded several times. It goes directly where it is needed, which also lowers transportation costs. These advantages are especially important when the product is bulky, unwieldy, and comparatively inexpensive. Thus, drop shipping is most commonly encountered for products such as coal, cement, building blocks, and logs.

Because the drop shipper does not physically handle any products, no investment in warehousing facilities or equipment is required. In fact, so little equipment of any sort is needed that these wholesalers often get by with little more than a small office, a desk, and a telephone. For this reason, they are also called desk jobbers.

Rack Jobber
Limited-service wholesaler that contracts with a retailer to place display racks in a store and to stock those racks with merchandise.

Rack Jobbers. **Rack jobbers** are merchant wholesalers that came to prominence in the 1930s when supermarkets began to practice scrambled merchandising and started selling cosmetics and other items they had not previously carried. To do this easily, they contracted with wholesalers willing to come to the store, set up a display rack, stock and replenish it, and give the supermarket operator a percentage of the sales. Now rack jobbers sell many different product lines, such as work gloves, paperback books, magazines, toys, cosmetics, and panty hose. The attraction of this system to the store operator is the chance to stock and sell certain items at little risk. The great attraction to the rack jobber is the chance to place merchandise in a high-traffic supermarket location. Like most relationships among channel of distribution members, theirs is a mutually beneficial one.

Agents

Agent
Wholesaler that does not take title to goods. Agents sometimes take possession of goods but function primarily to bring buyers and sellers together.

Agents, the second general category of wholesalers, may take possession of goods they deal in but do not take title to them. Agents, as a rule, do not carry an inventory or extend credit, but they may provide physical facilities for conducting business. They may help to arrange for delivery or credit as part of their services, which generally can be described as bringing buyer and seller together. Agents typically receive commissions based on the selling prices of the products they help to sell. The commission percentage varies tremendously depending on the industry. Agents are expected to have adequate product knowledge and be familiar with potential buyers and sellers. In short, they are expected to have an expert knowledge of the market in which they operate.

Brokers

Broker
Agent intermediary whose major role is placing buyers and sellers in touch with one another and assisting in contractual arrangements.

Brokers are agent intermediaries who receive a commission for putting sellers in touch with buyers and assisting with contractual negotiations. Brokers generally portray themselves as "neutral" in their selling process, working for both buyers and sellers. Brokers are found in many fields. Such commodities as coffee, tea, crude petroleum, and scrap metal are frequently brokered. So are the financial instruments handled by the familiar stock broker. Effective brokers are experts in the market for the products in which they deal. In effect, they sell their expertise. They have relatively low expenses. Their commissions also are small, likely 6 percent or less of the selling price.

Use of brokers holds particular appeal for sellers because brokers work strictly on commission and do not enter into long-term relationships with the companies that use them. A broker can be used only when needed and does not tie sellers to continuous expenses the way a full-time sales force does. Because they commonly are used on a sporadic basis, brokers as a group do not constitute a major selling force in the day-to-day marketing activities of most organizations. A notable exception is the food broker who represents a number of manufacturers of food products on a consistent basis and actively attempts to sell their products to wholesalers or supermarkets. Such an operation violates the standard description of a broker because food brokers may be seen as working more for the seller than the buyer. In many ways, food brokers better fit other categories of agents. By tradition as much as anything else, however, they continue to be referred to as brokers.

Commission Merchants

Commission Merchant

Agent intermediary similar to a broker but having certain additional decision-making powers, such as the power to make price adjustments.

The **commission merchant** is an agent intermediary similar to a broker. Unlike brokers, however, commission merchants are usually given certain powers by sellers. For example they might be empowered to attempt to bid up the selling price or to accept a selling price as long as it is above a previously agreed-on floor. Commission merchants thus perform a pricing function and more clearly work in league with the seller than do most brokers. They are most commonly found representing producers of agricultural products. Commission merchants, despite the name, do not take title to the goods they sell. However, they often take possession of those goods for inspection by potential buyers. Once a sales agreement has been reached, the commission merchant deducts a commission from the selling price and returns the balance to the producer.

Auction Company

Agent intermediary that brings together buyers and sellers. Auction companies often assemble merchandise for sale in a central location and sell it by means of a bidding process.

Auction Companies

Auction companies are agent intermediaries that perform valuable services in the buying and selling of livestock, tobacco, and other commodities, as well as artwork and used mechanical equipment. In a sense, these companies take possession of the goods they deal in, because frequently they provide some special place in which the auction can be held. The auction company receives a commission based on the final, highest bid offered for an item or product, provided that this bid is above a minimum agreed-on figure.

Auction companies offer a certain convenience

in bringing buyers together in one spot and expediting a bidding process that might otherwise take a long time. Some industries, such as the tobacco industry, have traditionally used auction companies and continue to do so. The operation of the auction system also provides some less-than-obvious advantages: (1) products generally can be examined by potential buyers; (2) sellers and buyers may, if they choose, remain anonymous; (3) buyers may enjoy the thrills involved with the auction and savor their victory over other bidders. This last factor may not be important to a tobacco buyer, but it is to a patron of art auctions.

Manufacturers' Agents and Selling Agents

Manufacturer's Agent
Independent agent intermediary that represents a limited number of noncompeting suppliers in a limited geographical area. Also called a manufacturers' representative.

Manufacturers' agents, also called manufacturers' representatives, are independent intermediaries that specialize in selling and are available to producers that do not want to perform sales activities themselves. These agents operate in geographically limited areas, such as a few states or a portion of a state, representing two or more noncompeting producers and spreading selling costs over all of them. Suppose a maker of photocopy equipment wants to employ a sales force only in major markets, not in smaller cities or rural areas. It might decide to hire a series of manufacturers' agents to cover areas with low market potential and to let the company's own sales force take the more important markets.

The existence of markets with low market potential is not the only good reason to use manufacturers' agents. Their familiarity with local markets is often an advantage. Another reason is that the producer may lack the interest or expertise to perform sales and marketing functions. Still another is finances: A company that has relatively few financial resources is more likely to use an agent because the agent need not be paid until a sale is made.

Selling Agent
Independent agent intermediary similar to a manufacturers' agent but representing a given product in every area in which it is sold, rather than in a limited geographical area.

Selling agents also are paid a commission and are expected to be familiar with the products they handle and the markets they serve. However, they differ from manufacturers' agents in one major respect. They sell the products they represent in all the areas in which the products are sold rather than only one geographic area. Because in effect they function as sales and marketing departments, they often are given more responsibility than manufacturers' agents. They may be permitted to handle the advertising and pricing of the products sold and determine any conditions of sale to be negotiated. When a selling agent is utilized, the manufacturer obtains what might be called an external marketing department.

Manufacturers That Do Their Own Wholesaling

Throughout this section, we have been considering wholesaling as if it were performed entirely by independent organizations other than manufacturers. Actually, although the various agent and merchant intermediaries are extremely important, especially in particular industries, many manufacturers perform the wholesaling functions themselves. Some manufacturers have become disenchanted with wholesalers for a number of reasons. The feeling is widespread among them that wholesalers that handle the products of many manufacturers cannot promote any one manufacturer's product as that producer feels it should be promoted.

Sales Office
Wholesaling establishment maintained by a manufacturer that does not carry an inventory of the product.

When manufacturers do their own wholesaling, whether to retailers or industrial users, they may use sales offices, sales branches, or both. (The U.S. Department of Commerce classifies sales branches and sales offices as wholesalers even though, according to our definition, they are not independent intermediaries.) **Sales offices** and **sales branches** are wholesaling establishments maintained by producers of the products, and both may serve as headquarters for "outside" salespeople or as offices for "inside" salespeople. The central difference between the two is that the sales branch carries an inventory of products, while the sales office does not. The bulk of the product, the need for fast delivery, the technical aspects of the prod-

Sales Branch
Wholesaling establishment maintained by a manufacturer that carries an inventory of the product.

uct, and the opportunity to sell a standardized product rather than a custom-made one all contribute to the decision whether to use offices or branches.

The reason manufacturers choose to do their own wholesaling can be expressed in one word: control. The maintenance of sales offices and branches permits manufacturers to control more effectively the flow of goods to their customers, the training and selling activities of their salespeople, and the flow of information returned to "headquarters" by a staff that is actually out in the field.

Wholesalers That Distribute Services

Some wholesalers specialize in the distribution of services. For example, your college library may use the services of BRS (Bibliographical Retrieval Service), Lexis/Nexis, or the Dow-Jones News Retrieval Service. These organizations are wholesalers that market information services.

Chapter 5 discussed global information systems, but not in the context of wholesaling and retailing. However, information and other services also flow through channels of distribution. In the 21st century, when interactive media, such as the Internet, are even more prominent, the distribution channels for information and entertainment services will become even more significant.

WHOLESALE MANAGEMENT STRATEGIES

Wholesalers, like all marketers, create marketing strategies. They analyze market segments, select target markets, and determine the competitive position they wish to occupy. To a great extent, the wholesaler's strategy is dominated by physical distribution concerns, the subject of the previous chapter. However, two other aspects of strategy have dimensions that deserve special attention, and we discuss them here. They are (1) selecting target markets and creating assortments and (2) developing strategic alliances.

Selecting Target Markets and Creating Assortments

We have seen that wholesalers sell to three basic classes of customers: retailers that resell the product, other wholesalers that resell the product, and organizations in the business market that use the product. Each of these markets has different needs. The wholesaler must determine which target markets to serve and what product mixes to offer. Further, the depth of the product lines offered must be matched to the needs of the target market. Consider this wholesaling strategy. Frieda's Finest is a produce grocery wholesaler that specializes in marketing uncommon fruits and exotic foods, such as tamarinds, babaco, and purple potatoes, to retailers. Its success with kiwi fruit is typical. Once the pioneering company succeeds in gaining market acceptance for the product, larger produce companies like Chiquita enter the market with their brands and become such formidable competitors that Frieda's Finest must exit the market. Then it once again attempts to pioneer the wholesaling of another rare food.

Organizational Collaborations for Long-Term Relationships

A wholesaler and its customer determine the extent to which the wholesaler will be involved in the operation of the customer's business. The customer expects the wholesaler to have an inventory of products in sufficient quantity to make rapid delivery possible. But in many situations, the wholesaler goes on to form a strategic business alliance with its customer.

Strategic Business Alliance
Commitment between a wholesaler and a customer to establish a long-term relationship.

A **strategic business alliance** is a commitment between a wholesaler and its customer to establish a long-term relationship. Such alliances may include arrangements to share or pool inventory information or interchange other databases so that purchase orders are executed automatically by computers. Vertical marketing systems are, of course, the strongest type of strategic alliance. However, wholesalers that are not part of such systems may also concentrate on building long-term relationships with their customers. For example, Fleming Foods offers many managerial services to grocery retailers because it considers them "partners." This wholesaler provides computer programs and other assistance to determine supermarket locations, design store layouts, and maintain the proper levels of on-shelf inventory.

 REGULATION OF RETAIL AND WHOLESALE DISTRIBUTION

In the United States, other countries, and international trade agreements, dealings in the area of distribution may be subject to numerous restrictions. For example, a manufacturer's ability to exercise power over wholesalers and retailers is often regulated in an attempt to preserve the independence of intermediaries and to assure that unfair competition does not result.

The Sherman Antitrust Act, the Clayton Act, the Federal Trade Commission Act, and other laws dealing with antitrust policy are the bases for much U.S. legislation influencing distribution. In the United States, the three main legal issues concerning wholesale and retail distribution are exclusive dealing, exclusive territories, and tying agreements.

Exclusive Dealing

Exclusive Dealing
Situation in which a distributor carries the products of one manufacturer and not those of competing manufacturers.

Exclusive dealing refers to a restrictive arrangement by which a supplier prohibits intermediaries that handle its product from selling the products of competing suppliers. A manufacturer may wish to deal only with those distributors that will agree to market only its brand. Would such an arrangement be legal? The answer to this question depends on whether the arrangement abuses the intermediary's right to act independently or the rights of other business competitors to succeed.

If a manufacturer restricts an intermediary from selling products that compete with that manufacturer's products, the activity is illegal if it tends to restrict competition. A new brand of automobile engine oil would never reach the marketplace if all makers of oil already in the market enforced exclusive dealing agreements with their wholesalers and retailers. Such arrangements, in blocking entry of a new product, would appear to be restricting competition.

An exclusive dealing arrangement is likely to lessen competition if (1) it comprises a substantial share of the market, (2) the dollar amount involved is substantial, or (3) it involves a large supplier and a smaller distributor, where the supplier's disparate economic power can be inherently coercive. Exclusive dealing arrangements generally are legal if it can be shown that the exclusivity is necessary for strategic reasons, such as a franchisor's need to protect a product's image. Exclusive dealing may also be legal if the supplier's own sales are restricted because of limited production capacity.

Exclusive Territories

Exclusive Territory
An area, defined by geographical boundaries or population, assigned to a retailer, wholesaler, or other dealer with the understanding that no other distributors will be assigned to operate in that area.

A manufacturer that grants a wholesaler or retailer an **exclusive territory** may be performing an illegal act. The key point, as in so many legal matters relating to business, is restriction of competition. If the granting of exclusive territories does not violate the statutes relating to this point, then limiting the number of outlets within an area or assigning exclusive territories may be considered proper. Again, in many cases, this evaluation must be made by the legal system.

What about Cadillac? This organization attracts dealers in part by promising that other dealers will not be set up within the same areas. A number of defenses might be offered on behalf of organizations engaged in this sort of practice. It might be argued that the investment expected from new dealers is so great that dealers could not be recruited unless they were offered some sort of exclusive territory. In this case, the defense is that the nature of the business demands such exclusivity. It also might be argued that the "image" associated with the product offered demands some exclusivity. Cadillac, for example, is portrayed as a luxury product. Excellent sales and service people are thus necessary. Cadillac dealers and mechanics are carefully selected and trained. If some exclusivity of territories were not maintained, if "everybody" could be a Cadillac dealer, then the quality of products and services would seem to diminish. If Cadillac dealerships were allowed to open on every other street corner, this might destroy the elite image Cadillac Motor Division is trying to create.

Tying Contracts

Tying Contract
Agreement tying the purchase of one product to the purchase of another.

Tying contracts require a channel intermediary or a buyer to purchase lines of merchandise that the seller sees as supplementary to the merchandise the purchaser actually wants to buy. The seller tells the buyer, in effect, "If you want to have this product (say, a printing press), you must also buy my other product (paper)." Thus, two or more products are tied together. The Clayton Act appears to make tying contracts illegal, but it is open to debate whether or not a particular agreement is, in fact, a tying contract. Certain tying agreements can be legal, but the matter is too complex to discuss here.

Legalities of International Distribution

The many restraints, limits, and problems associated with domestic retailing and wholesaling are compounded in the international marketplace. Domestic laws, the laws of the country to which goods are being shipped, the laws of the nations through which goods are being shipped, and the general conventions associated with international trade must all be obeyed.

The many-faceted aspects of international constraints on distribution are beyond the scope of this chapter, but the immense problems that flow from them should be recognized by all students of marketing.

SUMMARY

Retailing and wholesaling are the major distribution institutions that make our marketing system work.

sell, and help to physically distribute products through the economy.

Learning Objective 1
Describe the nature of retailing and wholesaling.
Retailers deal with ultimate consumers, people who buy products for their own use. Wholesalers deal with institutions that acquire products for use in organizations or for resale. Both types of intermediaries buy,

Learning Objective 2
Categorize the various types of retailers by ownership and prominent strategy.
The retail establishments in the United States may be classified by ownership, as independents, leased departments, chains, franchises, or ownership groups.

They also may be classified by retail strategy, as in-store retailers or direct marketing (nonstore) retailers. In-store retailers may be further classified as specialty stores, department stores, supermarkets, convenience stores, general mass merchandisers, or specialty mass merchandisers.

Learning Objective 3

Discuss the growth of direct marketing as a retail strategy.
Direct marketing involves the use of advertising, telephone sales, or other communications to elicit a direct response from consumers. Direct marketing in a retailing context also has been called nonstore retailing and direct-response retailing. The many means of direct marketing include direct-mail, door-to-door selling, computer interactive retailing, and vending machines.

Learning Objective 4

Explain the major premise of the wheel of retailing theory.
The wheel of retailing theory maintains that new retailing institutions enter the marketplace as low-status, low-margin, low-price operations and then move toward higher positions, leaving space for new low-position stores.

Learning Objective 5

Understand the nature of retailers' marketing mixes.
Retail marketers of all types must develop effective marketing mixes aimed at attracting and satisfying target markets. Merchandise assortment, location, atmospherics, customer service, and database management are of special importance to retailers.

Learning Objective 6

Distinguish between merchant wholesalers and agents and describe their functions in the distribution system.
Independent wholesalers are either merchants or agents. Merchants take title to the goods they sell, while agents do not. In addition, wholesaling activities by manufacturers using sales branches and offices represent an important aspect of wholesaling.

Learning Objective 7

Show how full-service and limited-service merchant wholesalers contribute to the marketing system.
Full-service merchant wholesalers can perform credit and delivery functions and provide managerial assistance and market information. Limited-service wholesalers perform some, but not all, intermediary functions, eliminating those that particular buyers do not require. These intermediaries can therefore lower their costs of doing business and the prices they must charge customers.

Learning Objective 8

Identify the marketing contributions of agent intermediaries, such as brokers, auction companies, and selling agents.
Agent intermediaries, such as brokers, auction companies, and selling agents, may offer expert knowledge of the marketplace, provide physical facilities for doing business, give advice to buyers and sellers, and help bring buyers and sellers together. They therefore play important roles in exchanges without actually taking title to the products.

Learning Objective 9

Understand the key elements of wholesalers' strategies.
To a large extent, the wholesaler's strategy is dominated by physical distribution strategies. However, selecting target markets, creating assortments for customers, and developing strategic alliances also are important aspects of wholesale strategy.

Learning Objective 10

Describe some of the legal concerns associated with the development and management of channels of distribution.
Several ethical issues arise concerning the macromarketing role of distribution. Many of these issues have been addressed by laws. Exclusive dealing arrangements can be seen as stopping the distribution of competitors' goods or services and are thus sometimes illegal. So are exclusive territorial arrangements, which may restrict free trade. Tying agreements, which tie purchase of one product to purchase of another, are in almost all cases illegal.

KEY TERMS

Retailing (p. 320)
Independent retailer (p. 320)
Leased department retailer (p. 320)
Chain store (p. 321)

Corporate chain (p. 321)
Ownership group (p. 321)
Specialty store (p. 322)
Department store (p. 323)

Supermarket (p. 324)
Scrambled merchandising (p. 324)
Convenience store (p. 324)
Mass merchandise retailer (p. 324)

General mass merchandisers
   (p. 324)
Specialty mass merchandisers
   (p. 325)
Catalog showroom (p. 325)
Warehouse club (p. 325)
Off-price retailer (p. 325)
Category discounter (p. 326)
Direct marketing (p. 326)
Computer-interactive retailing
   (p. 328)
Wheel of retailing (p. 329)
Store image (p. 330)
Atmospherics (p. 333)
Service level (p. 334)

Wholesaler (p. 335)
Merchant wholesaler (p. 335)
Full-service merchant wholesaler
   (p. 336)
General merchandise wholesaler
   (p. 336)
General line wholesaler (p. 336)
Specialty wholesaler (p. 336)
Limited-service merchant wholesaler
   (p. 336)
Cash-and-carry wholesaler (p. 336)
Truck wholesaler (p. 336)
Direct marketing wholesaler
   (p. 336)

Drop shipper (p. 337)
Rack jobber (p. 337)
Agent (p. 337)
Broker (p. 337)
Commission merchant (p. 338)
Auction company (p. 338)
Manufacturer's agent (p. 339)
Selling agent (p. 339)
Sales office (p. 339)
Sales branch (p. 339)
Strategic business alliance (p. 341)
Exclusive dealing (p. 341)
Exclusive territory (p. 341)
Tying contract (p. 342)

QUESTIONS FOR REVIEW AND CRITICAL THINKING

1. Give some examples of retailers in your area that fit the following categories.
   a. General mass merchandiser
   b. Specialty store
   c. Chain store
   d. Warehouse club

2. Which of the following retailers would tend to utilize free-standing locations? Why? Why would the others not use such locations?
   a. Kmart
   b. McDonald's
   c. Department store
   d. Popcorn shop

3. What are some advantages of data-based marketing?

4. What are some of the disadvantages of using vending machines as retail outlets?

5. What trends do you predict in direct marketing by retailers?

6. Research furniture marketing in the United States and discuss the evolution and development of retailing in this industry.

7. What are the key elements of a retailer's marketing mix? Provide an example.

8. Do executives in small independent retail organizations have the same growth orientation and business philosophy as executives in large corporations? Why or why not?

9. Find local examples of the following:

   a. Cash-and-carry wholesaler
   b. Rack jobber
   c. Manufacturer's sales office
   d. Auction company

10. What is the major difference between agents and merchant wholesalers?

11. What are the advantages and disadvantages of using manufacturers' agents in the following situations?
    a. New company marketing voice synthesizer for computers
    b. Large established company marketing truck axles
    c. West Virginia coal company selling coal in Pennsylvania

12. What are the most important aspects of a wholesaler's marketing strategies?

13. A wholesaler states: "Retailers are our customers. Our allegiance lies with them, not with the manufacturers that supply products to us." Do you agree?

14. Under what conditions is exclusive dealing legal?

15. Under what conditions are exclusive territories legal?

16. Form small groups as directed by your instructor. Each group is to function as a department store buying center for women's casual fashion for either the upcoming winter or the upcoming spring season. The group should come to a consensus and make a buying recommendation.

INTERNET INSIGHTS

Exercises

1. Go to

    http://www.hitech.retailer.com

    for the Wide World of Retailing.

2. RIC is a specialty food broker. Go to

    http://www.ricbrokers.com

    and read the information at this site. Describe the service RIC provides.

3. To learn what's hot in international retailing, go to the Imagine If . . . home page at:

    http://www.imagine-if.be/retail/

    Spend some time looking at the various options. What did you learn about international retailing?

Do you think it would be difficult to understand international retail markets? Why or why not?

Address Book

Corporate Intelligence on Retailing
http://www.cior.com

Shopping Center Industry and Research Databases
http://www.icsc.org

Space Mall
http://www.spacemall.com

Marketplace
http://www.marketplace.com

National Association of College Stores
http://www.nacs.org

ETHICS IN PRACTICE: TAKE A STAND

1. A Wal-Mart moves into a small town and many small retail establishments go out of business within a year. Is this right?

2. A major chain store has six supermarkets in a certain city but none on the poor side of town, where many minority-group consumers live. Should the store open a new branch on the poor side of town?

3. A wholesaler refuses to carry a lawn-mower manufacturer's product line because the wholesaler already represents a competitor's line. Is this legal? Ethical?

4. A manufacturer of office equipment used a manufacturer's agent on the West Coast to sell to wholesalers for six years. The agent did a good job, and sales volume reached a million dollars in the territory. When this happened, a sales representative was hired to replace the agent, and the long-standing relationship between manufacturer and agent was terminated. What obligation does the manufacturer have to the agent?

CASE 12–1

 EatZi's

At Brinker International Inc.'s latest restaurant innovation, you can hardly get a table—because there are only four of them indoors. Actually, EatZi's Market & Bakery located in Dallas, Texas, is a New York-style gourmet grocery aimed at the take-out crowd. It features the sort of sushi and pasta dishes favored by young professionals on the go, along with fresh produce, flowers and pastries.

It may not be going too far to say that EatZi's—a Dallas deli/grocery/restaurant referred to by the management as EatZi's concept—has generated a revolution in food service that will have far-reaching repercussions. To give you an idea of the impact this rambunctious, 8000-square-foot establishment has had on Dallas, just listen to what one customer said: "I've been here at least once a day for a month!"

Most people don't even go to their jobs that often. Here's what separates EatZi's from other grocery stores—it's really a restaurant. And don't let the fact that there are only four tables and two narrow counters on which to dine fool you either. EatZi's was created by restaurant genius Phil Romano and it is definitely in the business of serving food to its customers.

In fact, "Food for the Taking" is their slogan. Although it's not that big, EatZi's has everything you could ever want for dinner, and management goes to great lengths to suggest that the possibilities are endless. And—there's opera music (no German or English operas, they insist) merrily blaring away on the sound system.

Chefs in their tall white hats welcome customers outside; inside they hand out free samples of cheese, seafood salad, smoked salmon, and more in the executional areas where bread is baked and food to go is prepared. There are 140 produce items, EatZi's ripens its own apples, and a third

of EatZi's own produce goes to making the prepared food. The food bins are even custom-made, and everything but everything is for sale, even the baskets and totes. There are 700 specialty foods—oils, dressings, soy sauce, infused mayonnaise, roasted garlic, and even onion jam. In this world of plenty, the aisles have been made purposely narrow to create an intense atmosphere that's made even more intense because the chefs are constantly coming out from behind their counters to talk to the customers about the food.

In truth, much of the food EatZi's offers can be had at your local supermarket. But you won't feel as good shopping for it and you won't have nearly as much fun. And, you'll have to cook. Take-home offerings at EatZi's can be amazingly good, particularly because you know that most of the preparation has already been done for you. The focaccia topped with tomatoes and caramelized onions redolent with garlic has gotten raves as the best in town; pizza also gets top honors. Thuringer salami is spectacular. A basic like roasted chicken shows thoughtfulness in the preparation—even with crisply browned skin, the meat is still tender and succulent. If you live in Dallas you have likely been to EatZi's or are planning to go; out-of-towners can easily add it to their list of compelling tourist attractions. But if you don't want to join the masses just yet, wait a while—the EatZi's concept management team has plans to roll out EatZi's all over the country. Probably even in your own home town.

Questions
1. What prominent element is the basis for EatZi's retailing stragegy?
2. Explain EatZi's in terms of the wheel of retailing theory.

Muebleria La Unica

People often ask for Pichirilo, a general manager who offers deals so good they can't be for real, at the Muebleria La Unica furniture and appliance stores in western Puerto Rico.

Actually, Pichirilo himself isn't for real. This retailer with a soft spot for customers was created by MLU President Leandro Rodriguez for radio spot commercials, and he is so well known that many people think he exists. The spots have been a key weapon in a fight with chain stores for market share.

Rodriguez opened the first MLU store in Mayaguez in 1959, and his business grew as that city did. He opened two branch stores in smaller towns. Then two mainland U.S. chains moved into the area, followed by two more. Four Puerto Rican appliance/furniture chains also arrived. MLU's sales began to fall.

Volume-buying discounts allowed the newcomers to cut prices below locally owned stores' profit levels. MLU customers had been buying at good prices from salespeople they knew and trusted, but Rodriguez realized he couldn't count on customer loyalty alone to keep him in business. To get across the idea that MLU was as capable of offering low prices as the chains, he coined a slogan: "Ventas por millones, beneficios por centavos" ("sales by the millions, profits in pennies"). The slogan was incorporated in a catchy jingle for radio spots—which were enhanced by the introduction of Pichirilo.

Showrooms at MLU's stores were spruced up. Storage space at the main store was remodeled as an extra showroom, after a storeroom was rented in a separate building. A fourth MLU outlet was opened in a Mayaguez location convenient to areas where many MLU customers live. Thanks to an excellent record at banks, Rodriguez was able to get funds for expanding and remodeling—and for purchase volumes large enough to win better discounts.

Questions

1. What prominent element is the basis for Muebleria La Unica's retailing strategy?
2. Using the classification scheme in the chapter, what type of retailer is Muebleria La Unica?
3. Would Muebleria La Unica's strategy work in the continental United States?

PART 5

MARKETING COMMUNICATIONS AND PROMOTION STRATEGY

Chapter 13

Learning Objectives

After you have studied this chapter, you will be able to:

1. Discuss the three basic purposes of promotion.
2. Define the four major elements of promotion.
3. Describe the basic model for all communication processes, including promotion.
4. Explain the hierarchy of communication effects.
5. Explain how the elements of promotion can be used to support one another in a promotional campaign.
6. Identify the general promotional strategies known as push and pull strategies.
7. Discuss promotional campaigns and provide examples.
8. Be aware of arguments about the ethics of persuasion in society.

Cakebread Cellars of Rutherford, California, ranks as a small winery, producing 45,000 cases a year. But the brand, distributed by Kobrand Corporation of New York, has a steadfast following of 10,000 who receive its chatty food and wine newsletter. The quarterly routinely sings the praises of such off-beat pairings as peanut butter sandwiches and Cakebread Zinfandel. Through the mailing list, the vice president of sales/marketing Dennis Cakebread, son of winery founder Jack Cakebread, had no trouble rounding up 20 fans to go salmon fishing with him.

Cakebread and crew set off from San Francisco at 6 a.m., returning in the late afternoon. The outing wrapped up with a dinner of the day's catch

at Aqua, a local seafood restaurant. "We were all exhausted," recalled Cakebread. "But we forgot that as we all sat down and clinked our first glass."

Cakebread, which also has attracted Californians with fly-fishing seminars, is planning an out-of-state event in Chicago, where the winery is sponsoring a mushroom-foraging trip, complete with an appropriately wined dinner of the finds. It's a lot of effort for small groups of people, Cakebread admitted. "But I think we earn customers for life," he said. "The people on our fishing trip should go back to where they work and spend all day Monday talking about the trip. Every time they order salmon they should recount the trip. Every time they see a fishing boat, they should talk about the trip."

Small businesses like Cakebread Cellars often concentrate their promotional efforts on sales promotions and public relations. When properly planned and executed, these efforts can produce amazing results.

The purpose of this chapter is to explain how sales promotions and public relations can be important parts of an integrated communications plan. The chapter begins by describing sales promotions—both those aimed at members of the channel of distribution and those aimed at ultimate consumers. It then turns to a discussion of public relations and publicity, including how they differ and how publicity is managed. Several public relations topics of special interest conclude the chapter: crisis management, internal marketing, international public relations, and evaluating and monitoring public relations.

PROMOTION: COMMUNICATION WITH A PURPOSE

Effective marketers know that the old adage—"Build a better mousetrap and the world will beat a path to your door"—contains a basic flaw. If the "world" doesn't find out that there is a better mousetrap, the manufacturer will be a very lonely person, indeed. Having a great product is not enough. People must be made familiar with the product's benefits. Some form of promotion is necessary to make consumers, and other publics with which an organization interacts, aware of the existence of a product.

Promotion is applied marketing communication. Marketers use it to communicate both factual information and persuasive messages to prospective buyers. In the marketing mix, promotion serves three purposes:

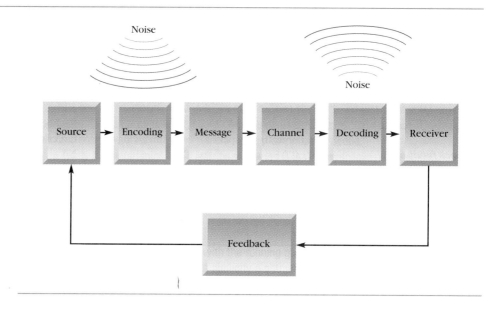

EXHIBIT 13–3
A Basic Model of the
Communication Process

wishes to communicate the notion that the Blazer is a durable, high quality product that helps drivers enjoy those special moments when driving in rugged terrain. This idea—not an easy one to get across—is the message of the advertisement. The message is communicated primarily in a visual and symbolic way, through the intriguing image of a Blazer easily handling a gravel road in the mountains. The sender's idea has been encoded by means of this picture. **Encoding** is the process of translating the idea to be communicated into a symbolic message consisting of words, pictures, numbers, gestures, or the like. This is a necessary step, because there is no way to send an idea from one person to another in its pure form.

As in the Blazer advertisement, nonverbal messages and nonrational symbolism are essential to the encoding process, because words can be hopelessly inadequate to express emotions. "There are just no words to express the various nuances of sensation and feeling, to express such things as mood and aesthetic impression. Try to describe to a child how a strawberry tastes compared to a raspberry, how a carnation smells, why it is pleasurable to dance, what a pretty girl looks like."[2] The emotional definition of a situation or the precise meaning of human feelings may be determined almost entirely from facial expressions; from movements of the body, such as the gestures of a traffic officer; from the general state of excitement, such as weeping, blushing, or laughter; or from involuntary exclamations and sounds, such as whistling or singing.

Notice that the word Chevrolet appears only in the Internet address shown in very small print. However, its nameplate symbol communicates that Blazer is part of the Chevrolet family of cars.

Encoding
In communication theory, the process by which the sender translates the idea to be communicated into a symbolic message consisting of words, pictures, numbers, gestures, or the like, so that it can be transmitted to the receiver.

Transmitting the Message through a Channel

Once the sender has created the message by encoding it into a transmittable form, it must be somehow conveyed to the receiver: It must be sent through a *channel of communication,* such as a magazine or other medium. Even our own casual conversations are sent in this way, though the medium is the less obvious one of vibrating vocal cords and movements of sound through air.

The message arrives at the receiver via the channel of communication. But some receivers will be more receptive than others. For example, some receivers

EXHIBIT 13–4
What is communicated in
this advertisement?

of the communication about Blazer will be elderly consumers who for one reason or another, have little interest in a rugged vehicle that facilitates driving in mountains and rough terrain. It is the sender's job to pick the medium that will reach a maximum number of target receivers and a minimum number of nontarget receivers.

Decoding the Message

Decoding
In communication theory, the process by which the receiver of a message interprets the message's meaning.

The message arrives and is viewed, heard, or otherwise sensed by the receiver. But in order for communication to occur, the receiver must decode it. **Decoding** is the mental process by which the receiver interprets the meaning of the message. A difficulty encountered at this stage of the communication process is that receivers may interpret the message in different ways, given their particular biases, backgrounds, and other characteristics. That is, selective perception operates as the message is decoded. We interpret messages with meaning drawn from our personal experiences and backgrounds (see Chapter 5). An advertisement for cigarettes may be viewed differently by different people, for example. Nonsmokers may pass over the message entirely; antismokers may be angered by it; smokers satisfied with another brand may note the advertisement only casually. Some who see the advertisement may not "get it" at all—the intended imagery may escape them completely.

In the Blazer advertisement, if the receiver interprets the message—like a rock—to mean that Blazers are tough, sturdy, and long-lasting, the communication has worked.

Feedback

Feedback
Communication of the receiver's reaction to a message back to the source.

Often the communication process includes **feedback,** communication of the receiver's reaction back to the source of the message. In a personal selling situation, the feedback may be direct and immediate, as when the customer raises questions about the product or states why no purchase will be made. Indeed, as mentioned, the great attraction of personal selling is that there can be a two-way conversation that will ensure greater understanding between the people involved.

Feedback from advertising, sales promotion, and publicity and public relations is in most cases slower and less direct. For instance, advertisers may conduct surveys, count coupon redemptions, or evaluate letters and telephone calls from consumers to learn the audience's reactions. Although advertisers can get delayed feedback about an advertisement's effectiveness, the feedback rarely provides all the desired information about the receivers' responses to the message.

Perfect Communication

Ideally, if perfect communication takes place, the message that is decoded and enters the mind of the receiver is exactly the same as the one the sender had in mind, encoded, and transmitted. If the sender and receiver share a common social background and have similar needs, they are more likely to similarly interpret the meaning of the words and symbols in the message. Perfect transmission, though, is never possible. Nevertheless, in many cases, the sender can develop messages that are decoded by the target audience in ways approximating what the sender had in mind.

Noise

In communication theory, any interference or distraction that disrupts the communication process.

It is likely—perhaps even inevitable—that any communication process will be interrupted or distorted by factors that communication experts term "noise." Noise is interference or distraction, and it may disrupt any stage of the communication process. **Noise** may come in the form of conflicting messages, misunderstood terminology, inadequacies in the channel of communication, and so on. A radio advertisement might not be heard because of loud traffic noises outside the car. In a cigarette advertisement, the Surgeon General's warning is noise. The sources of noise may be external to the individual, such as traffic noises, or internal, such as daydreaming that interrupts concentration on a sales presentation. Many advertising messages cause people to think of a competing product. Brand loyalties and past learning are internal distractions that may interfere with the decoding process.

THE HIERARCHY OF COMMUNICATION EFFECTS

Marketers have come to expect various responses to their communications. To understand the effects that promotion may bring about, we next discuss the promotion process as a force that moves people up a "staircase," or a series of steps, called the hierarchy of communication effects.[3] This promotion staircase is shown in Exhibit 13–5.

1. Near the bottom of the steps stand potential purchasers who are completely unaware of the existence of the product in question.
2. Closer to purchasing, but still a long way from the cash register, are those who are merely aware of its existence.
3. Up one step are prospects who know what the product has to offer.
4. Still closer to purchasing are those who have favorable attitudes toward the product—those who like the product.
5. Those whose favorable attitudes have developed to the point of preference over all other possibilities are up still another step.
6. Even closer to purchasing are consumers who couple preference with a desire to buy and the conviction that the purchase would be wise.
7. Finally, of course, is the step that translates this intention into actual purchase.

Thus, according to this somewhat idealized portrayal, consumers may move through a seven-step hierarchy, ranging from total ignorance of a brand's existence

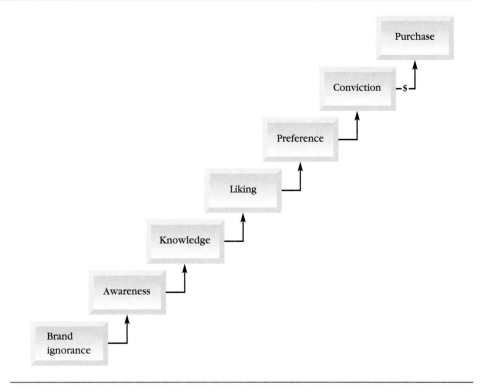

EXHIBIT 13–5
Promotion moves customers to ascend the seven steps of the hierarchy of communication effects.

to purchase of that brand. Eventually, a satisfied, or reinforced, customer is the result when the purchase decision leads to a reward.

The hierarchy model shown in Exhibit 13–5 suggests that communication may not be a one-step process. Marketers use promotion to induce buyers to change—that is, to move up the staircase. Communication may be aimed at any step, depending on the objective of the communication. The question is, what step should the marketer aim at?

Part of the answer comes from the nature of the product. Marketers of a totally new product, such as SoundTube stereo speakers, face a different set of communication problems than do marketers of tartar control toothpaste. The toothpaste communication need not include an extensive discussion of the fact that tartar buildup is to be avoided. Most consumers are already aware of that. In contrast, the seller of a near-revolutionary product may need to devote considerable effort to explaining what the product is, how it works, and even that it works.

The most important part of the answer, whatever the product, comes from the nature of the market. The organization seeking to create an effective promotional message must begin with one of marketing's most basic rules of action—identification of the target market or, in this case, the target audience.

The whole communications process must be built around the intended receiver of the message. A key question, then, is "What is the target audience's psychological state?" If the marketing organization is attempting to influence those who are currently on the awareness and knowledge steps, a primary promotional objective will be to provide factual information. According to many petroleum companies, most citizens are totally unaware of how oil company revenues are utilized. Some of these companies spend a good portion of their advertising budgets informing people of the true nature of the oil business. They demonstrate that a large portion of revenues are spent on additional exploration or on the development of products that enhance the lives of consumers.

Appealing to consumers on the liking or the preference step calls for promotional messages aimed at encouraging existing favorable feelings toward the good or service offered. For example, advertisements for many cosmetics, fashion items, soft drinks, and airlines emphasize the fun or sophistication associated with the products. The target audiences in these cases already know about the brands and probably know that the company is a respected manufacturer. Thus, the advertisement stresses emotional feelings toward the product.

Target customers who are on the conviction step of the model are very close to action, but they may need a little shove to get them to act. A bit of encouragement may be all that is required. Notification that now is the time to buy, that prices may go up, or that a two-for-one coupon is available may motivate these consumers to move up the staircase to the final step—the purchase.

As we've mentioned earlier, the sale is not the end of the line. The marketer may continue to use promotional messages to reinforce the buyer in the belief that a good buy was made or, later on, to remind the customer of the product and its value or effectiveness. For example, the advertisers of frequently purchased products like tomato sauce often remind buyers how satisfied they have been with the product. And a promotion for an infrequently purchased durable good might "advise" the buyer to tell a friend about his purchase or to remember that the company sells other fine products. Such efforts often reduce consumers' postpurchase dissonance.

Sophisticated consumer behavior research suggests that some consumer purchasing decisions, especially those made when consumers have low involvement in the product, do not follow the steps in the hierarchy of communication effects. Nevertheless, this approach is useful in understanding how many promotions work.

Since not all consumers are on the same step of the promotion staircase, and consumers on different steps will respond to different sorts of appeals, we might expect that different elements of the promotional mix will be more effective for different consumers. To some extent, they are. Exhibit 13–6 illustrates, in general

EXHIBIT 13–6
The relative importance of advertising and personal selling relates to the job to be done.

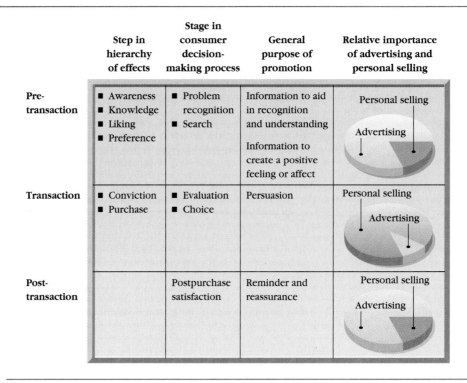

	Step in hierarchy of effects	Stage in consumer decision-making process	General purpose of promotion	Relative importance of advertising and personal selling
Pre-transaction	■ Awareness ■ Knowledge ■ Liking ■ Preference	■ Problem recognition ■ Search	Information to aid in recognition and understanding Information to create a positive feeling or affect	Personal selling Advertising
Transaction	■ Conviction ■ Purchase	■ Evaluation ■ Choice	Persuasion	Personal selling Advertising
Post-transaction		Postpurchase satisfaction	Reminder and reassurance	Personal selling Advertising

terms, the relative importance of advertising and personal selling at different steps in the hierarchy of effects, classified as pre-transaction, transaction, and post-transaction stages of the buying process. (The transaction may be roughly defined as the period in which the exchange agreement or the negotiation of the terms of sale becomes final.)

In the pre-transaction stage, the consumer becomes aware of a brand, acquires knowledge, and formulates likes, dislikes, and preferences. The purpose of promotion is informative, and advertising generally plays a larger role than personal selling. In the transaction stage, personal selling is important because the consumer must be persuaded to make a positive evaluation, develop a conviction, and actually make the purchase. In the post-transaction stage, advertising reminds and reassures consumers about their satisfaction.

This relationship is strongly influenced by the many forces that contribute to the purchase decision. The characteristics of the marketplace, the state of the economy, the nature of the product, and the seller's overall marketing strategy vary from case to case. And, of course, publicity and sales promotion play a part in moving consumers up the steps of the hierarchy. However, these general statements illustrate the roles advertising and personal selling play at each stage.

PUSH AND PULL STRATEGIES

The prime target of a promotional strategy may be either the ultimate consumer or a member of the distribution channel. Using this as a basis for classification, we can identify the basic strategies of push and pull. There is no single strategy of either type; but in general, they are described as follows.

Push Strategy
Promotional strategy whereby a supplier promotes a product to marketing intermediaries with the aim of pushing the product through the channel of distribution.

A **push strategy** emphasizes personal selling, advertising, and other promotional efforts aimed at members of the channel of distribution. Thus, the manufacturer of a product heavily promotes that product to wholesalers and other dealers. The wholesalers then promote the product heavily to retailers, who in turn direct their selling efforts to consumers. Not infrequently, the wholesalers and retailers are offered strong price incentives or discounts as part of this process. The term push comes from the fact that the manufacturer, with the help of other channel members, pushes the product through each level in the channel of distribution. The push strategy may be thought of as a step-by-step approach to promotion, with each channel member organizing the promotional efforts necessary to reach the channel member next in line (Exhibit 13–7).

EXHIBIT 13–7
Flow of Promotional Dollars and Effort in Push and Pull Strategies

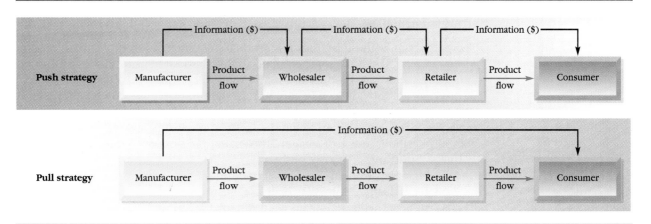

Pull Strategy
Promotional strategy whereby a supplier promotes a product to the ultimate consumer with the aim of stimulating demand and thus pulling the product through the channel of distribution.

When the **pull strategy** is used, the manufacturer attempts to stimulate demand for the product by aiming promotional efforts at the ultimate consumer or organizational buyer located at the other end of the channel of distribution. The goal is to generate demand at the retail level in the belief that such demand will encourage retailers and wholesalers to stock the product. If the customer is pulled into the store, each channel member will "pass back" the demand. In other words, the demand at the buyer end of the channel pulls the product through the channels of distribution.

Marketing organizations need not limit themselves to using only a push or only a pull strategy. Effective marketing often makes use of a combination of push and pull.

PROMOTIONAL CAMPAIGNS

So far we have considered the individual aspects of promotion while emphasizing that the parts of the promotional effort must fit together and complement each other. For example, a trade magazine mailed to owners of automobile muffler shops promotes itself to potential buyers of advertising space as the place to advertise to reach target customers. The magazine's management may sponsor race cars or make awards to outstanding people in the muffler business to build the magazine's image as a major force in the trade. All of these activities fit together into a unity of presentation that could be called the magazine publisher's total promotional effort or promotional mix.

Promotional Campaign
Series of promotional activities aimed at achieving a specific objective or set of objectives.

Military terminology is commonly used in football and business. We see this once again in the term **promotional campaign.** A promotional campaign is a part of a firm's promotional mix, just as a military campaign is a portion of a total war effort. Thus, a promotional campaign is a series of promotional activities with a particular objective or set of objectives.

The phrase "particular objective" is important here, because it is this objective that indicates the goal to be reached. The campaign must be constructed to achieve that goal. The task of introducing a new product requires a promotional campaign considerably different from one intended to increase the sales of an established or widely recognized product.

Because most products are in the mature stage of their product life cycles, this section focuses primarily on promotional campaigns for these products. However, aspects of these strategies can also be applied to product introductions or to products in the growth stage. There are four major approaches to developing a promotional campaign for a mature product: image building, product differentiation, positioning, and direct response.

Image Building

The product or brand image is an individual's net impression of what the product or brand is all about. It is the symbolic value associated with the brand. Buyers frequently prefer one product or brand over another because of its image. Brands or products are thus often purchased or avoided not because of what they cost or how they work but because of what they say about the buyer-user—how they symbolize that person's personality or lifestyle. Marketers are properly concerned with this symbolic value or image. Thus, many promotional campaigns are aimed at **image building.**

Image Building
Promotional approach intended to communicate an image and generate consumer preference for a brand or product on the basis of symbolic value.

For example, Holiday Inn is one of the most recognized brands in the hotel/motel industry. However, over the years, many of the chain's hotels and motels had been neglected. Many viewed Holiday Inn properties as old, rundown, roadside motels with coffee shops. Today, the company is trying to polish its tar-

For years, the Plymouth automobile appealed only to older consumers. The car had acquired a stodgy image. Marketers at Plymouth used a series of new product introductions and an advertising campaign with the tagline "One Creative Idea After Another" to overcome its image problems. Plymouth hopes to project an image of car that is youthful, fun, and affordable.

nished image and establish a more colorful, contemporary image that communicates it is a reinvigorated company.[4] Its new slogan is "On the Way. Every Holiday Inn as good as the Best Holiday Inn."

Not-for-profit organizations also are concerned with image building. For example, the image of a Girl Scout was one of dependability, trustworthiness, and honesty. However, in the MTV era, many young girls saw this positive image as being too squeaky-clean.[5]

Girl Scout membership had been dropping, especially in the 8–11 age group. Focus group research showed that these preteens perceived Girl Scouts as childish. So the organization's marketers decided that the Girl Scouts had to move away from the uniformed, goody-goody image and show that Girl Scout meetings were a fun, mature, cool place to be.

To overcome its image as an organization that was "locked in time," the Girl Scouts used a promotional campaign aimed at making the organization more relevant to the older age group while emphasizing the activities available to all girls who join. The new image portrayed Girl Scouts as more action-oriented. For example, cookie packages showed Girl Scouts engaged in outdoor games such as volleyball.

The not-for-profit organization developed an image-building advertising campaign that portrayed a hipper, more active organization. Using MTV-style graphics, TV advertising incorporated rap music and fantasy images, such as windsurfing, skiing, and parachuting, to suggest that the Scouts could offer girls a lot of fulfilling activities. One television ad closed with the line, "The Girl Scouts. As great as you want to make it."

In general, image-building promotional campaigns do not focus on product features but emphasize creating impressions. These may be impressions of status, sexuality, masculinity, femininity, reliability, or some other aspect of the brand's character thought to be alluring to target customers. Most advertisements for perfumes (such as Chanel No. 5 and Obsession) and clothing (Calvin Klein and Guess?) concentrate almost entirely on creating impressions.

Product Differentiation

Product Differentiation
Promotional approach in which the marketer calls buyers' attention to those aspects of a product or brand that set it apart from its competitors.

A promotional campaign aimed at developing **product differentiation** focuses on some dimension of the product that competing brands or competing products do not offer or accents some way in which using the product provides the solution to a consumer problem. For example, Samsonite's Piggyback suitcase advertising tries to convince frequent flyers that they should think of this suitcase with wheels and a telescoping handle as a luggage cart that doubles as a suitcase. The advertising shows how sturdy construction and tie down straps, which allow customers to pile on several other carry-on bags, make the Samsonite Piggyback suitcase different from regular bags. The promotional campaigns focused on attributes of the product, not its image or price.

Unique Selling Proposition (USP)
Unique characteristic of a product or brand identified by the marketer as the one on which to base a promotional campaign; often used in a product differentiation approach to promotion.

Product differentiation and related promotional efforts often take the form of the **unique selling proposition (USP).** As the name suggests, the basic idea of the USP is to identify and promote an aspect of the product that the competition does not offer or, because of patents or other reasons, cannot easily offer. Energizer batteries were the first to have "an on-battery tester." Initially, Everready and the Coppertop had no such feature and no such benefit. The on-battery testing feature provided Energizer with a unique selling proposition around which a promotional campaign has been built. The USP tells buyers that if they buy the product, they will receive a specific, exclusive benefit.

Generally, mature products are not truly unique, especially from the point of view of performance. Yet parity products—those with ingredients nearly identical to competitors' brands, such as Tylenol's brand of acetaminophen—are often promoted as if they were special. This can be done because products have aspects other than the strictly functional ones that can be promoted as effectively as functional features. Elmer Wheeler illustrated this fact in the classic statement "Don't sell the steak, sell the sizzle."[6] Keep in mind, though, that the point stressed in the unique selling proposition, whatever it is, must be meaningful to the potential buyer. It is possible to "sell the sizzle" only if the sizzle means something to the buyer—that is, if it satisfies a need. If buyers do not care about the USP, it does not influence the purchasing decision.

Positioning

You may recall that a brand's competitive position is the way consumers perceive it relative to its competition. The positioning approach, which promotes a brand's competitive position, is often the focal point of promotional campaigns. The campaign objective is to get consumers to view the brand from a particular perspective.

In launching such a campaign, the marketer assumes that consumers have so much information about other brands and similar products that it must create a distinct position for the brand in the prospect's mind. The Avis campaign advertising "We're only number two" is a classic example of this strategy. By positioning itself as the second-largest automobile rental company, Avis dramatically increased market share. Business was taken away from the smaller rent-a-car companies, rather than Hertz, because consumers remembered both the Avis and Hertz positions. Customers remembered that, while Hertz was number one, Avis was in the number-two slot, where a company has to "try harder." Today, Xerox, long thought of as "the copier company," positions itself as "the documents company," involved in faxing, scanning, copying, and printing. It wants to hold a position unoccupied by other competitors.

POSITIONING BY	EXAMPLE
Image of user	Arch Delux *The burger with the grown-up taste.*
Image of price and/or quality	Hallmark *When you care enough to send the very best.*
Suave	*When you know beautiful hair doesn't have to cost a fortune.*
Product attribute or benefit	Kellogg's Pop-Tarts *Frosted strawberry with Smuckers real fruit.*
Use or application	Arm & Hammer Baking Soda *Try adding Arm & Hammer along with your laundry detergent for a cleaner, fresher wash.*
Product class	Raid Baits *There's no better way to kill bugs dead.*
Competitor	Snapple *We want to be #3.*

EXHIBIT 13–8
Positioning Strategies

SOURCE: The idea for this exhibit comes from David A. Aaker and John G. Meyers, *Advertising Management,* 3rd ed. (Upper Saddle River, N.J.: Prentice-Hall, 1987), p. 375; George E. Belch and Michael A. Belch, *Introduction to Advertising and Sales Promotion* (Homewood, Ill.: Irwin, 1990), pp. 213–222.

How do marketers go about positioning their brands? As Exhibit 13–8 illustrates, there are many positioning strategies. It suggests that brand image campaigns and product differentiation campaigns can be thought of as ways to position the product. Positioning strategies often communicate what the product does. Such strategies may promote a single product attribute—"the car dealer with the lowest prices in town"—or multiple attributes—"the high-performance luxury car." Sometimes the promotional campaign positions a brand by its users—for the working woman. In general, the important point about positioning is not what "selling point" is used as the basis of positioning but the idea that promotion can be used to position a brand relative to the competition. Note, too, that promotional campaigns that stress positioning are highly interrelated with the market segmentation strategy and the overall positioning strategy.

Direct-Response Campaigns

Recall our discussions in earlier chapters about direct channels of distribution in which the manufacturer of a good or the producer of a service deals directly with the customer. The purpose of this "direct marketing" is to obtain a direct response, such as a sale.

Direct-Response Campaign
Promotional approach intended to elicit a direct, measurable response, such as an order.

A **direct-response campaign** is conducted specifically to elicit a direct, measurable response, such as an order, a donation, an inquiry, or a visit to a store or showroom.[7] For example, a mail order company such as L. L. Bean engages in a direct-response campaign by sending out its catalog. Of course, most personal selling fits this category. However, the recent availability of highly targeted computerized databases has brought increased prominence to direct-response promotions conducted via mail, telephone, and other media.

A direct-response campaign, like the other major promotional campaigns, may be used in conjunction with other strategies. We address the advertising and personal selling tactics associated with direct-response campaigns in the next two chapters.

COMPETITIVE STRATEGY: WHAT WENT RIGHT?

Got Milk?

The television commercial opens with a security-camera's fish-eyed view of a convenience store and a strung-out young man in the cold cereal aisle. Looking furtively over his shoulder, he takes boxes of Cheerios, Wheaties, and Trix to check out, where a cashier laughingly says, "Trix? Trix are for kids."

The edgy customer tosses the money at her and flees. Back at his apartment, he triple locks himself inside and tosses the Wheaties and Cheerios to the floor. The kitchen table awaits with an empty bowl and an open carton of milk. "Finally," he gasps, "after all these years of 'Trix are for kids! Trix are for kids!' Well, today. . . they're for rabbits! Hah hah hah hah!" Thanks to computer animation, the guy reachs back and unzips his face. What we now realize was a remarkable costume is peeled away to reveal a familiar cartoon character: the Trix rabbit himself.

Cackling with glee, the rabbit takes the carton and begins to pour milk onto the cereal he has been waiting 30 years to eat, but to his horror and frustration only a few drops dribble out. Then comes the title card and the voice of an announcer saying: "Got milk?"

The commercial is a recent entry in a marketing campaign created by the advertising agency of Goodby, Silverstein & Partners and sponsored by the California Fluid Milk Processor Advisory Board. An earlier commercial in the series featured an Aaron Burr-obsessed history buff who blows a chance at radio-quiz riches because his mouth is full of peanut butter when he has to answer who shot Alexander Hamilton. The point in both advertisements is clear: you'd better have milk around!

Before the "Got milk?" series debuted, reminding consumers of milk's health and nutritional benefits, there had been an uninteresting belaboring of obvious ideas like "Milk does a body good" that accompanied a steady decline in per capita milk consumption.

The "Got milk?" message defied conventional dairy-marketing wisdom by positioning milk not as a life essential but as a lifestyle essential—something you need to have on hand, if only to go with the foods you need to have it on hand for. The consequence of this marketing effort has been a sharp increase in sales and the first leveling off of per capita milk consumption in years.

THE ETHICS OF PERSUASION

Of all the macromarketing issues involving promotion, the use of persuasion has attracted the most attention. Advertising is the most common target of critics of promotions aimed at persuasion, but every element of promotion has been criticized at one time or another.

An important aspect of this issue involves the difference between informative and persuasive promotion. Most people would grant that some advertising or other promotion is needed, or we wouldn't know where to buy a product we want, whether a gas station will accept a credit card, or what freeway exit leads to a motel. Thus, critics often maintain that informative advertisements are fine. They argue, however, that it is not right to use marketing skills, psychology, and expensive commercials to persuade consumers to buy a product, vote for a particular candidate, or give to a certain charity. In summary, the basic argument is that persuasive advertisements are wasteful and manipulative.

A common defense reminds us that advertisements for an inferior product are almost certain to sell the product only once. Even the richest companies with the best sales records sometimes lose millions of dollars introducing products that fail in the marketplace. In fact, the quickest way to kill a poor product is to promote it aggressively. People will find out about its inferior nature just that much quicker.

Your own answer to questions about the proper use of persuasiveness will be influenced by your view of whether people are, or should be, able to exercise freedom of choice. Are consumers able to control their own destinies? Do you ever not buy products you see advertised? Have you ever said no to a salesperson? Why? Rethinking our discussions of the hierarchy of needs, selective perception, and other aspects of consumer behavior should help you to make a decision on this issue. Chapters 14 and 15 address several specific issues involving the ethics of advertising, publicity and public relations, personal selling, and sales promotion.

SUMMARY

Promotion consists of four elements: personal selling, advertising, publicity and public relations, and sales promotion. All must be integrated in the promotional mix.

Learning Objective 1
Discuss the three basic purposes of promotion.
Promotion is communication designed to inform, persuade, and remind buyers about the existence and benefits of a good, service, or idea. Without promotion, buyers would have less information on which to base informed buying decisions.

Learning Objective 2
Define the four major elements of promotion.
Personal selling occurs when a seller directly communicates a persuasive message to the buyer. Advertising includes any persuasive message carried by a nonpersonal medium and paid for by an identified sponsor. Publicity involves an unpaid message with no identified sponsor delivered through a mass medium. Sales promotion consists of nonroutine, temporary promotional efforts designed to stimulate buyer purchases or dealer effectiveness in a specified time period.

Learning Objective 3
Describe the basic model for all communication processes, including promotion.
The communication process occurs when a source encodes a message and sends it through a channel to a receiver, who must decode it and may respond with feedback. Noise may interfere. Each element in the process plays an essential role in the transference of a message from the source to the receiver.

Learning Objective 4
Explain the hierarchy of communication effects.
Consumers often move through a seven-step hierarchy in relation to a product: ignorance, awareness, knowledge, liking, preference, conviction, and purchase. Consumers at different steps have different communication needs.

Learning Objective 5
Explain how the elements of promotion can be used to support one another in a promotional campaign.
The effective marketer integrates all the elements of promotion—advertising, personal selling, publicity and public relations, and sales promotion—into a promotional mix. Such a mix is planned to meet the information requirements of all target customers. Each element of the mix performs a task. Some elements may be aimed at the target customer at a lower stage of the hierarchy of communication effects, while others may be aimed at potential customers near the top of the staircase. Advertising's strength is in creating awareness and spreading information to a wide audience. Personal selling is best at moving buyers from liking, to conviction, to purchase.

Learning Objective 6
Identify the general promotional strategies known as push and pull strategies.
A push strategy is directed toward members of a channel of distribution. A pull strategy is directed toward consumers in order to stimulate demand for the product.

Learning Objective 7
Discuss promotional campaigns and provide examples.
A promotional campaign consists of promotional activities designed to achieve specific objectives. An image-building approach stresses the symbolic value associated with the product. A product differentiation approach emphasizes unique product features. A positioning approach promotes a brand in relation to competing brands. A direct response campaign seeks a direct measurable response.

Learning Objective 8
Be aware of arguments about the ethics of persuasion in society.
Every element of promotion has been criticized at one time or another. Although most people would grant that some advertising or other promotion is needed

to provide information, critics argue that it is not right to use promotional efforts to persuade consumers. A key issue here is whether people are, or should be, able to exercise freedom of choice.

KEY TERMS

Personal selling (p. 352)
Advertising (p. 352)
Publicity (p. 353)
Public relations (p. 353)
Sales promotion (p. 354)
Promotional mix (p. 355)
Integrated marketing communications (p. 355)

Communication (p. 355)
Receiver (p. 355)
Source (p. 355)
Encoding (p. 356)
Decoding (p. 357)
Feedback (p. 357)
Noise (p. 358)
Push strategy (p. 361)

Pull strategy (p. 362)
Promotional campaign (p. 362)
Image building (p. 362)
Product differentiation (p. 364)
Unique selling proposition (USP) (p. 364)
Direct-response campaign (p. 365)

QUESTIONS FOR REVIEW AND CRITICAL THINKING

1. Identify the type of promotion and comment on the effectiveness of each of the following:
   a. Chicago Cubs announcer Harry Caray wears a Budweiser jacket during a televised game.
   b. A TV ad says "CNN Headline News: If you don't have it, call your cable operator to get it."
   c. A Special Olympics representative telephones at 7:00 p.m. while you are watching your favorite TV show and asks you to make a donation.
   d. As a forward receives the basketball, the announcer says "Here comes the Windex man."
   e. At the supermarket, a banner announces a scratch-and-win bingo game.
   f. During a corporate takeover attempt, a corporate executive invites television reporters from major cities to question him during a live satellite news conference. Reporters are allowed to splice in film of themselves for the evening news, so it appears that each local reporter has spoken to the executive in an exclusive interview rather than via a satellite hookup.

2. What is sales promotion? Give some creative examples of sales promotion.

3. Using the communication model in Exhibit 13–3, give examples of the encoding and decoding that might take place during the personal selling process.

4. What is "noise" in the communication process?

5. How does selective perception enter into the communication process?

6. How does a push strategy differ from a pull strategy?

7. Comment on the following: "Promotion mirrors the values and lifestyles of its target consumers."

8. For each of the following brands, indicate whether the primary promotional strategy is image building, positioning, or unique selling proposition.
   a. Mountain Dew soft drink
   b. Cooper tools (for example, crescent wrenches, Lumpkin measuring tapes, Nichols saws)
   c. Sunlight dishwashing liquid
   d. BMW convertibles

9. Form small groups as directed by your instructor. Outline a promotional campaign for your college or university business department, school, or college. Be sure to keep your promotional budget in mind.

INTERNET INSIGHTS

Exercises

1. The promotional mix and promotional strategy should be an integrated marketing communication. Follow the instructions below to take a look at Mama's Cucina, an Internet site brought to you by 'net heads at Ragú.

   http://www.eat.com or http://www.Ragu.com

   This Web site is constantly changing. However, you should find selections such as Mama's New Sauces, Mama's Italian Cookbook, Goodies from Mama, Learn to Speak Italian, and What's New at Mama's.

   Select several options from the menu and evaluate Ragú's promotional efforts. Answer the following questions and bring your answers to class:
   a. Why does a spaghetti sauce have a site on the Internet?
   b. Why does Ragú have recipes on this Web site?
   c. Why did Ragú use the personality of Mama rather than the authority of the company?
   d. Explain the messages communicated on the Ragu Web page in terms of the communication model presented in Exhibit 13–3.

2. To learn the advertising news of the day go to

   http://www.adage.com

   Write a short summary of the article you read.

3. Go to the PRNewswire Web site at

   http://www.prnewswire.com

   Select two news releases. What do they have in common?

Address Book

Integrated Marketing Communications, Inc.
http://www.intmark.com

KPMG Executive Communicator
http://www.kpmg.ca/hr/xcomm/xc_iss.htm

Communications Arts Magazine
http://www.commarts.com

ETHICS IN PRACTICE: TAKE A STAND

1. Because showing a brand in a movie offers some promotional benefits, some movie studios charge fees to feature products. For example, a studio may charge $20,000 simply to show the product, $40,000 to show the product and have an actor mention the brand name, and $60,000 to have an actor actually use the product. Is this right?

2. A tobacco company hands out free samples of a smokeless tobacco (snuff) at a college football game. Is this ethical?

3. Public television stations don't allow commercials, but they mention the names of sponsors of programs at the ends of programs. Should this practice be stopped?

4. H. G. Wells claimed that "advertising is legalized lying." Do you agree?

VIDEO CASE 13-1

International Management Group

The seeds for the International Management Group (IMG) sprouted when a college golfer named Mark McCormack realized he wasn't as good as one of his teammates. After concluding that he had no future as a professional golfer, McCormack decided to embark on another career. His college teammate Arnold Palmer became his first client, and McCormack became a manager—a sports agent.

When McCormack began, most athletes were amateurs, and television carried mostly black-and-white programming. However, as the business developed, McCormack anticipated the connection between sports, television, and global marketing. He thought of sports as a product; and ultimately, he created a multimillion-dollar operation based on sports marketing.

Today, McCormack's IMG represents hundreds of top athletes, including Joe Montana, Jim Courier, and Greg Norman, as well as sports announcers John Madden and Bob Costas. The company manages golfers, tennis players, NFL football players, and other athletes and entertainers. It negotiates contracts with many sporting organizations, including auto racing teams and organizations. And it works for clients like Martina Navratilova and Andre Agasi to obtain endorsement agreements with the marketers of consumer goods and services.

IMG even sponsors and manages its own tournaments and sporting events. It has created television shows such as "The Battle of the Network Stars" and "The Skins Game." Many times IMG athletes participate in these events.

Questions

1. Mark McCormack is a sports agent and a manager in charge of sports marketing. How important is personal selling in a job like this? What personal characteristics do you think would be important in a job like McCormack's?
2. What promotional opportunities are available for athletes who wish to lend their names to goods or services? How might a marketer like Fila, Wilson, or Nike use McCormack's services?
3. What might IMG look for in an athlete it agrees to manage?
4. How global is the sports marketing business?

ADVERTISING AND PUBLIC RELATIONS

Chapter 14

Learning Objectives

After you have studied this chapter, you will be able to:

1. Understand the purpose of product advertising, direct-action advertising, and institutional advertising.
2. Differentiate between primary and selective demand advertising.
3. Discuss the stages in the development of an advertisement.
4. Analyze the role of communication goals in the advertising process.
5. Show how advertisements for a product are likely to change over the course of the product's life cycle.
6. Define advertising appeal and describe several commonly used execution formats.
7. Compare the advantages and disadvantages of various advertising media.
8. Explain how advertising effectiveness is measured.
9. Describe the nature of public relations and explain how publicity should be managed.
10. Discuss several ethical issues involving advertising and public relations.

A Snickers television commercial is set in a football locker room, where a gruff, crew-cut head coach announces, "Listen up. This year we gotta be a little more 'politically correct' with the team prayer. (He turns to a priest, standing behind him.) Hit it, Padre."

"Let us take this moment to look inside and reflect on our good fortune," the priest says, but before he can go on, the coach butts in—to introduce a second clergyman. "All right, Rabbi. Let's go."

"And may victory be with you," the rabbi says, before he too is cut off.

"Come on Shaman, let's move. (This time it's a Native American spiritualist, who utters one word, 'Minika.') That was very touching. Come on, Bagwan."

Then, as the Indian mystic steps to the fore, the voice-over says, "Not going anywhere for a while? Grab a Snickers." Which one of the kneeling players does, as the Eastern Orthodox priest, black preacher, Hare Krishna et al., wait for their turns. "Stay in line," the coach says.

As the title card fills the frame, we hear the team chanting its mantra: "Ommmmmmmmmmm. . . ."

As funny as this gentle satire of diversity fever is, it pales next to the one about the end-zone painter, an elderly Chiefs employee whom we see painstakingly reproducing the team logo beneath the goalposts. As he steps back finally to admire his work, a player walks up behind him.

"Hey, that's great," says the lineman, "but who are the Chefs?"

Yeah, he left out the "i," which is amusing, but his reaction is hilarious.

(SFX: TEAM TALKING) COACH: Listen up. This year we gotta be a little more politically correct

COACH: All right, rabbi, let's go. RABBI: And may victory be with you.

MALE VO: Not going anywhere for a while? COACH: Stay in line, no pushing. Next.

TEAM: Ah-mmm.

"Great googily moogily!" the employee says. Then, consoling himself in a Snickers bar as he contemplates starting from scratch, the player tries to help.

"You spell it . . . ." But the old guy just snarls, "Yahhhh!" and takes another bite. Yahhhh. It's not even a word, and you have to hear it to appreciate it.

These two commercials are part of Snickers' "Not going anywhere for a while? Grab a Snickers" advertising campaign. It may be taken as comedy for comedy's sake but beneath the jokes is a very serious selling proposition: what to eat when there's no access to real food. Therein is the big promotional idea.

The power of advertising can be amazing. It is a creative marketing tool whose influence may go far beyond the marketer's intended purpose. This chapter explores the captivating world of advertising and public relations.

The chapter begins with a general discussion of the purpose of advertising. Next, it outlines the stages in an advertising campaign. It examines communication goals and advertising objectives, creative strategy, media strategy, and the use of research to evaluate these strategies. It then discusses public relations as an element of the promotional mix. The chapter closes with a consideration of ethical issues.

THE NATURE OF ADVERTISING

Chapter 13 defined advertising as a persuasive message carried by a nonpersonal medium and paid for by an identified sponsor. This definition points out two basic parts of advertising: the message and the medium. Both work together to communicate the right ideas to the right audience.

Traditional advertising promotes goods, services, and ideas in mass media, such as television, radio, newspapers, and magazines, to reach a large number of people at once. Increasingly, advertising also is used to promote a custom message to a single prospect using direct-response media or interactive media; such advertising is often a critical component of direct marketing efforts.

Advertising serves as a substitute for a salesperson talking to an individual prospect. But because mass media advertising is a one-way communication, advertisers cannot receive direct feedback and immediately handle objections. Advertisers do control the exact nature of the one-way message that will be communicated to the target audience, however, as well as the timing and degree of repetition. These features often provide benefits that far outweigh disadvantages associated with imperfect feedback.

Advertising supports other promotional efforts. It may communicate information about a sales promotion or announce a public relations event. Advertising helps the salesperson "get a foot in the door" by preselling prospects. A salesperson's job can be made much easier if advertising informs the prospect about unique product benefits or encourages prospects to contact a salesperson. Without advertising, the salesperson's efforts may be hindered because the prospect does not know about the company or its products. Advertising can also stimulate people to talk about a brand. Its power to influence word-of-mouth communication can be a great asset to a marketer.

Advertising can be subdivided into many different categories. A very basic scheme classifies advertising as product advertising or institutional advertising.

Product Advertising

Product Advertisement
Advertisement promoting a specific product.

Advertisements for Nike Air Jordan shoes, Hilton hotels, Special-K cereal, and many other brands are intended to persuade consumers to purchase a particular product—indeed, a particular brand. These are product advertisements. An advertisement for Ford trucks that declares "Ford trucks—the best never rests" and suggests that viewers go down to the local Ford dealership is a **product advertisement** because it features a specific product.

Direct-Action Advertisement
Advertisement designed to stimulate immediate purchase or encourage another direct response. Also called a direct-response advertisement.

If the Ford advertisement also recommends that viewers go to the showroom for a test drive during an inventory reduction sale—that is, suggests an immediate purchase—it is also a **direct-action advertisement,** or **direct-response advertisement.** Many television advertisements and many direct-mail advertisements are of this type. An increasing number of these involve direct marketing, which includes both direct-action advertising and a direct channel of distribution.

Indirect-Action Advertisement
Advertisement designed to stimulate sales over the longer run.

Advertisements designed to build brand image or position a brand for an eventual sale rather than to sell merchandise right this minute are **indirect-action advertisements.** For example, consider an advertisement portraying the romance and adventure of Jamaica. The advertiser knows the consumer is not likely to run directly to a travel agency after seeing such an advertisement. The objective is to provide information so that the next time the family is considering a vacation, Jamaica will be among the spots considered.

FOCUS ON QUALITY

Scotch-Brite Never Rust

Comparative advertising doesn't have to be scientific and dull. Scotch-Brite Never Rust soap pads from 3M associates its competitor Brillo with a dinosaur to illustrate its brand's quality.

"Steel wool," intones a voice-over, in a television commercial, "a creature from a prehistoric age." On-screen the viewer sees a steel wool pad metamorphose into a tyrannosaurus rex. ". . . terrorizing us with splinters (the tyrannosaurus-rex shakes itself, and thousands of steel fragments fly off like shrapnel), dripping with rust (the stalking dinosaur

leaves a disgusting trail of rusty, sooty water).

"Enter a superior species," the voice-over continues, "the new Scotch-Brite Never Rust soap pad. (Here the viewer sees the product in action, scouring grimy pots and pans). It's made from an innovative fiber that never rusts or splinters, and no steel wool pad cleans better. The old dinosaur is history." (Now the tyrannosaurus-rex melts like the Wicked Witch of the West in a ruddy puddle and is wiped away with a Scotch-Brite pad.)

---

these commercials center on some personal, household, or business situation, such as an attractive neighbor's visit next door to borrow some Taster's Choice coffee. The slice-of-life format is essentially a dramatized variation on the problem-solution format.

Demonstration

Demonstration Format
Advertising format in which a clear-cut example of product superiority or consumer benefits is presented.

The **demonstration format** dramatically illustrates product features or proves some advertised claim. For example, the Master Lock advertisement in which bullets are repeatedly fired into a lock that does not open is suspenseful and self-explanatory. **Comparative advertising,** which directly contrasts one brand of a product with another, inferior brand, is a form of demonstration advertising.

Comparative Advertising
Type of demonstration advertising in which the brand being advertised is directly compared with a competing brand.

Testimonial

Testimonials and endorsements show a person, usually a prominent show business or sports figure, making a statement establishing that he or she owns, uses, or supports the brand advertised. The idea is that people who identify with the celebrity will want to be like that person and use the same product.

Testimonial
Advertising format in which a person, usually a well-known person, states that he or she owns, uses, or supports the product being advertised.

A variation on the testimonial appeal is the use of a spokesperson. The **spokesperson** represents the company and directly addresses the audience, urging them to buy the company's product. The spokesperson, often the commercial's central character, need not be a real person. The Poppin' Fresh Dough Boy for Pillsbury and the Keebler elves are well-known animated spokespersons.[1]

Spokesperson
Person who, representing the advertiser, directly addresses the audience and urges them to buy the advertiser's product. Using a spokesperson is a variation on the use of testimonials.

Lifestyle

Lifestyle Format
Advertising format that reflects a target market's lifestyle or hoped-for lifestyle.

The **lifestyle format** combines scenes or sequences of situations intended to reflect a particular target market's lifestyle. Young people might be shown enjoying some outdoor activity and topping off a perfect day with a Mountain Dew, for example.

Still Life

Still-Life Format
Advertising format that makes the product or package its focal point, emphasizing a visually attractive presentation and the product's brand name.

The **still-life format** portrays the product in a visually attractive setting. The product or package is the focal point of the advertisement. Reminder advertising often uses still-life formats because the most important aspect of the message is to reinforce the brand name.

Association

Association Format
Advertising format that uses an analogy or other relationship to stimulate interest and convey information.

The **association format** concentrates on an analogy or other relationship to convey its message. This creative strategy often "borrows interest" from another, more exciting product or situation. Thrilling activities, such as skydiving or windsurfing, and scenes of beautiful places, such as the coast of Maine or a mountain wilderness, are used in this way. The purpose of such analogies is to create an emotional mood. **Fantasy** is a special associative format. The long-lived series of advertisements for Chanel perfume is a perfect example of the fantasy approach. The fantasy appeal seeks to associate the product not merely with a glamorous setting but with the target buyer's wildest hopes and dreams.

Fantasy
In the context of advertising, a type of association format in which the intention is to link the product with the target buyer's wildest dreams and hopes.

Montage

Montage Format
Advertising format that blends a number of situations, demonstrations, and other visual effects into one commercial to emphasize the array of possibilities associated with product usage.

The **montage format** blends a number of situations, demonstrations, and other visual effects into one commercial. The effect may be one of a swirl of colors or an exciting array of possibilities associated with product usage. Several of Pepsi's GenerationNext advertisments follow this format.

Jingle

Commercial Jingle
Song or other short verse used in an advertisement as a memory aid.

"My bologna has a first name . . . it's O-S-C-A-R." Can you remember the rest of this jingle? Probably so. **Commercial jingles** are musical verses with "memory value." They can have a significant effect on product recall.

Other Formats

This short list of advertising formats is far from exhaustive. Animation and special effects, for example, have not been mentioned. However, this discussion should help you to think of other advertising formats and of the ways they work in an effective marketing program.

Global Advertising Campaigns

Many multinational marketers with world brands have attempted global advertising campaigns that use standardized advertising executions in all markets. The logic is that the same advertising, adjusted for language differences, will work everywhere in a world that has become very homogeneous.

For example, Avon's Far Away positioning is intended to speak to women around the world.[2] Avon's marketing research for Far Away indicated that in most countries women felt the need to escape to someplace away from the wear and tear of everyday life. So Far Away's advertising agency created an advertisement showing a woman drifting peacefully on a boat, surrounded by flowers. The ad can be used worldwide because the image of retreating to a private place is one that most women can relate to.

However, Chanel No. 5, Parker Pen, and other global advertisers have experienced major disappointments because their advertising was too standardized. The idea of a global advertising campaign is tempting for a brand seeking a unified image, but even though companies such as these may market world brands, customers live, buy, and consume in local environments. It's crucial to keep regional sensibilities in mind. For example, it is considered inappropriate to show a full body shot of a woman in Muslim countries. Global marketers should always consider the need to adjust their advertising executions in a relevant and meaningful way to fit the context of the cultures of a particular county.

PRODUCING AN EFFECTIVE ADVERTISEMENT

Advertisements consist of verbal elements, visual elements, and auditory elements.[3] The exact combination of these elements depends on the people who design the advertisement and the advertising medium used.

Copy—The Verbal Appeal

Copy
In the context of advertising, any words contained in an advertisement.

The term **copy** refers to the words in an advertisement. The words may be printed or verbalized by an announcer or by a character in a commercial. In certain advertisements, such as in radio, the copy makes the biggest contribution to the advertisement's effectiveness. Even in a visual medium, such as television, copy is likely to retain its supremacy, because many of the claims an advertiser makes must be supported by the comments of the announcers or the characters. For example, advertisements for laundry detergents may show two piles of wash. It is the copy that assures viewers that the pile washed in Tide is whiter.

Art—The Visual Appeal

Art
In the context of advertising, any aspect of an advertisement other than copy, including pictures, layout, and white space.

The term **art** is used broadly to mean all aspects of an advertisement other than its verbal portions. Thus, pictures, graphs and charts, layout (the arrangement of the visual elements), and even white space (places where neither pictures nor words appear) fall under the heading of art.

The function of pictures in an advertisement is to illustrate a fact or idea or to attract attention. White space and layout are more subtle in their purposes. Layout can be effectively used to focus the viewer's attention on the picture of the product. It also can be used to draw attention to the brand name, the price, or the place of sale. White space can be used in similar ways but is more commonly used to suggest high quality. Notice that many newspaper and magazine advertisements employ considerable white space to accent the product. A great deal of white space says that the pictured item is special, probably expensive, and certainly of high quality. It implies that the product deserves the spotlight given it by a plain field that accents its appeal.

An effective advertisement draws attention immediately. Portraying novel or humorous situations is a proven attention-getting device.

Ever see a strawberry and a kiwi smile?

New Strawberry-Kiwi flavor Island Twists from Kool-Aid.

Copy and Art Working Together—The AIDA Formula

Most advertisements, with the exception of radio advertisements, feature both copy and art. The two elements must work together and complement each other to accomplish the communication objectives set by management. To do this, most advertisers follow a model known as the AIDA formula. **AIDA** stands for attention, interest, desire, and action.

AIDA
An acronym for attention, interest, desire, and action. The AIDA formula is a hierarchy of communication effects model used as a guideline in creating advertisements.

Attention

An effective advertisement must draw attention from the very first glance or hearing. Whatever follows will prove of little use if the target viewer has not been influenced to pay attention. Copy can be used to accomplish this, as when radio advertisements start out sounding like soap operas or mystery stories to draw attention. The copy can be enhanced by visual illustration. Often a person, representing the target customer, is shown in situations that make the viewer think, "What's going on here?" or "What happened to these people?" For example, to attract the attention of luggage users, Samsonite has for years run advertisements showing such things as suitcases falling out of airplanes and suitcases supporting automobiles that have flipped over on top of them. Humor is another proven attention-getting device.

Interest

After attention has been attracted, interest must be aroused. If the attention-getter is powerful enough, interest should follow fairly automatically. However, it may be necessary to focus the viewers or listeners on how the product or service being advertised actually pertains to them.

Desire

Next comes an attempt to create a desire for the product. A TV commercial for ChemLawn demonstrates this. The viewer sees one homeowner carrying tools and bags of lawn chemicals. One of the bags breaks, and the exhausted do-it-yourselfer looks on helplessly. The viewer at home sees, however, that the unfortunate fellow's neighbor has a very nice-looking lawn but does not look harried and sweaty. The viewer is interested in this story: Why is one fellow miserable while his neighbor smilingly pities him? The contented homeowner is a subscriber to the ChemLawn service, of course. The viewer is treated to some scenes of the ChemLawn man applying liquid lawn chemicals in one easy step. The ChemLawn people know what and when to spray—another load off the homeowner's mind. Thus, interest in and desire for the product are established in nearly simultaneous steps.

Action

Action is the last part of the AIDA formula. In the ChemLawn example, the last thing in the commercial is a call to action. In effect, the advertisement urges viewers to phone the local ChemLawn dealer for an estimate of what it will take to make them as happy as the man who has a nice lawn with no effort. Thus, the means to act is provided. Usually, the advertiser makes the action seem as effortless as possible by giving a phone number or closing with a note that credit cards are accepted.

How the AIDA Formula Works

The AIDA formula is based on a consumer behavior theory that closely parallels the hierarchy of communication effects model discussed in Chapter 13. The formula describes consumers' behavior and serves as a guideline for creating advertising. AIDA makes good sense as an advertising tool and is widely known and followed.

It must be understood that it is not possible for every advertisement to move the reader or viewer through the four stages to action with a single exposure. Repetition is usually necessary so that the advertisement's message can "sink in." Repetition also increases the chance that the target customer will see or hear the message at a time when there are no distractions. Finally, repetition recognizes the buyer's ever-changing environment. The target buyer who has just been paid or has received a tax refund may perceive an already-seen advertisement in a different light. Eventually, if the advertisement is an effective one aimed at the proper people, buyers are likely to move psychologically through the AIDA stages and then

Media Selection Strategy
Strategy involving the determination of which media are most appropriate for an advertising campaign.

act. As we have already indicated, developing a creative strategy and developing a **media selection strategy** are interrelated, and the planning of these activities occurs simultaneously. We now turn our attention to the selection of media.

 MEDIA SELECTION

Suppose you decide to open a retail store. You decide to have a Yellow Pages advertisement but are undecided about whether to use radio, television, or newspaper advertising as well. This choice is a matter of selecting a communications channel for your message. In making the choice, you are determining a media strategy, which must take account of the message you wish to transmit, the audience you want to reach, the effect you want to have, and the budget you have to support this effort.

Developing a media strategy requires answers to two questions: (1) Which media will efficiently get the message to the desired audience? (2) What scheduling of these media will neither bore people with too-frequent repetition of the message nor let too many people forget the message? Before we address these questions, let's look briefly at what the term *media* includes.

Mass Media, Direct-Marketing Media, and Interactive Media

When we think of advertising, we normally think of mass media, such as radio and television. However, we must remember direct-marketing media and interactive media as well. Exhibit 14–3 shows the individual advertising media in each of these classifications. Advances in technology have changed the nature of direct-marketing media in recent years. Direct mail advertising has been in existence for more than a century, for example, but modern computer technology has improved the selectivity of this medium. Now computers can access databases to customize what materials will be sent and to personalize the direct-response advertising message to a household or an individual.

The Baywatch program appeals to certain distinct demographic and psychographic market segments. An objective of the media selection strategy is to choose media that reach the desired segment.

EXHIBIT 14–3
Mass Media, Direct-
Marketing Media and
Interactive Media

Mass Media
Broadcast media
- Network television
- Cable television
- Radio

Print media
- Newspapers
- Magazines
- Directory/Yellow pages

Outdoor
- Billboards
- Posters

In-Store
- Point-of-purchase displays
- Video presentations

Other
- Movie theater
- Transit

Direct Media
- Letters and pamphlets
- Catalogs
- Bill inserts
- Flyers

Phone/Fax
- Computerized calls
- Fax advertisements

Interactive Media
- Internet
- Commercial on-line services
- Electronic mail

There are two important points to mention about strategies stressing direct-marketing media. First, new products and services, such as fax machines and computer voice-recognition systems, are used in much the same way as direct mail always has been used. That is, a list containing many individuals' names is used to directly contact potential buyers. New technologies may replace the postal service, but the process is essentially the same.

Second, as mentioned, computers are used to develop databases that can customize the message any individual consumer or household receives. For example, a personalized greeting may appear on a letter that, in addition to conveying an advertising message, indicates the name of a local retailer that sells the brand being advertised. If the database records the ages of the children in households, an advertiser using direct marketing can send coupons only to those households with, say, children in diapers. Furthermore, if the database also indicates the brand of diapers a consumer regularly purchases, then an advertiser like Huggies can limit the mailing list to consumers who are loyal to Pampers or other competitive brands.

Interactive media allow an individual to seek information, ask questions, and get answers without the direct assistance of a human being. For instance, The World of Clinique Web site (www.clinique.com) offers on-line skin-type consultation on the Internet.[4] Consumers can find answers to frequently asked questions about color and make-up and learn tips on topics such as sun protection. As the consumers interactively learn about skin care, they, of course, learn Clinique cosmetics products are appropriate for their own situation. Advertising on the Internet is ideal for consumers who want details about specific products. Interactive media can provide large amounts of information.

Also, advertising "banners" may be purchased on search engines and commercial Web sites. For example, a marketer of garden tools might work out an arrangement with the Yahoo search engine company to display its banner on the results

The PointCast Network is a pioneer in the development of personalized Web pages. PointCast's software can "surf the Web" and automatically send personalized information to an individual's computer. Users get stock quotes, news, sports, weather, and other information. Advertising messages, for products which coincide with the computer user's interests, appear in the upper right-hand corner of each screen.

page whenever the key word "garden" is entered as a search term. The advantage of this type of on-line Internet advertising is that the audience has self-selected the topic and the marketer message reaches an involved, highly targeted market.

Which Media?

Certain media lend themselves to certain tasks. If we assume, for the moment, that budget considerations can be set aside, certain factors become dominant in choosing the medium to carry a sales message. If demonstration or visual comparison of one brand with another is the goal, television becomes the most logical contender. If a lengthy explanation of sales points is required, print advertisements (magazines and newspapers) come to mind. If consumers require a message to remind them of package identification or a short sales idea, outdoor advertising (billboards) makes sense. Thus, before a marketing planner starts thinking about what medium to use, he or she must know what is to be said. Once what is to be said has been decided, the marketer's attention can turn to which media form can best say it. Ultimately, several different media may be selected to carry the multiple messages the marketer wants to communicate.

Several media may appear to be able to do a particular job. When this is so, the marketing planner can narrow the choice by considering which media will hit the all-important target market. At this point, the media expert becomes a market expert. Knowing the target market—who are the heaviest buyers, what are their demographic and psychographic characteristics—leads to a determination of which media will deliver these prospects. For example, the media planner in the insurance industry may be trying to target young males between the ages of 18 and 34; a European airline may be targeting well-educated, high-income men and women between the ages of 25 and 49; the primary customers for a sun-block cream may be youthful, fashion-conscious women. What media will reach each of these targets most effectively?

Most products can be related to a demographic profile. The data gathered pertaining to media are geared to that same profile information. Thus, if the target audience includes men and women, and it has been decided that television will do the best job and that the media budget permits such an expensive choice, the media planner may go for prime-time television—from 8 p.m. to 11 p.m. The next question becomes which television shows have audiences whose profiles most clearly match those of the target customer.

Careful analysis of any organization's marketing communication efforts might show that what appears to be the most appropriate advertising medium is, in fact, inappropriate. Where should one advertise a product like children's crayons? Saturday morning television shows, with their ability to show happy children drawing and coloring, and with their excellent demographics, would seem to be an obvious choice. But when Crayola's marketing managers discovered that mothers were the prime factors in the purchase of crayons, they shifted a large portion of their advertising budget out of children's TV and into women's magazines. The copy theme they developed, "Give them a fresh box of crayons and see how they grow," reflected the shift in audience and the new media strategy. The TV advertisements were still useful, but the TV advertisements coupled with women's magazine advertisements were better.

Media Advantages and Disadvantages

Each medium has its advantages and disadvantages. Direct-marketing media, such as direct mail, can be very selective and can reach a clearly defined market, such as all families within a certain zip code area, individuals with upcoming birthdays, or all holders of American Express cards. But it can also end up in the wastepaper basket.

Television reaches a mass audience. However, specialization by type of show is possible. For example, *Moesha* appeals to preteens and teenagers, and *Seinfeld* appeals to a range of young-to-middle-aged adults. Television allows advertisers to show and tell, because it can involve sight, sound, movement, cartoons, actors, and announcers. The strengths of television may be outweighed by its relative expensiveness. Cable television, with advertising rates lower than network television's, can be a good alternative for many products. Even when the advertising rates for a particular program or station are relatively low, however, the costs to develop and produce a commercial keep many potential users away from TV.

Newspapers have the advantages of mass appeal within selected geographical markets, a general respect in the community, and a short lead time (that is, newspaper advertisements can be inserted, withdrawn, or altered quickly). Magazines have relatively long lead times but offer the advantages of selectivity of audience and far better reproduction of print and pictures than can be found in newspapers. Radio provides geographic and demographic selectivity because the programming of different stations attracts different types of listeners. Its lead time is short, and its use as a means to expose listeners to frequent messages is obvious.

Exhibit 14–4 highlights the general characteristics of several media. In 1997, the top 100 U.S. advertisers spent approximately $50 billion to place advertisements in various media.[5]

Newspapers

Advantages

Geographic market selectivity

Flexibility—ease of ad insertion and change

Editorial support

Disadvantages

Lack of permanence of advertising message

Poor quality of print production

Limited demographic orientation

Magazines

Advantages

Demographic market selectivity

Long-life ad capability

Good quality of print production

Editorial support

Disadvantages

Lack of flexibility—difficult to make last-minute changes

Limited availability

Expensive—especially for color

Radio

Advantages

Geographic and demographic market selectivity

Flexibility

Inexpensive on a relative basis

Disadvantages

Lack of permanence—perishability

Clutter

Lack of visual support

Limited impact—background medium

Television

Advantages

Show and tell—demonstration is possible

Geographic market selectivity

Market penetration due to large viewing audience

Disadvantages

Perishable ad message unless repeated

Expensive on a relative basis

Clutter—message may become lost in group of advertisements

Direct mail

Advantages

Highly selective

Easy to measure results

Lengthy copy possible

Reader governs exposure

Disadvantages

Expensive—especially on a cost-per-person basis

Little or no editorial support

Limited reader interest

Internet/Interactive

Advantages

Easy to measure audience

Lengthy copy possible

Readers read what interests them

Readers can request additional information

Inexpensive—especially on a cost-per-person basis

Disadvantages

Cannot reach consumers without Internet access

No advanced knowledge of audience

Point-of-purchase

Advantages

Promotes impulse buying

"Sells" in nonpersonal selling environment

Ties together product and ads

Disadvantages

Difficult to obtain desired placements

Clutter

Limited creative possibilities

Directory

Advantages

Permanence—long life

High reach and frequency potential

Disadvantages

Limited customer usage

Market coverage limited to phone customers

Outdoor

Advantages

High reach and frequency potential

Market selectivity

High impact due to size

Inexpensive on a relative basis

Disadvantages

Brevity of message

Image is thought to be poor for certain markets

Clutter is often present

Location choices may be limited

EXHIBIT 14–4
Selected Advantages and Disadvantages of Some Advertising Media

SOURCE: The idea for this table is based on William H. Bolen, *Advertising*, 2nd ed. (New York: John Wiley & Sons, 1984), pp. 601–602.

FOCUS ON TRENDS

Narrowcasting

Lately, there has been a lot of talk about phone companies merging with cable television companies to create interactive television systems. Fiber optics and telecommunications technologies will soon allow viewers to select from 500 channels. Consumers will not just receive programming; they will control it. Effective marketers are planning for a change from broadcasting to "narrowcasting" by which they will be able to direct fine-tuned messages to very specific groups of consumers. For example, a 24-hour golf channel is available in some markets. An average commercial on this channel may reach as few as 30,000 people, but it's highly likely that these viewers will be good prospects for golf shoes, clubs, and balls. And the viewers will be able to interact with their TV sets to place orders. The trend away from mass marketing will have a tremendous impact on media selection strategies.

What Scheduling?

Media Schedule
Schedule identifying the exact media to be used and the dates on which advertisements are to appear. Also called media plan.

The **media schedule,** or **media plan,** is a time schedule identifying the exact media to be used and the dates on which advertisements are to appear. Media planners not only select the general media category (such as magazines and cable television) but also the specific media vehicles (such as *Sports Illustrated* and *Star Trek: Voyager*). Selecting specific vehicles requires managers to consider reach and frequency.

Reach
The number of people exposed to an advertisement carried by a given medium.

Reach—that is, the number of people exposed to an advertisement in a given medium—is an important factor in determining which media to use. Obviously, the advertiser who wishes to reach the largest number of people in the target audience must take cost into consideration. A major aspect of the media selection job is making cost comparisons—evaluating whether, for example, *Sports Illustrated* has a lower cost per thousand readers than *Inside Sports*.

Frequency
The number of times an advertisement is repeated in a given medium within a given time period, usually a month.

Another cost, and another strategy consideration, relates to repetition, or **frequency,** of the advertising message in a given medium within a given time period, typically a month. Frequency reflects the number of times an individual is expected to be exposed to an advertiser's message. Reach may be traded off for frequency. Two advertisements in *Forbes,* for example, may be more cost-effective than a single advertisement in *Fortune*. Although cost is an important consideration, strategy considerations may be equally important in choosing between reach and frequency. For example, frequency may be more important than reach when repetition will help the audience learn something new. If the advertising objective for a new brand is to establish awareness or to communicate a new product feature, then the benefits of frequency may outweigh the benefits of reach. Because the trade-off between reach and frequency is a complex issue, marketing managers often use marketing research to help them choose the best media schedule.

MEASURING THE EFFECTIVENESS OF ADVERTISING

An advertiser about to commit $1,200,000 for a 30-second commercial on the Super Bowl or for the development of a series of advertisements created especially for the Christmas season will want some way to measure the effectiveness of those advertisements. Measuring the effectiveness of advertisements in terms of the sales dollars generated is difficult. Despite that fact, several approaches to measuring effectiveness have been developed. These research techniques do not provide exact measures of effectiveness, but they do provide a systematic means by which advertisers can develop and test advertisements to determine whether they are accomplishing their intended objectives. Advertising research may be divided into two phases: (1) the pretesting stage of development and refinement of advertising content and copy and (2) the posttesting stage that evaluates its effectiveness.

Developing Messages and Pretesting Advertisements

Pretesting
In the context of advertising, research on the effectiveness of an advertisement that begins at the earliest stages of development and continues until the advertisement is ready for use.

Before advertisements are put on TV or in magazines, they may have gone through several stages of testing. The purpose of **pretesting** is to limit, or even eliminate, mistakes. Pretesting may be conducted in the earliest stages of the development of an advertisement and continues virtually until the advertisement is printed or broadcast. First, the basic appeal of an advertisement, or the concept around which it will be built, may be tested. Then a headline, picture, or slogan can be tested. A "rough" version of the advertisement, featuring still photos in the case of a television commercial or a story acted out by nonprofessional actors in the case of a radio advertisement, can be assembled rather inexpensively and shown to a sample audience to measure its appeal and believability.

Videotaping possible spokespersons for products and showing these tapes to panels of consumers in an attempt to determine the appropriateness of the spokesperson is a worthwhile pretest. Consider, for example, the manufacturer of a hair-coloring kit that developed an advertisement featuring Raquel Welch endorsing the product. Tests of rough commercials showed that, while Welch was easily recognized and was perceived as an outstanding personality, she was not seen as an authority on the product or as a user of a home hair-coloring kit. The pretesting indicated that, to enhance believability, advertisements for home-use products such as this should feature "real people" rather than movie stars. Later in her career, when she reached middle age, research showed Welch to be a very credible spokesperson for Bally Fitness Centers, because the target audience associated the need for fitness with movie stars of a "certain age" who must keep in shape.

Many of the marketing research tools discussed in Chapter 5 are used to pretest advertisements. Focus group discussions with consumers can be especially helpful.

Posttesting Advertisements

Posttesting
In the context of advertising, testing that takes place after an advertisement has been run to determine whether it has met the objectives set for it by management.

Once an advertisement has been developed and has run in the chosen media, **posttesting** should be done to determine if it has met the objectives set by management. Posttests usually measure brand awareness, changes in attitudes toward the product, or generation of inquiries about the product.

Measuring Brand Recall and Recognition

Recall Test
In the context of advertising, a research tool used to determine how much people remember about an advertisement.

Because advertisers must gain the attention of buyers and have them remember the names of brands or the stores in which they can be found, many posttests are designed to evaluate recognition or recall.

Recall tests can take many forms. For example, a telephone survey may be conducted during the 24-hour period following the airing of a television commercial to measure day-after recall. In such studies, the telephone interviewer first poses a question such as this:

> *"Did you watch* Sixty Minutes *last night?"*

If the answer is positive, the next question might be:

event sponsorship. However, sponsors of a global event such as the Wimbledon tennis championship, the PGA championship, or the World Series can expect to receive media coverage and considerable publicity around the world.

NationsBank Corporation spent approximately $120 million on its sponsorship of the 1996 Olympic Games in Atlanta. Besides choice seats and hospitality tents, what did the bank get for its $40 million sponsorship fee?[11] The bank received national name recognition beyond what any advertising campaign could buy because the Olympics reaches a wide spectrum of ages and allows a sponsor to cut across all socioeconomic lines. The heart of NationsBank's strategy was to associate the bank as often as possible with world-class athletes and teamwork. It expects its effort will yield a healthy boost for employees and investors alike.

When a marketer, such as Yukon Jack, actually creates a special event to sponsor, such as the Yukon Jack Wrestling Championship, the company is the title sponsor and the activity is called **event marketing.** The accompanying Competitive Strategy feature explains how the Chemical Bank Corporate Challenge has grown into a major event. You can probably see that event sponsorship can be an integrated marketing communication that is both a public relations effort and a sales promotion effort. This matter is discussed next.

Event Marketing
Marketing when the title sponsor creates the event and activity

PUBLIC RELATIONS GOES BEYOND PUBLICITY: AN INTEGRATED MARKETING COMMUNICATIONS APPROACH

Although management of an organization's public image through publicity is the cornerstone of public relations, all forms of promotion may influence an organization's relationship with the general public. Thus, managers should not overlook the coordination of public relations efforts with other promotional efforts. Many of the objectives of publicity are the same as the objectives for other promotions. Indeed, these activities may be carried out by the public relations department. For example, the Macy's Thanksgiving Day parade is a sales promotion event that enhances Macy's public image. And the lobbying effort by the Friends of Kuwait is a form of personal selling, even though the public relations workers involved have titles other than sales representative. (The term *public relations* may be used in preference to the term *sales* by government officials who would rather go to lunch with a lobbyist than a salesperson or by a charity that prefers to discuss its fund raising as something other than a sales promotion.)

Exhibit 14–5 illustrates the fact that public relations to enhance organizational image and to communicate product information includes more than just publicity. It also illustrates that public relations efforts have various target audiences—not just consumers but also stockholders, government bodies, environmental groups, and the like—which can be reached in various ways.

Public relations campaigns—like all promotional campaigns—should use an integrated marketing communications approach. Each promotional element should be employed so its unique characteristics can help communicate a unified message. Because integrated marketing communication is so important, large public relations companies, such as Hill & Knowlton and Ketchum PR, are as familiar with using advertising as they are with using publicity to tell a company's story.

Crisis Management

Crisis Management
Public relations effort to manage an emergency that urgently requires dissemination of information.

Sometimes a tragic event, such as an airplane crash, or some other occurrence, such as criticism from an activist group like Greenpeace, creates a public relations crisis. **Crisis management** is a public relations effort to manage an emergency that urgently requires dissemination of information.

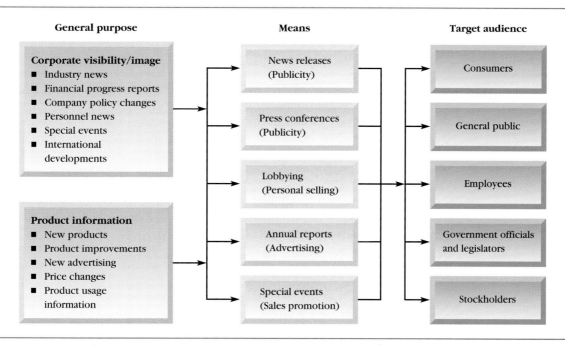

EXHIBIT 14–5
The Scope of Public
Relations

Public relations specialists believe managers should make themselves available to journalists as quickly as possible after a crisis strikes. In the case of a plane crash or a health care scare, the public has an urgent need for information. Thus, the company should not delay—it should respond immediately.

Another guideline for crisis management is for top executives to be visible when a crisis occurs. Top executives can be very effective as company spokespersons. Public relations efforts during a crisis should use executives to communicate something very important about company policy. Experience shows that it is vital that these executives tell the truth rather than using subterfuge to postpone dealing with the problem. It is also wise for them to apply the K.I.S.S. formula—which stands for "keep it short and simple" (or "keep it simple, stupid")—to their remarks. A message that is not understood because it is too complicated can defeat the purpose of crisis management. Sometimes, rumors about a company's operations or products reach near-crisis proportions. When the company wants to cope with untrue rumors, it should develop a plan of action for rumor control. The following steps are recommended:[12]

1. Create a rumor center and appoint a person to be responsible for its operation on a constant basis. Have the rumor center trace the rumors' origins.
2. Send out the correct facts. Don't just deny the rumor; demonstrate the truth to dispel the rumor.
3. Hold press conferences when appropriate.
4. Ask a respected third party, such as an outside expert, to comment on the rumor.
5. Deal with the rumor locally when appropriate.

Internal Marketing and Employee Relations

One of an organization's most important publics consists of its managers and employees. Employees who feel that they are important parts of a worthwhile activity, who identify themselves with the creation of good products for others, who

Internal Marketing
Public relations efforts aimed at a company's own employees.

take pride in the delivery of outstanding service, and who understand the workings of the organization are likely to be satisfied employees.[13] Giving employees a sense of identification and satisfaction with the company should thus be a priority for every organization. The term **internal marketing** often is used by marketers when referring to public relations efforts aimed at their own employees.

Internal marketing may be especially important for employees who have contact with ultimate consumers or who have a direct effect on ultimate consumers' satisfaction with the product. The objective of internal marketing directed toward these employees may be to help them recognize their role in the organization's effort to create customer satisfaction; these employees should understand that the level of service they provide is essential to the firm's existence.

When Delta Airlines created its "We love to fly and it shows!" advertising campaign, the company combined advertising with an internal marketing effort. Consider one ad in this campaign: a television commercial for Delta Airlines that portrays the soldiers of the U.S. Army's "Company B."[14]

The ad opens with a troop of soldiers in the pouring rain being dismissed by a stern sergeant. Whooping with joy, the men stampede to the nearest telephone booth. "Even when Company B heads for the telephone," says an announcer, "it's no problem for Gail Godfrey." Godfrey, a real Delta reservationist, keeps her cool as the phone is passed from one soldier to another. Hailing from all over the country, they're all anxious to fly home. As the last soldier hangs up, a fellow reservationist asks Godfrey if she's answered many calls that afternoon. "One," Godfrey replies, looking a little sheepish.

This advertisement was designed to communicate what Delta believes is its unique competitive advantage—the service provided by its frontline personnel. The advertisement illustrates how Delta employees go beyond the call of duty. Delta realized that before it aired the ad campaign, internal marketing would be necessary to ensure that its employees would deliver on the promise. Delta produced an employee video for the campaign, and every employee got a cassette explaining how important he or she was to the campaign's success.[15]

FOCUS ON TRENDS

Ritz-Carlton's Employee Empowerment

Building customer loyalty requires empowerment with an entrepreneurial twist. It's easy to tell employees to do whatever it takes to satisfy a customer, as long as there is no cost. The Ritz-Carlton Hotel Co. brings an entrepreneurial dimension to it. Employees can spend up to $2,000 to redress a guest grievance. They have permission to break from their routine for as long as needed to make a guest happy. Expensive, perhaps, but customers who have problems resolved are more loyal than those who didn't have a problem at all, reports Jay Marwaha, a senior vice president with Technical Assistance Research Programs, a customer-service consultancy.

Recently a member of the Ritz-Carlton cleaning staff at the Dearborn, Michigan, hotel noticed a guest waiting for the gift shop to open. The staffer, failing to find a key, kept watch until the shop opened, picked up what the guest had wanted, and camped outside a hotel conference hall to personally deliver the goods.

There is cold calculation behind such warm and fuzzy hospitality: Guests remember this level of service and tell their friends and colleagues. Says Patrick Mene, vice president of quality: "People don't have a rational understanding of quality. Personalized service is our method of driving retention." More than 90 percent of Ritz-Carlton's customers return, and the rate is even higher for customers who hold meetings there."

VIDEO CASE 14–1

 Lee Jeans

During the 1980s, as the baby boom generation aged into thirtysomething and fortysomething groups, marketers of denim jeans saw a steady decline. From a demographic perspective, the number of teenagers, the heavy user segment, had declined. Many denim jeans marketers concentrated on marketing high-fashion jeans.

Lee's business hadn't been built on one key market segment. Its sales volume reflected market sales in general. Consequently, as the product category declined, so did Lee's business. Furthermore, the market segment with the strongest brand loyalty to Lee, women aged 25–54 years, was not perceived as a desirable group for a denim company in a fashion-driven market. Thus, in the 1980s, Lee began to target younger consumers with fashion jeans in an attempt to restore brand loyalty with retailers and consumers. This fashion focus resulted in production and delivery problems, which alienated retailers. As a result, retailers began to carry only one or two styles. Many used the Lee jeans as a loss leader. Others stopped carrying the brand altogether. Market share declined as consumers could no longer identify with the brand or find it at retail outlets.

The company faced several problems: how to stop sales volume and market share from declining, how to restore the power of the Lee brand, and how to impact retail distribution. Marketing research was conducted with woman aged 24–54. It found that these women were still very loyal to the Lee brand. The research uncovered that this loyalty was based on the belief that Lee offered a superior-fitting, well-made, high-quality product. It also showed that Lee had failed to establish an emotional relationship with female consumers. There was a rational reason to buy Lee, but no emotional reason. However, no other brand had built an emotional bond with female consumers, either. When given a choice, these consumers picked Lee as the brand they would most like to associate with.

The research also showed that women saw jeans in several ways, as work jeans, those worn for work in the house or out in the yard; casual jeans, for shopping, school, and other regular activity; and dress-up jeans, for social occasions. Lee concluded that it was the only brand that could function for all three purposes. The company also knew that there was a great deal of discomfort associated with wearing many brands of jeans. Lee was the brand that fit the best. Lee jeans provided working women with a sense of relaxation as well as a sense of energy. Women believed that coming home to their jeans after a day at work in a uniform or office attire was a pleasurable experience.

Questions
1. What overall marketing mix objectives would you set for Lee jeans?
2. What creative strategy for advertising would you recommend?
3. What media strategy would you recommend?

CASE 14-2

 TV3

The first night Swedish copywriter Michael Malmborg's commercial ran on Sweden's TV3, the TV station was flooded with calls from viewers, most of them outraged, some in tears. By the time the news media picked up the story, Malmborg more than once had heard himself called a "murderer."

The source of the stir was a commercial showing a goldfish that suffers a dramatic death by detergent right before our eyes. The commercial, opening with a stark white-on-black written question—"Are you taking overdoses?"—starts out innocently enough as a man prepares to do his laundry.

As a voice-over explains how 10,000 tons of excess washing powder pollutes Swedish waters, the man takes a heaping cup of detergent, pushes the excess on top into the goldfish bowl, and pours the rest into his washing machine.

The big, beautiful fish thrashes, and it seems to stare into the camera in horror as it gasps for air. Its demise dramatized by sound effects, the fish gives a final shudder and sinks to the bottom of the cloudy bowl with a thud. Then, ending with a flourish to show the potential polluter how his habits come back to haunt him, the man in the commercial picks the fish out of the tainted bowl and throws it into a sizzling frying pan. "It's all going to end up on your own plate," concludes the announcer.

Of course, there was no way for TV viewers to know that the fish in question (four altogether) were killed relatively humanely during this shoot. (Detergent truly would have caused a slow, tortured death.) Outraged reactions caused TV3 to move the spot from its original prime-time airing to a later time slot. Morkman Film, a production company that had donated its services to get the ad produced, got an unpleasant surprise when it sent out an updated reel that included the "Goldfish" spot. One Danish agency reportedly objected so strongly that it said it would never hire the production house.

Yet the commercial's most rewarding ramifications were manifested when Michael Malmborg's neighbors came up to him outside his house in a Stockholm suburb and told him that they thought of that goldfish every time they stood over their washing machines measuring out powder and resisted the urge to overdo it. This was just the type of reaction that Malmborg had dreamed of when the project began.

Questions

1. Do you find this commercial objectionable? Why?
2. If a similar ad were produced in the United States, should it be allowed to run during prime-time viewing hours?
3. When the purpose of an advertisement is to create a better society for everyone, does the end justify the means?

PERSONAL SELLING, SALES MANAGEMENT, AND SALES PROMOTION

Chapter 15

Learning Objectives

After you have studied this chapter, you will be able to:

1. Describe the role of personal selling and relationship management.
2. Identify marketing situations in which personal selling would be the most effective means of reaching and influencing target buyers.
3. Show how the professional salesperson contributes to a modern marketing firm.
4. Outline the steps involved in making a sale.
5. Explain why the marketing process does not stop when the sale is made.
6. Characterize the major aspects of the sales manager's job.
7. Classify the various forms of sales compensation.
8. Identify some of the ethical issues facing sales personnel.
9. Identify the purposes of sales promotion and explain how the major sales promotion tools work.

"I see them everywhere, and I have come to understand that they are among the bravest of us. They face on a daily basis what we all dread the most: flat, cold rejection. Even the best of them hears 'No' more than he hears 'Yes'. . . . Yet all of them get up each morning and go out to do it again." So says Bob Greene, describing salespeople in his book *American Beat*. Probably many of us share Greene's image of what salespeople's lives are like.

But salespeople don't just make sales. For many, if not most, salespeople, servicing accounts—working with existing customers—is a big part of the job. That means they hear questions like "Can you help me solve this?" as often as questions with simple "Yes" and "No" answers. To prosper, most

salespeople need to know more than the customer does about some aspects of the customer's own business. Today's salesperson is often a cross between a consultant and a vendor.

Also, many of today's salespeople are women— 28 percent of sales jobs are held by women, according to a recent survey of sales forces. More than 80 percent of salespeople have at least some college education. On average, salespeople (including sales managers) work 49 hours a week and earn almost $50,000 a year. Christine Sanders, a top sales representative for Eastman Kodak copiers, typifies today's successful salesperson. Selling and leasing machines that cost from $18,000 to $105,000, Sanders may spend up to six months to close a sale. Her commissions range from a few hundred to a few thousand dollars. The sales she feels best about are the ones "you earn because you really understood a customer's applications or because you worked hard or were persistent in the face of a lot of competition," she says.

At Northwestern University, Sanders earned a bachelor's degree in a special program that combined economics and communications. She didn't plan on a sales career, but she effectively trained for one through extracurricular activities that often involved fund-raising.

After recruiting her in a campus interview, Kodak sent Sanders to a 10-week training program that included classroom work, real and simulated sales calls, and many sessions probing the innards of the copiers she would eventually sell. The training was "intense," she recalls, "good preparation for the real world."

Sanders shone in the suburban Chicago territory she was given and quickly advanced, eventually to a territory that includes a handful of major accounts in downtown Chicago. Forty-hour workweeks are uncommon for Sanders; the job typically demands 50 to 60. "Whatever it takes to satisfy the customer," she says.

Companies that buy or lease Kodak copiers get a package of services along with their hardware. Training is one of these services, and if a customer with 24-hour administrative operations needs to conduct late-night training sessions, a Kodak sales representative may oblige. For one such session, Sanders got up at 4 a.m. and drove to the customer's office. No trainees appeared that morning. "But I was there," she says, "and the customer will never forget that."

Her advice to newcomers in the sales profession is to know their product, their competitors' products, and their customers. That way, they can sell the benefits of their product without slamming a rival firm. A salesperson may need to understand what bothers a prospective customer about a competing product, Sanders says, "but you don't need to harp on that. I'd rather sell the benefits of my company and myself than ever bad-mouth the competition, because I think it's unprofessional and it doesn't really buy you anything—and it could come back to haunt you."

This chapter begins by explaining the nature of personal selling in organizations and its importance in our economy. It discusses the various types of personal selling jobs and then describes the creative selling process and the tactics that order-getting salespeople use in each stage of this process. After describing the basic principles of sales management, it addresses some ethical issues facing both salespeople and sales managers. The chapter ends with a discussion of sales promotion.

PERSONAL SELLING DEFINED

Personal selling, as noted in Chapter 13, is a person-to-person dialogue between the prospective buyer and the seller. Thus, it consists of human contact and direct communication rather than impersonal mass communication. Personal selling involves developing customer relationships, discovering and communicating customer needs, matching the appropriate products with these needs, and communicating benefits.[1]

Personal selling is the most widely used means by which organizations communicate with their customers. Almost every marketing organization, even the one-person machine shop, deals with clients through some kind of personal contact and sales effort. And although you may not have thought of it in this way, accountants, stockbrokers, dentists, lawyers, and other professionals are personal salespeople in that they deal with clients and sell a service. Robert Louis Stevenson was not far from the mark when he said, "Everyone lives by selling something."

Why is personal selling so important? The answer is that the salesperson is the catalyst that makes our economy function. The old adage "nothing happens until a sale is made" reflects the importance of personal selling in all aspects of business. Few of us have ever purchased a car from a plant engineer or a financial manager; we buy cars from salespeople. Salespeople stimulate economic activity and produce revenue for the organization. They keep the economy going.

The salesperson's job may be to remind, to inform, or to persuade. In general, the salesperson's responsibility is to keep existing customers abreast of information about the company's products and services and to persuasively convey a sales message to potential customers. Salespeople also are expected to be aware of changes in the markets they serve and to report important information to their home offices. Professional sales personnel are vitally important as "front-line troops in the battle for customers' orders."[2] A salesperson communicates the company's offer and shows prospective buyers how their problems can be solved by the product.

Many different businesses—farms, factories, retailers, banks, transportation companies, hotels, and many others—use personal selling. Each faces personal selling tasks that are unique. Various methods of personal selling may be used to accomplish these tasks.

We are all familiar with **retail selling**—selling to ultimate consumers. Field selling, telemarketing, and inside selling are the three basic methods for personal selling in business-to-business transactions. **Field selling** is performed by an "outside" salesperson, who usually travels to the prospective account's place of business. **Telemarketing** involves using the telephone as the primary means of communi-

Retail Selling
Selling to ultimate consumers.

Field Selling
Nonretail selling that takes place outside the employer's place of business, usually in the prospective customer's place of business.

Telemarketing
Using the telephone as the primary means of communicating with prospective customers. Telemarketers often use computers for order taking.

Inside Selling
Nonretail selling from the employer's place of business.

cating with prospective customers. **Inside selling** is similar to retail selling by store clerks; here, salespeople sell in the employer's place of business.[3] For example, the typical plumbing wholesaler employs inside sales personnel to assist customers—plumbers—who travel to the wholesaler's place of business to obtain fixtures, tools, or parts.

 ## THE CHARACTERISTICS OF PERSONAL SELLING

Two basic characteristics that contribute to the importance of personal selling are its flexibility and its value in building relationships. We will look more closely at these characteristics and then discuss the disadvantages of personal selling.

Personal Selling Is Flexible

Perhaps the key word to describe personal selling's advantages over other means of promotion is *flexibility*. Flexibility means that the salesperson can adapt a sales presentation to a specific situation. When a sales prospect has a particular problem or series of problems to solve, the professional salesperson can adjust the presentation to show how the product or service offered can solve these problems and satisfy the individual needs of the potential customer. Similarly, the salesperson can answer questions and overcome objections. The salesperson can even "read" the customer. Sensing that the client agrees with a certain aspect of the presentation or is not interested in a given point, for example, the salesperson can shift gears and move to another consumer benefit or adjust in some other way the manner in which the sales talk is presented.

All this is possible because personal selling entails a two-way flow of communication. Direct and immediate feedback is elicited. Consider the following examples of how feedback allows the salesperson to gather as well as give information.

- The salesperson discovers in casual conversation that potential buyers have problems that no products on the market can solve.
- A customer suggests how existing products can be modified to better suit client needs.
- A customer provides the salesperson with new sales leads by mentioning other firms that could use the salesperson's merchandise.

Personal selling also is flexible because it allows the carrier of an organization's message to concentrate on the best sales prospects. In contrast, a television advertisement might be seen by just about anyone, including many people who will never be interested in the product offered for sale. This "waste circulation," as marketers call it, can be reduced or even eliminated by effective personal sellers. With personal selling, large-volume buyers can be visited or called frequently. Personal selling allows efforts to be concentrated on the profitable accounts because it is a selective medium.

Personal Selling Builds Relationships

Throughout this book we have emphasized that the relationship between marketer and buyer does not end when the sale is made. Long-term success often depends on the sales force's ability to build a lasting relationship with the buyer. This is especially true in business-to-business marketing. For many business-to-business marketers, the relationship intensifies after the sale is made. How well the marketer

Relationship Management
Sales function of managing the account relationship and ensuring that buyers receive appropriate services.

manages the relationship becomes the critical factor in what buying decision is made the next time around.[4]

The term **relationship management** refers to the sales function of managing the account relationship and ensuring that buyers receive the appropriate services. The goal of relationship management is to help customers expand their own organizational resources and capacities through the relationship. The salesperson is the key in relationship management, for it is the salesperson who makes sure the product solves the customer's problems and contributes to the success of the customer's organization.

FOCUS ON TRENDS

IBM's Virtual Sales Office

Out in the heartland of America, IBM has eviscerated that most sacred of corporate perks: the corner officer. Today, all the company's salespeople and sales managers in the midwestern region, as well as in other locations, are no longer assigned specific offices. They work from home, where extra phone lines, computer, fax equipment, desks and chairs have been provided at IBM expense. And they work from their cars, with cellular phones and laptops. None of the sales teams, a total of 15,000 employees and growing, have fixed work locations provided by IBM.

If they need an office for the day they go to one of a series of "office hotels." These are scattered throughout the region of eight (plus portions of three more) midwestern states. Each has been designed to be nearly interchangeable "to minimize disruption on the road." Mail rooms are in the same place (near the entry), physical components such as paint, color schemes and cubicle layouts are similar; check-in procedures are identical. Check in for the day, get an assigned cubicle or team or conference room, have all your telephone calls routed automatically to your new desk and get to work.

Some Limitations of Personal Selling

Our emphasis on the advantages of personal selling as an effective communication tool should not overshadow its major limitations. Personal selling cannot economically reach a mass audience and therefore cannot be used efficiently in all marketing situations. Face soaps, such as Ivory and Dove, may be used by tens of millions of people; millions more are potential users. Reaching these target customers by personal selling would be too expensive. Advertising via mass media is the appropriate tool in cases like these because it can reach a mass audience economically. (Personal selling does, however, play a role in marketing these products when sales representatives call on the major retailers and wholesalers that distribute them.)

Personal selling is expensive because it involves one-on-one communication. The cost per thousand viewers and cost per sale for a high-priced TV advertisement are quite small, since the ad is seen by a vast audience. In contrast, the average cost per call for personal selling exceeds $300 for many organizational products. The high cost results from the fact that recruiting, training, and paying salespeople costs the marketer a great deal. Each salesperson, because of the nature of the job, talks to only one or a few people at a time and may spend many hours driving to and from appointments and waiting in reception rooms. When we realize in addition that many sales calls may be needed to generate a single sale, we can see that the cost per sale can be tremendously high. The advantages of personal selling, however, often offset the high cost per sale. In some cases, as in selling custom-made machinery, personal selling is the only way a sale can be made.

THE TYPES OF PERSONAL SELLING TASKS

The importance of personal selling varies considerably across organizations. Some organizations may rely almost entirely on their sales forces to generate sales, while others use them to support a pulling strategy based on advertising. Some organizations employ salespeople who do little professional selling, such as store clerks at SportsTown and Kmart, while others employ engineers and scientists as technical sales representatives. Clearly, these two types of sales representatives are not comparable.

Because of this diversity, it is useful to differentiate among selling tasks. The marketing manager must do this, for example, in deciding which selling skills and job descriptions are appropriate to the sales objectives to be accomplished. To assign a highly skilled salesperson to a task that could be accomplished just as efficiently by a less skilled individual or an interactive databased marketing system would waste an important resource.

Order Taking

Order Taker
Salesperson who is primarily responsible for writing up orders, checking invoices, and assuring prompt order processing.

Suggestive Selling
Suggesting to a customer who is making a purchase that an additional item or service be purchased.

Millions of people are employed in sales jobs of a routine nature. These people, who do very little creative selling, are called **order takers.** They write up orders, check invoices for accuracy, and assure timely order processing. The term *order taking* is appropriate here because the customer decides on the products and prices and then tells the salesperson what the order is to be. The order taker's job is to be pleasant and helpful and to ensure that the order truly satisfies the customer's needs. The order taker may engage in **suggestive selling** by suggesting that the customer purchase an additional item ("Would you like French fries with your hamburger?")

In general, order-taking salespeople are divided into the "inside" sales group and the "outside," or field, sales group. Inside order takers are exemplified by auto parts salespeople. Here, the customer has come to the shop seeking the part; the salesperson has not sought out the customer. The inside salesperson may provide some advice on product quality or installation and may even suggest that additional parts or tools would make the job easier or that the customer might as well change the oil filter while handling the other repairs. However, the order taker typically does not substantially modify the basic order presented by the customer.

Telemarketing is becoming a major activity of many inside order-taking sales representatives. Telemarketing involves the use of telephone selling in conjunction with computer technology, which is used for order taking. Of course, all salespeople telephone prospects and customers, and telephone selling is an important part of many order-getting sales jobs. However, as indicated earlier, we will use the term telemarketing to mean using the telephone as the primary means of communication.

Outside, or field, salespeople may also be order takers. Manufacturer or wholesaler representatives selling such well-known products as Campbell's soups find themselves in this position. The question they ask their customers is essentially "How much do you want?" Some sales representatives holding positions of this sort do a better job than others in enlarging order size, tying the product to special sales promotions, and so on. Such efforts are likely to be rewarded with a promotion or a bonus.

Order Getting

Order Getting
Adaptive selling process that tailors sales efforts and product offerings to specific customer needs. Order getters seek out customers and creatively make sales. Also called creative selling.

In **order getting**—also called **creative selling**—the sales job is not routine. Order getters must seek out customers, analyze their problems, discover how the products for sale might solve those problems, and then bring these solutions to the customers' attention.

Creative selling calls for the ability to explain the product and its auxiliary dimensions in terms of benefits and advantages to the prospective buyer and to persuade and motivate the prospect to purchase the right quality and volume of products or service. Whereas the order taker's job is to expedite the sale, the order getter's job is to make the sale. Put another way, the primary function of the creative salesperson is to generate a sale that might not occur without his or her efforts. Creative salespeople generally invest far more time and effort in making a sale than do order takers. And, while it is possible to engage in creative selling in either an inside or a field environment, it is far more common for creative salespeople to go to the customer's place of business to evaluate the needs to be addressed. This process can take a very long time. An IBM salesperson attempting to demonstrate that a particular computer networking system is the best available to meet the needs of a state government, for example, can spend years preparing to make a sale.

Pioneer
In sales, a person who concentrates on selling to new prospects or on selling new products.

Account Manager
In sales, a person who concentrates on maintaining an ongoing relationship with existing customers.

Order getters may specialize in certain types of selling. For example, some organizations have sales personnel, often called **pioneers,** who concentrate their efforts on selling to new prospects or selling new products. Selling an established product or service for the first time to a new customer or selling an innovative product new to the market to an existing customer generates new business for the organization. In contrast, **account managers** concentrate on maintaining an ongoing relationship with existing customers and actively seek additional business for reorders or for other items in the product line. Although pioneering and account management activities may be specialized in some organizations, in many instances the creative salesperson may be involved in both.

An order-getting salesperson's primary responsibility is, of course, selling. However, order getters, especially account managers, may spend a great deal of time engaged in other activities. Exhibit 15–1 classifies the job activities of order getters.

Sales Support and Cross-Functional Teams

Missionary Salesperson
Salesperson who visits prospective customers, distributes information to them, and handles questions and complaints but does not routinely take orders. Missionaries serve as customer relations representatives.

Many salespeople hold jobs whose titles suggest that they are involved in special selling situations. One commonly encountered salesperson of this sort is the so-called **missionary.** Pharmaceutical manufacturers, for example, employ missionaries, called *detailers,* to call on doctors and provide them with information on the latest prescription and nonprescription products. Detailers do not take orders; sales occur only when the doctor prescribes medication for patients. Missionary sales personnel in fact rarely take or actively seek orders; their primary responsibility is to build goodwill by distributing information to customers and prospective customers and by "checking in" to be sure that buyers are being satisfactorily serviced by company representatives and other relevant channel members such as wholesalers.

Even missionary salespeople working for consumer goods companies and calling on retailers do not directly sell anything. If a retailer insisted on placing an order, the missionary would not refuse to accept it but would simply pass it on to the salesperson who regularly handles the retailer's account. Missionaries are, in effect, employed by the manufacturer to perform a public relations function.

Other specialized sales support people are found in industries in which scientists and engineers serve as technical specialists to support the regular field sales force. The credentials and expertise of these sales engineers, applications pro-

Salespeople should be aware of nonverbal communication. This is especially true in international sales, where nonverbal communication can take on unfamiliar meanings because of cultural differences. A navy blue suit is inappropriate for sales presentations in Hong Kong, for example, because it signifies mourning.

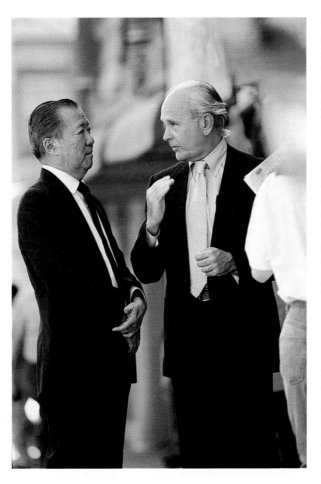

and enter that information into the computer. Within minutes, the computer can yield output that shows exactly how the salesperson's product will affect the prospect's business operations.

It should be noted that some of the communication in the sales presentation may not be verbal. Many successful salespeople use body language, seating arrangements, and clothing colors to communicate important nonverbal messages to their clients.

Step Five: Handling Objections

In most sales presentations, the salesperson does not make a one-way presentation while the customer passively listens. The customer, no matter how friendly or interested in the product, may have reservations about committing money or other resources in a purchase agreement. Questions or strong objections are likely to arise. Because objections explain reasons for resisting or postponing purchase, the salesperson should listen and learn from them.

Indeed, the sales call should be a dialogue or conversation in which questions are welcomed and direct feedback elicited. It is undesirable to have the prospect sit quietly until the end of the talk and then say "No" without any explanation. Effective salespeople encourage prospects to voice reasons why they are resisting the purchase. Even though the well-prepared sales presentation covers such topics as the quality of the product, the reputation of the seller, post-sale services, and the like, the objection or question reveals to the salesperson what points the customer views as most important.

Handling Objections
The step in the creative selling process wherein the salesperson responds to questions or reservations expressed by the prospect.

There are many means of **handling objections.** When an objection indicates that the prospect has failed to fully understand some point that was made, the salesperson can comment on the area of uncertainty. A question about a product characteristic may mean that the prospect has not grasped how the product works or seen the benefits it can provide. A salesperson who encounters an objection of this type can go on to provide additional persuasive information, clarify the sales presentation, or offer the basic argument for the product in a different manner.

Objections also can be turned into counterarguments by experienced sales representatives. A stockbroker might say: "You are right, Dr. Williams. The price of this stock has dropped 50 percent in the last six months. That is exactly why I am recommending it to you. At this low price, it is now underpriced and is an excellent buy in the opinion of our analysts."[5]

COMPETITIVE STRATEGY: WHAT WENT RIGHT?

SOQ NOP

The senior regional sales manager from John Deere was wearing an odd tie tack. It was in the shape of a cross. The vertical letters spelled out DEERE; the horizontal, SOQ NOP. When asked what the letters stood for, his reply was "Sell on quality, not on price." He added, "It's my toughest job, in down markets, to make my own people realize that the objective is to sell the benefits, not just resort to price. I tell them a story. I was going after a sale some years ago. It came down to two final contenders. The fellow making the buy called me in to give me one last chance. His message in a nutshell: 'You're just too high on the price side. No hard feelings, and we hope we can do business with you again in the future.' I was about to walk out the door, unhappy to say the least. Then I had an inspiration. I turned and said, 'Those are nice-looking boots you've got on.' He was a bit surprised, but said, 'Thanks,' and he went on to talk for a minute or so about those fine boots, what was unique about the leather, why they were practical as well as fine. I said to him, at the end of this description. 'How come you buy those boots and not just a pair off the shelf in an Army-Navy store?' It must have taken twenty seconds for the grin to spread all the way across his face. 'The sale is yours,' he said, and he got up and came around his desk and gave me a hearty handshake."

One tactic for handling objections is to agree with the prospect, as did the stockbroker mentioned above, accepting the objection with reservation. This is consistent with the marketing concept's prescription to sell the product from the customer's point of view. The salesperson's counterargument is intended to refute the objection. The purpose of this method of dealing with objections is to avoid getting into an argument with the prospect. If the customer says the price is high and the salesperson says it is low, the discussion goes nowhere fast. But if the salesperson responds, "Yes, it is priced higher than many, but our product quality is higher than the competitors', so you get more for your money," the salesperson has agreed and counterargued at the same time. More importantly, the seller has given a reason for the higher price. (Another approach to a price objection is described in the accompanying Competitive Strategy feature.)

The prospect's questions, objections, and other comments may reveal how close the prospect is to making a purchase decision. Good salespeople use such clues to determine whether they should attempt to enter the closing stages of the sales presentation.

Step Six: Closing the Sale

Closing
The step in the creative selling process wherein the salesperson attempts to obtain a commitment to buy from the prospect.

Ultimately, salespeople must make the sale. In selling, the term **closing** indicates that the sale is being brought to a finish. The main advantage of personal selling over other forms of promotion is that the salesperson is in a position to conclude negotiations by actually asking for an order.

Unfortunately, many salespeople are knowledgeable and convincing when making sales presentations, but they never get around to asking for the order. Sometimes this is due to the presenter's genuine belief in the product being offered—a belief so strong that he or she can barely stop talking about it. In other cases, worry about receiving a negative answer or misreading the client's willingness to deal may be the cause.[6] In any case, there comes a point when the presentation must be drawn to its logical conclusion.

Because closing the sale is so vital, experienced sales personnel constantly try to read prospects' reactions to the presentation for signs that a conclusion is in

Closing Signals
Signs from the prospect revealing that he or she is ready to buy.

Trial Close
A personal selling tactic intended to elicit from a prospect a signal indicating whether he or she is ready to buy.

order. Signs revealing that prospects are ready to buy are called **closing signals.** For example, a comment such as "These new machines should reduce the number of breakdowns we've been having" may indicate a readiness to purchase. Should a signal like this occur, the sales representative should quickly respond and ask for the prospect's signature on the order.

When the prospect's willingness to close is not clearly revealed, the salesperson may utilize what is called the **trial close.** A trial close is a tactic intended to draw from the prospect information that will signal whether a sale is imminent. For example, the salesperson may attempt to focus the conversation on closing the sale by asking whether the customer prefers the standard model or the deluxe (thus narrowing the alternatives to a choice). If the customer indicates a preference in a positive way, the sale may almost be made.

Salespeople often use standard closing techniques such as the following:

1. The direct, straightforward approach. The salesperson requests the order.
2. The assumptive closing technique. The salesperson takes out the order forms or in some other way implies that an agreement has been reached, saying something like, "Let's see here, you'll need 20 units by the first of the month."
3. The "standing-room-only" closing technique. Here the sales representative indicates that time is an important factor and supply is limited. Typical phrases used are: "We've been selling a lot of these lately, and I want to make sure that you get what you need."
4. The summative approach. Here, the salesperson summarizes, usually with pencil and paper, the benefits of buying the product, perhaps mentioning some disadvantages that the advantages overcome. When the product's benefits have been summarized, the salesperson asks for the order.

Step Seven: The Follow-up—Building Relationships

Marketers view the closing of the sale not as the end of a process but as the start of an organization's relationship with a customer. A satisfied customer will return to the company that treated it best if it needs to repurchase the same product at some time in the future. If it needs a related item, the satisfied customer knows the first place to look. The professional salesperson knows that the best way to get repeat business is to keep customers. And the best way to keep customers is to follow up after the sale.

Follow-up
The final step in the creative selling process, after the sale has been made wherein the salesperson contacts the buyer to make sure everything connected with the sale was handled properly.

During the **follow-up,** the salesperson makes sure that everything was handled as promised and that the order was shipped promptly and received on schedule. The salesperson should also check with the customer as to whether there were any problems such as missing parts or damage to the merchandise during shipping.

As noted earlier, the term relationship management refers to the sales function of managing the account relationship and ensuring that buyers receive the appropriate services. The goal is to help customer organizations expand their own resources and capacities through their relationships with the seller. The salesperson is the vehicle marketers use to achieve this goal. There are many ways a salesperson can affect relationships; showing appreciation, expediting delivery, and resolving complaints are but a few. Often, in managing relationships with customers, the salesperson obtains help from others in the organization. For example, WordPerfect Corporation has an extensive sales support service that offers customers technical assistance with software via a series of 800 telephone numbers.

FOCUS ON GLOBAL COMPETITION

Selling in Japan—A Lengthy Process

International sales negotiations can break down through failures in cross-cultural communications, even when both parties have much to gain from an agreement. Cultural understanding begins with a sensitivity to cultural differences and a willingness to learn more about the precise meaning of agreement in the host culture.

In Japan prospective clients allow plenty of time to gain trust in the salesperson. Thus, negotiating a sale with Japanese executives is a lengthy exercise, not only because of cultural gaps but also because the Japanese will not take a position until they have achieved an internal consensus among a great many organizational members. However, once an internal consensus is achieved, the Japanese or-

ganization can move very quickly. Patience, a virtue in Japan, can also be used as a valuable asset in obtaining the best sales terms, especially with impatient Americans. Misreading the situation, U.S. sales executives often make ill-considered concessions just to keep negotiations moving forward.

Ultimately, the Japanese prefer broad agreement rather than a detailed contract. "Like the Greeks, the Japanese do not view the signing of a contract as the end of negotiations. Japanese firms want long-term, exclusive business relations based on *Kan,* a word that can be translated as 'emotional attunement.'"

SALES MANAGEMENT

Sales Management
The marketing management activity that deals with planning, organizing, directing, and controlling the personal selling effort.

Sales management is the marketing management activity dealing with planning, organizing, directing, and controlling the personal selling effort. Sales managers are responsible for a number of administrative tasks. The major activities involved in operating a sales force are shown in Exhibit 15–3.

Sales personnel, like most employees, require some degree of supervision and management. However, the typical salesman or saleswoman, especially those operating in a business-to-business setting, are responsible for setting priorities and managing their own time. Although they maintain contact with sales management and may ask for advice or other support, most of the time they work away from their direct supervisors. For this reason, the job of the sales manager differs significantly from that of other managers.

The sales manager's responsibilities also may include selling activities. After all, virtually every sales manager earned the job by performing well "in the field." Sales managers may accompany less-experienced sales personnel during training periods or work with a veteran salesperson to sell a particularly significant account. Thus, while sales managers are responsible primarily for planning, organizing, directing, and controlling the sales force, they also have opportunity to engage in the personal selling process.

Setting Sales Objectives

Sales Objectives
The specific objectives that an organization's sales effort will attempt to meet. Sales objectives should be precise and quantifiable, should include a time frame, and should be reasonable in terms of the organization's resources.

All good managers, before setting out to accomplish a task, first give considerable thought to what that task should or must be. In other words, they set objectives. The reason a statement of sales objectives is so important is that much of sales management involves the assignment of resources. How can the manager know, for example, how many salespeople to hire unless the tasks to be accomplished are first understood?

Sales objectives should meet the criteria by which objectives generally are evaluated in the marketing world. They should be precise, be quantifiable, include

MANAGEMENT FUNCTION	SALES MANAGEMENT ACTIVITY	EXAMPLE OF THE SALES MANAGER'S TASK
Strategic planning	Setting sales objectives	Determine specific sales objectives that reflect the organization's overall strategy.
Organizing	Organizing sales activity	Determine if sales territories should be based on geography, customer type, or product line.
	Recruiting and selecting personnel	Determine the best individuals to hire.
Directing	Training and development	Determine knowledge sales personnel need to have about their company's products and customers' businesses.
	Managing compensation	Determine if a straight commission, a salary, or some combination is the best compensation plan.
	Motivating	Determine how much praise and reinforcement each salesperson needs.
Control	Evaluating and controlling	Determine if sales quotas have been met.

EXHIBIT 15–3
Managerial Activities of Sales Managers

a time frame, and be reasonable given the organization's resources, its overall promotional strategy, and the competitive environment in which it operates. If the objectives are not precise, neither managers nor salespeople will know what they are trying to accomplish. If they are not quantifiable, managers cannot know when an objective has been reached. If no time frame is included, the sales force has "forever" to reach the goals. If the objectives are not reasonable, time and effort will be wasted in a pursuit doomed to fail from the start.

Sales objectives can be expressed in many ways. Among these are sales totals in dollars, sales totals in units of products, increases over previous sales totals, market share, sales calls completed, sales calls on new customers, and dollar or unit sales per sales call made. An example of a sales objective stated in terms of sales volume is "to expand annual sales in the Virginia/West Virginia sales territory by 10 percent over last year's dollar volume." The sales forecast—which, depending on the organization, may or may not be the responsibility of the sales manager—strongly influences decisions about sales objectives.

Organizing Sales Activity

Because nonretail sales forces typically must contact their customers either face-to-face or by telephone, sales departments generally are organized so that sales personnel are responsible for certain accounts. Calling regularly on the same organizations and individuals leads to a better understanding of customers' problems and needs and provides the sales representative with an opportunity to develop a personal relationship with the client. The specific accounts and prospects assigned to a salesperson comprise the **sales territory.** A sales territory commonly is thought of as a geographical area. Territories are not always so defined, however. Sales territories may also be determined according to customer type or product line. Every method of creating territories has advantages and disadvantages. Whatever the method employed, the characteristics and needs of the customers to be served should always take precedence over the convenience of the sales force.

Sales Territory
The specific and prospective accounts assigned to a salesperson. They may be based on geographical divisions, customer types, or product lines.

Geographically Based Sales Territories
Sales personnel frequently are assigned to particular geographical sales territories. Exhibit 15–4 shows an organization chart for a company using this approach. Notice

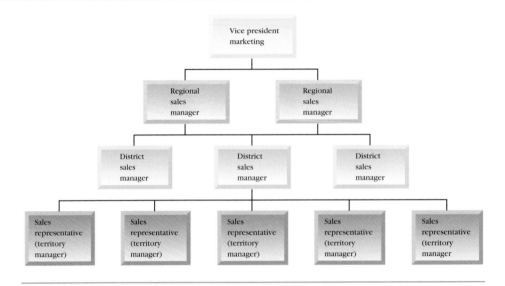

EXHIBIT 15-4
Example of a Geographic
Sales Organization

that as an individual manager moves higher in the organizational scheme, he or she becomes responsible for increasingly larger territories, with the vice-president for marketing ultimately responsible for the entire country, or even the world.

District sales managers and regional sales managers, who are held accountable for the activity of sales personnel operating within specific areas, are referred to as **field sales managers** because of their direct concern for salespeople "out in the field." Their primary concern is management of the field sales personnel who report to them.

Field Sales Manager
A district or regional sales manager, so-called because his or her main concern is the salespeople in the field.

Much attention has been paid to the design of geographic sales territories. A number of variables should be considered as the market is being "cut up" into sections for assignment to individual sales representatives. Even though each company's situation is different, similar factors must be weighed. A major concern is creating territories that are roughly equal in terms of the following variables: physical size, transportation within the territory, the number of current and potential customers within the territory, the general economic state of the territory, and the size of the territory's sales and sales potential.

FOCUS ON QUALITY

James River Corp.

James River Corp., which sells toilet tissue, napkins, Dixie cups, and the like, understands that when it puts its head together with its retailers', both sides benefit. Specifically, James River shares proprietary marketing information with its customers that enables them to sell more paper products. For instance, it told its West Coast client, Lucky Stores, how often shoppers generally buy paper goods and which items they tend to buy together. Lucky has since reshelved all its paper products and managed to win market share in the category from competing stores.

James River has reorganized the way it calls on customers. Previously, three or more salespeople would approach a company like Lucky Stores: one armed with plates, another with cups, and still another with toilet paper. If all three secured orders, Lucky was obliged to buy three full truckloads, one for each product, to get the lowest price from James River. Today, a unified team from James River will sell Lucky Stores one truckload with a mix of paper products at the lowest price.

Personnel problems result when one salesperson gets a "bad" territory and another gets the "best" territory. Thus, equality and fairness are important goals in this process.

Organization by Customer Type

When a sales organization specializes by customer type, two or more salespeople may cover the same geographical area. For example, a chemical manufacturer may have one sales representative call on users of petrochemicals in the Southwest and another representative call on users of other chemicals in this region. Similarly, a textbook publishing company may cover the Midwest with one sales representative who calls on business and engineering professors and another who deals with professors in colleges of arts and sciences. Notice that in both cases more than one representative of the same company may call on a single organization and the representatives may call on different individuals within these organizations. Obviously, the chemical company and the publisher both feel that the customer is better served by dealing with a salesperson who is a specialist rather than a generalist.

Even when salespeople are assigned by customer type, the matter of geography still enters the picture. The bookseller specializes by buyer type within a specific area, as do the chemical company's representatives. Thus, a combination of geography and customer type is in use. In fact, the inescapability of the geographic factor makes a combination approach to the assignment of sales territories the most commonly employed.

Organization by Product Line

Within large, multiproduct companies, each corporate division or product line may have its own sales force. As with organization by customer type, the emphasis is on specialization. Multiline organizations often find that their salespeople must know a great many technical details about their products and customers. The need to remember too many products and too many details will almost certainly reduce the salesperson's ability to sell a product effectively.

Recruiting and Selecting the Sales Force

Two shoe salespeople were sent to a poverty-stricken country. The first cabled, "Returning home immediately. No one wears shoes here." The second, more optimistic salesperson cabled, "Unlimited possibilities. Millions still without shoes."[7]

This apocryphal story illustrates one of the most important jobs sales managers perform—the personnel function. The personnel function starts with finding and hiring individuals for sales slots in the organization—persons who are both interested in sales jobs and qualified to fill them. An important point here is that no salesperson, whatever his or her qualifications, is universally acceptable in all selling situations. Thus, the sales manager must decide what characteristics a given sales position requires. These requirements must be carefully thought out and matched with job candidates, not only for the sake of the sales organization but also for the sake of the individuals hired. The task at hand is to get the right person for the job.

Because selling situations vary tremendously, the analysis of a sales position should include a list of traits that an appropriate applicant should have. Some traits and accomplishments commonly considered in recruiting sales personnel are educational background, intelligence, self-confidence, problem-solving ability, speaking ability, appearance, achievement orientation, friendliness, empathy, and involvement in school or community organizations. These things do not guarantee that an applicant will be a successful sales representative. They may, however, be used as indicators of otherwise difficult-to-determine attributes. For example, a friendly and helpful personality may be considered a meaningful trait, and membership in clubs and service organizations may suggest that trait is present.

Training the Sales Force

After sales personnel have been recruited and selected, they must be trained. Training programs vary from company to company. Some companies use an apprentice-type system by sending the newcomer into the field with an experienced salesperson to "learn the ropes." Others put the recruit through an intensive training program at headquarters or at a regional office before putting him or her out in the field. A few organizations believe in a "sink or swim" method whereby new people are sent out on their own to succeed or fail.

A typical sales training program for a recent college graduate hired by an office photocopier company is likely to cover the following areas: (1) company policies and practices, (2) industry and competitors' background, and (3) product knowledge and selling techniques. The graduate may receive several weeks of instruction at a center run by staff that specializes in training recruits. The instruction will probably feature guest lectures by both field salespeople and company executives. The next stage may require the graduate to work as an account service representative for several months, becoming familiar with customer needs and complaints and handling these by telephone or letter. The next phase may be on-the-job training that involves making sales presentations under the supervision and guidance of the sales manager or a senior salesperson. Programs like this usually are varied to suit the needs of the incoming employee. If the new person is experienced in sales, for example, less emphasis will be placed on selling skills than on company policies and product information.

In many successful sales organizations, training to develop the skills of sales personnel is an ongoing process. Most sales representatives can benefit from a refresher course, a few days learning about new products, or just a break from their regular schedules. Thus, ongoing training often is carried out at the home office, at sales conventions, or even at a local hotel or conference center.

Compensating the Sales Force

Sales work—unlike certain other business professions, such as accounting or personnel management—is generally highly visible. It involves the attempt to achieve quantifiable results: Did sales go up or did they fall? How many new accounts were opened? How many calls were made? For this reason, most sales managers feel that salespeople who achieve the highest performance in terms of some specific measure should receive the highest compensation. Financial incentives are not the only motivators, but they are important and deserve the sales manager's close attention.

What would be the ideal compensation plan for salespeople? It would be simple so that disagreements over the size of paychecks and bonuses might be avoided. It would be as fair as possible to avoid petty jealousies among the sales team members. It would be regular so that salespeople would be able to count on a reasonable reward coming to them steadily. It would provide security to the salesperson as well as a degree of incentive to work harder. It would give management some control over the sales representative's activities. Finally, it would encourage optimal purchase orders by the customer. (For example, a heavily incentive-based plan might encourage salespeople to engage in extra-hard-sell activities, including selling customers items that they really do not need. This is not optimal ordering; ordering should promote the development of a long-term profitable relationship with clients.) Based on the sales manager's objectives and the nature of the selling job, management must select from among the following types of compensation plans.

Straight Salary or Wage

Straight Salary
Compensation at a regular rate, not immediately tied to sales performance.

The **straight salary** method or an hourly wage plan offers the salesperson compensation that is not immediately tied to sales performance. Management has the greatest control over a salesperson's time and activity under this plan and the least uncertainty about selling expenses, because earnings are not tied to sales. Many creative salespeople dislike this plan, preferring to accept the risks of commission in the hope of achieving high earnings. However, there are some selling situations that require use of the straight wage or salary plan. The common denominator among these situations is management's desire to control a salesperson's time and activity. Straight salary is most likely when the job requires the salesperson to engage in nonselling activities. For example, retail sales personnel may be expected to arrange stock, clean up spills, feed the fish in the display tank, or fill in wherever an extra worker is needed. To pay these people on anything other than a straight wage or salary plan would reduce management's control.

Straight Commission

Straight Commission
Compensation based strictly on sales performance.

Unlike the salary plan, the **straight commission** plan rewards only one thing—sales performance. A clear-cut financial incentive is its prime advantage. On the surface, this plan would seem to have considerable appeal to most managements. However, the plan has a number of disadvantages. As suggested, salespeople paid this way cannot be expected to perform additional activities that do not lead directly to a sale. In other words, their activities are difficult to control. Furthermore, they may be reluctant to try to sell to new accounts that may develop slowly or to sell merchandise that is difficult to move, preferring instead to raise their short-term compensation by concentrating on products they know they can sell quickly. Management may decide to discourage this understandable behavior by lowering the commissions on easy-to-sell products and raising it on those harder to sell. This, however, destroys one of the straight commission plan's key advantages—simplicity. In addition, salespeople may resent changes that might reduce their incomes. Straight commission has other shortcomings, too. The salesperson has little security. If the economy slows down, or if sales fall off for some other reason beyond the salesperson's control, the "incentive" in the plan may be lost, because the sales representative may fail to achieve a satisfactory income over a period of a few weeks or more.

Quota-Bonus Plan

Quota-Bonus Plan
Compensation plan whereby a salesperson is paid a base salary related to achievement of a quota and a bonus for sales exceeding the quota.

Under the **quota-bonus plan,** each salesperson is assigned a sales quota—a specific level of sales to be achieved over a specified period. The incentive is built in because a bonus is offered to salespeople who exceed their quotas. A base salary is related to the quota total, while the bonus provides a commission-like incentive. This plan attempts to provide aspects of both straight salary and straight commission.

Salary Plus Commission

Salary Plus Commission
Compensation consisting of a regular salary plus a commission based on sales performance.

As the name suggests, the **salary plus commission** compensation plan combines two pay methods by granting the salesperson a straight salary or wage and a commission on sales. Typically, because a salary is provided, the commission is smaller than would be expected in a straight commission pay package. The intent of this plan is to allow management to ask salespeople to engage in nonselling work (since they are on salary) but also reward them for successful sales efforts (with a commission).

Motivating the Sales Force

Many salespeople work alone in the field, often at great distances from their home offices and far from direct supervision. This unique situation—the idea of working for oneself—draws many talented individuals into selling. But it can also create problems with respect to supervision.

Many salespeople are high achievers and may seldom require supervision from sales managers. For these people, the selling process itself is ample motivation. There is an intrinsic challenge in "making the sale" and a related challenge in trying to understand and solve customers' problems. Despite all this, most salespeople need at least occasional support from management. Sales personnel often are subject to broad fluctuations in morale and motivation, from the lows that may accompany a string of customer rejections or a sense of being alone on the road to the highs of obtaining major orders, enjoying peaks of success, and earning substantial commissions and bonuses. Sales personnel, especially young trainees, may become discouraged if they are not given proper help, supervision, and attention to morale. Because sales personnel do need a "listening ear" as well as direction and advice, telephone contact is helpful to the sales manager in supervising the sales force.

While experienced sales managers may know how, by words and actions, to properly reward and encourage salespeople to keep them fresh and interested in the job, many corporations use another element of their promotional mixes to help in this matter, the element of sales promotion. Sales contests, bonus plans, prizes and trips to be won, and sales conventions in exciting cities can all be of great help to the sales manager seeking to keep sales force motivation high. Periodic sales meetings also are useful, both for creating a feeling of group support and mutual interest and for providing a time for training and transmitting information.

Many sales organizations rely on sales meetings as the primary means of motivating the sales force. For example, the field sales manager of a New Jersey territory rented the Meadowlands football stadium. Corporate executives, family, and friends were assembled to cheer as each salesperson emerged from the players' tunnel. The electronic scoreboard bearing the salesperson's name and the cheering crowd motivated the salespeople to keep excelling at their jobs.

Evaluating and Controlling the Sales Force

An organization's overall marketing plan must be translated into a series of sales plans that specify regional, district, or territorial goals. Evaluation of a sales manager's or a sales representative's performance is based on whether he or she has met the appropriate goal or objective.

Objectives, especially those that a sales manager and a sales representative work out together, should be specific and measurable if they are to form the basis for reviewing the salesperson's performance and progress. The evaluation system must be fair and based on a mutual understanding of the performance standards and how they were determined. Note that the actual performance should be measured against predetermined standards, not standards set after the fact. It does little good to tell the sales representative that his or her performance this past year was "not too good" when no indication of what was expected was given at the start of the year. To minimize misunderstandings, the salesperson often is assigned a sales quota. During progress reviews, actual sales can be compared with the quota.

To do their jobs properly and meet their own objectives or quotas, sales managers must develop instruments of control that provide feedback from salespeople in the field. This feedback is not always expressed in terms of sales generated but may involve measures of effort, such as increases in the number of sales calls made per week, increases in the number of orders per sales call (the sales "batting average"), or reductions in selling expenses. Feedback tells managers if they should proceed with plans as scheduled, change course, look into particular problems, or check in with local sales personnel to take corrective action. For example, a simple but fundamental aspect of the sales manager's job is to assure that each salesperson calls on an appropriate number of customers. In most companies, therefore, sales representatives keep a log, call report, or activity report that must be filed, weekly or monthly, to indicate the number of calls made and to relate special information about accounts. Sales managers evaluate this "paperwork" to determine whether the sales representative is working at an appropriate intensity level.

ETHICAL ISSUES IN SALES AND SALES MANAGEMENT

Salespeople may be regularly confronted with decisions involving ethical and legal issues. These issues can range from violations of price discrimination and antitrust laws to "little white lies" about a competitor's product. The sales job is one of personal interaction, and because the range of interactions is so broad, the ethical issues confronting salespeople are innumerable. The basic starting point is for the sales force to know the law. Yet this is not enough, and companies that have adopted the marketing concept usually communicate to the sales force what ethical behavior is expected of them.[8]

Many organizations have codes of conduct for salespeople. At a very general level, most include statements similar to the following:

> *Salespeople should be honest and straightforward with prospects. They should keep their promises. They should use factual information and avoid misrepresentation and deception. They should not make statements that lead inadvertently to implied warranties. They should neither provide bribes or valuable gifts nor solicit them for themselves. They should not conspire with competitors.*

SALES PROMOTION

We turn now to the final major element of promotion—sales promotion. Recall that the typical purpose of a sales promotion effort is to bolster or complement other elements of the promotional mix during a specific time period. Thus, a sales promotion program—say, a contest—may be used as an incentive to motivate the sales force, may play a part in company advertising, or may serve as the basis for a publicity campaign. Here are some examples of sales promotions aimed at achieving a variety of objectives at various levels of the marketing channel:

- Sales promotions may be used to encourage a wholesaler's sales force to sell more aggressively to retailers. For instance, the salesperson with the highest sales volume for a particular period might win a trip to Hawaii.
- A sales promotion may be conducted to obtain retailers' cooperation with a consumer-targeted promotion. A marketer of videotaped movies wishing to reach consumers at the retail level could provide a special promotional allowance to retailers who agree to place displays at key locations in their stores.
- A sales promotion's objective may be to add an attention-getting quality to consumer advertising and to stimulate consumers to make an immediate purchase. Offering Jurassic Park: Lost World cups with a purchase at McDonald's gets the attention of members of a certain target market and stimulates them to act.

In the remainder of this chapter, we examine sales promotions in two general categories: promotions geared toward wholesalers and retailers and promotions aimed at ultimate consumers.

Sales Promotions Geared Toward Wholesalers and Retailers

Sales promotions targeted at wholesalers and retailers are generally intended either to motivate these channel members to make special efforts to market a product (for example, by giving the product more shelf space) or to increase the number of distributors and dealers handling the product. The major forms of sales promotion at the wholesale and retail level are trade shows, contests, point-of-purchase displays, cooperative advertising and promotional programs, and allowances.

Trade Shows

Trade Show
A meeting or convention of members of a particular industry where business-to-business contacts are routinely made.

Trade shows are extremely important in business-to-business marketing. Industrywide conventions and trade association meetings are scheduled throughout the year at hotels and convention centers across the country. The typical trade show features many "booths" where producers, suppliers, and other marketers display and provide information about their products, in effect using the booths as temporary bases of sales operations. You may be familiar with boat and auto shows, where hundreds and even thousands of products and services are shown and demonstrated. Most trade shows are organized along the same lines. Usually trade shows are not open to the general public because marketers use these shows to distribute literature, obtain sales leads, and sell products to wholesalers, retailers, organizational buyers, and other members of "the trade." The main purpose of a trade show is to serve as a central marketplace. Trade members, by making a single trip to the city in which the trade show is held, can view many products and discuss trends with many other professionals in the industry.[9]

Contests

Contest
In the context of a wholesaler's or retailer's sales promotion, a means of motivating a sales force by offering bonuses or prizes for sales performance.

Contests to motivate a manufacturer's sales force, or a wholesaler's or retailer's sales force, are very common sales promotion activities. The purpose of these contests is to increase sales levels by stimulating individual competition among salespeople. Competition is, of course, stimulated by the chance to win bonuses or prizes.

Sales contests add some excitement to regular activities and provide the opportunity for a salesperson to gain personal recognition as well as extra compensation and prizes. The major problem with sales contests is that the sales increases that result are often temporary. Furthermore, to improve their performance in a contest, salespersons often shift sales that would have occurred in another time period to the contest period.[10]

Display Equipment and Point-of-Purchase Materials

Point-of-Purchase Materials
Promotional items intended to attract attention to specific products in the places where those products are purchased. Signs and displays in supermarkets are examples.

Display equipment and other **point-of-purchase materials** are often provided to retailers and other members of distribution channels so that they can conveniently display or highlight the product to be sold. Such materials come in many forms. Convenience stores and bars almost always display clocks supplied by soft-drink or beer marketers, for example. Bookstore operators often receive new books in shipping packs that can be converted into book display racks.

Cooperative Advertising and Promotions

Cooperative Advertising
Advertising paid for jointly by a supplier and a customer—for example, by the manufacturer of a product and a retailer.

Cooperative advertising and other cooperative promotions are frequently used by manufacturers to increase promotional activity at local wholesale and retail levels. Programs vary, but the essence of all of them is that suppliers share promotional expenses with their customers. For example, suppose the manufacturer of La-Z-Boy chairs offers retailers a 50/50 co-op program. Half of the retailer's advertising expense will be borne by the manufacturer, so the retailer will pay just half of what the ad would ordinarily cost and will get to promote its own name as well as the La-Z-Boy brand name. The reward for the supplier who offers such a program is the active local support of dealers and the increased likelihood of immediate consumer purchases.

Allowances

Allowance

A reduction in price, a rebate, or the like given to a marketing intermediary in return for a large order or performance of a specific activity.

An **allowance** is a reduction in price, a rebate, merchandise, or something else given an intermediary for performance of a specific activity or in consideration for a large order. For example, a manufacturer may offer free merchandise to retailers that feature its product in point-of-purchase displays.

Sales Promotions Aimed at Ultimate Consumers

Like other forms of promotion, sales promotion at the consumer level can inform, remind, and persuade. Specific objectives of sales promotions may be to attract more in-store attention to a product, to serve as a reminder at the point-of-purchase, to help break down loyalty to competing brands, to add value to the product in the consumer's eyes, to make short-term price adjustments, to incent consumers to try a product for the first time, to offer an incentive for repeat purchases, or to induce large-volume purchases. The objectives of sales promotions are almost limitless, and their nature is bounded only by the marketer's imagination. For convenience, however, sales promotions can be grouped into these categories: product sampling, cents-off coupons, rebates, contests and sweepstakes, premiums, multiple-purchase offers, point-of-purchase materials, and product placements.

Product Sampling

Product Sampling

A sales promotion in which samples of a product are given to consumers to induce them to try the product.

The purpose of **product sampling** is to reach new customers by inducing trial use. A free trial or sample of the brand is given to consumers to stimulate product awareness, to provide first-hand knowledge about the product's characteristics, and to encourage a first purchase. Typically, miniature packages of the product are distributed to homes or in retail settings. Product sampling is expensive, but good for new brands in mature markets where strong brand loyalties may exist.

Coupons

Coupons, which generally offer price reductions of some kind, are one of the most widely used sales promotions. Like other kinds of price reductions, coupons have an established record of increasing short-term sales. They attract new users to a brand, encourage brand switching, and stimulate increased purchase among existing users. It should be noted that cutting prices occasionally with cents-off coupons does not damage a product's long-term quality or value image—many price-conscious consumers always clip coupons.

Coupons have an attention-getting quality and are often found as portions of print advertisements or free-standing inserts in newspapers. They may also be printed on packages or placed inside packages. Coupons are increasingly being distributed in stores and by direct mail. With the growth of data-based marketing, there have been changes in the nature of coupon distribution strategy. Coupons may be distributed selectively to consumers who are known to use particular competing brands or who are identified in the database as having certain purchasing behaviors of interest to the marketer. This helps minimize a major disadvantage of coupons—the fact that most coupon redemptions are made by consumers who already buy the brand.

COMPETITIVE STRATEGY: WHAT WENT RIGHT?

Oscar Mayer

What do Diana Ross, 50,000 kids, and the Wienermobile have in common? To Oscar Mayer they mean a 10 percent lift in market share.

That's what happened after Oscar Mayer's "Talent Search" promotion that tapped parents' egos and a nostalgic fondness for the Wienermobile and two classic advertising jingles. Approximately 50,000 kids flocked to Wienermobiles parked in supermarket lots to take their shot at fame by singing "I wish I were an Oscar Mayer wiener," or "My bologna has a first name." Local winners in 50 markets got $100; 20 of them won family trips to Orlando,

Florida, to compete in the finals. The winner, Trent South, introduced Diana Ross and the Super Bowl XXX halftime show and starred in Oscar Mayer's first-ever Super Bowl advertisement.

"Kids were lined up and down the block to sing," said David Rizzo, consumer promotion manager at Oscar Mayer Foods. "It was incredible."

The promotion boosted sales of Oscar Mayer's full portfolio, including bacon and Lunchables as well as hot dogs and lunchmeat. Volume sales were up an average 18 percent, with incremental volume up 40 percent.

Rebates

Rebate
A sales promotion wherein some portion of the price paid for a product is returned to the purchaser.

A **rebate,** like a coupon, is a price reduction designed to induce immediate purchase. However, with a rebate the consumer gets money back from the manufacturer rather than a price break at the retail level. Rebate offers often require that the consumer purchase multiple units (for example, three boxes of cereal). Typically, the consumer must then send in some proof of purchase, after which the company will send a check to the consumer. For many consumers, this time lag is less attractive than an immediate price reduction at the retail level. For the marketer, however, costs are lower, because rebate offers are typically printed on the packages or placed inside them and do not involve circulating materials by other means.

Contests and Sweepstakes

Contests and sweepstakes stimulate purchases by giving consumers a chance to be big winners. Certain types of consumers enjoy these exciting promotions. Contest participants have to complete some task, such as submitting a recipe to the Pillsbury Bake-Off, and are awarded prizes when their entries are judged to be among the best. Sweepstakes participants become winners based on chance. Sweepstakes are tied easily to repeat purchases of a brand when the chances of winning increase with each purchase. If sweepstakes promotions require the purchase of a unit of the product, however, state or local lottery laws may prohibit them.

Premiums and Self-Liquidating Premiums

Premium
A product offered free or at reduced charge if another product is purchased.

A **premium** is a product offered free or at a reduced price when another product, the key brand, is purchased. The premium, such as a baseball cap at an L.A. Dodgers game, is a giveaway; so consumers see themselves as getting something for nothing. Self-liquidating premiums are special types of premiums that consumers obtain by using proofs of purchase, trading stamps, cash, or a combination of these.

Multiple-Purchase Offers

Multiple-purchase offers, or two-for-one deals, are tied to price or to some other promotion. Offering four bars of Dial soap for the price of three is a typical example of a multiple-purchase offer; it encourages a bigger-than-normal purchase and helps maintain customer loyalty.

Point-of-Purchase Materials

Banners, pamphlets, coasters, and similar materials may be used to provide information at the point of purchase. Point-of-purchase materials serve as reminders. Reminding a shopper of an appeal used in advertising may trigger a sale. In-store videos, shopping-cart videos electronically started when the cart moves toward the aisle where the product is stocked, and other technological innovations are changing the nature of these sales promotions.

Product Placements

A product or company that appears in a movie scene is exposed to millions of movie viewers. If a certain brand of soft drink is consumed or if a certain brand of clothing is worn by a celebrity actor in a movie or television show, a very positive message can be communicated in what most consider a noncommercial setting. In recent years, movie studios have come to recognize that selling these **product placements** in their movies can be a profitable side business. Marketers of widely used consumer goods and services often are willing to pay large fees for product placements. In some cases, the product placements are tied in to other promotional efforts.

Exhibit 15–5 summarizes the major forms of consumer sales promotions. As a final note we should mention that sales promotions can be overused. For example, a number of sales promotions, such as coupons, rebates, and premiums, lower the price of the product or similarly enhance the product offering. If these special incentives are used regularly or if consumers can predict their timing, then consumers may buy only during sales promotions. Marketers who continually use this type of sales promotion risk the loss of traditional sales to price-conscious consumers.

Sales Promotion Tie-ins

A **tie-in** involves a collaborative effort between two or more organizations or brands that work as partners in a promotional effort. Tie-ins generally borrow interest value from movies, sporting events, or other marketing efforts. When McDonald's sells a Happy Meal that includes a *Hunchback of Notre Dame* toy, its sales promotion effort is based on a tie-in with the popular Disney movie. It expects its soft drink sales to benefit from the popularity of the movie.

Product Placement
Conveying a noncommercial, positive message by having a product or company appear in—or be used by a celebrity in—a movie or television show.

Tie-in
Collaborative effort between two or more organizations or brands that work as partners in a promotional effort.

ACTIVITY	DESCRIPTION	FEATURES	EXAMPLE
Product sampling	A sample of the brand is given to consumers.	Expensive, but good for new brands in mature markets where brand loyalties may exist.	Quilted Bounty Rinse and Reuse.
Cents-off coupons	A temporary price reduction coupon is most often found in an advertisement, but may be distributed in the store, in the package, or by direct mail.	Cutting price does not damage long-term quality or value image—many price-conscious consumers always clip coupons.	Save 25¢ on Cap'n Crunch's Crunch Berries Bars.
Rebates	Consumer is offered the opportunity to get money back from manufacturer rather than price break at retail level.	Lower cost than circulating coupons because rebate coupon is inside package.	Mail-in rebate for $5 on Black and Decker drill.
Contests and sweepstakes	Consumer is given a chance to be a big winner.	Liked by some consumers; may be tied to repeat purchase of a brand.	Safeway Bingo Game Sweepstakes.
Premiums and self-liquidating premiums	Another product is offered free or at a reduced charge if the key brand is purchased.	Consumers see themselves as getting something for nothing.	Oscar Mayer wiener whistle given away with each pack of hot dogs.
Multiple-purchase offers	Multiple purchases are tied to price or another promotion.	Induces heavier-than-normal purchase and maintains customer loyalty.	Four bars of Dial soap for the price of three.
Point-of-purchase materials	Banners, pamphlets, coasters, and similar materials are used to provide information at the point of purchase.	Reminders at the point of purchase may trigger a sale.	Cardboard display for Stephen King's latest book.
Product placements	Product appears in a movie or is used by a celebrity.	Conveys positive image in what most consider a noncommercial setting.	Ray Ban sunglasses in the blockbuster movie *Men in Black.*

EXHIBIT 15–5
A Summary of Consumer Sales Promotions

The benefits of tie-ins with premiums are easily appreciated, but contests, sweepstakes, coupons, and other sales promotional elements can also benefit from a tie-in approach. For example, The National Basketball Association (NBA) and Sprite's tie-in collaboration ranged from having NBA promotional information appear on special Sprite cans to a portable playground traveling to state fairs.

FOCUS ON RELATIONSHIPS

McDonald's and Disney

McDonald's has a ten-year multinational promotional alliance with Disney. McDonald's is Disney's primary promotional partner in the restaurant industry, sharing exclusive rights linked to Disney theatrical releases, theme parks, and home video releases in more than 93 countries.

SUMMARY

Professional selling is important to the success of most organizations. Selling is most effective when it is a flexible process involving identifying and fulfilling customer needs on an individual basis, thus reflecting the marketing concept. Sales promotion supports other elements of the promotional mix by stimulating sales over short periods of time.

Learning Objective 1

Describe the role of personal selling and relationship management.

Personal selling occurs when a seller personally attempts to persuade a prospective buyer to purchase a product. A salesperson is a professional who can effectively communicate the benefits of a product or service. The sales message must be flexible—adapted to the individual needs of each prospective buyer. Relationship management refers to the sales function of managing the account relationship and ensuring that the buyer receives the appropriate services.

Learning Objective 2

Identify marketing situations in which personal selling would be the most effective means of reaching and influencing target buyers.

Personal selling is effective because the salesperson can adjust the sales message on the basis of direct verbal and nonverbal feedback and close the sale. It works better than other forms of promotion for technical, expensive, innovative, or complex products and is effective in selling to organizational buyers. However, it is inefficient in reaching large numbers of consumers of frequently purchased products.

Learning Objective 3

Show how the professional salesperson contributes to a modern marketing firm.

There are three kinds of selling tasks: order taking, order getting, and sales support. Order takers perform routine sales tasks. The professional order-getting salesperson must apply the marketing concept by identifying customers' problems and solving them individually with the organization's products, terms of sale, and other benefits. Sales support personnel engage in special activities such as providing service and expertise.

Learning Objective 4

Outline the steps involved in making a sale.

The steps involved in making a sale are: (1) locating and qualifying prospects, (2) making the approach, (3) making the sales presentation, (4) handling objections, (5) closing the sale, and (6) following up.

Learning Objective 5

Explain why the marketing process does not stop when the sale is made.

Obtaining an order is the beginning of an organization's relationship with a customer. Satisfied customers provide repeat sales. To ensure an enduring buyer-seller relationship, sales personnel should follow up on orders to guarantee that they are delivered in proper condition on schedule and that post-sale services are provided.

Learning Objective 6

Characterize the major aspects of the sales manager's job.

Members of the sales force must be managed so that their efforts are directed toward organizational goals. A sales manager is responsible for (1) setting sales objectives, (2) organizing the sales force, (3) recruiting and selecting sales personnel, (4) training the sales force, (5) developing an effective compensation plan, (6) motivating the sales force, and (7) evaluating and controlling the sales force.

Learning Objective 7

Classify the various forms of sales compensation.

Sales personnel may be compensated by use of a straight salary method, a commission based on sales, or a combination of these plans, such as a quota-bonus plan or a salary plus commission.

Learning Objective 8

Identify some of the ethical issues facing sales personnel.

The ethical issues facing sales personnel are numerous because of the broad range of human interactions involved. In general, companies expect salespeople to comply with the law and be honest and straightforward in all their dealings.

Learning Objective 9

Identify the purposes of sales promotion and explain how the major sales promotion tools work.

Sales promotion programs support other promotional elements, which in turn support the sales promotion. At the wholesale and retail level, they include trade shows, contests, point-of-purchase displays, cooperative advertising, and allowances. Popular sales promotions at the consumer level are product sampling, cents-off coupons, rebates, contests and sweepstakes, premiums and self-liquidating premiums, multiple-purchase offers, and point-of-purchase materials.

KEY TERMS

Retail selling (p. 410)

Field selling (p. 410)

Telemarketing (p. 410)

Inside selling (p. 411)

Relationship management (p. 412)

Order taker (p. 413)

Suggestive selling (p. 413)

Order getting, or creative selling
   (p. 414)

Pioneer (p. 414)

Account manager (p. 414)

Missionary (p. 414)

Cross-functional sales team (p. 415)

Account service representative
   (p. 415)

Creative selling process (p. 415)

Prospecting (p. 416)

Qualifying (p. 417)

Preapproach planning (p. 417)

Approach (p. 417)

Sales presentation (p. 418)

Handling objections (p. 419)

Closing (p. 420)

Closing signals (p. 421)

Trial close (p. 421)

Follow-up (p. 421)

Sales management (p. 422)

Sales objectives (p. 422)

Sales territory (p. 423)

Field sales manager (p. 424)

Straight salary (p. 427)

Straight commission (p. 427)

Quota-bonus plan (p. 427)

Salary plus commission (p. 427)

Trade show (p. 430)

Contest (p. 430)

Point-of-purchase materials (p. 430)

Cooperative advertising (p. 430)

Allowance (p. 431)

Product sampling (p. 431)

Rebate (p. 432)

Premium (p. 432)

Product placement (p. 433)

Tie-in (p. 433)

QUESTIONS FOR REVIEW AND CRITICAL THINKING

1. For each of the following, tell whether you would expect the salesperson to be an order taker or an order getter.
   a. Selling cable TV subscriptions to homeowners
   b. Selling industrial power tools to purchasing agents in the aircraft industry
   c. Selling blocks of Oakland A's season tickets to businesses that entertain customers at the games
   d. Selling paper product supplies to office supply stores

2. For each of the following, tell how you would prospect and qualify customer accounts.
   a. Selling chain saws to hardware wholesalers
   b. Selling installations of cables for office computer networks
   c. Selling life insurance
   d. Selling executive jet aircraft

3. "Salespeople are born, not made." Comment.

4. What are the steps in the personal selling process? Which is the most important step?

5. Handle the following objections:
   a. "The price is too high."
   b. "I don't have enough money. I'll have to wait a month or two."
   c. "I'm just not certain if I need one or not."

6. Why do some college students avoid careers in personal selling?

7. What average cost per contact do you think is involved in having sales representatives personally visit customers?

8. How important are personal appearance and proper dress in personal selling?

9. The sales volume of a man with 25 years of selling experience begins to slip. How would you motivate him to work harder?

10. Many salespeople take clients to restaurants for lunch. What should a young salesperson be told about entertaining at lunch?

11. Some sales promotions are geared toward stimulating activity among wholesalers and retailers; others are geared toward influencing ultimate consumers. How do the objectives of these types of promotion differ?

12. What is internal marketing?

13. For each of the following sales promotion tactics, give your opinion on the promotion's likely effectiveness.
    a. A rebate offer on an automotive battery
    b. A four-unit package of panty hose for the price usually charged for a three-unit package
    c. A sweepstakes contest for a regional airline
    d. A free screwdriver with a can of WD-40 oil

14. Form small groups as directed by your instructor. Each group should brainstorm to get ideas for how

a local restaurant or college bar could creatively use a sales promotion. After 10 minutes of brainstorming, the group should evaluate the ideas suggested and select three for presentation to the class.

15. Field sales representatives often work in teams. Discuss the situations in which team selling is most likely.

INTERNET INSIGHTS

Exercises

1. Some tips on export etiquette can be found at

    http://www.cl.ais.net/jchevron/

    List at least three tips for sales representatives selling in Europe.

2. The Executive Woman's Travel Network offers tips on travel safety, health and fitness when traveling, and other travel information. It may be found at

    http://www.delta-air.com/womensexecs

What information do you think women sales representatives would find most useful?

Address Book

SalesLeads USA
http://www.lookupusa.com

U.S. Navy Observatory Time Service
http://tycho.usno.navy.mil

Canadian Professional Sales Association
http://www.cpsa.com

ETHICS IN PRACTICE: TAKE A STAND

1. Are the following sales activities ethical?
    a. A salesperson skips lunch but adds the typical $10 charge to her expense account. Is this ethical?
    b. In a hotel bar, a salesperson recognizes a sales representative from a competing company, and they discuss their companies' prices, discounts, and terms of sale. Is this a good business practice?
    c. A salesperson gives a Christmas gift worth $50 to a purchasing agent responsible for buying for a major account. Take a stand.
    d. A salesperson offers a "customer who is difficult to deal with" a higher discount than the typical prospect. Is this right?

2. A sales manager tells the sales force that he is under a lot of pressure to increase sales for the quarter, which ends in a week. Afterward, a salesperson calls a prospect who has recently mentioned that she is almost ready to place an order for a competitor's product and arranges to take her to dinner at an expensive restaurant. During the dinner, after the best of everything has been ordered, the salesperson says a number of negative things about the way the competitor does business. Some of these statements are not completely accurate. The salesperson normally would not be misleading but really wants to make a quick sale to help out the sales manager. Did the salesperson do the right thing?

Stone Hill Winery

Changing tastes in wines during the late '70s and early '80s were hard to swallow for vintners Jim and Betty Held.

Baby-boomer professionals were replacing older, blue-collar types as the predominant U.S. wine drinkers, and dry wines were replacing the sweet in consumer preferences. The Helds' Stone Hill Winery, of Hermann, Mo., wasn't suited to the shift. Its products were sweet or semisweet; Missouri's harsh winters were unfriendly to now-favored European grape varieties such as cabernet, chardonnay, and zinfandel.

With an onslaught of competition from new California wineries, and waves of advertising that put Stone Hill's low-budget advertising in the shade, Stone Hill wines went from top to bottom shelves in the stores.

Other Missouri wineries also suffered, and some went under. Not Stone Hill. The Helds charted a new course, aided by the expertise of three of their children, who had won grape-growing and wine-making degrees from the University of California, Fresno.

Investment in new vineyards and equipment would enable Stone Hill to compete with California wines—in price as well as quality, if the investment was large enough to provide economies of scale. To raise the money, Stone Hill had to grow significantly.

Questions

1. Suppose Stone Hill decided that sales promotion was the only way it could afford to promote its product. What sales promotion strategy would you recommend?

2. How would you implement this strategy?

PART 6

INTRODUCTION TO PRICING CONCEPTS

C h a p t e r   16

Learning Objectives

After you have studied this chapter, you will be able to:

1. Define price and discuss it.
2. Tell how price interacts with the rest of the marketing mix.
3. Analyze the role of price in our economy.
4. Outline the fundamentals of pricing strategy.
5. Characterize the relationship between price and organizational objectives.
6. Relate the demand in a target market to the prices charged.
7. Understand that demand and cost considerations influence pricing.
8. Differentiate among price elasticity, price inelasticity, and price cross-elasticity.

Long before there was an information superhighway, long before the emergence of the Internet, long before a sojourn in cyberspace, there was Western Union.

The financial services company, which pioneered mass telegram service and has long been synonymous with wiring money, is one of the oldest and remains one of the strongest brand names in the world despite recent financial woes. Now, its power is about to be put to the test in the opening salvo of what could become a money-transfer price war.

A brash competitor, the MoneyGram money wiring service, began a major television and radio advertising campaign in November 1994, proclaiming that sending money through its service is significantly cheaper. The MoneyGram ads attacked Western Union with sarcastic humor. In one ad, a fully dressed woman was sitting in a bathtub. As she was doused with gallons of water, the voiceover said, "Still using Western Union to wire money? Next time, go to MoneyGram and save up to 19 bucks. Because taking one bath a day is enough."

Using a competitive promotional pricing strategy, the MoneyGram service charged customers $10 to wire as much as $300, instead of its usual $18 rate; Western Union charged $29. This price effort is the most aggressive since the MoneyGram service was created in 1988.

MoneyGram is currently owned by American Express and managed by First Data, a New Jersey company. Ownership will pass to First Data in April 1997.

First Data is not just any rival. It is the most pesky of adversaries, a spurned suitor. In September 1994, First Data was one of three companies bidding for Western Union, which had filed for protection against creditors in U.S. Bankruptcy Court in Newark, New Jersey. First Data bid $1.13 billion, but First Financial Management emerged as the winner. "We felt our businesses would have been a good fit," says Rob Ayers, First Data's senior vice-president of marketing. "But since we couldn't come to an agreement, we felt a price-comparison campaign was the best way to get our message across."

The money-transfer business may not be glamorous—many who use it live in low-income urban areas and don't have bank accounts—but it does generate an impressive amount of business. Each year, $6 billion to $8 billion is wired, and that represents $500 million to $600 million in combined revenues for Western Union and the MoneyGram service.

Price, as the story about MoneyGram and the money-transfer business illustrates, plays a major role in the marketing mix. A lower price can be a means to enter a market or to gain a competitive advantage. A proper price can make the difference between success and failure.

This chapter focuses on the nature of price as a marketing mix variable and the role of price in our economy. The chapter provides a framework by examining the fundamental concepts underlying pricing strategy. It shows the interrelationship between overall organization and marketing objectives and the organization's pricing objectives. In doing this, it addresses target market considerations, supply and demand, price elasticity, and the nature of costs.

WHAT IS PRICE?

Value
The power of one product to attract another product in an exchange.

As we have seen, marketing involves exchanging things of value. **Value** is a quantitative measure of the power one good or service has to attract another good or service in an exchange. An auto mechanic could exchange four tune-ups for two months of coffee and doughnuts from a nearby diner. Such a trade is possible because the tune-ups, the coffee, and the doughnuts all have value. When products are exchanged for one another, the trade is called **barter.**

Barter
The exchange of products without the use of money.

While it would be possible to value every product in the world in terms of every other product, such a system would be complicated and unwieldy. It is far easier to express these many values in terms of the single variable of money. Price is thus a statement of value, because it is the amount of money or other consideration given in exchange for a product.

Price has many names. These names vary according to tradition or the interests of the seller. For example, rent, fee, and donation are terms used in specific exchange situations to describe price. Some sellers avoid using the word price in order to make what is offered for sale appear to be of a quality that price cannot fully describe. Thus, the student pays tuition, not a price, for education. The commuter pays a toll. The professor who gives an off-campus speech accepts an honorarium. The physician charges a fee for professional services. Universities, governments, professors, and doctors all sell their services for a price, no matter what that price is called.

In brief, marketing involves exchanges of things that have value. The name most commonly used to describe this value is *price.* In the United States, it is most commonly expressed in dollars and cents.

PRICE AS A MARKETING MIX VARIABLE

Price has a special significance in that it ultimately "pays" for all of the firm's activities. Because sales revenue equals price times unit sales volume, the price of a product is one of the prime determinants of sales revenues. If a price can be increased while unit volume and costs remain the same, revenues and profits will be increased. For this reason alone, pricing decisions are important. But price is important for another reason. It, like other marketing mix variables, influences unit sales volume. Thus, proper pricing of a product is expected to increase the quantity demanded. Price is perhaps the most flexible element of the marketing mix because it can be changed rapidly in response to changes in the environment.[1]

List Price
The basic price quote, before adjustment.

In setting prices, many marketers start with a basic price quote called a **list price.** Price adjustments can be made when the season changes, when a buyer makes a large-quantity purchase, or for another reason. Many marketers adjust list price with discounts or rebates. For example, retailers often mark down, or reduce, the list price when merchandise is out of season or moving slowly.

A list price functions as a communications tool by adding symbolic value to a good or service and by helping to position the brand in relation to competitors. A high price may suggest a high-status good, a low price may suggest a bargain, and a discount coupon or rebate may be used to encourage purchases by people who would otherwise not buy the product. Entire positioning strategies may revolve around price. For example, Tiffany's, a chain of exclusive jewelry stores, maintains an image of the highest quality by stocking reliable products and providing special services and also by charging comparatively high prices. Wal-Mart and Price Club stress bargains and must therefore keep prices at the lowest levels.

COMPETITIVE STRATEGY: WHAT WENT WRONG?

Sprint

AT&T and MCI, the leaders in the long-distance calling business, are constantly at loggerheads about who has the lowest long-distance prices. Third place Sprint, rather than directly entering the "our rates are the lowest" fray, chose to have a "Fridays Free" program. The company promised to give small-business customers free long-distance calling every Friday for a year. Many small businesses found the offer attractive and switched to Sprint. What could go wrong?

Plenty as it turned out. Sprint found that its Fridays Free promotion ran out of control. Its costs were too high. Many residential customers signed up for the service, even though the program originally was targeted at businesses. And many small businesses, as it turns out, do a lot of international marketing. Calling volumes to nine countries—China, India, Pakistan, Israel, Ecuador, Bolivia, Thailand, Iran, and Myanmar—increased 800 percent.

Startled by the high volume of free calls placed by its business customers in the promotion, Sprint beat a hasty retreat. It barred any free calls to overseas destinations for customers who newly sign up for the service. Moreover, for current customers, Sprint effectively banned freebie Friday traffic to those nine countries that became especially popular targets.

The move angered many customers, who accused the company of luring them to convert to Sprint with terms that have now been withdrawn. Some complained Sprint's actions were unprofessional.

Price is closely related to other marketing variables and cannot be discussed without simultaneous consideration of product, place, and promotion. Pricing strategies must be consistent with the firm's other marketing mix decisions and must support the firm's other marketing strategies. For example, the Maytag product strategy—ensuring that customers will have "ten years trouble-free operation"—stresses the quality and reliability that is highlighted in its advertising strategy, which is compatible with its premium pricing strategy. Although mechanical problems with its product are infrequent, Maytag's strategy requires the proper distribution system, including service technicians. The premium pricing strategy, which allows an adequate profit margin for intermediaries, helps support the distribution strategy.

Price bears a special relationship to promotion. One job of promotion is to show potential buyers that an item is worth the price demanded. We can all think of products we bought or services we used because we believed that we were getting a good deal, a bargain, or high-quality workmanship. But after a bit of thought, we might admit that the favorable price or statement of quality was identified with a familiar advertisement or a television salesperson's convincing presentation. In such instances, the consumer more willingly pays the asked-for price because promotion has convinced him or her that the price is justified.

Price Competition

Price Competition
Competition based solely on price. It is especially important in the marketing of products that are not distinctive, such as raw materials.

The degree of **price competition** influences the nature of the marketing mix. Intensive price competition exists in many industries. This is especially true with raw materials, such as crude petroleum. Because competing products are not distinctive, price becomes the key marketing variable. In other product categories, price may be less important to the consumer than a distinctive product feature or a differentiated brand image. In these categories, the firm that emphasizes low price exclusively may find that competitors easily meet this low price.

Shortly after Tylenol was introduced, its maker, Johnson & Johnson, built strong brand name recognition by emphasizing that acetaminophen is less irritating to the stomach than aspirin. Bristol-Myers then introduced Datril as a "me too" brand. The gist of its advertising campaign was that Datril was lower in price than the leading brand, Tylenol. Unfortunately for Datril, when Tylenol marketers felt Datril was becoming serious competition, Tylenol met Datril's price—and informed Bristol-Myers that all of the Datril advertising would have to be changed. The primary Datril strength, low price, was no longer an issue. Today, Datril is no longer an issue.

If price is the sole basis of competition, then competitors can easily take away the competitive advantage. Of course, if the low price is the result of technology and production efficiency that, in the short term, competitors cannot easily match, then a low-cost, lowest-price strategy may be effective.

Price and Marketing Effectiveness

Nonprice Competition
Competition emphasizing marketing variables other than price—for example, product differentiation.

As mentioned, in some competitive situations price may be less important than some other feature. Effective **nonprice competition** allows the marketer to charge premium prices. Indeed, price is often indicative of overall marketing effectiveness. Legos commands a price substantially above that of many of its competitors but nevertheless sells far more building-block toys than any of them. This is fairly substantial proof that its overall marketing strategy produces a product, promotion, and distribution mix consistent with and supportive of its pricing strategy. Legos is thus better off than its competitors. The ability to maintain prices and sales volume in the face of relatively stiff competition certainly indicates an excellent marketing strategy and an effective execution of that strategy.

PRICE IN THE ECONOMY

The main function of price in our relatively free market economy is to help allocate goods and services. Most items of value are distributed to those who demand them and have the means to pay for them. When products are scarce or in short supply, prices are high, and wealthier citizens are better able than poorer citizens to afford them. Thus, from a macromarketing perspective, price allocates available goods and services within our economy by determining who will get them. Price also determines the quantity of goods and services that will be produced and marketed. An economist's explanation of demand and supply helps us understand the role of pricing in the economy.

Demand Curve

Demand Curve
Graphic representation of the relationship between various prices and the amount of product that will be demanded at those prices. Also called a demand schedule.

Demand is the quantity of a product consumers are willing and able to buy at a given price. Usually, the quantity demanded changes as price changes. Thus, you might be willing to pay someone $10 to clean your untidy bedroom each week. But you might have the room cleaned only every two weeks if the price rose to $25, and not at all at a price of $100. At $100, you would either clean the room yourself or leave it dirty! This relationship can be shown as a table or a curve, as in Exhibit 16–1.

The **demand curve,** or *schedule of demand,* is a graphic representation of the relationship between the various prices sellers might charge for a product and the amount of that product that buyers will demand at each price. Clearly, it would be a great help to marketers to have access to a specific demand curve for their industry. While marketers seldom have an exact demand schedule showing how much they can sell at price 1, price 2, or price 3, they may have some demand information from marketing research. At the very least, when precise demand curves cannot be drawn, assumptions are made about them. A demand curve is repre-

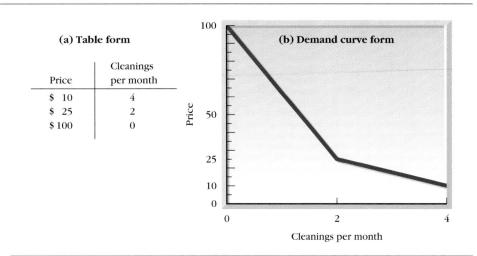

EXHIBIT 16–1
Changes in Room Cleanings
Demanded as Prices
Increase

(a) Table form

Price	Cleanings per month
$ 10	4
$ 25	2
$ 100	0

(b) Demand curve form

sented as the line labeled D in Exhibit 16–2. Note that as price (P_1) declines, more and more quantity (Q_1) of the product is demanded.

Supply Curve

Supply is the quantity of a product that marketers are willing and able to sell at a given price in a given time period. A **supply curve,** or *supply schedule* (labeled S in Exhibit 16–2), graphically represents the amount of goods or services marketers will supply at various prices.

A supply curve shows that as prices become more attractive to suppliers (marketers), those suppliers will try to provide more of the product. Thus, in most cases, as prices rise, suppliers are encouraged to supply more product; and as prices fall, they will prefer to supply less.

The intersection of the industry demand and supply curves establishes the market price (P_1) and the quantity produced (Q_1), or size of the market. Thus, economic theory shows how price determines how much will be produced and distributed to members of society.

We have focused here on price for an industry, not for an individual firm marketing a product. We now turn our attention to pricing strategy for a firm.

Supply Curve
Graphic representation of the relationship between various prices and the amount of product that will be supplied at those prices. Also called a supply schedule.

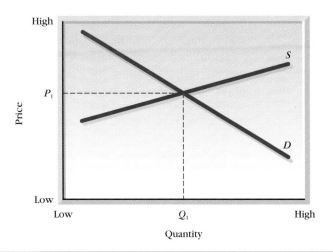

EXHIBIT 16–2
The Intersection of Supply
and Demand

FOCUS ON RELATIONSHIPS

 Hyatt Hotels

Large companies once were famous for ruthlessly driving down supplier prices. They would, for example, pit one against another or not pay bills at all until the supplier buckled under pressure. But Hyatt Hotels Corporation has a better idea. It believes that the best way to drive down supplier prices is to find additional customers for the supplier.

Rather than holding brutal negotiations with suppliers where both sides usually end up losing, Hyatt offers public testimonials and letters of support designed to create new business for its suppliers. Says Hyatt Hotels' president Darryl Hartley-Leonard, "The more money you help someone make, the more responsive they are going to be."

THE FUNDAMENTALS OF PRICING STRATEGY

Many mathematical tools can be used to determine the specific price that should be assigned to a particular product. Most marketing managers, however, would be reluctant to trust such an important matter as price exclusively to any mechanical technique. Company objectives, costs, and demand need to be considered. Further, there remains an important role to be played by managerial judgment supported by marketing research, knowledge of competitors' actions, and an understanding of the target market's reaction to prices. In setting prices, it is important to:

1. Determine your pricing objectives.
2. Know the importance of price to your target market.
3. Know your demand.
4. Understand your costs.
5. Determine your pricing strategy.

Of course, as in other marketing mix decisions, environmental forces also influence pricing decisions. Competitive forces and legal influences are extremely important factors. This chapter discusses the first four items listed above. Chapter 17 focuses on pricing strategies and tactics as well as the legal aspects of pricing.

PRICING OBJECTIVES

Pricing Objective
The desired result associated with a particular pricing strategy. The pricing objective must be consistent with other marketing objectives.

Although we are concerned here with pricing, we should mention again that **pricing objectives** must be coordinated with the firm's other marketing objectives. These must, in turn, flow from the company's overall objectives. Thus, if Toshiba seeks to become the leader in developing and marketing high-technology electronics products, all of its marketing objectives, including its pricing objectives, must be consistent with that broad company mission. For example, the objectives associated with a high level of product differentiation at the overall marketing level would not generally be compatible with an objective of always setting prices below competitors' prices.[2] The relationship of pricing decisions to organizational objectives is diagrammed in Exhibit 16–3.

With organizational objectives firmly in mind, marketers pricing a good or service must determine what specific objectives are to be accomplished with the pricing strategy. Managers should know why certain prices are being charged as well as why these prices might differ from buyer to buyer and from time to time. A firm may face any number of problems and opportunities, and these may give rise

ing campaign, positioning it as a gourmet coffee, or packaging the coffee in attractive reusable containers.

Stabilize Prices

Price Stabilization

Pricing objective aimed at avoiding widely fluctuating prices. The marketer with this objective sets prices to match competitors' prices or maintain existing price differentials.

A marketer may aim to match competitors' prices or maintain existing price differentials in order to avoid injurious price wars and help stabilize the general price level. This is a **price stabilization** strategy. It is fairly common, particularly in the retailing of gasoline and groceries. Though price wars in these fields are not unheard of, normally all gas stations in town charge roughly equal prices for fuel, and all grocery stores charge approximately the same price for milk. Thus, prices remain stable and predictable.

Objectives Related to Social Concerns

Many organizations, especially not-for-profit organizations, set pricing objectives on the basis of social concerns. For example, zoos might be able to raise prices but refuse to do so because the organizational mission stresses public education above profit maximization. Pricing objectives for other organizations, especially sole proprietorships, might simply be to make enough to meet the payroll. Pricing objectives based on social concerns are highly interrelated with the ethical and legal aspects of pricing. We discuss this topic further in Chapter 17.

TARGET MARKET CONSIDERATIONS

Pricing decisions are affected by many factors. The most significant of these is demand from the organization's target market. Even when a competitor making the same product changes price, target market considerations are important because the competitor's move may affect only the competitor's target market. In essence, the question the marketing manager faces is this: "Who are our customers and what do they want the price to be?"

Many market segments are price-conscious. Recall that Pillsbury's Oven Lovin' cookie dough, loaded with Hershey's chocolate chips, Reese's Pieces, and Brach's candies and packaged in a resealable tub, was a product failure. One reason for the failure was that price-conscious shoppers didn't think the product was worth 20 cents more than the company's conventional tube of dough, especially since the new package was 10 percent smaller.

Nevertheless, the notion that the customer wants the lowest price is not always correct. Diamonds and Rolls Royce automobiles are expensive partly because people expect them to be expensive. A $100 bottle of perfume may contain only $10 to $20 worth of scent; the rest of the price goes to advertising, packaging, distribution, and profit. When consumers buy such perfume, they are buying atmosphere, hope, the feeling of being someone special, and pride in having "the best."

Even frequently purchased products can exemplify the customer's willingness to pay a higher price rather than a lower one. Parents do not usually brag about buying bargain-priced baby food for their infants, nor do most hosts offer their guests a drink while discussing what an inexpensive brand of whiskey they've been able to buy.

When targeting certain markets, then, marketers can expect to sell more at a higher price than at a lower one. However, most successful marketers do not employ high prices to appeal to buyers. Instead, they offer reasonably priced products that prove popular to target markets.

FOCUS ON TRENDS

USA Today

An entirely new publishing and advertising economy is taking shape because of the Internet. It is changing the way information is priced to the market segment that uses the World Wide Web.

In April 1995, *USA Today* announced it would begin providing software for people to access its Web site, charging $12.95 per month for three hours of access to its online newspaper, $2.50 for every hour beyond that. But after four months, it managed to attract only about 1,000 subscribers, a disastrous showing for a newspaper with a daily print circulation topping 2 million. A post-mortem analysis indicated the paper's first mistake was the "unnecessary" quick move into the Internet access business, a commodity market well served by dozens of other companies. The second mistake was charging a subscription fee. In August 1995, *USA Today* began phasing out its software business and made its Web site free.

On the Internet consumers will rarely pay a subscription fee for access to a Web site. There are vast amounts of free time and users "treat information charges as damage, and route around them." In this sense, the Web is like cable TV: people will pay for delivery of the medium itself, but will pay extra for only one or two premium channels, if any.

KNOW YOUR DEMAND

Marketers need to know how many people will buy their products. How many people are willing to buy and how much they will buy are primarily functions of price. To describe how sensitive demand is to price, we discuss price elasticity.

Price Elasticity of Demand

Price Elasticity
Measure of the effect of a change in price on the quantity of product demanded.

Price elasticity measures the effect of a change in price on the quantity of a product demanded. Price elasticity refers to price sensitivity. Specifically, price elasticity measures what percentage change in quantity demanded is induced by a percentage change in price. Exhibits 16–5, 16–6, 16–7, and 16–8 illustrate the concept of *price elasticity of demand.*

Logic would lead us to predict that (1) a decline in the price of a product might lead to an increase in the quantity of it demanded and (2) the rate of increase might differ from case to case and from product to product. For example, we would expect that bread sales might increase as prices went down. However, the rise would be slight and would happen slowly, because bread is a common product that most people can afford and are already buying. Demand increases are also limited by the fact that there is a limit to how much bread people can eat.

This situation is demonstrated in Exhibit 16–5. A decrease in price from P_1 to P_2 increases demand from Q_1 to Q_2. The gap between the two Qs is far less than the gap between the two Ps. This illustrates relative price *inelasticity* of demand. That is, demand is not very flexible when price is changed. Thus, when price is raised rather than lowered, from P_2 back to P_1, demand does not decrease rapidly; it is price inelastic.

The opposite situation is shown in Exhibit 16–6, in which a downward change in price does increase demand significantly. More than that, the increase in demand appears to be greater than what the decrease in price might warrant. This curve might apply to, say, filet mignon. This product is very much in demand even though most families buy it in limited amounts because of its high price. The shopper finding that the price of the steak has been reduced is likely to stock up. Thus, the demand for the product is highly flexible, or elastic, in terms of price.

EXHIBIT 16–5
Demand Curve Showing
Relative Price Inelasticity

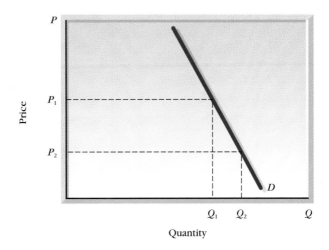

If the slope of the demand (*D*) line in Exhibit 16–5 increases, so as to make it straight up and down as in Exhibit 16–7, the line shows absolute and complete inelasticity of demand. Regardless of the price charged, be it high or low, the same quantity is demanded. No change in price will affect demand. The classic example of this phenomenon is medicine. Suppose a patient needs one dose per day of a certain drug—say, insulin—to stay alive. If the price fell, the patient would not buy more than the prescribed amount. If the price became extremely high, the same single treatment would be demanded, even if the patient had to resort to drastic measures to pay for it.

Another special case is shown in Exhibit 16–8. Here, the demand curve is perpendicular to the price axis. In this situation, there is a single price, and various quantities are demanded at that one price. Sometimes no goods may be demanded; sometimes many units of goods may be demanded. Whereas the vertical curve shows absolute price inelasticity, the horizontal line demonstrates total price elasticity—no change in price is needed to increase or decrease quantities demanded. The classic example of this situation involves the wheat farmer, who grows a prod-

EXHIBIT 16–6
Demand Curve Showing
Relative Price Elasticity

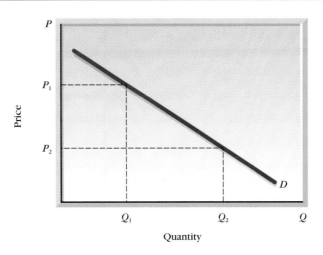

EXHIBIT 16–7
Demand Curve Showing
Total Price Inelasticity

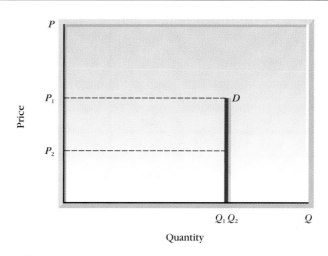

EXHIBIT 16–7
Demand Curve Showing
Total Price Inelasticity

uct that is nearly identical to that of all competitors and who is unable to influence market price. Such a farmer can only earn the going price and sell as much wheat as he chooses at that price.

The demand schedules for most products lie somewhere between the extremes of total price inelasticity and total price elasticity. It is the often-difficult task of the marketer to determine the nature of the demand curve for each product offered to the market. Information published by trade associations and information from other sources should assist in this chore. Experimentation with different price levels may also provide insights. Marketers experiment in this way every day. When items don't sell at one price, they charge a different price or offer a discount. They move, either consciously or unconsciously, to a new point on the demand schedule.

Cross-Elasticity
Elasticity in the demand for one product in relation to the prices of substitutable or complementary products.

Cross-Elasticity of Demand

One other aspect of elasticity of demand should be mentioned here. Many products depend partially on cross-elasticity for their sales. **Cross-elasticity** describes

EXHIBIT 16–8
Demand Curve Showing
Total Price Elasticity

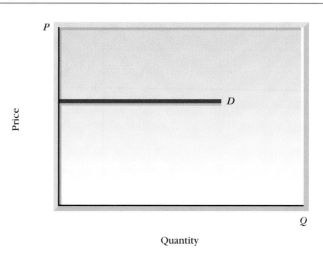

how demand for one product responds to changes in the price of another product. The demand for laser printers, for example, is closely related to the demand for personal computers—they are complementary products; they go together. Conversely, if the price of beef rises sharply, thereby reducing the demand for beef, the demand for lower-priced meat or for fish might increase. Effective marketers thus study not only their own product's demand schedule but also the demand schedules of substitute and complementary products.

KNOW YOUR COSTS

Pricing methods based only on the seller's costs fail to include the all-important buyer in the pricing effort. Nevertheless, the seller's costs are a major area of concern. Although some products may occasionally be sold at a loss, cost must be recouped sooner or later. Cost thus provides the "floor" on which to build a pricing strategy.

Marginal Analysis
Method for determining the costs and revenues associated with the production and sale of each additional unit of a product.

Marketers often use **marginal analysis** in examining costs. This measure allows them to determine the costs and revenues connected with the production and sale of each *additional* unit of a product. The concept of marginal analysis can be demonstrated by example: If only one unit of a product or service is produced, all the costs of production and marketing must be assigned to that single unit. Thus, the cost associated with the very first brake repair job performed by a Brakeman franchise would be immense. All the fixed costs (that is, the expenses associated with entering the business) would have to be covered by that first repair job. However, each *additional* brake repair would take over some portion of these costs. When there were many brake repair jobs, only a small portion of the fixed cost would have to be allocated to each one.

Marginal Cost
The net addition to a firm's total costs that results from the production of one additional unit of product.

The costs and revenues associated with the production of "one more unit" of a product are the marginal costs and marginal revenues. **Marginal cost** is the net addition to total costs created by the production of one more unit of a product. **Marginal revenue** is the net addition to the total revenue of the firm from the sale of one more unit of a product. The idea that these combine to create a point of maximum profitability for a firm is the basis of marginal analysis. As shown in Exhibit 16–9, that point is where marginal cost equals marginal revenue.

Marginal Revenue
The net addition to a firm's total revenue that results from the sale of one additional unit of product.

Average Cost
Total costs divided by the number of units produced.

Move a pencil point along the horizontal, or quantity, axis of Exhibit 16–9 and note the behavior of the variables shown. Begin by looking at **average cost,** which represents the total costs divided by the number of units produced. Moving from

---

EXHIBIT 16–9
Behaviors of Costs and
Revenues as Demand and
Quantity Produced Increase

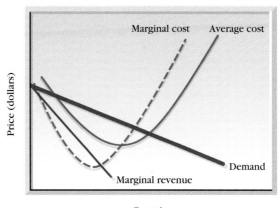

EXHIBIT 16–10
Intersection of Marginal Cost and Marginal Revenue Curves

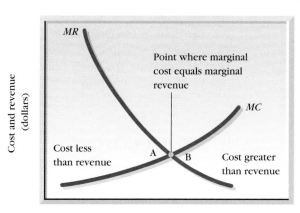

the extreme left, where the quantity produced and sold is zero, the average cost at first declines as quantity increases, because the cost of the first unit produced is far greater than the cost of the thousandth. The marginal cost also at first declines as we move along the quantity axis. In the case of the Brakeman franchise, this is because the same garage, using the same equipment and instruments, is handling an increasing number of cars. The marginal revenue declines because the revenue generated from each additional sale is an increasingly smaller portion of Brakeman's total income. The two cost curves eventually move upward because, after a certain level of output has been reached, production inefficiencies, such as overcrowding in the workplace, cause cost per unit to rise.

The important point is that profit is maximized where marginal cost equals marginal revenue (MC = MR). Consider Exhibit 16–10, which shows only these two variables. Suppose a seller of a good or service discovered that the cost of producing one more unit was less than the revenue to be realized by producing that unit (in other words, suppose the firm was at point *A*). Management would logically decide to produce and sell that additional unit. That is, there would still be some profit to be made, because the cost would be less than the revenue to be gained. However, if management discovered its operation to be at point *B*, where costs per unit are greater than revenue, it would realize that the "one more unit" would cost more than it would bring in—that a loss would be taken on that unit. The sensible thing to do would be to cut back—not to point *A*, where the cost is still less than the revenue to be made, but to the point where cost and revenue levels come together—that is, where *MC = MR*.

SUMMARY

Marketing involves the exchange of something of value. Value is generally represented by price. Price plays an important role in the marketing mix and in the attainment of marketing objectives.

Learning Objective 1
Define price and discuss it.
Price represents value, which is the power of one

product to attract another in an exchange. Price enables buyers and sellers to express the value of the products they have to offer.

Learning Objective 2
Tell how price interacts with the rest of the marketing mix.
In an effective marketing mix, product, distribution,

promotion, and price decisions must be consistent with and supported by one another. For example, high price is consistent with high product quality, an image-oriented promotion, and exclusive distribution in prestigious stores.

Learning Objective 3
Analyze the role of price in our economy.
Price plays a major role in the allocation of goods and services in market economies. In addition, price may encourage or discourage demand; it often gives products a symbolic value that can easily be perceived by buyers; it helps achieve financial or market-share objectives; and it can be used in a rapid-response adjustment to environmental changes.

Learning Objective 4
Outline the fundamentals of pricing strategy.
In setting prices, it is important to: (1) determine your pricing objectives, (2) know the importance of price to your target market, (3) know your demand, (4) understand your costs, and (5) determine your pricing strategy.

Learning Objective 5
Characterize the relationship between price and organizational objectives.
Organizational objectives are the basis for pricing strategies and are achieved partially as a result of those strategies. Price affects income generation, sales, competitive moves, and attainment of social objectives.

Learning Objective 6
Relate the demand in a target market to the prices charged.
The price of a product must suit the target market. For example, the decision to target potential buyers of extremely expensive jewelry means that the prices charged can be high if they are supported by the appropriate product quality, promotion, and distribution choices.

Learning Objective 7
Understand that demand and cost considerations influence pricing.
Marketers need to know how many people will buy their product and how much it will cost to meet this demand. Cost provides the "floor" on which to build a pricing strategy. Marginal analysis is a technique that helps marketers determine the cost and revenue associated with production and sale of each additional unit of a product.

Learning Objective 8
Differentiate among price elasticity, price inelasticity, and price cross-elasticity.
Price elasticity exists when the change in quantity demanded exceeds the change in price that brought it about. Price inelasticity exists when the change in quantity demanded is smaller than the change in price. Cross-elasticity exists when price changes for one product affect demand for another, as when a rise in the price of beef contributes to an increase in the demand for fish.

KEY TERMS

Value (p. 442)	Supply curve (p. 445)	Price elasticity (p. 452)
Barter (p. 442)	Pricing objective (p. 446)	Cross-elasticity (p. 454)
List price (p. 442)	Return on investment (ROI) (p. 447)	Marginal analysis (p. 455)
Price competition (p. 443)	Turnover (p. 449)	Marginal cost (p. 455)
Nonprice competition (p. 444)	Market share (p. 449)	Marginal revenue (p. 455)
Demand curve (p. 444)	Price stabilization (p. 451)	Average cost (p. 455)

QUESTIONS FOR REVIEW AND CRITICAL THINKING

1. What are some other names given to price? Why are these names used instead of price?

2. What is the main macromarketing function of price in the economy? Differentiate between that function and the role of price as a micromarketing tool.

3. "A high price policy needs supporting policies." Explain.

4. Give examples of situations in which price might not suit other aspects of a firm's marketing plan.

5. Why does the consumer often view price as the most important part of a transaction?

6. Consumers can rent everything from houses, yachts, and luxury cars to televisions and other home appliances. What price-related advantages might renting bring to consumers? What aspects of buyer behavior are brought into play when a consumer compares renting a TV or refrigerator with buying such items?

7. Days Inn of America, a chain of 325 motels, adopted a slogan for use in its advertisements: "Inexpensive. But not cheap." What does this slogan say about Days Inn motels, their prices, and the target market Days Inn is trying to attract?

8. The price a firm charges for its goods or services often depends primarily on how the customer is expected to react to the price charged. In what situations have you, as a customer or seller, encountered this approach to pricing?

9. Differentiate among organizational objectives, marketing objectives, and pricing objectives.

10. Why must managerial judgment play a role in determining prices even though many mathematical techniques for that purpose have been developed?

11. How can target market considerations affect a firm's pricing policies?

INTERNET INSIGHTS

Exercises

1. Much pricing theory is related to economics. AmosWorld is a guide to all things economic and the home of Mr. Economy. Go to

http://amos.bus.okstate.edu/

and you find, among other things, the AmosWorld Encyclopedic Glossary. It is a searchable, cross-referenced database of economic terms. You should find it quite useful. Search for an economics term from this chapter in the AmosWorld Glossary and compare the two definitions.

Address Book

The Economist Newspaper
http://www.economist.com

The Conference Board
http://www.conference-board.com

ETHICS IN PRACTICE: TAKE A STAND

1. Some roses-only stores import roses from South America. They sell imported roses at prices much lower than domestic roses. Some domestic rose growers believe that these low prices will increase the demand for roses and make roses widely available. They fear the market will become saturated and roses will lose their image as a special flower. Some suggest the government should pass laws to restrict the importation of roses into the United States. How would you feel about this if you were an American rose grower? A retailer who imports roses from South America? A consumer who wants to buy roses for her mother's birthday?

2. Supply-and-demand theory suggests that prices should find their own level—that is, they should represent "all that the traffic will bear." Is such pricing ethical? Is it good for society?

3. "Consumers want lower prices. If the marketing concept means being oriented toward the consumer, prices should be lowered." Comment.

CASE 16-1

 Toy Scalpers

It is 8 A.M., and a Target store [in Ypsilanti, Mich.] has just opened for business. Dennis Barger, who has been waiting in the parking lot since 7:30, races in to buy a toy.

A few minutes later, he is down the road at a Wal-Mart, then on to a Kmart and two Toys 'Я' Us stores. At 10:30, a weary Mr. Barger finds a coffee shop, sits down to an iced tea, and surveys his haul: one Captain Kirk, three Guinans, two Cygors, one Hamburger Head, one Worf, one Violator—13 action figures in all, from the world of Star Trek or Spawn comic books. Total price: $55.

Mr. Barger didn't get everything he was looking for, but not to worry. "I'll sell two figures and get my money back," he says. The entire purchase, he reckons, should fetch him more than $200. Mr. Barger, 24 years old, is a toy scalper. By staying alert to the latest fads, moving fast and using special purchasing channels, he makes his living buying toys that are in short supply and then selling them at huge markups to collectors, other resellers, or parents and children who are desperate to have them.

In the toy business, where shortages are increasing, the influence of scalpers is growing. For reasons that are hotly debated, temporary unavailability of certain toys has plagued consumers ever since the big run on Mighty Morphin Power Rangers began three years ago. Parents agonized when Mattel Inc.'s Happy Holiday Barbie sold out weeks before last Christmas morning. Not long before that, stores were cleaned out of Earring Magic Ken. More recently, Mattel's Treasure Hunt cars, Toy Biz Inc.'s Xena the Warrior, and the Cal Ripken Jr. replica from Hasbro Inc.'s Starting LineUp have been scarce.

Some buyers speculate that shortages are designed by manufacturers seeking to create cachet for toys and stir consumer interest. Others say supply problems are the result of a highly unpredictable market in which toy makers aren't really sure what products will become hot. "The penalty for overproducing product in the toy industry is so huge—many toy companies have gone out of business. And because of that, manufacturers would rather deal with a shortage than overproduction," says Sean McGowan, an analyst for Gerard Klauer Mattison Co., a New York investment bank.

Toy makers say their calculations have been upset by collectors, such as the Barbie devotees who gobbled up so many Happy Holidays last Christmas. Estimates on the number of collectors vary widely, from 200,000 to three million. Judging from ads in toy-collector magazines, there is a thriving business for scalpers as well.

A Toys 'Я' Us store in New Hampshire banned a collector—for the first time—from buying any more toys there. The company says the collector had become too frequent of a customer, purchasing thousands of dollars of hot figures.

While some stores set limits on the number of certain items each customer can purchase, "it's very hard to police" scalping, says Michael Goldstein, chairman of Toys 'Я' Us Inc., the nation's largest toy retailer. "Scalpers can easily sidestep the customer limit by having relatives or friends come in to buy for them."

Toys 'Я' Us has investigated a number of deals made between its employees and scalpers, Mr. Goldstein says, leading to the dismissal of some workers.

One of the biggest current squeezes is on Hasbro's new line of Star Wars figures linked to a re-release of the space-movie trilogy. At Toys 'Я' Us stores, characters such as Obi Wan Kenobi and Princess Leia retail for $4 to $5—if you can find them. Eleven-year-old Kilian Ellison couldn't. After what he calls "an endless search for the Princess," he ran into Mr. Barger at a comic-book store, and paid $55 for one. "I get $15 for mowing people's lawns," shrugs Kilian, who lives with his mom in Ann Arbor, Michigan. "So I'll mow a few more lawns." Mr. Barger has a wide reputation—and an eclectic clientele. During the Power Ranger drought, he sold scarce versions of the drop-kicking avengers for about $120 apiece to film stars Tim Robbins and Susan Sarandon, who gave them to their children for Christmas. Specialty shops paid plenty for his Earring Magic Kens, which had become a novelty item among gays. "He's like Indiana Jones," says Rex Schroeder, owner of Total Entertainment, a comic-book and video store in Ypsilanti. "If there's a Holy Grail in toys, he'll find it." But collectors are outraged at scalpers' prices. Mr. Barger's inventory includes a hard-to-get World War II G.I. Joe for $150, a replica of Los Angeles Dodgers pitcher Hideo Nomo for $35 and a Commander Riker Star Trek doll at $225. Each has, or had, a retail price of about $5. "When will the escalation end?" asks Sean MacIntre, a Dallas collector. "His type of price inflation we see in Argentina, not America." There is nothing illegal about what Mr. Barger does, but that doesn't make kids any happier when they can't find their favorites. "The adults beat us to the store every time," says Jon Iwata, 10, combing shelves for Star Wars and Hercules figures at a Caldor store in Braintree, Massachusetts "It's like little kids racing against these big adults in a 100-yard dash or something."

Mr. Barger says he doesn't feel guilty, reasoning that he deals mostly with adult collectors and owners of small toy stores. He blames toy makers for shortages, saying they don't make enough toys to go around. He adds that he makes donations to Toys for Tots and other children's charities as a way of saying to kids: "I'm sorry for buying up all your toys."'

A stocky figure with a penchant for black T-shirts and baseball caps worn backward, Mr. Barger graduated from Eastern Michigan University earlier this month with a major in marketing. He declines to discuss his income, but says he paid for college with scalping profits. "I almost never sell my stuff for less than a 100 percent markup," he says. "What stock on any of the exchanges offers that kind of return in just a few weeks?" Industry estimates are that a good scalper can make upward of $50,000 a year. Mr. Barger's biggest concern at the moment is moving his bulging inventory—which he values at $200,000 in street prices—to a larger home.

Questions

1. How important is price in a person's decision to buy a toy? A collector's item?
2. How do the forces of supply and demand operate in the toy industry?
3. In your opinion, are toy scalpers' activities ethical? Should toy scalping be illegal?

PRICING STRATEGIES AND TACTICS

Chapter 17

Learning Objectives

After you have studied this chapter, you will be able to:

1. Identify the various pricing strategies.
2. Discuss the nature of differential pricing strategies.
3. Describe skimming and penetration pricing.
4. Show how competition affects pricing activity.
5. Discuss the effects of inflation on pricing.
6. Discuss the nature of product-line pricing strategies.
7. Explain some of the psychological aspects of price.
8. Show how geography influences pricing decisions.
9. Discuss such pricing tools as list price and cash, trade, quantity, and other discounts.
10. Describe the major legal restrictions on pricing freedom.
11. Identify a major ethical issue related to price.

EXHIBIT 17–2
Kinked Demand Curve
Facing Marketers of
Products Sold at a
Traditional Price

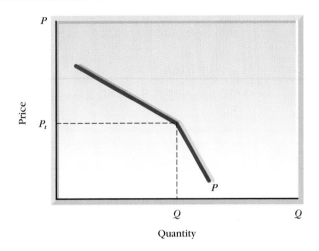

petitors. Unfortunately for Motorola, Apple, and IBM, Intel was too well established in the computer chip market to be dislodged strictly on the basis of price.

The logic of penetration pricing is that the strategy will reduce the threat of competitive imitation because the small profit margin discourages low-cost imitators from entering the market. Furthermore, by increasing the size of the total market or of its market share, the marketer establishes a strong brand loyalty and increases the brand's dominance in consumers' minds.

To restrict competitors, an organization trying to establish a monopoly might set prices low to eliminate competition and then raise prices after all competition had been eliminated. This **predatory pricing strategy** is illegal under the Sherman Antitrust Act and the Robinson-Patman Act.

Predatory Pricing Strategy
Illegal pricing strategy whereby a product is priced low to eliminate competition and then raised to a high level after competition has been eliminated.

Traditional Pricing

Certain prices are set largely by tradition rather than by individual marketers. These customary prices may remain unchanged for long periods. The ten-cent phone call, although now a thing of the distant past, was priced at the same level for decades. Today the traditional price is a quarter. Candy bars also tend to be priced at the level of coinage. As chocolate and sugar prices rose and fell, the bars got smaller or larger, but the price (at a nickle, dime, quarter, etc.) remained the same. It was only when the candy bar had diminished to near invisibility that manufacturers broke with tradition and raised the price. Until that time, only a few bars were priced higher than the traditional price, and these were bigger than the others or of better quality and were heavily promoted.

Exhibit 17–2 portrays the demand situation faced by firms in industries where prices have become established at particular levels. Should a company attempt to raise prices above the traditional level, the result will be considerably decreased sales. On the other hand, notice that a reduction of price will not produce sales increases that justify the price cut.

Demand is thus elastic above the traditional price (P_t) but inelastic below it. The resulting curve is "kinked." When this condition exists, it is because consumers' beliefs and habits are so ingrained that price reductions are attributed to some negative change, such as a perceived lowering of quality, rather than to competitive market pressures.

The kinked demand curve also characterizes oligopolistic markets in which a small number of marketers must price at traditional market levels to maximize profits. Oligopolists, which are highly sensitive to competitive price shifts, generally respond in kind to price reductions. Thus, there is no advantage in price reductions; they will only lead to a lower market price adhered to by all of the oligopolists.

Inflationary Pricing

Executives focus increased attention on pricing strategies when inflation rates are high. During periods of inflation, buying power declines for consumers as well as for many organizational buyers, and most buyers become more price conscious and sensitive to price changes. Heightened price awareness increases price competition. Products may be altered to permit the offering of lower-priced alternatives. For example, during an inflationary period, an airline may cut some of the "free" frills and extra services rather than increase price.

Organizations may react to inflation by changing the size or amount of the product sold. When the candy bar manufacturers raised prices and enlarged bar size, perceived value was enhanced even though price per ounce increased. Alternatively, distribution systems may be tightened in an effort to hold costs down. Advertising and personal selling messages can stress lower prices and better values when customers are known to be especially sensitive to price.

To make sure its brands offer value, Gillette's pricing is based on a market-basket approach. Marketing managers keep daily track of a collection of lowly items, including a newspaper, a candy bar, a can of Coke, all priced under a dollar. And then it never raises its prices at a faster rate than the price of the market basket. The company does not believe in an "all that traffic will bear" strategy. Gillette believes consumers have a relative-value consciousness. If the prices of certain goods get out of whack, consumers feel as if they are being ripped off.[3]

 ## PRODUCT-LINE PRICING STRATEGIES

Many pricing strategists consider the product line, rather than individual product items, to be the appropriate unit of analysis. The objective of product-line pricing is to maximize profits for the total product line rather than to obtain the greatest profits for any individual item in the line. Marketers who do this are said to focus on *total-profit pricing* rather than *item-profit pricing*.

Captive Pricing

Captive Pricing Strategy
Strategy whereby a basic product, such as a razor, is priced low but the profits from associated products needed for operating the basic product, such as razor blades, make up for the lack of profit on the basic product.

A camera manufacturer may set low prices on cameras in the hope of making significant profits on film. Firms such as Schick and Gillette sell their razors at low prices to encourage long-term purchase of blades that fit the razors. In a **captive pricing strategy,** the basic product is priced low, often below cost, but the high markup on supplies required to operate the basic product makes up for that low price.

Leader Pricing and Bait Pricing

Loss Leader
A product priced below cost to attract consumers, who may then make additional purchases.

A common pricing strategy that sacrifices item profit for total profit is *leader pricing*. Most consumers are familiar with the concept of the **loss leader,** the product that the seller prices at a loss so as to attract customers, who may then buy other goods or services from the seller. Consumers are perhaps less aware of similar strategies involving cost leaders and low-profit leaders. Here again, products are priced to attract bargain-hunting customers, who may make additional purchases. The leader items, however, are sold not at a loss but at the seller's cost (the cost leader) or at a very small profit (the low-profit leader). Such pricing strategies can be quite effective. For example, when Target discount stores priced selected popular video games at two-thirds the regular price, they tripled store traffic. Goods so priced are usually familiar, frequently purchased items that customers will be able to recognize as bargains. Reduced prices on caviar and goat meat would not accomplish the same objective.

Bait Pricing
A method of attracting customers by offering low-priced items for sale with the intention of selling more expensive goods.

Bait pricing involves attracting customers by advertising low-priced models of, for example, televisions. Although the bait item is available for sale in sufficient quantity, the marketer's expectation is to trade the customer up to a higher-margin model that is also available for sale. This strategy may be an effective means to sell higher-margin items.

The term *bait and switch,* however, is used when the merchant has no intention of selling the bait merchandise but only intends to lure the customer in to buy more expensive goods. In fact, the item used in the bait-and-switch scheme is sometimes referred to as the "nailed-down model," so unlikely is it that it will be sold. Bait and switch has an unsavory reputation and is often the target of attention from the Federal Trade Commission.

Pricing Lining

Price-Lining Strategy
Strategy whereby a seller prices products in a product line in accordance with certain "price points" believed to be attractive to buyers.

A marketer using a **price-lining strategy** prices the products in a product line according to a number of "price points." Price points are simply specific prices. A marketer selling a full product line establishes certain price points to differentiate the items in the line.

FOCUS ON QUALITY

Parker Pen

It would be tough to outflank Parker Pen in the arena of high-low marketing. On the low end, the Gillette Stationery Products subsidiary markets the refillable Jotter Ball Pen for $4.99. On the high end, Parker offers the Limited Edition Gold Snake Fountain Pen, yours for a mere $12,000. The Parker brand, by price, can quite obviously mean greatly different things to different scribblers.

But if Parker has the high and the low down pat, other price points in between have proven more problematic. It needed more of a compelling draw into the crucial $10–$40 range—a necessary next step in keeping the discerning pen-user in the brand franchise. Parker didn't just revise its existing product in the tier, the slim-barreled Classic, it launched a whole new subbrand, the Frontier Collection, a line of eight basic wide-barreled pens ranging in price from the $12.50 translucent ball pen to the $32.50 two-tone fountain pen with gift box. Initially, Parker expected to sell 250,000 units in 1996, but the brand more than doubled that projection, selling 580,000 pens throughout the gift-giving season. In 1997, the company will sell more than 1 million Frontier units, according to company estimates.

"The Frontier has helped bridge the gap between [Parker's] commodity pens and the high priced models," said Robert George, a merchandise buyer at office superstore Staples. "It's been a great seller for us."

Parker, in conjunction with British design firm Hollington Associates, constructed the new line to satisfy a variety of tastes and budgets while capitalizing on the "corporate casual" theme that's becoming increasingly popular in U.S. workplaces. The unifying brand strategy is to encourage consumers to trade up to higher price points, a classic Gillette strategy. The less expensive translucent models are generally sold on a counter display rack, while the more expensive two-tones are merchandised under glass. The line and in fact its breadth has become the bridge by which Parker hopes to usher consumers eventually to the next level of the brand, the Insignia Custom pen, a line that runs $40–$70, a point at which a writing instrument becomes, truly, an accoutrement of lifestyle, and the brand becomes a badge. Parker Pen's product line strategy is designed to keep customers for life.

Many retailers, especially clothing retailers, practice price lining. A dress store ordinarily does not stock dresses from $300 to $55, pricing them at $299.99, $299.87, $299.76, and so on, down to $55. Instead, the prices offered are, for example $299, $249, $199, and the like. These prices are believed by the store owner to be "strong price points," or prices that are greatly attractive to buyers. The assumption is that a good number of dresses will be sold at $249 but that, if the price is lowered, not many more will be sold until the price reaches the next strong price point, $199. Similarly, if the price is raised from $249, there will be a rapid drop in sales until the next strong price point is reached.

Price lining simplifies consumers' buying decisions. Shoppers can first select a price point and then choose from the assortment in the price line based on color, style, or other product characteristics. It also simplifies the retailer's decisions about what specific prices should be selected.

Price Bundling and Multiple-Unit Pricing

Price-Bundling Strategy
Strategy whereby the price of a set of products is lower than the total of the individual prices of the components would be. An example is a new car with an "options package."

Choosing a car with an "options package" is a reaction to a **price-bundling strategy.** The set of products sold as a bundle is offered at a price lower than the total of the individually priced items. The bargain price for the "extras" provides an incentive for the consumer.

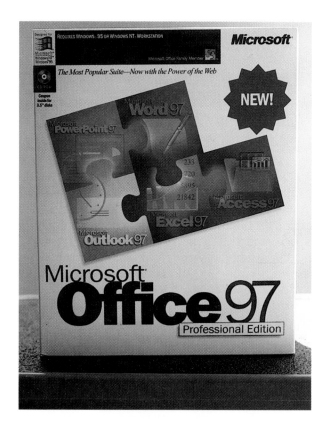

Microsoft Corporation pairs a price-bundling strategy with a product strategy in its Microsoft Office 97 software suite. Suites are bundles of applications— for example, spreadsheets, word processing programs, and graphics programs— sold together for a fraction of what they would cost if separately purchased. Microsoft Office 97 combines Microsoft Word, Microsoft Excel, Microsoft Power-point, Microsoft Access, and Microsoft Explorer.

The marketer benefits by increasing total revenues and, in many instances, reducing manufacturing costs. Inventory costs may also be reduced when marketers bundle slow-selling items with popular items to deplete inventory.

Multiple-Unit Pricing
Selling more than one unit of a product at a price lower than the sum of the individual units' prices, as in a four-for-the-price-of-three sale.

Price bundling differs from **multiple-unit pricing** (as in a two-for-one sale) and quantity discounts in that "enhanced" products or complementary products are sold rather than increased quantities of a particular product.

Multiple-unit pricing, in addition to attracting new customers through lower prices, may increase overall consumption of the product. Consumers who bring home two six-packs rather than a single six-pack may increase consumption, for example. The major disadvantage of multiple-unit pricing is that regular customers may stock up and store the product in their pantries, postponing future purchases until other "specials" appear.

 # PSYCHOLOGICAL AND IMAGE PRICING STRATEGIES

A price, like any other stimulus, may be selectively perceived by consumers. Consumers may infer something about a brand's value or image from its price. When brands are chosen by the message their prices send to consumers, a psychological or image pricing strategy has been chosen.

Reference Pricing

Reference Pricing Strategy
Strategy whereby a moderate price is set for a version of a product that will be displayed next to a higher-priced model of the same brand or next to a competitive brand.

Isolation Effect
An effect by which a product appears more attractive next to a higher-priced alternative than in isolation.

Retailers often use a **reference pricing strategy,** in which a moderate price is chosen for a version of a product that will be displayed next to a higher-priced model of the same brand or a competitive brand. This strategy is based on the **isolation effect,** which suggests that a choice looks more attractive next to a high-priced alternative than it does in isolation. Reference pricing is also used by catalog retailers such as Service Merchandise to convey the idea that they offer bargain prices. The catalog may show "reference price," "store price," and sometimes "sale price."

Odd versus Even Pricing

One seldom sees consumer packaged goods priced at $2.00, $5.00, or $10.00. Instead, they are normally priced at odd amounts such as $1.87, $4.98, and $9.99. Odd prices have, in fact, become traditional.

The logic that led to the use of odd prices is based on the belief that, for example, a price of $1.95 is seen by consumers as only a dollar plus some small change. Advocates of odd pricing assume that more sales will be made at certain prices than would have been made at prices just one or two cents higher. However, the published research findings in this area are inconclusive about the benefits of odd pricing. There are those who suggest that a price of $1.98 is seen as $2.00 and that deeper cuts—say, to $1.75—are necessary to achieve the intended psychological effect. The practice of odd pricing does have a practical purpose. It forces clerks to use the cash register to make change, thus creating a record of the sale and discouraging employee dishonesty.

Even prices are often used to good effect by the marketers of services and high-quality merchandise. A physician charges $175 for your annual check-up. A sapphire ring costs $1,000. Even prices are said to be most effective when the objective is to create an image of high quality or to position the product to upscale consumers.

Prestige Pricing

Prestige Price
A high price meant to convey an impression of high quality.

For many products, consumers use price to infer quality, especially when it is difficult to determine quality by inspection. Certain products are demanded in part because of their high prices. Perfumes, furs, and gems are among them. These products are high-status goods, and marketers often charge a high **prestige price** for them to portray an image of high quality.

FOCUS ON GLOBAL COMPETITION

Levi's

In the United States, Levi's 501 jeans sell for about $35 a pair. In foreign markets, a pair of Levi's is a status symbol, so Levi's uses prestige prices. In Tokyo, for example, a pair of 501 blues costs more than $60. In Paris, the price is about $90. Levi's is a savvy global competitor that has profit-oriented objectives for each international market it serves.

DISTRIBUTION-BASED PRICING STRATEGIES AND TACTICS

Many prices are based on the geographic distance separating the buyer from the point of sale or the point of production. The prices are not always higher as the buyer gets farther from the seller. However, in most cases, geographic pricing policies reflect management's attempt to recover some or all of the product shipping costs.

F.O.B.

F.O.B.
"Freight on board" or "Free on board"; together with further information, a term that identifies the point at which title passes from seller to buyer. For example, "F.O.B. factory" means that the buyer takes title at the factory and is responsible for all shipping charges.

A common form of geographic pricing is **F.O.B.,** which may be read as "freight on board" or "free on board." The letters never stand alone but are always followed by the name of a specific place, such as "F.O.B. factory" or "F.O.B. Baltimore." This place name tells the buyer the point to which the seller will be responsible for shipping. At that point, the buyer takes title to the goods and becomes responsible for shipping charges. A consumer in Kansas City might buy a Swedish auto "F.O.B. New York." This means that the price quoted includes shipment to New York. All other transportation costs will be extra.

Delivered Pricing

Delivered Pricing
Pricing that includes delivery within a specified area. Also called freight-allowed *pricing.*

When a department store advertises that the price of a sofa is "$1,500 delivered in our area," that store is practicing **delivered pricing,** or **freight-allowed pricing.** The delivery charges are built into the price paid by the consumer. Occasionally, ill will may develop when customers located just beyond the delivery zone lines must be charged a price higher than the advertised price.

Zone Pricing
Type of delivered pricing in which prices vary according to the number of geographic zones through which a product passes in moving from seller to buyer.

A variation on delivered pricing is **zone pricing,** whereby geographic zones are delineated and prices increase as the number of zone lines crossed in completion of the transaction accumulate. The parcel post system employs zone pricing, charging a customer mailing a package a rate that depends on the weight of the parcel and the number of zones it will travel through before arriving at its destination. "Slightly higher in Canada" is a phrase that reflects a zone pricing policy.

Uniform Delivered Pricing
Type of delivered pricing in which an organization charges the same price for a given product in all locations.

A company that views the entire country as its delivery zone, and charges the same prices in every location, is practicing a special form of delivered pricing called **uniform delivered pricing.** When you buy through a catalog, such as Land's End, you pay a postage-and-handling fee subject to uniform delivered pricing. Such prices are attractive to marketers because they simplify pricing and nationwide advertising.

EXHIBIT 17–3
Basing-Point Pricing

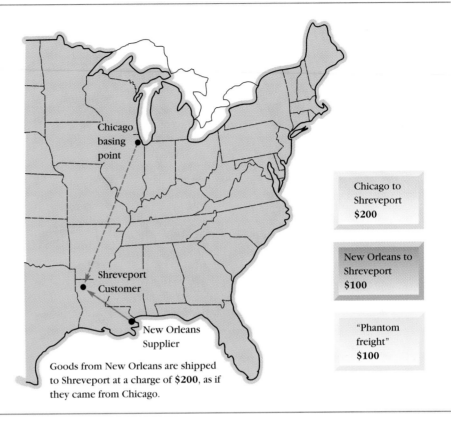

Chicago basing point

Chicago to Shreveport $200

New Orleans to Shreveport $100

"Phantom freight" $100

Shreveport Customer

New Orleans Supplier

Goods from New Orleans are shipped to Shreveport at a charge of **$200**, as if they came from Chicago.

Basing-Point Pricing

Another distribution-based pricing system involves the selection of one or more locations to serve as *basing points.* Customers are charged prices and shipping fees as if their orders were shipped from these points regardless of where the merchandise actually originates. For example, consider the situation shown in Exhibit 17–3. A buyer in Shreveport makes a purchase from a supplier in New Orleans. The goods are in fact shipped from New Orleans. However, Chicago has been specified as the basing point, so the buyer is charged as if the goods came from Chicago. The true shipping charge is $100, but the buyer must pay $200. The seller is able to pocket the extra $100 (known as phantom freight) because of this **basing-point pricing.**

Basing-Point Pricing

Charging for shipping from a specified basing point, or location, no matter where the shipment actually originates.

Because this system rarely is in the buyer's best interest, and because it smacks of collusion on the part of suppliers, it has been the subject of court cases for more than 70 years. Although Supreme Court rulings made in the 1940s forbid industrywide pricing systems that include phantom freight, cases involving basing-point pricing still are encountered.

ADDITIONAL PRICING STRATEGIES AND TACTICS

Pricing strategies represent logical responses to individual marketing situations. Because of this, a great number of pricing strategies and tactics can be identified. Here are some of the wide choices available to marketers in addition to those already discussed.

Many professionals, such as doctors and lawyers, often price their services at a figure that suggests they are committed fully to a client's case and therefore will

Pharmaceutical drugs are often based on ethical pricing strategies. The forces of supply and demand are ignored for humanitarian reasons.

present a bill that is free of itemized, penny-counting entries. Thus, the professional charges $2,000 for a gall bladder operation or $700 for a quick divorce. Such prices are called *professional prices* or *gentleman's prices.*

Another pricing tactic is the so-called *ethical price.* Supposedly, ethical prices are lower than what could have been charged. The marketer has chosen the lower prices for ethical or humanitarian reasons. Drug companies claim that they set the price of insulin at a reasonable level, even though more could be charged, because it is the right thing to do.

 ## ESTABLISHING THE EXACT PRICE

Marketers use many methods to assign specific prices to the products they sell. Here, we discuss the determination of several types of calculations: the markup on selling price or cost, the cost-plus and average-cost methods, target return pricing, and break-even analysis. (Also see Appendix C.)

Markup on Selling Price and Markup on Cost

Many marketers, especially retailers and wholesalers, rely on a comparatively uncomplicated method for determining their resale prices: The cost of the product is noted and a simple percentage markup is added to reach the selling price.

When a markup is expressed as a percentage of the selling price, it is called a **markup on selling price.** For example, a cost of $1.00 and a selling price of $1.50 means a markup on selling price of 33.3 percent. The 50-cent markup is 33.3 percent, or one-third, of the selling price of $1.50. When only the term markup is used, it refers to markup on selling price. However, in many industries, pricing focuses on costs.

Consider an example comparing a focus on selling price with a focus on cost. An item costs a retailer $50, and the retailer sells it for $100. Using a markup on

Markup on Selling Price
Markup expressed as a percentage of the selling price of an item.

selling price, we calculate the markup by dividing the amount added to the cost of the product by the selling price of the product:

$$\frac{\$50 \text{ added on}}{\$100 \text{ (selling price)}} = 50 \text{ percent}$$

Markup on Cost
Markup expressed as a percentage of the cost of an item.

In contrast, we calculate the **markup on cost** by dividing the amount added to the cost of the product by the cost:

$$\frac{\$50 \text{ added on}}{\$50 \text{ (cost)}} = 100 \text{ percent}$$

As you can see, using a markup based on cost makes it appear that the marketer's markup is higher (100 percent versus 50 percent here), even though the dollar figures are the same. Distinguishing between markup on selling price and markup on cost is important. Users of the markup method almost always use the selling price rather than the cost of the product in figuring the markup percentage. The reason is that many important figures in financial reports, such as gross sales, revenues, and so on, are sales figures, not cost figures.

The effective use of markup based on cost or selling price requires that the marketing manager calculate an adequate margin—the amount added to cost to determine price. The margin must ultimately provide adequate funds to cover selling expenses and profit. Once this is done, the markup technique has the major advantage of being easy to employ.

As Exhibit 17–4 shows, a series of markups is used as products move through channels of distribution. Certain industries have established traditional markups for the various channel members. The ultimate markup, that of the retailer, results in the price paid by the consumer.

The Cost-Plus Method

Manufacturers often use a pricing method, similar to markup, in which they determine what costs were involved in producing an item and then add an amount to the cost total to arrive at a price. Like markup, this cost-plus method is easy to use once an appropriate addition to the cost has been determined. Much government contracting is done on this basis, with the supplier of a good or service submitting the cost figures associated with a particular project and adding a reasonable profit margin to yield a total price for the project.

The Average-Cost Method

Identifying all the costs associated with the manufacturing and marketing of a good or the provision of a service should make it possible to determine what the average cost of a single unit of the good or service might be. Consider an example.

EXHIBIT 17–4
Markup through a Channel of Distribution

NOTE: At each step, markup is expressed as a percent of the selling price.

Manufacturer		Wholesaler		Retailer	
Cost	$20.00	Cost	$25.00	Cost	$29.41
20% Markup	$ 5.00	15% Markup	$ 4.41	41% Markup	$20.59
Selling price	$25.00	Selling price	$29.41	Selling price	$50.00

$$\frac{\text{All costs (\$80,000)}}{\text{Number of units produced (100)}} = \text{Average cost of a single unit}$$

$$= \$800$$

(Note that to do this, it is necessary to predict how much of the product will be demanded and produced.) Adding a margin for profit to the total cost figures allows calculation of a likely price for a unit of product.

$$\text{All costs (\$80,000)} + \text{Margin for profit (\$20,000)} = \$100,000$$

$$\frac{\$100,000}{100 \text{ units}} = \text{Average cost of a single unit including the profit margin}$$

$$= \$1,000$$

While the average cost method can suggest a price, there is a serious risk that the quantity demanded by the market might not match the predictions of the marketing manager. If in our example only 50 units were demanded at the price of $1,000, the firm's revenue would be only $50,000, while the costs of production and marketing would remain at $80,000. This demonstrates that it is extremely risky to base pricing decisions on costs alone. The market—the demand generated by customers—must be carefully considered in any calculation of price. Changes in demand can turn profit into loss.

Target Return Pricing

Total Cost
Fixed costs plus variable costs.

Fixed Cost
Cost that is a function of time and not of volume of production or sales.

Variable Cost
Cost that varies directly with an organization's production or sales. Variable costs are a function of volume.

Target Return Pricing
Setting prices to yield a particular target level of profit for the organization.

You probably remember from your accounting class that **total costs** are the sum of fixed and variable costs. **Fixed costs** are incurred with the passage of time regardless of volume. **Variable costs** fluctuate with some measure of volume. These costs are used in calculating a target return price.

A marketing manager using **target return pricing** first calculates a total fixed cost figure. This figure includes such items as executive salaries, rents, and other expenses that must be paid even when no units of a product are being produced. A target return, usually represented as a percentage of investment, is added to total cost to yield a figure representing total fixed costs and target return. To illustrate, assume a fixed cost of $400,000 and a target return of $100,000, for a total of $500,000.

Now the marketer must estimate demand. For an estimated demand of 1,000 units, given a total of fixed costs and target return of $500,000, each unit produced would cost $500 in fixed cost and target return.

$$\frac{\text{Fixed costs} + \text{Target return}}{\text{Units to be sold}} = \frac{\$500,000}{1,000} = \$500 \text{ per unit}$$

But production and sale of each unit involves variable costs as well. Suppose these costs are calculated to be $75 per unit. This figure is added to the already determined cost per unit of $500 to indicate that the price per unit should be $575.

$$\begin{array}{ccc}\text{Fixed costs and target return} & + & \text{Variable costs} \\ \text{per unit (\$500)} & & \text{per unit (\$75)}\end{array} = \begin{array}{c}\text{Suggested price} \\ \text{per unit (\$575)}\end{array}$$

As in the case of the average-cost method of pricing, a miscalculation of the demand for the product can be disastrous. If the firm's customers demanded only 500 units of the product, not the expected 1,000, the carefully calculated price of $575 would lead to a loss.[4]

EXHIBIT 17–5
Costs, Revenues, and the
Break-Even Point

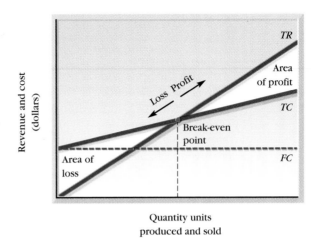

Break-Even Analysis

As we have seen, all marketers, whether of consumer goods, organizational goods, or services, face costs that must somehow be recovered. These include fixed costs and variable costs. Variable costs would be zero if no products were produced and marketed, but fixed costs would remain at their established level even if production and sales were zero.

Exhibit 17–5 portrays fixed costs as the horizontal line *FC*. Variable costs added to fixed costs give the total cost figures showed by the line marked *TC*. This curve rises to the right because total costs should increase as production and sales increase.

With regard to revenue, the hope is that each additional unit of goods manufactured and sold or each additional service performed and paid for will raise the firm's total revenue (total revenue equals price per unit times units sold). This is shown in Exhibit 17–5 by the total revenue curve labeled *TR*. Obviously, it is hoped that total revenue will exceed total costs, resulting in a profit. If total costs exceed total revenue, the result is a loss.

At the start of operations, zero units are being produced, and total revenue is zero because no sales are being made. However, fixed costs such as rent already are being incurred. Therefore, the company is suffering a loss at this point. If all goes well, however, and sales rise, revenue will also rise. Revenue will continue to rise, if the firm is successful, until it meets and exceeds the costs associated with production and marketing. Now, with revenue greater than costs, a profit is being made. The point at which costs and revenue meet is called, logically, the **break-even point.** At this point, the money coming in is equal to the money going out. (Appendix C, Marketing Arithmetic for Business Analysis, describes a formula for calculating the break-even point.)

Break-Even Point
Point at which an organization's revenues and costs are equal.

Price and Break-Even Analysis

Price plays an important role in break-even analysis. For example, raising the price of the product may enhance revenue, allowing revenue to catch up to cost more quickly, while lowering the price may have the opposite effect. It might also be demonstrated that a cost-control program would increase profit by lowering the total cost curve. In any case, every organization has a break-even point. If that point is achieved and surpassed, the organization makes a profit. Price has an impact that determines when the break-even point is met. The concept, though simple, is important.

Demand and Break-Even Analysis

Break-even analysis should deal with demand as well as cost. As price changes, the quantity demanded will change. It might be expected that a rise in price will lead to fewer sales and a drop in price will generate more sales. The marketing manager's problem in employing break-even analysis is to determine just what effect a change in price will actually have on demand. Simple manipulation of cost and revenue figures is not enough, nor are graphs (such as the one in Exhibit 17–5) that seem to portray ever-increasing profits as more and more units are sold. There is no built-in reason to assume that the product is going to sell at either a higher price or a lower price. An effective marketer, aware of the changes and uncertainties operating in the marketplace, knows that raising prices will not necessarily increase revenues and lower the break-even point.

In short, determining a break-even point is only the beginning. The analysis may be of most use in conducting preliminary studies to eliminate certain extreme pricing situations. For example, a restaurant might be so poorly run that its costs necessitate menu prices that start at $10 for a hot dog—a price at which few are likely to be sold. Break-even points are also of use in evaluating alternative pricing strategies. But the underlying problem of estimating demand remains no matter how carefully costs and revenues are portrayed on a graph. Thus, break-even analysis must be used with the customer in mind.

PRICE ADJUSTMENTS

Recall that the list price is the basic, "official" price of a product. In many industries, it is common for list prices to be adjusted with rebates or discounts.

Rebates reduce the list price by giving back to the consumer part of the amount paid. Rebates generally are reimbursements from the manufacturer rather than the retailer. A rebate policy, by passing savings on directly to the consumer, assures that the consumer, and not the retailer, will benefit from the price adjustment.

Discount
A reduction from list price or a reimbursement for performance of a specific task.

The most common price adjustments are **discounts,** reductions from the list price or reimbursements for performing a specific action, such as maintaining a sales force or carrying inventory. Common discount schemes are discussed briefly below. Notice that each discounting technique provides an incentive to potential buyers but also yields some advantage, such as speedier payment of bills, to sellers.

Cash Discounts

Cash Discount
Price discount that offers lower prices for early payment of bills.

Cash discounts may take the form of the common 2/10, net 30, payment scheme, which indicates that payment made within 10 days of the date on the invoice will be discounted 2 percent and that full payment, with no discount, must be made within 30 days. The amount of discount, the time allowed, and when the counting of days begins vary from industry to industry. The discount offered usually is large enough that it is worthwhile for the buyer to borrow from a bank to pay what is owed to the supplier. An **anticipation discount,** an additional discount to encourage even faster payment, may also be offered. The purpose of each form of cash discount is to encourage prompt payment of bills. All forms of cash discounts are legal if offered equally to all similar buyers.

Anticipation Discount
Discount over and above the regular cash discount, meant to encourage even faster payment.

Trade Discounts

Trade Discount

Discount given to whole-salers, retail dealers, or others in a particular trade as a repayment for the performance of certain functions; also called a functional discount.

Trade discounts are discounts given to members of the trade. Electricians receive discounts on wire and tape because they are in the electrical trade. Electrical distributors (wholesalers) get even larger discounts, because they must make a profit on the products they sell to electricians. Because the recipient of the discount is performing a function, such as holding an inventory of electrical parts, these discounts are also called *functional discounts*.

The types and sizes of discounts for wholesalers, retailers, or other tradespeople vary considerably by industry. Generally, the discount rate, which reflects the intermediary's percentage margin on the goods sold, increases as the intermediary's role in marketing to the customer increases. Thus, discounts are higher in the furniture industry than in the grocery industry.

Quantity Discounts

Noncumulative Quantity Discount

Price discount determined by the size of an individual purchase order. The larger the order, the larger the discount.

Cumulative Quantity Discount

Price discount determined by the amount purchased over some specified time period.

Seasonal Discount

Price discount intended to encourage purchase of products during a time of year when sales are traditionally low.

There are two types of quantity discounts, noncumulative and cumulative. In the case of **noncumulative quantity discounts,** each order is treated separately. The buyer's discount is calculated in terms of size of that single purchase, without consideration of past purchases or planned purchases. Obviously, the purpose of this discount is to encourage large orders.[5]

Cumulative quantity discounts, on the other hand, allow the buyer an ever-increasing discount with each purchase made over some period of time—say, a year. The more the buyer orders, the greater the discount becomes. The intent of the cumulative quantity discount is to keep the customer coming back. Stated another way, the supplier's aim is to build a relationship and to tie the buyer to the seller.

Seasonal Discounts

As one would guess, the **seasonal discount** is intended to help level out the marketing workload by encouraging buyers to make purchases and take delivery of

After December 25th, there is not much demand for Christmas decorations. Holiday products are subject to seasonal discounts.

out-of-season merchandise. Products such as bathing suits, winter clothing, paint, and lawn furniture are obvious candidates for seasonal discounting at various times during the year.

Chain Discounts

In many purchasing situations, a buyer qualifies for a series of discounts. A wholesale buyer quoted terms of 40/10/5, net 30, realizes that he or she will receive a series of discounts if all the appropriate options are utilized. For example, for a machine with a list price of $995, the chain discount mentioned above is calculated as follows:

List price	$995.00
Less trade discount (40 percent of $995)	−398.00
Balance	$597.00
Less seasonal discount (10 percent of $597)	− 59.70
Balance	$537.30
Less cash discount (5 percent of $537.30)	− 26.86
Price wholesaler pays	$510.44

Promotional Allowances

A manufacturer may partially reimburse wholesalers or retailers for promotional assistance at the local level. These reimbursements may be cash or merchandise, with the value commonly restricted to a percentage of sales or a discount off the list price. A summary of the various discounts and allowances is given in Exhibit 17–6.

EXHIBIT 17–6
Discounts and Objectives

DISCOUNT	OBJECTIVE
Cash discount	To encourage customers to pay their bills within a given period of time, such as 10 days
Anticipation discount	To encourage even faster payment of bills by offering additional discounts if the customer pays within, for example, 5 rather than 10 days
Trade or functional discount	To "reward" a customer for functions performed, such as for installing a particular brand of storm windows in houses being built or for stocking a particular brand of clothing in a store
Noncumulative quantity discount	To encourage buyers to place a larger order each time they buy merchandise
Cumulative quantity discount	To encourage buyers to return to a particular supplier for repeat business
Seasonal discount	To encourage buyers to make purchases during the "off season"—examples are house paint and bathing suits in the fall and winter and visits to winter resort areas during the summer
Promotional allowance	To encourage intermediaries to promote the product to their local customers

PRICING AND THE LAW

Because pricing strategies can be used in ways harmful to competition, and because price so clearly affects the consumer-citizen as well as the businessperson, a number of national and local laws have been passed which influence pricing practices. The Sherman Antitrust Act (1890) and the Clayton Act (1914) were early attempts to curb price fixing, restraint of trade, and other unfair and monopolistic practices. Additional legislation amended these acts. Here we discuss the Robinson-Patman Act, the fair trade acts and their repeal, and various state laws. Such laws, and court cases based on them, are so numerous that a service industry has grown up to supply companies with the latest information on legislation and litigation that may affect their pricing and other marketing plans.

Robinson-Patman Act

Robinson-Patman Act
U.S. federal law passed in 1936 and intended to halt discriminatory pricing policies by specifying certain limited conditions under which a seller may charge different prices to different buyers.

Price discrimination occurs when a manufacturer or supplier charges a lower price to one customer than to another, similar customer. The **Robinson-Patman Act** of 1936 is a federal law that makes it illegal to give, induce, or receive discriminatory prices except under certain conditions specified in the law. The act's sponsors believed it would wipe out chain stores. Under the law, a supplier of, say, meat products may not give a large discount to a supermarket chain just because that chain is an important customer. But the supplier may give the discount if a "proportional" discount is offered to the corner grocer. In the event of litigation, a judge must decide what is proportional and what is not.

The law also prohibits the granting of a *wholesaler's discount,* or *broker's discount,* to a business that does not meet criteria identifying it as a true wholesaler. The effect of this *brokerage provision* is that a large retailing organization cannot demand to be given a wholesaler's discount even though it may buy merchandise in larger quantities than do typical wholesalers. The law does allow for the offering of cooperative advertising and other promotional assistance if the promotional help is offered to all customers on proportionally equal terms.

The Robinson-Patman Act includes two provisions that can be used to defend prices that could appear to be discriminatory. One of these allows for the use of several prices if the competitive situation demands it. Thus, a lower price may be charged to one customer if this price is granted to meet the equally low price of a competitor. For example, a buyer in one city may be faced with a price war while a buyer in another city is not. The second provision is the so-called *cost-justification provision*. If the seller can prove that granting a lower price to one buyer simply represents passing on cost savings—for example, as a result of producing and shipping in large quantities—the seller has successfully employed the cost-justification provision.

The Robinson-Patman Act, along with the Federal Trade Commission Act (discussed in Chapter 3), is one of the most important laws affecting the daily dealings of marketers. But mere observance of its major provisions is not enough to avert legal troubles. As with all legislation, its content is open to interpretation and reinterpretation by the courts and government agencies.[6]

The Repeal of Fair Trade Acts

Before 1975, the states were empowered under federal law to pass *fair trade* or *resale price maintenance acts*. Most states enacted laws that allowed manufacturers to fix the prices of their goods and prohibited wholesalers and retailers from offering reduced or discount prices. Although it was argued that these laws would protect small companies by forcing all businesses to charge the same prices for goods, their main purpose was to stabilize prices at comparatively high levels. Enforcement of these laws was difficult, and growing consumer awareness that certain prices were being kept artificially high contributed to the passage of the Consumer Goods Pricing Act (1975), which repealed the right of individual states to allow price maintenance in interstate commerce.

Unfair Sales Practices Acts

Unfair Sales Practices Acts
State laws that limit or prohibit the use of certain sales and marketing techniques; most commonly, laws that require that certain types of merchandise be sold at prescribed markups.

Unfair sales practices acts are state laws commonly requiring that certain items be sold at prescribed markups. The markups may range from zero (thus eliminating loss leaders) to a relatively high percentage. Generally, some provision is made to allow for the sale of old or out-of-style merchandise at a reduced price. Dealers covered by such laws may charge more, but not less, than the specified markups allow. Thus, the laws are also termed *minimum markup laws*. These acts are intended to protect the small business using a relatively high markup by assuring that even a discount store must mark up its merchandise by the minimum amount. The smaller dealer then has a cushion that brings its price closer to that charged by the chain store.

Other State Laws and Local Laws

Many states and cities further restrict the pricing freedom of firms within their boundaries. For example, several states set limits on the number of times per year that wholesale beer prices may be changed. Many cities require that a "fire sale" actually follow a fire, and that "going out of business" sales be followed by a cessation of business operations.

PRICING AND SOCIAL RESPONSIBILITY

Our society believes that an organization's right to make a profit is important. And as our discussion of the legal aspects regulating price shows, society cares a great deal about the consumer's right to fair pricing. Laws define many ethical issues involving price. However, some legal pricing practices can create ethical dilemmas. For example, should zoos and museums be free to the public? If public institutions such as these do charge an admission fee, should it be waived for disadvantaged members of society?

Elsewhere in this book, we have discussed the complaint that certain marketing efforts, such as advertising, increase prices. This points to the fact that many ethical issues about price are not independent of other marketing mix decisions. Changing one marketing mix element may bring about higher prices. This fact leads us to one of the most fundamental questions concerning ethical pricing: the compatibility, or the lack thereof, between corporate social responsibility and the corporate profit motive.

It has been argued that "welfare and society are not the corporation's business. Its business is making money, not sweet music."[7] A number of managers believe that profit maximization is the only legitimate goal of business. Furthermore, they argue that business's pursuit of economic self-interest is what's best for the country.

Pursuing goals related to social responsibility may place a company at a competitive disadvantage. Consider some examples. Ingersol-Rand developed a quiet air compressor to silence noisy jack-hammers. Unfortunately, this product, which provided a clear social benefit in the form of noise abatement, had to be sold at a 25 percent premium because of its higher manufacturing cost. In effect, the question here is, "Would a buyer rather buy a jack-hammer for $5,000 or for $6,250?" And suppose a manufacturer of coal-mining equipment believes a certain safety feature will save lives. If this marketer adds the feature as standard equipment and increases the price of the equipment, but other competitors are not forced to do so, will the company be at a competitive disadvantage?

It is unlikely that one manufacturer will add an expensive safety feature to a product aimed at a price-conscious market segment unless all competitors are forced to do the same. Like it or not, this kind of problem is often settled by legislation requiring that socially desirable, but costly, features be added.

SUMMARY

Pricing is one of the most critical aspects of marketing. Prices must be used to appeal to buyers and offer them satisfaction. Costs and profit considerations are important, but prices that do not appeal to customers are of no use, no matter how they are determined. Effective marketers employ a combination of pricing strategies to arrive at prices that appeal to buyers first and then meet other organizational goals.

Learning Objective 1

Identify the various pricing strategies.
Broadly stated, there are five categories of pricing strategies: (1) differential pricing, (2) competitive pricing, (3) product-line pricing, (4) psychological and image pricing, and (5) distribution-based pricing.

Learning Objective 2

Discuss the nature of differential pricing strategies.
Maintaining a single fixed price for all buyers is a one-price strategy. Organizations that sell the same product at different prices to different buyers use a differential pricing strategy. Second-market discounting, skimming, periodic discounting, and random discounting are differential pricing strategies.

Learning Objective 3

Describe skimming and penetration pricing.
The skimming strategy involves charging a high price to "skim" the market. It is most appropriate when demand for a product is strong and there is little competitive pressure to lower price. The penetration strategy is employed by an organization seeking to enter a competitive market. By charging a low price, the organization hopes to quickly establish market share.

Learning Objective 4

Show how competition affects pricing activity.
Several types of prices are the direct results of the competitive structure of the marketplace. Charging the going rate, or pricing above or below that rate, are clearly responses to competition. Similarly, charging a traditional price or following the lead of the industry's leading firms are competition-influenced policies. Competition, though one of many variables affecting prices, is among the most powerful influences on pricing activity.

Learning Objective 5

Discuss the effects of inflation on pricing.
When inflation rates are high, buyers become increasingly price-conscious. Effective marketers can meet this challenge by attempting to maintain their prices or control their upward spiral. They can also alter their products, tighten distribution, and use promotional methods to help allay buyer concern over rising prices. The total marketing mix, not just price, can be adjusted to respond to high inflation rates.

Learning Objective 6

Discuss the nature of product-line pricing strategies.
Many pricing strategies consider the product line the appropriate unit of analysis. The objective of product-line pricing is to maximize profits for the total line rather than for an individual item in the line. Captive pricing, leader pricing, bait pricing, price lining, price bundling, and multiple-unit pricing are product-line pricing strategies.

Learning Objective 7

Explain some of the psychological aspects of price.
Price influences buyers psychologically, sometimes in ways that have little to do with the product or marketing mix. For example, to most buyers, a high price implies high quality, and a low price, lower quality. Odd prices and reference pricing suggest bargains. Prestige prices are used for high-status items.

Learning Objective 8

Show how geography influences pricing decisions.

Prices influenced by geography include the various forms of F.O.B. prices, delivered pricing, and basing-point pricing. In most cases, the greater the distance a product must travel to reach its buyer, the higher the product's price will be.

Learning Objective 9

Discuss such pricing tools as list price and cash, trade, quantity, and other discounts.

List price is the "official" price assigned by an organization to a product. The list price may be discounted in various ways to appeal to particular markets and to achieve certain marketing goals. The cash discount is used to encourage rapid payment by customers. The trade discount is used to reward channel intermediaries or members of specific trades by providing them with a margin of profit. Quantity discounts can be used to encourage large orders or to keep customers returning to a seller. Many other discounts, each with a specific purpose, are used by effective marketers.

Learning Objective 10

Describe the major legal restrictions on pricing freedom.

National, state, and local laws restrict the marketer's freedom to set prices. Pricing agreements among competitors are strictly forbidden. The Robinson-Patman Act limits the size of discounts a seller may offer a buyer. In most cases, such discounts must be proportional to the discounts offered to other, similar buyers. State unfair sales practices acts establish minimum markups that sellers must charge or in other ways restrict pricing freedom. In part because price is a visible element of the marketing mix and one that strongly affects buyers, it has been a frequent target of regulation at all levels of government.

Learning Objective 11

Identify a major ethical issue related to price.

A fundamental question concerning ethical pricing is whether corporate social responsibility is compatible with the corporate profit motive. Pursuing goals related to social responsibility may place a company at a competitive disadvantage. Ultimately, such questions often are settled by legislation requiring socially desirable, but costly, features.

KEY TERMS

Differential pricing strategy, or variable pricing strategy (p. 464)
One-price strategy (p. 464)
Second-market discounting (p. 465)
Skimming price (p. 465)
Periodic discounting (p. 466)
Random discounting (p. 466)
Meeting-the-competition strategy (p. 466)
Undercutting-the-competition strategy (p. 467)
Price leadership strategy (p. 467)
Follow-the-leader strategy (p. 468)
Penetration price (p. 468)
Predatory pricing strategy (p. 469)
Captive pricing strategy (p. 470)

Loss leader (p. 470)
Bait pricing (p. 471)
Price-lining strategy (p. 471)
Price-bundling strategy (p. 472)
Multiple-unit pricing (p. 472)
Reference pricing strategy (p. 473)
Isolation effect (p. 473)
Prestige price (p. 473)
F.O.B. (p. 474)
Delivered pricing, or freight-allowed pricing (p. 474)
Zone pricing (p. 474)
Uniform delivered pricing (p. 474)
Basing-point pricing (p. 475)
Markup on selling price (p. 476)
Markup on cost (p. 477)

Total cost (p. 478)
Fixed cost (p. 478)
Variable cost (p. 478)
Target return pricing (p. 478)
Break-even point (p. 479)
Discount (p. 480)
Cash discount (p. 480)
Anticipation discount (p. 480)
Trade discount (p. 481)
Noncumulative quantity discount (p. 481)
Cumulative quantity discount (p. 481)
Seasonal discount (p. 481)
Robinson-Patman Act (p. 483)
Unfair sales practices acts (p. 484)

QUESTIONS FOR REVIEW AND CRITICAL THINKING

1. What are the relative advantages and disadvantages of variable pricing and the one-price strategy?

2. In what competitive situations would you recommend using a penetration price? A skimming price?

3. What is the difference between periodic discounting and random discounting? How, if at all, do they differ in their purposes?

4. How might competitors influence a firm's pricing activities?

5. How does inflation affect consumers' perception of prices? How can marketers adjust their efforts to counter any negative perceptions of price?

6. Give three examples in which item profit is sacrificed for the sake of total profit.

7. Why are some prices based in part on the distances products must travel to reach the customer? Are prices always greater if the distance traveled is greater and lower if the distance is less?

8. If the manufacturing cost of an item is $250, the selling expenses associated with the item $75, and the required return 25 percent, what would the selling price of the item be?

9. Describe the concept behind break-even analysis. Briefly explain the limitations of break-even analysis.

10. From time to time, automobile makers offer sizable rebates to customers. Why not simply lower the price?

11. What is a trade discount? Why is it sometimes called a functional discount?

12. Name three products for which seasonal discounts are commonly offered. How do sellers use these discounts to sell products?

13. Using the average-cost method, what price would you recommend for a product if the costs associated with its production and marketing were $150,000, the margin for profit $50,000, and anticipated sales 5,000 units?

14. A marketer using the target return method made a mistake in predicting demand; the actual demand turned out to be half the expected demand. What would be the resulting loss per unit if the marketer used the following data to calculate price?

Expected demand	2,000 units
Fixed cost and target return	$200,000
Variable cost per unit	$100

15. Textbooks and courses in marketing, economics, accounting, and finance discuss price. In a major corporation, who are the individuals (by job title) involved in the pricing decision? What are some potential sources of disagreement or conflict among these individuals?

INTERNET INSIGHTS

Exercises

1. The Professional Pricing Society's home page is located at

    http://www.pricing-advisor.com

Each month excerpts from the Pricing Advisor Newsletter appear with information about things like value added pricing. What is the subject matter of the current newsletter?

Address Book

World Currency Exchange Rates
http://www.rubicon.com/passport/currency.htm
http://www.bloomberg.com/markets.wcv.htm

Consumer Price Index
http://stats.bls.gov/eag.table.htm

United States Trade Council
Usit.gov/tarffairs.hlm

ETHICS IN PRACTICE: TAKE A STAND

1. A retailer uses a 150 percent markup on cost for an item with a cost of $10. When the item is put on sale, the retailer advertises 50 percent off (markdown on selling price) and sells the item for $12.50. Is this deceptive?

2. A salesperson is allowed to vary the price a customer is charged by 10 percent. The salesperson sells 100 units to one wholesaler for $3,500. The next day, another wholesaler says he will buy 100 units only if the price is $3,000. The salesperson writes up the order and says "I hope this clears the order-processing department." Did the salesperson do the right thing?

3. A retailer's advertisement for fine china compares "our everyday price" with the "manufacturer's suggested retail price." A statement in small print at the bottom of the page says: "Manufacturer's suggested retail price is not a price at which our store offered or sold this merchandise and may not be a trade area price." Is this ethical?

4. An airline arranges with a national association to offer a special discount fare to association members who are attending a convention. A travel agent uses these group fares for regular clients, who are not association members, so they can get the lowest possible air fares. Is this good business?

5. For more than 30 years, StarKist Seafood packaged $6\frac{1}{2}$ ounces of tuna in its regular-sized can. During a period of inflation, the can's weight was reduced by $\frac{3}{8}$ ounce, but the price remained the same. Detecting this subtle change, which resulted in a 5.8 percent price increase, was a challenge for most consumers. The weight was clearly marked on the package but the size of the can did not change. Was this ethical?

VIDEO CASE 17–1

Pacific Paper Tube

The earthquake that struck the San Francisco area during the 1989 World Series gave Patrick Wallace's paper-tube manufacturing company quite a jolt—but it was nothing like the impact of strictly-business events that followed.

Wallace and his father had founded Pacific Paper Tube, Inc., that July in Oakland, Calif., across the bay from San Francisco. On October 17 they were reveling in news that a competitor was closing when the Cypress Freeway collapsed a block from their plant.

Crawling up into the structure, Wallace located two children, trapped in a car containing dead adults. Emergency crews couldn't complete the rescue until late that night.

The event attracted media attention, and precious days went by before Wallace could focus on his embryonic company. Other business delays were considerably longer: Demolition of the freeway disrupted transportation in the area, and closing of the Bay Bridge separated the company from many customers, primarily small businesses.

There was much more turmoil for the company when one of its two production employees quit, started a rival enterprise, and cut prices below break-even. Many customers were lured away.

Questions

1. Pacific Paper Tube's new environment has increased price competition. What should its pricing objective be?
2. What role will cost play in Pacific Paper Tube's marketing strategy?

APPENDIX A: CAREERS AND THE INTERNET

Marketing is a fascinating field. Students interested in a challenging career will find that it offers many opportunities that are hard to equal elsewhere. College students who have studied marketing provide a fresh source of talent for major corporations as well as smaller organizations.

The Zikmund and d'Amico home page (http://zikmund.swcollege.com) discusses a variety of marketing careers and provides a great deal of information about job opportunities available to students who major in marketing. It also provides tips on resume writing, job interviewing, and sources to learn about the availability of jobs.

The American Marketing Association is one of the most respected professional organizations for people working in the field of marketing. A visit to its home page (http:www.ama.org) will provide you with additional information about careers in marketing.

The remainder of this appendix provides some Internet exercises that will help you learn more about the jobs available to you.

INTERNET INSIGHTS

1. Use your Web browser to go to the CareerMosaic home page at the following address:

   http://www.careermosaic.com/cm/

   Read through the information on the home page to see what is going on at CareerMosaic this month. Then select College Connection to get information on internship opportunities, entry-level jobs, résumés, and the like. Select one of the companies on the list and find out what marketing-related employment opportunities are listed. If the company doesn't have any marketing jobs listed, select another company.

a.   What marketing jobs did you find available?

b.   What advice did the company post to potential employees?

Go back to the CareerMosaic home page and select Jobs Offered. Read the directions for entering a job search. Then enter a search on something like sales and marketing. Submit your search and let the computer do the work. Read through some of the many job postings to see if any look interesting to you.

2.   Use your Web browser to go to the Career Magazine home page at:

http://www.careermag.com

Select the Job Openings option and do a search for marketing-related jobs that have been posted on the Internet. Click on the Click Here icon to begin your Job Search. Leave the Location field empty, enter Marketing in the Skills field and enter Manager in the Title field. Then submit your search by clicking on the Submit Search button. Browse through the jobs you find.

Pick a job that looks interesting to you, write down the information, and bring it to class for discussion and to share with others.

3.   Go to the following address:

http://www.job-hunt.org

You will find a fantastic connection to career resources. At the home page, choose General. On the General Job Listings page, select College Grad Job Hunting. Take a look at Job Postings, Interviews and Negotiations, Résumé Writing Tips, and any other topics that interest you.

4.   The Internet's Online Career Center (OCC) is a wonderful resource for people seeking jobs, as well as companies seeking new employees. Check out the Online Career Center home page at:

http://www.occ.com/occ/

Once at the Online Career Center home page, choose Jobs. Then choose OCC Member Jobs for a listing of jobs posted by OCC members. You will find a wide range of companies, including AT&T, CNA Insurance, DowElanco, DuPont, Procter & Gamble, and SmithKline Beecham Pharmaceutical. Choose several companies and look at the jobs they have posted on the OCC. Keep looking at different companies until you find some marketing-related positions. Why are there so many technology-related positions on the OCC? Is this good target marketing? Why? Check out the other options at the OCC. You will find information under Résumés, Career Assistance, Recruiter's Office, and others that may help you find a job or internship.

5.   Use your Web browser to go to the JobNet home page at the following address:

http://www.westga.edu/~coop/

Read through the information on the JobNet home page to learn about the services available at JobNet. Select Employment Tips, Statistics, and General Information to find out more about the current condition of the job market. Select Employment Cost Index, Text Only to find out how quickly wages and benefits are rising in the current job market. Then go back and select Employment-Unemployment Statistics by State (text) to find out which states have the highest unemployment.

Return to the JobNet home page and select Subject to see a listing of jobs by subject.

6. Use your Web browser to go to the NPD Group, Inc., home page at:

http://www.npd.com

Choose the Employment Opportunities option to find out what a career in marketing research might look like. Look at the Getting Started at NPD in the Building a Career at NPD section. In what areas does the company hire new recruits? What qualifications is it looking for? What tasks is a research analyst expected to perform? What types of training does the company offer?

APPENDIX B: THE MARKETING AUDIT

A **marketing audit** is a comprehensive appraisal of the organization's marketing activities. It involves a systematic assessment of marketing plans, objectives, strategies, programs, activities, organizational structure, and personnel. Such a thorough study of a marketing operation requires an objective attitude. Thinking about bank auditors, whose cautious care makes them hard to fool, provides good insight into the marketing audit process. A good marketing audit, therefore, is:

Systematic. It follows a logical, predetermined framework—an orderly sequence of diagnostic steps.

Comprehensive. It considers all factors affecting marketing performance, not just obvious trouble spots. Marketers can be fooled into addressing symptoms rather than underlying problems. A comprehensive audit can identify the real problems.

Independent. To ensure objectivity, outside consultants may prepare the marketing audit. Using outsiders may not be necessary, but having an objective auditor is essential.

Periodic. Many organizations schedule regular marketing audits because marketing operates in a dynamic environment.

Managers often describe the audit process as costly, complex, and upsetting to organizations and individuals. This is because the audit emphasizes not only what is being done but why it is being done; it evaluates both current tactics and past strategies. Ideally, the audit should stress correcting procedures rather than assigning blame to individuals. Organizations that conduct regularly scheduled marketing audits can avoid problems by pointing out that the process is scheduled from time to time and is not aimed at criticizing an individual or a part of the organization.

Marketing audits typically begin with a meeting between the organization's officers and the outside people who are to conduct the audit. They decide on the audit's objectives, report format, timing, and other matters. A typical audit consists of numerous sections, as shown in Exhibit B–1.

EXHIBIT B–1
Sample of Items from a
Marketing Audit

Environment
How are environmental trends monitored?
What population trends are expected to affect existing and planned strategy?
What social and psychological patterns (attitudes, lifestyle, etc.) are expected to affect buyer behavior patterns?
How are present and pending legal developments affecting your operation?
What are the effects of competitors (their products, services, technologies) on your operation?

Objectives
Are the marketing objectives of your department consistent with overall company objectives?
Should these objectives be altered to fit changing environmental variables?
Are objectives consistent with one another?
How do objectives relate to marketing strengths and market opportunities?

Strategy
What is the relationship between objectives and strategies?
Are resources sufficient to implement the strategies?
What are the company's weaknesses?
How do you compare your strategies with those of competitors?

Product Decisions
How are new products developed within your business unit?
How are existing products evaluated?
How are products phased out of the line?

Pricing Decisions
How are pricing decisions made?
How do pricing decisions reflect the influences of competitors and the concerns of channel members?

Distribution Decisions
How are channel members selected, evaluated, and dropped if necessary?
How are channel members motivated?
How are decisions to modify channel structures reached?

Promotion Decisions
How are promotion mix decisions made?
How are salespeople selected, monitored, and evaluated?
How are payoffs associated with promotional efforts estimated?

Market Information
How is marketing research information transmitted to, and used within, the business unit?
Is a global information system in place?

Activities and Tasks
How are tasks scheduled, described, and planned? How are the responsibilities of individuals determined?
What spans of supervision, reporting relationships, and communication patterns exist? How are they evaluated?

Personnel
What level of competence has been attained by personnel in each position?
Are remedies to problems, if necessary, being planned? What are they?
What is the state of morale? Motivation? What are present plans in these areas?
Describe career development paths. Are replacements for personnel in key positions being groomed?

NOTE: This list of items is intended to represent matters typically treated in a marketing audit. It is not intended to be a complete checklist.

APPENDIX C: MARKETING ARITHMETIC FOR BUSINESS ANALYSIS

The marketing concept stresses profitability as well as consumer orientation. To achieve this aim and to accomplish other marketing objectives, which are often stated in financial terms, marketing managers need to know how to evaluate an organization's financial success. To do this, they must understand the operating statement and certain performance ratios from a marketing perspective.

THE PROFIT AND LOSS STATEMENT

Every manager needs to be able to interpret whether the organization or an organizational segment (strategic business unit, department, product line, or the like) is making a profit or contributing to profits. The basic equation for profit is:

Profit = Sales − Costs

The **profit and loss statement,** or **operating statement,** identifies an organization's sales revenues and costs over a given period—typically a year, quarter, or month. This statement allows a marketer to determine which elements are most strongly associated with profits or losses.

Exhibit C–1 shows a profit and loss statement for a retailer. The first item, **gross sales,** represents all sales revenues—that is, the total dollar amount the organization receives for the sale of its products. Retailers often refund money for returned goods or make allowances for damaged goods or for other reasons. These **returns** and **allowances** are subtracted to yield **net sales.**

Once net sales have been determined, costs are subtracted. In Exhibit C–1, the basic equation of profit = sales − costs is presented in greater detail:

$$E = \frac{(100 - 90)/100}{(5 - 6)/5}$$

$$= \frac{10/100}{-1/5}$$

$$= \frac{0.1}{-0.2}$$

$$= -0.5, \text{ or simply } 0.5$$

Unitary elastic demand occurs when elasticity equals 1. If demand is elastic, E will be greater than 1. In our example, elasticity is 0.5, which is less than 1, indicating that demand is inelastic.

Glossary

A

acceleration principle A principle describing the situation in which demand for a product that derives its demand from another product may either increase or decrease at a much higher rate than demand for the product from which demand is derived.

account manager In sales, a person who concentrates on maintaining an ongoing relationship with existing customers.

account service representative Contact at company headquarters who can answer customers' questions.

administered strategic alliance A vertical marketing system in which a strong channel leader coordinates marketing activities at all levels in the channel through planning and management of a mutually beneficial program.

adoption process The mental and behavioral stages through which an individual passes before making a purchase or placing an order: awareness, interest, evaluation, trial, and adoption.

advertising An informative or persuasive message carried by a nonpersonal medium and paid for by an identified sponsor whose organization or product is identified in some way.

advertising appeal The central theme or idea of an advertising message.

advertising theme An advertising appeal used in several different advertisements to give continuity to an advertising campaign.

agent intermediary A channel intermediary that does not take title to the product. Agent intermediaries bring buyers and sellers together or otherwise help to consummate a transaction.

AIDA An acronym for attention, interest, desire, and action. The AIDA formula is a hierarchy of communication effects model used as a guideline in creating advertisements.

aided recall test *See recall test.*

air freight A mode of transportation in which air carriers are used in the shipment of products.

allowance A reduction in price, a rebate, or the like given to a marketing intermediary in return for a large order or performance of a specific activity.

anticipation discount A discount over and above the regular cash discount, meant to encourage even faster payment.

antitrust legislation Federal laws meant to promote competition in United States markets; the major antitrust laws are the Sherman Antitrust Act (1890), the Clayton Act (1914), and the Federal Trade Commission Act (1914).

approach The step in the creative selling process wherein the salesperson makes initial contact and establishes rapport with the prospect.

art In the context of advertising, any aspect of an advertisement other than copy, including pictures, layout, and white space.

aspirational group In reference to an individual, a group to which the individual would like to belong.

assembler A marketing intermediary that performs a bulk-accumulating function.

association format An advertising format that uses an analogy or other relationship to stimulate interest and convey information.

assorting function An activity performed by marketing intermediaries, consisting of combining products purchased from several manufacturers to create assortments.

atmospherics Physical characteristics of a store's environment, such as appearance, layout, and displays.

attitude An individual's general effective, cognitive, and intentional responses toward a given object, issue, or person.

attribution theory A theory of learning stressing that a person must attribute an obtained reward to his or her action if the reward is to result in a repetition of the action.

auction company Agent intermediary that brings together buyers and sellers. Auction companies often assemble merchandise for sale in a central location and sell it by means of a bidding process.

autonomic decision making Process in which decisions are made individually by group members and vary from occasion to occasion.

auxiliary dimensions Aspects of a product providing supplementary benefits, including special features, aesthetics, package, warranty, repair service contract, reputation, brand name, or instructions.

average cost Total costs divided by the number of units produced.

B

backward channel A channel of distribution for recycling in which the customary flow from producer to ultimate user is reversed.

bait-and-switch advertising An unethical advertising technique, usually associated with retailers, whereby a product is offered at an extremely low price to attract customers, who are then told the product is unavailable and "switched" to a more expensive, higher-margin product.

bait pricing A method of attracting customers by offering low-priced items for sale with the intention of selling more expensive goods.

balance sheet A financial statement that reports assets, liabilities, and net worth at a given moment in time.

barter The exchange of products without the use of money.

basing-point pricing Charging for shipping from a specified basing point, or location, no matter where the shipment actually originates.

belief A conviction concerning the existence or the characteristics of something.

benefit segmentation A type of market segmentation by which consumers are grouped according to the specific benefits they seek from a product.

birdyback service *See piggyback service.*

black box A way of representing consumers' unobservable psychological processes. The black box concept suggests that researchers must focus on input to and output from the decision-making process, since they cannot observe the process itself.

boycott An action in which some group refuses to buy certain products. A government may enforce a boycott of the products of some other country.

brand A name or some other identifying feature that distinguishes one marketer's product; much competition is among brands.

brand equity The value associated with a brand. Where there is brand equity, market share or profit margins are greater because of the goodwill associated with the brand.

brand extension A product category extension or product line extension that employs a brand name already used on one of the company's existing products.

brand image The complex of symbols and meanings associated with a brand.

brand manager *See product manager.*

brand mark A unique symbol that is part of a brand.

brand name The verbal part of the brand; the part that can be spoken or written.

break-down method Forecasting starts with large-scale estimates (for example, an estimate of GDP) and works down to industrywide, company, and product estimates.

break-even point The point at which an organization's revenues and costs are equal.

broker Agent intermediaries whose major role is placing buyers and sellers in touch with one another and assisting in contractual arrangements.

build-up method Starts with smaller-scale estimates and works up to larger-scale ones.

bulk-accumulating function An activity performed by marketing intermediaries, consisting of buying small quantities of a particular product from many small producers and then selling the assembled larger quantities.

bulk-breaking function An activity performed by marketing intermediaries, consisting of buying products in relatively large quantities and selling in smaller quantities.

business analysis stage The stage in new product development when a new product is reviewed from all organizational perspectives to determine performance criteria and likely profitability.

business cycle Recurrent fluctuations in general economic activity. The four phases of the business cycle are prosperity, recession, depression, and recovery.

business market *See organizational market.*

business-to-business marketing Marketing aimed at bringing about an exchange in which a product or service is sold for any use other than personal consumption. The buyer may be a manufacturer, a reseller, a government body, a not-for-profit institution, or any organization other than an ultimate consumer. The transaction occurs so the organization may conduct its business.

buyer The buying-center role played by the organizational member who will actually use the product.

buyer for export Any customer or merchant intermediary that buys a mix of products in the domestic market for use or sale in other markets.

buying center An informal, cross-departmental decision unit for which the primary objective is the acquisition, dissemination, and processing of relevant purchasing-related information.

buying function Activities associated with making a purchase and thus effecting the transfer of ownership of a product.

buy phase One of the stages of the multistage process by which organizations make purchase decisions.

C

call report A salesperson's periodic report listing the number of sales calls made, sales closed, and other activities.

cannibalization A situation in which one item eats into the sales revenues of another item in the same line.

capacity management strategy See *demand management strategy*.

capital product Installations and accessory equipment.

captive pricing strategy A strategy whereby a basic product, such as a razor, is priced low but the profits from associated products needed for operating the basic product, such as razor blades, make up for the lack of profit on the basic product.

cash-and-carry wholesaler A limited-service wholesaler that does not offer delivery or credit.

cash cow High-market-share product in a low-growth market.

cash discount A price discount that offers lower prices for early payment of bills.

catalog showroom General mass merchandise outlet in which customers select goods from a catalog and store employees retrieve the selected items from storage.

category discounter Specialty mass merchandise outlet offering extensive assortment and depth in a specific product category. Also called a category killer.

census A survey of all the members of a group (an entire population).

chain store One of a group of two or more stores of a similar type, centrally owned and operated.

channel captain See *channel leader*.

channel conflict A situation in which antagonism exists between distribution channel members.

channel cooperation A situation in which the marketing objectives and strategies of distribution channel members are harmonious.

channel interdependency The interdependent relationships among the members of a channel of distribution.

channel leader A distribution channel member that is able to exert power and influence over other channel members. Also called the channel captain.

channel of distribution The complete sequence of marketing organizations involved in bringing a product from the producer to the consumer.

channel power The extent to which a channel member is able to influence the behavior of another channel member.

choice criteria The critical attributes a consumer uses to evaluate product alternatives.

closed door house See *warehouse club*.

close-out price A special price used to sell off remaining inventories of a discontinued, out-of-style, or otherwise unattractive product.

closing The step in the creative selling process wherein the salesperson attempts to obtain a commitment to buy from the prospect.

closing signals Signs from the prospect revealing that he or she is ready to buy.

closure An element of perception by which an observer mentally completes an incomplete stimulus.

cluster sample A probability sample resulting from a process by which certain geographical areas are selected on a chance basis and then probability sampling techniques are used to select samples within these areas.

co-branding The use of two brands on a single product.

code of conduct A statement establishing a company's or a professional organization's guidelines with regard to ethical principles and acceptable behavior.

coding Establishing meaningful categories for responses collected by means of surveys or other data collection forms so that the responses can be grouped into usable classifications.

coercive power Power based on threats of punishment.

cognitive dissonance In consumer behavior, the negative feelings that may occur after a commitment to purchase has been made. It describes the tension that results from holding two conflicting ideas or beliefs at the same time.

cognitive process The general term for the broad range of mental activities, such as perception, learning, thinking, information processing, and reasoning, that involve the interpretation of stimuli and the organization of thoughts and ideas.

collaborator Person or company that works with a marketing company. Collaborators help the company run its business without actually being part of the company.

combination organization An organizational structure based on more than one of the following: geography, product type, type of customer, or marketing functions.

commercialization The stage in new product development when the decision is made to launch a new product's full-scale production and distribution.

commercial jingle A song or other short verse used in an advertisement as a memory aid.

commission merchant Agent intermediary similar to a broker but having certain additional decision-making powers, such as the power to make price adjustments.

commission with draw Compensation based strictly on sales performance, but with the provision that the salesperson can borrow from a drawing account if necessary.

common cost *See indirect cost.*

communication The process of exchanging information with and conveying meaning to others.

communication function Buying and selling functions whose ultimate purpose is ownership transfer.

communication goals In the context of marketing, what the marketer wants the promotional message to accomplish: to gain attention, to be understood, to be believed, and to be remembered.

company The business or organization itself.

comparative advantage The position a country occupies when it uses its resources to make the goods it can produce most efficiently. In theory, when each country produces according to its competitive advantage and trades with others to obtain products it cannot produce efficiently, everyone benefits.

comparative advertising A type of demonstration advertising in which the brand being advertised is directly compared with a competing brand.

comparative parity method A method of setting a promotional budget in which the marketer tries to match competitors' expenditures.

competitor One or two or more rival companies engaged in the same business.

competitive advantage Superiority to or favorable difference from competitors along some dimension important to the market.

competitive position *See market position.*

computer-interactive retailing A retailing method through which consumers shop at home using personal computers and interactive computer services. It is called Internet retailing when the Internet is utilized.

concentrated marketing Developing of a marketing mix and directing of marketing efforts and resources to appeal to a single market segment.

concept testing Research procedures used to learn consumers' reactions to new product ideas. Consumers presented with the idea are asked if they like it, would use it, would buy it, and so on.

conspicuous consumption Consumption for the sake of enhancing social prestige.

consumer behavior The activities people engage in when selecting, purchasing, and using products so as to satisfy needs and desires.

consumer information-processing (CIP) approach A model of consumer decision making that focuses on the information-processing aspect of decision making. It looks at buyers as problem solvers who actively acquire the information they need.

consumer involvement The extent to which an individual attaches interest and importance to a product and is willing to expend energy in making a decision about purchasing the product.

consumer market Market consisting of buyers who use the product to satisfy personal or household needs.

consumer orientation First aspect of marketing concept; emphasizes the importance of consumers' needs.

contest In the context of a wholesaler's or retailer's sales promotion, a means of motivating a sales force by offering bonuses or prizes for sales performance.

continuous innovation A new product characterized by minor alterations or improvements to existing products and little change in consumption patterns.

contract manufacturing In international marketing, an agreement by which a company allows a foreign producer to manufacture its product according to its specifications; typically, the company then handles foreign sales of the product.

contractual vertical marketing system A vertical marketing system in which two or more channel members are connected through ownership.

control The process by which managers ensure that planned activities are completely and properly executed.

controllable variables *See four Ps of marketing.*

convenience product A relatively inexpensive, regularly purchased consumer product bought without much thought and with a minimum of shopping effort.

convenience sample A nonprobability sample made up of the subjects most conveniently available.

convenience store A small grocery store stressing quick service and typically charging higher prices than other retailers selling similar products.

conventional channel of distribution A channel of distribution characterized by loosely aligned, relatively autonomous marketing organizations that carry out a trade relationship.

cooperative advertising Advertising paid for jointly by a supplier and a customer—for example, by the manufacturer of a product and a retailer.

cooperative organization A group of independent retailers that combine resources and expertise to control their wholesaling needs, as through a centralized wholesale buying center.

copy In the context of advertising, any words contained in an advertisement.

core competency A proficiency in a critical functional activity—such as technical know-how or a particular business specialization—that helps provide a company's unique competitive advantage.

corporate chain A chain with 11 or more stores.

corporate strategic planning Long-term planning for the organization as a whole, carried out by top management.

corporate vertical marketing system A vertical marketing system in which two or more channel members are connected through ownership.

cost analysis The assignment of costs to strategic business units, departments, products, sales territories, customers, or other meaningful categories to determine and evaluate the use of resources.

cost of goods sold The purchase price of goods sold during a specified period, including transportation costs.

cost reduction strategy A product strategy that involves lowering costs, used especially during a product's maturity or decline; a product marketing strategy that involves redesigning a product to lower production costs.

countertrade Large-scale international barter.

creative process In the context of advertising, the generation of ideas and the development of the advertising message or concept.

creative selling *See order getting.*

creative selling process The six-step process by which creative selling is carried out: (1) locating and qualifying prospects, (2) approaching the prospect, (3) making the sales presentation, (4) handling objections, (5) closing the sale, and (6) following up.

credit function Provision of credit to another member of a distribution channel.

crisis management Public relations effort to manage an emergency that urgently requires dissemination of information.

cross-classification matrix A grid that helps isolate variables of interest in the market. For example, a geographic variable might be cross-classified with some other variable of interest, such as income.

cross-elasticity Elasticity in the demand for one product in relation to the prices of substitutable or complementary products.

cross functional sales team All the people in and organization involved in helping the salesperson to close the sale.

cross-functional terms Individuals from various organizational departments, such as engineering, production, finance, and marketing, working together and sharing a common purpose.

cultural environment That part of the environment, domestic or foreign or both, that is shaped by humankind.

culture The institutions, values, beliefs, and behaviors of a society; everything we learn, as opposed to that with which we were born.

cumulative quantity discount A price discount determined by the amount purchased over some specified time period.

customer Buyer or consumer of goods or services.

customer-based organization An organizational structure based on the specific needs of customer groups.

customization strategy International strategy in which marketers adapt product strategies to each country.

custom marketing A marketing effort in which the marketer seeks to satisfy each customer's unique set of needs. In effect, each customer is an individual market segment.

D

damage in transit Breakage, spoilage, and other injuries to products that occur while the products are being transported.

data Facts and recorded measures of phenomena.

data analysis Statistical and/or qualitative consideration of data gathered by research.

database Collection of data arranged in a logical manner and organized in a form to be stored and processed by a computer.

data based marketing The practice of maintaining customer data bases with the customer's names, addresses, phone numbers, past purchases, responses to previous offers, and demographic characteristics.

data collection system An organization's manner of systematically collecting data. It includes internal records and reports systems, a marketing research system, and a marketing intelligence system. The data collection system is part of the marketing information system.

deceptive advertising *See misleading advertising.*

decider The buying-center role played by the organizational member who makes the actual purchasing decision.

decision making A process aimed at the making of a valuative judgment. It includes the cognitive activities of memory, thinking, and information processing.

decision support system A computer system consisting of databases and software that stores and transforms data into accessible information for a business unit.

decline stage The stage in the product life cycle when the product loses market acceptance because of such factors as popularity, obsolescence, and market saturation.

decoding In communication theory, the process by which the receiver of a message interprets the message's meaning.

delivered pricing Pricing that includes delivery within a specified area. Also called freight-allowed pricing.

demand curve A graphic representation of the relationship between various prices and the amount of product that will be demanded at those prices. Also called a demand schedule.

demand management strategy A strategy used by service marketers and aimed at accurate forecasting of the need for services so that service supply is in line with service demand. Also called capacity management strategy.

demand schedule *See demand curve.*

demarketing Marketing strategy designed to discourage all or some customers from buying or consuming a product on either a temporary or permanent basis.

demographic category A grouping based on age, sex, educational background, income, or some other demographic variable.

demography The study of the size, composition, and distribution of the human population in relation to social factors such as geographic boundaries.

demonstration format An advertising format in which a clear-cut example of product superiority or consumer benefits is presented.

department store A departmentalized retail outlet, often large, offering a wide variety of products and generally providing a full range of customer services.

depth of product line The number of different items in a product line.

derived demand Demand for a product that depends on demand for another product.

desk jobber *See drop shipper.*

devaluation A government action decreasing the value of the domestic currency in relation to that of a foreign currency.

developed country An economically advanced country characterized by a high level of specialization, full-scale marketing structures and activities, large markets, and extensive possibilities for importing and exporting.

developing country A country characterized by social change and increased economic activity. Features include some specialization of resources, growth of certain industries, an emerging business-based middle class, and some export and import activity.

development stage The stage in new product development when a new product concept is transformed into a prototype. The basic marketing strategy also develops at this time.

dialectic theory In the context of marketing, the theory that an existing institution (the thesis) is challenged by another institution (the antithesis); the interaction of the two yields a new institution (the synthesis), which has some characteristics of both.

differential pricing strategy A strategy whereby different prices are charged to different buyers for the same product. Also called variable pricing strategy.

differentiated marketing A marketing effort in which the marketer selects more than one target market and then develops a separate marketing mix for each. Also called multiple market segmentation.

differentiation strategy Strategy in which the marketer offers a product that is unique in the industry, provides a distinct advantage, or is set apart from competitors' brands in some way other than price.

diffusion process The spread of a new product through society.

direct-action advertisement An advertisement designed to stimulate immediate purchase or encourage another direct response. Also called a direct-response advertisement.

direct cost A cost that is clearly identified with a particular segment of an operation and directly allocated to that segment.

direct exporting A practice by which domestic producers sell products directly to foreign buyers.

direct foreign investment Investment of capital in production and marketing operations located in a host foreign country.

direct marketing Marketing in which advertising, telephone sales, or other communications are used to elicit a direct response, such as an order by mail or phone. In a retailing context, also called direct-response retailing.

direct marketing wholesaler Limited-service wholesaler that uses catalogs, mail or telephone ordering, and mail delivery.

direct-response campaign Promotional approach intended to elicit a direct, measurable response, such as and order.

direct-response retailer A nonstore retail operation that sells goods by television or telephone and fills orders by mail.

disaggregated market A market containing no identifiable groups, or aggregates. The result is that products must be made to order for each buyer.

discontinuous innovation A product so new that no previous product performed an equivalent function. Such a product requires the development of new consumption or usage patterns.

discount A reduction from list price or a reimbursement for performance of a specific task.

distribution (place) An element of the marketing mix involving all aspects of getting products to the consumer in the right location at the right time.

distributor brand A brand owned by a retailer, wholesaler, or other distributor rather than by the manufacturer of the product. Also called a private brand.

diversification The strategy of marketing new products to a new market.

diversion in transit Direction of a rail shipment to a destination not specified at the start of the trip.

divisibility The characteristic by which a product provides the opportunity for consumers to sample small amounts.

dog Low-market-share product in a low-growth market.

domestic environment The environment in an organization's home country.

drop shipper A limited-service wholesaler, often dealing in bulky products, that takes customer orders and arranges for shipment of merchandise from the producer directly to the customer. Also called a desk jobber.

dumping Selling large quantities of a product in a foreign market at prices below their fair market value in the domestic market.

durable good A physical, tangible item that functions over an extended period.

dynamically continuous innovation A product that is different from previously available products but that does not strikingly change buying or usage patterns.

E

early adopter A group of consumers who purchase a product soon after it has been introduced, but after the innovators.

early majority A group of consumers, usually solid, middle-class people who purchase innovation more deliberately and cautiously than early adopters.

economic order quantity (E.O.Q.) A mathematically determined purchase order size that yields the lowest total cost of order processing and inventory holding.

economic system The system through which a society allocates its scarce resources.

economic utility The ability of an organization marketing a product to satisfy a consumer's wants or needs; includes form utility, place utility, time utility, and possession utility.

editing Checking questionnaires or other data collection forms for omissions, incomplete or otherwise unusable responses, illegibility, and obvious inconsistencies.

80/20 principle In marketing, a principle describing the situation in which a relatively small percentage of customers accounts for a disproportionately large share of the sales of a product.

electronic catalog An interactive videotext system in which consumers see products on their home TV screens but use touch-tone phones to control the order in which the products are shown and to place orders.

embargo A government prohibition of trade, especially for a particular product.

emotion State involving subjectively experienced feelings of attraction or repulsion.

encoding In communication theory, the process by which the sender translates the idea to be communicated into a symbolic message consisting of words, pictures, numbers, gestures, or the like, so that it can be transmitted to the receiver.

enhanced model A model that extends the product line because of its distinctive features, which consumers perceive as better.

entrepreneur A risk-taking individual who sees an opportunity and is willing to undertake a venture to create a new product or service.

environmental monitoring Tracking certain phenomena to detect the emergence of meaningful trends.

environmental scanning Information gathering designed to detect changes that may be in their initial stages of development.

ethical dilemma A predicament in which a marketer must resolve whether an action that benefits the organization, the individual decision maker, or both, may be considered unethical.

ethnocentrism Belief in the superiority of one's own culture.

European Union (EU) A 15-member community of European nations within which all barriers to trade between members have been eliminated; formerly called the Common Market.

event marketing Marketing when the title sponsor creates the event and activity.

exchange process The interchange of something of value between two or more parties.

exchange rate The value of one currency in relation to that of another.

exclusive dealing A situation in which a distributor carries the products of one manufacturer and not those of competing manufacturers.

exclusive distribution A distribution strategy in which only one outlet in a given area is allowed to sell a product.

exclusive territory An area, defined by geographical boundaries or population, assigned to a retailer, wholesaler, or other dealer with the understanding that no other distributors will be assigned to operate in that area.

execution The carrying out of plans, also called implementation.

execution format The style in which the advertising message is delivered.

expected service-perceived service gap The situation where consumers' expectations do not match the perceived level of service received. A gap can be negative or positive.

experiment A research method in which the researcher changes one variable and observes the effects of that change on another variable.

expert power Power issuing from expertise and knowledge.

exploratory research Research to clarify the nature of a marketing problem.

export department An organizational unit developed to deal directly or indirectly with foreign customers.

exporting Selling domestically produced products in foreign markets.

export management company A company that specializes in buying from sellers in one country and marketing the products in other countries. Such companies typically take title to the products.

extensive problem solving In-depth search for and evaluation of alternative solutions to a problem.

F

fad A passing fashion or craze that many people are interested in for only a short time.

family A group of two or more persons related by birth, marriage, or adoption and residing together.

family branding The practice of using a single brand name to identify different items of a product line.

family life cycle A series of stages through which most families pass.

fantasy In the context of advertising, a type of association format in which the intention is to link the product with the target buyer's wildest dreams and hopes.

fashion A style that is current or in vogue.

fashion obsolescence The pattern of products becoming out of date because of changes in the preferences for particular styles.

Federal Trade Commission (FTC) Federal agency established in 1914 by the Federal Trade Commission Act to investigate and put an end to unfair methods of competition.

feedback Communication of the receiver's reaction to a message back to the source.

field sales manager A district or regional sales manager, so called because his or her main concern is the salespeople in the field.

field selling Nonretail selling that takes place outside the employer's place of business, usually in the prospective customer's place of business.

financial resources The organization's capital and cash flow.

fishyback service *See piggyback service.*

fixed cost A cost that is a function of time and not of volume of production or sales.

flanker brand An item that extends the product line in order to deny shelf space to competitors.

F.O.B. "Freight on board" or "Free on board"; together with further information, a term that identifies the point at which title passes from seller to buyer. For example, "F.O.B. factory" means that the buyer takes title at the factory and is responsible for all shipping charges.

focus group interview A loosely structured interview in which a group of 6 to 10 people discuss a product or focus on some aspect of buying behavior.

follow-the-leader strategy A pricing strategy whereby an organization sets prices at the level the market leader has established; especially common for organizations in weak competitive positions.

follow-up The final step in the creative selling process, wherein the salesperson, after the sale has been made, contacts the buyer to make sure everything connected with the sale was handled properly.

foreign environment The environment outside an organization's home country.

form utility Utility created by conversion of raw materials into finished goods or service processes that meet consumer needs.

four Cs An acronym for the microenvironmental participants who perform essential business activities: company, customers, competitors, and collaborators.

four Ps of marketing The basic elements of the marketing mix: product, place (distribution), price and promotion; also called the controllable variables of marketing because they can be controlled and manipulated by the marketer.

franchise A contractual agreement between a franchisor and a franchisee by which the franchisee distributes the franchisor's product.

freight allowed pricing See *delivered pricing*.

frequency The number of times an advertisement is repeated in a given medium within a given time period, usually a month.

full-function wholesaler See *full-service merchant wholesaler*.

full-line strategy The product line strategy that involves offering a large number of variations of a product. Also called a broad strategy.

full-service merchant wholesaler Merchant wholesaler that provides a complete array of services, such as delivery, credit, marketing information and advice, and managerial assistance. Also called a full-function wholesaler.

functional discount See *trade discount*.

functional organization An organizational structure whereby a firm's efforts are specialized and expended according to the business functions involved.

G

gap analysis The type of analysis marketers use to identify the sources of the consumer's expected service-perceived service gap.

gatekeeper A group member who controls the flow of information to the decision maker; the buying-center role played by the organizational member who controls the flow of information related to the purchase.

General Agreements on Tariffs and Trade (GATT) A series of agreements reached by a number of trading nations around the world and intended to encourage international trade

general line wholesaler Full-service merchant wholesaler that sells a full selection of products in one product line.

general mass merchandisers Mass merchandisers that carry a wide variety of merchandise cutting across product categories.

general merchandise wholesaler Full-service merchant wholesaler that sells a large number of different product lines.

general-specific-general theory Theory describing the development of retailing as a cyclic process in which general merchandisers are replaced by specialty merchandisers, which in turn are replaced by general merchandisers, and so on.

generation X Americans born between 1965 and 1976.

generic brand See *generic product*.

generic demand Demand for a product class as a whole, without regard to brand. Also called primary demand.

generic name A brand name so commonly used that it is part of the language and is used to describe a product class rather than a particular manufacturer's product.

generic product A product that carries neither a manufacturer nor a distributor brand. The goods are plainly packaged with stark lettering that simply lists the contents. Also called a generic brand.

geodemographic segmentation A type of market segmentation by which consumers are grouped according to demographic variables, such as income and age, and as identified by a geographic variable, such as zip code.

geography-based organization An organizational structure in which the market area is divided into territories, and marketing efforts are specialized and expended by geographic area.

global information system An organized collection of telecommunications equipment, computer hardware, software, data, and personnel designed to capture, store, update, manipulate, analyze, and immediately display information about worldwide business activity.

globalization strategy A plan by which a marketer standardizes its marketing strategy around the world.

green marketing Marketing activities beneficial to the physical environment.

gross domestic product (GDP) The total value of all the goods and services produced by capital and workers in a country.

gross margin Net sales minus cost of goods sold over a specified period. Also called gross profit.

gross margin percentage The percentage of revenues available to cover expenses and provide a profit: gross margin/net sales.

gross national product (GNP) The total value of all the goods and services produced by a nation's residents or corporations, regardless of location.

gross profit *See gross margin.*

gross rating points (GRPs) A measure combining reach and frequency. GRP equals reach (in percentage points) times frequency.

gross sales Total sales over a specified period, before deduction of returns and allowances.

growth stage The stage in the product life cycle when sales increase at an accelerating rate.

H

handling objections The step in the creative selling process wherein the salesperson responds to questions or reservations expressed by the prospect.

head-to-head competition Positioning a product to occupy the same market position as a competitor.

heterogeneity The degree of variability among services provided.

horizontal cooperative promotion An approach whereby channel members at the same level jointly sponsor particular promotions.

human resources The number and quality of an organization's employees.

hypermarket A mass merchandise outlet featuring an especially large variety of products and an especially large size. Also called a superstore.

hypothesis An unproved proposition that can be supported or refuted by marketing research. Research objectives are often stated as hypotheses.

I

idea generation usage The stage in new product development that involves a continuing search for product ideas consistent with target market needs and the organization's objectives.

image building A promotional approach intended to communicate an image and generate consumer preference for a brand or product on the basis of symbolic value.

import quota A limit set by a government on how much of a certain type of product can be imported into a country.

incentive Something believed capable of satisfying a particular motive.

independent retailer A retail establishment that is not owned or controlled by any other organization.

indirect cost A cost that is not directly traceable to a particular segment of operation. Also called a common cost.

indirect exporting Exporting through an intermediary.

indirect-action advertisement An advertisement designed to stimulate sales over the longer run.

individual brand A brand assigned to a product within a product line that is not shared by other products in that line.

individual factor With reference to perception, a characteristic of a person that affects how the person perceives a stimulus.

influencer A group member who attempts to persuade the decision maker; the buying-center role played by organizational members (or outsiders) who affect the purchase decision by supplying advice or information.

information Data in a format useful to decision makers.

information search An internal or external search for information carried out by the consumer to reduce uncertainty and provide a basis for evaluating alternatives.

innovator A member of the first group of customers to buy a new product.

inseparability A characteristic of services referring to the fact that production often is not distinct from consumption of a service.

inside selling Nonretail selling from the employer's place of business.

institutional advertisement An advertisement designed to promote an organizational image, stimulate generic demand for a product, or build goodwill for an industry.

intangibility A characteristic of services referring to the customer's inability to see, hear, smell, feel, or taste the service product.

intensive distribution A distribution strategy aimed at obtaining maximum exposure for the product at the retail or wholesale level.

internal marketing Public relations efforts aimed at a company's own employees.

international department An organizational unit that manages the firm's international marketing operations.

international franchising A form of licensing in which a company establishes foreign franchises. Franchising involves a contractual agreement between a franchisor, often a manufacturer or wholesaler, and a franchisee, typically an independent retailer, by which the franchisee distributes the franchisor's product.

international marketing *See multinational marketing.*

integrated marketing communications A term to remind managers that all elements of the promotion mix should be coordinated and systematically planned to be in harmony with each other.

Internet A worldwide network of computers that give individuals access to electronic mail and vast amounts of information and documents from distant sources.

intranet A company's private decision support system that uses Internet standards and technology.

intrapreneurial organization An organization that encourages individuals to take risks and gives them the autonomy to develop new products as they see fit.

introduction stage The stage in the product life cycle when the new product is attempting to gain a foothold in the market.

inventory control The activities involved in decisions relating to inventory size, placement, and delivery.

inventory turnover ratio *See stock turnover ratio.*

isolation effect An effect by which a product appears more attractive next to a higher-priced alternative than in isolation.

J

jobber A wholesale intermediary in a channel of distribution for an organizational good.

joint decision making Decision making shared by all or some members of a group. Often, one decision maker dominates the process.

joint ownership venture In international marketing, a joint venture in which domestic and foreign partners invest capital and share ownership and control.

joint venturing In international marketing, an arrangement between a domestic company and a foreign host company to set up production and marketing facilities in a foreign market.

judgment sample A nonprobability sample chosen according to the judgment and experience of the selector.

just-in-time (JIT) inventory system A materials management system in which inventory arrives just in time for use.

K

keystoning Retailers' practice of doubling the wholesale price of an item and making this the regular retail price.

L

label The paper or plastic sticker attached to a container to carry product information. As packaging technology improves, labels become incorporated into the protective aspects of the package rather than simply being affixed to the package.

laboratory experiment An experiment in a highly controlled environment.

laggard A member of the group of final adopters in the diffusion process.

Lanham Act A U.S. law declaring that brand names cannot be confusingly similar to registered trademarks.

late majority A group of consumers who purchase a product after the early majority, when it is no longer perceived as risky.

learning Any change in behavior or cognition that results from experience or an interpretation of experience.

leased department retailer An independent retailer that owns the merchandise stocked but leases floor space from another retailer and usually operates under that retailer's name.

legal environment Laws and regulations and their interpretation.

legitimate power Power based on legal agreement.

less-developed country A country in which small, low-technology companies may be developing but in which marketing mechanisms typically do not exist.

license A contractual arrangement by which a firm may use another firm's trademark.

licensing In international marketing, an agreement by which a company (the licensor) permits a foreign company (the licensee) to set up a business in the foreign market using the licensor's manufacturing processes, patents, trademarks, trade secrets, and so on in exchange for payment of a fee or royalty.

lifestyle An individual's activities, interests, opinions, and values as they affect his or her mode of living.

lifestyle format An advertising format that reflects a target market's lifestyle or hoped-for lifestyle.

limited-function wholesaler See limited-service wholesaler.

limited-line strategy The product line strategy that involves offering a smaller number of product variations than the full-line strategy.

limited problem solving An intermediate level of decision making between routinized and extensive problem solving in which the consumer has some purchasing experience but is unfamiliar with stores, brands, or price options.

limited-service merchant wholesaler Merchant wholesaler that offers less than full service and charges lower prices than a full-service merchant wholesaler. Also called a limited-function wholesaler.

line extension See product line extension.

list price The basic price quote, before adjustment.

location-based competition Competition based on providing place utility by delivering the product where the consumer wants it.

logistics The activities involved in moving raw materials and parts into the firm, in-process inventory through the firm, and finished goods out of the firm.

logo A brand name or company name written in a distinctive way; short for logotype.

loss leader A product priced below cost to attract consumers, who may then make additional purchases.

M

macroenvironment Broad societal forces that shape every business and nonprofit marketer including the physical environment, sociocultural forces, demographic factors, economic factors, scientific and technical knowledge, and political and legal factors.

macromarketing The aggregate of marketing activities in an economy or the marketing system of a society, as opposed to micromarketing.

Magnuson—Moss Warranty Act Federal law requiring that guarantees provided by sellers be made available to buyers before purchase and that they specify who the warrantor is, what products or parts of products are covered, what the warrantor must do if the product is defective, how long the warranty applies, and the obligations of the buyer.

mail-order wholesaler A limited-service wholesaler that uses catalogs, mail or telephone ordering, and mail delivery.

majority fallacy The error caused by a marketing effort that blindly pursues the largest, or most easily identified, or most accessible market segment. The error lies in ignorance the fact that other marketers will be pursuing the same segments.

manufacturer brand A brand owned by the maker of the product. Sometimes called a national brand or a world brand.

manufacturers' agent Independent agent intermediary that represents a limited number of noncompeting suppliers in a limited geographical area. Also called a manufacturers' representative.

marginal analysis A method for determining the costs and revenues associated with the production and sale of each additional unit of a product.

marginal approach In setting the promotional budget, a method whereby the marketer attempts to spend resources until additional expenditures would not be justified by the additional sales and profits they would generate.

marginal cost The net addition to a firm's total costs that results from the production of one additional unit of product.

marginal revenue The net addition to a firm's total revenue that results from the sale of one additional unit of product.

market A group of potential customers that may want the product offered and that has the resources, the willingness, and the ability to purchase it.

market development The strategy by which an organization attempts to draw new customers to an existing product, most commonly by introducing the product in a new geographical area.

market factor A variable associated with sales that is analyzed in forecasting sales.

market factor index A number of variables that in a combined index are associated with sales.

marketing The process of planning and executing the conception, pricing, promotion, and distribution of ideas, goods, and services to create exchanges that will satisfy individual and organizational objectives.

marketing audit A comprehensive review and appraisal of the total marketing operation; often performed by outside consultants or other unbiased personnel.

marketing concept Organizational philosophy that stresses consumer orientation, long-range profitability, and the integration of marketing and other organizational functions.

marketing ethics The principles that guide an organization's conduct and the values it expects to express in certain situations.

marketing intelligence system A network of diverse sources that provide data about the marketing environment; part of an organization's data collection system.

marketing management The process of planning, executing, and controlling marketing activities to attain marketing goals and objectives effectively and efficiently.

marketing mix The specific combination of interrelated and interdependent marketing activities in which an organization engages to meet its objectives.

marketing myopia Failure to define organizational purpose from a broad consumer orientation.

marketing objective The level of performance the organization, SBU, or operating unit intends to achieve. Objectives define results in measurable terms.

marketing opportunity analysis The interpretation of environmental attributes and change in light of the organization's ability to capitalize on potential opportunities.

marketing organization The part of an organization to which marketing responsibilities are assigned.

marketing orientation Organizational philosophy that focuses on satisfying consumers' wants and needs better than the competitors.

marketing plan A written statement of the marketing objectives and strategies to be followed and the specific courses of action to be taken when (or if) certain events occur.

marketing program All of the activities associated with marketing research and the implementation and control of the individual elements of the marketing mix.

marketing research The systematic and objective process of generating information for use in marketing decision making.

marketing strategy A plan identifying what marketing goals and objectives will be pursued and how they will be achieved in the time available.

market manager An individual responsible for administering all marketing activities that relate to a particular market, including forecasting, product planning, and pricing.

market penetration The strategy by which sales of an established product grow because of increased use of the product in existing markets.

market position The way consumers perceive a product relative to its competition. Also called competitive position.

market potential The upper limit of industry demand. That is, the expected sales volume for all brands of a particular product during a given period.

market/product matrix A matrix containing the four possible combinations of old and new products with old and new markets. The purpose of the matrix is to broadly categorize alternative opportunities in terms of basic strategies for growth.

market segment A portion of a larger market, identified according to some shared characteristic or characteristics.

market segmentation Dividing a heterogeneous market into segments.

market share The percentage of total industry sales accounted for by a particular firm, or the percentage of sales of a given product accounted for by a particular brand.

markup on cost A markup expressed as a percentage of the cost of an item.

markup on selling price A markup expressed as a percentage of the selling price of an item.

and component products that go into the manufacture of a final product.

profit analysis A study that organizes profits by particular segments of the marketing operation in order to evaluate them.

profit and loss statement A statement listing net sales, costs, expenses, and profit or loss for a specified period. Also called an operating statement.

promotion The element of the marketing mix that includes all forms of marketing communications.

promotional campaign A series of promotional activities aimed at achieving a specific objective or set of objectives.

promotional mix The organization's combination of personal selling, advertising, publicity and public relations, and sales promotion; the total promotional effort.

prospecting In sales, identifying likely customers. In prospecting, the salesperson may search lists of previous customers, trade association lists, government publications, and many other sources.

psychographics Quantitative measures of lifestyles.

psychological/social needs Needs stemming from people's interactions with the social environment.

publicity A message about a product, organization, or event carried by a nonpersonal medium but not paid for by a sponsor. Publicity involves a third party who determines whether the message is newsworthy enough to transmit and what the nature of the transmitted message will be.

public relations The activities involved in actively seeking to manage the nature of the publicity an organization receives.

puffery The practice of exaggerating a product's good points in advertising or selling.

pull strategy A promotional strategy whereby a supplier promotes a product to the ultimate consumer with the aim of stimulating demand and thus pulling the product through the channel of distribution.

purchase satisfaction The feeling on the part of the consumer that the decision to buy was appropriate.

pure competition A market structure characterized by free entry, a homogeneous product, and many sellers and buyers, none of whom controls price.

push strategy A promotional strategy whereby a supplier promotes a product to marketing intermediaries with the aim of pushing the product through the channel of distribution.

Q

qualifying In sales, evaluating a prospect's potential. Key questions are whether the prospect needs the product, can pay for it, and has the authority to make, or at least contribute to, a decision to buy.

quality-based competition Competition based on product quality; associated with form utility.

quality of life The sense of well-being perceived by people in a society.

quota-bonus plan Compensation plan whereby a salesperson is paid a base salary related to achievement of a quota and a bonus for sales exceeding the quota.

quota sample A nonprobability sample whose members' characteristics match a predetermined quota.

R

rack jobber A limited-function wholesaler that contracts with a retailer to place display racks in a store and to stock those racks with merchandise.

railroads In relation to physical distribution, a mode of transportation by which products are shipped by train over railways.

random discounting A pricing strategy whereby discounts are offered occasionally and unpredictably.

random sampling error Inaccuracy of results associated with random sampling and caused by chance variation.

reach The number of people exposed to an advertisement carried by a given medium.

rebate A sales promotion wherein some portion of the price paid for a product is returned to the purchaser.

recall test In the context of advertising, a research tool used to determine how much people remember about an advertisement. Unaided recall tests give those being tested no clues as to the specific material to be remembered. Aided recall tests provide such clues. Related recall tests measure recall of specific messages or images.

receiver In communication theory, the one at whom a message is aimed.

reference group A group that influences an individual because that individual is a member or aspires to be a member of the group.

reference pricing strategy A strategy whereby a moderate price is set for a version of a product that will be displayed next to a higher-priced model of the same brand or next to a competitive brand.

referent power Power based on leadership and admired characteristics.

reinforcement Reward; reinforcement strengthens a stimulus-response relationship.

related recall test *See recall test.*

relationship marketing Marketing activities aimed at building long-term relationships with parties, especially customers, that contribute to the company's success.

relationship management The building and maintaining of long-term relationships with the parties that contribute to the organization's success; the sales function of managing the account relationship and ensuring that buyers receive appropriate services.

relative advantage The characteristic of offering clear-cut advantages over competing offerings.

repositioning Changing the market position of a product.

research design A master plan that specifically identifies what tools and techniques and procedures will be used to collect and analyze data relevant to the research problem.

response A reaction called forth by a stimulus.

retailer cooperative organization A group of independent retailers that combine resources and expertise to control their wholesaling needs, as through a centralized wholesale buying center.

retailing All business activities concerned with the sale of products to the ultimate users of those products.

retail selling Selling to ultimate consumers.

return on investment (ROI) The ratio of profits to assets (or net worth) for an organization, a unit of an organization, a product line, or a brand. Also called the profit target.

returns Goods sent back to the seller because of damage, late delivery, or some other reason.

returns and allowances percentage Percentage of returns and allowances for each sales dollar: returns and allowances/net sales.

reward power Power based on the ability to give economic rewards.

right to be informed The consumer's right to obtain the information that is required to make an intelligent choice from among the available products.

right to choose The consumer's right to have viable alternatives from which to choose.

right to safety The right consumers have to expect that the products they purchase are free from unnecessary dangers.

risk-taking function Assumption of the responsibility for losses when the future is uncertain.

Robinson—Patman Act U.S. federal law passed in 1936 and intended to halt discriminatory pricing policies by specifying certain limited conditions under which a seller may charge different prices to different buyers.

role A cluster of behavior patterns considered appropriate for a position in a social setting.

routinized response behavior The least complex type of decision making, in which the consumer bases choices on past behavior and needs no other information.

S

salary plus commission Compensation consisting of a regular salary plus a commission based on sales performance.

sales analysis A detailed study of sales records or the aggregation and breaking down of sales information to reveal patterns that can be used to evaluate the effectiveness and efficiency of marketing efforts.

sales branch Wholesaling establishment maintained by a manufacturer that does not carry an inventory of the product.

sales forecast The actual sales volume an organization expects during a given period.

sales forecasting The process of estimating sales volume for a product, an organizational unit, or an entire organization over a specific future time period.

sales management The marketing management activity that deals with planning, organizing, directing, and controlling the personal selling effort.

sales objectives The specific objectives that an organization's sales effort will attempt to meet. Sales objectives should be precise and quantifiable, should include a time frame, and should be reasonable in terms of the organization's resources.

sales office Wholesaling establishment maintained by a manufacturer that does not carry an inventory of the product.

sales orientation Organizational philosophy that emphasizes selling existing products, whether or not they meet consumer needs, often through aggressive sales techniques and advertising.

sales potential The maximum share of the market an individual organization can expect during a given period.

sales presentation The step in the creative selling process wherein the salesperson attempts to persuasively communicate the product's benefits and to explain appropriate courses of action.

sales promotion Promotional activities other than personal selling, advertising, and public relations intended to stimulate buyer purchases or dealer effectiveness over a specific time period.

sales team The sales representative and those who support his or her efforts in making sales and servicing accounts. Support personnel may include technical specialists, missionary salespeople, sales correspondents, and others.

sales territory The specific and prospective accounts assigned to a salesperson. They may be based on geographical divisions, customer types, or product lines.

sample A portion or subset of a larger population.

sampling Any procedure in which a small part of the whole is used as the basis for conclusions regarding the whole. The small part is called the sample; and the whole, the population.

science The accumulation of knowledge about humans and the environment.

scrambled merchandising The offering of products for sale in a retail establishment not traditionally associated with those products.

screening stage The stage in new product development that involves analysis of ideas to determine their appropriateness and reasonableness in relation to the organization's goals and objectives.

seasonal discount A price discount intended to encourage purchase of products during a time of year when sales are traditionally low.

secondary data Data previously collected and assembled for some purpose other than the one at hand.

secondary group A group, generally larger than a primary group, whose influence on members is not as strong as the influence of primary groups.

second-market discounting A differential pricing strategy whereby a product is sold at one price in the core target market and at a reduced price in a secondary market.

selective attention A perceptual screening device whereby a person does not attend to a particular stimulus.

selective demand advertising Advertising aimed at stimulating demand for a particular brand.

selective distribution A distribution strategy in which the product is sold in a limited number of outlets.

selective exposure The principle describing the fact that individual, selectively determine whether or not they will be exposed to certain stimuli.

selective interpretation A perceptual screening device whereby a person distorts a stimulus that is incompatible with his or her values or attitudes.

selective perception The screening out of certain stimuli and the interpretation of other stimuli according to personal experience, attitudes, or the like.

selective retention The process by which a person remembers information in which he or she is interested and forgets information that is of little interest.

self-concept The individual's perception and appraisal of himself or herself.

selling agent Independent agent intermediary similar to a manufacturers' agent but representing a given product in every area in which it is sold, rather than in a limited geographical area.

selling function Activities associated with communicating ideas and making a sale, thus effecting the transfer of ownership of a product.

service A task or activity performed for a buyer or an intangible that cannot be handled or examined before purchase.

service encounter A period during which a consumer interacts with a service provider.

service function Activities performed by channel members that increase the efficiency and effectiveness of the exchange process. Repair services and management services provided by intermediaries are examples.

service level Extent of extra services provided to customers; often related to price.

service mark A symbol that identifies services. It distinguishes a service in the way a trademark identifies a good.

service quality A comparison of customers' expectations with the performance of service providers.

shopping product A product for which consumers feel the need to make comparisons; seek out more information; examine merchandise; or otherwise reassure themselves about quality, style, or value before making a purchase.

simple random sample A probability sample selected in such a way that all members of the sampled population had an equal chance of being selected.

simplicity of usage Ease of operation; a product benefit that can offset the complexity of the product itself.

single-product strategy The product line strategy that involves offering one product item or one product version with very few options.

single-sourcing Purchasing a product on a regular basis from a single vendor.

situational analysis The interpretation of environmental attributes and change in light of the organization's ability to capitalize on potential opportunities.

skimming price A relatively high price, often charged at the beginning of a product's life. The price is systematically lowered as time goes by.

slice-of-life format An advertising format that dramatizes a "typical" setting wherein people use the product.

social audit A means for reviewing whether an organization is accomplishing its mission in society; an investigation of the firm's place in the macromarketing environment.

social class A group of people with similar levels of prestige, power, and wealth who also share a set of related beliefs, attitudes, and values in their thinking and behavior.

social institution A stable cluster of values, norms, roles, and other means that have developed over time to fulfill a central purpose of a society.

socialization process The process by which a society transmits its values, norms, and roles to its members.

social marketing Activities aimed at enhancing the acceptability of social causes, ideas, or desirable behaviors; sometimes used to refer to not-for-profit marketing.

social and psychological need Need stemming from people's interactions with the social environment.

social responsibility The ethical consequences of a person's or an organization's acts as they might affect the interests of others.

social value A value that embodies the goals a society views as important and expresses a culture's shared ideas of preferred ways of acting.

societal marketing concept Organizational philosophy that stresses the need for marketers to consider the collective needs of society as well as individual consumers' desires and organizational profits.

sociology The science that studies cultures, social institutions, groups, and social interactions.

sorting function An activity performed by marketing intermediaries in which accumulated products are classified as to grade and size, then grouped accordingly.

source In communication theory, the one who sends a message.

specialty mass merchandisers Mass merchandisers that carry a product selection limited to one or a few product categories.

specialty product A consumer product that is not frequently bought, is likely to be expensive, and for which great care in purchase is likely.

specialty store A retail establishment that sells a single product or a few related lines.

specialty wholesaler Full-service merchant wholesaler that sells a very narrow selection of products.

spokesperson A person who, representing the advertiser, directly addresses the audience and urges them to buy the advertiser's product.

Standard Industrial Classification (SIC) system A numerical coding system developed by the U.S. government and widely employed by organizational marketers to classify organizations in terms of the economic activities in which they are engaged. It is being replaced by the North American Classification system.

star High-market-share product in a high-growth market.

still-life format An advertising format that makes the product or package its focal point, emphasizing a visually attractive presentation and the product's brand name.

stimulus Some aspect of the environment that triggers a behavioral response.

stimulus factor A characteristic of a stimulus—for example, the size, colors, or novelty of a print advertisement—that affects perception.

stock turnover ratio The number of times inventory, or stock, is turned over, or sold, over a specified period: net sales/average inventory or cost of goods sold/average inventory. Also called inventory turnover ratio. Turnover measures the speed with which inventory is sold.

storage The holding and housing of goods in inventory for a certain period of time.

store image Everything consumers see and feel about a store. Store image is affected by such things as personnel, merchandise, external and internal appearance, prices, and services.

storyline format An advertisement that gives a history or tells a story about the product.

straight commission Compensation based strictly on sales performance.

straight rebuy A type of organizational buying characterized by automatic and regular purchase of familiar products from regular suppliers.

straight salary Compensation at a regular rate, not immediately tied to sales performance.

strategic alliance An informal partnership or collaboration between a marketer and an organizational buyer.

strategic business unit (SBU) A distinct unit, such as a company, division, department, or product line, of the overall parent organization with a specific marketing focus and a manager who has the authority and responsibility for managing all unit functions.

strategic corporate goals Broad organizational goals related to the long-term future. The organization's primary strategic corporate goal is identified in its organizational mission statement.

strategic gap The difference between where the organization wants to be and where it is.

strategic marketing process The entire sequence of managerial and operational activities required to create and sustain effective and efficient marketing strategies.

strategic planning Long-term planning dealing with the organization's primary goals and objectives, carried out primarily by top management.

strategic window of opportunity A limited time during which an organization's capabilities, resources, or competitive position provide it with certain advantages over the competition.

stratified sample A probability sample resulting from a process by which the population is divided into subgroups based on characteristics of interest and then a simple random sample is taken from each subgroup.

style A distinctive execution, construction, or design of a product class.

subculture A group within a dominant culture that is distinct from the culture. A subculture will typically display some values or norms that differ from those of the overall culture.

suggestive selling Suggesting to a customer who is making a purchase that an additional item or service be purchased.

supermarket Any large, self-service, departmentalized retail establishment but especially one that primarily sells food items.

supplier An organization that provides raw materials, component parts, equipment, services, or other resources to a marketing organization; also called a vendor.

supply curve A graphic representation of the relationship between various prices and the amount of product that will be supplied at those prices. Also called a supply schedule.

survey Any research effort in which data are gathered systematically from a sample of people by means of a questionnaire. Surveys are conducted through face-to-face interviews, telephone interviews, and mailed questionnaires.

SWOT Acronym for internal Strengths and Weaknesses and external Opportunities and Threats. In analyzing marketing opportunities, the decision maker evaluates all these factors.

systematic bias A research shortcoming caused by flaws in the design or execution of a research study.

systems concept The idea that elements may be strongly interrelated and may interact toward achieving a goal.

T

tactics Specific actions intended to implement strategies.

target market A specific market segment toward which an organization aims its marketing plan.

target population The population of interest in a marketing research study; the population from which samples are to be drawn.

target return pricing Setting prices to yield a particular target level of profit for the organization.

tariff A tax imposed by a government on an imported product.

task force A group within an organization whose membership spans its functional departments and ensures that a new project gets appropriate departmental support and resources. The group gives its full attention to the new product from start to finish.

task method *See objective and task method.*

technological obsolescence The pattern of products becoming out of date because of technological improvements in competing products.

technology The application of science to practical purposes.

telemarketing Using the telephone as the primary means

of communicating with prospective customers. Tele-marketers often use computers for order taking.

television home shopping A cable television shopping service in which consumers see a product on their home TV screens and place orders by telephone.

testimonial Advertising format in which a person, usually a well-known person, states that he or she owns, uses, or supports the product being advertised.

test marketing A controlled experimental procedure that provides an opportunity to test a new product under realistic market conditions in a limited geographical area.

tie-in Collaborative effort between two or more organizations or brands that work as partners in a promotional effort.

time-based competition Competition based on providing time utility by delivering the product when the consumer wants it.

time utility Utility created by making goods and services available when consumers want them.

total cost Fixed costs plus variable costs.

total cost concept In relation to physical distribution, a focus on the entire range of costs associated with a particular distribution method.

total product The wide range of tangible and intangible benefits that a buyer might gain from a product after purchasing it.

total quality assurance A differentiation strategy that promises customers' satisfaction with product quality.

total quality management (TQM) A management principle that seeks to instill the idea of customer-driven quality throughout the organization and managing all employees so that there will be continuous improvement in quality.

trade discount A discount given to wholesalers, retail dealers, or others in a particular trade as a repayment for the performance of certain functions; thus also called a functional discount.

trademark A legally protected brand name or brand mark. Its owner has exclusive rights to its use.

trade show A meeting or convention of members of a particular industry where business-to-business contacts are routinely made.

transportation In relation to physical distribution, the physical movement or shipment of products to locations in the distribution channel.

trialability The ability to be tested by possible future users with little risk or effort.

trial close A personal selling tactic intended to elicit from a prospect a signal indicating whether he or she is ready to buy.

trial sampling The distribution of newly marketed products to enhance trialability and familiarity; giving away free samples.

truck wholesaler A limited-service wholesaler that sells a limited line of items (often perishable goods) from a truck, thus providing immediate delivery. Also called a truck jobber.

turnover Sales divided by average inventory. Turnover measures the speed with which merchandise is sold.

tying contract An agreement tying the purchase of one product to the purchase of another.

U

unaided recall test *See recall test.*

uncontrollable variable In marketing, a force or influence external to the organization and beyond its control.

undercutting-the-competition strategy A pricing strategy whereby an organization sets prices at levels lower than those of competitors.

undeveloped country A country in which the standard of living is low and the economy is largely based on the land and agriculture.

undifferentiated marketing A marketing effort not targeted at a specific market segment but designed to appeal to a broad range of customers. This approach is appropriate in a market that lacks diversity of interest.

unfair sales practices acts State laws that limit or prohibit the use of certain sales and marketing techniques; most commonly, laws that require that certain types of merchandise be sold at prescribed markups.

uniform delivered pricing A type of delivered pricing in which an organization charges the same price for a given product in all locations.

unique selling proposition (USP) A unique characteristic of a product or brand identified by the marketer as the one on which to base a promotional campaign; often used in a product differentiation approach to promotion.

Universal Product Code (UPC) The array of black bars, readable by optical scanners, found on many products. The UPC permits computerization of tasks such as checkout and compilation of sales volume information.

user The buying-center role played by the organizational member who will actually use the product.

V

VALS-2 A psychographic classification scheme that divides consumers into groupings according to values, attitudes, and lifestyles.

value The power of one product to attract another product in an exchange.

value chain Chain of activities by which a company brings in materials, creates a good or service, markets it, and provides service after a sale is made. Each step creates more value for the consumer.

variable cost A cost that varies directly with an organization's production or sales. Variable costs are a function of volume.

variable pricing strategy *See differential pricing strategy.*

vendor analysis The rating of alternative suppliers on attributes such as product quality, reliability, delivery speed, and price.

venture team A group of specialists in an organization who operate in an entrepreneurial environment to develop a new business without being a closely controlled part of the organization. The team independently develops, tests, and commercializes new products.

vertical cooperative promotion An approach whereby channel members at different levels jointly sponsor particular promotions.

vertical marketing system A vertical network of marketing establishments operating as a centrally coordinated distribution system.

voluntary chain A group of independent retailers linked to a wholesale supplier in a system instituted by the wholesaler.

voluntary membership group Membership group to which an individual has chosen to belong.

W

warehouse club General mass merchandise outlet in which only "members" are allowed to shop. Also called a closed door house.

warehouse retailer A mass merchandiser that sells products from showrooms that double as storage places for stock.

warehousing All the activities necessary for the holding and housing of goods between the time they are produced and the time of shipment to buyers.

water transportation In relation to physical distribution, the use of ships, boats, or barges in the shipment of products.

wheel of retailing A theory positing that new forms of retail institutions enter the marketplace as low-status, low-margin, low-price operations and then gradually trade up, opening a market position for a new low-end retailer.

wholesaler An organization or individual that serves as a marketing intermediary by facilitating transfer of products and title to them. Wholesalers do not produce the product, consume it, or sell it to ultimate consumers.

width of product mix The number of product lines within a product mix. Wide indicates a high diversity of product types; narrow indicates little diversity.

world brand A product that is widely distributed around the world with a single brand name common to all countries and recognized in all its markets.

Z

zone pricing A type of delivered pricing in which prices vary according to the number of geographic zones through which a product passes in moving from seller to buyer.

Endnotes

Chapter 1

1. Elizabeth Sanger, "Morphin Rangers Overpower Rivals," *New York Newsday,* June 27, 1994; and Carol Wolf, "Zapped by High Demand: Shortage of Power Ranger Toys Tests Parents, Stores," *Crain's Cleveland Business,* June 6, 1994.

2. Jennifer Cody, "Power Rangers Take On the Whole World," *Wall Street Journal,* March 23, 1994.

3. For a full treatment of the exchange process, see Franklin S. Houston and Julie B. Gassenheimer, "Marketing and Exchange," *Journal of Marketing,* October 1987, pp. 3–18.

4. For an excellent discussion of not-for-profit marketing issues, see P. Rajan Vardarajan and Anil Menon, "Cause-Related Marketing: A Coalignment of Marketing Strategy and Corporate Philosophy," *Journal of Marketing,* July 1988, pp. 58–74.

5. This is the American Marketing Association's definition of marketing as reprinted in *Marketing News,* March 1, 1985, p. 1. For a philosophical discussion about the nature of marketing see Shelby D. Hunt, "Marketing Is...," *Journal of the Academy of Marketing Science,* Fall 1992, pp. 301–311 and Gerald Albaum, "What Is Marketing? A Comment on Marketing Is...," *Journal of the Academy of Marketing Science,* Fall 1992, 313–316.

6. This will be explained in greater detail in the section on the marketing concept.

7. Regis McKenna, "Marketing Is Everything," *Harvard Business Review,* January–February 1991, pp. 65–79.

8. The word marketing derives from the Latin *mercatus* (marketplace), which, in turn, comes from the word *mercari* (to trade).

9. Neil H. Borden, "The Concept of the Marketing Mix," *Journal of Advertising Research,* June 1964, pp. 2–7.

10. William D. Perreault, Jr. and E. Jerome McCarthy, *Basic Marketing: A Managerial Approach,* 12th ed. (Homewood, Ill.: Richard D. Irwin, 1996).

11. When one or more elements of the marketing mix are altered or controlled, as by a law or other environmental influence, the other elements of the mix, as well as consumer behaviors, are affected.

12. Matt Murray, "What Kids Eat: Snacks, Meals, Snacks, Snacks," *Wall Street Journal,* October 20, 1994.

13. For a seminal work on historical marketing philosophies, see Ronald A. Fullerton, "How Modern Is Modern Marketing? Marketing's Evolution and the Myth of the 'Production Era,'" *Journal of Marketing,* January 1988, pp. 108–125. Also see D. G. Brian Jones and David D. Monieson, "Early Development of Marketing Thought," *Journal of Marketing,* January 1990, pp. 102–113, and Terence Nevett, "Historical Investigation and the Practice of Marketing," *Journal of Marketing,* July 1991, pp. 13–23.

14. Although the marketing concept has clear applications to many situations, the point has been made that it need not be applied to every possible situation. Franklin S. Houston, "The Marketing Concept: What It Is and What It Is Not," *Journal of Marketing,* April 1986, pp. 81–87. See also Bernard J. Jaworski and Ajay K. Koli, "Market Orientation: Antecedents and Consequences," *Journal of Marketing,* July 1993, pp. 53–70 and Stanley F. Slater and John C. Narver, "Does Competitive Environment Moderate the Market Orientation-Performance Relationship?" *Journal of Marketing,* January 1994, pp. 46–55.

15. Fred J. Burch, "The Marketing Philosophy as a Way of Business Life," in *The Marketing Concept, Its Meaning to Management,* Marketing Series no. 99. See also Theodore Levitt, "Marketing Myopia," *Harvard Business Review,* July–August 1960, pp. 45–56.

16. Mary Kuhn and Kitty Kevin, "The 1995 New Product Hit Parade," *Food Processing,* November 1, 1995.

17. Theodore Levitt, "Marketing Myopia," *Harvard Business Review,* July–August 1960, pp. 45–56.

18. For discussions on this contemporary issue, see George Day, "The Capabilities of Market-Driven Organizations," *Journal of Marketing,* October 1994, pp. 37–52; John C. Narver and Stanley F. Slater, "The Effect of

Marketing Orientation on Business Profitability," *Journal of Marketing,* October 1990, pp. 20–35; Bernard Jaworski and Ajay Kohli, "Market Orientation: Antecedents and Consequences," *Journal of Marketing,* July 1993, pp. 53–70; George S. Day and Prakash Nedungadi, "Managerial Representations of Competitive Advantage," *Journal of Marketing,* April 1994, pp. 31–44; Gary L. Frankwick, James C. Ward, Michael D. Hutt, and Peter H. Reingen, "Evolving Patterns of Organizational Beliefs in the Formation of Strategy," *Journal of Marketing,* April 1994, pp. 96–110.

19. Theodore Levitt, "Marketing Myopia," *Harvard Business Review,* July–August 1960, pp. 45–56. For an excellent discussion of customer value, see Robert B. Woodruff, "Customer Value: The Next Source for Competitive Advantage," *Journal of the Academy of Marketing Science,* Spring 1997, pp. 138–153; A. Parasuraman, "Reflections on Gaining Competitive Advantage through Customer Value," *Journal of the Academy of Marketing Science,* Spring 1997, pp. 154–161; Stanley F. Slater, "Developing a Customer Value-Based Theory of the Firm," *Journal of the Academy of Marketing Science,* Spring 1997, pp. 162–167.

20. Paul Mazur, "Does Distribution Cost Enough?" *Fortune,* November 1947, p. 138.

21. Major League Baseball's owners made a proposal for a revenue-sharing arrangement with the players during the off season in the winter of 1993/1994. The owners' proposal asked players to accept a cap on overall team payrolls as part of a new collective bargaining agreement, similar to arrangements in pro basketball and football. The owners' proposal for a salary cap unleashed sharp opposition from the major league players' association's rank and file. The players wanted salary arbitration changed from three years to two years. The disagreements between players and owners led to a strike in August 1994.

Chapter 2

1. See, for example, Richard L. Daft, *Management,* 3rd ed. (Ft. Worth: Dryden Press, 1996), p. 8.

2. Mission statement of The Limited Corporation reprinted by permission.

3. Theodore Levitt, "Marketing Myopia," *Harvard Business Review,* July–August 1960, p. 45.

4. Michael E. Porter, *Competitive Strategy* (New York: Free Press, 1980).

5. Janice Castro, "Making It Better," *Time,* November 13, 1989, pp. 78–81; David A. Gavin, "Competing on the Eight Dimensions of Quality," *Harvard Business Review,* November–December 1987, pp. 101–108.

6. "Burger King Opens Customer Hot Line," *Marketing News,* May 28, 1990, p. 7.

7. Marshall Loeb, "How to Grow a New Product Every Day," *Fortune,* November 14, 1994, p. 269.

8. Gene Bylinsky, "Manufacture for Reuse," *Fortune,* February 6, 1995, pp. 110, 112.

9. Michael A. Hitt, R. Duane Ireland, and Robert E. Hoskisson, *Strategic Management: Competitiveness and Globalization* (St. Paul: West Educational Publishing, 1995), p. 46.

10. Based on a speech by Dan Robertson at the 1983 ABSEL Convention, Tulsa, Oklahoma, February 1983.

11. Peter D. Bennett, *Marketing Terms* (Chicago: American Marketing Association, 1988), p. 189.

12. Ray Billington, *Living Philosophy: An Introduction to Moral Thought* (London: Routledge, 1988), p. 17.

13. See Geoffrey P. Lantos, "An Ethical Base for Marketing Decision Making," *Journal of Business and Industrial Marketing,* Spring 1987, pp. 11–16; R. Eric Reidenbach, Donald P. Robin, and Lyndon Dawson, "An Application and Extension of a Multidimensional Ethics Scale to Selected Marketing Practices and Marketing Groups," *Journal of the Academy of Marketing Science,* Spring 1991, pp. 90–91. For formal theories of marketing decision making and ethical dilemmas, see Shelby D. Hunt and Scott Vitell, "A General Theory of Marketing," *Journal of Marketing,* Spring, 1986, pp. 5–16; O. C. Ferrell, Larry G. Gresham, and John Fraedrich, "A

Synthesis of Ethical Decision Models for Marketing," *Journal of Macromarketing,* Fall 1989, pp. 87–96.

14. For a general discussion of ethical dilemmas in business, see John R. Schermerhorn, Jr., James G. Hunt, and Richard N. Osborn, *Managing Organizational Behavior* (New York: John Wiley & Sons, 1991), p. 27. See also Anusorn Singhapakdi and Scott J. Vitel, "Marketing Ethics: Factors Influencing Perceptions of Ethical Problems and Alternatives," *Journal of Macromarketing,* Spring 1990, pp. 4–18.

15. John R. Schermerhorn, Jr., James G. Hunt, and Richard N. Osborn, *Managing Organizational Behavior* (New York: John Wiley & Sons, 1991).

16. For investigations of ethical awareness and values among marketing executives, see David J. Fritzche, "An Examination of Marketing Ethics: Role of the Decision Maker, Consequences of the Decision," *Journal of Macromarketing,* Fall 1988, pp. 29–39; M. M. Pressley, D. J. Lincoln, and T. Little, "Ethical Belief and Personal Values of Top Level Executives," *Journal of Business Research,* December 1982; Shelby D. Hunt, Van R. Wood, and Lawrence B. Chonko, "Corporate Ethical Values and Organizational Commitment in Marketing," *Journal of Marketing,* July 1989, pp. 79–90; R. Eric Reidenbach, Donald P. Robin, and Lyndon Dawson, "An Application and Extension of a Multidimensional Ethics Scale to Selected Marketing Practices and Marketing Groups," *Journal of the Academy of Marketing Science,* Spring 1991, pp. 83–92; and Jerry R. Goolsby and Shelby D. Hunt, "Cognitive Moral Development and Marketing," *Journal of Marketing,* January 1992, pp. 55–68. For a discussion of green marketing ethics see Noah Walley and Bradley Whitehead, "It's Not Easy Being Green," *Harvard Business Review,* May–June, pp. 46–52. See also commentary from various individuals in "The Challenge of Going Green," *Harvard Business Review,* July–August 1994, pp. 46–55.

Chapter 3

1. See, for example, Terry Clark, "International Marketing and National Character: A Review and Proposal for an Integrative Theory," *Journal of Marketing,* October 1990, pp. 66–79; Duane Davis, Michael Morris, and Jeff Allen, "Perceived Environmental Turbulence and Its Effect on Selected Entrepreneurship, Marketing, and Organizational Characteristics in Industrial Firms," *Journal of the Academy of Marketing Science,* Winter 1991, pp. 43–52; Leopoldo G. Arias Bolzmann, "Retailing in a Developing Economy: A Case Study of the Peruvian Retailing Economy," in *Advances in Marketing,* ed. Joseph F. Hair, Jr., Daryl O. McKee, and Daniel L. Sherrell (Baton Rouge, La.: Southwestern Marketing Association, 1992), pp. 250–258; and Ravi S. Achrol, "Evolution of the Marketing Organization: New Forms of Turbulent Environments," *Journal of Marketing,* October 1991, pp. 77–92.

2. Elaine Underwood, "Green Jeans and Pop Bottles," *Brandweek,* October 10, 1994, p. 8.

3. For related articles see James A. Roberts, "Green Consumers in the 1990s," *Journal of Business Research,* July 1996, pp. 217–232, and Ajay Menon and Anil Menon, "Enviropreneurial Marketing Strategy: The Emergence of Corporate Environmentalism as a Marketing Strategy," *Journal of Marketing,* January 1997, pp. 51–67.

4. Ian Robertson, *Sociology* (New York: Worth Publishing, 1987), pp. 64–65.

5. Unless otherwise noted, the statistics in this section are from the U.S. Bureau of the Census. See *http://www.census.gov* for updated information.

6. Peter Francese, "America at Mid-Decade," *American Demographics,* February 1995, p. 28.

7. *Ibid.*

8. Larry S. Lowe and Kevin McCrohan, "Gray Marketing in the United States," *Journal of Consumer Marketing,* Winter 1988, pp. 45–51 and Haya El Nasser and Andrea Stone, "Study: 2020 Begins Age of the Elderly," *USA Today,* May 21, 1996, p. 4A.

9. Cheryl Russell, "The Aging of Two Generations," *Marketing Power,* November 1995, p. 6 and Melinda Beck, "Next Population Bulge Shows Its Might," *The Wall Street Journal,* February 3, 1997, p. B1.

10. Peter Francese, "America at Mid-Decade," *American Demographics,* February 1995, p. 26.

11. References for this section include: U.S. Department of Labor, Bureau of Labor Statistics, "Outlook 2000," bulletin 2352, April 1990 (Washington D.C.: Government Printing Office, 1990) and from the following publications of the U.S. Bureau of the Census (all published by the Government Printing Office): "Household and Family Characteristics," March 1990 and 1989, "Current Population Reports," series P-20, no. 447; "How We're Changing: Current Population Special Studies," series P-23, no. 170, December 1990, and series P-23, January 1990; *Statistical Abstract of the United States: 1990*, pp. 444–445, and 451–453; and "Consumer Income," *Current Population Reports*, series P-60, no. 157, July 1987, p. 15.

12. Paul Overberg, "Rich Earn More than All of the Middle Class," *USA Today*, June 20, 1996, p. A-1.

13. U.S. Bureau of the Census, "U.S. Population Estimates, by Age, Sex, Race, and Hispanic Origin: 1989," *Current Population Reports*, series P-25, no. 1057 (Washington, D.C.: Government Printing Office, 1990), pp. 2–7; and Peter T. Kilborn, "The Middle Class Feels Betrayed, but Maybe Not Enough to Rebel," *New York Times*, January 12, 1992, p. 1e.

14. GNP and other measures of the economy are not always accurate. Unmeasured, or "underground," activities take place throughout the economy. See Kevin F. McCrohan and James D. Smith, "A Consumer Expenditure Approach to Estimating the Size of the Underground Economy," *Journal of Marketing*, April 1986, p. 48.

15. Kenneth G. Hallgren, "Marketing in an Electronic Age: Profession in Transition," *Proceedings of the Midwest Marketing Association* (1993), pp. 43–47.

16. Kevin Goldman, "Video Explosions Sell Technology to Teens," *The Wall Street Journal*, October 25, 1993.

17. Michael D. Hutt and Thomas Speh, *Industrial Marketing Management* (Hinsdale, Ill.: Dryden Press, 1988), p. 39.

18. Tim Friend, "Cosmetic Ads Must Tone Down Claims," *USA Today*, April 5, 1988, p. 1D.

19. For a survey of this topic, see Bruce D. Fisher and Michael J. Phillips, *The Legal, Ethical and Regulatory Environment of Business* (St. Paul: West Publishing Company, 1992), pp. 627–893.

Chapter 4

1. The "Four Cs of Business" concept is copyrighted by William G. Zikmund, 1991. Use of this conceptual scheme elsewhere is not permitted without written permission from William G. Zikmund. For an alternative conceptualization, see Kenichi Ohnae, *The Mind of the Strategist* (New York: Penguin Books, 1982), p. 91.

2. See Michael H. Morris and Joan M. Jarvi, "Making Marketing Curriculum Entrepreneurial," *Marketing Educator*, Fall 1990, pp. 1 and 8.

3. Patricia Sellers, "John Bryan's Sara Lee," *Fortune*, February 6, 1995, p. 24.

4. However, it should be noted that economic price theory is *ceteris paribus*. That is, all things other than price are assumed to remain the same.

5. Thomas A. Stewart, "Welcome to the Revolution," *Fortune*, December 13, 1993, p. 76.

6. John A. Byrne, "The Futurists Who Fathered the Ideas," *Business Week*, February 8, 1993, p. 103.

7. For an alternative view of this concept, see Michael E. Porter, *Competitive Advantage* (New York: Free Press, 1985), pp. 36–43.

8. Rosabeth Moss Kanter, "Collaborative Advantage: The Art of Alliances," *Harvard Business Review*, July–August 1994, p. 97.

9. James Brian Quinn and Frederick G. Hilmer, "Strategic Outsourcing," *Sloan Management Review*, Summer 1994, p. 43.

10. Peter F. Drucker, "The Information Executives Really Need," *Harvard Business Review*, January–February 1995, p. 59.

11. Shawn Tully, "You'll Never Guess Who Really Makes," *Fortune*, October 3, 1994, p. 127.

12. Harry Berkowitz, "Here Comes a Whopper for One Agency," *New York Newsday*, March 21, 1994.

13. Kenichi Ohmae, "The Equidistant Manager," *Express Magazine*, Fall 1990, pp. 10–12.

14. Philip R. Cateora, *International Marketing* (Homewood, Ill.: Richard D. Irwin, 1990), p. 2.

15. Laurel Wentz, "Multinationals Tread Softly While Advertising in Iran," *Advertising Age International*, November 8, 1993, p. I-21.

16. Bill Montague, "Worst Fears of Free Trade Have Cooled," *USA Today*, November 25, 1994, p. B-1.

17. "Boone Set for Showdown with Japanese Business Culture," *Tulsa World*, June 27, 1990, p. 2B.

18. Geoffrey Lee Martin, "P&G Puts Nappies to Rest in Australia," *Advertising Age*, September 19, 1994, p. I-31.

Chapter 5

1. This chapter presents many of the concepts outlined in William G. Zikmund, *Exploring Marketing Research*, 6th ed. (Ft. Worth: Dryden Press, 1997).

2. See Thomas G. Exter, "The Next Step Is Called GIS," *American Demographics Desk Reference*, May 1992, p. 2.

3. Thomas A. Stewart, "The Netplex: It's a New Silicon Valley," *Fortune*, March 7, 1994, p. 98.

4. Nathaniel Sheppard, Jr., "Information Service Links Professors," *Tulsa World*, February 5, 1995, p. 12.

5. Parts of this section borrow heavily from Patrick A. Moore and Ronald E. Milliman, "Application of the Internet in Marketing Education," paper presented to the Southwest Marketing Association, Houston, Texas, 1995.

6. Rick Tetzeli, "The Internet and Your Business," *Fortune*, March 7, 1994, p. 92.

7. Ralph H. Sprague, Jr., and Hugh J. Watson, *Decision Support Systems: Putting Theory into Practice* (Englewood Cliffs, N.J.: Prentice-Hall, 1986), p. 1. See also Jim Bessen, "Riding the Marketing Information Wave," *Harvard Business Review*, September–October 1994, pp. 150–160.

8. "Three Visions of an Electronic Future," *New York Times*, March 24, 1996, p. 22F.

9. Paul Schneider, "Behind Company Walls: It's the Intranet," *Arizona Business Gazette*, March 7, 1996.

10. "Technology: Sun Microsystems Planning to Unveil Intranet Products," *The Wall Street Journal*, March 26, 1996.

11. Adapted from the definition of research in the report of the committee on Definitions of Marketing Research, 1987. The official AMA definition is as follows: "Marketing research is the function that links the consumer, customer, and public to the marketer through information—information used to identify and define marketing opportunities and problems; generate, refine, and evaluate marketing actions; monitor marketing performance; and improve understanding of marketing as a process. Marketing research specifies the information required to address these issues; designs the method for collecting the information; manages and implements the data collection process; analyzes the results; and communicates the findings and their implications." See also Morris B. Holbrook, "What Is Marketing Research?" and Shelby D. Hunt, "Marketing Research: Proximate Purpose in Ultimate Value," both in *Proceedings, 1987 Winter Educators' Conference*, ed. Russell W. Belk and Gerald Zaltman (Chicago: American Marketing Association, 1987).

12. P. J. Runkel and J. E. McGrath, *Research of Human Behavior: A Systematic Guide to Method* (New York: Holt, Rinehart and Winston, 1972), p. 2.

13. A. Einstein and L. Infeld, *The Evolution of Physics* (New York: Simon and Schuster, 1942), p. 95.

14. Quote from David Walker, "Rubbermaid Tries Its Hand at Bristles and Wood," *Adweek Marketing Week*, March 5, 1990, pp. 20–21.

15. For further insight into problems associated with surveys, see Philip E. Down and John R. Kerr, "Recent Evidence on the Relationship between

Anonymity and Response Variables for Mail Surveys," *Journal of the Academy of Marketing Science,* Spring 1986, pp. 72–82; Jon M. Hawes, Vicky·L. Crittenden, and William F. Crittenden, "The Effects of Personalization, Source, and Offer on Mail Survey Response Rate and Speed," *Akron Business and Economic Review,* Summer 1987, pp. 54–63; and three articles in Joseph F. Hair, Jr., Daryl O. McKee, and Daniel L. Sherrell, eds., *Advances in Marketing* (Baton Rouge, La.: Southwest Marketing Association, 1992): Robert E. Stevens, David London, and C. William McConkey, "Does Questionnaire Color Affect Response Rates?," pp. 80–85; Ronald D. Taylor and Michael Richard, "Mail Survey Response Rates, Item Omission Rates, and Response Speed Resulting from the Use of Advanced Notification," pp. 67–72; and David Strutton and Lou Pelton, "Surveying the Elderly," pp. 264–268.

16. "You Say Tomato, I Say Tomahto," *Express Magazine,* Spring 1992, p. 19.

17. "The Honomichl 50," *Marketing News,* June 5, 1995, p. H4.

Chapter 6

1. William L. Wilkie, *Consumer Behavior,* 2nd ed. (New York: John Wiley & Sons, 1990), p. 12.

2. Kurt Lewin, *A Dynamic Theory of Personality* (New York: McGraw-Hill, 1935).

3. This model is a variation of that discussed by John C. Mowen in *Consumer Behavior,* 4th ed. (New York: Macmillan, 1997).

4. William L. Wilkie, *Consumer Behavior,* 2nd ed. (New York: John Wiley & Sons, 1990), pp. 220–225. See also Mark E. Slama and Armen Tashchian, "Validation of the S-C-R Paradigm for Consumer Involvement with a Consumer Good," *Journal of the Academy of Marketing Science,* Spring 1987, pp. 36–45; Joseph J. Belonax, Jr., and Rajshekhar G. Javalgi, "The Influence of Involvement and Product Class Quality on Consumer Choice Sets," *Journal of the Academy of Marketing Science,* Summer 1989, pp. 209–216.

5. For a related article see Jeffrey B. Schmidt and Richard A. Spreng, "A Proposed Model of External Consumer Information Search," *Journal of the Academy of Marketing Science,* Summer 1996, pp. 232–245.

6. Marketers are interested in dissatisfaction as well as satisfaction; but since complaints are only one measure of dissatisfaction, this result is difficult to measure. Marsha Richins, "A Multivariate Analysis of Responses to Dissatisfaction," *Journal of the Academy of Marketing Science,* Fall 1987, p. 24.

7. A. Maslow, *Motivation and Personality* (New York: Harper & Row, 1954), p. 92.

8. Matthew Grimm, "Coors Serves Taste-Test Results in Ads," *Adweek,* July 1, 1991, p. 9. For related studies on perception in marketing, see R. I. Allison and K. P. Uhl, "Impact of Beer Brand on Taste Perception," *Journal of Marketing Research,* August 1964, pp. 36–39; Gordon L. Patzer, *The Physical Attraction Phenomena* (New York: Plenum Publishing, 1985); William L. Rhey, Hemant Rustogi, and Mary Anne Watson, "Buyers' Perceptions of Automobile Saleswomen: A Field Study," *Advances in Marketing,* eds. Joseph F. Hair, Jr., Daryl O. McKee, and Daniel Sherrell (Baton Rouge, La.: Southwest Marketing Association, 1992), pp. 41–46. Donald R. Lichtenstein, Nancy M. Ridgway, and Richard Netermeyer, "Price Perceptions and Consumer Shopping Behavior," *Journal of Marketing Research,* May 1993, pp. 234–245.

9. A review of the 25-year history of subliminal cues is found in Sid C. Dudley, "Subliminal Advertising: What Is the Controversy About?" *Akron Business and Economic Review,* Summer 1987, pp. 6–18. See also Robert E. Widing II, Ronald Hoverstad, Ronald Coulter, and Gene Brown, "The VASE Scales: Measures of Viewpoints about Sexual Embeds in Advertising," *Journal of Business Research,* January 1991, pp. 3–10.

10. Debra L. Nelson and James Campbell Quick, *Organizational Behavior: Foundations, Realities, and Challenges* (St. Paul: West Educational Publishing, 1994), pp. 112–113.

11. Kenneth R. Evans, Tim Christiansen, and James D. Gill, "The Impact of Social Influence and Role Expectations on Shopping Center Patronage Intentions," *Journal of the Academy of Marketing Science,* Summer 1996, pp. 208–218.

12. See, for example, Van R. Wood and Roy Howell, "A Note on Hispanic Values and Subcultural Research," *Journal of the Academy of Marketing Science,* Winter 1991, pp. 61–67.

13. Studies indicate that the importance of reference groups, opinion leaders, friends, and other such influences may be greater than was recognized in the past. See Dennis L. Rosen and Richard W. Olshavsky, "The Dual Role of Informational Social Influence: Implications for Marketing Management," *Journal of Business Research,* April 1987, pp. 123–144.

14. See Lawrence F. Feick and Linda L. Price, "The Marketing Maven: A Diffuser of Marketplace Information," *Journal of Marketing,* January 1987, pp. 83–97.

15. Sanford Grossbart, Lee Carlson, and Ann Walsh, "Consumer Socialization and Frequency of Shopping with Children," *Journal of the Academy of Marketing Science,* Summer 1991, pp. 155–164.

16. H. L. Davis and B. P. Rigaux, "Perception of Marital Roles in Decision Processes," *Journal of Consumer Research,* June 1984.

Chapter 7

1. This paragraph is based on F. E. Webster, Jr., and Y. Wind, *Organizational Buying Behavior* (Englewood Cliffs, N.J.: Prentice-Hall, 1972), p. 1.

2. A good discussion of derived demand is found in William S. Bishop, John L. Graham, and Michael H. Jones, "Volatility of Derived Demand in Industrial Markets and Its Implications," *Journal of Marketing,* Fall 1984, pp. 95–103. This article suggests marketing strategies that might dampen the powerful effects of derived demand on sales performance.

3. Claudia H. Deutsch, "A Matter of Supplier-Customer Trust," *New York Times,* February 17, 1991, p. F25.

4. Though these three situations are common and widely recognized, some research has been done that offers alternative viewpoints and "improvements." See Erin Anderson, Wujin Chu, and Barton Weitz, "Industrial Purchasing: An Empirical Exploration of the Buyclass Framework," *Journal of Marketing,* July 1987, pp. 71–86; Morry Ghingold, "Testing the Buygrid Buying Process Model," *Journal of Purchasing and Materials Management,* Winter 1986, pp. 30–36.

5. It appears that organizational buyers and sellers develop mental "scripts," which they tend to follow in dealing with each other. Salespeople should devote some effort to understanding these "cognitive scripts." See Thomas W. Leigh and Arno J. Rethans, "A Script-Theoretic Analysis of Industrial Purchasing Behavior," *Journal of Marketing,* Fall 1984, pp. 22–32.

6. It has been suggested that there is a "marketing strategy center," the seller's equivalent of the "buying center." See Michael D. Hutt and Thomas W. Speh, "The Marketing Strategy Center: Diagnosing the Industrial Marketer's Interdisciplinary Role," *Journal of Marketing,* Fall 1984, pp. 53–61.

7. R. D. Buzzell, R. E. M. Nourse, J. B. Matthews, Jr., and T. Levitt, *Marketing: A Contemporary Analysis* (New York: McGraw-Hill, 1972), pp. 205–206.

8. Sue Davis, "New Product Pioneers Garner Grand Awards," *Prepared Foods,* April 15, 1993.

9. Adapted from Press Release, Executive Office of the President, Office of Management and Budget, Washington, D.C. 20603.

Chapter 8

1. Steven L. Goldman, Roger N. Nagel, and Kenneth Preiss, "Why Seiko Has 3,000 Watch Styles," *New York Times,* October 9, 1994, p. F9.

2. Joseph Pine II, Bart Victor, and Andrew C. Boynton, "Making Mass Customization Work," *Harvard Business Review,* September–October 1993, p. 118.

3. Alex Taylor III, "Porsche Slices Up Its Buyers," *Fortune,* January 16, 1995, p. 24.

4. Pricing information from Wilton Woods, "Not Priced for the Nineties," *Fortune,* September 22, 1993, p. 87.

5. "Hot Spot: Ethan Allen," *Advertising Age,* January 13, 1997, p. 38.

Chapter 9

1. Theodore Levitt, *The Marketing Imagination* (New York: Free Press, 1986), p. 79.

2. Peter D. Bennett, *Dictionary of Marketing Terms,* (Chicago: American Marketing Association), 1995.

3. Estimates of the importance of services vary because definitional problems exist. For example, U.S. government statistics omit transportation from the definition of services and thus estimate services to account for approximately 30 percent of the gross national product.

4. Based on the concept presented in G. Lynn Shostack, "Breaking Free from Product Marketing," *Journal of Marketing,* April 1977, p. 76, and a more detailed depiction of this concept, in matrix form, found in Martin Bell, "Some Strategy Implications of a Matrix Approach to the Classification of Marketing Goods and Services," *Journal of the Academy of Marketing Science,* Spring 1986, pp. 13–20.

5. The description presented here varies somewhat from Copeland's classification, which only classified goods. It should also be noted that Copeland's work was influenced by Charles Parlin's 1912 work. Although Copeland's classification is the most commonly used, others have been proposed. These are reviewed, and a new system proposed, in Patrick E. Murphy and Ben M. Enis, "Classifying Products Strategically," *Journal of Marketing,* July 1986, pp. 24–42.

6. Suzanne Oliver, "New Personality: Black and Decker's DeWalt Line of Industrial Power Tools," *Forbes,* August 15, 1994, p. 114.

7. Leonard L. Berry, Valerie Zeithaml, and A. Parasuraman, "Responding to Demand Fluctuations: Key Challenges for Service Business," in *A.M.A. Educators' Proceedings,* eds. R. Belk et al. (Chicago, American Marketing Association, 1985), pp. 231–234. Mary Jo Bitner, "Evaluating Service Encounters: The Effects of Physical Surroundings and Employee Responses," *Journal of Marketing,* April 1990, pp. 68–82. See also Ruth N. Dolton and James H. Drew, "A Longitudinal Analysis of the Impact of Service Changes on Customer Attitudes," *Journal of Marketing,* January 1991, pp. 1–9; Keith B. Murray, "A Test of Service Marketing Theory," *Journal of Marketing,* January 1991, pp. 10–25; Raymond P. Fisk, Stephen J. Grove, and Mary Jo Bitner, "Dramatizing the Service Experience: A Managerial Approach," in *Advances in Services Marketing and Management: Research and Practice,* eds. Teresa A. Swartz, Stephen W. Brown, and David E. Bowen (*JAI Press,* 1992); William H. Davidow and Bro Uttal, "Service Companies: Focus or Falter," *Harvard Business Review,* July–August 1989, p. 83.

8. Adapted from R. A. Baron and P. B. Paulus, "Group Seekers and Avoiders: How Well-Suited Are You for Working in Groups?" in *Understanding Human Relations,* 2d ed., pp. 286–287. © Copyright 1991 by Allyn & Bacon. Reprinted by permission.

Chapter 10

1. For a complete discussion of this issue, see C. Merle Crawford, *New Products Management* (Homewood, Ill.: Irwin, 1991).

2. Kevin J. Clancy and Robert S. Shulman, *The Marketing Revolution* (New York: Harper Business, 1991), p. 6.

3. E. M. Rogers and F. F. Shoemaker, *Communication of Innovation* (New York: Free Press, 1971). See also Vijay Mahajan, Eitan Muller, and Frank M. Bass, "New Product Diffusion Models in Marketing: A Review and Directions for Research," *Journal of Marketing,* January 1990, pp. 1–26; Fareena Sultan, John V. Farley, and Donald R. Lehmann, "A Meta-analysis of Diffusion Models," *Journal of Marketing Research,* February 1990, pp. 70–77.

4. Gene Sloan, "Steering Drivers to Restaurants, Hotels, by Satellite," *USA Today,* Januray 16, 1997, p. D1.

5. Robert G. Cooper and Elko J. Kleinschmidt, "Resource Allocation in the New Product Process," *Industrial Marketing Management 17* (1988), pp. 249–262.

6. Robert G. Cooper and Elko J. Kleinschmidt, "An Investigation into the New Products Process: Steps, Deficiencies, and Impact," *Journal of Product Innovation Management,* June 1986, pp. 71–85; William L. Moore, "New Product Development Practices of Industrial Marketers," *Journal of Product Innovation Management,* December 1987, pp. 6–20. See also Gary L. Frankwick, James C. Ward, Michael D. Hutt, and Peter Reingen, "Evolving Patterns of Organizational Beliefs in the Formation of Strategy," *Journal of Marketing,* April 1994, pp. 96–110.

7. "Listen to the Voice of the Marketplace," *Business Week,* February 21, 1983, p. 90.

8. The systematic integration of research and development and marketing is essential for innovation success. Ashok K. Gupta, S. P. Raj, and David Wilemon, "A Model for Studying R&D-Marketing Interfaces," *Journal of Marketing,* April 1987, p. 7.

9. See Michael H. Morris and Joan M. Jarvi, "Making Marketing Curriculum Entrepreneurial," *Marketing Educator,* Fall 1990, pp. 1, 8.

10. For examples of marketing implications of life cycle stages, see Stanley R. Schultz and S. R. Rao, "Product Life Cycles of Durable Goods for the Home," *Journal of the Academy of Marketing Science,* Spring 1986, pp. 7–12. Peter N. Golder and Gerald J. Tellis, "Pioneer Advantage: Marketing Logic or Marketing Legend?" *Journal of Marketing Research,* May 1993, pp. 158–170.

11. Ellen Neuborne, "Price Wars Give Shoppers Holiday Bonus," *USA Today,* December 6, 1991, pp. B1–B2; Robert F. Hartley, ed., *Marketing Mistakes,* 3rd ed. (New York: John Wiley & Sons, 1986), pp. 77–87; Ellen Neuborne, "Girls Putting 'Boys-Only' Toys on Their Lists," *USA Today,* January 4, 1994, p. B5.

12. For the original conceptualization of this process, see Evert M. Rogers, *Diffusion of Innovations* (Glencoe, Ill.: Free Press, 1962). Although we are discussing primarily the diffusion of consumer goods, technology and organizational products are also subject to the same process. See Thomas S. Robertson and Hubert Gatigon, "Competitive Effects on Technology Diffusion," *Journal of Marketing,* July 1986, pp. 1–12. See also Christopher M. Miller, Shelby H. McIntyre, and Murali K. Mantrala, "Toward Formalizing Fashion Theory," *Journal of Marketing Research,* May 1993, pp. 142–157.

13. Jean Halliday, "Hush Puppies," *Advertising Age,* June 24, 1996, p. S3.

14. David A. Aaker, *Managing Brand Equity* (New York: Macmillan, 1991), p. 99.

15. See David M. Andrus and D. Wayne Norvell, "The Effect of Foreign Involvement on the Standardization of International Marketing Strategies: An Empirical Study," *International Journal of Management,* December 1990, pp. 422–431; and Subash C. Jain, "Standardization of International Marketing Strategy: Some Research Hypotheses," *Journal of Marketing,* January 1989, pp. 70–79.

16. Subash C. Jain, "Standardization of International Marketing Strategy: Some Research Hypotheses," *Journal of Marketing,* January 1989, pp. 70–79.

17. Warren E. Leary, "Out of the Lab, into the Grocery Store," *New York Times,* May 22, 1994, p. 2e; Michael Unger, "FDAs Nod Has Calgene Ripe to Grow," *Newsday,* April 8, 1994.

Chapter 11

1. James C. Johnson and Donald F. Wood, *Contemporary Physical Distribution and Logistics* (New York: Macmillan, 1990), Chapter 1.

2. Wroe Alderson, *Marketing Behavior and Executive Action* (Homewood, Ill.: Richard D. Irwin, 1957).

3. This definition is adapted from David A. Revzan, "Marketing Organization through the Channel," in *Wholesaling and Marketing Organizations* (New York: John Wiley & Sons, 1961), pp. 107–142; and Ralph F. Breyer, "Some Observations on Structural Formation and Growth in Marketing Channels," in *Theory in Marketing,* eds. R. Cox, W. Alderson,

and S. Shapiro (Homewood, Ill.: Irwin, 1963), pp. 163–175. For a more recent discussion of channels of distribution see Robert A. Robicheaux and James E. Coleman, "The Structure of Marketing Channel Relationships," *Journal of the Academy of Marketing Science,* Winter 1994, pp. 38–51, and Saul Klein, "Satisfaction with International Marketing Channels," *Journal of the Academy of Marketing Science,* Winter 1993, pp. 39–43.

4. For an excellent discussion of the environmental forces that affect channel length, see Arun Sharma and Luis Dominguez, "Channel Evolution: A Framework for Analysis," *Journal of the Academy of Marketing Science,* Winter 1992, pp. 1–16.

5. Prodigy interactive personal service, January 12, 1994.

6. "Caterpillar—Sticking to the Basics to Stay Competitive," *Business Week,* May 4, 1981, p. 74.

7. A detailed discussion of conflict within the channel of distribution can be found in John F. Gaski, "The Theory of Power and Conflict in Channels of Distribution," *Journal of Marketing,* Summer 1984, pp. 9–29. For more recent research in this area, see Gary L. Frazier and Raymond C. Rody, "The Use of Influence Strategies in Interfirm Relationships in Industrial Product Channels," *Journal of Marketing,* January 1991, pp. 52–69; Jakki Mohr and John R. Nevin, "Communication Strategies in Marketing Channels: A Theoretical Perspective," *Journal of Marketing,* October 1990, pp. 36–51; James C. Anderson and James A. Narus, "A Model of Distributor Firm and Manufacturer Firm Working Partnerships," *Journal of Marketing,* January 1990, pp. 42–59. Shankar Ganesan, "Negotiation Strategies and the Nature of Channel Relationships," *Journal of Marketing Research,* May 1993, pp. 183–203; Kaushik Mitra, Samantha J. Rice, and Stephen A. LeMay, "Postponement and Speculation in Exchange Relationships: A Transaction Cost Approach," *Advances in Marketing,* eds. Joyce A. Young, Dale L. Varble, and Faye W. Gilbert (Terre Haute, IN: Southwestern Marketing Association, 1977), pp. 18–26; Joyce A. Young, Faye W. Gilbert, and Faye S. McIntyre, "Examining the Partnership Mentality," *Journal of Marketing Management,* Spring/Summer 1996, pp. 39–45.

8. See also Pratibha A. Dabholkar, Wesley J. Johnson, and Amy S. Cathey, "The Dynamics of Long-Term Business-to-Business Exchange Relationships," *Journal of the Academy of Marketing Science,* Spring 1994, pp. 130–159.

9. See, for example, J. L. Grimm and J. B. Spaulding, "Is Channel(s) Theory Lagging?" in *Theoretical Developments in Marketing,* eds. C. W. Lamb and P. M. Dunne (Chicago: American Marketing Association, 1980), pp. 255–258. See also L. A. Crosby and J. R. Taylor, "Consumer Satisfaction with Michigan's Container Deposit Law—An Ecological Perspective," *Journal of Marketing,* Winter 1982, pp. 47–60.

Chapter 12

1. It is common to use sales figures to differentiate between retailers and other intermediaries. If an intermediary makes more than 50 percent of sales to consumers, that intermediary is counted as a retailer in the U.S. government's *1992 Economic Census Retail Trade.*

2. U.S. Bureau of the Census, *1992 Economic Census Retail Trade, Nonemployer Statistical Series* (Washington, D.C.).

3. The convenience shopping style, the price trade-off, and the convenience shopper are examined in Joseph A. Bellizzi and Robert E. Hite, "Convenience Consumption and Role Overload," *Journal of the Academy of Marketing Science,* Winter 1986, pp. 1–9.

4. Consumers perceive mail-order buying as more risky than in-store shopping. In fact, catalog buying is among the riskiest shopping methods as perceived by consumers. Those who have had a favorable experience with this nonstore shopping method are more favorably inclined toward it. See Troy A. Festervand, Don R. Snyder, and John D. Tsalikis, "Influence of Catalog vs. Store Shopping and Prior Satisfaction on Perceived Risk," *Journal of the Academy of Marketing Science,* Winter 1986, p. 37; Jon M. Hawes and James R. Lumpkin, "Perceived Risk and the Selection of a Retail Patronage Mode," *Journal of the Academy of Marketing Science,* Winter 1986, p. 37.

5. Ronald D. Taylor and Blaise J. Bergiel, "Chain Store Executives' Ratings of Critical Site Selection Factors," *Journal of Midwest Marketing,* Fall 1988, pp. 37–49.

6. For an interesting discussion of this issue, see Mary Jo Bitner, "Servicescapes: The Impact of Physical Surroundings on Customers and Employees," *Journal of Marketing,* April 1992, pp. 57–71; and Joseph A. Bellizzi, Ayn E. Crowley, and Ronald W. Hasty, "The Effects of Color on Store Design," *Journal of Retailing,* Spring 1983, pp. 21–57.

7. Ellen Neuborne, "Stores Say Remodeling Boosts Sales," *USA Today,* April 19, 1993, p. B2.

8. U.S. Bureau of the Census, *1992 Economic Census Wholesale Trade.*

9. As a percentage of dollar sales volume. Ibid.

Chapter 13

1. H. D. Lasswell, *Power and Personality* (New York: W. W. Norton, 1948).

2. Pierre Martineau, *Motivation in Advertising* (New York: McGraw-Hill, 1957), p. 134.

3. The hierarchy of communication effects model has been portrayed in several other forms. A common one is as follows: awareness, interest, evaluation, trial, and adoption. Another model includes attention, interest, desire, and action (AIDA). The nature of the model depends on consumer involvement.

4. Mark Gleason and Alan Salomon, "Fallon's Challenge: Make Holiday Inn More 'In,'" *Advertising Age,* September 2, 1996, p. 14.

5. Adapted from Jane Weaver, "Girl Scout Campaign: Shedding Old Image for MTV Cool," *Adweek,* September 11, 1989, p. 68. (c) ADWEEK, L.P. Used with permission from *Adweek.*

6. Elmer Wheeler, *Tested Sentences That Sell* (Englewood Cliffs, N.J.: Prentice-Hall, 1937).

7. Herbert Katzenstein and William Sacks, *Direct Marketing,* 2nd ed. (New York: Macmillan, 1992), p. 5.

Chapter 14

1. For more on the attractiveness of spokespersons, see Elizabeth C. Hirschman, "People as Products: Analysis of a Complex Marketing Exchange," *Journal of Marketing,* January 1987, pp. 98–108. See also Maureen Morrin, "Advertising and the Self: Is Negative Affect Effective?" pp. 64-71, and Joseph A. Bellizzi, Lauri Minas, and Wayne Norvell, "Tangible and Intangible Copy in Industrial Print Advertising," p. 55, in 1992 *A.M.A. Educators' Proceedings: Enhancing Knowledge Development in Marketing,* ed. Robert P. Leone, V. Kumar, Peter J. Gordon, and Bert J. Kellerman (Chicago: American Marketing Association, 1992).

2. "Border Crossings: Brands Unify Image to Counter Cult of Culture," *Brandweek,* October 31, 1994.

3. In some instances, as in the use of scratch-and-sniff technology, the senses of touch and smell may be taken into consideration in developing advertisements.

4. "Clinique," *Brandweek,* June 24, 1996, p. 18.

5. *Advertising Age,* (Dataplace, September 30, 1996, www.adage.com).

6. Randall L. Rose, Paul W. Minard, Michael J. Barone, Kenneth C. Manning, and Brian D. Till, "When Persuasion Goes Undetected: The Case of Comparative Advertising," *Journal of Marketing Research,* August 1993, pp. 315–330.

7. Scott M. Cultip, Allen H. Center, and Glen M. Broom, *Effective Public Relations* (Englewood Cliffs, N.J.: Prentice Hall, 1985), p. 4.

8. Adapted from "Campbell Soup Company Introduces Convenient, 32-Ounce Resealable Carton for Swanson Chicken Broth," *PRNewswire,* October 31, 1996, PRODIGY® interactive personal service, November 1, 1996.

9. "Tony Bennett," *Advertising Age,* July 4, 1994, p. S25.

10. Terry Lefton, "MasterCard World Cup Promotion," *Brandweek,* September 19, 1994, p. 34.

11. Robert Morris, "Banking on the Olympic Games," *Business Journal-Charlotte,* August 15, 1994.

12. Philip Lesley, ed., *Lesley's Handbook of Public Relations and Communications,* 4th ed. (New York: AMACOM, American Management Association, 1991), p. 340.

13. Ibid., p. 15.

14. Debbie Seaman, "In Company B, Delta Snaps to Attention," *Adweek's Marketing Week,* April 11, 1988, p. 26.

15. "What's Ahead for Travel Industry," *Advertising Age,* January 22, 1990, p. 22.

16. Steve J. Grove and William E. Kilbourne, "A Mertonian Approach to the Analysis of Advertising's Role in Society: From Polemics to Discourse," in *1992 A.M.A. Educators' Proceedings: Enhancing Knowledge Development in Marketing,* ed. Robert P. Leone, V. Kumar, Peter J. Gordon, and Bert J. Kellerman (Chicago: American Marketing Association, 1992), p. 441.

17. "14 States Sue Mazda Over Ads," *Tulsa World,* p. E-6.

18. See, for example, Srivatsa Seshadri and C. P. Rao, "Considerations in Advertising Directed toward Children," and Les Carlson, Russell N. Lacznink, and Darrel D. Muehling, "Antecedents of Mothers' Perceptions of Toy-Based Programming—An Empirical Investigation," in *1992 A.M.A. Educators' Proceedings: Enhancing Knowledge Development in Marketing,* ed. Robert P. Leone, V. Kumar, Peter Gordon, and Bert J. Kellerman (Chicago: American Marketing Association, 1992), p. 234.

Chapter 15

1. Gerald L. Manning and Barry L. Reece, *Selling Today: A Personal Approach* (Boston: Allyn and Bacon: 1990), p. 6.

2. D. J. Dalrymple and L. J. Parsons, *Marketing Management* (New York: John Wiley & Sons, 1980), p. 538.

3. Thomas N. Ingram and Raymond W. LaForge, *Sales Management: Analysis and Decision Making* (Hinsdale, Ill.: Dryden Press, 1993), p. 37.

4. Theodore Levitt, *The Marketing Imagination* (New York: Macmillan, 1986), p. 111.

5. Albert W. Frey, *Marketing Handbook* (New York: Ronald Press, 1965), pp. 9-24–9-25.

6. Experienced salespeople know that they will hear the word "No" most of the time, or at least more than they hear "Yes." Rejection is never a source of enjoyment, but there are many times when the sales representative is better off accepting a negative response gracefully and moving on to prospects who may be more likely to buy.

7. Eric Sevareid, *Enterprise: The Marketing of Business in America* (New York: McGraw-Hill, 1983), p. 13.

8. For an excellent discussion of some of these issues, see Karl A. Boedecker, Fred W. Morgan, and Jeffrey J. Stoltman, "Legal Dimensions of Salesperson's Statements: A Review and Managerial Suggestions," *Journal of Marketing,* January 1991, pp. 70–80.

9. Trade shows are evaluated in Roger A. Kerin and William L. Cron, "Assessing Trade Show Functions and Performance: An Exploratory Study," *Journal of Marketing,* July 1987, pp. 87–94.

10. William H. Murphy, "Even Roses Have Thorns: Functional and Dysfunctional Effects of Sales Contests on Sales Personnel," in *1992 A.M.A.*

Educators' Proceedings: Enhancing Knowledge Development in Marketing, eds. Robert P. Leone, V. Kumar, Peter J. Gordon, and Bert J. Kellerman (Chicago: American Marketing Association, 1992), p. 402.

Chapter 16

1. During periods of inflation, price's importance in the marketing mix is rated higher by managers. See Saeed Samiee, "Pricing in Marketing Strategies of U.S. and Foreign-Based Companies," *Journal of Business Research,* February 1987, pp. 17–30.

2. See Hugh M. Cannon and Fred W. Morgan, "A Strategic Pricing Framework," *Journal of Consumer Marketing,* Summer 1990, p. 62. The relationship of price and product quality over time is discussed in David J. Curry and Peter C. Riesz, "Prices and Price/Quality Relationships: A Longitudinal Analysis," *Journal of Marketing,* January 1988, pp. 36–51. See also Jerry B. Gotlieb and Dan Sarel, "The Influence of Type of Advertisement, Price, and Source Credibility on Perceived Quality," *Journal of the Academy of Marketing Science,* Summer 1992, pp. 253–260.

Chapter 17

1. This chapter has been strongly influenced by the work of Gerald J. Tellis. The authors strongly suggest that readers review his important paper on pricing strategy. Because our purpose differs from his, terminology employed here differs somewhat. See Gerald J. Tellis, "Beyond the Many Faces of Price: An Integration of Pricing Strategy," *Journal of Marketing,* October 1986, pp. 146–160.

2. Some prices are actually "consumer negotiated." See Kenneth R. Evans and Richard F. Beltramini, "A Theoretical Model of Consumer Negotiated Pricing: An Orientation Perspective," *Journal of Marketing,* April 1987, pp. 58–73.

3. Erin M. Davies, "The Brand's the Thing," *Fortune,* March 4, 1996.

4. The per-unit loss is $300. The fixed cost per unit is $400,000/500 = $800. The variable cost per unit remains at $75. However, because there is a loss, there is no target return per unit. The total per-unit cost (fixed cost + variable cost) is thus $875. Subtracting the selling price of $575 yields a $300 per-unit loss. Calculating the target return at 500 units would have yielded a selling price of $1,075: Fixed cost and target return per unit ($1,000) + variable cost per unit ($75) = suggested price per unit ($1,075).

5. Care must be taken that discount schedules are not structured in ways that encourage buyers to purchase more product than they need and sell the excess on the "black market." See James B. Wilcox, Roy D. Howell, Paul Kuzdrall, and Robert Britney, "Price Quantity Discounts: Some Implications for Buyers and Sellers," *Journal of Marketing,* July 1987, pp. 60–70.

6. For an excellent discussion of the Robinson-Patman Act, see James C. Johnson and Kenneth C. Schneider, "Those Who Can, Do . . . and Those Who Can't . . . : Marketing Professors and the Robinson-Patman Act," *Journal of the Academy of Marketing Science,* Summer 1984, pp. 123–138.

7. Theodore Levitt, "The Dangers of Social Responsibility," *Harvard Business Review,* September–October 1958, p. 47.

Acknowledgments

Chapter 1

Opening vignette, pp. 3-4: Adapted from Jill Lieber, "In Focus: Baseball's Newest Stadium," *USA Today*, April 3, 1997. Copyright 1997, USA TODAY. Reprinted with permission.

Competitive Strategy box, p. 16: Excerpted with permission from Jaclyn Fierman, "The Death and Rebirth of the Salesman," Fortune, July 25, 1994, p. 86. © 1994 Time Inc. All rights reserved.

Focus on Trends box, p. 19: Excerpted from Faye Rice, "The New Rules of Superlative Service," *Fortune,* Autumn-Winter 1993, pp. 50-53. © 1993 Time Inc. All rights reserved.

Video Case 1-1, p. 24: Information from *Total Baseball* (New York: Harperperennia, 1993) and *Total Baseball* (New York: Harper and Row, 1990); Dave Price, "Revenue-Sharing May Be Ticket for Twins," Minneapolis-St. Paul *Citybusiness,* February 11, 1994; "Baseball Salaries Show 6.1 Percent Increase This Year," *Tulsa World,* April 6, 1994, p. 5.

Video Case 1-2, p. 25: Excerpted with permission from *Insights and Inspiration: How Businesses Succeed,* pp. 3-4. Copyright 1995 by MassMutual—The Blue Chip Company.

Chapter 2

Opening vignette, pp. 27-28: Reprinted with permission from Brian O'Reilly, "The Rent-A-Car Jocks Who Made Enterprise #1," *Fortune,* October 28, 1996, pp. 125-128. © 1996 Time Inc. All rights reserved.

Competitive Strategy box, p. 37: Adapted with permission from T. L. Stanley, Karen Benezra, Betsy Spethmann, Gerry Khermouch, Elaine Underwood, "Brand Builders. (Promotion Marketing Association of America's Reggie Awards)," *Brandweek,* March 11, 1996, Vol. 37, No. 11. © 1996 ASM Communications Inc.

Focus on Relationships box, p. 40: Adapted with permission from Faye Rice, "The New Rules of Superlative Service," *Fortune,* Autumn-Winter 1993, pp. 50-53. © 1993 Time Inc. All rights reserved.

Focus on Global Competition box, p. 43: Adapted with permission from Thomas A. Stewart, "Welcome to the Revolution," *Fortune,* December 13, 1993, pp. 66-67. © 1993 Time Inc. All rights reserved.

Competitive Strategy box, p. 47: Reprinted with permission from "Computer Firm Lists Wrong No.," *AP Online,* June 21, 1996.

Case 2-1, p. 54: Reprinted with permission of Lanier Worldwide, Inc., from "Lanier: Customer Vision Gives Clear Market Focus," *Managing Office Technology,* July 1993.

Video Case 2-2, p. 55: Excerpted with permission from *Real World Lessons for America's Small Business,* pp. 10-11. Copyright 1992 by MassMutual—The Blue Chip Company.

Chapter 3

Opening vignette, p. 57: Excerpt reprinted with permission from Karl Schoenberger and Melanie Warner, "Motorola Bets Big on China," *Fortune,* May 27, 1996. © 1996 Time Inc. All rights reserved.

Competitive Strategy box, p. 61: Adapted from "Japanese Like Seafood Really Fresh," *Tulsa World,* April 27, 1991, p. C2. Used with permission of The Associated Press.

Focus on Trends box, p. 67: From Antonia Barber, "Take-out Has Bigger Place on Home Tables," *USA Today,* January 27, 1997, D1. Copyright 1997, USA TODAY. Reprinted with permission.

Focus on Trends box, p. 73: All but the first paragraph excerpted from "Technology to Watch," *Fortune,* September 5, 1994, p. 109. © 1994 Time Inc. All rights reserved.

Focus on Global Competition box, p. 74: Adapted from Patty Cignarella, "A New Pepsi Challenge in India," *Adweek,* April 30, 1990, p. 17. © 1990, ASM Communications, Inc. Used with permission from *Adweek.*

Video Case 3-1, p. 80: Excerpted with permission from *Real World Lessons for America's Small Business,* pp. 181-182. Copyright 1992 by MassMutual—The Blue Chip Company.

Case 3-2, p. 81: Adapted from Margot Hornblower, "Learning to Earn," *Time,* February 24, 1997, p. 34. © 1997 Time Inc. Reprinted by permission.

Chapter 4

Opening vignette, p. 83: Information in first paragraph from Rita Koselka, "Red Faces in Michigan," *Forbes,* August 2, 1993; rest of material adapted by permission from Al Wrigley, "Whirlpool Shifts toward China," *American Metal Market,* June 28, 1993. © ABC MEDIA INC., 1993

Competitive Strategy box, p. 93: Excerpt from *Do's and Taboos Around the World* by Roger E. Axtel, 3rd edition. Copyright 1992 by Parker Pen Company; published by The Benjamin Company, Inc., distributed by John Wiley & Sons, Inc. Used by permission.

Video Case 4-1, p. 101: Excerpted with permission from *Insights and Inspiration: How Businesses Succeed,* pp. 106-107. Copyright 1995 by MassMutual—The Blue Chip Company.

Video Case 4-2, p. 102: Reprinted by permission from *Real-World Lessons for America's Small Business: Insights*

from the Blue Chip Enterprise Initiative. Copyright 1994 by MassMutual—The Blue Chip Company.

Chapter 5

Opening vignette, p. 105: Information from Karen Benezra, "Fritos Around the World," *Brand Week,* March 27, 1995, p. 32; "Chinese Cheetos," *New York Times,* November 27, 1994, p. 31; and "Chee-tos Make Debut in China but Lose Cheese in Translation," *USA Today,* September 2, 1994, p. B-1.

Focus on Trends box, p. 111: Excerpt reprinted with permission from Amy Cortese, "Here Comes the Intranet," *Business Week,* February 26, 1996. Copyright 1996 McGraw-Hill, Inc., Number 3464.

Competitive Strategy box, p. 117: Adapted with permission from Doug Stewart, "In the Cutthroat World of Toy Sales, Child's Play Is Serious Business," *Smithsonian,* December 1989, pp. 76-78.

Focus on Global Competition box, p. 126: Adapted from Thomas J. Meyer, "Slicing the Japanese Pie," *American Way,* November 1989, pp. 40-43. © Thomas J. Meyer, 1989. Reprinted by permission of the author and *American Way,* the magazine of American Airlines, copyright 1989 by American Airlines.

Chapter 6

Opening vignette, pp. 135-136: From "Babies as Dolls," *Forbes,* February 27, 1995, p. 79. Reprinted by permission of FORBES Magazine © Forbes Inc., 1995.

Competitive Strategy box, p. 140: Adapted by permission of Faulkner & Gray from Edward DiMingo, "The Fine Art of Positioning," *Journal of Business Strategy,* March–April 1988, p. 37.

Focus on Quality box, p. 142: Information from Wilton Woods, "A PC Learns How to Kiss," *Fortune,* September 5, 1994, p. 107. © 1994 Time Inc. All rights reserved.

Focus on Global Competition box, p. 148: Adapted from Damon Darlin, "Where Trademarks Are Up for Grabs: U.S. Products Widely Copied in South Korea," December 5, 1989, p. B1. Reprinted by permission of the *Wall Street Journal,* © 1989 Dow Jones & Company, Inc. All Rights Reserved Worldwide.

Focus on Global Competition box, p. 153: Adapted from Sally Goll, "China's 'Only' Children Get the Royal Treatment," *Wall Street Journal,* February 8, 1995. Reprinted by permission of the *Wall Street Journal,* © 1995 Dow Jones & Company, Inc. All Rights Reserved Worldwide.

Focus on Relationships box, p. 157: Adapted from Noreen O'Leary, "Goodbye to the Middle Class," *Adweek,* February 24, 1992, p. 19. © 1992 ASM Communications. Used with permission from *Adweek.*

Chapter 7

Opening vignette, pp. 165-166: Information from Roberta Maynard, "Striking the Right Match," *Nation's Business,* May 1, 1996, pp. 18-20. Reprinted by permission, *Nation's Business,* May 1996. Copyright 1996, U.S. Chamber of Commerce.

Competitive Strategy box, p. 173: Adapted from Calmetta Y. Coleman, "Fliers Call Electronic Ticketing a Drag," January 17, 1997, p. B1. Reprinted by permission of the *Wall Street Journal,* © 1997 Dow Jones & Company, Inc. All Rights Reserved Worldwide.

Focus on Global Competition box, p. 174: Reprinted with permission from Ronald Henkoff, "The Hot New Seal of Quality: ISO 9000 Standard of Quality Management," *Fortune,* June 28, 1993, pp. 116-117. © 1993 Time Inc. All rights reserved.

Focus on Quality box, p. 175: Adapted from "At DEC, Someone Is Breathing on the Phone Line," *Time,* February 17, 1997, p. 70. © 1997 Time Inc. Reprinted by permission.

Video Case 7-1, p. 180: Excerpted with permission from *Insights and Inspiration: How Businesses Succeed,* pp. 135-136. Copyright 1995, by MassMutual—The Blue Chip Company.

Video Case 7-2, p. 181: Adapted from Peter P. Donker, "Nypro Molds Successful Future," *Worcester (Massachusetts) Telegram & Gazette,* September 15, 1994, and Peter P. Donker, "Local Firms Keep Eye on Trade Tiff; China-U.S. Discord Hass Ripple Effect," *Worcester (Massachusetts) Telegram & Gazette,* February 8, 1995. Reprinted with permission of the Worcester Telegram & Gazette. Some information from Tom Peters, "In a Complex World Businesses Find 'Tis a Gift to Be Simple,'" *St. Louis Business Journal,* February 20, 1995; Paul Hyman, "Improving Purchasing's Image: Would You Do Business with You?" *Electronic Buyers' News,* August 2, 1993.

Chapter 8

Opening vignette, pp. 183-184: Reprinted with permission from Jack Russell, "Working Women Give Japan Culture Shock," and Jack Russell, "At Last a Product That Makes Japan's Subways Safe for Men," *Advertising Age,* January 16, 1995, p. I24. Copyright Crain Communications, Inc. 1995.

Focus on Trends, p. 186: Adapted from Rene Stutzman, "Sports Marketers Focusing on Women," *Tulsa World,* October 9, 1994, Business section, p. 7. Reprinted by permission of The Associated Press.

Competitive Strategy box, p. 194: Reprinted from Cleveland Horton, "A Car or a Club?" *Advertising Age.* Reprinted with permission from the November 8, 1993, issue of *Advertising Age.* Copyright Crain Communications, Inc. 1993.

Focus on Global Competition box, p. 196: Information from Julie Liesse Erickson and Kate Fitzgerald, "Ralston Lures Barbie to the Breakfast Table," *Advertising Age,*

August 14, 1989, p. 2; Pauline Yoshahashi, "Mattel Shapes a New Future for Barbie," *Wall Street Journal,* February 12, 1990, p. B1.

Competitive Strategy box, p. 201: Adapted with permission from Alex Taylor III, "Porsche Slices Up Its Buyers," *Fortune,* January 16, 1995, p. 24. © 1995 Time Inc. All rights reserved.

Case 8-1 and Case Exhibits 8-1 and 8-2, pp. 208-209: Adapted by permission of SRI International from "The VALS™ 2 Typology," © 1994 SRI International.

Case 8-2, pp. 210-211: Reprinted with permission from Diane Toroian, "Making the Point a Collection of Savvy and Irrepressible Staffers have Turned KPNT into One of the Top Alternative Radio Stations in the Nation," EVERYDAY MAGAZINE, *St. Louis Post-Dispatch,* November 9, 1996.

Chapter 9

Opening vignette, p. 215: Reprinted with permission from Ronald Henkoff, "Service Is Everybody's Business," *Fortune,* June 27, 1994, p.48. © 1994 Time Inc. All rights reserved.

Competitive Strategy box, p. 224: From Rita Koselka, "Hope and Fear as Marketing Tools," *Forbes,* August 29, 1994, p. 78. Reprinted by permission of FORBES Magazine © Forbes Inc., 1995.

Competitive Strategy box, p. 227: Information from Bruce I. Knoviser, "A Czech Entrepreneur Makes Names for Himself," *New York Times,* February 19, 1995, p. 4F.

Focus on Quality box, p. 228: Information from John Gilbert, "Fans Love That Moose," *Minneapolis Star Tribune,* April 22, 1995, pp. 1D-2D.

Focus on Global Competition box, p. 230: Adapted with permission from "Sony," *Express Magazine,* a publication of Federal Express Corporation, Winter 1992, p. 14.

Focus on Global Competition box, p. 236: Reprinted with permission from Rahul Jacob, "Why Some Customers Are More Equal Than Others," *Fortune,* September 14, 1994, p. 215. © 1994 Time Inc. All rights reserved.

Video Case 9-1, p. 243: Excerpted with permission from *Insights and Inspiration: How Businesses Succeed,* pp. 116-117. Copyright 1995, by MassMutual—The Blue Chip Company.

Case 9-2, p. 244: Package label from Dirty Potato Chips reprinted courtesy of Chickasaw Foods.

Chapter 10

Opening vignette, p. 247: Adapted with permission from Allison Sprout, "Blood Test While You Wait," *Fortune,* June 27, 1994, p. 125. © 1994 Time Inc. All rights reserved.

Focus on Global Competition, p. 254: Adapted from Gary Hamel and C. K. Prahalad, Competing for the Future (Cambridge, Mass.: Harvard Business School Press, 1994), as it appeared in Gary Hamel and C. K. Prahalad, "Seeing the Future First," *Fortune,* September 5, 1994, p. 70.

Focus on Trends box, p. 263: Adapted from Michael Ceiply, "Popularity of Compact Disks and Cassettes May Take Record Out of Record Industry," October 16, 1986, p. 3. Reprinted by permission of the *Wall Street Journal,* © 1986 Dow Jones & Company, Inc. All Rights Reserved Worldwide.

Competitive Strategy box, p. 269: Adapted with permission from Alan Deutschman, "The Managing Wisdom of High-Tech Superstars," *Fortune,* October 17, 1994, p. 200. © 1994 Time Inc. All rights reserved.

Focus on Quality box, p. 270: Adapted from "No Deodorant? No Sweat!" Tulsa World, December 18, 1991, p. A1. Reprinted by permission of The Associated Press.

Competitive Strategy box, p. 274: Adapted with permission from Ronald Henkoff, "Service Is Everybody's Business," *Fortune,* June 27, 1994, p. 60. © 1994 Time Inc. All rights reserved.

Case 10-1, p. 283: Adapted from "New Twist on an Old Cup of Joe; Caffeinated Water Joins Beverage Fray." *Dallas Morning News,* April 16, 1996, Copyright 1996. REPRINTED WITH PERMISSION OF THE DALLAS MORNING NEWS.

Video Case 10-2, p. 284: Excerpted with permission from *Real-World Lessons for America's Small Business: Insights from the Blue-Chip Enterprise Initiative 1994,* pp. 91-92, Copyright 1994, by MassMutual—The Blue Chip Company.

Chapter 11

Opening vignette, p. 287: Adapted with permission from John Labate, "Companies to Watch," *Fortune,* May 2, 1994, p. 79. © 1994 Time Inc. All rights reserved.

Focus on Global Competition box, p. 302: Excerpted from Peter T. White, "The Power of Money," *National Geographic,* January 1993, p. 83.

Focus on Relationships, p. 307: Based on "Caterpillar's Backbone: A Long Dealer Network, *Business Week,* May 4, 1981, p. 77; Geoffrey Brewer, "Industrial & Farm Equipment: Caterpillar Inc.," *Sales & Marketing Management,* September 1, 1993; Hillary Durgin, "The Caterpillar's Meow: Growing Economy Has Manufacturer," *Crains Chicago Business,* March 21, 1994; Bob Bouyea, "This Competitive Edge No Longer Seems Jagged," *Peoria Journal Star,* October 19, 1993, "Cat Signs New Joint Venture, Puts Down More Roots in CIS," *Peoria Journal Star,* February 8, 1994; "Cat Joins with Russian Truck Maker," *Peoria Journal Star,* December 4, 1993.

Competitive Strategy box, p. 310: Excerpted from Debra Sparks, "The Card Game," *FW (Financial World),* July 5, 1994, pp. 28-29. Used with permission of *Financial World.*

Video Case 11-1, p. 317: Excerpted with permission from *Strengthening America's Competitiveness,* p. 56. Copyright 1991, by MassMutual—The Blue Chip Company.

Video Case 11-2, p. 317: Excerpted with permission from *Real-World Lessons for America's Small Business,* pp. 52-52. Copyright 1992, by MassMutual—The Blue Chip Company.

Chapter 12

Opening vignette, p. 319: Adapted with permission from Stephen Bennett, "Natural Foods: A Fad No More," *Progressive Grocer,* May 1, 1994.

Focus on Global Competition box, p. 327: Information from Beverly Martin, "Machine Dreams," *Brandweek,* April 26, pp. 17-22. © 1996 ASM COMMUNICATIONS.

Focus on Trends box, p. 328: Excerpted with permission from Alex Taylor III, "How to Buy a Car on the Internet—and Other New Ways to Make the Second-biggest Purchase of a Lifetime," *Fortune,* March 26, 1996, p. 163. © 1996 Time Inc. All rights reserved.

Competitive Strategy box, p. 329: Adapted from M. R. Kropko, "Card Makers Struggling with Computer Kiosks," *Marketing News,* June 3, 1996, p. 6. Adapted with permission from the American Marketing Association; and Erin Flynn, "American Greeting Cards Creates a New Card Pitch," *Brandweek,* November 14, 1994, p. 24. © 1994 ASM Communications.

Competitive Strategy box, p. 333, adapted with permission from Patricia Sellers, "Look Who Learned About Value," *Fortune,* October 18, 1993, pp. 75 and 78; with updates from Andrew Serwer, "McDonald's Conquers the World," *Fortune,* October, 1994, pp. 108-117. © 1994 Time Inc. All rights reserved.

Case 12-1, p. 346: Reprinted with permission from and *Texas Monthly's* Internet Web site located at http://www. Texasmonthly.com/resto/onthemenu/thread.html. Information in first paragraph from *Wall Street Journal Interactive Edition,* "Marketplace Front, Latest Restaurant Innovation Looks a Lot Like a Grocery,"

Video Case 12-2, p. 347: Adapted with permission *from Insights and Inspiration: How Businesses Succeed,* pp. 100-101. Copyright 1995, by MassMutual—The Blue Chip Company.

Chapter 13

Opening vignette, p. 351: Adapted with permission from John Labate, "Companies to Watch," *Fortune,* May 2, 1994, p. 79. © 1994 Time Inc. All rights reserved.

Competitive Strategy box, p. 354: Information from Victoria Griffith, "The Power of the Plug," *The Financial Times,* April 1, 1997, London Edition, p. 19 and David Bauder, "Scope Learns It's Not Nice to Cross Rosie," The Associated Press, March 20, 1997.

Competitive Strategy box, p. 366: Adapted with permission from Bob Garfield, "Mild Board's Cereal Tie-in Really Does the Trix," *Advertising Age,* April 3, 1995, p. 3. Copyright Crain Communications, Inc. All rights reserved.

Chapter 14

Opening vignette, p. 373: Adapted from Bob Garfield, "Snickers Ads Grab the Elusive 'Big Idea', *Advertising Age.* Reprinted with permission from the September 2, 1996, issue of Advertising Age. Copyright Crain Communications Inc. 1996.

Competitive Strategy box, p. 375: Based on information from *Brandweek,* June 10, 1996—"BrandWeek Magazine Salutes the 1996 Effies," Special Advertising Supplement Sponsored by *People* Magazine.

Focus on Quality box, p. 381: Adapted from Bob Garfield, "A Powerful Message," *Advertising Age.* Reprinted with permission from the September 16, 1996, issue of *Advertising Age.* Copyright Crain Communications Inc. 1996.

Competitive Strategy box, p. 395: Information from Chuck Stogel, "Chemical Bank Corporate Challenge," *Brandweek,* September 19, 1994, p. 43. © 1994 ASM Communications, Inc.

Focus on Trends, p. 398: Excerpted with permission from Rahul Jacob, "Why Some Customers Are More Equal than Others," *Fortune,* September 19, 1994, p. 224. 1994 Time Inc. All rights reserved.

Case 14-2, p. 406: Excerpted with permission from Debbi Seaman, "Carpe Dyin'," *Advertising Age,* special creativity insert, January 1991, pp. 8-9. Copyright Crain Communications, Inc. All rights reserved.

Chapter 15

Opening vignette, pp. 409-410: Adapted from Kevin McManus, "Selling," pp. 48-56. Reprinted by permission from the October 1990 issue of *Changing Times Magazine.* Copyright © 1990 The Kiplinger Washington Editors, Inc.

Focus on Trends box, p. 412: Excerpted from Jeffery Young, "Hit the Road, Jack: IBM's Wandering Tribe," *Forbes ASAP,* August 28, 1995, p. 93. Reprinted by permission of FORBES Magazine, © Forbes Inc. 1995.

Competitive Strategy box, p. 420: Adapted from Tom Peters and Nancy Austin, *A Passion for Excellence* (New York: Random House, 1985), p. 51.

Focus on Global Competition box, p. 422: Adapted from Franklin R. Root, *Entry Strategies for International Markets* (Lexington, Mass: Lexington Books, 1987), pp. 252-255.

Focus on Quality box, p. 424: Excerpted with permission from Jaclyn Fierman, "The Death and Rebirth of the Salesman," *Fortune,* July 25, 1994, pp. 86, 88. © 1994 Time Inc. All rights reserved.

Competitive Strategy box, p. 432: Adapted with permission from T. L. Stanley, Karen Benezra, Betsy Spethmann, Gerry Khermouch, Elaine Underwood, "Brand Builders (Promotion Marketing Association of America's Reggie Awards)," *Brandweek,* March 11, 1996, Vol. 37, No. 11, ISSN: 1064-4318.

Video Case 15-2, p. 438: Adapted by permission from *Insights and Inspiration: How Businesses Succeed,* pp. 27-28. Copyright 1995 by MassMutual—The Blue Chip Company.

Chapter 16

Opening vignette, p. 441: Adapted from Kevin Goldman, "A Telegram for Western Union: MoneyGram Wants Market Share," *Wall Street Journal,* November 25, 1994. Reprinted by permission of the *Wall Street Journal,* © 1994 Dow Jones & Company, Inc. All Rights Reserved Worldwide.

Competitive Strategy box, p. 443: Adapted with permission from Gautam Naik, "Sprint Scales Back Fridays Free Plan," *Wall Street Journal,* April 11, 1996. Reprinted by permission of the *Wall Street Journal,* © 1996 Dow Jones & Company, Inc. All Rights Reserved Worldwide.

Focus on Relationships box, p. 446: Adapted from "Business 2000: The New World Order" (Special Advertising Section), *Inc.,* December 1993, p. 51.

Focus on Trends box, p. 452: Adapted with permission from Evan I. Schwartz," ELECTROSPHERE - Advertising Webonomics 202," *Wired,* April 2, 1996. (4.02— http://www.wired.com/) Copyright 1996 Wired Ventures Ltd. Compilation copyright 1996 HotWired Ventures LLC. All rights reserved.

Case 16-1, p. 459: Excerpted from "Toy Scalpers Buy Scarce Items, Then Resell Them at a Profit," *Wall Street Journal Interactive Edition,* June 24, 1996. Reprinted by permission of *Wall Street Journal,* © 1996 Dow Jones & Company, Inc. All Rights Reserved Worldwide.

Chapter 17

Opening vignette, p. 463: Adapted from Barbara Woller, "Long-distance Callers Cash in on Incentives," *USA Today,* July 27, 1995, pp. 1c-2c. Copyright 1995, USA TODAY. Reprinted with permission.

Competitive Strategy box, p. 467: Information from Jeffrey A. Trachtenberg, "Sony, Unfazed by Flops, Rolls Out MiniDisc for Third Time in U.S." *Wall Street Journal,* July 24, 1996, p. B5; Wayne Thompson, "Sony Tries Once Again to Maximize the MiniDisc, which has Superior Recording Abilities," *The Oregonian;* and the Sony Web site, July 21, 1997: http://www.sel.sony.com

Focus on Quality, pp. 471-472: Excerpted with permission from Becky Ebenkamp, "Drawing a New Frontier," *Brandweek,* May 5, 1997, p. 17. © 1997 ASM Communications Inc.

Video Case 17-1, p. 488: Adapted by permission from *Insights and Inspiration: How Businesses Succeed,* pp. 37-38. Copyright 1995, by MassMutual—The Blue Chip Company.

Photo Credits

Chapter 1

3   © Robert Ginn/Atlanta
5   © PhotoEdit/Michael Newman/PhotoEdit
6   Walter Thompson Co.—Chicago/Brookfield Zoo
9   © AP Photo/Bebeto Matthews/AP/Wide World
11 © Unicorn/John Schakel, Jr./Unicorn Stock Photos
18 © PhotoEdit/Dwayne E. Newton/PhotoEdit
20 © Unicorn/Jim Shippee/Unicorn Stock Photos

Chapter 2

27 © Unicorn/Jim Shippee/Unicorn Stock Photos
29 © Parmalat/Parmalat
30 © Unicorn/Eric R. Berndt/Unicorn Stock Photos
33 © Unicorn/Jim Shippee/Unicorn Stock Photos
34 © Unicorn/Jeff Greenberg/Unicorn Stock Photos
36 © Unicorn/Jeff Greenberg/Unicorn Stock Photos
38 © Courtesy of Morton Salt/Morton Salt
39 © Courtesy of Warner Bros. Studio Store/Freeman
    Public Relations—Warner Bros. Studio Store
45 © VISA U.S.A. Inc. 1994, all rights reserved.
    Reproduced with the permission of VISA U.S.A.

Chapter 3

57 © Bradshaw/SABA
60 © Unicorn/Batt Johnson/Unicorn Stock Photos
66 © PhotoEdit/Tony Freeman/PhotoEdit
72 © IBM Corporation
76 © Tony Stone Images

Chapter 4

83 © Tony Stone Images/Don Smetzer
86 © Tony Stone Images/Ralph Mercer
87 © 1994 Robert Tinney CAD/CAM
89 © PhotoEdit/Dwayne E. Newton/PhotoEdit
90 © Tony Stone Images/Howard Grey
91 © 93 Dilip Mehta
94 © James L. Fly/Unicorn Stock Photos

Chapter 5

105 Courtesy of PepsiCo Foods International
107 © PhotoEdit/Tony Freeman
108 © PhotoEdit/Tony Freeman
116 Courtesy of Focus Suites

Chapter 6

135 © PhotoEdit/Michael Newman
137 Courtesy of the Wm. Wrigley Jr. Company
143 Courtesy of Straight Status, Inc.
147 © 1994 Time Inc.
148 Courtesy of Ferrari
150 © Stephen Frink/Tony Stone Images
155 © Tony Stone Images/Robert Daemmrich

Chapter 7

165 © Courtesy of New Pig Corporation, Tipton PA
    16684 Phone 1-800-HOT-HOGS® (468-4647)/New Pig
168 © Greg Pease/Tony Stone Images
171 © Gary D. Landsman/Tony Stone Images

Name Index

A

Aaker, David A., 527n.14, 271; 271; 365
Achrol, Ravi S., 524n.1, 58
Agasi, Andre, 370
Albaum, Gerald, 523n.5, 7
Alderson, Wroe, 527n.2, 290; 527–528n.3, 291
Alfano, Kathleen, 117
Allen, Jeff, 524n.1, 58
Allison, Bob, 24
Allison, R. I., 526n.8, 147
Anderson, Erin, 526n.4, 169
Anderson, James C., 528n.7, 312
Andrus, David M., 527n.15, 275
Arnow, Fred, 194
Astin, Alexander, 81
Atkinson, Lee, 47
Ayers, Rob, 441

B

Barad, Jill, 37
Barger, Dennis, 459–460
Barkley, Charles, 98
Baron, R. A., 527n.8, 241

Barone, Michael J., 528n.6, 393
Bass, Frank M., 527n.3, 251
Beck, Melinda, 524n.9, 64
Belch, George E., 365
Belch, Michael A., 365
Belk, Russell W., 525n.11, 112; 527n.7, 235
Bell, Martin, 527n.4, 219
Bellizzi, Joseph A., 528n.3, 324; 528n.6, 333; 528n.1, 381
Belonax, Joseph J., Jr., 526n.4, 138
Beltramini, Richard F., 529n.2, 465
Ben, Ray 434
Bengston, Roger A., 253
Bennett, Peter D., 524n.11, 48; 527n.2, 218
Bennett, Tony, 394
Berg, Greg, 210
Bergiel, Blaise J., 528n.5, 332
Berkowitz, Harry, 525n.12, 89
Berry, Leonard L., 527n.7, 235
Bessen, Jim, 525n.7, 109
Billington, Ray, 524n.12, 48
Bishop, William S., 526n.2, 167
Bitner, Mary Jo., 527n.7, 235; 528n.6, 333

Boedecker, Karl A., 529n.8, 429
Bolen, William H., 388
Bolzmann, Leopoldo G. Arias, 524n.1, 58
Borden, Neil H., 523n.9, 8
Bourne, Geoff, 284
Bowen, David E., 527n.7, 235
Breyer, Ralph F., 527–528n.3, 291
Britney, Robert, 529n.5, 481
Broom, Glen M., 528n.7, 393
Brown, Gene, 526n.9, 147
Brown, Michele, 186
Brown, Stephen W., 527n.7, 235
Burch, Fred J., 523n.15, 15
Burnett, Leo, 235
Burr, Aaron, 366
Buzzell, R. D., 526n.7, 171
Bylinsky, Gene, 524n.8, 41
Byrne, John A., 525n.6, 87

C

Cakebread, Dennis, 351
Cakebread, Jack, 351
Cannon, Hugh M., 529n.2, 446
Cantalupo, James, 333

Carew, Rod, 24
Carey, Mariah, 210
Carlson, Lee, 526n.15, 158
Carlson, Les, 529n.18, 401
Castro, Janice, 524n.5, 36
Cateora, Philip R., 525n.14, 91
Cathey, Amy S., 528n.8, 312
Center, Allen H., 528n.7, 393
Charles, Ray, 147
Chauhan, Ramesh, 74
Chonko, Lawrence B., 524n.16, 50
Christiansen, Tim, 526n.11, 154
Chu, Wujin, 526n.4, 169
Clancy, Kevin J., 527n.2, 250
Clark, Terry, 524n.1, 58
Clinton, Bill, 111
Cody, Jennifer, 523n.2, 6
Coleman, James, E., 527–528n.3, 291
Connor, Chris, 283
Cooper, Robert G., 527n.5, 252; 527n.6, 252
Copeland, Melvin T., 527n.5, 219; 219–222
Cornelius, Julie, 133
Costas, Bob, 370
Costello, Elvis, 210

Coulter, Ronald, 526n.9, 147
Courier, Jim, 370
Cox, R., 527–528n.3, 291
Crawford, C. Merle, 527n.1, 248
Crawford, Cindy, 354
Crittenden, Vicky L., 525–526n.15, 120
Crittenden, William F., 525–526n.15, 120
Croke, Sara, 180
Cron, William L., 529n.9, 430
Crosby, L. A., 528n.9, 313
Crowley, Ayn E., 528n.6, 333
Cultip, Scott M., 528n.7, 393
Curry, David J., 529n.2, 446

D

Dabholkar, Pratibha A., 528n.8, 312
Daft, Richard L., 524n.1, 29
Dalrymple, D. J., 529n.2, 410
Daniels, Sky, 210–211
Davidow, William H., 527n.7, 235
Davies, Erin M., 529n.3, 470
Davis, Duane, 524n.1, 58
Davis, H. L., 526n.16, 158
Davis, Sue, 526n.8, 174
Dawson, Lyndon, 524n.13, 48; 524n.16, 50
Day/Day, George S., 523–524n.18, 17
Delano, James, 80
Deutsch, Caludia H., 526n.3, 169
Dietrich, Frank, 111
Dolton, Ruth N., 527n.7, 235
Dominguez, Luis, 528n.4, 302
Donahue, Phil, 102
Donaldson, Yvonne, 47
Down, Philip E., 525–526n.15, 120
Drew, James H., 527n.7, 235
Drucker, Peter F., 525n.10, 88
Dudley, Sid C., 526n.9, 147
Dunne, P. M., 528n.9, 313

E

Edgy, Lance, 215
Einstein, Albert, 114; 525n.13, 114
Ellis, Peter, 328
Enis, Ben M., 527n.5, 219
Evans, Doug, 165–166
Evans, Kenneth R., 526n.11, 154; 529n.2, 465
Exter, Thomas G., 525n.2, 106

F

Farley, John V., 527n.3, 251
Feick, Lawrence F., 526n.14, 157

Ferrell, O. C., 524n.13, 48
Festervand, Troy A., 528n.4, 326
Fisher, Bruce D., 525n.19, 76
Fisk, Raymond P., 527n.7, 235
Ford, Henry, 15; 32; 189
Fortun (brothers), 317
Fraedrich, John, 524n.13, 48
Francese, Peter, 524n.6, 63; 524n.10, 65; 68
Frankel, Steven, 224
Frankwick, Gary L., 523–524n.18, 17; 527n.6, 252
Frazier, Gary L., 528n.7, 312
Frey, Albert W., 529n.5, 419
Fridstein, Stanley, 135
Friend, Tim, 525n.18, 76
Fritzche, David J., 524n.16, 50
Fujii, Toshio, 61
Fullerton, Ronald A., 523n.13, 14

G

Gandhi, Rajiv, 74
Ganesan, Shankar, 528n.7, 312
Gardner, John, 81
Garvin/Garvin, David A., 271
Gaski, John F., 528n.7, 312
Gassenheimer, Julie B., 523n.3, 7
Gaston, Jim, 102
Gatigon, Hubert, 527n.12, 265
Gavin, David A., 524n.5, 36
George, Robert, 472
Ghingold, Morry, 526n.4, 169
Gilbert/Gilbert, Faye W., 528n.7, 312
Gill, James D., 526n.11, 154
Gleason, Mark, 528n.4, 363
Godfrey, Gail, 398
Golder, Peter N., 527n.10, 264
Goldman, Kevin, 525n.16, 73
Goldman, Steven L., 526n.1, 192
Goldstein, Michael, 459
Goolsby, Jerry R., 524n.16, 50
Gordon, Peter J., 528n.1, 381; 529n.16, 399; 529n.18, 401; 529n.10, 430
Gotlieb, Jerry B., 529n.2, 446
Graham, John L., 526n.2, 167
Greene, Bob, 409
Gresham, Larry G., 524n.13, 48
Grimm, J. L., 528n.9, 313
Grimm, Matthew, 526n.8, 147
Grossbart, Sanford, 526n.15, 158
Grove, Stephen J., 527n.7, 235; 529n.16, 399
Gupta, Ashok K., 527n.8, 257

H

Hair, Joseph F. Jr., 524n.1, 58; 525–526n.15, 120; 526n.8, 147

Hallgren, Kenneth G., 525n.15, 72
Halliday, Jean, 527n.13, 268
Hamilton, Alexander, 366
Hartley, Robert F., 527n.11, 265
Hartley-Leonard, Darryl, 446
Hasty, Ronald W., 528n.6, 333
Hawes, Jon M., 525–526n.15, 120; 528n.4, 326
Held, Jim and Betty, 438
Henn, Kathleen, 47
Hill, Grant, 393
Hilmer, Frederick G., 525n.9, 88
Hirschman, Elizabeth C., 528n.1, 381
Hite, Robert E., 528n.3, 324
Hitt, Michael A., 524n.9, 42
Holbrook, Morris B., 525n.11, 112
Holder, Ruth, 463
Hoskisson, Robert E., 524n.9, 42
Houston, Franklin S. 523n.3, 7; 523n.14, 15
Hovserstad, Ronald, 526n.9, 147
Howell, Roy D., 526n.12, 154; 529n.5, 481
Hoynton, Andrew C., 526n.2, 193
Hunt, James G., 524n.14, 49; 524n.15, 50
Hunt, Shelby D., 523n.5, 7; 524n.13, 48; 524n.16, 50; 525n.11, 112
Hutt, Michael D., 523–524n.18, 17; 525n.17, 75; 526n.6, 170; 527n.6, 252

I

Infeld, L., 525n.13, 114
Ingram, Thomas N., 529n.3, 411
Ireland, R. Duane, 524n.9, 42
Irwin, Richard D., 525n.14, 91
Isakson, Mike, 274

J

Jain, Subash C., 527n.15, 275; 527n.16, 276
Jarvi, Joan M., 525n.2, 84; 527n.9, 258
Javalgi, Rajshekhar G., 526n.4, 138
Jaworski, Bernard J., 523n.14, 15; 523–524n.18, 17
Johnson, James C., 527n.1, 288; 529n.6, 483
Johnson, Wesley J., 528n.8, 312
Jones, Brian, 181
Jones, D. G. Brian, 523n.13, 14

Jones, Michael H., 526n.2, 167
Jordan, Michael, 98; 149

K

Kanter, Rosabeth Moss, 525n.8, 88
Kasten, Stan, 3
Katzenstein, Herbert, 528n.7, 365
Kellerman, Bert J., 528n.1, 381; 529n.16, 399; 529n.18, 401; 529n.10, 430
Kennedy, John F., 50
Kerin, Roger A., 529n.9, 430
Kerr, John R., 525–526n.15, 120
Kevin, Kitty, 523n.16, 16
Kijowski, John, 211
Kilborn, Peter T., 525n.13, 67
Kilbourne, William E., 529n.16, 399
Killebrew, Harmon, 24
King, Stephen, 434
Klein, Saul, 527–528n.3, 291
Kleinschmidt, Elko J., 527n.5, 252; 527n.6, 252
Koli, Ajay K., 523n.14, 15; 523–524n.18,17
Kuhn, Mary, 523n.16, 16
Kumar, V., 528n.1, 381; 529n.16, 399; 529n.18, 401; 529n.10, 430
Kurth, Terry, 25
Kuzdrall, Paul, 529n.5, 481

L

Lacznink, Russell N., 529n.18, 401
LaForge, Raymond W., 529n.3, 411
Lamb, C. W., 528n.9, 313
Landon, Alf, 123
Lankton, Gordon B., 181
Lantos, Geoffrey P., 524n.13, 48
Lasswell, H. D., 528n.1, 355
Lavalle, Nye, 186
Leary, Warren E., 527n.17, 277
Lefton, Terry, 528n.10, 395
Lehmann, Donald R., 527n.3, 251
Leigh, Thomas, 526n.5, 170
LeMay, Stephen A., 528n.7, 312
Leone, Robert P., 528n.1, 381; 529n.16, 399; 529n.18, 401; 529n.10, 430
Lesley, Philip, 529n.12, 397
Levitt, Theodore, 523n.15, 15; 523n.17, 16; 524n.19, 17; 524n.3, 33; 526n.7, 171; 527n.1, 216; 529n.4, 412; 529n.7, 484
Lewin, Kurt, 526n.2, 136
Lichtenstein, Donald R., 526n.8, 147

Lincoln, D. J., 524n.16, 50
Lipshultz, Alfred, 317
Lipshultz, Mitchell, 317
Little, T., 524n.16, 50
Loeb, Marshall, 524n.7, 39
London, David, 525–526n.15, 120
Lowe, Larry S., 524n.8, 63
Luke, Alex, 211
Lumpkin, James R., 528n.4, 326
Lynn, C. Stephen, 101

M

MacIntre, Sean, 459
Madden, John, 370
Mahajan, Vijay, 527n.3, 251
Mahre, Bill, 24
Malmborg, Michael, 406
Manning, Gerald L., 529n.1, 410
Manning, Kenneth C., 528n.6, 393
Mantrala, Murali K., 527n.12, 265
Marcheschi, David, 283
Martin, Billy, 24
Martin, Geoffrey Lee, 525n.18, 95
Martineau, Pierre, 528n.2, 356
Marwaha, Jay, 398
Maslow, Abraham, 144; 526n.7, 144
Mathews, J. B., Jr., 526n.7, 171
Mazur, Paul, 524n.20, 19
McCarthy, E. Jerome, 523n.10, 8
McConkey, C. William, 525–526n.15, 120
McCormack, Mark, 370
McCracken, Ed, 269
McCrohan, Kevin F., 524n.8, 63; 525n.14, 70
McGowan, Sean, 459
McGrath, J. E., 525n.12, 113
McGuinn, Jim, 211
McIntyre, Faye S., 528n.7, 312
McIntyre, Shelby H., 527n.12, 265
McKee, Daryl O., 524n.1, 58; 525–526n.15, 120; 526n.8, 147
McKenna, Regis, 523n.7, 8
McNeal, James, 135
Mellencamp, John, 210
Mene, Patrick, 398
Menon, Ajay, 524n.3, 59
Menon, Anil, 523n.4, 7
Menon, Anil, 524n.3, 59
Meyers, John G., 365
Miller, Christopher M., 527n.12, 265
Milliman, Ronald E., 525n.5, 108
Minard, Paul W., 528n.6, 393
Minas, Lauri, 528n.1, 381

Mitra, Kaushik, 528n.7, 312
Mohr, Jakki, 528n.7, 312
Molinaro, Tony, 173
Moncrief, William C., 415
Monieson, David D., 523n.13, 14
Montague, Bill, 525n.16, 93
Montana, Joe, 370
Moore, Patrick A., 525n.5, 108
Moore, William L., 527n.6, 252
Morgan, Fred W., 529n.8, 429; 529n.2, 446
Morissette, Alanis, 210
Morita, Akio, 230
Morrin, Maureen, 528n.1, 381
Morris, Michael H., 524n.1, 58; 525n.2, 84; 527n.9, 258
Morris, Robert, 528n.11, 396
Mowen, John C., 526n.3, 136
Muehling, Darrel D., 529n.18, 401
Muller, Eitan, 527n.3, 251
Murphy, Patrick E., 527n.5, 219
Murphy, William H., 529n.10, 430
Murray, Keith B., 527n.7, 235
Murray, Matt, 523n.12, 14

N

Nader, Ralph, 16
Nagel, Roger N., 526n.1, 192
Nap, Rick, 283
Narus, James A., 528n.7, 312
Narver, John C., 523n.14, 15; 523–524n.18, 17
Nasser, Haya El, 524n.8, 63
Navratilova, Martina, 370
Nedungadi, Prakash, 523–524n.18, 17
Nelson, Debra L., 526n.10, 150
Nelson, Robert, 283
Nemec, Marek, 227
Netemeyer, Richard, 526n.8, 147
Neuborne/Neuborne, Ellen, 527n.11, 265; 528n.7, 333
Nevett, Terence, 523n.13, 14
Nevin, John R., 528n.7, 312
Nomo, Hideo, 459
Norman, Greg, 370
Norvell, D. Wayne, 527n.15, 275; 528n.1, 381
Nourse, R. E. M., 526n.7, 171

O

O'Donnell, Rosie, 354
Ohmae Kenichi, 525n.1, 84; 525n.13, 90
Oliver, Suzanne, 527n.6, 223
Olshavsky, Richard W., 526n.13, 156
Opie, John, 43
Osborn, Richard N., 524n.14, 49; 524n.15, 50

Ostoich, Vladimir, 247
Overberg, Paul, 525n.12, 67

P

Paddock, Barbara, 395
Palmer, Arnold, 370
Parasuraman, A., 524n.19, 17; 527n.7, 235
Parlin, Charles, 527n.5, 219
Parsons, L. J., 529n.2, 410
Pascual, Camilo, 24
Patzer, Gordon L., 526n.8, 147
Paulus, P. B., 527n.8, 241
Pelton, Lou, 525–526n.15, 120
Perper, Cynthia, 173
Perreault, William D., Jr., 523n.10, 8
Petersen, Randy, 173
Phillips, Michael J., 525n.19, 76
Pine, Joseph, II, 526n.2, 193
Pohlad, Carl, 24
Porter, Michael E., 524n.4, 35; 525n.7, 87
Preiss, Kenneth, 526n.1, 192
Pressley, M. M., 524n.16, 50
Price, Linda L., 526n.14, 157
Pryde, Neil, 284
Puckett, Kirby, 24

Q

Quick, James Campbell, 526n.10, 150
Quinn, James Brian, 525n.9, 88

R

Raj, S. P., 527n.8, 257
Rao, C. P., 529n.18, 401
Rao, S. R., 527n.10, 264
Reece, Barry L., 529n.1, 410
Reidenbach, R. Eric, 524n.13, 48; 524n.16, 50
Reingen, Peter, 523–524n.18, 17; 527n.6, 252
Rethans, Amo J., 526n.5, 170
Revson, Charles, 224
Revzan, David A., 527–528n.3, 291
Rhey, William L., 526n.8, 147
Rice, Samantha J., 528n.7, 312
Richard, Michael, 525–526n.15, 120
Richins, Marsha, 526n.6, 141
Ridgway, Nancy M., 526n.8, 147
Riesz, Peter C., 529n.2, 446
Rigaux, B. P., 526n.16, 158
Riley, John, 16
Rizzo, David, 432
Robbins, Tim, 459
Roberts, James A., 524n.3, 59
Robertson, Dan, 524n.10, 46
Robertson, Ian, 524n.4, 61
Robertson, Thomas S., 527n.12, 265

Robicheaux, Robert A., 527–528n.3, 291
Robin, Donald P., 524n.13, 48; 524n.16, 50
Rodriguez, Leandro, 347
Rody, Raymond C., 528n.7, 312
Rogers, Evert M., 527n.3, 251; 527n.12, 265
Romano, Phil, 346
Roosevelt, Franklin, 123
Rose, Randall L., 528n.6, 393
Rosen, Dennis L., 526n.13, 156
Ross, Diana, 432
Runkel, P. J., 525n.12, 113
Russell, Cheryl, 524n.9, 64
Rustogi, Hemant, 526n.8, 147
Ryo, 183

S

Sacks, William, 528n.7, 365
Salomon, Alan, 528n.4, 363
Samiee, Saeed, 529n.1, 442
Sanders, Christine, 409
Sanders, Deion, 395
Sanger, Elizabeth, 523n.1, 6
Sarandon, Susan, 459
Sarel, Dan, 529n.2, 446
Schaub, Bernie, 117
Schermerhorn, John R., Jr., 524n.14, 49; 524n.15, 50
Schmidt, Eric, 211
Schmidt, Jeffrey B., 526n.5, 139
Schneider, Kenneth C., 529n.6, 483
Schneider, Paul, 525n.9, 111
Schroeder, Rex, 459
Schultz, Stanley R., 527n.10, 264
Seaman, Debbie, 529n.14, 398
Seinfeld, Jerry, 379
Sellers, Patricia, 525n.3, 84
Seshadri, Srivatsa, 529n.18, 401
Sevareid, Eric, 529n.7, 425
Shapiro, S., 527–528n.3, 291
Sharma, Arun, 528n.4, 302
Sheppard, Nathaniel, Jr., 525n.4, 107
Sherrell, Daniel L., 524n.1, 58; 525–526n.15, 120; 526n.8, 147
Shoemaker, F. F., 527n.3, 251
Shore, Pauly, 210
Shostack, G. Lynn, 527n.4, 219
Shulman, Robert S., 527n.2, 250
Singhapakdi, Anusorn, 524n.14, 49
Slama, Mark E., 526n.4, 138
Slater, Stanley F., 523n.14, 15; 524n.19, 17; 523–524n.18, 17
Slezinger, Herbert, 173
Sloan, Gene, 527n.4, 252
Smidt, Valerie, 40
Smith, James D., 525n.14, 70

Smith, Troy, 101
Snyder, Don R., 528n.4, 326
Spanier, Barry, 284
Spaulding, J. B., 528n.9, 313
Speh, Thomas W., 525n.17, 75; 526n.6, 170
Sprague, Ralph H., Jr., 525n.7, 109
Spreng, Richard A., 526n.5, 139
Spring, James, 81
Stevens, Robert E., 525–526n.15, 120
Stevenson, Robert Louis, 410
Stewart, Thomas A. 525n.5, 86; 525n.3, 107
Stoltman, Jeffrey J., 529n.8, 429
Stone, Andrea, 524n.8, 63
Stroy, Gary, 247
Strutton, David, 525–526n.15, 120
Sultan, Fareena, 527n.3, 251
Swartz, Teresa A., 527n.7, 235

T

Tashchian, Armen, 526n.4, 138
Taylor, Alex, III, 526n.3, 200
Taylor, J. R., 528n.9, 313

Taylor, Ronald D., 525–526n.15, 120; 528n.5, 332
Tellis, Gerald J., 527n.10, 264; 529n.1, 464
Tetzeli, Rick, 525n.6, 108
Thompson, J. Walter, 98
Till, Brian D., 528n.6, 393
Tsalikis, John D., 528n.4, 326
Tully, Shawn, 525n.11, 89
Tyler, Steve, 210

U

Uehara, Sunao, 61
Uhl, K. P., 526n.8, 147
Underwood, Elaine, 524n.2, 59
Unger, Michael, 527n.17, 277
Uttal, Bro, 527n.7, 235

V

Varble, Dale L., 528n.7, 312
Vardarajan, P. Ranjan, 523n.4, 7
Veit, Gae, 55
Victor, Bart, 526n.2, 193
Viola, Frank, 24

Virgin, Tim, 210–211
Vitell, Scott J., 524n.13, 48; 524n.14, 49

W

Walker, David, 525n.14, 117
Wallace, Patrick, 488
Walley, Noah, 524n.16, 50
Walsh, Ann, 526n.15, 158
Wantz, Sherman, 16
Ward, James C., 523–524n.18, 17; 527n.6, 252
de Wardener, Max, 243
Warrick, Sandy, 284
Watson, Hugh J., 525n.7, 109
Watson, Mary Anne, 526n.8, 147
Weaver, Jane, 528n.5, 363
Webster, F. E., Jr., 526n.1, 167
Weitz, Barton, 526n.4, 169
Welch, Raquel, 391
Wentz, Laurel, 525n.15, 91
Wheeler, Elmer, 528n.6, 364
Whitehead, Bradley, 524n.16, 50
Whitwam, David R., 83

Widing, Robert E., II, 526n.9, 147
Wilcox, James B., 529n.5, 481
Wilemon, David, 527n.8, 257
Wilkie, William L., 526n.1, 136; 526n.4, 138
Wind, Y., 526n.1, 167
Wolf, Carol, 523n.1, 6
Wood, Donald F., 527n.1, 288
Wood, Van R., 524n.16, 50; 526n.12, 154
Woodruff, Robert B., 524n.19, 17
Woods, Wilson, 527n.4, 201

Y

Yates, John, 174
Young/Young, Joyce A., 528n.7, 312
Yukon, Jack, 396

Z

Zaltman, Gerald, 525n.11, 112
Zeithaml, Valerie, 527n.7, 235
Zikmund, William G., 525n.1, 84; 525n.1, 106

process, 415–422
Creative strategy, 378–382
Credit function, 301
Crisis management, 396–397
Cross-classification matrix, 187
Cross-elasticity, 454
    of demand, 454–455
Cross-functional
    buying center, 170–172
    sales team, 415
    teams, 36
    teams, sales support and,
        414–415
Culture, 59, 154
Cumulative quantity discount,
    481
Custom marketing, 191
    and data-based marketing: to
        each his own, 191–194
Customer service, 234, 333–334
Customer type, organization
    by, 425
Customer value, 17
Customers, 84–85
    keeping and building rela-
        tionships, 7–8
    survey of, 129
    the era of the global con-
        sumer, 91–93
Customization strategy, 238,
    275

D

Data, 107
    analysis, 125
    analyzing, 124–125
    and information, 107
    collecting, 124
    primary, 107
    secondary, 107
Database, 109
    management, 334–335
Data-based marketing, 112
    to customize promotional
        materials, 191
Deceptive and misleading
    practices, 399–400
Decider, 172
Decision maker, 158
Decision support systems, 109
    and intranets, 109–111
Decision-making process,
    136–142
    individual factors that shape,
        142–152
    interpersonal influences on,
        152–158
Decline stage, 262–265
Decoding, 357
Deep-line (full-line) strategy,
    273
Delivered pricing (freight-al-
    lowed pricing), 474
Demand, 452–455

and break-even analysis, 480
curve (demand schedule),
    444–445
cross-elasticity of, 454–455
inelasticity of, 453
management strategies, 236
price elasticity of, 452–454
Demarketing, 37
Demographic segmentation,
    196–198
Demographics, 62–69
Demography, 62
Demonstration format, 381
Department store, 323
Depth of product line, 223
Derived demand, 167
Desk jobber (drop shipper),
    337
Development stage, 255–256
Differential pricing strategies,
    464–466
Differentiated marketing, 191
Differentiation
    strategy, 35
    total quality management to
        achieve, 35–37
Diffusion process, 265
    adoption and, 265–267
Direct channel
    for consumer goods and ser-
        vices, 302
    in business-to-business mar-
        keting, 305
Direct exporting, 96
Direct foreign investment, 95
Direct marketing, 326
    media, 385–387
    wholesalers, 336
Direct-action advertisement,
    374
Direct-response
    advertisement, 374
    advertising, 327
    campaign, 365
    retailing, 326
Discontinuous innovation, 249
Discount, 480
    anticipation, 480
    broker's, 483
    cash, 480
    chain, 482
    quantity, 481
    seasonal, 481
    strategies, 324
    trade (functional), 481
    wholesaler's, 483
Discounting
    periodic, 466
    random, 466
    second-market, 465
Display equipment and point-
    of-purchase materials, 430
Distribution, 9
    channel of, 9, 290–291
    conventional channel of, 291

costs, 313
delivers a standard of living
    to society, 288
exclusive, 311
extent of, 310–311
intensive, 310
legalities of international,
    342
managing the channel of,
    308–311
physical, 288–290
regulation of retail and
    wholesale, 341–342
reverse, 313
selective, 310
typical channels of, 302–306
Distribution defined, logistics
    and physical, 288–289
Distribution functions
    integration of the physical,
        299–300
    physical, 293–300
Distribution management, ethi-
    cal, political, and legal
    forces in, 313
Distribution-based pricing
    strategies and tactics,
    474–475
Distributor (private) brand, 229
    manufacturer brands versus,
        229–230
Diversification, 40
Divisibility, 251
Dog, 224
Domestic environment, 57–58
Domestic laws, 342
Door-to-door selling, 327
Downstream activities, 88
Downtowns, 332
Drawing conclusions and
    preparing the report, 125
Drop shipper, 337
Durable good, 218
Dynamically continuous inno-
    vation, 249–250

E

Early adopters, 266
Early and late majorities—rid-
    ing the bandwagon, 266
Early majority, 266
Eating patterns, American, 67
Ecology, quality of life and,
    277–278
Economic and competitive
    forces, 69–71
Economic community, multina-
    tional, 91
Economic conditions, 70–71
Economic system, 69–70
Economic utility, 85
Economy, price in, 444–445
Editing, 124
Effective marketing, 7

information—the basis of,
    106
80/20 principle, 190
Electronic ticketing by airlines,
    173
Element(s)
    art of blending, 12–13
    first—product, 8–9
    fourth—promotion, 11
    second—place, 9–10
    third—price, 11
Embargo, 94
Emotion, motivation and, 144
Employee empowerment, Ritz-
    Carlton's, 398
Encoding, 356
    the message, 355–356
Entrepreneur, 84, 258
    role of, 258
Environment
    domestic, 57–58
    foreign, 57–58
    legal, 73
    physical, 58–59
    political, 73
Environmental factors, other,
    309
Environmental monitoring, 42
Environmental scanning, 42
Ethical considerations associ-
    ated with product strategy,
    276–278
Ethical dilemma, 49
Ethical issues
    in advertising and public re-
        lations, 399–401
    in sales and sales manage-
        ment, 429
Ethical price, 476
Ethics of persuasion, 366–367
Evaluating results, controlling
    efforts and, 46–47
Evaluation
    of alternatives, 141
    postpurchase consumption
        and, 141–142
Event marketing, 396
Event sponsorship, 395–396
Exact price, establishing,
    476–480
Exchange process, 7
Exclusive dealing, 341
Exclusive distribution, 311
Exclusive territory, 341–342
Execution, 45
    format, 380
    of the appeal, how to say it,
        379–382
    opinion, 128
    planning and control are in-
        terrelated, 47–48
    poor, 257
Experiment, 122
Exploratory research, 115
Export Administration Act, 73

Export management companies, 97
Exporting, 96
External environmental criteria, 309
External search, 140

F

F.O.B., 474
Facilitating functions, 301
Factory outlet, 325
Fad, 272
Fair Debt Collection Act (1980), 77
Fair trade, 483
  acts, the repeal of, 483–484
Family, 157–158
  branding, 230
  brands and individual brands, 230–231
  life cycle, 197
Fantasy, 382
Fashion, 272
Federal Antitampering Act (1983), 77
Federal Hazardous Substances Act (1960), 75
Federal Trade Commission (FTC), 75
Federal Trade Commission Act (1914), 75, 77, 278, 341, 399, 483
Feedback, 357–358
Field sales manager, 424
Field selling, 410
Fieldwork, 124
Fixed cost, 478
Flexibility, 411
Focus group interview, 116
Follow-the-leader strategy, 468
Follow-up—building relationships, step seven, 421
Following up, 125
Forecasting
  break-down and build-up, 127
  conditional, 128
  options, 128–129
  sales, 127
  three levels of, 127–128
  by time periods, 128
Foreign environment, 57–58
Form utility, 85
Formal marketing plan, preparing, 44–45
Forward invention, 275
Four Cs, 84
  in a global economy, microenvironments and, 90–98
  microenvironment, 83–87
Four Ps of marketing, 8
Franchise, 3085

Freight-allowed pricing (delivered pricing), 474
Frequency, 390
FTC Improvement Act (1980), 77
Full-function wholesalers, 336
Full-line strategy, 273
Full-service merchant wholesalers, 336
Functional discount, 481

G

Gatekeeper, 159–172
General line wholesalers, 336
General mass merchandisers, 324
General merchandise wholesalers, 336
Generation X, 64
Generic brand, 230
Generic name, 227
Generic or primary demand, 377
Generic product, 230
Gentleman's prices, 476
Geodemographic segmentation, 202
Geographic segmentation, 195–196
Gestures, 93
Glasnost, 74
Global advertising campaigns, 382
Global collaborations, 97–98
Global economy, microenvironments and the four Cs in, 90–98
Global information system (GIS), 106
  in the 21st century, 106–107
Globalization strategy, 275
Goods, durable and nondurable, 218
Graying of America, 63
Green marketing, 59
Green River Ordinance, 77, 327
Gross domestic product (GDP), 70
Gross margin percentage, 497
Gross national product (GNP), 70
Gross sales, 496
Growth in the Sunbelt, 63
Growth stage, 260–261

H

Handling objections, 419–420
Head-to-head competition, 203
Health Care and Social Assistance Sector, 177
Heterogeneity, 238

Heterogeneous shopping products, 220
High-tech packaging, 73
Homogeneous shopping products, 220
Host, 108
HOTBOT, 110
House and Senate legislation, 108
Household income, family and, 67
Households
  changing American, 65
  single-parent, 66
  single-person, 65

I

IBM's virtual sales office, 412
Idea generation, 253–254
Image building, 362–364
Image pricing strategies, psychological and, 473–474
Import quota, 94
In-store retailing, 322
Incentive, 143
Income, family and household, 67
Income-oriented objectives, 447–449
Independent retailers, 320
Indirect exporting, 96
Indirect-action advertisement, 374
Individual brand, 231
  family brands and, 230–231
Individual factor, 146
Industrial, 166
Inflationary pricing, 470
Influencer, 159, 172
Informal partnerships, 87
Information, 107
  the basis of effective marketing, 106
  data and, 107
  search for alternative solutions and, 139–140
  sector, 177
  systems in the 21st century, global, 106–107
InfoSeek, 109–110
Innovation
  continuous, 250
  discontinuous, 249
  dynamically continuous, 249–250
Innovators, 266
Inseparability, 236–237
Inside selling, 411
Institutional advertising, 375
Instrumental services, 234
Intangibility, 235
Integrated marketing communications, 355

approach, 395–398
  the promotional mix, 355
Integrated marketing effort, 17
Intensive distribution, 310
Interactive marketing, 326
Interactive media, 385–387
Interest, 384
Intermediaries
  agent, 291, 335
  fit in channels, how, 292–293
  marketing functions performed by, 292
  merchant, 291, 335
  nature and availability of, 309
Intermodal transportation, 298
Internal marketing, 398
  and employee relations, 397–398
Internal search, 140
International distribution, legalities of, 342
International franchising, 97
International laws, 78
International marketer, the company as, 95–97
International markets, modifying product offerings for, 275–276
International marketing, 90, 195
International public relations, 399
Internet, 62, 72, 107–109, 111, 116, 119, 140, 328, 356, 386, 441, 452
  a new means of global communication, 107–109
  advertisements, 392
  advertising, 386–387
  careers and, 491
  retailing, 328
Interpersonal influences, 152
Intranet, 111
  decision support systems and, 109–111
Intrapreneurial, 258
  organization, 84
Introduction stage, 259–260
Inventory control, 298–299
Inventory management, 288
  opportunities for organizational collaboration, reliable delivery and, 175–176
Inventory turnover ratio, 499
Investment
  direct foreign, 95
  return on (ROI), 447
  target return on, 447
ISO 9000, 174
ISO 14000, 174
Isolation effect, 473
Item-profit pricing, 470

J

Jingle, 382
Jobber, 305
  desk, 337
  rack, 337
  truck, 336
Joint decision making, 158–159
Joint ownership venture, 98
Joint venturing, 97
Justification provision, 483

K

Kefauver-Harris Drug
    Amendment (1962), 75
Keiretsu, 93
KISS (Keep It Simple Stupid)
    formula, 142, 397
Korea, copying in, 148

L

Label, 233
Labeling—telling about the
    product, 233
Laboratory experiment, 122
Laggard, 267
  bringing up the rear, 267
Late majority, 266
Law(s)
  federal level, 75
  international, 78
  local level, 76
  markup, 484
  other state and local, 484
  politics and, 73–78
  pricing and, 483
  state level, 76
  three levels of U.S., 75–78
Leader pricing, 470
  and bait pricing, 470–471
Learning, 149–150
  occurs, how, 149
  social, 149
  theories and marketing, 150
Leased department retailer, 320
Legal environment, 73
Licensee, 97
Licensing, 97, 232
Licensor, 97
Lifestyle, 199, 381
  format, 381
  psychographic segmentation
    and, 199–201
Likert scale, 120
Limited problem solving, 137
Limited-line retailers, 322
Limited-line strategy, 273
Limited-service merchant (cash-
    and-carry) wholesalers,
    336
Line extension (product line
    extension), 274

Links, 111
List price, 442
Literary Digest fiasco of 1936,
    123
Location, 332
Location-based competition, 86
Logistics, 288–289
Logo, 226
Long-term profitability, 17
Long-term relationships, orga-
    nizational collaborations
    for, 340–341
Loss leader, 470

M

Macroenvironment, 58
Macromarketing, 19
Magnuson-Moss Warranty Act
    (1975), 77, 234
Mail-order catalogs, 326
Majority
  early, 266
  fallacy, 190
  late, 266
Management
  crisis, 396–397
  database, 334
  inventory, 288
  marketing, 28–29
  materials, 288
  relationship, 7, 89–90, 412
  sales, 422–429
  total quality (TQM), 18, 36
Management strategy and total
    quality, 268, 272
Management's perspective on
    new products, 248–249
Manager, account, 414
Managerial ethics and socially
    responsible behavior,
    48–50
Manufacturer, 9, 293
  brands versus distributor
    brands, 229–230
  national) brand, 229
Manufacturer-retailer-consumer
    channel, 304
Manufacturer-wholesaler-orga-
    nizational user channel,
    305
Manufacturer-wholesaler-re-
    tailer-consumer channel,
    304
Manufacturer's agent, 339
Manufacturers and wholesaling,
    339–340
Marginal analysis, 455
Marginal cost, 455
Marginal revenue, 455
Market, 8
  classifying products by the
    nature of, 217–222

consumer, 43
characteristics, 309
development, 38
and market segmentation,
    184–188
modifying product offerings
    for international, 275–276
organizational, 43
penetration, 38
position, 44
potential, 127
share, 449
target, 44
Market differences, identifying,
    194–202
Market factor, 129
  index, 129
  analysis of, 129
Market segments, 44
  and selecting target markets,
    analyzing, 43–44
  choosing meaningful,
    185–186
  cross-classification matrix,
    187
Market segmentation, 44
Market-related strategies
  for existing products, 38
  for new products, 39
Market/product matrix, 38
Marketer(s)
  not-for-profit organizations,
    6–7
  the company as an interna-
    tional, 95–97
  use the marketing concept,
    modern, 14–17
Marketer's product portfolio,
    223–225
Marketing, 4–7, 19–21, 98
  agents in business-to-
    business, 305
  analysis and performance ra-
    tios, 497–499
  arithmetic for business
    analysis, 496–501
  audit, 46, 494–495
  business-to-business, 166
  channels of distribution for
    business-to-business,
    304–306
  concentrated, 189
  custom, 191
  data-based, 112, 191
  definition of, 7
  differentiated, 191
  direct, 326
  effective, 7
  effects on our daily lives, 4
  ethics, 48
  event, 396
  four Ps of, 8
  green, 59
  interactive, 326

international (multinational),
    90, 195
learning theories and, 150
management, 28–29
myopia, 33
objective, 45
perception and brand image,
    147
person, 395
relationship, 7, 168
society and, 18–19
strategy, 29–30
test, 255
undifferentiated, 189
Marketing concept, 15
  modern marketers use,
    14–17
  the foundation of a market-
    ing orientation, 15
Marketing effectiveness, price
    and, 444
Marketing effort, integrated,
    17
Marketing environment—coping
    with the uncontrollable,
    13–14
Marketing functions performed
    by intermediaries, 292
Marketing group, multinational,
    78
Marketing mix, 8–13
  positioning: the basic focus
    for, 203–205
Marketing mix strategy, 308
  planning a market position
    and developing, 44
Marketing mix variable, price
    as, 442–444
Marketing orientation, 15, 17
  the marketing concept—the
    foundation of, 15
Marketing plan, 44–45
Marketing research, 112–113
  as a global activity, 125–126
Markup on cost, 477
Markup on selling price, 476
Maslow's hierarchy of needs,
    144
Mass customization, 192
Mass merchandise retailers, 324
Materials handling, 288
Materials management, 288
Maturity stage, 261–262
Media
  advantages and disadvan-
    tages, 389
  mass, direct-marketing, and
    interactive, 385–387
  schedule or media plan, 390
  which, 387–389
Media selection, 385–390
  strategy, 385
Meeting-the-competition strat-
    egy, 466

Membership group, 156
Memory, 149
Merchandise assortment, 331–332
Merchant intermediaries, 291, 335
Merchant wholesalers, 335–337
Microenvironment, 58
    and the four Cs in a global economy, 90–98
    the four Cs, 83–87
Middle managers plan strategies for SBUs, 34–40
Migration, 62
Minimum markup laws, 484
Misleading or deceptive advertising, 399–400
Missionary salesperson, 414
Modified rebuy, 169
Monopolistic competition, 70
Monopoly, 70
Montage, 382
    format, 382
Moral behavior, 48
Mosaic, 111
Motivation, 142–145
    and emotion, 144
    and needs defined, 143
Motives, classifying needs and, 143
Motor carrier, 297
Multicultural population, 67
Multinational economic community, 91
Multinational (international) marketing, 195
Multinational marketing group, 78
Multiple market segmentation (differentiated marketing), 191
Multiple-purchase offers, 432
Multiple-unit pricing, 472

N

NAFTA, 77, 92, 93, 176
Narrowcasting, 390
National (manufacturer) brand, 229
Needs, 143
    and motives, classifying, 143
    defined, motivation and, 143
    Maslow's hierarchy of, 144
    physiological, 143
    social and psychological, 143
Net income ratio, 498
Net profit, 497
    percentage, 498
Net sales, 496
Networks, 87
New product(s), 248
    development, 252–256
    failure of, 257–258

management's perspective on, 248–249
New task buying, 170
Newness
    consumer's perspective on, 249–250
    observability, 251–252
News release, 393–394
Nielsen TV ratings survey, 123
Noise, 358
Nonadopter, 267
Noncumulative quantity discount, 481
Nondurable good, 218
Nonprice competition, 444
Nonprobability sample, 124
Nonstore retailing, 326
Norms, 48, 153
    roles and social values, 152–154
North American Free Trade Agreement (1993), *see* NAFTA
North American Industry Classification System (NAICS), 176–177
Not-for-profit organizations, 6–7

O

Observability, 251–252
Observation research, 121
Off-price retailers, 325
Oligopoly, 70
One-price policy versus variable pricing, 464–465
One-price strategy, 464
Operant conditioning, 150
Operating expenses, 497
Operating product, 222
Operational planning, 31
Opinion leaders, 157
Opportunities
    identifying and evaluating, 41–43
    problems can be, 114
Order getting (creative selling), 414
Order processing, 288
Order taker/taking, 413
Organizational, 166
    buying behavior, 166–167
    market, 43
    resources, 308
Organizational collaborations
    for long-term relationships, 340–341
    reliable delivery and inventory management, 175–176
Organizational mission, 31–33
Organizational products, 221–222
Organizations buying, 172–176

Orientation
    consumer, 15–17
    marketing, 15, 17
    production, 15
    sales, 15
Outsourcing, 88
Ownership group, 321

P

Packaging, 232
    containerization and, protective, 289
    legal guidelines for, 233
    packing and, 232–233
Peer pressure 156
Penetration pricing, 468–469
Perceived risk, 139
Perception, 145–148
    and brand image marketing, 147
    selective, 146
    subliminal, 147
Perestroika, 74
Perfect communication, 358
Performance ratios, marketing analysis and, 497–499
Periodic discounting, 466
Perishability, 235
Person marketing, 395
Personal relationship, 417
Personal selling, 352
    and building relationships, 411–412
    characteristics of, 411–413
    defined, 410–411
    flexibility of, 411
    some limitations of, 412–413
    tasks, types of, 413–415
Personality, 152
    and self-concept, 151–152
    theory evaluated, 152
    what is, 151
Persuasion, ethics of, 366–367
Physical distribution, 288
    defined, logistics and, 288–289
    the objectives of, 289–290
Physical distribution functions, 293–300
    integration of, 299–300
Physical environment, 58–59
Physical obsolescence, 278
Physiological needs, 143
Pioneers, 414
Pipeline, 298
Place (distribution), 9
    the second element, 9–10
    utility, 85
Plan, executing, 45–46
Planned obsolescence, 278
Planning, 30
    business-unit growth strategies, 38–40

designing a framework for the future, 30–31
developing advertising campaigns and, 376–378
execution, and control are interrelated, 47–48
inadequate or inferior, 257
a market position and developing a marketing mix strategy, 44
operational, 31
preapproach, 417
strategic, 30
Point-of-purchase materials, 430, 433
Poison Prevention Labeling Act (1970), 75
Political environment, 73
Politics and laws, 73–78
Population, 123
    multicultural, 67
    target, 123
    U.S., 62–68
    world, 68–69
Positioning, 44, 364–365
    the basic focus for the marketing mix, 203–205
Possession utility, 85
Postpurchase consumption and evaluation, 141–142
Posttesting, 391
    advertisements, 391–392
Preapproach planning, 417
Predatory pricing strategy, 469
Premium, 432
Premiums and self-liquidating premiums, 432
Press conference, 394
Prestige price, 473
Pretesting, 124, 390
Price(s), 11, 175, 442
    adjustments, 480–483
    break-even analysis and, 479
    competition, 86, 443–444
    establishing the exact, 476–480
    ethical, 476
    gentleman's, 476
    in the economy, 444–445
    leaders and followers, 467–468
    leadership strategy, 35, 467
    list, 442
    marketing effectiveness and, 444
    as a marketing mix variable, 442–444
    professional, 476
    skimming, 465
    stabilization, 451
    the third element, 11
Price elasticity, 452, 500–501
    of demand, 452–454
Price-bundling strategy, 472
Price-lining strategy, 471

Price-reduction strategies, other, 466
Pricing
  bait, 471
  basing-point, 475
  captive, 470
  delivered (freight-allowed), 474
  inflationary, 470
  item-profit, 470
  and law, 483–484
  leader, 470
  lining, 471
  multiple-unit, 472
  objectives, 446–451
  odd versus even, 473
  penetration, 468–469
  prestige, 473
  reference, 473
  and social responsibility, 484–485
  target return, 478
  total-profit, 470
  traditional, 469–470
  uniform delivered, 474
  zone, 474
Pricing strategies
  an overview of, 464
  competitive, 466–470
  differential, 464–466
  fundamentals of, 446
  product-line, 470–473
  psychological and image, 473–474
Pricing strategies and tactics
  additional, 475–476
  distribution-based, 474–475
Primary activities, 88
Primary characteristic, 216
Primary data, 107
  research designs, 119
Primary demand
  advertising, 377
  generic or, 377
Private (distributor) brand, 229
Pro forma profit and loss statements, 497
Probability sample, 123
Problem(s)
  children, 224
  defining, 114–118
  recognition, 138–139
Problem solving
  extensive, 137
  solving, limited, 137
Product(s), 8, 215–217
  advertising, 374
  capital, 222
  class, 85
  classifying consumer, 218–219
  classifying organizational, 221–222
  convenience, 219
  concept, 216

design, 271
development, 39
differentiation, 217, 364
eliminating old, 276
enhancement, 270
failure of, 257–258
the first element, 8–9
generating inquiries about, 392
generic, 230
heterogeneous shopping, 220
homogeneous shopping, 220
item, 223
labeling, 233
management's perspective on new, 248–249
market-related strategies for existing, 38
market-related strategies for new, 39
measuring changes in attitudes about, 392
modification, 149, 267
new, 248
new-to-the-world, 248
obsolescence, 278
offerings for international markets, modifying, 275–276
operating, 222
organizational, 221
placement, 433
production, 222
quality, 173–174
sampling, 431
shopping, 220
specialty, 221
strategies for modifying existing, 267–273
total, 216
total service, 239
uses and problem solutions, 380
warranty, 233–234
Product category, 85
  extensions, 274, 248
Product life cycle, 259–265
  advertising objectives and, 377–378
  do all products follow, 263–264
Product line, 223
  extension, 249, 274
  depth of, 223
  organization by, 425
  product mix and, 223, 274–275
Product line strategy, 273
  matching products to markets, 273–276
Product mix, 223
  strategies for expanding the product line or, 274–275
  width of, 223

Product portfolio, 224
  analysis, 224
  the marketer's, 223–225
Product strategy, 216
  ethical considerations associated with, 276–278
Product superiority or uniqueness, inadequate, 257
Product-line pricing strategies, 470–473
Production orientation, 15
Production product, 222
Professional prices, 476
Professional, scientific, and technical services sector, 177
Profit and loss statement, 496–497
Profit maximization, 449
Profitability, long-term, 17
Promotion, 11
  communication with a purpose, 351–352
  cooperative advertising and, 430
  elements of, 352–355
  the fourth element, 11
  sales, 354
Promotional allowances, 482
Promotional campaign, 362–366
Promotional mix, 355
Prospecting, 416
Psychographic segmentation, lifestyle and, 199–201
Psychographics, 199
Psychological and image pricing strategies, 473–474
Public Health Smoking Act (1970), 75
Public relations, 353, 393–396
  ethical issues in advertising and, 399–401
  evaluating and monitoring, 399
  going beyond publicity, 395–398
  international, 399
Public standards, 400–401
Publicity and public relations, 353
Puffery, 400
Pull strategy, 362
Purchase decisions and the act of buying, choice, 141
Purchase satisfaction, 141
Purchases, unsought, 221
Pure competition, 69
Push and pull strategies, 361–362
Push strategy, 361

Q

Qualified prospects, locating, 416–417

Qualifying, 417
Quality assurance strategy, 268
Quality of life and ecology, 277–278
Quality, managing service, 272
Quality-based competition, 86
Quantity discount, 481
  cumulative, 481
  noncumulative, 481
Quota, import, 94
Quota sample, 124
Quota-bonus plan, 427

R

Rack jobber, 337
Railroad, 296
Random discounting, 466
Reach, 390
Rebate, 432
Recall tests, 391
Receiver, 355
Recognition, measuring brand recall and, 391–392
Recording industry, 263
Reducing transactions, 295–296
Reference group, 156–157
Reference pricing strategy, 473
Reinforcement, 150
Relationship management, 7, 89–90, 412
Relationship marketing, 7, 168
Relative advantage, 251
Repositioning strategies, 205, 268
Resale price maintenance acts, 483
Research about the future, sales forecasting, 127–129
Research design, 118
  planning, 118–122
  primary data, 119
  secondary data, 118
  selecting, 122
Research, observation, 121
Research objective, 117
Research process, stages in, 113–125
Retail and wholesale distribution, regulation of, 341–342
Retail management strategies, 330–335
Retail selling, 410
Retailer(s), 10, 293
  classifying by ownership, 320–321
  classifying by prominent strategy, 321–329
  cooperative organization, 307
  independent, 320
  leased department, 320
  limited-line, 322
  mass merchandise, 324

off-price, 325
sales promotions geared toward wholesalers and, 430–431
single-line, 322
Retailing, 320
computer-interactive, 328
direct-response, 326
importance of, 320
institutions—toward a system of classifications, 320–329
in-store, 322
internet, 328
nonstore, 326
supermarket, 324
wheel of, 329–330
Return on investment (ROI), 447, 499–500
Returns and allowances, 496
percentage, 499
Reverse distribution, 313
Right to be informed, 276–277
Right to choose, 278
Right to safety, 276
Risk-taking function, 301
Robinson-Patman Act (1936), 77, 278, 465, 469, 483
Roles, 153
social values and norms, 152–154
Routinized response behavior, 136

S

Salary plus commission, 427
Sales, 396
advertisement effectiveness and, 392–393
branch, 339
ethical issues in, 429
forecast, 127
management, 422–429
office, 339
potential, 127
presentation, 418–419
support and cross-functional teams, 414–415
Sales activity, organizing, 423–425
Sales force
composite, 129
compensating, 426–427
evaluating and controlling, 428–429
motivating, 428
recruiting and selecting, 425–426
training, 426
Sales forecasting, 127
research about the future, 127–129
Sales manager, field, 424
Sales objectives, 422
setting, 422–423

Sales orientation, 15
Sales promotions, 354, 429–434
aimed at ultimate consumers, 431–434
geared toward wholesalers and retailers, 430–431
tie-ins, 433
Sales territories, 423
Sales-oriented objectives, 449–450
Sample, 123
convenience, 124
nonprobability, 124
probability, 123
quota, 124
selecting, 122–124
simple random, 124
Sampling, 122
Science and technology, 71–73
Scrambled merchandising, 324
Screening stage, 254
Search engine, 109
Seasonal discounts, 481–482
Second-market discounting, 465
Secondary data, 107
research designs, 118
Segmentation
by behavioral patterns, 201–202
benefit, 202
demographic, 196–198
geodemographic, 202
geographic, 195–196
lifestyle and psychographic, 199–201
socioeconomic bases of, 198–199
Selective attention, 146
Selective demand advertising, 377
Selective distribution, 310
Selective exposure, 146
Selective interpretation, 146
Selective perception, 145–146
Self-concept, 152
how we see ourselves, 152
personality and, 151
Selling
agent, 339
characteristics of personal, 411–413
defined, personal, 410–411
field, 410
function, 300
inside, 411
in Japan, 422
price, markup on, 476
retail, 410
suggestive, 413
Semantic differential, 120
Server, 108
Service(s), 218
are products too, 234–239
characteristics of, 234–238

consummatory, 234
encounter, 238
function, 301
instrumental, 234
level, 334
mark, 227
Service quality, managing, 272
Sherman Antitrust Act (1890), 75, 77, 278, 341, 469, 483
Shopping products, 220
Silicon Junction, 111
Simple random sample, 124
Simplicity of usage, 252
Single-line retailers, 322
Single-product strategy, 273
Single-sourcing, 175
Situation analysis, 41–42
Skimming price, 465–466
Slice of life format, 380
Social and psychological needs, 143
Social class, 155
Social concerns, objectives related to, 451
Social learning, 149
Social responsibility, 48
Social situations, 158
Social value, 60, 153
norms, and roles, 152–154
Socialization process, 157
Societal marketing concept, 19–20
Sociocultural forces, 59–61
Socioeconomic bases of segmentation, 198–199
SOQ NOP, 420
Sorting function, 294
Source, 355
Specialty mass merchandisers, 325
Specialty product, 221
Specialty store, 322
Specialty wholesalers, 336
Spokesperson, 381
Standard Industrial Classification (SIC), 176–177
Standardization, strategy of, 238
Star, 224
STAT-USA/ Internet, 110
Statistical Abstract of the United States, 62
Still-life format, 381
Stimulus factor, 146
Stock turnover ratio, 499
Storage, 298
and inventory control, 298
transportation and, 296–299
warehousing and, 288
Store image, 330
Storyline format, 380
Straight commission, 427
Straight rebuy, 169
Straight salary or wage, 427

Strategic alliance, 169
Strategic business alliance, 341
Strategic business unit (SBU), 33
establishing, 33–34
middle managers plan strategies for, 34–40
Strategic corporate goals, 31
Strategic gap, 43
Strategic marketing process, 40–47
Strategic planning, 30
Strategic plans, 31–34
Strategy of customization, 238
Strategy of standardization, 238
Style, 272
Subculture, 154
cultures within cultures, 154–156
Subliminal perception, 147
Success, 250–252
Suggestive selling, 413
Sunbelt, growth in, 63
Super Bowl, 120, 432
Supermarket, 324
and convenience stores, 323
retailing, 324
Supplier, 87
Supply curve (supply schedule), 445
Supportive activities, 88
Survey, 119
Sweepstakes, 432
SWOT, 42
Systematic bias, 120
Systems concept, 299

T

Tactics, 29
Tangibility and durability, 218
Target market(s), 44, 184–185
analyzing market segments and selecting, 43–44
and creating assortments, selecting, 340
considerations, 451
matching the mix to, 188
Target marketing, four strategies for, 188–194
Target population, 123
Target return on investment, 447
Target return pricing, 478
Tariff, 92
Technical problems, 258
Technology, 71
Telemarketing, 327, 410
Television home shopping, 327
Test marketing, 255
Testimonial, 381
Tie-in, 433
Time utility, 85
Time-based competition, 86
Timing, poor, 258

Total cost concept, 299, 478
Total product, 216
Total quality management
(TQM), 18, 36
to achieve differentiation,
35–37
Total quality management
strategies, 268–273
Total service product, 239
Total-profit pricing, 470
Trade discount, 481
Trade show, 430
Trademark, 226
Traditional pricing, 469–470
Transportation, 296
intermodal, 298
outbound, 289
storage and, 296–299
water, 297
Trends, projection of, 129
Trial close, 421
Trial sampling, 251
Trialability, 251
the opportunity for buyer
testing, 251
Truck wholesalers, 336
Turnover, 449
Tying contracts, 342

U

U.S. Bankruptcy Court, 441
U.S. Government Information
Servers, 109
U.S. population, 62–68

Ultimate consumer, 293
sales promotions aimed at,
431–434
Unaided recall, 392
Uncontrollable variable, 13
Undercutting-the-competition
strategy, 467
Undifferentiated marketing, 189
Unfair sales practices acts, 484
Uniform delivered pricing, 474
Uniform Resource Locator
(URL), 109
Unique selling proposition
(USP), 364
Universal product code (UPC),
233
Unsought purchases, 221
Upstream activities, 88
Urbanization, 62
Usage, simplicity of, 252
User, 158, 172
Utility
economic, 85
form, 85
place, 85
possession, 85
time, 85

V

VALS 2, 208–209
Value, 442
Value chain, 87–88
Variable pricing
one-price policy versus,
464–465

strategy, 464
Variables
controllable, 8
uncontrollable, 13
Vending machines, 328
Verbal appeal, copy, 383
Vertical marketing system,
306–308
contractual, 307
corporate, 306
Virtual corporations, 87
Virtual memory, 87
Visual appeal, art, 383
Voluntary chain, 308
Voluntary membership group,
156

W

Wall Street Journal Interactive,
109
Warehouse, 299
Warehouse club, 325
Warehousing and storage, 288
Water transportation, 297
Web browsers, 109
Wharton forecast, 127
Wheel of retailing, 329–330
Wheeler-Lea Act (1938), 77,
278
Wholesale distribution, regula-
tion of retail and, 341–342
Wholesale management strate-
gies, 340–341
Wholesale trade, census of,
335

Wholesaler(s), 9, 335
and retailers, sales promotions geared toward,
430–431
classifying, 335–340
direct-marketing, 336
discount, 483
distribution of services, 340
full-service merchant, 336
general line, 336
general merchandise, 336
limited-service merchant, 336
merchant, 335–337
specialty, 336
Wholesaling, 335
manufacturers that do their
own, 339–340
Width of product mix, 223
Women, working, 66
World brand, 229
World of Clinique Web, 386
World perspective, 57–58
World population, 68–69
World Series, 120
World Wide Web, 109, 328,
452

Y

Yahoo, 109, 110, 386

Z

Zone pricing, 474
31